The Book of Charlatans

Letter from the General Editor

The Library of Arabic Literature makes available Arabic editions and English translations of significant works of Arabic literature, with an emphasis on the seventh to nineteenth centuries. The Library of Arabic Literature thus includes texts from the pre-Islamic era to the cusp of the modern period, and encompasses a wide range of genres, including poetry, poetics, fiction, religion, philosophy, law, science, travel writing, history, and historiography.

Books in the series are edited and translated by internationally recognized scholars. They are published as hardcovers in parallel-text format with Arabic and English on facing pages, as English-only paperbacks, and as downloadable Arabic editions. For some texts, the series also publishes separate scholarly editions with full critical apparatus.

The Library encourages scholars to produce authoritative Arabic editions, accompanied by modern, lucid English translations, with the ultimate goal of introducing Arabic's rich literary heritage to a general audience of readers as well as to scholars and students.

The Library of Arabic Literature is supported by a grant from the New York University Abu Dhabi Institute and is published by NYU Press.

Philip F. Kennedy
General Editor, Library of Arabic Literature

كتاب المختار في كشف الأسرار

جمال الدين عبد الرحيم بن عمر بن أبي بكر الدمشقيّ

المعروف بالجوبريّ

LIBRARY OF
المكتبة
ARABIC
العربية
LITERATURE

The Book of Charlatans

Jamāl al-Dīn
ʿAbd al-Raḥīm al-Jawbarī

Edited by
Manuela Dengler

Translated by
Humphrey Davies

Foreword by
S. A. Chakraborty

Volume editor
Maurice A. Pomerantz

NEW YORK UNIVERSITY PRESS
New York

NEW YORK UNIVERSITY PRESS
New York

Library of Congress Cataloging-in-Publication Data

Names: Jawbarī, ʿAbd al-Raḥmān ibn ʿUmar, active 1216-1222, author. | Dengler, Manuela, editor. | Davies, Humphrey T. (Humphrey Taman) translator. | Chakraborty, S. A., other. | Jawbarī, ʿAbd al-Raḥmān ibn ʿUmar, active 1216-1222. Mukhtār fī kashf al-asrār wa-hatk al-astār.
Title: The book of charlatans = Kitāb al-Mukhtār fī kashf al-asrār / Jamāl al-Dīn ʿAbd al-Raḥīm al-Jawbarī ; edited by Manuela Dengler ; translated by Humphrey Davies ; foreword by S. A. Chakraborty.
Other titles: Mukhtār fī kashf al-asrār wa-hatk al-astār. English | Kitāb al-Mukhtār fī kashf al-asrār
Description: New York : New York University Press, 2020. | Includes bibliographical references and index. | Summary: "a comprehensive guide to trickery and scams as practiced in the thirteenth century in the cities of the Middle East, especially in Syria and Egypt"-- Provided by publisher.
Identifiers: LCCN 2020017851 (print) | LCCN 2020017852 (ebook) | ISBN 9781479897636 (hardcover) | ISBN 9781479810185 (ebook) | ISBN 9781479869442 (ebook)
Subjects: LCSH: Swindlers and swindling--Islamic Empire. | Quacks and quackery--Islamic Empire. | Impostors and imposture--Islamic Empire.
Classification: LCC HV6699.N4 J3813 2020 (print) | LCC HV6699.N4 (ebook) | DDC 364.16/309569209022--dc23
LC record available at https://lccn.loc.gov/2020017851
LC ebook record available at https://lccn.loc.gov/2020017852

New York University Press books are printed on acid-free paper, and their binding materials are chosen for strength and durability.

Series design by Titus Nemeth.

Typeset in Tasmeem, using DecoType Naskh and Emiri.

Typesetting and digitization by Stuart Brown.

Manufactured in the United States of America
c10 9 8 7 6 5 4 3 2 1

Table of Contents

Foreword

In the city of Ḥarrān in the year 613 [1216–17], there occurred a most extraordinary scene.

It was a Friday, the Muslim day of communal prayer, and the city's mosques were packed with the faithful, completing their ablutions and rolling out prayer mats. But one of those faithful was not like the rest. He was an ape, dressed in the clothing of princes and perfumed like royalty, riding upon a mule in a saddle of finely worked gold. Indian slaves escorted him, carrying his prayer mat and shoes as the creature made his way down the street and into the mosque, performing his ablutions and then greeting the mosque by performing the customary salutation prayer, before busying himself with prayer beads, the very picture of piety.

But if the sight of the ape was enough to render worshippers speechless, the story his slaves spun was even more astonishing. According to them, the ape was not truly an ape—he was a prince from one of the richest kingdoms of India, his beastly appearance the result of a jealous wife's curse. As the ape prince wept tears like rain, a handkerchief pressed to his eyes, his loyal servants continued his tragic account, telling the growing crowd how handsome and devout the young man had once been. They related how his wife was now holding his life in ransom, swearing not to reverse the curse until she was paid a handsome amount of gold. And what good fortune, for the assembled kings of India had nearly gathered the hefty sum—they just needed a little bit more: money the good people of Ḥarrān could offer in return for blessings on such a holy day.

The scam worked, the "prince" and his companions collecting a tidy fortune and then presumably vanishing. But they weren't the only travelers to Ḥarrān—and their trick hadn't worked on everyone. Watching from the sidelines was a self-proclaimed, self-taught scholar from Damascus, an explorer and seemingly quite the veteran of cons himself: Jamāl al-Dīn ʿAbd al-Raḥīm ibn ʿUmar ibn Abī Bakr al-Dimashqī, known as al-Jawbarī.

Al-Jawbarī would later recount the tale of the well-trained ape—among dozens of others—in a book he claimed he was pressured to write by a Turkmen ruler. The text must have been popular, considering the number of copies that have survived into the modern era. And its popularity shouldn't be surprising—the book is incredibly entertaining, told by a natural storyteller whose tales of lecherous highwaymen, knockout drugs delivered via sweaty armpits, and the best way to construct a fire-breathing, booby-trapped snake would captivate a modern audience as surely as they did his medieval ones.

While no one enjoys being swindled, people have long devoured tales of con artists and their schemes. From ancient tricksters such as Anansi and Loki, to their medieval counterparts Scheherazade and Robin Hood, to the blockbuster heists that dominate summer movie theaters, there is a peculiar thrill in following the transgressions—criminal or otherwise—of shrewd, audacious men and women. Indeed, it is impossible to read al-Jawbarī's text and not notice how cleverly he skewers many of the magical tropes of contemporary fantasy tales such as *The Thousand and One Nights* and *Tales of the Marvelous and News of the Strange*, pulling back the curtain to examine how one might manufacture an "ancient" treasure map, make a severed head appear to speak, and disable the sword-bearing automatons known to guard jewel-stuffed tombs. Al-Jawbarī takes clear delight in his knowledge—he boasts throughout that there is hardly a book he hasn't read and that the astonishingly comprehensive list of tricks he shares is but a mere fraction of what he knows.

And what tricks! There are recipes to manufacture fake ginger and lapis lazuli so precise one could attempt a recreation (though I would suggest you avoid doing the same with the many poisons and drugs also listed). False holy men who fill hairnets with glowworms to give themselves the appearance of the blessed and others who use remarkable engineering to make it appear that the Nile is rising. Appropriately for the medieval setting, there are over a dozen accounts of alchemists, though al-Jawbarī openly mocks the famed craft, pointing out—quite rightly—that if anyone had solid knowledge of turning ordinary metals into gold, they not only wouldn't need a partner, they'd be a fool to spill such a lucrative secret.

Al-Jawbarī's narration is as entertaining as the text. This is the kind of historical account that brings the past alive, and both al-Jawbarī and his twelfth-century audience leap from the page. It is a product of its age—modern readers will no doubt notice that al-Jawbarī has far sharper words for con artists who are female, Jewish, or Zoroastrian than he has for Muslim and Christian men. But in al-Jawbarī's silver-tongued telling, we get a glimpse of the lives of people who don't show up in the annals of sultans and scholars, and see a world that was about to be irrevocably changed; indeed, Ḥarrān, a city that had thrived for millennia, would be destroyed by the Mongols only a few decades after the incident of the royal ape above.

That darkness, however, is little seen in al-Jawbarī's account, even among tales of murderers and thieves. Though he curses the worst offenders, he seems more often amused by the charlatans he encounters, and eager to learn their tricks. This begs the question: What kind of trickster was al-Jawbarī? For he relates many of his stories in the oily, teasing tone of his two-timing characters—he *could* tell you a hundred other tricks, but he would hate to bore you! For a book purportedly about laying bare deceptions and dodges, there are tricks listed here that are so complex, time-consuming, and unnecessarily convoluted—Solomon's ant and the unfortunate boy come to mind—that they strain belief. Are we to believe that al-Jawbarī, clearly a clever man well aware of the power of stories, bought everything he's selling here? Or might our self-taught master have learned there was just as fine a life to be had in the telling of criminal deeds as in committing them? It's tempting to imagine al-Jawbarī in the well-appointed salons of the rich rulers of his day, winking as he collected his coins and spun increasingly elaborate fictions.

Readers will have to find their own line between truth and falsehood. However, as you make your way from Morocco to India in the company of al-Jawbarī's sly hustlers and devious tomb raiders, you may find, like the many enthralled audiences that have come before you, that sometimes it's a bit more fun to believe in the magic.

S. A. Chakraborty
New York City

Acknowledgments

The editor and translator would like to thank Paul Chevedden, Emily Cottrell, George Kiraz, Christian Mauder, Everett Rowson, Kevin van Bladel, and Luke Yarborough, all of whom contributed to the untying of knots, and to express our sincere appreciation for the input of Maurice Pomerantz, our project editor, without whose dedication and insight the production of this edition and translation would have been an almost impossible task. Special thanks is owed to Daniel Jacobs for his research on plant names. Our heartfelt thanks for their efficient support go also to the administrative team at the Library of Arabic Literature, both in New York and in Abu Dhabi: Chip Rossetti, Lucie Taylor, Stuart Brown, and Amani Al-Zoubi.

Introduction

From the third/ninth century on, medieval Muslim men of letters developed an interest in the lives of simple people and marginal groups. This produced some remarkable works. In various literary forms, and to a greater or lesser extent, these works focused on the manners and customs of wandering professional beggars. They include the list of beggars in the *Book of Misers* (*Kitāb al-Bukhalāʾ*) of the essayist and encyclopedist al-Jāḥiẓ (d. 255/868); the *Beggars' Poem* (*al-Qaṣīdah al-Sāsāniyyah*) of the doctor, globetrotter, and poet Abū Dulaf (fl. fourth/tenth c.); the *Assemblies* (*Maqāmāt*) of the courtier and scribe Badīʿ al-Zamān al-Hamadhānī (d. 398/1008); the *Shadow Plays* (*Khayāl al-ẓill*) of the eye doctor Ibn Dāniyāl (d. 710/1310), especially that entitled *ʿAjīb wa-Gharīb*, which not only depicts scenes of the everyday life of vagabonds but also contains elements of the jargon of the Banū Sāsān; and a further *Beggars' Poem* (*Qaṣīdah Sāsāniyyah*) by the poet Ṣafī al-Dīn al-Ḥillī (d. ca. 750/1339). All these texts provide diverse glimpses of the colorful daily life of the various sorts of beggars, swindlers, charlatans, and vagrants generally known in the Arabic of the time as the Banū Sāsān ("Sons of Sāsān")—followers, according to the best-known account, of a certain Shaykh Sāsān, usurped heir to the throne of Persia, who traveled the world and gathered around him a band of like-minded roamers.[1] C. E. Bosworth drew on many of these literary genre paintings for his pioneering *The Mediaeval Islamic Underworld* (1976), which reproduces, translates, and discusses in detail the *qaṣīdah sāsāniyyah*s of both Abū Dulaf and al-Ḥillī.

Within this subgenre of Arabic literature, a book that has attracted little attention is *The Book Containing a Selection Concerning the Exposure of Secrets* (*Kitāb al-Mukhtār fī kashf al-asrār*), rendered here as *The Book of Charlatans*. Written in the mid-seventh/-thirteenth century, *The Book of Charlatans* describes a wide range of beggars' and charlatans' groups, with examples of their various tricks, and portrays the mentality and morals of this secret subculture. It thus provides a sketch of the social reality of the professions of begging and swindling, making *The Book of Charlatans* one of the most important literary representations of underworld customs in medieval Islamic civilization. Al-Jawbarī recorded unique aspects of the charlatans' milieu with the eyes and knowledge of an initiate, opening a window onto the daily life of the medieval Islamic underworld that would otherwise be effectively closed to us, as these are rarely described in other historical sources. *The Book of Charlatans* is also important because of its language, a form of Middle Arabic[2] shot through with jargon and rare words, an invaluable source for linguistic analysis of the sociolect of professional beggars and charlatans.

The Author and the Work

There is little in the relevant Arabic biographical and bibliographical literature about al-Jawbarī and his literary activity except for two short entries in the *Removal of Doubt Concerning the Names of Books and Arts* (*Kitāb Kashf al-ẓunūn ʿan asāmī l-kutub wa-l-funūn*) of Ḥājjī Khalīfah (d. 1067/1657) and one entry each in the *Gift of the Knowledgeable* (*Hadiyyat al-ʿārifīn*) of Ismāʿīl Pāshā al-Baghdādī (d. 1335/1920) and the *Dictionary of Authors* (*Muʿjam al-muʾallifīn*) of ʿUmar Riḍā al-Kaḥḥālah (d. 1407/1987). Ḥājjī Khalīfah characterizes al-Jawbarī's *Book of Charlatans* as "an amazing book, unique . . . . Its author has torn away the liars' veils and stripped naked the impudent of every sort"[3] and bestows on the author the honorifics "unique imam" and "shaykh," implying that Ḥājjī Khalīfah considered al-Jawbarī to be a scholar of a certain level of attainment.[4] Al-Kaḥḥālah, presumably following Ismāʿīl Pāshā,[5] notes that al-Jawbarī was an adherent of the Shāfiʿī school of Islamic law and that he was still alive in 613/1216. He describes him as an occultist (*ʿālim rūḥānī*) and lists his works as *The Book Containing a Selection Concerning the Exposure of Secrets and the Rending of the Veils* (*al-Mukhtār fī kashf al-asrār wa-hatk al-astār*), *The Straight Path to the Science of the Celestial Bodies and the Astrologers' Craft* (*al-Ṣirāṭ al-mustaqīm fī ʿilm al-rūḥāniyyah wa-ṣināʿat al-tanjīm*), and *The Drawing Aside of the Veils of the Artful and [the Exposure] of the Illusions of the Artificers* (*Kashf asrār al-muḥtālīn wa-nawāmīs al-ḥayyālīn*).[6] The only source to provide more specific information for al-Jawbarī's biography is his partly autobiographical *Book of Charlatans*, the sole work of his known to have survived.

Al-Jawbarī's full name is Jamāl al-Dīn (or Zayn al-Dīn) ʿAbd al-Raḥīm (or ʿAbd al-Raḥmān) ibn ʿUmar ibn Abī Bakr al-Dimashqī al-Jawbarī. He was from al-Jawbar, at that time a village in the Ghouta (the irrigated ring of gardens encircling Damascus) and now a suburb of the city. Based on the limited internal and external evidence, the exact dates of al-Jawbarī's birth and death cannot be ascertained with precision, but all dates specified or implied in the work as occurring within the author's lifetime fall between 613/1216–17 and 646/1248.

Al-Jawbarī nowhere refers to a teacher and was therefore in all likelihood self-taught. If his remark that he had studied more than three hundred books (§0.4) is to be believed, he was unusually well read for his time. The vast majority of the authors to whom he refers, and who range from the apocryphal (such as Adam and Solomon) to contemporaries, wrote on the sciences, whether occult or natural (§§0.3–6). Despite occasional references in the text to the poetry of al-Ḥallāj (d. 309/922) (§2.3) and to literary figures such as al-Ḥarīrī (d. 516/1122) (§14.10) and al-Jāḥiẓ (§30.13), he was not a product of the classical literary and religious curriculum typically followed by the educated of his day, a fact that is reflected in his writing style (see the Note on Translation below). The two works that he claims to have written himself—namely, *The Straight Path to the Science of the Celestial Bodies and the Astrologers' Craft* (*al-Ṣirāṭ al-mustaqīm fī ʿilm al-rūḥāniyyah wa-ṣināʿat al-tanjīm*) (§0.6) and a short treatise in verse on geomancy (§§0.6, 12.25)—confirm the focus of his interests. Nothing certain is known today of either text.[7]

According to his own account (§0.7), al-Jawbarī wrote *The Book of Charlatans* at the request of a ruler of the Turkmen Artuqid Dynasty, al-Malik al-Masʿūd Rukn al-Dīn Mawdūd (r. 619–29/1222–32).[8] In his preface, al-Jawbarī recounts how, during a salon at the ruler's court, talk turned to the *Deceit Disrobed and Doubt Dispelled* (*Fī kashf al-dakk wa-īḍāḥ al-shakk*) of Ibn Shuhayd (d. 426/1035).[9] Rukn al-Dīn asked for a copy to be brought and was impressed. After asking al-Jawbarī his opinion of it, he ordered him to compile a new work along the lines of Ibn Shuhayd's, but "shorter and easier to understand" (§0.7). Despite al-Jawbarī's conventional and pro forma demurral, Rukn al-Dīn continued to insist, and the author eventually accepted the commission, undertaking to put down in writing secrets that, he claimed, no one before him had uncovered or divulged. It may be assumed that al-Jawbarī received the commission while al-Malik al-Masʿūd Rukn al-Dīn Mawdūd was in power—that is, between 619/1222 and 629/1232.[10]

Al-Jawbarī's sometimes extremely precise descriptions of tricks and recipes give the impression that he was familiar with many different areas of knowledge, including alchemy, chemistry, pharmaceutics, medicine, geomancy, astrology, and mechanics, although it is far from certain that he mastered them all. This raises the question of his professional life and to what extent he was involved in the activities he describes. He says nothing about how he earned a living during his travels (which ranged from western Morocco to India and included Tunis, Egypt, Cyprus, Syria, Anatolia, Mesopotamia, the Hejaz, and Yemen) beyond mentioning that at a certain point he was involved in treasure seeking in Egypt (§27.26). On one occasion, he admits he was tempted to participate in nefarious activities, but his better self refused to allow him to do so (§13.24). At the same time, the author's repeated claim that his reports are based on personal observation ("I have direct experience of these matters" (§6.1); "there isn't a single art of theirs that I have failed to study or a single science of theirs of which I lack direct experience" (§6.25), and so on) should be treated with caution (even if we set aside the clearly fantastic nature of many of them). For example, the story of the pious ape whose behavior the author claims to have witnessed with his own eyes "when I was in Ḥarrān in the year 613" (§6.5) is cited, with differences of detail, by the tenth/seventeenth-century bibliographer Ḥajjī Khalīfah as an example of "things [done by the Banū Sāsān] that the mind is incapable of grasping."[11] Ḥājjī Khalīfah then adds, "This story is also mentioned in the *History* of Mīr Khūnd,"[12] referring to a ninth/fifteenth-century Persian-language work. Though it is of course possible that Mīr Khūnd took the story directly or indirectly from al-Jawbarī, it seems more likely that the latter was using a story that was in general circulation and attempting to add credence to it by claiming that he—or, in other cases, a friend (§6.24)—had witnessed the events in question.

Certainly, al-Jawbarī's attitude to the activities of the charlatans he describes is in some cases ambiguous. While in many cases he condemns them for the heinousness of their crimes, in others he expresses his admiration for their skill, even remarking on how "smart" a given trick is (e.g., §27.11, 27.55–60) or how closely an ersatz or adulterated substitute for a certain food or mineral either resembles the original (a certain recipe makes "a lovely high-grade tutty that couldn't be bettered" [§10.8]) or even improves on it ("The result is spicier and better than real ginger" [§10.4]). Occasionally, he mentions tricks he has invented himself: He describes how he once devised a new means to expose a thief (§§13.22–23); on another occasion, he cannot conceal his pride at having invented a new way to make fake pepper (§27.12).

The possibility that al-Jawbarī was himself, wholly or in part, a "charlatan"—that is, someone who practiced one or more of the activities described in the work—must be entertained. That said, the author emphasizes throughout the work the difference between genuine, though hermetic, disciplines such as alchemy (a skill that he implies he has himself mastered; see, e.g., §§9.17–27 and §25.7), astrology, and magic; and practices such as the staging of illusions and other chicanery intended to deceive. In doing so, he reflects a tradition among Muslim theologians, who "discussed the possibility of distinguishing between magic and tricks on the one hand and the genuine divine miracle on the other."[13] What the author most violently condemns in *The Book of Charlatans* are the deceitful practices of false astrologists, geomancers, and alchemists, who abuse these sciences for their own nefarious ends. Lower forms of chicanery—to which the greater part of the book is devoted—he approaches with the attitude that, however remarkable the trick may seem, it is just that: a deception that can be picked apart and whose ingenuity may even be worthy of admiration. It is this "spirit of suspicious scepticism, always on the look-out wherever supernatural forces seemed to put gold, lust, or power into all too easy reach" that caused Stefan Wild to suggest that *The Book of Charlatans* should be seen as "a first and important step in something like an enlightenment literature in Islam."[14]

The Book of Charlatans is an extremely rich source for the cultural, social, and psychological history of medieval Islam. It has documentary value as a mirror of medieval Islamic religious and social life in the seventh/thirteenth century, providing a wealth of material that has yet to be exploited. Khawam describes al-Jawbarī well when he says that "he looks at society with the eyes of a sociologist avant la lettre—a hundred years before Ibn Khaldūn—but a sociologist who is less interested in society's structures than in its flesh. His favorite method is close to a social survey; he has a flair for mingling with the different milieus he studies and getting people to talk; he compares their accounts and, if necessary, he does not hesitate to play Sherlock Holmes, sometimes with considerable talent."[15]

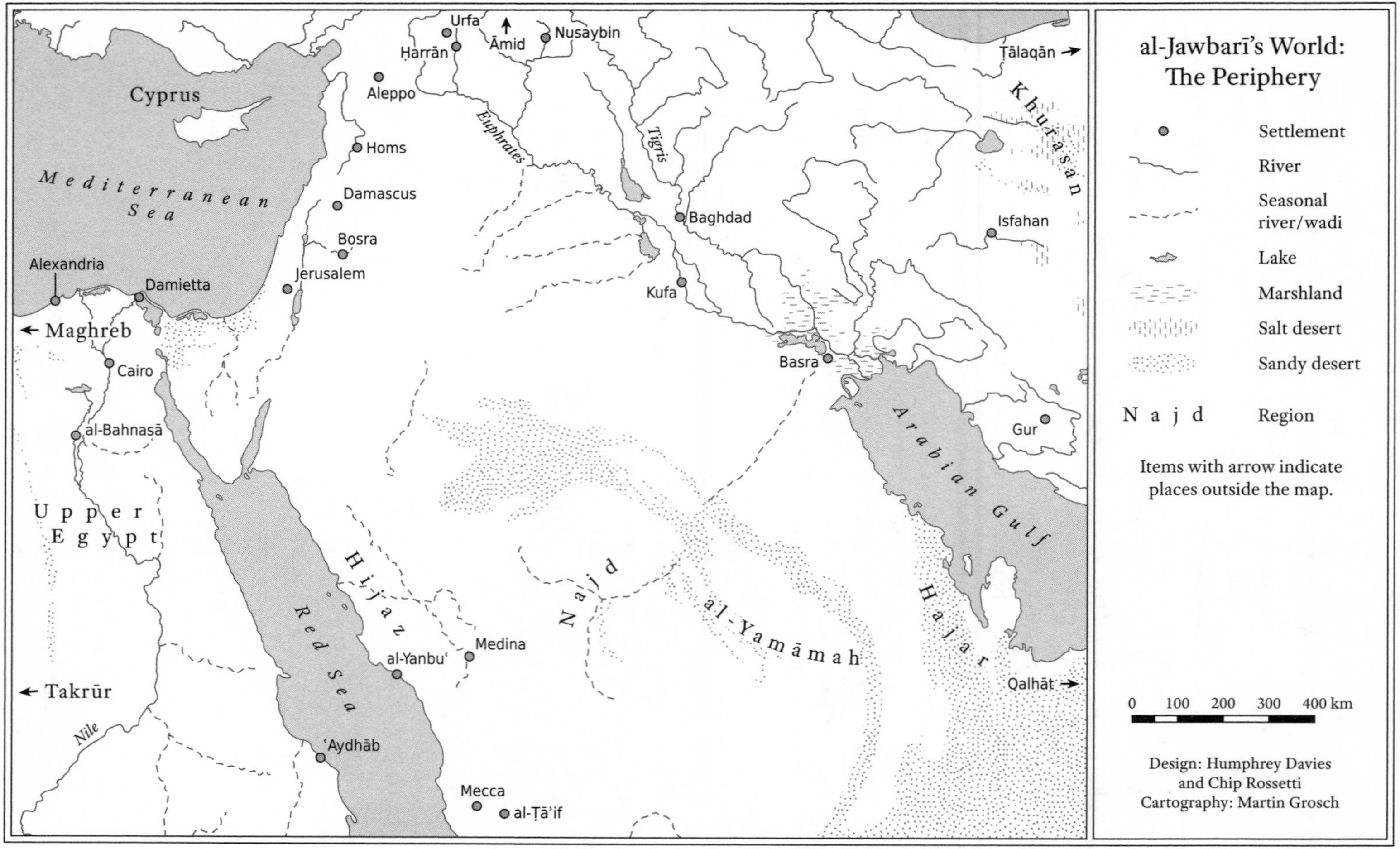

al-Jawbarī's World:
The Periphery
Settlement
River
Seasonal river/wadi
Lake
Marshland
Salt desert
Sandy desert
N a j d
Region
Items with arrow indicate places outside the map.
0 100 200 300 400 km
Design: Humphrey Davies and Chip Rossetti
Cartography: Martin Grosch
Cyprus
Mediterranean Sea
Alexandria
Damietta
Maghreb
Cairo
al-Bahnasā
Upper Egypt
Takrūr
Nile
Jerusalem
Bosra
Damascus
Homs
Aleppo
Ḥarrān
Urfa
Āmid
Nusaybin
Euphrates
Tigris
Baghdad
Kufa
Basra
Ṭālaqān
Khurasan
Isfahan
Gur
Arabian Gulf
Hajar
Qalhāt
al-Yamāmah
Najd
Hijaz
Red Sea
al-Yanbuʿ
Medina
ʿAydhāb
Mecca
al-Ṭāʾif

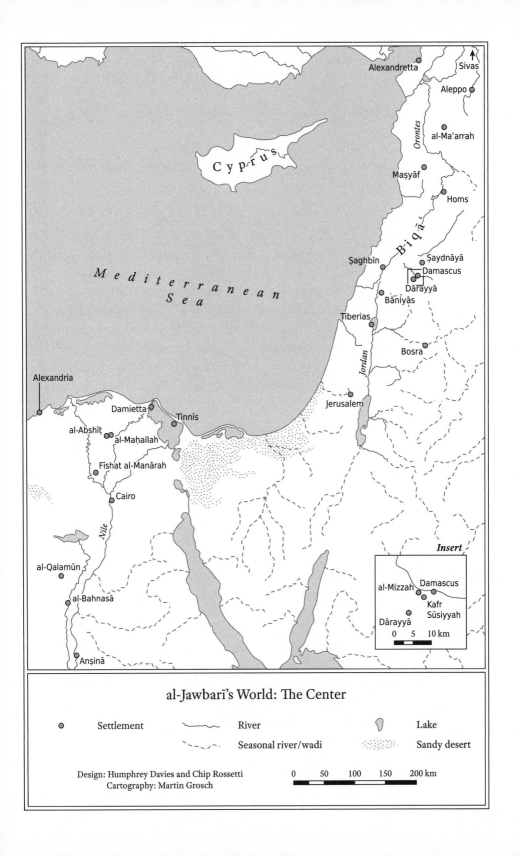

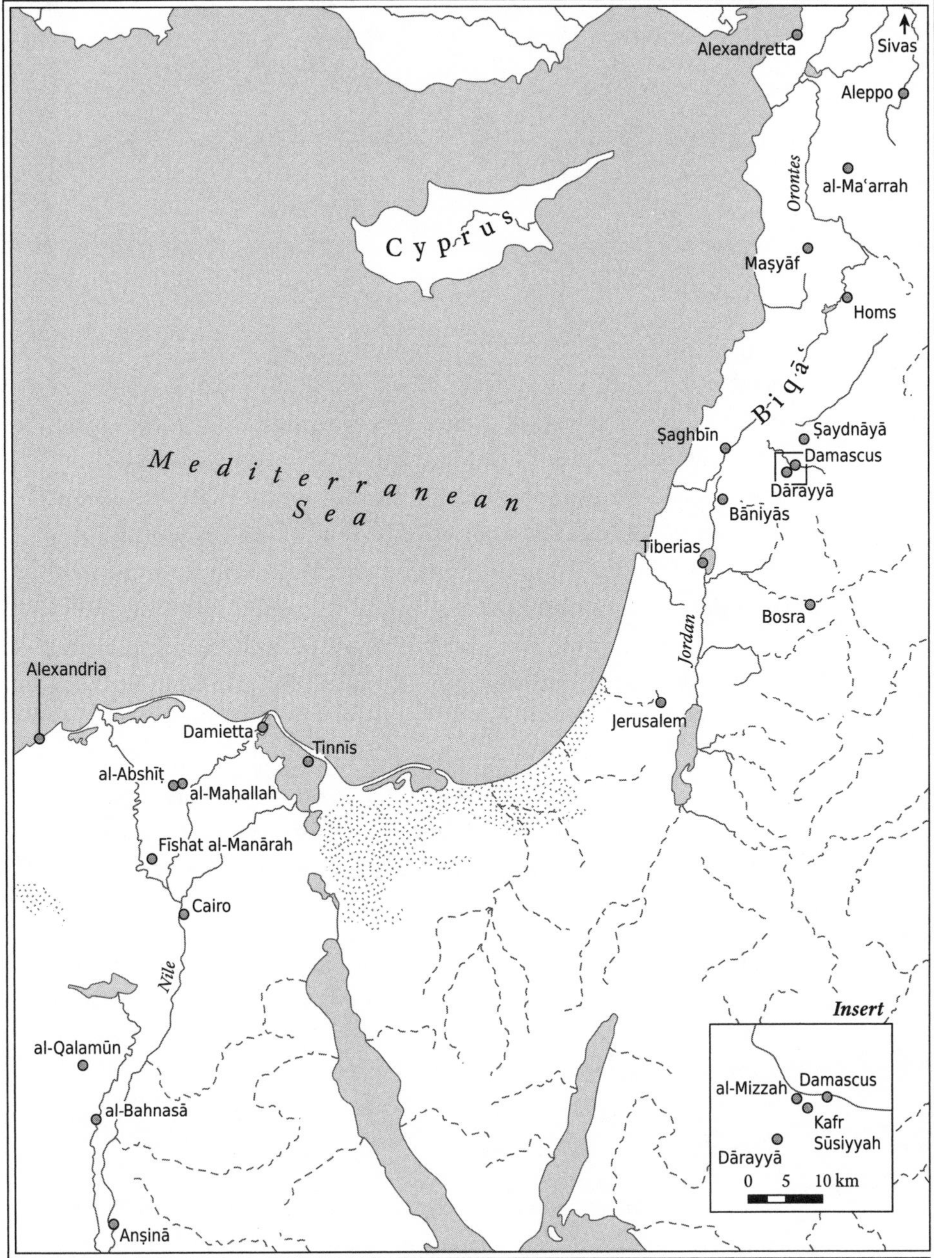

al-Jawbarī's World: The Center

Settlement	River	Lake
	Seasonal river/wadi	Sandy desert

Design: Humphrey Davies and Chip Rossetti
Cartography: Martin Grosch

0 50 100 150 200 km

Note on the Text

The Edition

The number of copies, some of which are in excellent condition, made over the centuries, and the number of modern printed versions are testimony to the great and continuing popularity of this work up to the early twentieth century. The present edition revises an earlier one submitted as a doctoral dissertation at the University of Cologne in the summer of 2004 and subsequently published in 2006 by Klaus Schwarz Verlag.[16] The two manuscripts used in the preparation of that edition are the longest, and in all probability earliest, surviving manuscripts of the work: Istanbul, Süleymaniye Library, Karaçelebizade 253 (microfilm no. 71) and Leiden, University Library, Or 191 (CCO 1222). The Leiden copy was made in 714/1314 and that now in Istanbul in 717/1317–18.[17] These two manuscripts are also in a Middle Arabic likely close to the original; they retain, for example, the charlatans' jargon in roughly hewn form, whereas later copies register a more grammatically polished language, purified and abridged in content and with arcane lexical items sometimes replaced by the copyists' vocabulary. Sigla used in this edition are:

- ش indicates readings from the 2006 Schwarz edition, based on the Leiden and Istanbul manuscripts; departures from the 2006 edition are due to the need to produce translationally viable, as opposed to stemmatically oriented, readings
- في الأصل indicates questionable readings in the manuscripts used as the basis for the 2006 Schwarz edition

Since the plentiful and grammatically and orthographically diverse linguistic characteristics of *The Book of Charlatans*, such as the colloquialisms and the terms drawn from professional jargon, are a determining feature of the work, they have been retained and corrected as little as possible.[18] Some of the main morphological and syntactical features are:

1. incongruence of gender, e.g., هذه الأبريق for هذا الأبريق, الأرجوزة الذي for الأرجوزة التي;
2. final ي as a feminine ending, e.g., عنكي for عنكِ, تأكلي for تأكلين;
3. little distinction between the moods of the imperfect, e.g., يدقوا الجميع for يدقون الجميع, أن يعملون for أن يعملوا, ولم يذكرون for ولم يذكروا;
4. كان together with another verb is not conjugated, e.g., كان اجتمعت for كانت اجتمعت;
5. use of long vowels in the imperative, e.g., قوم for قم, امشي instead of امش;
6. elision of a final consonant, e.g., بينا for بيننا;
7. fluid use of the plural, e.g., هما for هم, هم for ها, هؤلاء القوم for هذا القوم;
8. use of أخير for خير and أشرّ for شرّ;
9. little distinction between case endings, e.g., أيها الخدّام الصالحين for أيها الخدّام الصالحون, له بكرتين for له بكرتان, ذكروه بني موسى for ذكروه بنو موسى, رأيت بدمشق رجل for رأيت بدمشق رجلاً, أشدّ الناس خبث for أشدّ الناس خبثًا, رأيت رجل نجّار مجوسيًا for رأيت رجلاً نجّارًا مجوسيًا, and occasional apparent copyist's hypercorrection, e.g., أسودًا for أسْوَدَ;
10. use of the article with both terms of an *iḍāfah*, e.g., الطير الحمام for طير الحمام, فهذه الأبيات الخمسة for فهذه الخمسة أبيات;
11. irregular agreement in numerals, e.g., سبعة عشر شريعة for سبع عشرة شريعة, خمس الدراهم for خمسة دراهم, أربعة عشر شيخ for أربعة عشر شيخًا;
12. unexpected prepositions with verbs, e.g., تغافل على for تغافل عن.

In other sources, the charlatans' jargon is usually referred to as "the language of Shaykh Sāsān" (*lughat al-Shaykh Sāsān*), "the language of the beggars" (*lughat al-mukaddīn*), "the language of the wonder-workers" (*lughat al-ghurabā'*), or simply "the language" (*al-lughah*).[19] Al-Jawbarī himself uses none of these terms and only rarely draws attention to jargon. When he does so, he typically simply says, "they call [the item in question] X"; thus, speaking of amulets, he says, "There are two kinds of amulet—the smaller, which they call 'slices,' and the larger, which they call 'temples'" (§12.2). The frequent use of jargon without explanation suggests that al-Jawbarī assumed his reader was either already familiar with it or, more likely, could be counted on to deduce meanings from context.[20] He nowhere implies that such terms are intended to be incomprehensible to outsiders.

Al-Jawbarī does, however, single out one particular variety of language as being used for concealment. This variety he refers to as *al-Sīn*, literally "the S."[21] He describes *al-Sīn* as a "form of communication they use for speaking to one another that only they and those who hang out with them understand," and he associates it specifically with astrologers (§27.32). The passage in which he describes it is very brief and the sole example that he provides is, as one might expect, incomprehensible. *Al-Sīn* would indeed appear to be, in contrast to the charlatans' jargon, a "cant" or an "argot," in the sense of a "jargon of criminals and other groups whose professional activities depend on secrecy."[22]

According to Bosworth's classification, four elements play a part in the creation of the beggars' and charlatans' vocabulary: first, phonetic modifications such as assimilation, dissimilation, metathesis, and other substitutions of phonemes; second, morphological modifications such as remodeling the morpheme, extending it with prefixes, infixes, or suffixes, or a combination of all three, shortening words in initial or final positions, or creating onomatopoeic formations; third, semantic modifications such as specialization and severe restriction of meaning, and also using words in a metaphorical, metonymic, euphemistic, opposite, or ironic sense; and fourth, the adoption of loanwords not only from foreign languages but also from the everyday and literary languages contemporary with the jargon speakers, and from urban and rural dialects.[23] Enno Littman, a German scholar of Semitic languages (d. 1958), was of the view that the vocabulary also drew on the jargon of the Romani,[24] noting apropos of beggars' and swindlers' jargon:

> It must be observed to start with that we are here on exceptionally uncertain ground. The words in the charlatans' and vagabonds' language are intentionally and arbitrarily rendered unrecognizable either in form or, when the form is maintained, in meaning. The changes in form are of many kinds . . . . Consequently, the explanation of many words becomes much more difficult. In some cases, one will never get beyond a more or less probable interpretation, and so the reader of my explanations will say, as I do myself: "It could also be quite different."[25]

Furthermore, it is often not possible to be certain whether a given word was specific to a given group and thus qualifies as "jargon." A number of unfamiliar lexical items occurring in the work may be words that occur rarely in the written record simply because they were used by "subalterns" or in environments that were not usually written about. The interested reader will find a vocabulary of rare words occurring in *The Book of Charlatans*, including references to their occurrences in other sources, in an online appendix.[26]

The Translation

Fragments of this work taken from a variety of manuscripts and printed editions have been published previously in English, German, and French, in translation or paraphrase.[27] René Khawam published a complete translation into French in two volumes in 1979–80 but did not identify the four manuscripts on which he states that he relied.[28] This is the first complete translation of the work into English.

The "voice" of the text alternates between formality and informality at the level of narrative structure and at the level of language. Short programmatic descriptions, running from a few dozen to a few hundred words and often introduced by "Example," or "Another Example," or "Exposé" dominate and, with the detailed chapter and subject headings, lend the text an impression of scientific rigor. They are, however, supplemented by much longer illustrative passages, either in the form of anecdotes drawn from the author's life (e.g., §§6.22, 25.2–6), or of edifying tales, perhaps well known at the time (such as that of the enchanted ape, §§6.5–9), or of extended, complex narratives with multiple characters, not unlike short stories (e.g., the tale of "Those Who Work Solomon's Ant," §§7.2–16); many of these include lengthy passages of highly vernacular dialogue. As a result, a tension exists in the book between its scientific aspirations and its down-to-earth pictures from real life, which draw on both the realia and the idiom of the author's day.

A further tension exists in the text between, on the one hand, the presence of Middle Arabic forms, colloquialisms, and grammatical liberties (or errors), and, on the other, a linguistic matrix that aspires to correctness and even, on occasion, to an elevated style. The latter is represented by the deployment of semi-rhyming formulas (typically at the beginning and/or end of a passage, e.g., §§23.1, 27.1) and the use of high-flown vocabulary and grammar, as when a shaykh adjures a mythical creature (§7.2) or the author himself exhorts his readers (§2.34). There are also, as is to be expected, quotations from the Qur'an and Hadith.

In order to capture in the translation this unusual, uneven voice, which gives the book its quirkiness, freshness, and tonal distance from most of the literature of the time, an unadorned idiom tending to the oral has been adopted for passages that do not aspire to grammatical correctness or high style, including the use of contracted verbal forms, anachronistic terms and phrases such as "MO" (for modus operandi), and slang such as "Wise up!" and "Hit me!" (as when dealing cards). However, though anachronisms have been used in nontechnical passages, an opposite logic has been applied to the names of many of the apothecary's ingredients mentioned by the author, whether plant-derived or mineral. For these, archaic terms such as realgar, orpiment, and galia moschata have been used to translate Arabic words that are likely as unfamiliar to an Arabic readership as their equivalents are to an English; English terms of this sort are, however, included in the Glossary.

A feature of the author's style that required special attention is his frequent failure to specify a subject or object for a verb, using instead simple pronoun suffixes. This is especially true of the narrative passages, where the lack of specification perhaps has its origin in the oral nature of these stories, which may have been composed for performance before a live audience, allowing the storyteller to use gestures to clarify the meaning. An example is the story of "Those Who Work Solomon's Ant" (§§7.2–16), with its elaborate sexual choreography, in which it can be unclear to the reader which of four characters is doing what to whom at any given moment. To mitigate this tendency in the text, identifications have often been supplied (e.g., §7.7).

Plants—so frequently referred to in this book—pose a special problem in that any given species may bear many common names, while the scientific names have often changed over the years, especially recently, with the introduction of classifications based on DNA. Plants and fungi mentioned in the translation are listed alphabetically in an online appendix, where all English names in reasonably common usage are given, beginning with the one most widely used, which is also that used in the translation; also included are the item's Arabic name, references to its occurrence in the text, its accepted binomial Latin name (verified using The Plant List and The International Plant Names Index), and a list of the sources, published and online, used to identify it.[29]

Notes to the Introduction

1 For further details and other versions of Shaykh Sāsān's story, see Bosworth, *Underworld*, 22–24.

2 We use this term in the sociolinguistic sense described in Fischer, "What Is Middle Arabic?"

3 Ḥājjī Khalīfah, *Kashf al-ẓunūn*, 2:148.

4 Ḥājjī Khalīfah, *Kashf al-ẓunūn*, 2:1487, 1623; the work mentioned by Ḥājjī Khalīfah, *Kashf al-ẓunūn*, 2:148, under the title *Kashf asrār al-muḥtālīn wa-nawāmīs al-ḥayyālīn* by ʿAbd al-Raḥīm ibn ʿUmar al-Dimashqī al-Ḥarrānī, corresponds to the title of the Karshūnī MS Oxford/Bodleian 73 (Uri 111) in which al-Jawbarī is mentioned by the name of Zayn al-dīn ʿAbd al-Raḥīm ibn ʿUmar al Dimashqī, known as al-Ḥawrānī, of which Steinschneider, "Gauberi's 'entdeckte Geheimnisse,' eine Quelle für orientalische Sittenschilderung," 565–66, observes: "Evidently the Syriac transcriber read الحوراني for جوبري." It thus refers to the *Kashf al-asrār* by al-Jawbarī. On the title "shaykh," see "Shaykh" (E. Geoffroy) in *EI2*.

5 Al-Baghdādī, *Hadiyyat al-ʿārifīn*, 1:524, where the title *Kashf asrār al-muḥtālīn wa-nawāmīs al-khabbālīn* is mistakenly given as a separate work by al-Jawbarī. See preceding note.

6 On this title, which is erroneously listed as a separate work, see n. 4 above.

7 It has been suggested that a manuscript fragment of an *urjūzah* on geomancy preserved in the Forschungsbibliothek in Gotha (MS orient. A 1315) contains the poem referred to here by the author, though the lines quoted in the text (§12.25) are not to be found in that manuscript. See Pertsch, *Die arabischen Handschriften der Herzoglichen Bibliothek zu Gotha*, 2:487.

8 Al-Malik al-Masʿūd Rukn al-Dīn Mawdūd, the last independent ruler of his dynasty, ruled from 619/1222 to 629/1232 over Ḥiṣn Kayfā and Āmid (Diyarbakir) in what is today southeastern Turkey.

9 Aḥmad ibn ʿAbd al-Malik Ibn Shuhayd al-Ashjaʿī was a writer, poet, and vizier born in Cordoba who was nicknamed "the Jāḥiẓ of al-Andalus." His *Fī kashf al-dakk wa-īḍāḥ al-shakk*, which evidently served as a model for al-Jawbarī, has not survived. See "Ibn Shuhayd" (Ch. Pellat) in *EI2*.

10 Thus al-Jawbarī apparently continued to work on his book after Rukn al-Dīn's fall from power in 629/1232 (see n. 8 above).

11 Ḥājjī Khalīfah, *Kashf al-ẓunūn*, 1:694–95.

12 I.e., his *Rawḍat al-ṣafā*, see Ḥājjī Khalīfah, *Kashf al-ẓunūn*, 1:307.

13 Wild, "A Juggler's Programme in Mediaeval Islam," 357.

14 Wild, "Juggler's Programme," 62.

15 Khawam, *Le Voile arraché*, 1:16.

16 Höglmeier, *Al-Ǧawbarī und sein Kašf al-asrār*. For a complete list of surviving cataloged manuscripts and known printed editions, as well as a detailed description of the manuscripts that served as the basis for this edition, see pp. 51–53. The most recent printed edition listed there dates from 1918.

17 Cf. Wild, "Juggler's Programme," 59: "Suffice it to say that the best and most complete text is preserved in two manuscripts now at Leiden and Istanbul."

18 Stefan Wild characterizes the language as "careless Middle Arabic." See "Al-Djawbarī" (S. Wild) in *EI2*.

19 See Bosworth, *Underworld*, 158.

20 Given the tradition in Arabic sources of referring to jargon as *lughah sirriyyah* ("secret language"), it is worth keeping in mind Bosworth's caution (*Underworld*, 153) that "it seems safest to view the evolution of jargons as one manifestation amongst several of social cohesiveness within a special group, rather than of secretiveness." See "Jargon" (E. M. Bergman) in *EALL*, 2:468.

21 *Sīn*, the twelfth letter of the Arabic alphabet, is the first letter of *sīmiyā'*, meaning "natural magic," which may explain its use, as here, to mean "argot, cant."

22 "Jargon," in *EALL* 2:468.

23 Cf. Bosworth, *Underworld*, 154–55

24 Cf. Littmann, *Zigeuner-Arabisch: Wortschatz und Grammatik der arabischen Bestandteile in den morgenländischen Zigeunersprachen*, 23–24.

25 Cf. Littmann, *Zigeuner-Arabisch*, 5.

26 Appendix 1: Vocabulary of Rare Words and Phrases Occurring in *The Book of Charlatans*, www.libraryofarabicliterature.org/extra-2/.

27 The following partial translations and paraphrases are listed in the order in which the passages appear in the original text—introductory material: Cheikho/Wiedemann, "Die Auswahl über die Enthüllung der Geheimnisse al Maschriq (arabisch)," 386–90; Chapter 2: Wild, "Jugglers and Fraudulent Sufis," 60–61; Chapter 4: Wiedemann, *Aufsätze zur arabisch-islamischen Wissenschaftgeschichte* 1:356–59; Chapter 5: Wiedemann, *Aufsätze* 1:769–72; Bosworth, "Jewish Elements in the Banū Sāsān," 10–13; Chapter

6: Horovitz, "Spuren griechischer Mimen im Orient," 23–26; Bosworth, *Underworld* 110; Chapter 8: Wiedemann, *Aufsätze* 1:198, 677–79; Chapter 9: Wiedemann, *Aufsätze* 1:194–97; Wiedemann, *Gesammelte Schriften zur arabisch-islamischen Wissenschaftsgeschichte* 1:263; Abrahams, "Al-Jawbari on False Alchemists," 84–88; Chapter 10: Behrnauer, "Mémoire sur les institutions de police chez les Arabes, les Persans, et les Turcs," 12–14; Wiedemann, *Aufsätze* 1:679–82, 773–74; Wiedemann, *Schriften* I, 306–7; Chapter 14 and Chapter 15: Wiedemann, *Aufsätze* I, 750–69; Wiedemann, *Schriften* 2:764–77; Chapter 16: Wiedemann, *Aufsätze* 1:766–69, note 2; Chapter 17 and Chapter 18: Wiedemann, *Schriften* 1:476–80; Chapter 20: Wiedemann, *Aufsätze* 1:683–85; Chapter 21: Wiedemann, *Aufsätze* 1:772–73; Chapter 23: Wiedemann, *Aufsätze* 1:207–8; Wild, "Juggler's Programme," 354–56; Chapter 24: Wiedemann, *Schriften* 1:278–80, Cheikho/Wiedemann, "Auswahl," 389–90; Chapter 25: Wiedemann, *Aufsätze* 1:106–8; Chapter 27: Wiedemann, *Aufsätze* 1:685–88, 773; Wiedemann, *Schriften* 1:209–10, 301–2; Chapter 29: Bosworth, *Underworld*, 117–18.

28 Khawam, *Le Voile arraché*, 9.

29 Appendix 2: Plants and Fungi Mentioned in *The Book of Charlatans*, www.libraryofarabicliterature.org/extra-2/.

كتاب المختار في كشف الأسرار

The Book of Charlatans

مـــمّا ألّفه الشيخ الفاضل جمال الدين عبد الرحيم بن عمر بن أبي بكر الدمشقيّ المعروف ١،٠
بالجوبريّ وهو يشتمل على ثلاثين فصلاً وعدّة الفصول مائتان وتسعة وسبعون باباً
كاملاً والحمد لله حقّ حمده وصلواته على محمّد خير خلقه وآله وسلّم وشرّف ومجّد وكرّم
صلّى الله عليه وقال مؤلّفه [كامل]

يَا نَاظِـرًا فِيمَا قَـصَدْتُ بِجَمْـعِـهِ   أَعْـذِرْ فَإِنَّ أَخَا ٱلْفَضِيلَةِ يَعْـذِرُ
عِلْمًـا بِأَنَّ ٱلْـمَـرْءَ لَوْ بَلَغَ ٱلْـمَدَى   فِي ٱلْعُمْـرِ فَاتَ ٱلْعُمْـرُ وَهُوَ مُقَصِّرُ
سِيَّمَا وَقَدْ رُمْتُ ٱلْعُلُومَ فَمَا حَصَلَ   إِلَّا ٱلْقَلِيـلُ وَغَابَ عَنِّي ٱلْأَكْثَرُ
وَٱلْعُـذْرُ فِي ٱلتَّقْصِيرِ عَنْ إِدْرَاكِهِ   فِي ٱلْعِـلْمِ مَنْـظُومًا وَفِيمَا يَنْـثُرُ
فَإِذَا ظَـفِـرْتَ بِـزَلَّةٍ فَافْـتَحْ لَهَا   بَابَ ٱلتَّجَـاوُزِ وَٱلتَّجَاوُزُ أَجْدَرُ
وَمِنَ ٱلْمُحَالِ بِأَنْ يُرَى أَحَدٌ حَوَى   وَصْفَ ٱلْكَمَـالِ وَوَصْفُهُ مُتَعَذِّرُ
وَٱلنَّقْـصُ فِي نَفْسِ ٱلطَّبِيعَةِ كَامِنٌ   فَبَنُو ٱلطَّـبِيعَـةِ نَقْصُهُمْ لَا يُذْكَرُ

بسم الله الرحمن الرحيم

وما توفيقي إلّا بالله الحمد لله الملك الأعظم مظهر الموجودات بعد العدم جاعل الأنوار ٢،٠
والظلم ومبدع اللوح والقلم ليصرّفهما في إثبات ما تأخّر من حكمته وتقدّم وصلّى الله
على نبيّه الأكرم المبعوث بالشرع المعظّم والكلم الوجيز المنظّم فصلّى الله عليه وسلّم وكرّم
صلاة يحيّي ويعرّف نسيمها النعيم ويتّقد بنورها من المحلّ الفاني المظلم إلى المحلّ المشرق
المسلم قال العبد الفقير إلى الله تعالى عبد الرحيم بن أبي بكر الدمشقيّ المعروف بالجوبريّ
عفا الله عنه

This is a work of Erudite Shaykh Jamāl al-Dīn ʿAbd al-Raḥīm ibn Abī Bakr al-Dimashqī, known as al-Jawbarī. It consists of thirty chapters made up of a total of 279 sections.[1] God be praised, as is His due, and may He bless Muḥammad, the best of His creation, and cherish him and likewise his family, and honor and ennoble him, peace be upon him! The author of this work says: 0.1

You who look at what I have attempted overall,
excuse my failings, for the virtuous man to such gives no consideration.
He knows that, should a man live life
to its fullest span, yet, when it's over, he still will have fallen short of expectation—
Especially since, though I coveted learning, little of it
was my lot, while the greater part escaped my attempts at appropriation;
And excuse the shortcomings of your servant
in scholarship, be it in mastery of verse or of prose narration,
And when you find indeed a slip, let it slip
through pardon's door, for lenience is worthier of your station.
It is not possible that any will be found to have achieved
the attribute of perfection—an attribute impossible of realization—
For imperfection is in man's very nature ensconced
and nature's children's imperfection defies delineation.

In the Name of God, the Merciful, the Compassionate

—any success I may have being through His agency alone, praise be to Him, the Mightiest King, Who makes existent all that once was nonexistent, Who is the Maker of Light and Dark, Who created the Tablet and the Pen[2] that He might employ them in the establishment of His wisdom, now and of yore! And God bless His noblest prophet, sent with the mighty Law and the succinct well-ordered Word; God bless him, keep him, and ennoble him, with a blessing whose exquisite zephyr both revitalizes and aromatizes, while its light illumines that expanse which lies between the dark land of ephemerality and the bright land of surrender to God's intentionality! 0.2

God's slave, needy of His mercy, ʿAbd al-Raḥīm ibn Abī Bakr al-Dimashqī, known as al-Jawbarī, God excuse him his sins, declares:

٣،٠ أمّا بعد فإنّه لمّا طالعت كتب الحكماء والسادة المتقدّمين من العلماء رأيت ما قد وضعوه من العلوم وقرأت ما وقع إليّ من الكتب من سائر العلوم والفنون مثل علوم الرياضة وغيرها وحصّلت كتب ينبوع الحكمة لآصف بن بَرَخْيا بن شَمْوِيل العشرة الموجودة في زمن نبيّ الله سليمان بن داود عليهما[1] السلام مثل كتاب الطوالق والأَصْطَنّة والجمهرة وسرّ السرّ والمصحف الخفيّ والمصابيح والأفاليق وذات الدوائر وغاية الآمال والأجناس والعهد الكبير فطالعت هذه الكتب العشرة وحللت رموزها ثمّ بحثت على أصول العلوم فوجدت أصل ذلك في كتب الأسفار الخمسة وهو سفر الخفايا وسفر المستقيم المخلّفة عن أبونا آدم عليه السلام ثمّ سفر شيث بن آدم عليه السلام ثمّ سفر نوح عليه السلام ثمّ سفر إبرهيم عليه السلام فحصّلت هذه الأسفار الخمسة ثمّ طالعتها وحللت رموزها ثمّ بحثت عن الأصول فطلبت كتب هِرْمِس المثلّث وهو إدريس عليه السلام ويقال المثلّث بالحكمة لأنّ بعض الحكماء كان ملك وحكيم مثل بَطْلِمُيوس والإسكندر ولاذَن وغيرهما ولم يكن لهما درجة النبوّة ويقال المثلّث لأنّه كان له ثلاثة أسماء اسمه في الأصل أخنوخ وسمّي إدريس لكثرة دراسته الكتب فطالعت له عشرة كتب أوّلها كتاب الهاديطوس وآخرهما الميلاطيس الأكبر ولولا خوف الإطالة وتوسّع الدائرة وإلّا لذكرت جميع أسماء الكتب وذكرت كلّ كتاب وما يقتضي وما يختصّ ولكن قصدنا الاختصار

٤،٠ ثمّ طالعت كتب الحكماء المتقدّمين مثل طُمْطُم الفيلسوف وشرف وبَليناس ودَعْميوس ولاذن وإِسْطَخْر[2] وأفلاطون ومارِية وإشراسيم وسيرا وكَنْكَه وأراطو[3] وأَرِسطوطاليس وهُرْمُزان وصَصَه وابن تميم وبمثلهما من العلماء الكبار وأصحاب الهياكل ممّن لم أسمّه خوف الإطالة وأمّا العلماء المتأخّرون مثل ابن سينا وابن وَحْشيّة وجابر بن حيّان والخوارزميّ وابن خطيب الريّ وصالح بن أبي صالح المُدَيْبِريّ وابن قَنّان ولَوْهَق بن عَرْفَجة وابن عصفور وخلف بن سعيد بن يوسف وعبد الله بن هلال الكوفيّ والعبادلة فهم خمسة وقد ذكرهم الفخر الرازيّ في كتابه السرّ المكتوم ومثل أبو القاسم ذا النون

١ ش: عليه. ٢ ش: أراسطو وإسطخر. ٣ ش: وأراسطو.

When I perused the books of the sages and scholarly gentlemen of old, I looked into all the scientific fields they had established and read all I could of the various arts and sciences, such as mathematics and the like. I obtained the ten books—those founts of wisdom!—of Āṣaf ibn Barakhyā ibn Shamwīl, which already existed at the time of God's prophet Solomon, son of David, eternal peace be theirs, and which consist of the following:[3] *The Released, The Aṣṭannah,*[4] *The Multitude, The Innermost Secret, The Concealed Codex, The Lamps, The Wonders, That of the Circles, The Ultimate Hope and the Kinds,* and *The Great Covenant.* I studied these, deciphered their symbols, and then went searching for the fundamentals of those same sciences, finding them in the Five Codices:[5] *The Codex of Hidden Things, The Codex of the Straight Path* (left to us by our father Adam, eternal peace be his), *The Codex of Seth* (who was the son of Adam, eternal peace be his), *The Codex of Noah* (eternal peace be his), and *The Codex of Abraham* (eternal peace be his). These five works I acquired too and studied, and likewise deciphered their symbols. Then I went looking for what lay behind these and searched for the works of Hermes Trismegistus, who is Idrīs, eternal peace be his, also known as Trismegistus—the Threefold-in-Wisdom—because he was one of those sages, such as Ptolemy, Alexander, Lādhan, and others, who were kings and wise men but did not have the rank of prophethood. Another reason for his being called the Threefold is that he had three names: His original name was Akhnūkh, and he was also called Idrīs because he studied so many books.[6] I studied ten works of his, the first being *The Book of al-Hādīṭūs,* the last *The Book of al-Mīlāṭīs the Great.* If I weren't afraid of boring you and anxious to stick to the matter at hand, I'd list them all by name, with a description of each, what it requires by way of preparatory study, and what it's about. I am determined, however, to keep things concise. 0.3

I then studied the books of such ancient sages as Ṭumṭum the Philosopher, Sharaf, Apollonius, Daʿmiyūs, Lādhan, Isṭakhr, Plato, Māriyā, Ishrāsīm, Sīrā, Kanakah, Aratos, Aristotle,[7] Hurmuzān, Ṣaṣah, Ibn Tamīm, and other similar outstanding scholars and masters of the great magic formulas, whom I haven't listed for fear of boring you. I also studied modern scholars such as Ibn Sīnā, Ibn Waḥshiyyah, Jābir ibn Ḥayyān, al-Khawārazmī, Ibn Khaṭīb al-Rayy, Ṣāliḥ ibn Abī Ṣāliḥ al-Mudaybirī, Ibn Qannān, Lawhaq ibn ʿArfajah, Ibn ʿUṣfūr, Khalaf ibn Saʿīd ibn Yūsuf, ʿAbd Allāh ibn Hilāl al-Kūfī, and the five ʿAbd Allāhs mentioned by Fakhr al-Dīn al-Rāzī in his *Well-Kept Secret,* as well as others, 0.4

المصريّ الإخْميميّ وغيرهما ممّن لم أسمّه فحصّلت كتب هؤلاء العلماء وغيرهما إلى أن حصلت نيف وثلاثمائة كتاب

٥،٠ ثمّ قرأت جميع الكتب الموضوعة في فنون النواميس مثل حيل بني موسى ونواميس أفلاطون وكتاب الباهر وغيرهما من النواميس ثمّ أخذت في كشف دكّها وقرأت كتاب ابن شُهَيد المغربيّ في كشف الدكّ وإيضاح الشكّ ثمّ كتاب ابن شهيد النيسابوريّ مثله ثمّ كتاب إرخاء الستور والكِلَل في كشف المِدكّات والحيل فطالعت هذه الكتب

٦،٠ ثمّ بعد ذلك طالعت كتب علم الرمل فحصّلت منها أربعة عشر كتاباً لأربعة عشر شيخ أوّلهم طُمْطُم ثمّ الزَناتيّ وآخرهم أبو الخير وكان أعلم علماء الرمل في زمانه وقد اجتمعت به وصاحبته ثمّ قرأت الكتب المتعلّقة بعلم الفلك من علم الأزياج والأحكام وأحكام الدرج بشيء يعجز عن معرفة أسمائها فضلا عن معرفتها وما يتضمّن كلّ كتاب منها من العلوم فلمّا طالعت هذه الكتب سألني بعض أصحابي أن أصنف له مدخلاً في علم التنجيم والروحانيّة ففعلت ذلك وعملت كتاباً في علم التنجيم ووسمته بالصراط المستقيم في علم الروحانيّة وصناعة التنجيم ثمّ صنعت كتاباً ملخّصاً منظوماً في علم الرمل يحتوي على أصول الرمل وفروعه

٧،٠ ثمّ لمّا جرى في مجلس مولانا السلطان الأعظم الملك المسعود أعزّ الله أنصاره ذكر كتاب ابن الشهيد وما كشف فيه من ذكر أرباب الصنائع والعلوم فأحضر الكتاب ثمّ طالعه وتعجّب من ذلك وقال لي ما تقول فيه وما اقصر فقلت ما كان إلّا فاضل وما عسى أن يقال في الفضلاء فقال اعمل كتاباً تحذو فيه حذوه وتسلك فيه طريقته بل يكون أقلّ مسلك وأوضح معاني فاستقلت[١] من ذلك فلم يقلني

٨،٠ فلمّا لم أجد بدّاً من ذلك بدأت على اسم الله وحسن عونه وعملت هذا الكتاب ووسمته بكتاب المختار في كشف الأسرار وهو يشتمل على ثلاثون فصلاً كلّ فصل

---

١ ش: فاقتلت.

such as Abū l-Qāsim Dhā l-Nūn al-Ikhmīmī, whom I will not list. In the end, I got up to around three hundred books.

Next, I read all the compilations on the arts of illusion, such as the Banū Mūsā's *Book of Ingenious Devices*, Plato's *Book of Illusions*, a book called *The Brilliant*, and others. Then I began to look into and expose the chicanery associated with these arts and read Ibn Shuhayd al-Maghribī's *Deceit Disrobed and Doubt Dispelled*, followed by Ibn Shuhayd al-Nīsābūrī's work on the same subject, as well as *The Book of the Drawing Aside of Curtains and Screens to Expose Deceptive and Crafty Schemes*. Every one of these books I studied. 0.5

I next studied books on geomancy. I got hold of fourteen of these, by fourteen shaykhs—the first Ṭumṭum, another al-Zanātī, and the last Abū l-Khayr, the most knowledgeable geomancer of his day; I met him, spent time with him, and took him as my teacher. After that, I read so many books related to astronomy—including the science of astronomical tables, of astrology, and of astronomical degrees—that I can no longer remember their names or even what they were and what each was about! Once I'd studied these books, a friend asked me to put together for him an introduction to the science of astrology and the celestial bodies, so I wrote such a book and called it *The Straight Path to the Science of Celestial Bodies and the Astrologers' Craft*.[8] I then composed a summary in verse of the science of geomancy, covering both its fundamentals and its branches.[9] 0.6

Later, when Ibn Shuhayd's book, with its exposés of "the masters of the crafts and sciences,"[10] cropped up in conversation at the salon of Our Lord, Mightiest of Sultans, al-Malik al-Masʿūd, God lend strength to his supporters, he had the book brought, looked through it, and was astounded. "What do you think of it?" he asked me. "What did he leave out?" "He was certainly a great authority, and what can one say about great authorities?" I replied. "Put together a book," he said, "that follows his method and takes the same approach, but make it shorter and easier to understand." I asked him to excuse me, but he wouldn't let me off. 0.7

When I saw there was no getting out of it, I set to, invoking God's name and asking for His gracious help, and put together this book, which I have titled *The Book Containing a Selection Concerning the Exposure of Secrets*. 0.8

منها يحتوي على عدّة الأبواب والفصول مائتان وتسعة وسبعون باباً

الفصل الأوّل أربعة عشر باباً في كشف أسرار الذين يدّعون النبوّة
الفصل الثاني أربعة وعشرون باباً في كشف أسرار الذين يدّعون المشيخة
الفصل الثالث أربعة أبواب في كشف أسرار الوعّاظ وما يعملون
الفصل الرابع خمسة أبواب في كشف أسرار الرهبان وما يعملون
الفصل الخامس خمسة أبواب في كشف أسرار اليهود وفعلهم
الفصل السادس ثمانية أبواب في كشف أسرار بني ساسان وفعلهم
الفصل السابع بابين في كشف أسرار الذين يمشّون بالنملة السليمانيّة
الفصل الثامن سبعة أبواب في كشف أسرار أصحاب السلاح والحرب
الفصل التاسع تسعة أبواب في كشف أسرار أهل الكاف وهو الكيمياء
الفصل العاشر اثنا عشر باباً في كشف أسرار العطّارين
الفصل الحادي عشر خمسة أبواب في كشف أسرار أصحاب الميم وهو المطالب
الفصل الثاني عشر تسعة أبواب في كشف أسرار المنجّمين أرباب الطريق
الفصل الثالث عشر ثلاثة عشر باباً في كشف أسرار المعزّمين وفعلهم
الفصل الرابع عشر اثنا وعشرون باباً في كشف أسرار أصحاب الطريق في الطبّ
الفصل الخامس عشر ستّة أبواب في كشف أسرار الذين يخرجون الدود من الضرس
الفصل السادس عشر باب واحد في كشف أسرار أصحاب الحديد من الكحّالين
الفصل السابع عشر ستّة أبواب في كشف أسرار الذين يصبغوا الخيل

It comprises thirty chapters—each divided into sections, of which there are a total of 279—as follows: [11]

Chapter One, in Fourteen Sections: Exposé of the Tricks of Fake Prophets
Chapter Two, in Twenty-Four Sections: Exposé of the Tricks of Fake Shaykhs
Chapter Three, in Four Sections: Exposé of the Tricks of Fire-and-Brimstone Preachers and What They Get Up To
Chapter Four, in Five Sections: Exposé of the Tricks of Monks and What They Get Up To
Chapter Five, in Five Sections: Exposé of the Tricks of Jews and Their Doings
Chapter Six, in Eight Sections: Exposé of the Tricks of the Banū Sāsān and Their Doings
Chapter Seven, in Two Sections: Exposé of the Tricks of Those Who Work Solomon's Ant
Chapter Eight, in Seven Sections: Exposé of the Tricks of Those Who Bear Arms and Practice War
Chapter Nine, in Nine Sections: Exposé of the Tricks of "the People of *Kāf*," That Is, Alchemists
Chapter Ten, in Twelve Sections: Exposé of the Tricks of Apothecaries
Chapter Eleven, in Five Sections: Exposé of the Tricks of "the People of *Mīm*," That Is, Treasure Hunters
Chapter Twelve, in Nine Sections: Exposé of the Tricks of Astrologers Who Ply Their Trade on the Highway
Chapter Thirteen, in Thirteen Sections: Exposé of the Tricks and Doings of Spirit Conjurors
Chapter Fourteen, in Twenty-Two Sections: Exposé of the Tricks of Those Who Practice Medicine on the Highway
Chapter Fifteen, in Six Sections: Exposé of the Tricks of Those Who Extract Worms from Teeth
Chapter Sixteen, in One Section: Exposé of the Tricks of Eye Doctors Who Use Metal Instruments
Chapter Seventeen, in Six Sections: Exposé of the Tricks of Those Who Dye Horses

الفصل الثامن عشر عشرة أبواب في كشف أسرار الذين يصبغون بني آدم
الفصل التاسع عشر ثلاثة أبواب في كشف أسرار الذين يلعبون بالنار
الفصل العشرون ثمانية أبواب في كشف أسرار الذين يعملون الطعم
الفصل الحادي والعشرون خمسة أبواب في كشف أسرار الذين يمشّون بالعلفات
الفصل الثاني والعشرون ستّة أبواب في كشف أسرار الكتّاب أصحاب الشروط
الفصل الثالث والعشرون ثمانية أبواب في كشف أسرار المشعوذين
الفصل الرابع والعشرون احدى عشر باباً في كشف أسرار الجوهريّة وأعمالهم
الفصل الخامس والعشرون ستّة أبواب في كشف أسرار الصيارف والدكّ عليهم
الفصل السادس والعشرون باب واحد في كشف أسرار الذين يدبّون على المردان
الفصل السابع والعشرون اثنان وثلاثون باباً في كشف أسرار أرباب الصنائع مجمل
الفصل الثامن والعشرون ثلاثة أبواب في كشف أسرار اللصوص الهجّامين
الفصل التاسع والعشرون أربعة أبواب في كشف أسرار اللصوص أصحاب النقوب
الفصل الثلاثون بابين في كشف أسرار النساء وما لهم من الدهاء والمكر وقلّة الحياء وهو خاتمة الكتاب

الفصل الأوّل

أربعة عشر باباً

في كشف أسرار الذين يدّعون النبوّة

اعلم وفّقك الله ورعاك أنّ الأنبياء صلوات الله عليهم والمرسلين فلا طعن عليهم ولا في نبوّاتهم وإرسالهم إلى الأمم مع ما قد أمدّهم الله عزّ وجلّ من القوّة والتقدّم في الأمور الصعاب فهذه قوّة متّصلة بهم من الله عزّ وجلّ وهي المادّيّة الإلهيّة منها صبروا على المجاهدة وأداء الرسالة وتبلّغها لطفاً من الله عزّ وجلّ وبهم عرفت الطريق إلى الخالق جلّت قدرته وإن كانت الشرائع مختلفة فمن سلك سبيل ذلك النبيّ الذي أرسل إليه وإلى قومه وتبع شريعته ولم يبدّل ولم يغيّر ولم يتبع الهوى فقد تبع الحقّ لأنّ الأنبياء صلوات الله عليهم لم يبعثهم الله عزّ وجلّ بالباطل وما جاءوا إلّا بالحقّ من الله عزّ وجلّ ١،١

وقد قال النبيّ صلّى الله عليه وسلّم إن لله مائة وسبعة عشر شريعة من وافاها بخلق رضيّ دخل الجنّة واعلم أنّ الأنبياء لم تزل تأتي بما أمرهم الله عزّ وجلّ به إلى أن بعث سيّد الأوّلين والآخرين محمّد خاتم النبيّين صلّى الله عليه وسلّم وشرّف وكرّم فنسخت شريعته جميع الشرائع فلزم كلّ من كان على شريعة أن يتركها ويتبع شريعة سيّد المرسلين ثمّ أنزل عليه الكتاب العزيز الذي لا يأتيه الباطل من بين يديه ولا من خلفه فنسخ جميع الكتب وقد قال تعالى مخبرًا عن دين نبيّه ﴿إِنَّ ٱلدِّينَ عِندَ ٱللَّهِ ٱلْإِسْلَٰمُ﴾ ٢،١

Chapter One, in Fourteen Sections:

Exposé of the Tricks of Fake Prophets

Know, God grant you prosperity and protection, that the prophets, God's blessings upon them, and those whom God has sent as messengers are beyond reproach, as are their missions to all nations and the strength and drive with which God, Mighty and Exalted, has endowed them, in order that they might see difficult affairs through to their end. This strength they derive directly from God, Mighty and Exalted; it is the Divine Materiality—a grace bestowed by God, Mighty and Exalted, through which they find the patience they need to struggle, carry out their mission, and transmit their message. Through them the road to the Creator, may His power be exalted, can be known, though the paths may differ. Anyone who walks the way of the prophet who was sent to him and his people and follows his path without switching or changing or running after his own whims, follows the truth, because God, Mighty and Exalted, does not dispatch His prophets, God's blessings upon them, to bring falsehood; they bring from God, Mighty and Exalted, only truth. 1.1

The Prophet, God bless him and cherish him, has said, "There are 117 paths to God; anyone who follows any of them faithfully, with a willing heart, will enter Paradise."[12] Prophets kept on coming, bringing whatever God commanded them to bring, up to the time when He sent the Lord of all Humankind, from first to last—Muḥammad, Seal of the Prophets, God bless, cherish, honor, and ennoble him! His path superseded all others, and anyone who followed another was required to leave it and follow that of the Lord of Messengers. God then revealed to him the Precious Book, which admits of no falsehood from anywhere and which has superseded all other revelations. Speaking of the religion brought by His prophet, God has said, «Surely, the true religion in God's sight is Islam.»[13] 1.2

٣،١ فأمّا من ادّعى بعد نبيّنا صلّى الله عليه وسلّم النبوّة فقد كذّبه الله عزّ وجلّ إذ قال ﴿وَلَٰكِن رَّسُولَ ٱللَّهِ وَخَاتَمَ ٱلنَّبِيِّۦنَ﴾ وقال النبيّ عليه السلام لا نبيّ بعدي فمن ادّعى هذا المقام بعده فقد طعن في نبيّنا عليه السلام وإنّ الله أظهره على ما يكون بعده فأخبر عنه فكذّب دعوى من ادّعى النبوّة بعده فقال لا نبيّ بعدي فقال إنّ الذي يأتي بعدي فاحصبوه علماً بمن يدّعي بعده النبوّة

الباب الأوّل في كشف أسرارهم

٤،١ أوّل من ادّعى النبوّة رجل يُعرف بنَجدة بن عامر الحنفيّ الخارج باليمامة ويقال له أبو ثمامة ومسيلمة الكذّاب وكان خبيراً بالمخيّلات فأوراهم المخَرَقات وتبعه خلق كثير وقتله خالد بن الوليد رحمه الله

الباب الثاني في كشف أسرار من ادّعى النبوّة

٥،١ وقد كان ظهر في آخر خلافة السفّاح بإصفهان رجل يُعرف بإسحٰق الأخرس فادّعى النبوّة وتبعه خلق كثير وسلك[١] إلى البصرة وعمان وفرض على الناس فرائض وفسّر لهم القرآن على ما أراد ثمّ قُتل وكان من حديثه أنّه نشأ بالمغرب فتعلّم القرآن ثمّ قرأ التوراة والإنجيل والزبور وجميع الكتب المنزّلة ثمّ قرأ الشرائع ثمّ حلّ الرموز والأقلام ولم يخلّ من علم حتّى أتقنه ثمّ ادّعى أنّه أخرس وسافر فنزل إصفهان وخدم قيّم في مدرسة فأقام بها عشر سنين وعرف جميع أهلها وكبارها

٦،١ ثمّ بعد ذلك أراد الدعوة فعمل له أدهان إذا دهن منها وجهه لا يمكنه أن ينظر أحد إليه من شدّة الأنوار ثمّ نام في المدرسة وغلق عليه الأبواب فلمّا ناموا الناس

---

١ ش: ملك.

It follows that anyone who comes after our prophet, God bless him and keep him, and claims prophethood, denies God's truth, for the Mighty and Exalted has said, «but the Messenger of God and the Seal of the Prophets»[14] and the Prophet, God bless him, has said, «There will be no prophet after me.»[15] Anyone, then, who lays claim to that station after him defames our prophet, God bless him. God had shown him what would happen after him, and he conveyed this by saying, "There will be no prophet after me," to give the lie to anyone who might thereafter lay claim to prophethood. He also said, knowing what the fake prophets who came after him would be like, "Anyone who claims to succeed me should be stoned!"[16] 1.3

Section One of the Exposé of Their Tricks

The first person to claim to be a prophet was a man called Najdah ibn ʿĀmir al-Ḥanafī, who led his revolt in al-Yamāmah; he was also called Abū Thumāmah and Musaylimah the Liar. He was an expert at producing illusions and showed the people conjuring tricks. Large numbers followed him. He was killed by Khālid ibn al-Walīd, God have mercy on the latter's soul. 1.4

Section Two of the Exposé of the Tricks of Fake Prophets

In the last days of the caliphate of al-Saffāḥ, a man known as Isḥāq the Mute[17] appeared in Isfahan. He claimed to be a prophet and attracted a large following. He made his way to Basra and Oman, where he imposed certain religious obligations on people,[18] interpreting the Qur'an for them as he pleased, but was killed soon after.[19] He claimed to have been born in northwest Africa and to have studied the Qur'an, the Torah, the Gospel, the Psalms, and all the other revealed texts. After these, he claimed to have studied the legal rulings of the various religions and deciphered symbols and writing systems till there was not a science left that he hadn't mastered. He then traveled to Isfahan, where he settled, working as a head monitor at a school and claiming to be mute. He lived there ten years and got to know everyone, including the city's notables. 1.5

He then decided the time had come to spread his message. He concocted ointments that prevented anyone from looking him in the face when he applied them because they gave off such a bright light. Then he went to the schoolhouse 1.6

وهدت الحواسّ قام فدهن وجهه من ذلك الدهن ثمّ أوقد شمعتان مصبوغة لها أنوار ليست كالشمع ثمّ صرخ صرخة أزعج الناس ثمّ أتبعها ثانية وثالثة ثمّ انتصب في المحراب يصلّي ويقرأ القرآن بصوت أطيب ما يكون بنغمة ألذّ من النسيم فلمّا سمعوا الفقهاء تواثبوا وأشرفوا عليه وهو على تلك الحالة لحارت أفكارهم من ذلك ثمّ أعلموا المعشر المدرّس ذلك فأشرف عليه وهو على تلك الحالة

٧،١ فلمّا رآه خرّ مغشيّاً عليه فلمّا أفاق عمد إلى باب المدرسة ليفتحه فلم يقدر على ذلك فخرج من المدرسة وتبعه الفقهاء حتّى انتهى إلى دار القاضي والمدينة قد شاشت فأخبر القاضي بذلك فخرج القاضي واتّصل الخبر بالوزير واجتمع الناس على باب المدرسة وهو قد فتح الأقفال وترك الأبواب غير مفتّحة فلمّا صار القاضي والمدرّس وكبراء البلد إلى الباب اطّلع عليه الفقهاء وقالوا بالذي أعطاك هذه الدرجة افتح لنا الباب فأشار بيده إلى الباب وقال تفتّحي أيّتها الأقفال فسمعوا وقع الأقفال إلى الأرض فدخل الناس وسأله القاضي عن ذلك فقال إنّه له منذ أربعين يوماً يرى في المكان أثر دليل ويطّلع على أسرار الخلق ويراها عياناً

٨،١ فلمّا كان في هذه الليلة أتاني ملكان فأيقظاني وغسّلاني ثمّ سلّما عليّ بالنبوّة فقالا السلام عليك يا نبيّ الله فخفت من ذلك وطلبت أن أردّ عليهم السلام فلم أطق وجعلت أتململ على ردّ الجواب فلم أقدر على ذلك فقال أحدهما افتح فاك وقل بسم الله الأزليّ ففتحت فمي وأنا أقول في قلبي بسم الله الأزليّ فجعل في فمي شيئاً أبيض ما أعلم ما هو بل أبرد من الثلج وأحلى من العسل وأذكى من المسك فلمّا وقع في أمعائي نطق لساني فكان أوّل ما قلت أشهد أنّ لا إله إلّا الله وأشهد أنّ محمّداً رسول الله فقالا[١] جميعاً وأنت رسول الله حقّاً فقلت ما هذا الكلام أيّها السادة فقالا إنّ الله قد بعثك نبيّاً فقلت وكيف ذلك والله قد أخبر عن سيّدنا محمّد أنّه خاتم النبيّين فقالوا صدقت ولكن أراد الله بذلك أنّه خاتم النبيّين الذي على غير ملّته وشريعته فقلت

١ ش: فقال.

to sleep and locked himself in. When all were asleep, and none could hear a peep, he set about applying some of the said ointments. Then he lit two dyed candles that gave off a different light from ordinary candles and uttered a great cry that woke everyone up, following it with a second cry and a third. Then he stood in the prayer niche, praying and reciting the Qur'an in a most exquisite voice and to a tune sweeter than any breeze. When the men of religion heard, they leapt up and went, all agog, and looked in on him through the window, and didn't know what to make of it. The crowd informed the schoolteacher of what was going on and he too observed him in that state.

Now, when the schoolteacher saw the man, he fell to the ground in a faint. 1.7 On coming around, he made straight for the schoolhouse door but couldn't open it, so he left the school and made for the judge's house, followed by the men of religion, the city being now in an uproar. He told the judge what had happened, so the judge came down from his house. Word reached the vizier too, and everyone gathered at the schoolhouse door. Isḥāq had unlocked the door but left it closed. When the judge, schoolteacher, and notables got there, the men of religion caught sight of him and said, "In the name of the One who has granted you this standing, open the door to us!" at which the man gestured with his hand toward the door and said, "Open, ye locks!" and they heard the locks fall to the ground. Everyone entered and the judge asked him what was going on. He answered that for the past forty days he had found evidence in that place that pointed to his being a prophet: He had been able to observe people's secret doings and see these with his naked eye.

"And last night," he went on, "two angels came. They woke me and washed 1.8 me and then saluted me as one would a prophet, saying, 'Greetings to you, Prophet of God!' This frightened me and I tried to return their greeting but couldn't produce a sound and, as I tried without success to respond, I began to writhe. One of them then said, 'Open your mouth and say, "In the name of God, Whose Eternity Has No Beginning!"' so I opened my mouth and said, in my heart, 'In the name of God, Whose Eternity Has No Beginning!' and some white stuff formed in my mouth. I don't know what it was, but it was cooler than ice, sweeter than honey, more fragrant than musk. When it reached my insides, my tongue broke its silence, the first thing I said being, 'I bear witness that there is no god but God and I bear witness that Muḥammad is the messenger of God,' to which they both responded, in unison, 'And you too are a messenger of God, for sure.' 'What are you saying, gentlemen?' I asked, and they replied, 'That

إنّي[1] لا أدّعي ذلك فلا أصدّق ولا لي معجزات بها فقالا جميعاً فوقع في قلوب الناس صدقك بعد أن كنت أخرس منذ خلقت

٩،١ وأمّا المعجزات التي أعطاك الله عزّ وجلّ فهي معرفة كتبه المنزّلة على أنبيائه ومعرفة شرائعه ومعرفة الألسن والأقلام ثمّ قالا اقرأ القرآن فقرأته كما أنزل ثمّ قالا اقرأ التوراة والإنجيل والزبور والصحف فقرأت الجميع كما أنزل فقالا قم فانذر الناس ثمّ انصرفوا عنّي فقمت وأنا أصلّي وهذا آخر خبري فمن آمن بالله وبمحمّد ثمّ بي ﴿فَقَدْ فَازَ﴾ ومن كذّب فقد عطّل شريعة محمّد وهو كافر والسلام فعند ذلك سمع له خلق كثير وكان ظهر الدرس الذي له وقام وسلك[2] إلى البصرة وعمان فاستفحل أمره ولم يزل كذلك حتّى قتل وله شيعة بعمان إلى يومنا هذا

الباب الثالث في كشف أسرار من ادّعى النبوّة

١٠،١ وقد ظهر في سنة اثنين وخمسين ومائتين رجل يقال له أبو سعيد الحسن بن سعيد الجنّابيّ القرمطيّ وادّعى النبوّة وملك هجر والبحرين وعمان ونهب وسبى وهتك حرم الإسلام وكان مع ذلك مريضا قد بطل شقّه الأيسر وكان يحمل حملا فيوضع على ظهر فرسه واختلف الناس في اسمه فقال قوم قرمط رجل انتمى إليه أبو سعيد فعرف به وقال قوم قرمطونة قرية خرج منها أبو سعيد فكان أعرف الناس بنواميس أفلاطون وأكثر مخاريقه وذُبح أبو سعيد في الحمّام سنة ثلاثمائة وخلّف سبع بنين وهم سعيد

١ ش: إنّه. ٢ ش: ملك. ٣ ش: القبطيّ.

God has sent you as a prophet.' 'How can that be,' I said, 'when God Himself has declared that Our Lord Muḥammad is the seal of all the prophets?' 'True,' they said, 'but what he meant was that he was the seal of the prophets *who were not of his own religious community or path.*' 'I cannot claim to be one,' I said, 'for I do not speak God's word and have performed no miracles,' to which they replied, in unison, 'Men have accepted in their hearts that you speak God's word because, from the day you were born until today, you were mute.

"'As for the miraculous powers granted you by God, Mighty and Exalted, they are knowledge of the books He revealed to His prophets, knowledge of His revealed paths, and knowledge of languages and writing systems.' Then they said, 'Recite the Qur'an!' and I recited it as it was revealed. Then they said, 'Recite the Torah, the Gospel, the Psalms, and the other scriptures!' and I recited them all as they were revealed. 'Arise and preach to the people!' they said, and left. So I arose, praying the whole time, and that's the long and the short of it. Whoever believes in God, Muḥammad, and then me «will surely triumph»[20] and anyone who calls me a liar has abandoned the path of Muḥammad and is an infidel, and that's all there is to it." At this, many heeded him, his studies paid off, and he set out for Basra and Oman, where he became a formidable presence and remained so until he was killed. He has partisans in Oman to this day. 1.9

Section Three of the Exposé of the Tricks of Fake Prophets

In the year 252 [866–67], a man called Abū Saʿīd al-Ḥasan ibn Saʿīd al-Jannābī al-Qarmaṭī appeared, claiming to be a prophet and the king of Hajar, Bahrain, and Oman. He looted, took captives, and violated Islam's sacred precinct, even though he was an invalid (his left side was paralyzed and he had to be lifted onto his horse). People differed over his name, some saying that Abū Saʿīd had belonged to a man called Qarmaṭ, whose name he then adopted, others that he mounted his revolt from a village called Qarmaṭūnah. He was well versed in Plato's *Book of Illusions* and performed many of the conjuring tricks described in it. He was slaughtered in a bathhouse in 300 [912–13], leaving seven sons—Saʿīd, al-Faḍl, Ibrāhīm, Yūsuf, Aḥmad, al-Qāsim, and Sulaymān. 1.10

والفضل وإبرٰهيم ويوسف وأحمد والقاسم وسليمان ولمّا ادّعى أبو سعيد النبوّة قال فيه شاعره القِفْطيّ[2] الشيبانيّ شعر [بسيط]

فَمَنْ لَهُ[1] ٱلْوَحْيُ مَكْتُوبٌ صَحَائِفُهُ   مُنَظَّمٌ بِكَلَامِ ٱللهِ تَنْظِيمَا
وَمَنْ بِهِ ٱلْأَرْضُ مُشْتَدٌّ مَرَاكِزُهَا   لَوْلَاهُ أَصْبَحَ وَجْهُ ٱلْأَرْضِ مَهْدُومَا

وهي قصيدة طويلة ورأيت له عقب لهم[2] مالاً حسناً يعرفون بالسادة

الباب الرابع في كشف أسرار من ادّعى النبوّة

١١،١ وقد ظهر في خلافة المعزّ بالديار المصريّة رجل ادّعى النبوّة ونزل بتِنّيس وكان يُعرف بفارس بن يحيى الساباطيّ وسلك مسلك عيسى بن مريم عليه السلام وأحيى الميّت وأبرأ الأبرص والأجذم والأعمى وبنى له صومعة بتنّيس على البحر شماليّ البلد وهي باقية إلى يومنا هذا ثمّ أحيى لهم الميّت

الباب الخامس

١٢،١ وذلك أنّه فيلسوف فأخذ من كفن ذلك الميّت الذي أراد أن يحييه جزء ومن حبّ النارجيل جزء ومن الجُنْدبادَسْتَر جزء ثمّ جعله فتيلة وأوقده قدّام أهل ذلك الميّت الذي قد أخذ من كفنه فخيّل لهم أنّ ميّتهم قد قام من قبره يمزق أكفانه وهو على هيئته فسألوه عمّا أرادوا فخيّل لهم أنّه يخاطبهم بما يسألوه عنه فحارت فيه الأفكار ولم يبق أحد بتنّيس إلّا حمل ميّته وطرحه تحت الصومعة رجاء أن يحييه له فيخاطبه فلم يفعلها ثانية

١ ش: لد.   ٢ أضيف للسياق.

When Abū Saʿīd laid claim to prophethood, his poet, al-Qifṭī al-Shaybānī, recited the following lines:

> He for whom divine revelation is ordained, his scriptures are,
> by God's words, most well deployed,
> And without Him by whom Earth's pillars are held firm,
> Earth's face would be destroyed.

They're part of a longer poem. I've met descendants of his. They have considerable wealth and are known as "the Sayyids." [21]

Section Four of the Exposé of the Tricks of Fake Prophets

A man claiming to be a prophet appeared in Egypt during the caliphate of al-Muʿizz. He took up residence in Tinnīs and was known as Fāris ibn Yaḥyā al-Sābāṭī. He adopted the way of Jesus son of Mary, eternal peace be his, raising the dead and curing people with vitiligo as well as lepers and the blind. A hermitage was built for him at Tinnīs, north of the town, where it still stands. It was there that he raised their dead. **1.11**

Section Five

Exposé: He was a philosopher.[22] He'd get hold of one part shroud of the person he wanted to bring back to life, one part coconut, and one part castoreum grains. He'd make these into a wick and light it in front of the family of the deceased from whose shroud he'd taken the piece. Then he'd trick them into thinking that their dear departed had risen from the grave, tearing his wrappings asunder, and was as he had been in life. They'd ask him anything they wanted to know and he'd trick them into thinking he was relaying the dead's man's answers. People were completely taken in by him, and there wasn't a soul in Tinnīs who didn't bring the body of a loved one and toss it under his hermitage with the request that he bring that person back to life. The man would then talk to the deceased, though only once. **1.12**

الباب السادس في كشف أسرار برء الأبرص

وذلك أنّ هذا النبيّ المذكور كان يأخذ أصول الكرفس ونعنع الماء من كلّ واحد جزء ثمّ يدقّها ويدفنها في الزبل الرطب حتّى يصير منه دودًا أبيضًا فيأخذ ذلك الدود ويجعله في إناء زجاج فإذا أراد أن يبرص إنسانًا أخذ من ذلك الدواء وسيّره[1] مع ثقته إلى الحمّام فمن اتّفق له من عظماء البلد لصق إليه ثمّ لطخه منه فأيّ مكان لمسه به أبرص من يومه فإذا أتى إلى النبيّ يزيله يأخذ من الشيطَرَج الهنديّ ثمّ يدقّه ويعجنه بخلّ حاذق ويطلي به كفّ نفسه فإذا أتاه الأبرص يمرّ بيده عليه ثمّ يمسح مكان البرص بكفّه فلا يرفع يده عنه إلّا وقد برئ وزال ذلك ١٣،١

الباب السابع

من ذلك وقد كشفت عن ذلك فوجدت له غير ذلك وإنّه كان يأخذ النعنع فيرضّه ثمّ يحشو به فُقّاعة ويسدّ رأسها ويدفنها في الزبل أربعة عشر يومًا ثمّ يخرجها ويكسرها فيجد خنافس بيض فيأخذهم وينقعهم في زيت فلسطين ويعلّقه في شمس حارّة سبع أيّام ثمّ يفعل بها مثل ذلك ١٤،١

الباب الثامن في كشف أسرار إزالة الجذام

وذلك أنّه يأخذ ورق العِظْلِم وباذَروج وكَبابة وورق اليَبْروح وقَلْقَنْد من كلّ واحد جزءًا ثمّ يغليهم حتّى يذهب ربع الماء ثمّ يغسل به جماعة من رهطه ويبعثهم في البلاد فإذا سمعوا به قد ظهر يحضرون إليه بعد أن عُرفوا في البلاد بأنّهم أهل البلاء فلمّا حضروا ١٥،١

---

[1] ش: ستره.

Section Six: Exposé of a Trick for Curing Those with Vitiligo

Exposé: The abovementioned prophet would take one part each celery root 1.13
and water mint. He'd pound this and bury it in moist pigeon droppings till it turned into white worms. Then he'd take the worms and put them in a glass container. To make someone look as though they had vitiligo, he'd take some of this preparation with him to the bathhouse, accompanied by an accomplice—some town notable with whom he'd previously made an agreement, who would stick close to him—and he'd daub him with it, and any place he touched would instantly take on the mottling of vitiligo. When the man went to the prophet later to have the discoloration removed, the prophet would take some pepperwort from India, pound it, make it into a paste with extra-sour vinegar, and spread it over the palm of his hand. When the supposedly afflicted person arrived, he'd pass the palm of his hand over the patches of vitiligo, leaving it there until the man was "cured" and everything was gone.

Section Seven

Another example (this one I was able to get to the bottom of myself, and I uncov- 1.14
ered other methods too): He'd take mint, bruise it, fill a mug with it, seal its top, and bury it in pigeon droppings for fourteen days. Then he'd take the mug out and break it, revealing white beetles. These he'd steep in unripe olive oil, hanging the oil out in the hot sun for seven days, before using as described above.

Section Eight: Exposé of a Trick for Getting Rid of Leprosy

Exposé: He'd take one part each of woad, basil, cubeb, mandrake leaves, and 1.15
green vitriol, boil them till a quarter of the water was gone, then bathe a few of his followers in it and send them out into the villages. When people heard that the disease had appeared, and it became known in the country that there were lepers about, those same men would come to him and he'd "cure" them as follows: He'd order them to bathe in hot water, which they would, after he'd

إليه أبرأهم وذلك أنّه أمرهم أن يغتسلوا بماء حارّ فاغتسلوا به بعد ما جعل يده في الماء فإنّ ذلك الجذام زال فأخرق عقول الناس

الباب التاسع في معجزاته وكشف أسراره

١٦،١ وذلك أنّه كان يمشي على الماء على ساحل البحر فيطلع السمك من البحر إليه ويقبّل أقدامه وذلك أنّه كان يأخذ من خرء الآدميّ جزء ومن الباذروج جزء ومن حبّ القنّا جزء ثمّ يدقّهم ناعماً ويعجنهم بدهن الياسمين ويلطخ به أقدامه ثمّ يمشي على الماء أعني على ساحل البحر فيطلع السمك على رائحة الدواء ويلحس أقدامه فيتوهّم فيه الأوهام بالنبوّة وغيرها

الباب العاشر في كشف أسرار الذين يدّعون النبوّة[١]

١٧،١ فلا يصدّقوا وينفر منه[٢] العوامّ ولم يذعنوا له[٣] بالطاعة فيظهر النبيّ أنّه طالع إلى الجبل يسأل الله في عذابهم فيصعد إلى أحدا الجبال كأنّه يدعو على قومه فيأخذ سمكة يقال لها الدُخَس[٤] في البصرة وفي مصر تسمّى الدرفيل يأخذ شحمها وشحم سامّ أبرص في لونه وهي الوَزَغة وشحم بنت سالامندرا وهي سامّ أبرص في لونه ويسمّونه المصريّين الحِرْذَوْن وعلامتها أنّك إذا طرحتها على النار تطفئ النار تأخذ شحمها ومن كلّ واحد من هذه الشحوم ثلاثة أجزاء ومن الزجاج الفرعونيّ جزءاً مكلّس ومن الزَنْجفور جزءاً ومن الزيبق جزءاً ومن الزِنْجار جزءاً وتأخذ مثل نصف هذه الأجزاء أخثاء البقر وهو ثلاث ونصف جزء ومثل ربع هذه الأجزاء والشحوم وهي سبعة أجزاء من شعر نواصي الخيل وهي جزء ونصف وربع جزء

١٨،١ فتصير الجملة اثنا عشر جزءاً وربع جزء يدقّوا الجميع وينخلوا ويعجنوا بتلك الشحوم الثلاثة وتهيأ حبّاً ويجفّفوا في الظلّ ويبخّر بها في الليل في مكان مرتفع فإنّه يظهر في الأفق

---

١ ش: النيل. ٢ ش: منهم. ٣ ش: لهم. ٤ ش: الدخن.

first put his hand into the water, and the "leprosy" would disappear. This was how he hoodwinked people.

Section Nine: On His Miracles, and an Exposé of His Tricks

Another example: He'd walk on the water at the very edge of the beach, and the fish would come up out of the sea and kiss his feet. Exposé: He did this by taking one part human feces, one part basil, and one part galbanum granules, pounding them till fine and then kneading them together with oil of jasmine, and smearing his feet with the resulting preparation. Then he'd walk on the water—meaning, of course, at the sea's edge—and when they smelled the preparation, the fish would emerge and nibble at his feet, and he'd pretend he was a prophet and so on. **1.16**

Section Ten of the Exposé of the Tricks of Fake Prophets

All the same, people would refuse to believe in him and the common folk would cold-shoulder him and refuse to obey his orders, so the prophet would put out the word that he was going to the mountaintop to ask God to torment them, and he'd set off up some mountain as though on his way to curse his people. He'd get hold of a fish, the kind called *dukhas* in Basra and *darfīl* ("dolphin") in Egypt, and take some of its fat plus the fat of a certain poisonous and patchily colored creature—namely, a gecko—along with that of a stellion (what the Egyptians call a *ḥirdhawn*), which is also poisonous and patchy in color (its distinguishing characteristic is that if you throw it onto a fire, it puts it out). You take three parts of each of these fats plus one part each of pharaoh glass (calcined), cinnabar, quicksilver, and verdigris. Then you take cow dung equal to around half of these quantities—that is, three and a half parts, plus around a quarter of the first-mentioned parts (which comes to seven parts including the fats, thus one and three-quarter parts) of hair from horses' forelocks. **1.17**

The whole comes to twelve and a quarter parts,[23] all of which, including the three fats, are pounded, sifted, kneaded together, and formed into granules, then dried in the shade and used at night in an elevated place as one would **1.18**

كلّه وقد احمرّ والهواء كلّه نار وترى فيه خيولاً شهباء ودهماء وعليها رجال من نار وبأيديهم حراب من نار وبعضهم يكرّ على بعض في الهواء حتّى يضجّ الناس ويفزعوا ويظنّون أنّ العذاب قد حلّ بهم فيكون منها تأثير عظيم فيتوهّم الناس أنّه قد دعا عليهم النبيّ وأنّه صادقًا ولا يزال كذلك حتّى تهدأ النار وتكون ناره بعزّ الجمال

الباب الحادي عشر في كشف أسرار الذين يدّعون النبوّة ولا يصدّقوا ولا يطاعوا

١٩،١ فإذا أراد رباطهم أظهر أنّه طالع إلى الدعاء على القوم فيدخّن بهذه الدخنة فتظلم الدنيا وترى النجوم كلّها والقمر نهارًا حتّى يخاف العالم من ذلك وذلك أنّه يأخذ بعقول الناس ويتوهّمون فيه الأوهام

الباب الثاني عشر في كشف أسرار الذين يدّعون النبوّة

٢٠،١ وكان قد ظهر بالشام رجل راعي فادّعى النبوّة وادّعى أنّ موسى بن عمران عليه السلام إنّما كان مبشّرًا بظهوره ولم يعرف لهذا الرجل اسم ولا نسب فسمّوه اليهود راعيًا لأنّه كان راعي ونزل طَبَرِيّة وسلك مسالك موسى عليه السلام وكانت معجزته العصا الذي كان يرعى بها الغنم كان في أوقات القيظ والهواجر يغرسها فتورق بأغصان وأوراق فتظلّه من حرّ الهجيرة وهذا العكّاز قد ذكروه بني موسى في كتبهم وهو مشهور وكان يسوق السباع والوحوش بتلك العصا مثل الغنم وتذعن له في الطاعة وكان يلقيها من يده فتسعى بين يديه وكان يعمل المخاريق من المخيّلات

٢١،١ وهذه صفة العصا إذا أرادت أن تسوق بها الوحوش والسباع مثل الغنم فتكون العصا قد حرّك بها إنسانا قد أحرق ثمّ إنّها تُجعل في رماد ليلة وتكون قد نالت منها

incense. The resulting smoke fills the whole horizon, turning it red and making the entire sky look as though it's enveloped in flames, and in the midst you'll see jet-black, curvetting horses ridden by fiery men holding fiery lances, some charging one another in the air. By this time, the people will be in an uproar. They panic, believing that God's punishment has fallen upon them, and the impression it makes on them is so overwhelming that they're deluded into thinking the prophet was telling the truth and has cursed them. The whole thing goes on until the fire dies down. The fire produced by these granules is very beautiful.

Section Eleven of the Exposé of the Tricks of Fake Prophets Who Are Neither Believed nor Obeyed

When a fake prophet of this sort wants to win people over, he makes them **1.19** believe he's going up the mountain to curse them and makes smoke as described above. Everything goes dark and all the stars can be seen, as well as the moon, even in daylight. Exposé: Everyone gets scared, which is how he fools people and deludes them into believing him.

Section Twelve of the Exposé of the Tricks of Fake Prophets

A shepherd appeared in Syria claiming to be a prophet and asserting that Moses **1.20** son of Amram, on whom eternal peace, had foretold his coming. The man had no name or pedigree, so the Jews called him the Shepherd because he was one.[24] He took up residence in Tiberias and followed the way of Moses, eternal peace be his. His miracle lay in the staff that he used to herd his flocks. At the peak of the summer's heat and at the hottest time of day, he'd plant this staff in the ground, and branches and leaves would break out and shade him from the heat. The Banū Mūsā mention such a staff in their books;[25] it's well known. He used to herd lions and wild beasts with it as though they were flocks of sheep and goats, and they would obey him; or he'd throw it on the ground and it would run around in front of him. He created illusions using conjuring tricks.

This is how the staff worked: If he wanted to herd wild beasts and lions as **1.21** though they were flocks of sheep and goats, he would first use the staff to prod the charred corpse of a human, then at night he'd place it in the remains of a

النار وهذه العصا متى أراد يسوق بها السباع وجميع الوحوش فإنّه إذا أومأ إلى سائر الوحوش انساقت قدّامه مثلما تنساق الغنم وهي تتكسكس قدّامه خوفاً منه ورؤوسها في أيديها وأذنابها بين أرجلها وهذا سرّ لا يعلمه إلّا الله عزّ وجلّ فإذا أرادها أن تسعى ترصد في أعظم ما يكون من الحرّ فيلقي العصا فإنّها إذا حميت سعت مثل الثعبان وهذا ممّا يخرق العقول واعلم أنّي وضعت في هذا الكتاب أسراراً لم أسبق إلى كشفها ومعرفتها

الباب الثالث عشر في كشف أسرار الذين يدّعون النبوّة ويزعمون أنّ الوحي ينزل عليهم ويكذبون على الله عزّ وجلّ

وذلك أنّهم يأخذون من القُسْط الحلو جزء ومن المرّ جزء ومن الصَبِر جزء ومن حبّ ٢٢،١
الباذروج جزء يدقّ الجميع مع جزء من فُقّاح الإذْخِر ومن الكبابة جزء ومن السيكران جزء ثمّ يبخّر به بين يديه عند النوم فإنّه يرى في منامه جميع ما يحدث به في العالم في المستقبل فيخبّر به قبل وقوعه فيتوهّم فيه أنّ الوحي نزل عليه

الباب الرابع عشر في كشف أسرارهم

وقد ظهر في خلافة المأمون رجل يُعرف بعبد الله بن ميمون بن مسلم بن عَقيل وادّعى ٢٣،١
النبوّة وحبسه المأمون ومات في الحبس وكان من سواد الكوفة وأورى الناس المخاريق من النارنجيّات ثمّ أوراهم انشقاق القمر فأخرق عقولهم وارتبطوا عليه إلى يومنا هذا وذلك أنّه أخذ رأس جمل كبير فجفّفه وأخذ مخّه فعجنه من دم سنّور أسود شديد السواد ومثله من شجرة يقال لها مسكترم وهي على مثال الكرّاث لا زائد ولا ناقص وهي موجودة كثيرة في الحشائش أخذ هذه الحشيشة فجفّفها ودقّها ناعماً وعجنها مع

fire, to be partially burned by the embers. When he wanted to herd the lions or the other wild beasts, he'd wave it at them and they would move along ahead of him just like flocks, and they'd fall into line before him, covering their heads with their paws and with their tails between their legs. Only God, Mighty and Exalted, knows how this trick works. And when he wanted the staff to run around in front of him, he'd wait for the hottest part of the day and then throw it on the ground; once it had heated up, it would slither around like a snake. This is one of the things he used to do to fool people. (Note: I have included a few tricks in this book that I haven't been able to get to the bottom of or understand yet.)

Section Thirteen of the Exposé of the Tricks of Fake Prophets and Those Who Claim That Divine Inspiration Has Descended upon Them but Who Lie Before God, Mighty and Sublime

Exposé: They take one part sweet costus, one part bitter costus, one part aloe, 1.22
and one part basil seed. Everything is pounded together with one part flowers of fever grass, one part cubeb, and one part stinking nightshade. This is burned before him like incense when he goes to sleep, and in his dreams he sees everything that will happen in the future and he announces it before it happens. This deludes people into thinking he is inspired by God.

Section Fourteen of the Exposé of Their Tricks

During the caliphate of al-Ma'mūn, a man called ʿAbd Allāh ibn Maymūn ibn 1.23
Muslim ibn ʿAqīl appeared, claiming to be a prophet. Al-Ma'mūn put him in prison, where he died. He was from the countryside around Kufa, where he had bewitched people with his conjuring tricks. Later, he dumbfounded them by showing them that he could split the moon; as a result, they have remained his followers to this day.

Exposé: He would take the head of a large camel, dry it, and remove its brains. These he would knead with the blood of a jet-black cat and an equal amount of the bush called dittany, a common plant that is exactly like a leek, neither larger nor smaller. He'd take this plant, dry it, pound it till smooth, and knead all these medicinal ingredients with the brains, which he'd then

تلك الأدوية بالمخّ ثمّ عمل منها حبّاً على مثال الحمّص ثمّ جفّفها في الظلّ ثمّ رفعها في حُقّ واحترز عليه من الهواء

٢٤،١ فلمّا أراد العمل بها أخذ فحماً من حطب المُقْل من شجرة ثمّ أوقد ناراً في مجمرة جديدة ثمّ وضع عليه مثل حبّتين من ذلك الحبّ فلمّا دخّن ذلك صعد لها دخاناً عظيماً وأورى الناس أنّ القمر قد انشقّ وانقسم نصفين وكان ذلك والقمر زائد النور وهذه معجزة لم يعطها الله لأحد من الأنبياء إلّا نبيّنا محمّد صلّى الله عليه وسلّم فلمّا عجزوا عن درجة النبوّة رجعوا إلى النواميس ومع ذلك فإنّها من الأسرار والمعجزات واعلم أنّ هذه الدخنة تعمل غير ذلك من العجائب إذا عُملت والقمر زائد النور وقد اختصرت في ذكر من ادّعى النبوّة خوف الإطالة بل والله لهم عندي ألف باب مختلفة الصفات لا يمكن شرحها فافهمْ ذلك واعلم أنّي لم أترك شيئاً ممّا وضعته الحكماء المتقدّمين

make into granules the size of chickpeas, dry in the shade, and store in an airtight box.

When he wanted to use the granules, he'd take bdellium charcoal, set a fire in a new brazier, and put a couple of them into it. When these were producing copious quantities of rising smoke, he'd invite the people to observe that the moon had been split and divided into two halves; it had to be done when the moon was very bright. As a miracle, this has been granted by God only to our prophet Muḥammad, God bless and keep him, among all the prophets.[26] However, when people of the sort we are describing find themselves incapable of doing things of this kind that are appropriate only to those of the rank of prophet, they resort to illusions, which are themselves, at the same time, tricks and miracles. The same smoke will work other marvels so long as it is made when the moon is very bright. 1.24

I have kept my account of fake prophets to a minimum for fear of boring you. In fact, I know a thousand more tricks of theirs, but they would take too long to explain. Wise up to these things—and don't forget: There isn't a single work of the ancient sages I haven't examined!

الفصل الثاني

وهو أربعة وعشرون بابًا

في كشف أسرار من يدّعي المشيخة وأصحاب النواميس من الفقراء والمشايخ ومن الصالحين

١،٢ فأمّا المشايخ والصالحين فإنّا لا نطعن في شيء منهم ولا من كراماتهم فإنّها غير مخفيّة عن العالم ولا طعن في كرامات الصالحين قدّس الله أرواحهم وذلك أنّهم الطريق إلى الله عزّ وجلّ مثل الجُنَيد وإبرٰهيم بن أدهم والحسن البصريّ وسريّ السقطيّ ومعروف الكَرْخيّ وسليمان الدارانيّ وغيرهما من المشايخ قدّس الله أرواحهم ممّن لم أسمّه ومنهم من لم يشهر ولم يعرف وهو أكرم على الله عزّ وجلّ من الملٰئكة وقد قال صلّى الله عليه وسلّم رُبّ أشعث أغبر ذا طِمْرَيْن لا يؤبه له لو أقسم على الله عزّ وجلّ لأبرّ قسمه

٢،٢ فإنّ أصحاب هذه الدرجة لا شكّ فيهم أنّ لهم عند الله قدم صدق فصدّقهم وصفاء قلوبهم اطّلع الله على أسرارهم وصفاء قلوبهم فلمّا علم ذلك منهم أسكنهم في جواره وكشف لهم ما يكون قبل كيانه وأُلحقوا بالعالم العلويّ لطفًا من الله تعالى فعند ذلك خبّروا بالمغيّبات وحصلت لهم الكرامات فهذه درجة الصالحين من المشايخ رحمة الله عليهم أجمعين وأمّا الدرجة التي هي دون ذلك فهي درجة المشايخ من أصحاب الرياضة وعلم السيمياء والعمل بالأسماء المقدّسة الذي إذا سُئل الله بها أعطى وإذا دُعي بها أجاب مثل عَبادان وبُهلول وجحا والشيخ قديم والشيخ أبو العبّاس والشيخ يس وغيرهما ممّن لم أسمّه خوف الإطالة

Chapter Two, in Twenty-Four Sections:

Exposé of the Tricks of Fake Shaykhs and Illusionists[27] among the Dervishes, the Shaykhs, and "the Righteous"

2.1 We do not impugn the miraculous deeds of true Sufi shaykhs and the genuine Righteous:[28] They are well known to all. Such people, God sanctify their souls, cannot be impugned. They are the path to God, Mighty and Exalted, and include such shaykhs as al-Junayd,[29] Ibrāhīm ibn Adham, Ḥasan al-Baṣrī, Sarī al-Saqaṭī, Maʿrūf al-Karkhī, Sulaymān al-Dārānī, and others I won't list, God sanctify their souls. Though some of them never achieved fame or became well known, such people are held in greater esteem by God, Mighty and Exalted, than the angels. The Prophet Muḥammad, God bless and keep him, has said, "Many a man with matted hair, covered in dust, wearing just two old, ragged wraps, to whom none pays heed, should he swear an oath in God's name, God, Mighty and Exalted, will ensure that it is fulfilled."[30]

2.2 As there can be no doubt that those who hold this rank have «a sure footing»[31] with God, have faith in their words and in the purity of their hearts. God Himself, having observed their secret thoughts and the purity of their hearts, and seeing their nature, brought them to dwell at His side, where he revealed to them what was before He brought the universe into existence, and, as an act of grace, granted them access to the Upper World. They then reported on things that otherwise would have been hidden and performed miraculous acts. This is the rank of the Righteous among the shaykhs, may God show them all mercy. The next rank down is that of the shaykhs who undertake spiritual exercises, practice alchemy, and perform magic using the Holy Names—those names in response to which God gives when solicited and answers when called.[32] These are such shaykhs as ʿAbādān, Buhlūl, Juḥā, Shaykh Qadīm, Shaykh Abū l-ʿAbbās, Shaykh Yāsīn,[33] and others I won't list for fear of boring you.

وقد ظهر ببغداد في سنة ثلاث وثلاثمائة رجل يُعرف بالحسين بن منصور الحلّاج وكان يدعو الناس إلى عبادة الله عزّ وجلّ فوشوا به إلى علي بن عيسى الوزير فأحضره وضربه ألف عصاً ثمّ فصّل أعضاءه وقيل إنّه لم يتأوّه وكان كلّما قُدّ له عضوًا يقول [سريع] ٣،٢

وَحُرْمَةِ ٱلْوُدِّ ٱلَّذِي لَمْ يَكُنْ   يَطْمَعُ فِي إِفْسَادِهِ ٱلدَّهْرُ
مَا نَالَنِي عِنْدَ نُزُولِ ٱلْبَلَا   جَهْدٌ وَلَا مَسَّنِي ٱلضُّرُّ
مَا قُدَّ لِي عُضْوٌ وَلَا مِفْصَلٌ   إِلَّا وَفِيهِ لَكُمُ ذِكْرُ

الباب الأوّل

رأيت الشيخ حسين وقد سمع قارئًا يقرأ فوجد لقراءته ورقص ورأيته وقد ارتفعت رجلاه على الأرض وهو يرقص ويقول [بسيط] ٤،٢

مَنْ أَطْلَعُوهُ عَلَى سِرٍّ فَبَاحَ بِهِ   لَا يَأْمَنُوهُ عَلَى ٱلْأَسْرَارِ مَا عَاشَا
وَعَاقَبُوهُ عَلَى مَا كَانَ مِنْ زَلَلٍ   وَأَلْزَمُوهُ مَكَانَ ٱلْأُنْسِ إِيحَاشَا

وكلّ هذا من أصحاب علم السيمياء الذي يجلبوا بالأسماء الخير ويدفعون بها الضرّ فهم يعدّون من الصالحين لأنّهم يحضرون الأشياء في غير أوانهم وفي أوقات لم يمكن أن توجد فيها

ولهم عمل الإخفاء عن أعين الناس فهذا سرّ ربّانيّ وللحلّاج في الإخفاء قصيدة يطول شرحها وإنّما نذكر منها شيئًا يسيرًا يقول [رجز] ٥،٢

In Baghdad in 303 [915–16], a man called al-Ḥusayn ibn Manṣūr al-Ḥallāj appeared and summoned people to the worship of God, Mighty and Exalted. People slandered him to the vizier ʿAlī ibn ʿĪsā, who had him brought and given a thousand strokes of the cane, after which his limbs were severed from his body.[34] It is said he never uttered a cry and that every time a limb was cut off, he would say: 2.3

By the sanctity of that love that
time to spoil has never dared,
Never, when subjected to ordeal, have I been pushed too far,
nor has harm my body neared.
Each time a limb or joint is cut,
By that limb or joint Your name's declared.

Section One

I saw this same Shaykh Ḥusayn in a dream. He'd just been listening to someone reciting from the Qurʾan. The recitation had sent him into ecstasy and he danced, his feet leaving the ground as he did so, and declaimed: 2.4

One whom others have let in on a secret and who reveals it
they'll not trust with another for the rest of his life's duration.
They'll punish him for his every slip
and make him feel, where once was friendship, desolation.[35]

This kind of thing is typical of those who understand the science of letters[36] and attract good and repel evil by invoking the names of God. Such persons are regarded as belonging to the Righteous because they can make things appear at other than their appointed times and at seasons when they ought not to be available.[37]

They also know how to make themselves vanish before people's eyes, which is a form of divine grace. Al-Ḥallāj has a poem on invisibility that it would take too long to go through and explain. We shall mention here only a small part, where he says:[38] 2.5

قَدْ طَالَمَا غِبْنَا عَنْ أَشْبَاحِ ٱلنَّظَرِ   بِنُقْطَةٍ يَحْكِي ضِيَاؤُهَا ٱلْقَمَرْ
مِنْ سِمْسِمٍ وَشِيرَجٍ وَأَحْرُفٍ   وَيَاسَمِينٍ فَوْقَ جَبِينٍ قَدْ سَطَرْ
تَمْشُوا وَنَمْشِي وَنَرَى أَشْخَاصَكُمْ   وَأَنْتُمُ لَيْسَ تَرَوْنَا يَا دَبَرْ

والقصيدة طويلة وإنّما هذا المقدار كافي للفطن اللبيب

وأمّا الدرجة الثالثة فهم أصحاب الدُخَن المختلفة والتباخير الهيولا واعلم أنّ هذه الدرجة لم يتعلّق بها إلّا من يأكل الدنيا بالدين ويدخل الشبهة في قلوب المسلمين وقد آن أن نشرح كشف سرّ كلّ واحد منهم واعلم أنّ كلّ واحد من أهل هذه الدرجة ظاهره ظاهر صدّيق وباطنه باطن زنديق يستحلّون المحارم ويجهّلون العالم فمنهم المباحيّة الذين يبيحون مباحات النسوان والخلوة مع المردان ثمّ يبيحون السماعات ويخلوا بالنسوان ويطعموهم القنبس ويتوسّمون عليهم بعقد المنديل وطرف المقنعة فإنّهم يعقدون طرف مقنعة الإمرأة ثمّ يقولون إن كان أمرها يؤول إلى الصلاح ويحلّ عنها أمر صعب فحلّوا هذه المقنعة ثمّ يقولون لها انفضي المقنعة فتنفضها فلا تجد فيها عقدة فيقولون الآن قد رضي الله عنكي وحلّ عنكي كلّ أمر عسير وقد جعل كلّ صعب عليكي هيّن يسير وقد وجب عليكي الشكران لهذه النعمة ثمّ يعملون معها القبائح المنكرة ٦،٢

الباب الثاني في كشف أسرارهم

ومنهم من يظهر في جسد المرأة من الكتابة من تحت قماشها ولبسها ويقول إنّ قد ظهر لي فيك على العضوّ الفلانيّ سرّ وهو إشارة من عند الله عزّ وجلّ يتضمّن كذا وكذا فاكشفي عن هذا العضوّ تجديه مكتوبًا كما ذكرنا لك فإذا كشفت بان لها الكتابة ٧،٢

How many a time we've distanced ourselves from the ghosts of sight
by means of a drop[39] whose light is like the lunar sphere—
Of sesame, sesame oil, cresses, and jasmine—
that He has traced upon a forehead clear.
Walk on! We too shall walk and see your shapes
but you'll not see us, you men of yesteryear!

The poem is long but the above should suffice the enquiring mind.

The third rank consists of the shaykhs who employ various kinds of smoke and mote-filled incense. Only people who are willing to make a living by abusing religion and planting doubt in the minds of Muslims belong to it, and the time has now come for us to reveal the tricks of each and every one of them. Members of this rank are all up-front and truthful on the outside but furtive and heretical on the inside. They declare that things that are forbidden are in fact allowed and would like to take the world back to the days of religious ignorance and barbarism. They include "the Permissivists," who deem illicit women licit and take beardless boys on retreat with them.[40] They also declare that listening to music is allowed[41] and will seclude themselves with a woman, feed her hempseed, and offer to tell her fortune by making a knot in her handkerchief or the end of her veil: They make a knot in the end of the woman's veil and say, "If things are going to go well for her and such and such a difficult situation is going to be resolved, loose this veil!" Then they tell her, "Shake out the veil!" and when the woman does so, she finds there's no knot in it, so they tell her, "God is pleased with you and has relieved you of all difficulties and made everything that was hard easy. You should be grateful for such blessings!" They then practice forbidden abominations with her. **2.6**

Section Two of the Exposé of Their Tricks

There are shaykhs who make writing appear on a woman's body, under her shift and her garments, and say, "I see something hidden on this or that part of your body. It is a sign from God, Mighty and Exalted, and reads thus and so. Expose the part and you'll see that what I have described is written there." When she does as he says, the writing is there for her to see, and he makes up whatever story he cares to about it and then says, "You ought to be grateful, **2.7**

فيقول فيها ما شاء أن يقول ثمّ يقول وجب لها الشكران وإن توجد بنا راحة ويفعلون من هذا النوع أشياء يطول شرحها

الباب الثالث في كشف أسرار أصحاب الزوايا من أهل هذه الدرجة

أمّا مشايخ هذه الدرجة فمنهم من يتعانى النزول في التنّور وقد أوقد فيه قنطار من الحطب فينزل فيه ويغيب ساعة ثمّ يطلع وعلى يده طاجن سمك محشيّ أو دجاج مطجّن أو خروف مشويّ أو ما اتّفق من ذلك فيخرق عقول الناس ويذهلهم ذلك وذلك أنّ هذا النوع ثلاثة أنواع الأوّل منه أن يكون هذا التنّور أعلاه مربّص فتكون حرارة النار أعلى التنّور وأسفله بارد إلّا أنّ هذا التنّور يكون محكم البناء وله صاج من الحديد في أسفله ولذلك الصاج خُلُوّا في حائط التنّور مهندم محكم من حيث أنّ النار جميعها تكون في الصاج وبمقدار ما يضع يده على حافة التنّور يسيخ ذلك الصاج بما عليه من النار في ذلك الخلوّ ويبقى أسفل التنّور خاليًا من النار بارد فيقعد فيه ويكون نزوله بمقدار ما يعلم أنّ ذلك المعلوم قد استوى ممّا ذكرناه فإذا طلع أخذه وأطعمه لمن حضر وإذا كان هو أسفل التنّور كان أعلى التنّور لا يقدر أحد يقابله من وهج النار لِما قد دبّره من اللزقات وهذه الصفة الأولى من التنّور ٨،٢

الباب الرابع

وأمّا الثاني فإنّه أعجب من هذا وذلك أنّ التنّور يكون بنيانه محكم وذلك أنّ بنيانه على نحو ما يعمل تنانير الشوي ويكون من تحته عضادة تحت الأرض تخرج إلى البرّية وهذا التنّور لا يكون عمله إلّا في زاوية ظاهر المدينة أو في قرية أو مستند إلى جبل فإذا كان كذلك وعمل السماع أحمى التنّور ولا بدّ من الصاج في أسفله على ما ذكرناه ٩،٢

and we're all on our own." They do so many things of this sort that I can't go through them one by one.[42]

Section Three: Exposé of the Tricks of Those of This Rank Who Have Lodges

Some shaykhs of this rank go so far as to descend into a baking pit[43] after a hundredweight of firewood has been lit inside. He descends, disappears for a while, and comes back out holding a pot of stuffed fish, a chicken casserole, some roast mutton, or whatever else it may be. This fools everyone and leaves them speechless. 2.8

Exposé: There are three ways of doing this trick. The first is to have the upper part of the pit fireproofed. This means that the heat of the fire is contained within the upper part of the pit while the lower part remains cool. The pit must be well constructed and have a metal sheet at the bottom. The sheet has an empty space in it next to the pit wall that is made so precisely and tightly that the fire is kept strictly within the confines of the sheet, and as long as the shaykh keeps his hand on the edge of the pit, the sheet is held steady around the empty space, along with the fire above it, and the bottom of the pit is kept cool and free of fire. The man stays there for as long as he knows it takes the dish in question to be done. On his way back, he picks it up, and then feeds those in attendance. No one can go near the pit while he's in its lower part: He will have prepped it with tarry substances and the heat will be too great. This is the first type of pit.[44]

Section Four

The second type is even more extraordinary. 2.9

Exposé: The pit is very well constructed, meaning that it's made like a grill pit. Beneath it is an underground tunnel that debouches into the countryside. Such a pit can only be made in a lodge on the outskirts of the city or in a village or on the side of a hill. When the pit has been constructed as described and a musical gathering is about to be held, the pit is heated, but the metal sheet at

فإذا طاب الشيخ صاح وخرج من السماع طالب الجبل أو البريّة إلى أن ينتهي إلى الموضع سرب العضادة فيدخل فيه ثمّ يمشي تحت الأرض إلى التنّور ويكون المغنّي قد وقف قرب التنّور ثمّ يرفع الشيخ رأسه ويطلع وهو يرقص فيذهل من رآه ويذهب عقله ويتوهّم فيه الأوهام هكذا رأيناه فافهم ذلك ممّا أشرت به إليك وابعد عن هؤلاء المشايخ السوقة وكن فريداً

الباب الخامس

١٠،٢ وأمّا الثالث فليس لهم فيه حيلة بل يكون الشيخ قد ربّص جميع جسده بالترابيص التي تمنع النار وفعلها وهذا كشف أسرار الترابيص التي يعملونها تمنع النار وحرّها عنهم فمن ذلك تأخذ الضفدع ثمّ تسلقها حتّى يتهرّأ لحمها ولا يبقى لها أثر ثمّ ترفعها عن النار حتّى تبرد فإذا بردت جمد الدهن على وجه الماء فيأخذ ذلك الدهن ثمّ يضيف إليه شيئاً من البارود الثلجيّ ثمّ يلطخ به جميع جسده وجميع أعضائه ويدخل النار فلا تضرّه شيئاً

الباب السادس في كشف الترابيص

١١،٢ فمنهم من يأخذ الطلق المحلول[١] ويجعله على صَلاية ثمّ يضيف إليه مُغْرة مدنيّة وحشيشة حيّ العالَم[٢] وزنبق أبيض[٣] ويسحقه بماء الكُسْفَرة الخضراء إلى أن يعود مثل المرهم ثمّ يجفّفه في الظلّ فإذا جفّ عاد إلى السحق بدهن الضفدع ويسحقه سحقاً بالغاً ثمّ يرفعه عنده على هيئة دهن الشمع فإذا أراد النزول في التنّور والوقوف على السندال وهو محمّى لُطخ من ذلك الدهن فلا يضرّه شيئاً فافهم ما لهم من الدهاء والمكر والحيل والخداع ولولا خوف الإطالة شرحت في هذا الفنّ مائة نوع ولكن هذا القدر كاف وبه يستدلّ على غيره

١ ش: المحلوب. ٢ ش: حشيشة الحيّ علم. ٣ ش: البيض.

the bottom has to have been prepared as described. When the shaykh feels the time is ripe, he cries out and exits the gathering, making for the hill or the countryside, and keeps going until he reaches the place where the tunnel begins. He enters and moves along underground till he gets to the pit, close to which the singer will have taken up position.[45] The shaykh now pokes out his head and emerges, dancing. Everyone who sees him is astonished and they all get deluded ideas about him. I saw it done this way myself. Take note of what I've alerted you to, stay away from these vulgar shaykhs, and keep your distance!

Section Five

The third type involves no subterfuge on their part. The shaykh just smears his **2.10**
whole body with agents that protect against fire and its effects. The following is an exposé of their tricks regarding the agents they concoct so as to protect themselves from the heat of the fire. One method is to take frogs and boil them until their flesh falls apart and not a trace of it is left. They take the remaining liquid off the fire to cool. When it has done so, the fat congeals on the surface of the liquid, and they take it and add a little saltpeter. If they daub their bodies and their limbs all over with this and enter the fire, it won't harm them.

Section Six: Exposé of the Tricks Involved in the Production of Fireproofing Agents

Others take loose talc and place it in a stone mortar, add hematite from **2.11**
Medina, houseleek, and white jasmine, and grind these with an infusion of fresh cilantro till the mixture takes on the consistency of an ointment. They put this out in the shade to dry and when it has done so, grind it a second time, very thoroughly, with frog fat. They store the result at home in the form of candle wax and when they want to descend into the baking pit and stand on the hot beaten-metal sheet, they smear themselves with the fat, and this keeps them safe from any harm. Note their cunning, their craftiness, their subterfuges, and their deceptions!

If I weren't afraid of boring you, I'd explain a hundred more examples of this art. But enough: The rest can be inferred.

الباب السابع في كشف أسرارهم

١٢،٢ ومن هذا المشايخ من إذا عمل السماع أخلى الزاوية من الماء فإذا دار السماع ورقصوا عطشوا فشكوا إلى الشيخ ذلك فيقول هاتوا شيء وخذوا ماء اشربوا فيعطوه إمّا إبريق أو جرّة أو كوز أو ما كان فيأخذه بيده ويفتح باعه ثمّ يدور في الطابق دورة ثمّ يدفع لهم الوعاء ملآن ماء مبخّر ممسّك فيقول هذا من نهر الكوثر فتشرب الجماعة من ذلك الماء فتحيّر عقولهم من ذلك

١٣،٢ كشف سرّ ذلك أنّه يأخذ سرداب غنميّ فيدبغه بعد غسله ثمّ ينقعه في الماورد سبعة أيّام وبعد ذلك يأخذه فيربط طرفه الواحد ربطًا جيّدًا ثمّ يجعل في طرف الآخر عقدة قصب ثمّ ينفخه حتّى يجفّ في الهواء فإذا جفّ رفعه عنده فإذا أراد العمل به أخذه فملأه ماء قد جعل فيه قليل مسك وماورد ثمّ جعله في قميصه وقد عمل له حمّالات من تحت القميص من كمّه الشمال إلى كمّه اليمين فإذا أراد أن يسقي الجماعة الماء جعل رأس السرداب في فم الوعاء وهو دائر من حيث لا يعلم به أحد ثمّ فرك رأس السرداب بظفره فقطعه ونزل الماء في الوعاء ثمّ يدفع لهم الوعاء ويمّس ما أراد وكيف يشاء

الباب الثامن في كشف أسرارهم

١٤،٢ ومن ذلك أنّ الشيخ يكون في السماع فأيّ من أومأ إليه بيده سقط إلى الأرض وهو بعيد عنه وذلك أنّه يأخذ من البنج الأزرق جزء ومن الأفيون جزء ومن بزر الخسّ جزء ومن بزر السَيكُران جزء ومن بزر الرشاد جزء ومن الغبيراء جزء ومن لبن التين جزء ثمّ يأخذ الجندبادستر ويسحقه به حتّى يعود مثل الغالية ثمّ إنّ الشيخ يلطخ به تحت إبطه ثمّ يجعل معه قطنة مسقيّة من دهن البنفسج العراقيّ فإذا أراد أن يشير إلى من أراد فيدور معه في الطابق ثمّ يعانقه ويجعل رأسه تحت إبطه

Section Seven of the Exposé of Their Tricks

Some of these shaykhs make sure there is no water available in the lodge when they hold a musical gathering. When the party is in full swing and everyone's dancing, the Sufis get thirsty, so they complain to the shaykh that there's no water. He says, "Give me something to hold it in and I'll give you water to drink." So they give him a pitcher or a water jar or a jug or whatever is to hand and he takes it and opens his arms wide.[46] Then he makes a round of the floor and returns the vessel to them full of incense-scented, musk-flavored water, saying, "This is from the River Kawthar." Everyone drinks, at a loss to explain what happened. **2.12**

The trick exposed: He takes a goat-hide waterskin,[47] washes and tans it, and steeps it in rosewater for seven days. Then he takes it, ties off one end of it well, and inserts a length of cane into the other. Now he inflates the skin so that it can dry in the air, and when it's dry, sets it aside at home. When he wants to use it, he takes it and fills it with water into which he has put a little musk and rosewater, then places it inside his shirt, having first provided it with straps that pass from his left sleeve to his right, beneath the shirt. To give the assembled crowd water to drink, he places the top end of the waterskin in the mouth of the vessel, moving as he does so from place to place so no one can see what he's up to. Then he scratches the top end of the waterskin with his fingernail, breaking it open, and the water descends into the vessel. He offers them the vessel, reproducing the illusion at will. **2.13**

Section Eight of the Exposé of Their Tricks

Another example: The shaykh is at a musical gathering and anyone he points at falls to the ground, even if he's at a distance from him. **2.14**

Exposé: He takes one part each of blue henbane, opium, lettuce seed, stinking nightshade seed, cress seed, marijuana, and fig milk. Then he takes some castoreum and grinds it into the mixture till it takes on the consistency of galia moschata. The shaykh then smears this under his armpit and takes a cotton boll soaked in oil of Iraqi violets.[48] When the shaykh wants to point at whoever it is he's selected, he takes a turn around the floor with the man, gives him a hug, tucking his head under his arm, and continues making the rounds with

ويدور معه بمقدار ما يعلم أنّ بخار الدواء قد تصعّد إلى دماغه ثمّ يتركه فيروح يقف ناحية وقد لعب دماغه هذا والشيخ يتربّص ويرقبه فإذا رآه قد اضطرب أشار إليه بيده فلا يزال يومئ إليه بالوقوع حتّى يقع إلى الأرض مغشيّاً عليه فيتوهّم فيه الأوهام فافهم وكن خبيراً بما يفعلون

الباب التاسع في كشف أسرارهم

١٥،٢ ومن ذلك أنّ الشيخ إذا طاف في السماع تقدّم إلى الشمعة فأطفأها أو إلى المصباح فمدّ إليه أصابع يده العشرة فأشعلها فاشتعلت كما يشعل الشمع فإذا أشعلها طفئ ما كان من الشمع أو السُرُج ولا يزال يرقص وأصابعه تشعل حتّى تضجّ الناس ثمّ يدنو من الشمعة فيشعلها ويطفئ أصابعه وهذا ناموس عظيم فافهم ذلك وتميّز

١٦،٢ والسرّ في ذلك أن يأخذ من ذلك الدواء الذي ذكرناه في باب نزول التنّور فيلطخ أصابعه جميعاً إلى العقد ويدعها حتّى تجفّ ثمّ يأخذ النفط ويلبّسه على ذلك الدهن ثمّ يشعل فيه النار فلا يزال يشعل حتّى ينفد النفط ولا يدرك يده شيء من حرارة النار فافهم ذلك ومنهم من يدهن يده من ذلك الدهن ويعمل له عشرة قموع من اللِبَد الأحمر الطالقانيّ ثمّ يلبّسها أصابعه العشرة ثمّ يسقيها بالنفط الجوريّ ويشعل فيها النار فلا يضرّه منها شيئاً وكلّ ذلك تمويه على الخلق ومخادعة لله ورسوله

الباب العاشر في كشف أسرارهم

١٧،٢ ومن هؤلاء المشايخ من يظهر الفواكه في غير أوانها وفي أوقات لا يمكن وجودها مثل المشمش والقراصيا والخوخ والتوت والتين الأخضر والعنب وجميع أجناس الفواكه

him for as long as is needed to make sure that the fumes from the preparation rise and enter the man's brain. Then the shaykh leaves him and goes and stands to one side. The mixture works on the man's brain and the shaykh keeps out of sight and watches. When he sees the man becoming unsteady, he points at him and keeps motioning at him to fall until the man collapses on the ground in a faint. This gives people deluded ideas about the shaykh. Wise up to these things! Be "aware of the things they do"![49]

Section Nine of the Exposé of Their Tricks

Another example: When the shaykh is making the rounds of the gathering, he goes up to a candle and extinguishes it, or does the same to a lamp. Then he extends his ten fingers toward it and they ignite like candles. Once he's lit them, he extinguishes any other candles or lights and keeps dancing, his fingers on fire, till everyone's in an uproar. Now he approaches the candle, relights it, and extinguishes his fingers. This is a powerful illusion. Wise up to these things! Discriminate! 2.15

The trick lies in the shaykh's taking some of the preparation described in the section on descending into baking pits.[50] He smears his fingers with this up to the knuckles and lets them dry. Then he takes bitumen and puts a layer of it over the grease and sets it alight, and it keeps burning till the tar is used up without the heat from the flames reaching his hand. Wise up to these things! Some of them wipe their hands with the same grease and, having had ten tubes made out of red Ṭālaqān felt, place these over their ten fingers, then dip them in tar from Gur and set them on fire; they will remain completely unharmed. All these things are just ways to pull the wool over people's eyes and attempts to put one over God and His messenger. 2.16

Section Ten of the Exposé of Their Tricks

Some of these shaykhs cause fruits—apricots, cherry plums, plums, mulberries, green figs, grapes, and fruit of every other kind, not to mention roses—to appear out of season and at times when they ought not to be available. When they do so, those who see the fruit are amazed and mistakenly believe that 2.17

التي لا إقامة لها في غير أوانها والورد فيظهرونه فيبهت من يراه ويتوهّم فيه الخير وهو بعيد منه وذلك أنّهم يعملون جميع الأجناس ويظهرونها في غير أوانها فمن ذلك تعمير الورد ويظهرونه في مثل كانون كأنّه جنى وقته وذلك أنّه يأخذ وعاء فخّار أحمر جديد يكون قد نقع في ماء الورد يوماً وليلة ثمّ يجفّفه بعد تفريغه ثمّ يجعل فيه ذلك الورد الزرّ بحيث أن لا يكبسه ثمّ يسدّ رأس الوعاء ويستوثق منه لئلّا يدخل إليه الهواء ثمّ يجعل الوعاء معلّقاً في بئر يكون قريباً من الماء فإنّه يقيم على حاله ستّة أشهر وأكثر ما لم يسلّط عليه الهواء فإذا أراد إحضاره أخرجه كأنّه في وقته

الباب الحادي عشر في كشف أسرارهم في تعمير المشمش وإظهاره في غير وقته

وذلك أنّهم يأخذون المشمش وفيه قوّة ثمّ يأخذون مُخْفِيَة زجاج ولها غطاء محكم عليها ١٨،٢
فيفرش فيها[١] الزعفران الشعر ثمّ يصفّون المشمش عليه ولا يلصق شيء بشيء ثمّ يجعل بينهم شيء من الزعفران ويلحفه ثمّ يردّ عليه الغطاء ويشمّع الوصل وخبأه فمتى أراد أحضره كأنّه جنياً جُنى وقته باللون والطعم ثمّ الرائحة ولولا خوف الإطالة لذكرت من هذا المعنى مائتي باب

الباب الثاني عشر في كشف أسرارهم

وقد ظهر بدمشق رجل يقال له المفقود وادّعى المشيخة وكان يظهر الأثمار في ١٩،٢
أوقات لا يمكن أن توجد فيها فاستجلب له خلق كثير فلمّا استفحل أمره ادّعى النبوّة وأنّه عيسى بن مريم فربط جماعة من كبراء البلد ومن جملتهم أهل سوق المَناخِليّين[٢] وكفرسوسيّة وأهل المِزّة فلمّا كثر الرهج فيه طلب ظاهر البلد والقلعة بمكان يُعرف

١ ش: فيفرشها في. ٢ ش: سوق المرحليّين.

God's bounty must be these men's to dispose of as they want, though nothing could be further from the truth.

Example: They make all these different kinds of fruit and produce them out of season, including making roses last a long time and producing them, as fresh as if they had just been gathered in, for example, December or January.

Exposé: They take a new container of red earthenware that has been steeped in rosewater for a day and a night, then emptied and dried. In this they arrange closed rosebuds in such a way as to ensure that they aren't squashed together, then seal the top of the container, making certain it's airtight. Then they hang the container in a well, close to the surface of the water. The roses will remain unchanged for six months or more, so long as they aren't exposed to the air. When the shaykh wants to display them, he takes them out, just as they were when in season.

Section Eleven: Exposé of Their Tricks for Making Apricots Last and for Producing Them out of Season

Exposé: They get the apricots while still fresh, then take a glass jar with a tightly fitting lid and spread its bottom with turmeric, arranging the apricots on it in rows in such a way that none of them is touching another. Then the shaykh puts more turmeric both around the apricots and in a layer on top of them. Finally, he puts the lid back on the jar, seals the join with wax, and hides it. Then he produces the apricots at will, as though they had just been picked, with the right color, taste, and even smell. If I weren't afraid of boring you, I could describe two hundred variants of this trick. 2.18

Section Twelve of the Exposé of Their Tricks

Once, a man called "the One Sought" appeared in Damascus. He claimed to be a shaykh and used to produce different kinds of fruit at times when it was impossible for them to be around. Many were drawn to him, and when he'd become the talk of the town, he claimed to be a prophet, and that he was Jesus, son of Mary. He won over a group of the city's notables, among them the people of the Sieve-Makers' Market and of Kafr Sūsiyyah, as well as of al-Mizzah. When the brouhaha around him became too much, he made 2.19

بالصفصاف وذلك في دولة الملك العادل أبو بكر بن أيّوب وذلك مشهور بدمشق يقال نبيّ الصفصاف

الباب الثالث عشر في كشف أسرارهم

٢٠،٢ ومنهم من يبقى أربعون يوماً لا يشرب ماء ولا يأكل شيئاً ويدّعون أنّ طعامهم التسبيح وشرابهم التقديس وأنّ الله تعالى يبعث لهم من طعام الجنّة ليس في الظاهر بل هو في أفكارهم فينمّسون على الناس ويأكلون أموالهم ويستحيون أولادهم وحريمهم فافهم وكن فطناً

٢١،٢ فمن ذلك من أراد أن يقيم الشهر والاثنين لا يأكل ولا يشرب الماء ولا يحتاج إليه فمن ذلك أن يأخذ بزر الرجلة الحمقاء ثمّ يسحقها ناعماً ثمّ ينقعها في خلّ ثقيف في الشمس فيتركها حتّى تشرب الخلّ ثمّ يسقيها خلّ ثاني في الشمس ثمّ يتركها حتّى تشربه ثمّ يسقيها لم ثالث فإذا شربته جففها ثمّ يستفّ منها على الريق مثقال فيبقى أيّاماً لا يشرب الماء ولا يحتاج إليه ومنهم من يأخذ كبد الغزال العطشان ويجفّفها في الظلّ ثمّ يسحقها ويسقيها فإنّه يقيم ستّة أشهر لا يطلب الماء ولا يشربه ولا تطلبه نفسه وبهذا يسلكون في البرور

٢٢،٢ وظهر بالديار المصريّة رجل يُعرف بأبي الفتح الواسطيّ في سنة خمسة عشر وستّمائة ونزل ببلدة يقال لها فيشة المنارة على بحر الإسكندريّة وادّعى المشيخة وادعى أنّه يبقى ستّة أشهر لا يحتاج إلى شرب الماء فلمّا شاع ذلك عنه أخذه صاحب تلك البلدة وكان يقال له عزّ الدين بَلَبان أمير شِكار الملك الكامل فحبسه في بيت داره وجعل له ترابة برسم التيمّم للصلاة وجعل المفتاح مع نفسه فكان كلّ يوم يفتح عليه الباب ويقعده إلى جانبه على سماطه ويطعمه كلّ مأكول حريف يحتمل شرب الماء مثل الأسماك والجبن والخِلاط والقُبّار وما أشبهه ثمّ يعيده إلى مكانه ويقفل عليه

for the outskirts of the city, for the citadel at a place called al-Ṣafṣāf. This was during the reign of al-Malik al-ʿĀdil Abū Bakr ibn Ayyūb. He's still remembered in Damascus, where they call him the Prophet of al-Ṣafṣāf.

Section Thirteen of the Exposé of Their Tricks

Some of them go for forty days without drinking or eating, claiming that their food consists simply of saying "Glory to God!" and their drink of saying "God sanctify his soul!," and that the Almighty sends them food from Heaven, not tangibly but in their minds. By such means they trick people with illusions, eat up their money, and seduce their children and women. Wise up to these things! Get smart! 2.20

Example: Some like to show they can live for one or two months without eating or drinking water, and that they have no need for either. Such a shaykh will take purslane seed, crush it till smooth, then steep it in strong vinegar in the sun, leaving it till it has soaked up all the vinegar. Then he gives it a second dose of vinegar and leaves it in the sun till that has been absorbed, and then a third. When it has soaked up the last dose, he dries it. Then, if he swallows a mithkal of it on an empty stomach without chewing, he can go for days without drinking or needing water. Some take the liver of a thirsty gazelle, dry it in the shade, crush it, and add water; then they can go for six months without either asking for or drinking water and without feeling any craving for it. It is enough to keep them going as they roam the countryside. 2.21

In Egypt, in 615 [1218–19], a man called Abū l-Fatḥ al-Wāsiṭī appeared and took up residence in the town of Fīshat al-Manārah on the Alexandrian branch of the Nile. He claimed he was a shaykh and that he could go for six months without needing to drink water. When this got out, the lord of the town, who was called ʿIzz al-Dīn Balabān and was al-Malik al-Kāmil's master of the hunt, imprisoned the man in a room in his own house, made him a heap of sand to use for his ablutions before prayer, and put the key in his pocket. Every day, he'd open the door, make the man sit beside him on his dining cloth, and feed him every kind of salty dish that calls for water—fish, cheese, salmagundi,[51] capers, and so on. Then he'd go back to wherever he'd come from, shutting the door on the man and not opening it again until the same time the next 2.22

ولا يفتح عليه إلى مثل ذلك الوقت من اليوم الثاني فأقام ستّة أشهر ولم يتغيّر عليه شيء من أحوال نفسه

فلمّا رأى ذلك منه أقبل عليه إقبال كلّيّ ثمّ نال منه شيء كثير وبنى له زاوية في البلد ثمّ أطلق له أرض مزدرع يتحصّل منها خمسمائة درهم ثمّ شاع ذكره بمصر ونواحيها فحملت إليه الهدايا والتحف والفتوحات إلى أن تموّل وأزوجه الأمير وجاءته الأولاد ومات بها سنة تسع وعشرين وستّمائة وخلّف من البقر والغنم والخيل مبلغ عظيم القدر وله عقب يعرفون بأولاد الشيخ ولولا خوف الإطالة ذكرت فنون يعجز عن إدراكها الناس ٢٣،٢

الباب الرابع عشر في كشف أسرار الذين يقيمون أربعين يوماً لا يأكلون

٢٤،٢ واعلم أنّهم أكثر دهاء ومكر وحيلة وذلك أنّهم يأخذون كبود الخراف ثمّ يسلقونها ويجفّفونها فإذا جفّت يسحقونها وينخلونها ويضيفون إليها سويق مغسول وشيء من سمسم مقشور ومصطكاء وزرّ ورد ثمّ يعجنونه بدهن لوز مقشور ثمّ يضيفون إليه مثل الجميع سكّر طَبَرْزَد ويقرّص أقراص وزن مثقال ثمّ يتناولون منه كلّ يوم قرص فهو يغنيهم عن الطعام ذلك اليوم إلى مثل ذلك الوقت ولهم من هذا النوع جمل لا تعدّ ولا تحصى

الباب الخامس عشر في كشف أسرارهم في نبع الماء من الحصى

٢٥،٢ ويقول هذا سرّ الله الأعظم الذي لا يطلع عليه إلّا من هو من خاصّته ويكذب خذله الله ويأخذ بعقول الناس ويذهل أفكارهم من شدّة الوهم ويفعلون ما أرادوا

day. The man stayed there for six months and his physical condition remained completely unchanged.

When ʿIzz al-Dīn saw what the man could do, he accepted him without reserve. The man exercised great influence over him and ʿIzz al-Dīn built him a lodge in the town, then leased some farmland to him for his personal upkeep, from which he was able to collect five hundred silver pieces in taxes. Soon, his reputation spread throughout Egypt and a variety of presents, valuable objects, and gifts in kind were brought to him by the camel load. He ended up a wealthy man and the emir married him to one of his daughters, by whom he had children. He died there in 629 [1231–32], leaving cattle, sheep, goats, and horses worth a huge sum. He has descendants, who are known as the Sons of the Shaykh. 2.23

If I weren't afraid of boring you, I could tell you more tricks of this type that ordinary people are incapable of understanding.

Section Fourteen: Exposé of the Tricks of Those Who Go for Forty Days without Eating

These are the craftiest, most cunning, and most artful. 2.24

Exposé: They take sheep's livers, boil them, and dry them. When the livers are dry, they pulverize them, sieve them, and add gruel of washed barley, a little shelled sesame, mastic, and rosebuds. They knead this with oil of shelled almonds, add an equal amount of rock candy, and form it into pills, each weighing about one mithkal. They take one of these daily and it obviates the need for them to eat until the following day at the same time. They have too many compounds of this sort to number, too many to count.

Section Fifteen: Exposé of Their Tricks for Making Water Seep from Stones

Shaykhs of this sort claim that this trick is God's greatest secret and that He reveals it only to His elect, but they lie, God dash their hopes, and deceive the 2.25

وذلك أنّهم يأخذون الحصى الفراتيّ ويجعلون بينهم حصى البارود ثمّ يجعله الشيخ في يده ويشغل الناس ساعة بالحديث فإنّه يذوب ذلك البارود ويقطر الماء من بين أصابعه فيذهل القوم ويتوهّم فيه الصلاح ومن ذلك أن يأخذ حصى يُعرف ببصاق القمر ويجعل معه حصى ملح وبارود ويجعله في كفّه ويشغل القوم ساعة فإذا حمي الحصى في يده ذاب الملح والبارود فيقطر الماء من بين أصابعه فيتوهّم فيه الصلاح وهو بضدّ ذلك

الباب السادس عشر في كشف أسرارهم

وذلك أنّ لهم بيوت العبادات قد يسمّونها كما أرادوا فمن ذلك بيت إذا دخلته في ٢٦،٢
الليل رأيت الشمس فيه مثل النهار وهذا البيت رأيت في هندبار رجل قد عمله وكان يقول بعبادة الشمس ورُبِطَ عليه خلق كثير وصار دينهم[١] به وهو من أعجب النواميس ورأيت جماعة من المشايخ يعملونه وذلك أنّه يأخذ صفار البيض فيسحقه وحده[٢] ثمّ يصيّره في دم ابن آدم ثمّ يعلّق في إناء زجاج يوماً فإنّه يصير دودا فيأخذ ذلك الدود ويجعله في صفار البيض المعزول ثمّ يتركه حتّى يأكل بعضه بعضاً ولا يبقى منه إلّا دودة واحدة فتترك في شيء حتّى تموت فتؤخذ وتسحق وهي طريّة ويطلى بها جام زجاج ويجعل ذلك الجام في طاقة في البيت ويغطّى بإجّانة ثمّ يؤخذ وزن دانق ذراريح فيبخّر به البيت فمن دخله يرى فيه ضوءاً أعظم من ضوء الشمس فافهم ذلك ترشد

١ ش: ديانهم. ٢ ش: فيسحقه وحده ثمّ يسحق سحقًا جيّدًا وحده.

people, whose thoughts, given how susceptible they are to delusion, are paralyzed, so that the shaykhs can do with them as they like.

Exposé: They take lumps of bitumen[52] and mix grains of saltpeter into them. The shaykh holds some in his hand and distracts his audience for a while with talk. While he does so, the saltpeter dissolves and the liquid drips from between his fingers. This amazes everyone, and people are deluded into thinking that he is one of the Righteous. A shaykh will also take the pebbles known as moon spittle, put grains of salt and saltpeter with them, and take them in his palm, while he keeps people distracted for a little. As the grains warm in his hand, the salt and the saltpeter dissolve and the liquid drips between his fingers. People are deluded into thinking he's one of the Righteous when in fact he's the opposite.

Section Sixteen of the Exposé of Their Tricks

Another example: They have houses of worship that they call by whatever name takes their fancy. One such is a house in which, if you enter at night, you will see the sun shining as though it were day. In Hindibār, I saw a man who had made a house like this and called on people to worship the sun. Many were won over by him and gave him their allegiance. It's one of the most extraordinary illusions, and I saw a group of shaykhs who perform it. **2.26**

Exposé: A shaykh of this sort will take egg yolks and beat them on their own. Then he brines it[53] in human blood and hangs it in a glass vessel for one day. This turns into worms, which he takes and puts into the egg yolk that was set aside. He leaves this till the worms have eaten one another and just one is left, which he leaves on something till it dies, then takes and crushes while still moist and uses to coat a glass vessel, which he places in a niche in the house and covers with a glass bowl. Then he takes a *dānaq*'s weight of Spanish fly and censes the house with it, and anyone who goes inside beholds a light more powerful than the sun's. Wise up to this and you won't get taken for a ride!

الباب السابع عشر في كشف أسرارهم

٢٧،٢ ومن ذلك أن يكون الشيخ مسافرًا أو سائرًا ورائحًا في الليل في أشدّ ما يكون من الليل والظلام فيظهر من جبينه عمود نور إلى عنان السماء فيضيء لمن يمشي معه مثل النهار وهذا من أعظم الدهاء منهم والمكر والحيل وذلك أن يأخذ من الدود المعروفة بالطَيبُوثة وهي تَسْرُج بالليل في أيّام الربيع ولهم فيها أمور كثيرة فيأخذ منها أربعين دودة عدد ثمّ يجعلها في خرقة شعر رفيعة ثمّ يربطها ويوسّع عليها الرباط ثمّ يجعلها على جبينه طرفها تحت عمامته فإنّه يظهر لها نور عظيم يذهل العقول وكذلك إذا وقف في المحراب يصلّي يظهر لها نور عظيم من جبينه فتضيء الزاوية وكلّ ذلك مسطّرة على أموال الناس وأكلها والفسق بنسائهم وأولادهم فنعوذ بالله من هذه المشايخ فافهم

الباب الثامن عشر في كشف أسرارهم في سجود الشجر لهم وإذعانها وخضوعها

٢٨،٢ وهذا شيء يخرق العقول وذلك الشيخ يقف يصلّي تحت الشجرة فهو يسجد والشجرة تخرّ إليه حتّى يصير رأسها عند رجليه ولا تزال كذلك حتّى يأمرها أن تعود إلى حالها الأوّل وذلك أن يأخذ دماغ سنّور وعظم حيّة سوداء وعظم إنسان أجزاء متساوية ثمّ يبخّر بها تحت شجرة السرو أو الأثل أو الطرفاء فإنّها تنحني إليه وهو واقف يصلّي حتّى يصير رأسها عند رجليه فيتوهّم فيه الأوهام ومنهم من يأخذ من عظم ابن آدم من أضراسه ومن دماغ سنّور وعظم حيّة سوداء أجزاء سواء ثمّ يدفنها في الأرض أربعين يوماً ثمّ يخرجها وتكون عنده فإذا أراد ذلك بخّر بها تحت الشجرة ويقف يصلّي فإنّها تخرّ حتّى يلصق رأسها بين رجليه وهذا ناموس عظيم فافهم

Section Seventeen of the Exposé of Their Tricks

Another example: When the shaykh is on a journey, or out walking, or on his way home by night (and even in the darkest part of the night), a column of light appears, coming out of his forehead and piercing the highest heavens. It provides as much light to the people walking with him as though it were day. This is one of the most powerful examples of craftiness, cunning, and subterfuge they perform. 2.27

Exposé: The shaykh takes the worms known as *ṭaybūthah*[54] that glow at night during the spring and that these shaykhs use in a number of different ways. He takes forty of these worms and puts them in a finely woven hairnet, which he ties loosely and places on his forehead with the end under his turban; it gives off such a powerful light that people are astounded. Likewise, when he stands in the prayer niche to lead the prayer, his forehead gives off so much light that it lights up the whole prayer chamber. All this is carefully designed to get at people's money, which they consume, and to open the way to depravity with their women and children. We seek refuge with God from these shaykhs. Wise up to these things!

Section Eighteen: Exposé of the Tricks They Use to Make Trees Bow Down to Them, Obey Them, and Be Submissive to Them

This is truly amazing. The shaykh stands, praying, under a tree. He performs a prostration,[55] and the tree bends over toward him till its crown is at his feet, and it stays like that till he commands it to go back to the way it was. 2.28

Exposé: He takes equal parts of the brain of a cat, the bones of a black snake, and human bones. Then he burns an incense made of these beneath a cypress, or an athel or Nile tamarisk, which then bows to him as he stands praying, till its crown touches his feet. As a result, people conceive deluded ideas about him. Some of these shaykhs take equal parts of human bones and teeth, cat brain, and black snake bones, and bury them in the ground for forty days. Then the shaykh takes them out and keeps them at home. To perform the trick, he burns them as incense beneath the tree and stands and prays. The tree then bows down till its crown touches the ground before his feet while he stands in prayer. This is a powerful illusion. Wise up to these things!

الباب التاسع عشر في كشف أسرارهم

٢٩،٢ وذلك أنّ من هذه المشايخ من إذا كان جالس في الزاوية وعنده جماعة من الذي يحضرها ثمّ اشتهى كلّ واحد من الجماعة على الشيخ شهوة[١] فإنها تحضر على الوصف الذي طلب وقد كان اجتمعت في بلد الحجاز بشيخ يُعرف بسليمان وكان من أهل المغرب كنّا عنده ذات يوم ثمانية أنفس فاشتهى كلّ واحد منّا على الشيخ شهوة فقام إلى بيت الخلوة ليصلّي ثمّ دعا وخرج فما لحق يخرج إلّا والذي طلبنا قد حضر من حيث لم يخرج أحد من الزاوية فخرق عقول الناس وشاع ذلك عنه وجاءته الفتوحات من كلّ إقليم

٣٠،٢ وكشفت عن هذا السرّ فوجدت الشيخ له قعيدة في فتر المدينة وعند الشيخ في بيت الخلوة طير حمام شاطر على بيت القعيدة الذي له فإذا اشتهى كلّ واحد ما في قلبه قام الشيخ إلى بيت الخلوة ثمّ كتب جميع ما طلبوه الجماعة في بطاقة ثمّ علّقها على الطير ثمّ أرسله فإنّه ينزل على القعيدة وما كان قد طلب منه يرسله ولا يشعرون به إلّا وقد حضر فيذهل كلّ من كان حاضر عنده ويرويه عنه في البلاد فافهم أسرار هؤلاء القوم ودهاءهم

٣١،٢ واعلم وفّقك الله أنّ أهل هذه الدرجة من المشايخ كلّهم مجمعون على بطلان معجزات الأنبياء عليهم السلام وكرامات الصالحين من هذا النوع الذي قد سلكوه ويكذبون والله بل إنّ الله عزّ وجلّ قد اختصّ أنبياءه وأولياءه بمعجزات وكرامات ثمّ إنّ أهل هذه الدرجة مجمعون على أكل الحشيشة واستباحة حريم المسلمين والفسق بأولادهم ولهم في ذلك فنون وبعض مشايخهم يقول [كامل]

١ ش: وعنده جماعة ثم اشتهى كلّ واحد من الجماعة على الشيخ شهوة ومن الذي يحضرها.

Section Nineteen of the Exposé of Their Tricks

Another example: There are shaykhs of this type who will be seated in the lodge with a group of those who frequent it, each of whom will ask him to provide him with something for which he has a fancy. That thing will then arrive, exactly as the man described it. In the Hejaz, I met a shaykh called Sulaymān, from the Maghreb. One day, eight of us were at his place and each asked the shaykh to provide an item of this type. The shaykh rose and went to say the ritual prayer in the cell where he held his retreats. Then he emerged, uttering the final blessings, and barely had he done so than what we'd asked for arrived, even though no one had left the lodge. Everyone was astounded, and the news spread, and gifts in kind came to the shaykh from every land. 2.29

I exposed the trick. I found that the shaykh had accomplices in the heart of the city. He also had messenger pigeons in his cell trained to fly to the house of these accomplices. When each of those present had stated what it was that he'd set his heart on, the shaykh would go off to his cell, where he would write down on a piece of paper everything they'd asked for. He would hang this around the neck of the bird, which he would then dispatch. The bird would alight at the accomplices' place and they'd send him whatever people had asked for, while the latter would have no idea of what was going on until the things arrived. Everyone who was there would be astounded and spread the word through the surrounding towns. Wise up to the tricks of this company and their cunning! 2.30

Just so you know, God grant you success, shaykhs of this rank are all of the same mind when it comes to declaring invalid both the miracles of the prophets, eternal peace be theirs, and the miraculous acts performed through God's grace by the righteous members of that same path that they themselves claim, mendaciously, to follow. The fact is, however, that God, Mighty and Exalted, has granted the power to perform such miracles and miraculous acts to His prophets and wards alone. Shaykhs of this rank are equally of the same mind when it comes to the eating of "weed"[56] and the permissibility of violating the sanctity of Muslim women and performing depraved acts with their children, for which they have a number of techniques. One of their shaykhs has written:[57] 2.31

وَمُهَفْهَفٍ بَادِي ٱلنُّفُورِ رَأَيْتُهُ   لَا أَلْتَقِيهِ قَطُّ غَيْرَ مُعَبِّسِ
صَادَفْتُهُ بَعْضَ ٱللَّيَالِي ضَاحِكًا   سَهْلَ ٱلْعَرِيكَةِ رَائِضًا فِي ٱلْمَجْلِسِ
عَيْنَاهُ تَخْطُبُ عَاشِقًا مُتَجَاسِرًا   وَٱلسُّكْرُ يُحْسِنُ لِلْمُحِبِّ وَلَا يُسِيءْ
قَضَيْتُ مِنْهُ مَآرِبِي وَشَرِكْتُهُ[1]   إِذْ صَارَ مِنْ بَعْدِ ٱلتَّنَافُرِ مُؤْنِسِي
فَأَجَابَنِي لَا تَشْكُرَنَّ خَلَائِقِي   وَٱشْكُرْ شَفِيعَكَ فَهُوَ خَمْرُ ٱلْمُفْلِسِ
فَحَشِيشَةُ ٱلْأَفْرَاحِ تَشْفَعُ عِنْدَنَا   لِلْعَاشِقِينَ لِبَسْطِهَا لِلْأَنْفُسِ
فَإِذَا هَمَمْتَ بِصَيْدِ ظَبْيٍ نَافِرٍ   فَٱجْهَدْ بِأَنْ يَرْعَى حَشِيشَ ٱلْقُنْبُسِ
هَبْ إِنَّهُ مُتَحَفِّظٌ فِي يَقْظَةٍ   مَا صُنْعُهُ فِي نَوْمِهِ ٱلْمُتَعَرِّسِ
وَسَلِ ٱلْمُجَرِّبَ لِلْأُمُورِ وَخَلِّنِي   مِنْ حُسْنِ ظَنِّ ٱلنَّاسِكِ ٱلْمُتَنَمِّسِ
وَٱشْكُرْ عِصَابَةَ حَيْدَرٍ إِذْ أَظْهَرُوا   لِذَوِي ٱلْخَلَاعَةِ مَذْهَبَ ٱلْمُتَخَمِّسِ[2]

فإذا كانت هذه مشيختهم فما عسى أن يقال فيهم فإنّهم كما قال الله تعالى في كتابه ﴿وَجَعَلْنَٰكُمْ شُعُوبًا وَقَبَآئِلَ﴾

الباب العشرون في كشف أسرارهم

فمنهم الرِفاعيّة وهم الذين كراماتهم أكل الحيّات والنار فوالله لو فعل هذا قدّام ٣٢،٢
الأطفال لضحكوا على من يفعله فيا عميان القلوب هذه كرامات الصالحين فانتبهوا
يا نيام وتيقّظوا

١ ش: تركته. ٢ ش: المتحمّس.

A slender boy I saw, feigning aversion—
    I never met him when he wasn't scowling!
One night, I came across him at a gathering
    laughing, compliant, easygoing,
His eyes engaging a lover's glances in mutual daring
    (for intoxication makes a boy kinder to the beloved, not less caring).
I got from him what I wanted and thanked him,
    for, after avoidance, he'd become my cozy darling.
He responded, "Don't thank my natural disposition,
    thank the one who pled your cause—the tipple of the poorling:
In our world, the cheerful herb pleads
    on the lover's behalf, it being to our spirits so relaxing."
If, then, you're bent on hunting a gazelle who's standoffish,
    make your play while he's on hempseed grazing.
Suppose he's reticent while waking,
    such won't be his way in his nuptial drowsing.
Ask those who know how the world works (spare me
    the good opinion of the ascetic, calumniating![58])
And thank Ḥaydar's band, for they've revealed to the licentious
    how to practice the art of quintupling![59]

If this is the sort of shaykh they are, what can one say of them? They are like the people of whom the Almighty says in His book «and We have appointed you races and tribes.»[60]

Section Twenty of the Exposé of Their Tricks

They include the Rifāʿīs,[61] whose "miraculous acts" consist of eating serpents and fire. If they did such things in front of children, I swear they'd laugh at them! People's hearts are so blind! Things like these are the exclusive prerogative of the Righteous. Pay attention, you sleepers, and rouse yourselves! 2.32

الباب الحادي والعشرون في كشف أسرارهم

ومنهم ضروب الحيْدَريّة وهم الذين يحلقون لحاهم ويلبسون الحديد ثمّ يثقبون به ويتسوّرون ويثقب الواحد منهم ذكره ويجعل فيه حلقة وكلّ ذلك مسطّرة على أموال الناس والفسق بأولادهم والدليل أنّ أحدهم لا يبقى يوم واحد بلا أكل الحشيش فإذا أكله اختلط عقله وسوّلت له نفسه كلّ قبيح وهذا الحشيش فهو من أعظم المُسْكِرات[1] وكلّ مسكر حرام فإذا أكل الحرام فعل كلّ قبيح وكلّ منهيّ عنه فإذا أكل الحشيش وأدمن أكلها استولى الهوس على دماغه وتشعّب منه أمور تودّي إلى أن يمرق أحدهم وربّما مرق أكثرهم فنعوذ بالله من ذلك ٣٣،٢

الباب الثاني والعشرون في كشف أسرارهم

ومنهم الجَوالقيّة الذين يلبسون الجوالق ويحلقون لحاهم أيضاً وهذه بدعة ابتدعوها ثمّ إنّهم لا يصومون ولا يصلّون ولا يؤدّون شيئاً من الفرائض ولا يغتسلون من الجنابة فيا أهل الإيمان هذه صفات الصالحين فتدبّروا كلامي واعقلوه ٣٤،٢

الباب الثالث والعشرون في كشف أسرارهم

ومنهم الحَريريّة وهم ثلاث فرق وقد كان ظهر في دمشق رجل يُعرف بالشيخ عليّ الحريريّ وسكن أرض حَوْران وادّعى المشيخة وأتبعه خلق كثير وأتلف أولاد أهل دمشق وقد كان أصل مذهبه أنّه يقول لمن يتلمذ له لا تمنع النفس شيئاً من حظّها فما طلبت نفسك فهو حظّها فابلغها ذلك وله أحاديث كثيرة وعجيبة وهذا الرجل ظفر به السلطان الملك الأشرف قدّس الله روحه وحبسه في حصن عربا ٣٥،٢

---

١ ش: المنكرات.

Section Twenty-One of the Exposé of Their Tricks

They include too the various species of Ḥaydarīs, who are the ones who shave off their beards and wear iron, which they pierce themselves with, and who put on metal rings; they even pierce their penises and insert rings through them.[62] All of this is carefully designed to allow such shaykhs to get their hands on people's money and practice depravity with their young sons, the proof being that not one of them can go a day without eating "weed," which addles his brain and incites his carnal soul to do ugly things. This "weed" is a most powerful intoxicant, and anything that intoxicates is forbidden by religion. If he eats this forbidden intoxicant, the fake shaykh will perform the ugliest acts and do everything he is prohibited from. When such people develop an addiction to the eating of "weed," they become demented, with ramifying consequences that may lead one, or even most, of them to abandon the true faith (God protect us!). 2.33

Section Twenty-Two of the Exposé of Their Tricks

They also include the Sack Men,[63] who wear sacks, and shave their beards too, which is a reprehensible innovation they have introduced. They don't fast or perform the ritual prayers or any other religious duty and they don't wash after sex. Does this, O ye faithful, sound like a description of the Righteous? Take what I'm telling you seriously and use your common sense! 2.34

Section Twenty-Three of the Exposé of Their Tricks

In addition, there are the Ḥarīrīs, who are divided into three subsections. A man known as Shaykh ʿAlī al-Ḥarīrī appeared in Damascus and took up residence in Ḥawrān, where he claimed to be a shaykh. He gained lots of followers and corrupted the sons of its inhabitants. The basis of his doctrine was to tell his pupils, "Don't deny your appetites their due—and what they're due is whatever they ask for, so make sure they get it!" Many extraordinary things were reported of him. Sultan al-Malik al-Ashraf, God sanctify his soul, seized him and imprisoned him in the fortress of ʿArabā, in the district of Jubbat ʿAssāl, 2.35

من جُبّة عسّال فأقام حتّى مات السلطان وله أمور كثيرة قباح لا يلاقي[1] يدي النجدة بذكرها

٣٦،٢ الفرق من أصحابه الفرقة الأولى يقال لهم المُتَمَيِّزة وهم الذين يعانون الحسن من ملابيس الفقراء ويعاشرون أبناء الكبراء من الناس فلا يزالون عليهم بالمواظبة حتّى يطعمونهم القنبس فإذا أكله أصلى شبكته وشوى في الحريق سمكته ولا يزال عليه حتّى يخرج من المدينة إلى ظاهرها ثمّ يطعمه الحشيشة مبنجة ثمّ يعمد إلى رأسه فيحلقها ويشوّه بخلقته ويخلّعه ما عليه وكذلك يعمل بنفسه ويودّر الثياب ويسعطه الكندس والخل فيفيق فإذا أفاق تناوم هو فينبّهه الصبيّ فيجده بتلك الحالة رأسه قد حُلق وقماشه قد راح فيطير عقله خوفًا من أهله ولا يطيق الرجوع إلى أهله من الخوف فينتبه صاحبه

٣٧،٢ فإذا قعد صاح صيحة واحدة وقال أيش هذا القالب من فعل بنا هذا وأين قماشنا فيقول الصبيّ والله لا أعلم إلّا أنّي انتبهت وجدت روحي على هذه الصفة فيتوجّع ويتأسّف على ما تمّ عليهم ثمّ يفكّر ساعة زمانيّة ويقول للصبيّ كيف يكون العمل أنا ما خوفي إلّا عليك إن رأوك أهلك بهذه الحالة لا آمن عليك أن يقتلوك وأنا مسافر من وقتي هذا بل والله إنّني أخاف عليك ومتأسّف عليك فابصر أيش تعمل في نفسك فيتحيّر الصبيّ ويقول والله ما أعلم ما يكون عملي

٣٨،٢ فيقول له نقوم حتّى نسافر إلى المكان الفلانيّ ونبصر ما يكون من أخبار أهلك فإن كانت نيّتهم لك جيّدة سمعنا وإن كان غير ذلك سمعنا فإن سمعنا أخبار طيّبة قعدنا حتّى يطلع شعرك ونحصّل لك شيء تكتسي به ونأخذ هديّة وننزل والساعة لا تعمل إلّا ما تريد وأنا لا أوحش الله منك ودبّر رأيك بنفسك ثمّ يولّي عنه فيتحيّر الصبيّ ويقول شيء ما علينا ونحن حفاة كيف نسافر فيقول أنا أعبر أتجسّس عن أخبار أهلك فإن كانت نيّاتهم لنا جيّدة تحيّلت منّا في شيء نلبس وجئت أخذتك وعبرت إليهم

---

١ ش: يليق.

where he stayed until the sultan died. He did many things so ugly I cannot bring myself to speak of them.

The first of its subsections is that of the so-called "Distingués." These are the ones who are careful to wear the smartest dervish outfits and to mix with young men of good family, whom they visit regularly to persuade them to eat hempseed. Once one of them eats, the shaykh's net is set, his fish as good as fried, and he keeps feeding the youth with the drug till he can leave the city with him for the suburbs, where the shaykh feeds him "weed" laced with something to put him to sleep. The shaykh now takes the young man's head, shaves it, puts dirt on his face, removes his clothes and his own, gets rid of the clothes, and then wakes the youth by putting Egyptian soapwort and vinegar up his nose. As the young man revives, the shaykh pretends to fall asleep. The boy tries to wake him but finds himself as described, head shaven and clothing gone. Fear of his parents drives him crazy and he's so scared he can't bear the thought of going back to them. His companion now comes to. 2.36

The latter, sitting up, lets out a great cry and says, "This is a fine kettle of fish! Who has done this to us, and where are our clothes?" The boy replies, "I swear I have no idea! I came to just now and found myself like this," and the shaykh moans and groans over what has happened to them. After a while, he says to the boy, "What to do? My concern is entirely for you. If your parents see you like this, I can't be sure they won't kill you. I'm getting out of here right now, but I must say, I'm afraid for you and feel terrible about what might happen to you. What on earth are you going to do with yourself?" The boy, at his wits' end, declares, "I swear I have no idea!" 2.37

The shaykh then says to him, "Let's get moving and go to such and such a place. We'll see if there's any word from your parents. If their intentions toward you are good, we'll find out, and if not, we'll find that out too. If we hear good news, we can stay put until your hair grows back and find you something to cover yourself with and take a present with us and go back to the city. Now, it's up to you to do what you think best, though me, personally, I'd hate to see you go. Make up your mind." Then he turns away from him, and the boy, who's at his wits' end, says, "But what are we to do when we don't even have shoes? How can we go anywhere?" The other says, "I'll go spy out how things stand with your parents. If their intentions are good, I'll rustle up something for us to wear, come and get you, and we can go to them. If I hear they're plotting something bad for us, I'll get us some clothes and something to put on our feet 2.38

وإن سمعت أنّهم مضمرين لنا سوء حصّلت لنا شيء نلبس وشيء في رجلينا واتّكلنا على الله ثمّ سافرنا فيقول الصبيّ افعل فيتركه وقد أوصاه أن لا يظهر صورته لأحد من الناس

٣٩،٢ ثمّ يغيب عنه يوم ويجيء ومعه جبّة صوف وشَمْلة وزَرْبول وجراب فيه الحشيشة فيقول اشكر الله الذي ما جزت قد راح أبوك أو عمّك أو من يعلم أنّه حاكم عليه إلى عند الوالي وقال له ولدي فلان قد أخذ لي كذا وكذا درهم وراح وهذا قد خرج عن يدي فأريد تمكّني منه إذا وقع لأفعلن فيه الواجب فإنّ نحن قوم مستورين لا يشبه بنا أن نحضر في مثل هذه الأشياء قدّام والي وقد أذن له الوالي أن يفعل بك ما يريد وأنا رائح إلى عند فلان لعلّ آخذ منه شيء من الدراهم نتسفّر إلى الموضع الفلانيّ وقد لقيته ومعه غلامكم فلان ومعه قيد وزنود وهم رائحين إلى الدار وقال لي فلان أيش عليك من فلان فقلت جرى علينا كذا وكذا فقال احذر أن تخلّيه يقع في عينه فهو يتلفه فاعمل معه عمل الرجال فما يعرف الصاحب إلّا في الشدّة وفي مثل هذه الأشياء فقلت والله ما تطير رأسي إلّا قدّامه ولا يزال يحدّثه من هذه الأقاويل وهو يسأله أن يأخذه ويروح فهذه أوصاف المتميّزين

٤٠،٢ ومنهم طائفة تعرف بالبَحْرِيّة نذكرهم في كشف أسرارهم اعلم وفّقك الله ورعاك أنّ هؤلاء الطائفة لا ينبغي لهم أن يدخلوا إلى هذا المكان أو أيّ مكان كان ويخرجوا منه بلا شيء يفتخروا به ويفتّشوه منه لو كان ما كان حتّى أنّهم إذا دخلوا إلى المسجد أخذوا زيته من القناديل فإن غلبوا عنه أخذوا منه طاقة أو سلاسل القناديل أو باب أو ساقطة أو سكّرة ومن لا يفعل هذا ومثله لا يقدر على معاشرتهم وهو ساقط القدر عندهم وهم من ضروب الهجّامين فإنّهم أنجس هذه الطائفة

and we'll put our trust in God and get out of here." "Do as you think best," the boy says. So the shaykh leaves him, after instructing him not to show his face to anyone.

The man stays away for a day and comes back bringing a woolen jubbah, a mantle, leather slippers, and a bag of "weed." He says, "Thank God I didn't go through the city! Your father (or your uncle or whoever it is he knows has authority over the boy) went to the governor and told him, 'My son so-and-so took such and such a sum from me in silver pieces and made off. He has fled my authority, and I want to get my hands on him. When that happens, I'll give him what he's got coming to him. We're respectable folk and no one would ever have thought we'd find ourselves standing in front of the governor on a matter like this!' So the governor has given him permission to do what he likes with you, and while I was on my way to so-and-so's so that maybe I could get some money off him so we could make tracks to such and such a place, I ran into your father. He had with him your slave so-and-so, who was carrying a shackle and handcuffs, and they were on their way to the house. And someone asked me, 'What's going on with you and so-and-so?' and I said, 'This and that,' so he told me, 'Mind you don't let his father catch sight of him or he'll give him hell and let him have it like a real man! A friend only shows his true colors at moments like these, when the going gets tough.' I told him, 'I swear, I'd rather put my head on the chopping block than let him down!'" He keeps on feeding him this line till the boy asks the shaykh to take him away with him and get him out of there. This is the MO of the Distingués. 2.39

They also include a tribe of charlatans known as the Baḥriyyah whom we should mention in our exposé of their tricks. You should be aware, God grant you success and hold you in his keeping, that its members believe they shouldn't enter this or any other place unless they can take something with them on the way out, to show off with, and they'll forage around for it, whatever it may be, till they find it. They'll even enter a mosque and take the oil from its lamps, and if that's too difficult for them, they'll take a hoop,[64] or the iron lamp chains, or a door, or a door latch, or a wooden door lock. Anyone who doesn't do this or something similar isn't allowed to go around with them and has no standing among them. They are a kind of sneak thief, the most despicable of all this tribe. 2.40

الباب الرابع والعشرون في كشف أسرارهم

ومنهم طائفة يقال لهم الغواة وهم الذين لا يعفّون عن شيء ولا يتّقون نجساً أو يعملونه ٤١،٢
من أكل أو شرب أو قمار وضراب وزطاط وهذه الطائفة قد جمعت كلّ ما تفرّق
في الناس من العيوب والشرّ فافهم ولولا خوف الإطالة لذكرت فيهم بعض صفاتهم
كما قيل وعندي لهم دفاتر مرقومة يحيّر فيها الناظر فافهم ذلك

Section Twenty-Four of the Exposé of Their Tricks

There is also a tribe called "the Enthusiasts." They are the ones for whom nothing is too revolting and who have no fear of suffering or engaging in any defilement, whether it be the eating or drinking of impure things, or gambling, or whoring, or vagabondage. This sect combines all the vices and evils that are more thinly distributed among the rest of the population. **2.41**

Wise up to these things! If I weren't afraid of boring you, I'd list more of their characteristic features, as already mentioned; I have major dossiers on them that would leave anyone who takes a look quite disturbed. Wise up to these things!

الفصل الثالث

أربعة أبواب

في كشف أسرار الوعّاظ

اعلم أنّ هذه الطائفة صناعتهم أجلّ الصنائع وهي أعلى مرتبة بني ساسان وهي الذي وضع ساسان أساسها ونوّع أنواعها وأجناسها فأوّل ما لهم من الأعمال أنّهم يرتّبون من يطرح المسائل عليهم فيجيبون عنها على قدر ذلك ثمّ إنّهم يرتّبون القرّاء يقرؤون ما يقع على قافية الخطبة ثمّ إنّهم يذكروا الله عزّ وجلّ بما هو أهله ثمّ يوردون[1] أخبار النبيّ عليه السلام ثمّ أخبار الصالحين وغيرهم فيزهّدون الناس في الدنيا ويرغّبوهم في الآخرة وإذا أنت اطّلعت عليهم لولّيت منهم فرارًا ولملئت منهم رعباً إلّا أنّهم في الظاهر يذكرون أحوال الجنّة وما أعدّ الله لأهلها وكذلك النار وما فيها من الأحوال والأهوال ﴿وَأَنَّهُمْ يَقُولُونَ[2] مَا لَا يَفْعَلُونَ﴾ فافهم ذلك وكن بنفسك منفردًا ١،٣

الباب الأوّل في كشف أسرارهم

ومن دهائهم أنّهم يطلعون على المنبر بخشوع وسكينة فإذا شرعوا في الكلام وذكروا أهوال يوم القيامة وما أعدّ الله فيها للمجرمين يبكون بدموع أحرّ من الجمر فإذا أرادوا ذلك يأخذون الخردل فيسحقونه ثمّ ينقعونه في الخلّ يوماً وليلة كاملة ثمّ يسقون به المنديل الذي يمسحون به وجوههم ثمّ يتركونه حتّى يجفّ فإذا حصل على المنبر ثمّ أورد ٢،٣

١ ش: يردون. ٢ ش: وَيَقُولُونَ.

Chapter Three, in Four Sections:

Exposé of the Tricks of Fire-and-Brimstone Preachers

The trade practiced by this tribe of charlatans[65] is the most exalted of them all and has the highest status among the Banū Sāsān. It is a trade whose foundations were laid and branches and categories elaborated by the Banū Sāsān themselves. Their first order of the day is to organize people to pose them the questions to which they will fit their answers. Next, they organize the repeaters, who will echo the rhyme words of the sermon. This done, they invoke the name of God, Mighty and Exalted, as is proper, then introduce reports of the words and deeds of the Prophet, God bless and keep him, followed by those of the Righteous, and others. They urge the congregation to renounce the things of this world and encourage them to set their sights on the next, but if you were to get a close look at them, you'd turn and run, your heart filled with terror. The irony is that they talk about Paradise and what God has prepared for those who will enter it, and likewise of the Fire, with its terrors and conditions dire, yet «they say that which they do not.»[66] Wise up to these things and keep your distance! 3.1

Section One of the Exposé of Their Tricks

An example of their wiliness is that they mount the pulpit with reverence and tranquility of spirit. Then, when they reach the bit about the terrors of the Day of Resurrection and the things God has in store there for criminals, they weep tears hotter than embers. To be able to do so at will, they take mustard seed and crush it, steep it in vinegar for a day and the whole of the following night, then wet with it the handkerchief they use to wipe their faces and leave it to dry. When one of them gets to the pulpit and is passing the terrors 3.2

أهوال يوم القيامة مسح بذلك المنديل وجهه فتنزل دموعه مثل المطر وهو أوّل ما لهم من الدهاء والمكر

الباب الثاني في كشف أسرارهم

٣،٣ ومن ذلك أنّهم يجهّزون بعض نسائهم في زيّ أصحاب البيوتات وقد أخنى عليها الزمان فلا تقدر تبذل ماء[١] وجهها إلى الخلق فيعطف عليها القلوب ويردّد الكلام في ذلك المعنى ويورد فيه خبر ويجيب فيه حكاية ثمّ يخلع فَوقانيّته ويرميها عليها ويقول والله لو ملكت يدي شيء من النفقة لكنت أنا أحقّ بهذه المثوبة ولكن العذر واضح فأستعيني بثمن هذا الثوب وأصبري على جور الزمان عسى الله أن يأتي بالفتح أو أمر من عند الله فإذا رأوا الجماعة ذلك لم يبق أحد حتّى يرفدها بشيء من عنده على قدره ومكنته في ذلك الوقت وما تحصّل فهو للواعظ

الباب الثالث في كشف أسرارهم

٤،٣ من ذلك أنّهم إذا كانوا متوجّهين إلى بعض البلاد يجهّزون من يسبقهم إلى ذلك البلد فيدّعي أنّه نصرانيّ أو يهوديّ فإذا سمع أنّه قد ورد واعظ[٢] يقال له الواعظ الفلانيّ وأنّه يجلس في الموضع الفلانيّ فيتركه في المجلس الأوّل ولا يقربه وإذا كان في المجلس الثاني حضر في المجلس فإذا طاب في المجلس قام الذي ادّعى أنّه ذمّيّ فيشقّ الخلق ويتعلّق بالمنبر ويقول افتح[٣] الباب ويصعد إلى عند الواعظ ثمّ يتعلّق به ويقول أنا رجل كذا وكذا من البلد الفلانيّ رأيت البارح سيّد المرسلين وخاتم النبيّين محمّد صلّى الله عليه وسلّم

١ أضيف للسياق. ٢ ش: ووعظ. ٣ ش: فتح.

of the Day of Resurrection in review, he wipes his face with the same handkerchief and the tears fall like rain. This is the first example of their craftiness and cunning.

Section Two of the Exposé of Their Tricks

Another example: They deck out one of their women in the sort of clothes that might be worn by the mistress of a prosperous household who has fallen on hard times and cannot face the shame of being seen by people. Men feel sorry for her, and the charlatan preacher harps on this theme, quoting now a hadith of the Prophet, now a pious anecdote. Then he takes off his mantle and throws it to her, saying, "Had I any money on me to give away, I would have been the one to claim the heavenly reward for doing so, but one can only do what one can do. Use what you get for this garment and endure the tyranny of fate. Haply, God may make things easier for you or send you something." When those present see this, in no time each and every one of them will have given her some assistance, according to his means and what he has on him at the time. Whatever she collects goes to the preacher. 3.3

Section Three of the Exposé of Their Tricks

Another example: Before setting off for some country, they will dress up someone whose job is to go on ahead of them to the land in question, where he claims to be a Christian or a Jew. When he hears that Preacher So-and-so has arrived and set up shop in such and such a place, he steers clear of him and doesn't go near him, but when the preacher sets up shop in a second place, he attends the gathering.[67] If all goes well, the person pretending to be one of the People of the Book pushes his way through the crowd and clings to the pulpit, exclaiming, "Open the door!" Then he climbs up to where the preacher is and throws his arms round him, saying, "I'm from such and such a town and yesterday I dreamt I saw the Lord of Messengers and Seal of Prophets, Muḥammad, God bless and keep him." 3.4

فإذا كان دعواه أنّه نصرانيّ يقول رأيت محمّداً صلّى الله عليه ومعه عيسى بن مريم فقال لي النبيّ صلّى الله عليه وسلّم يا فلان إلى كم هذه الغفلة استيقظ من هذا الذي أنت فيه وهذا الاعتقاد المفسود وارجع إلى دين الحقّ فقلت وما دين الحقّ فقال تقول أشهد أنّ لا إله إلّا الله وأنّ محمّد رسول الله فقلت له لا أقدر على ذلك خوفاً من عقوبة يسوع[١] المسيح فقال يا عيسى ما تقول في ذلك قال لي عيسى عليه السلام قل ما يقول لك سيّد المرسلين وخاتم النبيّين تنجو من عذاب يوم الدين وأنا أقول معك أشهد أنّ لا إله إلّا الله وأشهد أنّ محمّداً رسول الله فقلت لعيسى يا روح الله ما أنت قلت إنّك إله فقال كذبوا عليّ أنا عبد من عبيد الله ولا إله إلّا الله ثمّ قال لي النبيّ عليه السلام إذا كان في الغد امض إلى مجلس أخي فلان وخصّه عنّي بالسلام وقل له قال لك رسول الله بأمارة كذا وكذا جدّد إسلامي على يديك وعلّمني فرائض الصلاة وحدود الإسلام فإذا سمعوا الناس ذلك توهّموا في الواعظ أنّه من الأفراد فعند ذلك تدور له رحاية المعيشة فافهم ذلك ٥،٣

الباب الرابع في كشف أسرارهم

وقد كان لي صاحب واعظ من أهل حلب بالديار المصريّة يُعرف بقطب الدين صحبته سنة ثلاث وعشرين وستّمائة وسنة أربع وكان أظرف أهل زمانه وأشدّهم خلاعة وكان معتكف على الخمر لا يصبر عنه يوماً واحداً وكان مجلسه يوم الثلاثاء بجامع الأزهر[٢] وكان مجلس عظيم محتفّ بالخلق من النساء والرجال وكانوا ينزلون الخلق من مصر ليحضره إلى مجلسه فقال لي في بعض الأيّام والله أقدر آكل وأشرب وألعب بالطَرَبْروب أفعل هذا على المنبر في المجلس فقلت هذا لا يقدر عليه أحد ٦،٣

١ في الأصل: يوشع. ٢ في الأصل: الأزلي.

If pretending to be a Christian, he then says, "I beheld Muḥammad, God bless him, and Jesus son of Mary was with him, and the Prophet, God bless and keep him, asked me, 'So-and-so, how much longer will you persist in this foolishness? Break free of this nonsensical and corrupted creed that you're caught up in and return to the true faith!' 'And what is the true faith?' I asked him, and he replied, 'That you should say, "There is no god but God and Muḥammad is the Messenger of God."' I said, 'I cannot, for fear of being punished by Jesus Christ.' Then the Prophet said, 'What do you have to say to that, Jesus?' and Jesus, eternal peace be his, told me, 'If you say what the Lord of the Messengers and Seal of the Prophets tells you to, you will be saved from the torment of the Last Day, and I will say along with you, "I bear witness that there is no god but God and I bear witness that Muḥammad is the Messenger of God"!' So I said to Jesus, 'O Spirit of God,[68] did you not say that you are a god?' to which he replied, 'They put lies in my mouth. I am but a slave of God, other than whom there is no god.' Then the Prophet, eternal peace be his, told me, 'Tomorrow, go to the gathering of my brother so-and-so, give him my best, and tell him, "The Messenger of God (and you will know by virtue of such and such a sign that he's the one who has sent me) says you're to renew my Islam[69] through your good offices and to instruct me in the fundamentals of the prayer and the punishments set by Islam."'" When the congregation hears this, they are deluded into believing that the preacher is a man apart, and the millstone of his livelihood begins to turn. Wise up to these things! 3.5

Section Four of the Exposé of Their Tricks

When I was in Egypt, I was friends with a preacher from Aleppo who went by the name of Quṭb al-Dīn. I hung out with him during 623 and 624 [1226–27]. He was the most amusing man of his day, and the most dissolute. He was a dedicated drinker of wine, which he couldn't go without for a single day. He held court on Tuesdays at the mosque of al-Azhar and they were huge gatherings, crammed with people—women as well as men—who'd come from Miṣr to be with him in his assembly.[70] One day, he said to me, "I swear I could eat, drink, and play the ukulele[71] while in the pulpit during the gathering!" "No way could anyone do that!" I responded, to which he replied, "I swear 3.6

فقال والله أفعله وأسلب الناس عقولهم فيكون مجلس أعظم من[1] المجالس الذي تقدّمت نخاطرنا على ذلك

٧،٣ فلمّا كان يوم الثلاثاء قال نحنا على الشرط قلت نعم فقال للنقيب روح دقّ لي أوساط خاثونيّة بحوائجها الجميع واحضرها إليّ ففعل ذلك وكان عندنا سراحيّة تسع رطل بالمصريّ فأملأها خمر وسدّ رأسها ودفعها للنقيب ثمّ قال له تكون معك فإذا طلبتها منك ادفعها وكان عندنا شيخ تركمانيّ اسمه بدل وكان يلعب بالطربروب وكان خليع الوقت فقال له إذا طاب المجلس وشرعت في نشيد الشعر خذ هذا الطربروب واصعد إلى عندي على المنبر حتّى أفرّجك يا شيخ نحس على عجيب ثمّ وثب وأنا معه والمنديل الذي فيه الأوساط في عبّه فصعد إلى المنبر فسلّم وجلس وجعل رأسه في زيقه

٨،٣ فلمّا شرعوا القرّاء في القراءة شرع هو في أكل الأوساط فأكلها فلمّا فرغوا القرّاء جميعهم أخرج رأسه وشرع في الخطبة فجعل يظهر الخلط والبلغم ويسعل ويتوقّف في الخطبة ثمّ قال يا أصحابنا اعذروني فإنّي قد حدث عندي هذا الخلط إلى أن صرت أعجز عن الكلام وقد شكوت ذلك للحكيم فعبأ لي نقوع وقال لي إذا حدث عليك هذا المرض تناول من هذا فإنّه يصرف الخلط والبلغم فبدستوركم أشربه وإن كان لا يحسن في هذا المكان فللضرورة أحكام وفي الضرورات تباح المحظورات[2] فقال من حضر أيّ والله اشرب فقال للنقيب هات ما معك فناوله السراحيّة فأخذها ويجعل يجلوها على الناس وشربها عن آخرها وقال الحاضرون جعله الله صحّة وضجّوا له بالدعاء ثمّ شرع فيما هو فيه حتّى طاب المجلس

٩،٣ فلمّا طاب وشرع الناس يتوبون قام الشيخ بدل ومعه الطربروب فصعد إليه وهو يقول أهلاً أهلاً يا عاشق فتح الحبيب الباب يا أهل المحبّة تجلّى المحبوب ومثل ذلك ثمّ جعل رأس الشيخ في حجره وهو يقول كيف ترى يا شيخ نحس والشيخ يقول يا قوّاد

---

١ أضيف للسياق. ٢ ش: المحذورات.

I will do so, and send the crowd crazy too! Then my gathering will outshine any that went before!" So we made a bet on it.

When Tuesday came, he said, "Do we have a deal?" "Indeed we do," I replied. Then he said to the mosque attendant, "Go pound me up some pork bellies[72] with all the trimmings and bring them to me," and the man did so. We also had with us a demijohn that held nine pints by the Egyptian measure. This he filled with wine, stoppered, and gave to the servant, telling him, "Keep this with you and give it to me when I ask for it." Staying with us was a Turkmen shaykh called Badal, who played the ukulele and was the most dissolute shaykh of his day. My friend told him, "When things have started jumping and I begin reciting poetry, take this ukulele, climb up to where I am in the pulpit, and I'll show you, Shaykh Calamity, something that will surprise you!" Then he jumped up, I along with him, the kerchief containing the pork bellies in the front of his robe, greeted the crowd, and sat, burying his face in the neck of his robe. 3.7

As the Qur'an readers began reciting, he began eating the bellies and got through the lot. Then, when the readers were done, he pulled his face out and started in on his sermon, at which point he began producing bile[73] and phlegm from his mouth and coughing and pausing in his preaching. "Forgive me, friends!" he said. "This bile got to be so bad I couldn't go on preaching, so I took my complaint to the doctor, who made me up an infusion and told me, 'If it comes back, take some of this. It makes the bile and phlegm go away.' So, if you don't mind, I'll go ahead and drink some, even though I really shouldn't in a place like this. Still, 'in cases of necessity, prohibitions are set aside.'"[74] "Go ahead, by God, and drink!" responded the congregation. So he said to the attendant, "Bring me that thing you have with you!" and the man handed him the demijohn, and the preacher took it, showed it around to everyone, and drank it all, while the congregation said, "God make it a cure for you!" and raised a prayerful uproar on his behalf. Then he went on with his sermon till the place was jumping. 3.8

With things now at fever point, and the people repenting of their sins, Shaykh Badal stood, holding his ukulele, and climbed up to the preacher, who said to him, "Welcome, welcome, the Lover! The Beloved[75] has thrown open the door! People of Love, the Beloved has revealed himself!" and suchlike. Then he took the shaykh's head in his lap, saying, "So what do you say, Shaykh Calamity?" to which the shaykh replied, "You pimp! You really know 3.9

ما أشدّ أخذك قلوب الناس ثمّ تركه وأشار إلى الناس وقال تعلمون أيش يقول هذا الشيخ قال والله قد ضجرت ممّا أقول تبت وكلّما أبصرت هذا الطربروب أنكث التوبة بالله عليك اكسره ثمّ قطع شعره ولبّسه طاقيّة ثمّ أخذ الطربروب وجعله في حجره وقال تعلمون لسان حاله أيش يقول [طويل]

سَرَتْ نَسْمَةٌ فِيهَا لِأَهْلِ ٱلْهَوَى نَشْرُ ... فَبِتْنَا نَشَاوَى حِينَ فَاحَ لَنَا ٱلنَّشْرُ
سَرَتْ تَسْتَزِيدُ ٱلْعَاشِقِينَ مِنَ ٱلْأَسَى ... فَعَاوَدَنَا مِنْهَا ٱلصَّبَابَةُ وَٱلسُّكْرُ
لَقَدْ حَمَلَتْ عَنْ أَهْلِ يَثْرِبَ رِسَالَةً ... فَأَدَّتْ كَلَامًا لَا يُكَيِّفُهُ ٱلذِّكْرُ

١٠،٣ فلمّا انتهى إلى هذا البيت ضرب بالطربروب الأرض فكسره فعند ذلك ضجّت الخلق وطلبوا المنبر أفواجًا يتعلّقون ويضجّوا فتوّب ذلك اليوم خلقًا كثيرًا ووقع عليه أحد وعشرون خلعة وكان له مجلس لم يكن له مثله وحملوه حمل بالمنبر إلى بيته فانظر إلى هذه النواميس وكيف تدخل على الناس فافهموا يا عميان القلوب

how to grab them by the hearts and minds!" at which the preacher let go of the shaykh, gestured to the people, and said, "You know what this shaykh just said? He said, 'I swear I'm fed up with saying "I repent!" and then going back on it every time I see this ukulele. I beg you, break it!'" Then the preacher cut off the shaykh's hair, put a cap on his head,[76] and taking the ukulele on his lap said, "This is the ukulele speaking! Do you know what it's saying? It's saying:[77]

> A breeze passed by that, for Love's People, contained a certain odor,
> and so we passed the night, once that scent had reached us, in intoxication.
> In passing, it increased the lovelorn in their grief
> yet restored to us at last our passionate inebriation!
> From Yathrib's folk I come, charged to bring a message,
> but one conveying words too heady for declamation."

When he got to the end of the last line, he struck the ukulele against the 3.10
ground and smashed it. Everyone broke into applause and moved in waves, applauding, toward the pulpit. That day he moved many to repent, twenty-one robes were thrown over his back, his gathering outdid any that had gone before, and they carried him to his house in his pulpit. Observe these conjuring tricks and the way they deceive people and wise up, ye blind of heart!

الفصل الرابع

خمسة أبواب

في كشف أسرار الرهبان

١،٤ اعلم أنّ هذه الطائفة أعظم الأمم كذب ونفاق ودهاء وذلك أنّهم يلعبون بعقول النصارى ويستحيون نسائهم وينزلون عليهم الباروك ولا يعلم أحد أحوالهم وهم ألعن الخلق وهم أخير من غيرهم لكنّهم إذا خلوا بأنفسهم يعلمون أنّهم على الضلالة وقد غيّروا الأقوال والأفعال ولهم أعمال عظيمة لا تحدّ ولا تحصى وهم قوم يأكلون الأموال بالباطل ويزيّنون الكذب وزخاريف المقال وهم أكذب الخلق على كلّ حال فمنهم من عمل للأديرة عيد وجعله ناموس من بعض النواميس يأكل به أموال النصارى ويستبيح نسائهم وأنا أثبّت لك شيئًا من ذلك

الباب الأوّل في كشف أسرارهم

٢،٤ اعلم أنّ هؤلاء الأقوام أعظم ناموس لهم قنديل النور في كنيسة قُمامة من بيت المقدس وهو من عمل بيت الرهبان الملاعين قد ارتبط عليه جميع النصارى وأجناسهم وقد كان الملك المعظّم بن الملك العادل قدّس الله روحه دخل إلى القمامة يوم سبت النور فقال للراهب لا براح حتّى أبصر هذا النور كيف ينزل فقال الراهب أيّما أحبّ إليك هذا المال الذي يتحصّل لك من هذا الوجه أو اطّلاعك عليه فإنّه إن كشفت

Chapter Four, in Five Sections:

Exposé of the Tricks of Monks

For your information, this tribe of charlatans is the most mendacious, hypocritical, and cunning nation of all. They mess with the minds of Christian men, seduce their women, and infect them with the clap without anyone being aware of what they're up to. They are the most despicable of people but cleverer than the rest, even though among themselves they know they are on the wrong path. They have changed sayings and deeds,[78] and get up to terrible things too numerous to count or calculate. They are a company who get their hands on people's money for nefarious purposes and dress up lies with fancy rigmarole; by any standard, they are the most barefaced liars there are. To further these ends of theirs, some of them have established festivals, held in monasteries, and turned these into yet another means to fool people, get their hands on the Christians' money, and make fair game of their women. I shall now provide you with some of the evidence. 4.1

Section One of the Exposé of Their Tricks

The most powerful illusion practiced by these bands is that of "the Lamp of Light" in the Qumāmah Church[79] in Jerusalem. It's one of the things faked up by the accursed order of monks, and all the various kinds of Christians have been taken in by it. Al-Malik al-Muʿaẓẓam, son of al-Malik al-ʿĀdil, God sanctify his soul, entered the Qumāmah Church on the Saturday of Light and told the monk who was there, "No one goes anywhere till I've seen how the light comes into being!"[80] The monk asked him, "Which do you prefer, to have all the money that accrues to you from it, or to observe how it appears? If you expose the secret, the money will disappear, so leave it be, protected and 4.2

سرّه عدمت هذا المال فاتركه مستور مصان وتربح هذا المال العظيم فلمّا سمع ذلك علم باطن قول الراهب فتركه على حاله وخرج

٣،٤ وذلك أنّ هذا القنديل هو أعظم النواميس الذي صنعوها الأوائل وذلك أنّ له في رأس القبّة حُقّ من حديد والرزّة الذي للسلسلة الذي هو معلّق فيها وهو مهندم في هلال القبّة لا يطّلع عليه أحد إلّا الراهب والسلسلة لها فيه خلوّ فإذا كان ليلة سبت النور صعد الراهب إلى الحُقّ وجعل فيه مطبوخ الكبريت على مثال السنبوسكة وجعل تحتها ناراً موقّتة إلى الساعة التي يريد أن ينزل فيها النور ثمّ يدهن السلسلة بدهن البَلَسان فإذا جاء الوقت أوقدت النار يطفّ المطبوخ على رزّة السلسلة في ذلك الحُقّ المهندم فاستمدّ من تلك النطفة دهن البلسان وسرى مع السلسلة نازل إلى القنديل فعلقت النار في فتيلة القنديل وتكون مسقيّة أوّلاً بدهن البلسان

الباب الثاني في كشف أسرارهم

٤،٤ ومن ذلك دير الصنم وهو مشهور وهو من العجائب وهو صنم من الحديد واقف في قبّة بين الهواء والفضاء لا يسقط إلى الأرض ولا يرتفع إلى فوق ولا يميل ميمنة ولا ميسرة ولا خلف ولا قدّام وقد ارتبط عليه الإفرنج والروم واليونان وجميع أجناس النصارى وهذا الصنم من صنعة الحكيم بَلينوس وذلك أنّه بنى قبّة من حجر المغناطيس ثمّ إنّه عمل الصنم بحكمة على مقدار ما تأخذ كلّ جهة من هواء الحديد ثمّ أوقفه في القبّة فأخذ هواءه من علوّ القبّة والعلوّ لا يتركه ينزل وهواء الأركان لا يتركه يميل أخذت كلّ جهة حقّها فبقي واقف في وسط القبّة لا يطلع ولا ينزل ولا يميل وذلك من جملة الدهاء والمكر فافهم ومن ذلك دير المعصم وهو

preserved, and profit by all that money!" When al-Malik al-Muʿaẓẓam heard this, he grasped what the monk was hinting at, so he let him be and left the church.

4.3 This lamp is the greatest illusion the ancients ever fabricated.

Exposé: At the top of the dome there is a small iron pot with a U-bolt for the chain from which the lamp is hung. This is carefully concealed within the curvature of the dome and no one except the monk in charge can see it. The chain has an end that hangs free inside the lamp. When the Saturday of Light comes, the monk climbs up to the pot and places inside it a lump of prepared sulfur the size of a small meat pasty, beneath which he puts a little kindling, ready for use at the moment when he needs the light to descend. Then he anoints the chain with oil of Meccan balsam and, when the time comes, he lights the kindling, and the condensate runs down onto the U-bolt from which the chain is suspended and which is attached to the carefully concealed pot. The oil of balsam catches fire from this dribble and the fire keeps going down the chain until it reaches the lamp, at which point the fire sets light to the lamp's wick, which has previously been soaked in oil of balsam.

Section Two of the Exposé of Their Tricks

4.4 Another example: The Monastery of the Idol, which is well known and a recognized marvel. It holds an idol[81] made of iron that stands upright under a dome with no visible means of support and that neither falls nor rises nor tilts right, left, backward, or forward. All the various kinds of Christian, from Franks to Romans to Greeks, have been taken in by it. The idol was made by the sage Apollonius.

Exposé: He built a dome out of magnetic rock, then cleverly made the idol so that each side was equal in terms of the iron's magnetic field. Then he stood it under the dome and it found its position in relation to the height of the dome within the latter's magnetic field, the magnetic field from above preventing it from descending and the magnetic field of the pillars preventing it from tilting, each side taking its due share; as a result, it remained upright under the dome, neither rising nor falling nor tilting. This is just one example of their craftiness and cunning. Wise up to these things!

كفّ ومعصم وهذا حديد أيضاً معلّقاً بين الفضاء والهواء وهو عمل الصنم وهذا المعصم في كنيسة في بلاد الكُرج وتدبيره مثل الصنم سواء

الباب الثالث في كشف أسرارهم

ومن ذلك الكنيسة التي بصَيْدَنايا من أرض دمشق وهي من دهاء الرهبان وقد جعلوا لها عيداً يحجّه الرهبان وقد جعلوا لها عيداً يحجّه المسلمون والنصارى في كلّ سنة ولهم فيه البركة الزيت يؤخذ منها في ذلك اليوم شيئاً كثيرًا وقد ارتبطوا عليها جميع الطوائف وذلك أنّهم أخذوا قرمة نخلة ثمّ نزلوا عليها بالمدقّات مع الطول حتّى رجعت مثال السفنج ثمّ غشّوا عليها بثوب شعر مثل المنخل ثمّ وضعوها في ذلك الموضع فإذا جاء العيد الذي لها سقوا تلك القرمة بالزيت المغسول ثمّ ثقّلوها بثقل ما توازن كما ينزز من ذلك إنّها تبقى ذلك اليوم ترشح طول النهار والناس يأخذون منها البركة وقد ربطوا الناس على أنّ هذا الزيت يزيل الأمراض والعلل فصار لها ذكر وشأن عظيم ٥،٤

الباب الرابع في كشف أسرارهم

ومن ذلك رأيت بالديار المصريّة قريب من المَحَلّة دير يُعرف بالأَبْشِيط وله راهب شيخ ملعون داهية من الدواهي وقد صنع عنده في الدير بئرًا محكم فإذا كان قبل العيد بثلاثة أيّام اجتمع إليه أهل البلد وذلك الإقليم وخرجت إليه الباعة والسوقة وضربوا الخيام وهرعت إليه الناس من كلّ جانب والراهب يطلع إليهم ويحادثهم بما قد زخرف لهم فإذا كان يوم العيد نزل وفتح باب الدير والرهبان حوله ثمّ يأذن لهم بالدخول ٦،٤

Another example: The Monastery of the Wrist, where there are a hand and a wrist, likewise made of iron and suspended without visible means of support. It's the same idea as the idol. This wrist is in a church in Georgia and is made on exactly the same principles as the idol.

Section Three of the Exposé of Their Tricks

Another example: The church at Ṣaydnāyā in the region of Damascus, which 4.5
is another example of the wiliness of the monks, who have established a festival there to which they themselves go on pilgrimage. They also hold a festival there to which both Christians and Muslims make an annual pilgrimage to gain blessing. Quantities of oil are taken away from there daily and all the different religious communities have been taken in by it.

Exposé: They take a palm log and hammer at it with mallets along its length till it becomes spongy. They then drape it in a covering made of hair, like a sieve. They keep it that way until it's time for the festival, when they soak the log in strained oil, then weigh it down with weights on either side so that the oil oozes out and it weeps oil, which people take away, all day long, as a form of blessing. They have fooled everyone into believing that the oil cures sickness and disease, and as a result it has become much talked about, and a big fuss is made over it.[82]

Section Four of the Exposé of Their Tricks

Another example: In Egypt, close to al-Maḥallah, I saw a monastery known 4.6
as the Monastery of al-Abshīṭ, which had an accursed old monk who was a wily rascal and had dug a tightly sealed well in his cell in the monastery. Three days before the festival, the people of the town and the surrounding region would congregate at the monastery, vendors and market people would go out there and pitch tents, and people would hurry there from all parts. The monk would go out to greet them, engage them with pretty speeches he'd prepared, and then, when the day of the festival arrived, he'd go down, surrounded by the monks, open the monastery door, and give the people permission to enter.

فإذا اجتمعوا عند ذلك البئر تقدّم الراهب والمبخرة معه بيده على رأس البئر ثمّ نزل بدرج إلى البئر وهو ناشف وأرضه مفروشة بالحصى قد نقلها من كلّ موضع فإذا حصل في الدرجة السفلى منه بخّر ثمّ تكلّم بما شاء من الهذيان فإذا فعل ذلك صعد الماء إلى تلك الدرجة التي هو عليها واقف ثمّ يرتفع إلى الدرجة التي تليها فيصعد الماء إلى الدرجة ولا يزال كذلك حتّى تمتلئ البئر فيأخذون الناس منه في القناني والكيزان فيغتسلون منه ويدّخرونه عندهم لكلّ مرض وألم ويرفع الراهب منه شيئاً كثيرًا وهو من جملة دهائه ٧،٤

فإذا كان آخر النهار نزل الراهب وأذن للناس بالدخول ثمّ يلبس ثيابا من الصوف الرفيع ويأخذ المبخرة والعكّاز ويقف على رأس البئر ثمّ يبخّر ويتكلّم بما أراد ويدقّ العكّاز على الدرجة فيهبط الماء عن تلك الدرجة فينزل الدرجة الأخرى ويفعل كذلك والماء يهبط درجة بعد درجة حتّى يهبط الجميع وينشف البئر ثمّ يصعد ويقفل عليه ولا يرجع يفعل ذلك إلى مثل ذلك اليوم من السنة الثانية فيحصل له كلّ يوم من أيّام العيد شيئاً كثيرًا وتأتيه نذورًا لا تحدّ وباقي أيّام السنة كلّ من مرض أو حمّ أو وجعه رأسه أو عيناه أو حدث عليه مرض يطلبوا له من الماء الذي عند الراهب فما يطلب أحد منه وزن خمس الدراهم حتّى يهدي إليه شيئاً يسوى درهمين ثلاثة وأصل ما ربط عليه الناس أنّ من التمس من هذا الماء شيئاً بلا قربان الدير ليس ينفعه ما أخذه من الماء فانظر إلى دهاء هذا الرجل وكيف ربط العالم من سائر الملل والأجناس واعلم أنّ هذا البئر هو ثلاث آبار كلّ واحد ينفذ إلى الآخر فافهم ذلك ٨،٤

When they had assembled around the well in question, the monk would approach its mouth, censer in hand, and descend its steps. The well would be dry, its bottom spread with a layer of pebbles that the monks had brought in from wherever they could find them. When the monk reached the lowest step, he would cense it and say whatever nonsense might come into his head. As soon as he did so, the water would rise as far as the step on which he was standing. Then he would go up to the next step, and the water would rise to the level of that step, and it would go on like that till the well had filled with water, which the people would take away in bottles and jugs to use for washing, and which they would store in their houses to be used against any illness or pain. The monk made a lot of money out of this, though it was only one example of his craftiness. 4.7

At the end of the same day, the monk would go out again and permit the people to enter. Then he'd put on fine woolen clothes, take his censer and his crosier, and stand at the mouth of the well. He would cense the place, say whatever nonsense came into his head, and then strike the crosier against the step, and the water would retreat from that step. Then he'd go down to the next step and do the same and the water would sink, step after step, until it had all drained away and the well was dry. Then he'd go back up, close the well, and not revisit it or do as described until the same day the following year. Each day of the festival he took in lots of money and votive offerings. Afterward, throughout the rest of the year, anyone who fell ill or had a fever or a headache or whose eyes hurt or who contracted a disease would try to get hold of some of the water from the monk. No one would ask him for even five dirhams' weight of it without giving him in return the equivalent of two or three silver pieces. The most important part of how he duped the people was making them believe that if anyone obtained any of the water but didn't make an offering to the monastery, the water he'd taken would do him no good. Observe the craftiness of the man and how he managed to delude people of every conviction and kind! The fact is this well consists of three wells, each opening onto the other. Wise up to these things! 4.8

الباب الخامس في كشف أسرارهم

وذلك أنّي رأيت في قبرص دير في جانب جبل الصليب وفي ذلك الدير صنم يُعرف الدير بدير الصنم وفيه راهب اسمه مَيْرون ما على وجه الأرض ألعن منه ولا أدهى ولا أخبث وقد جعل لذلك الدير عيداً يجتمع إليه أهل البلاد وجميع من في تلك الجزيرة وهذا الصنم قد جعله الملعون كما زعم أنّه عبد المسيح على الناس ٩،٤

فإذا كثر فيهم الفساد وانقطعت زيارة الديورة فإنّ ذلك الصنم يبكي بدموع مثل المطر وإذا كان المسيح راضي عن الناس ابتسم ذلك الصنم وكان قد ربطهم أنّ يوم العيد إن ابتسم الصنم فهو يخبر عن المسيح برضاه عنهم وأنّهم ينصرون في تلك السنة على عدوّهم إلّا أن أحدثوا معصية باطنة أو ظاهرة وعيده سبع أيّام فيحصل فيهم شيئاً كثيراً وكلّ من راح وجاء لا بدّ له من زيارة هذا الدير وكلّ من أراد أن يعلم أنّ المسيح عليه راضي أو ساخط لا يعلم ذلك إلّا من الصنم وأيّ ملك أراد المُلك وملاقاة الأعداء لا بدّ له من هذا الدير ويسأل الراهب يسأل الصنم وكلّ الملوك من بعد منهم ومن قرب يحمل لهذا الدير كلّ سنة جملة وكلّ امرأة تريد تعلم ما يكون منها من جميع ما تحاول تحضر إلى عند الراهب وما تنزل ولا تروح حتّى ينزل عليها الباروك من الراهب والرهبان الذين معه في الدير ١٠،٤

وهذا الصنم فيه صناعة دقيقة وهندسة محكمة وذلك أنّ هذا الصنم مجوّف الرأس والبدن في رأسه سَخّانة لطيفة ولها بُزال إلى عيني الصنم فإذا أراده يبكي ملأ تلك السخّانة ماء ثمّ سخنّه حتّى يمنع الكفّ منه ثمّ هندم البزال فتهمل دموعه مثل المطر ويهزّ رأسه مثل المنتحب وذلك أنّ في رأسه زيبق فإذا سخن الماء وحمي الزيبق في رأس الصنم فإنّه يحرّك بمقدار ما فيه من الزيبق ١١،٤

ثمّ من جملة لعنة هذا الراهب أنّه قد عمل لهذا الصنم مقصورة ولها شبابيك من الحديد وهي على هندام القفص والصنم في وسطها على كرسيّ وهو شاخص نحو ١٢،٤

Section Five of the Exposé of Their Tricks

Another example: In Cyprus, I saw a monastery on the side of the Mountain of the Cross[83] and in that monastery was an idol. The monastery is known as the Monastery of the Idol, and in it is a monk called Mayrūn than whom there is no one more despicable, wilier, or more malignant on the face of this earth. He has established a festival at the monastery that attracts the people of the surrounding towns and everyone on the island. The accursed man made this idol while still pretending to everyone that he was a worshipper of Christ! 4.9

If corruption grows among them and people stop visiting the monasteries, this idol weeps tears like rain, but if Christ is pleased with the people, the idol smiles. The monk has duped them into believing that if the idol smiles on the day of the festival, it is letting the people know that Christ is pleased with them and that they will be victorious over their enemies that year, unless they commit any kind of sin, covert or overt. This festival of his lasts seven days, during which he collects masses of money. Everyone coming and going on the road is bound to visit the monastery, anyone who wants to know if Christ is pleased or angry with him has to go to the idol to find out, and any king who wants to be strong and confront his enemies has to visit the monastery and ask the monk to question the idol. Likewise, kings far and near all send the monastery large sums of money and every woman who wants to know what lies in store for any of her endeavors goes to the monk and by the time she leaves will have caught the clap, either from the monk or from the other monks who are with him in the monastery. 4.10

The idol in question is precision engineered to a fine tolerance. 4.11

Exposé: Its head and body are hollow. There is a cleverly designed water heater in its head that has a faucet opening into the idol's eyes. When the monk wants it to weep, he fills the heater with water and heats it till it is too hot to touch. Then he adjusts the faucet and the idol's tears flow like rain and it moves its head from side to side like someone moaning.

Exposé: The head contains mercury, so when the water is heated and the mercury inside it heats up, the head moves in proportion to the quantity of mercury it contains.[84]

One despicable thing this monk has done is to make an enclosure for the idol with iron windows. This is as precisely constructed as a cage, with the idol sitting in the middle on a throne, gazing at the sky and covered with masses of 4.12

السماء وعليه من الذهب والفضّة شيء كثير فإذا كان يوم العيد دخل الراهب إلى المقصورة ويبخّر بأنواع الطيب ثمّ يشرع في تلاوة الإنجيل المبدّل فإن كان المراد البكاء الصنم دبّر السخّانة كما ذكرنا ويجتمع الخلق إليه حول المقصورة وهو يدور حول الصنم ويأخذ من دموعه بالقطن ويدفعه للناس ويضجّ إليهم بالسجود والتضرّع إلى المسيح بالرضى عنهم وإن كان راضياً عنهم فإنّ عنده صنم كأنّه الصنم الأوّل لا يغيّب منه شيئاً ولا يشكّ فيه أنّه إيّاه وهو مفترّة شفتاه ضاحكاً فإذا كان الليلة التي صبحتها يجتمع الناس وهو يوم العيد وضع ذلك الصنم على الكرسيّ ورفع الصنم الذي يبكي ونومس بما أراد من زخاريف الكلام وعمل شغله

gold and silver. On the day of the festival, the monk goes inside the enclosure and censes it with different kinds of sweet-smelling perfume, then starts reciting from the Gospels (in their corrupted form).[85] If his intention is to have the idol weep, he prepares the water heater as described and gathers everyone around him at the enclosure while he walks round the idol in circles, taking samples of its tears with a bit of cotton, giving these to the people, and shouting at them to prostrate themselves and beg Christ to be pleased with them. If Christ is to appear pleased, the monk has on hand another idol just like the first; nothing is missing and no one would doubt it was one and the same, except for the fact that its lips are parted in a smile. During the night before the morning when the people are to gather—that is, the morning of the day of the festival—the monk puts this other idol on the throne, removes the idol that weeps, mumbles at length whatever rigmarole he cares to, and gets down to business.

الفصل الخامس

وهو خمسة أبواب

في كشف أسرار اليهود وغيرهم

اعلم أنّ هذه الطائفة ألعن الخليقة وأخبثهم وأشدّهم كفراً ولعنة وهم أشدّ الناس ١.٥
خبث في أفعالهم وأظهرهم ذلّة ومسكنة وهذا عين اللعنة والدهاء وهم إذا خلوا بإنسان أهلكوه ودكّوا عليه المرقد في الطعام ثمّ إنّهم يقتلوه وذلك أنّهم إذا أرادوا هلاك واحد جعلوا له في طعامه المرقد حتّى ينام ثمّ يثبون إليه وقد تمكّنوا منه ثمّ يقتلوه

الباب الأوّل في كشف أسرارهم

ومن ذلك أنّهم يعملون من بزر البنج الأسود ووسخ الأذن وبصل الفأر من كلّ واحد ٢.٥
جزء ثمّ يجعلوه في أيّ طعام كان فإنّه ينام من وقته وساعته فيتمكّنون منه ويقتلوه في مكان لا يؤبه له فافهم فإنّهم أكثر الخلق خبثاً وكفراً ولعنة وإيّاك ومصاحبتهم فما لهم قول ولا دين ولا أمانة وهذه صفة أحبار اليهود وأمّا الجمهور منهم فإنّهم جميعهم يتعلّقون بالعطر ولهم أوصاف يأتي ذكرها

Chapter Five, in Five Sections:

Exposé of the Tricks of Jews and Others

This sect is the most hateful and malignant of all creation, just as it is the most tenacious in its misbelief and the most intolerable as an affliction. They are also the most vicious in their behavior and, in outward appearance, the most abject and miserable, though it is here that the essence of their hatefulness and cunning lies. If they find themselves alone with someone, they will do him in by slipping a knockout drug into his food and then killing him. 5.1

Exposé: To do someone in, they put a knockout drug in his food, jump on top of him, and, once they have him in their clutches, finish him off.

Section One of the Exposé of Their Tricks

Example: They make a mixture of one part each stinking nightshade seed, earwax, and sea squill, and put it into any food. Anyone who eats it will fall asleep immediately, which means that they have him under their control and can kill him in some inconspicuous place. You have to understand that they are the most malignant, godless, and hateful of people. Beware of taking them as friends! Their word cannot be trusted, and they have neither conscience nor honesty. What I have just said describes their rabbis. The ordinary members of the community all make their living as perfumers and apothecaries, and have characteristics that I shall now describe. 5.2

الباب الثاني في كشف أسرارهم

٣،٥ وذلك أنّ جميع العطر يزغلوه ويحكوه ويبيعوه على المسلمين ولا يؤبه لهم فمن ذلك أنّهم يعملون الهَليلَج والفلفل والزعفران والمسك والعود والكافور والمصطكاء وكلّ ما يتعلّق بالعطر وسوف أذكر ذلك في الموضع الذي يليق به وأكشف أسراره وأعماله إن شاء الله وأثبّت بعضه

الباب الثالث في كشف أسرارهم

٤،٥ ومن ذلك الأطبّاء الطبائعيّة منهم فإنّهم أشدّ كفرًا ونفاقًا ولهم أسرار لا يقف عليها غيرهم فمن ذلك تقريب البعيد وتهوين الشديد فإذا أرادوا أن يداووا إنسانًا ويبرئوه فيبادروا قبل كلّ شيء على حفظ قوّته ثمّ يعمل له دواء موافق لذلك المرض فيبرئه في أيّام قلائل وإن أراد أن يخبث عليهم تغافل على حفظ القوّة أوّلا فيسقط بعضها ثمّ يعمل له دواء نافع لذلك المرض ثلاثة أيّام ثمّ يحرف عليه بما يهيج عليه مرض آخر ولا يزال كذلك يدخله في شيء ويخرجه من شيء فيجعله مقثأة يأكله

٥،٥ وإن كان المريض له شيء من أحوال الدنيا وكان له وارث أشار إلى الحكيم بما يعمل ويجعل له فيحرف عليه ويضعفه قليلاً قليلاً إلى أن يقتله وذلك إن كان له زوجة تريد موته فتشير إليه وتقول يا حكيم بالله عليك إن كان عليه موت فبشّرني ولك عندي الحلاوة الوافرة فيقول أمّا مرضه فسالم بل يقدر الحكيم يسقيه شيئًا يسقط قوّته ثمّ يهلك فإذا سمعت المرأة ذلك مع قلّة عقلها ودينها وشهوتها لموته تقول يا حكيم ابصر أيش تعمل وأيش ما أردت عندي فيقول هذا الأمر لا أجسر أن أقدم عليه فلا تزال عليه وتوعده بما يريد فيقول هذا الأمر لا يتمّ بأجل بل يتمّ بالنقود فيأخذ منها ما يتّفق بينها وبينه فإن كانت مليحة وأرادها فيتركها ذلك اليوم

Section Two of the Exposé of Their Tricks

Example: They produce fake versions and imitations of all the apothecary's products, sell these to Muslims, and don't give a damn. They make fake versions of, for example, myrobalan, pepper, saffron, musk, agar, camphor, mastic, and everything else related to the apothecary's trade. I shall discuss this in the proper place, providing an exposé of their tricks and their operations, God willing, and furnishing, in many cases, irrefutable evidence. 5.3

Section Three of the Exposé of Their Tricks

Another example: Their physicians. These are the most irreligious and hypocritical among them and know tricks nobody else has ever studied, including, for example, how to achieve quick and easy results that ought to require a great deal of time and that seem difficult to achieve. Thus, when they want to treat a person properly and cure him, they take the utmost pains to preserve his strength, preparing him a concoction appropriate to the sickness in question, curing him in a matter of days. But when they want to exercise their malice against someone, they pay no attention, initially, to the preservation of his strength, allowing it to decline somewhat. They then concoct him an antidote that works for the disease in question for three days. Then they destroy his health again, using things that cause some other disease to attack him. They keep him going like this, first contracting a disease and then escaping it, and by so doing turn him into a nice little pumpkin patch that they can crop. 5.4

If the patient has worldly goods and there is an heir, the latter will give the doctor a nod and a wink as to what to do and give him gifts. The doctor then gives the patient something to make him sick and weakens him little by little until he kills him off. This is what happens when the patient has a wife who wants him dead: She gives the doctor a hint with the words: "I beg you, doctor, if he's about to die, just let me know the good news and you'll get a good bonus from me." To this the doctor replies, "Actually, from the medical perspective, he's fine, though a doctor could always give a man something that will destroy his strength, in which case he'd be a goner." When the women hears this, due to her lack of either intelligence or godliness, as well as her lust 5.5

ثمّ يقول اعلمي أنّ هذا الأمر لا يتمّ إلّا بمواصلتك لأدبر له من المنى دواء وقد انقضى الشغل ولا يزال عليها حتّى تجيبه إلى ذلك فانظر إلى هذا المكر والدهاء والخبث وكيف يستحلّون أموال الناس ويستحيون نسائهم فافهم ذلك وكن خبيرًا بالأمور لا يدخل عليك شيء

الباب الرابع في كشف أسرارهم

٦،٥ فمن ذلك البوارز والخرّازين الذين يدورون بالبيوت والضياع والبساتين فإنّ لهم أمر لا يقف عليه أحد ولا يعدّ ولا يحدّ فمن ذلك أنّهم يعملون بالنساء القبائح ويفتحون لهم أبواب لا تكيّف بل يبيعونهم بما يخلّطون به عقل الرجل ويدمغه ويبهته حتّى أنّه إذا رأى أحدا عند إمرأته لا ينطق وإن راحت إلى موضع لا يقول لها شيء وأيّ شيء قالت صدّقها فمن ذلك مخّ الجمل فإنّ له في هذا الباب فعل عظيم وكذلك مخّ الرخم ومخّ الحمار وأشياء كثيرة يطول شرحها ثم إنهم لهم أفعال كثيرة فافهم ذلك

الباب الخامس في كشف أسرارهم

٧،٥ وذلك أنهم يركّبون لهم دواء إذا أطعمته المرأة الرجل يبقى باهت لا يعلم ما يقال له ولا ينطق ولا يعلم ما هو فيه ولا ما يتمّ عليه فإذا أرادوا ذلك فإنّهم يأخذون من الكاكنج

to see her husband dead, she says, "Doctor, do the necessary and whatever you ask of me is yours." He responds, "I would never dare do such a thing!" but she keeps at him and keeps promising him whatever he wants until he says, "Stuff like that doesn't happen when things are just allowed to take their course; they happen when someone pays cash!" and he takes off her whatever sum they agree on. If she's pretty and he wants her, he leaves her be on that occasion, but tells her later, "It's not going to happen till I've had intercourse with you, so that I can make him a concoction from the sperm." Then things are put on hold while he keeps after her until she gives in. Observe this cunning, craftiness, and malice, and how they make free with people's wealth and seduce their wives. Wise up to these things! Be aware of how things are so you don't get taken!

Section Four of the Exposé of Their Tricks

Another example: Hawkers and cobblers who make the rounds of houses, 5.6
farms, and plantations, and do things no one knows about and that are too numerous to count or calculate.

Another example: Doing dirty things with women and opening to them possibilities they would never have imagined. They sell them stuff to addle and disturb their husbands' minds and make them so befuddled that even if a husband in this state sees someone with his wife he doesn't say a word, and if she goes off somewhere he says nothing to her and believes everything she says.

Another example: Camel's brain, which is highly effective in such cases, the same going for vulture's brain and donkey's brain and a number of other things it would take too long to describe. There are all sorts of other things they get up to over and above this, so wise up!

Section Five of the Exposé of Their Tricks

Another example: They make the women a concoction which, when they give 5.7
it to their husbands to eat, leaves the latter befuddled, incapable of understanding what is being said to them or speaking or grasping what's going on around them or where things are heading.

جزء ومن حبّ البَلاذُر جزء ومن الغاريقون جزء فيدقّ الجميع دقًّا ناعمًا ويطعم في طعام فإنّه إذا أكله يبقى باهت ولا يعلم ما يتمّ في العالم

Exposé: To make it, they take one part each alkekengi, anacardium nut, and agarikon. These are pounded together till fine, and put into food. When the husband eats this, he becomes befuddled and has no idea what's going on around him.

الفصل السادس

ثمانية أبواب

في كشف أسرار بني ساسان

اعلم أنّ هذه الطائفة يدخل فيها جميع الطوائف ويتعلّق بها أكثر الخلق وذلك أنّها ١،٦ صناعة واسعة الدائرة تحتمل أمور شتّى وهم أصحاب الدهاء والمكر والمحال ولهم الجسارة على كلّ ما يفعلونه ولهم ألف باب من أبواب المكر ولولا الإطالة ذكرتها جميعها بل ذكرت منها شيئاً يستدلّ به العاقل على الكلّ فمنهم أصحاب النواميس والفقراء والمُدَرْوِزين وأصحاب البلاء من الزُطّ وغيرهم وأصحاب الوحوش مثل الدباب والقرود والذين يعلّمون التيوس والحمير ويؤلّفون بين القطّ والفأر ويعملون اللحى للنساء والذين يدّعون أنّهم كانوا مأسورين والذين يدّعون العمى وكلّ مرض يظهرون الاستسقاء والقروح والخراجات ولهم أشياء كثيرة مثل ذلك ولهم الجّ الذي يركبون الجمل وأمّا الوعّاظ فهم أعلى مرتبة بني ساسان ولهم الدهاء والمكر والحيل ومع ذلك فإنّ الإنسان إذا احتاج احتال وقد قال الشيخ ساسان الحيلة عليهم ولا الحاجة إليهم إلّا أنّ بني ساسان أسرع تقدّماً إلى هذه الأفعال وقد ذكر أن كان على عصا ساسان من جسر أيسر ومن هاب خاب فاعلم ذلك وقد أتيت لك من اختلاف أجناسهم ما تكتفي به عن غيرهم وسوف أكشف لهم بعض أسرارهم لتقف عليها وتعلم أنّي قد مارست الأمور وعرفت حقائق الأشياء وبواطنها

Chapter Six, in Eight Sections:

Exposé of the Tricks of the Banū Sāsān

The tribe of charlatans so named encompasses all others of this type. 6.1

Exposé: Most such people belong to it, as it is a craft that encompasses many diverse skills: Anyone who practices cunning, deceit, and trickery is a member.[86] They go about everything they do audaciously and know a thousand ways to deceive—ways I'd list one by one if I weren't afraid of boring you; instead, I shall give just a few examples, from which the intelligent reader will be able to deduce the rest. By way of example, then, they include illusionists; dervishes and pseudo-dervishes; lepers (be they vagabonds[87] or others); handlers of wild animals such as bears and apes,[88] and the ones who train goats and donkeys to perform tricks, persuade cats and mice to be friends, and make women grow beards; also, those who pretend to have been prisoners of war and the fake blind, as well as fakers of every other morbid condition who put their dropsical limbs, ulcers, and abscesses on display. They have lots of things like that. They also have pilgrims who ride camels. The highest ranking of the Banū Sāsān are the fire-and-brimstone preachers, who have their own forms of craftiness and cunning and their own subterfuges. That said, "Everyone resorts to tricks when caught in a fix," and Shaykh Sāsān himself has said, "These folk feel they have to play tricks even if they're not in a fix!" since the Banū Sāsān are quicker than others to initiate such acts. It is said that written on Sāsān's staff are the words, "Who dares does, who fears fails." Bear this in mind, then. I have provided you with enough examples of their different practices to suffice. I shall now provide exposés of some of their tricks, for you to study and to make you aware that I have direct experience of these matters and have gotten to the bottom of what they are really about and of their inner workings.

الباب الأوّل في كشف أسرار الذين يدّعون العمى

٢،٦ وذلك أنّهم يعمون من غير عمى وإذا أرادوا ذلك يأخذون من دم القراد جزءًا ومن الصمغ العربيّ جزءًا ثمّ يكتحلون به على أطراف جفونهم فتنطبق وتلزق فلا يشكّ من رآهم أنّهم عميان وإذا أرادوا أن يفتحوها فيأخذون الصابون ثمّ يغسلون به أعينهم فإنّها تنفتح فاعلم ذلك

الباب الثاني في كشف أسرار الذين يدّعون الجذام

٣،٦ وقد سبق ذلك في ادّعاء النبوّة فإذا أرادوا أن يظهرون أنّهم جذمة فيأخذون من ورق العظلم جزء ومن الباذروج جزء ومن الكابة جزء ومن القلقند جزء ثمّ يغلوا الجميع حتّى يذهب الربع ثمّ إنّهم يستحمون بذلك الماء فيتخيّل للآدميّ أنّه جذام أو برص وليسوا من ذلك شيء وإنّما هو حيل ومكر ومغاش

الباب الثالث في كشف أسرار الذين يدّعون الاستسقاء والصفار والعلل الباطنة

٤،٦ وذلك أنّهم إذا أرادوا ذلك فإنّهم يأخذون ماء التبن وبيض النمل فيغلوا الجميع حتّى ينقص الربع ثمّ يشربونه فتكبر بطونهم وتصفرّ وجوههم حتّى يخيّل لمن رآهم كان بهم علّة الاستسقاء فإذا أرادوا أن يُذهبوا ذلك شربوا ماء الهِندِباء بسكّر الطبرزد فإنّه يذهب

الباب الرابع في كشف أسرارهم

٥،٦ ومن ذلك رأيت بحرّان سنة ثلاثة عشر وستّمائة رجل من بني ساسان قد أخذ قردًا وعلّمه السلام على الناس والتسبيح والسواك والبكاء ثمّ رأيت من هذا القرد

Section One: Exposé of the Tricks of Those Who Fake Blindness

Example: They act blind when they aren't. To do this, they take one part ticks' blood and one part gum arabic and anoint the edges of their eyelids. These then join and stick together. It is impossible to look at a person who has done this and not be convinced that he's blind. To open them again, they take soap and wash their eyes, and they open again. Wise up to these things! 6.2

Section Two: Exposé of the Tricks of Those Who Fake Leprosy

We spoke about this earlier when discussing fake prophets. To give the appearance of being lepers, they take one part woad, one part basil, one part cubeb, and one part vitriol. They boil these together till they are reduced by a quarter, then bathe with the resulting juice, and the mark thinks they have leprosy, or vitiligo, when they have nothing of the sort and it's all just subterfuge, deceit, and fakery. 6.3

Section Three: Exposé of the Tricks of Those Who Fake Dropsy, Jaundice, and Internal Diseases

Exposé: To do this, they take water in which straw has been steeped, plus ants' eggs, and boil them together till reduced by a quarter. Then they drink this concoction and their bellies grow so big and their faces turn so yellow that anyone who sees them thinks they must be suffering from dropsy. To get rid of it, they drink endive water with sugar candy and it goes away. 6.4

Section Four of the Exposé of Their Tricks

Another example: When I was in Ḥarrān in the year 613 [1216–17], I saw one of the Banū Sāsān who'd taken an ape and taught it to make salaams to people, as well as tell prayer beads, use a tooth-cleaning stick, and weep. Then I watched as the ape performed an illusion no human could have pulled off. It was a 6.5

من الناموس ما لا يقدر عليه أحد من الناس فإذا كان يوم الجمعة أرسل عبداً هندياً نظيف الملبوس وهو حسن الشمائل جاء الجامع إلى عند المحراب بسط سجّادة حسنة ثمّ راح فإذا كان في الساعة الرابعة لبّس القرد ملبوس خاصّ جيّد من ملابيس أولاد الملوك وجعل في وسطه حياصة لها قيمة ثمّ طيّبه بأنواع الطيب ثمّ ركّبه بغلة بمركب ذهب محلّى ثمّ مشّى في ركابه ثلاث عبيد هنود بأفخر ملبوس الواحد يحمل الوَطاء المصلّى والآخر يحمل الشَرْموزة والآخر يطرق قدّامه هذا والقرد يسلّم على الناس طول الطريق

٦،٦ فإذا دخل إلى باب الجامع لبّسوه الشرموزة وعضدوه ونزل والعبد قدّامه بالوطاء ويطرق له وهو يسلّم على الناس وكلّ من يسأل عنه يقال له هذا ابن الملك الفلانيّ من أكبر ملوك الهند وهو مسحور ولا يزال كذلك حتّى يصل إلى الموضع الذي فيه السجّادة فيفرش له العبد الوطاء فوقها ويحطّ له سبحة ومسواك فيقلع القرد ملبوسه ومنديله من وسط الحياصة ويضعه قدّامه ثمّ يستاك بالمسواك ويصلّي ركعتين شكر الوضوء وركعتين تحيّة المسجد ثمّ يأخذ المسبحة ويسبّح

٧،٦ فإذا فعل ذلك قام نهض العبد فسلّم على الناس وقال يا أصحابنا من أصبح معافى فإنّ لله عليه نعمة لا تحصى واعلموا أنّ ابن آدم هدف للبلاء فمن ابتلى فليصبر ومن عوفي فليشكر واعلموا أنّ هذا القرد الذي ترونه بينكم والله لم يكن في زمانه أحسن منه شباباً وهو ابن الملك الفلانيّ صاحب الجزيرة الفلانيّة سبحان من سلبه الحسن والملك ومع ذلك لم يكن في زمانه أرحم منه قلباً ولا أطوع منه لله تعالى

٨،٦ ولكن المؤمن ملقى لقضاء الله من القضاء المقدّر أنّه أزوجه والده بابنة الملك الفلانيّ فأقام معها مدّة كذا وكذا ثمّ نقلوا إليها أنّه قد عشق مملوكاً له فسألته عن ذلك فحلف بالله أنّ هذا شيء ما كان فتركته فزاد عليها القول في ذلك ثمّ لحقها من الغيرة ما يلحق أمثالها ولم تجد عن ذلك صبراً فطلبت منه دستوراً تروح تزور أهلها وأمّها شهرين

Friday, and the man sent an Indian slave, smartly dressed and personable, to the mosque. On reaching the prayer niche, he laid out a handsome carpet, after which he left. At the fourth hour, the man dressed the ape in exclusive clothes of the most luxurious sort, of the kind worn by the sons of kings, and put an expensive belt round its waist. Then he perfumed the ape with perfumes of all kinds, mounted it on a mule with a saddle decorated in gold, and assigned three Indian slaves wearing the finest clothes to walk at its stirrup. The first carried its prayer mat and the second its overshoes, while the third strutted along before it, and the ape made salaams to everyone, from one end of its route to the other.

Once the ape reached the door of the mosque, they put the overshoes on its feet and gave it their arm, and it dismounted, the slave with the prayer mat strutting along in front, the ape making salaams. If anyone asked who it was, he was told, "This is the son of King So-and-so, one of the greatest of the kings of India, but the man is under a spell." The ape made its way like this till it came to the carpet. There the slave laid the ape's prayer mat down on the carpet and placed the prayer beads and tooth-cleaning stick in its hands. The ape now removed its clothes,[89] pulled its handkerchief out of its cummerbund, and placed it in front of him. It rubbed its teeth with the stick and performed two prostrations of thanks for ablution and two of greeting to the mosque. Then it took the prayer beads and busied itself telling them. 6.6

The moment it did so, the slave jumped up, made his salaams to the people, and said, "Friends! To any who rises of a morning in good health God has granted blessings incalculable! Know, however, that man is a target of misfortune, and any who suffers misfortune should be patient, while any who enjoys good health should be grateful. Know too that, in its day, this ape that you see among you was the handsomest of youths and that he is the son of King So-and-so, ruler of the Island of Such-and-such, glory be to Him who has stripped him of both good looks and princely status! Moreover, there was none in his day with a more merciful heart or more obedient to God Almighty. 6.7

"The believer, though, is subject to God's foreordained decrees. Now, his father married him to the daughter of King So-and-so, and he lived with her for such and such a length of time. Then men passed word to her that he'd fallen in love with one of his slave boys. She asked him about this and he swore to God there was no truth to the matter, so she let him be. Later, she heard more to the same effect, was overtaken by the jealousy to which her sex is so prone, and, 6.8

من الزمان فأذن لها في ذلك وجهّزها كما يجب لمثلها فلمّا حصلت عند أهلها سحرته كما ترون فلمّا علم والده ذلك قال هذا اختلق به بين الملوك فأمر بإخراجه من ذلك الإقليم فأُخرج

وقد سألنا زوجته بجميع الملوك فادّعت أنّها خلفت عنده أثاث قيمته مائة ألف دينار ولا تردّه إلى صورته إلّا بها وقد تعصّبوا له الملوك وساعده كلّ منهم بشيء وقد حملها لها تسعين ألف دينار وقد تخلّف عليه عشرة ألف دينار من يساعده بشيء من ذلك وارحموا هذا الشابّ الذي قد عدم الملك والأهل والوطن وأُخرج من صورته إلى صورة القردة هذا والقرد قد جعل المنديل على وجهه وجعل يبكي بدموع مثل المطر فترقّ قلوب الناس لذلك وما منهم إلّا من يرفده بشيء فما يخرج من الجامع إلّا بشيء كثير وهو يدور به البلد على هذه الصفة فافهم ذلك ونبّه فكرك فيما يعملون بني ساسان من الدهاء والمكر ٩،٦

الباب الخامس في كشف أسرارهم

ومن ذلك أنّي كنت في قونية من بلاد الروم في سنة ستّة عشر وستّمائة فمررت ببعض الشوارع فرأيت إنسانًا عليه خَلَق وهو مرميّ على جنبه وهو معصّب بشَرْموط وهو يئنّ أنين ضعيف ويقول شهوتي رمّانة فنظرت إليه فقلت وعزّة الله من بني ساسان ولا بدّ أن أبصر إلى أين يؤول مآله فجلست قريبًا منه بحيث أراه ولا يراني جعلت الفلوس والدراهم تنهال عليه ولم يزل كذلك إلى القائلة انقطعت الرجل من الرائح والجائي فلمّا أن رأى ذلك التفت يمينه وأيسره فلم يجد أحدًا فوثب مثل البعير المُنْشَط من العقال وجعل يخرق الأزقّة وأنا خلفه إلى أن انتهى إلى دار حسنة البنيان عالية الأركان فطرق الباب ففتح له فهو قد همّ أن يدخل وأنا قلت سلام ١٠،٦

unable to bear it any longer, asked his permission to go and visit her family and her mother for two months. He granted her that permission and equipped her for the journey in accordance with her status. When she reached her family, she cast a spell on him, as you can see. When he heard what had happened, the youth's father declared, 'This creature is an interloper among us kings!' and ordered that he be driven from that region of the world, and so he was.

"Now his wife has come begging to us, as well as all the other kings, claiming that she left furnishings at his house worth one hundred thousand gold pieces and she refuses to restore him to his former shape till she has been paid that sum. The kings have all banded together and helped him, each and every one contributing something, and he has sent her ninety thousand gold pieces, leaving him with ten thousand still to pay. Who will help him with some part of that amount? Who will have mercy on this youth whose princely status, family, and homeland have all been lost to him, and who has been changed from his true form into that of this ape?" (Throughout all this, the ape, handkerchief to face, wept tears like rain.) Everyone's heart was moved and each gave him something and, by the time he left the mosque, he'd collected a tidy sum. The man took him all over town pulling the same ruse. Wise up to these things and be alert to the cunning and deceitful deeds of the Banū Sāsān! 6.9

Section Five of the Exposé of Their Tricks

Another example: When I was in Konya, a city in Anatolia, in 616 [1219–20], 6.10
I was going along a street when I saw a man dressed in rags lying on his side, his head bound with a piece of cloth. He was moaning feebly and saying, "I have to have a pomegranate!" Looking at him, I said to myself, "He's got to be Banū Sāsān! I must watch and see where he's going with this," so I sat myself down close by, where I could see him but he couldn't see me. Copper and silver pieces now began raining down on him and kept doing so till midday, when the foot traffic let up. Noticing this, he looked right and left and, seeing no one, jumped up like a camel released from its tether and set off through the alleyways, with me in pursuit. Eventually, he came to a handsomely built pile and knocked on the door. The door opened and he was about to go in when I accosted him with a "Peace be upon you!" to which he replied, "And upon you be peace!" "Do you have room for a guest?" I asked. "Sure I do!" he replied.

عليك قال وعليك السلام فقلت تقبل ضيفاً قال نعم ومرحباً بمن أتى ثمّ أخذ يدي في يده ثمّ قال على خير مَقْدَم ثمّ دخلنا إلى دار حسنة فنظرت فيها بُسُط وطُرُح لا تصلح إلّا لبعض السعداء

١١،٦ فقال اصعد فصعدت على طرّاحة حسنة فأمّا صاحبي فإنّه رمى من رقبته شَلّاق فيه مقدار عشرة أرطال خبز وفيه فلوس ودراهم شيئاً كثيراً ثمّ شدّ في وسطه بوشيّة تسوى دينارين وخلع ذلك الخلق وقدمت إليه الجارية سخّانة من ماء بطشت فتغسّل ورأيت له شعراً زائداً عن الوصف ثمّ لبس قميصاً رفيعاً وسراويل وقباء وشاش ثمّ رشّ عليه ماورد وطلع جلس إلى جانبي وقال يا فلانة هاتي ما عندك ولا تتكلّفي للضيف بل حسب العادة فأحضرت مائدة عليها أربع زبادي أربعة ألوان طعام حامض[1] وخبز مختلف ألوانه ونقل من جميع النقول ثمّ أُحضر كل حريف ومالح وحامض[2] وغير ذلك فأكلنا وقال اعذرني فإنّك جئتنا على غفلة ولكن الكرام تسامح

١٢،٦ فأكلنا حسب الكفاية ثمّ رفعت المائدة وغسلنا أيدينا ثمّ أتانا بطبق فيه أنواع الحلوى فتحلّينا ثمّ شرع في الحديث وأنا متعجّب منه فقلت له لو فتحت لك دكّان بزار كان خيراً لك من هذه الحرفة فقال إذا كان تاجراً إمّا مسافراً وإمّا صاحب دكّان وكان رأس ماله خمسة آلاف دينار فكم كان يقع مكسبه في كلّ يوم بطّال عمّال فقلت لعلّ نصف دينار أو دينار فقال أنا يقع لي كلّ يوم خمسة وعشرة وأكثر أيش أعمل أنا بالدكّان مع أنّ التاجر ما يخلو من الخسارة في بعض الأوقات ويكون عليه كلف وأنا فرح بلا خسارة فقلت له فهذا الخبز الذي حصل لك ما أراك تأكل منه شيء فما تصنع به قال يجمعوه ويعملوه فتيت فيجيء التجّار من أنطاكية فيشتريه وسفّار المراكب في البحر فتحصّل منه كلّ سنة ما يكفي البيت كسوة فتعجّبت منه

١٣،٦ ثمّ قال تقول بها فقلت وبكلّ من ينتمي إليها فقال وا لك يا فلانة أحضري لنا شيئاً نشتغل به فأحضرت آنية الشرب تصلح للسعداء من الناس فعملت مجلساً لم يغيّبه[3]

١ ش: خاصّ. ٢ ش: خاصّ. ٣ ش: يغيّره.

"Welcome one and all!" and he took me by the hand, said, "Best foot forward!" and ushered me into a fine house where I beheld rugs and carpets of a sort that could only belong to someone well heeled.

"Come on up!" he said, so I climbed onto a handsome carpet,[90] while my friend flung down off his neck a garbage sack containing ten pounds or so of bread plus a great quantity of copper and silver pieces. Tying a wrapper worth two gold pieces round his waist, he threw off the rags he was wearing, and a slave girl brought him a jug of hot water along with a washbasin, and he washed. I noticed that he had amazingly long hair. He then dressed himself in a fine shift, drawers, a robe with full-length sleeves, and a long piece of muslin that he wrapped round his head and sprinkled with rosewater, after which he climbed up and sat down next to me. "Girl," he commanded, "fetch us whatever you happen to have and don't go to any trouble for the sake of our guest. Just bring us the usual." The girl brought a table on which were set four crocks containing four different kinds of savory food, as well as all sorts of bread and nibbles. Then more spicy, salty, and savory dishes of every type were brought, and we ate. "You must excuse me," the man said, "but you come to us unannounced. As a gentleman, however, you will make allowances." 6.11

We ate till we'd had enough, and then the slave girl removed the table and we washed our hands. Then he had a plate of sweetmeats brought and we had our dessert. He now opened the floor for conversation. I was amazed by him and asked, "Wouldn't you do better opening a store in the bazaar than practicing this profession?" to which he responded, "If a merchant, be he itinerant or the owner of a store, has a capital of five thousand gold pieces, how much profit will he make in a day, taking the rough with the smooth?" "Maybe half a gold piece, or a gold piece," I answered. "I," he declared, "make five, ten, or even more, so what use would a store be to me? And don't forget that a merchant sometimes actually loses money and has expenses; for me, though, it's pure profit." "But I don't see you eating any of this bread that you've earned, so what do you do with it?" I asked. "They collect it all," he replied, "and break it into bits, and merchants from Antioch and those who sail the sea in ships come and buy it, and we make enough money off it each year to spare the house the cost of new cushion covers, and so on." I was astounded at him. 6.12

"Are you a fan of this profession?" he then asked, to which I replied, "And of all who belong to it!" So he said, "You, girl! Bring us something to put us in a good mood!" and she brought a flagon of wine of a kind only somebody well 6.13

شيئاً ممّا يحتاج إليه فشربنا ساعة ثمّ قال يا فلانة اتركي فلانة تجيء تطيّب عيشنا فنزلت جارية أحسن ما يكون من النساء ومعها عود زاوية فلعبت به ساعة لعب كالدرّ ثمّ أرمت العود وأخذت الجُنُك فلعبت به نوبة ولم تزل تبدّل الملاهي حتّى انقضى المجلس فلمّا أردنا النوم فقال وا لك افرشي لسيّدك في المخدع وأغلقي عليه ففرشت لي فرشاً حسناً وأوقدت عليّ قنديل ثمّ أتتني بطشت ومِسينة فاغتسلت ونمت ولم أزل نائم إلى باكر

١٤،٦ فانتبهت فإذا به قد دخل عليّ فقال الضيافة ثلاثة أيّام فلا تبرح مكانك حتّى أعود إليك ثمّ قال للجارية هاتي العدّة فأتته بذلك الخلق الشلّاق والعصابة فلبس وعصب رأسه وخبأ شعره ثمّ اتته بمخلاة وفيها تراب مطحون وجعلت تنفض عليه ثمّ ودّعني وخرج ولم تزل الجارية تفتقدني بالطيب والطيّبات إلى الظهر

١٥،٦ فإذا به قد جاء وفعل كما فعل بالأمس فأقمنا إلى يوم الجمعة فقال للجارية خذي سيّدك إلى الحمّام واتركي فلان يخدمه ثمّ قال لي أريد منك اليوم لا تصلّي إلّا عند المنبر فإنّ لي في ذلك غرض ثمّ تعود إلى هاهنا بعد الصلاة ثمّ لبس وخرج فأتت الجارية وأخذت معها البساط ثمّ عبت حوائج الحمّام مكمّلة ثمّ أخذتها وراحت ثمّ عادت وقالت يا سيّدي بسم الله فنهضت معها فدخلت فوجدت بساط وعليه بوشيّة وبقجة فخلعت قماشي ودخلت والبلّان قدّامي إلى المقصورة فخدمني خدمة حسنة ثمّ سبّحت فجاءني بمنشفة روميّ مخمل مبخّرة معطّرة ثمّ خرج خلفي بالطاسة فصعدت على البساط وجاءتني الجارية بقدح شراب شربت ورجعت إلى الدار

١٦،٦ فدخلت والجارية قدّامي فجلست وقدّمت لي شيء أكلت وقدّمت لي سجّادة وقالت بسم الله فخرجت جئت الجامع فبسطت تحت المنبر كما أمر صاحبي فلمّا امتلأ الجامع وصعد الخطيب على المنبر فلم أشعر إلّا وصاحبي قد خرق الصفوف وهو

off could afford and set up a cozy get-together for us that lacked for nothing. We drank for a bit and then he said, "Girl, tell so-and-so to come and show us a good time!" and a slave girl appeared, pretty as a woman could be, who brought with her an oud and played on it for a bit, stringing her compositions together like pearls on a necklace. Then she set the oud aside and took up a harp and played on that for a bit and went on switching instruments till the party was over. When we wanted to sleep, he said, "You there, put out bedding for your master in the bedchamber and close the door on him," so she set out some quality bedding for me and lit me a candle. Then she brought me a washbasin and a copper dipping bowl and I washed and slept and didn't wake till early morning.

I woke to find him entering my room and saying, "Hospitality is good for three days, so don't stir till I come back!" Then he told the girl, "Get the kit!" and she brought him the rags, the garbage sack, and the headband, and he dressed and tied the band round his head, hiding his hair. Next, she appeared with a bag containing fine dust and busied herself scattering it over him. He then said goodbye to me and left, but the girl kept looking in on me regularly with perfumes and tasty dishes till it was noon. 6.14

Soon enough he was back and did the same as the day before, and we stayed there till Friday, when he said to the girl, "Take your master to the baths and have so-and-so take care of him." To me he said, "Today I want you to pray next to the pulpit and nowhere else. I have a reason for this. After the prayer, come back here." He dressed and left, and the girl came, bringing the mat, and prepared a complete set of bath things, and took them and went away, and then came back and said, "Master, let's be off!" So I rose and went with her and entered the baths and found the mat with a waist wrap and a bundle full of bath things on it. I took off my clothes and went on in, the bath attendant leading the way, till we got to the partitioned area, where he gave me a good going over. Then I took a bath in the pool and he brought me a velvety Turkish towel, censed and perfumed, and followed me out with the copper dipping bowl, and I climbed onto the mat and the girl brought a cup of wine and I drank and went back to the house. 6.15

I entered the house, the girl ahead of me, and sat, and she offered me food and I ate and she brought me the prayer mat and said, "On your way!" I left and went to the mosque and spread the prayer mat at the foot of the pulpit as my friend had told me to. When the mosque had filled and the preacher had climbed up into the pulpit, my friend suddenly appeared, making his way through the rows of worshippers clothed in his usual rags. Climbing up the 6.16

بذلك الخلق ثمّ صعد إلى المنبر إلى عند الخطيب وأخرج من عبّه كيس أطلس أحمر وقال للخطيب يا سيّدنا أنا رجل فقير ولي عائلة ووالله لنا اليوم يومين لم نطعم طعام وقد مضّنا الفقر فلمّا أن كان اليوم قالوا لي العائلة اليوم يوم الجمعة قم إلى الجامع لعلّ يفتح الله عزّ وجلّ بشيء نتقوّت به فقد هلكنا من الجوع

١٧،٦ فخرجت طالب الجامع فأنا في الزقاق الفلانيّ وأنا لا أقشع شيئًا من الجوع فعثرت بهذا الكيس وأنا لا أعلم ما فيه فسوّلت لي نفسي أن آخذه وأرجع إلى البيت ثمّ قلت يا نفس ملعونة تريدين أن تجرّئيني على أكل الحرام والله لا طاوعتك على ذلك أبدًا ولو تلفت جوعًا وما عند الله خير وأبقى وقد حملته لتفعل به ما يجب ثمّ ناوله الكيس

١٨،٦ فلمّا رآه الخطيب فتحه وإذا فيه حلي يساوي جملة مال فتعجّب الخطيب من أمانة هذا الرجل مع ما هو فيه من الفقر والحاجة ثمّ أشار إلى الناس وقال أيّها الناس إذا كان الرجل هذه أمانته وعفّته على ما هو عليه من الفقر والحاجة يكون أحد أعفّ من هذا فإذا كان مكفّى غير محتاج كيف تكون أمانته ودينه ومثل هذا لا يصلح أن يكون فقيرًا بين ظهور المسلمين الواجب على كلّ مسلم إعانته وبرّه وأن تبرّوه بشيء وأن يغني فقره فأريد أن تغنوا فقره كلّ على قدره وما يمكنه

١٩،٦ فجعلت الدراهم والذهب تنهال عليه إلى أن قدرت ما تحصل له أن يكون بالتقريب مائتي دينار هذا وأنا ألومه وأنا أقول قد حصل له شيء يساوي ألف دينار فباعه بهذا المبلغ وما بأصدق أن تنقضي الصلاة ونحن في السنّة والضجّة قد أخذتنا من صحن الجامع وإذا بامرأة عجوز وهي تصيح وتقول والله يا مسلمين ما أملك قوّتي في هذا اليوم وقد كان معي حلي أحمل من ناس إلى ناس وقع منّي والخلق يقولون لا باس قد وصل إلى عند الخطيب خرّت مغشيّة عليها ساعة ثمّ أفاقت وقالت يا مولاي العفو ارحمني الله عزّ وجلّ وردّ لهفتي لله تعالى

stairs of the pulpit to where the preacher was, he produced from the folds of his clothes a red satin purse and said to the preacher, "Master, I'm a poor man with a family to support, and I swear it's two days now since we ate a thing, and poverty has made our lives a misery. Today, the wife said to me, 'It's Friday, so go to the mosque. Who knows, maybe God, Almighty and All-Powerful, will send you something to feed us with, for we are about to perish of hunger.'

"So I left, making for the mosque, and was walking down such and such an alley, blinded by hunger, when I stumbled over this purse, of whose contents I am completely ignorant. My evil appetite urged me to take it and go home, but I said, 'Accursed appetite, would you have me fill my stomach from ill-gotten gains? Never, I swear to God, shall I obey you in such a thing though I die of hunger! Whatever God may have in store for me is better and of more lasting worth.' So I've brought it to you to do with it what's proper," and he handed him the purse. 6.17

When the preacher saw it, he opened it and to his surprise found jewelry worth a huge sum. Marveling at the man's honesty in the face of his poverty, the preacher gestured to the congregation and said, "Good people, could any man show greater honesty and integrity than this, despite his poverty and need? Were he free of want and in need of nothing, how might his honesty and respect for the principles of his religion be then? It is not right that a man such as he should go poor among his fellow Muslims. It is the duty of each and every Muslim to help him and give him alms, and to treat him charitably and relieve him of his poverty. I therefore ask you all to do so, each according to his ability and his means." 6.18

At this, the gold and silver rained down upon him until it amounted, as I reckoned, to about two hundred gold pieces. I thought it was a shame, though, and said to myself, "He'd gotten his hands on something worth a thousand gold pieces, and he gave it away for only that much?" Before I knew it, however, the prayer was over and we had entered the period of the extra prayers. Suddenly we heard a racket from the courtyard of the mosque and an old woman appeared, crying, "I swear, good Muslims, I've been worn to a frazzle today! I had a purse full of jewelry with me that I was taking from certain people to certain other people. I dropped it, but everyone told me, 'Don't worry, it's with the preacher.'" Then she fell down in a swoon and remained so for a bit before reviving and saying, "Pardon me, Master! Have pity on me for the sake of God, the Almighty, the All-Powerful, and let my anguish be the Almighty's to assuage!" 6.19

فقال الخطيب على مهلك ما الذي عدم منك فقالت كيس فيه كذا وكذا وشرابته كذا وكذا وفيه من الحلي كذا وكذا قطعة وفيه إسورة كذا وخواتم كذا ومنها حلق كذا ومنها عقد نعته كذا ولم تزل تنعت ذلك قطعة قطعة قدّام الجماعة من العدول كلّما نعتت شيء قد أخرجه الخطيب من الكيس إلى أن نعتت الجميع وصحّ ما قالت فسلم إليها الكيس بما فيه فأخذته ومضت والخلق يدعوا لصاحبي فتعجّبت من حسن دينه وأمانته ٢٠،٦

ثمّ انصرفت وجئت إلى الدار كما أوصاني فوجدته قاعدا يزن ما تحصّل له في ذلك اليوم فقلت أنا لائمك على ذلك قال وَلِمَ قلت وقع لك شيء يساوي ألف دينار بذلته بهذا القدر فقال أتعرف الكيس والإمرأة الذي أخذته فقلت إذا أبصرته عرفته فقال خلّوا العجوز تأخذ الكيس وتنزل فنزلت والكيس في يدها فقال هذا الكيس وهذا العجوز وهي حماتي والحلي لبنتها وأنا سيّرتها بهذه الحيلة فلو أقمت طول النهار كم مقدار ما كان يحصل لي فلمّا أن وعيت ذلك تعجّبت منه ثمّ انصرفت من عنده متعجّباً ٢١،٦

الباب السادس في كشف أسرارهم

ومن ذلك أن كان لي صاحب من أهل دمشق يُعرف بالجمال محمّد بن عتمة فغاب عنّي مدّة ولا أعلم ما كان منه فلمّا دخلت الروم اجتمعت به في بازاركوى[1] وهو راكب على بغلة وعليه ثياب برد حرير وعلى رأسه عمامة شَرَب وعلى أكتافه بردة حرير وحوله نفر من أهل الحجاز بذلك الزيّ فلمّا رآني عرفني ولم أعرفه فسلّم عليّ وقال ما تعرفني فقلت ولا أنكرك فقال أنا صاحبك محمّد بن عتمة فعند ذلك عرفته ثمّ أخذني إلى منزله فأضافني فقال[2] توافقني فيما أعمل فقلت وما الذي تعمل وما هذا الدَسْت الذي أنت فيه فأحضر صندوق من خشب الأبنوس وعليه شيء كثير من أستار ٢٢،٦

١ في الأصل: بارالملوى. ٢ ش: فقلت.

"Take your time," said the preacher. "What is it you've lost?" "A purse," she replied, "containing this and that and with a tassel thus and so, holding such and such a number of pieces of jewelry, including a bracelet of this description, rings of that description, and a necklace of another description," and she went on describing the contents of the purse piece by piece before that company of honest witnesses, and every time she described something, the preacher would pull it from the purse, till in the end she'd described everything, and everything she'd said was correct. At this, he handed the purse with its contents to her, and she took it and went her way, while the congregation called down blessings on my friend and I marveled at his extraordinary piety and honesty. 6.20

I left and went back to the house as he'd asked me to do, and I found him sitting there, weighing his earnings for the day. "I'm disappointed in you!" I said. "How so?" he responded. "You came into possession," I said, "of something worth a thousand gold pieces, and you sacrificed it for this paltry sum?" "Would you recognize the purse and the woman who went off with it?" he asked me. "If I saw it, I'd know it," I answered. "Have the old woman get the purse and come down and see us," he ordered, and she came down, purse in hand. "Here's the purse," he said, "and here's the old lady. She's my mother-in-law, the jewelry belongs to her daughter, and it was me who put her up to this subterfuge. If I'd spent the whole day begging, how much do you think I would have made?" I was amazed and left his house marveling. 6.21

Section Six of the Exposé of Their Tricks

I had a friend from Damascus called al-Jamāl Muḥammad ibn ʿAtamah. For a while I lost all track of him and had no idea what he was up to. Then, when I went to Anatolia, I came across him in Pazarköy,[91] riding a mule and wearing silk garments, with a turban of byssus linen on his head, a silk mantle over his shoulders, and a troop of people from the Hejaz similarly dressed surrounding him. When he saw me, he knew me, though I didn't know him. He greeted me and said, "Don't you know me?" "No," I said, "I've no idea who you are." "I'm your friend Muḥammad ibn ʿAtamah," he said, and then I recognized him. He took me to his house, invited me to be his guest, and asked, "Will you come in with me on my scam?" to which I replied, "And what might your scam be, and what are all these fancy clothes you're wearing?" He then fetched an ebony 6.22

الكعبة التي تكون على الكعبة وعليه ثوب أطلس وعليه قفل ذهب وسواقطه من الفضّة وكذلك مساميره وقد أخذ نعل وهو على صفة نعل رسول الله صلّى الله عليه وسلّم وشراكه من الخوص وقد سمّره في أرض الصندوق بمسامير من الذهب والفضّة وجعل فيه من أنواع الطيب وقد زعم أنّ هذا قدم النبيّ صلّى الله عليه وسلّم وهو دائر به في بلاد الروم وهو على فرس والصندوق على رؤوس تلك العبيد وقد ادّعوا أنّه من بني شَيْبَة وقد حصل به جملة فإذا نزل بقوم سُنّة ادّعى أنّه عَدَويّ وإذا نزل بقوم إماميّة ادّعى أنّه علويّ وهو على تلك الحالة فسألني أن أصحبه فأبيت ذلك ثمّ انصرفت طالب سيواس

الباب السابع في كشف أسرارهم

٢٣،٦ ومن ذلك أنّي رأيت بآمِد أقوام على هذه الصفة ومعهم صندوق على صفة الصندوق الذي تقدّم وفيه خلق عباءة مطيّبة بأنواع الطيب وقد زعموا أنّها العباءة التي كانوا يتغطّون بها أهل البيت صلوات الله عليهم وهم دائرين في البلاد وقد تحصّل لهم بها جمل فافهم ذلك واعلم أنّ بني ساسان لا تعدّ صفاتهم

الباب الثامن في كشف أسرارهم

٢٤،٦ ومن ذلك ما حكى لي بعض أصحابي قال رأيت في بلاد العجم جماعة من أهل الحجاز من بني ساسان ومعهم صندوق كذلك وفيه قطعة من عباءة وقد ربطوا بها الناس أنّها العباءة التي تخلّل بها أبو بكر الصدّيق رضي الله عنه وقد داروا بها البلاد وحصلوا عليها جملة

٢٥،٦ ولو شرحت ما لهم من الدهاء والمكر والحيل والتسلّط والجرأة على أموال الناس لطال الشرح ولكن هذا القدر كاف للعاقل اللبيب وقد يستدلّ بهذا القليل على

casket adorned with pieces of the covering of the Kaaba. It had a satin wrapper and a gold lock, and its clasps and nails were all of silver. He'd gotten hold of a pair of sandals fitting the description of those of the Prophet, God bless and keep him, with a thong made of palm leaf, fastened it to the bottom of the casket with nails of gold and silver, and perfumed it with various kinds of perfume. He was claiming that this was the footwear of the Prophet, God bless and keep him, and was going around the towns of Anatolia riding a horse, the casket borne on the heads of the aforementioned slaves, who put out that he was a member of the Banū Shaybah. He'd made a bunch of money from it. When he was staying among Sunnis, he'd claim he was an ʿAdawī and when he was staying among Imāmīs, he'd claim he was an ʿAlawī, which was what he was currently passing for. He asked me to go with him but I refused and left town, making for Sivas.

Section Seven of the Exposé of Their Tricks

Another example: At Āmid, I saw several people of this kind who had with them caskets of the sort described above that contained rags scented with all kinds of perfumes and who claimed that they were mantles that the members of the Prophet's family, blessings upon them, used to wrap themselves in. They were going around the towns and had made loads of money. Wise up to this and note that the Banū Sāsān come in innumerable forms. 6.23

Section Eight of the Exposé of Their Tricks

Another example: A friend of mine told me the following story. "In Persia, I saw a company of Banū Sāsān from the Hejaz. They had a casket of the same type with them and in it a piece of a cloak that they'd fooled people into thinking was the famous 'pinned' cloak of Abū Bakr al-Ṣiddīq,[92] may God be pleased with him. They'd been touring the towns and had made a bunch of money off it." 6.24

It would take me forever to describe to you all the cunning, craft, subterfuge, effrontery, and daring they use to get their hands on other people's money, but this should be enough to allow anyone with intelligence and insight to deduce the many from the few. Everyone who peruses this book of 6.25

الكثير منه فليعلم من وقف على كتابي هذا أنّي لم أترك فنّا من الفنون ولا علم من العلوم إلّا وقد باشرته وقد كشفت سرّه وسرّ من ذهب إليه وقد بيان ذلك في أثناء الكلام وفي تنويع هذه الفصول وما يتضمّن بها الأسرار وما قد كشفت بها للعالم كيما لا ينطلي عليه محال فافهم

mine should bear in mind that there isn't a single art of theirs that I have failed to study or a single science of theirs of which I lack direct experience, or whose tricks and the tricks of whose practitioners I have not exposed. This should be clear from my own statements, from the diversity of the subjects I cover in the various sections of the work, from the tricks these contain, and from everything I have revealed to the public to prevent charlatans putting anything over them. Wise up to these things!

الفصل السابع

بابان

في كشف أسرار الذين يمشّون بالنملة السليمانيّة

اعلم وفّقك الله لِما تحبّ أنّ هذه الطائفة هي نوع من بني ساسان إلّا أنّ لهم كتاب قائم بذاته يُعرف بكتاب العزيز وهؤلاء القوم قد تسلّطوا على أخذ أموال الناس والفسق بأولادهم ولهم الدهاء والمكر وهم أخير من غيرهم ومن أفعالهم الفسق بالصبيان وأخذ أموالهم إلّا أنّهم أقلّ مكسب من سائر الناس ولا يقعون على طائل أكثر من الفسق بأولاد الناس ١٠٧

الباب الأوّل في كشف أسرارهم

وذلك أنّهم يكونوا ثلاثة أنفس الواحد بعيد منهم والآخر المتكلّم وهو الشيخ والآخر طالب فإن كان مرادهم بعض المردان فإنّهم يخرجون إلى ظاهر المدينة إلى الحاضر الذي لها فإذا عاينوا مليحًا يقول الشيخ عليها ثمّ يأخذ منديله يلفّه ويمشي وصاحبه يتبعه فإذا قربوا من الأمرد يقول صاحب الشيخ بالله عليك يا سيّدي أوريني إيّاها فيقول يا ولدي هذه نملة سليمانيّة وزنها خمسمائة درهم وجهها وجه ابن آدم وما هي ابن آدم عينها عين ابن آدم وما هي ابن آدم وخلقتها خلقة ابن آدم وما هي ابن آدم تسبيحها أن تقول سبحان الله خالق الليل والنهار سبحان مخرج الماء من الأحجار سبحان عالم الأسرار لعن الله قطّاع الحجر وذبّاح البقر وراكب ذكر الذكر لقيتها في قبر ٢٠٧

Chapter Seven, in Two Sections:

Exposé of the Tricks of Those Who Work Solomon's Ant

You should be aware, God grant you success in all you desire, that this tribe of charlatans is a subgroup of the Banū Sāsān but has a book of its own, known as *The Book of the Mighty One*. This company is daring in making off with people's money and practicing debauchery with their sons; they are crafty and cunning and cleverer than any of the others. Their MO is to debauch boys and make off with people's money, but they make less than others and all they get out of it is the pleasure of debauching people's sons. 7.1

Section One of the Exposé of Their Tricks

Exposé: There are three of them—one who keeps at a distance from the other two, one (the shaykh) who does the talking, and a third, who is a student. When they want a beardless boy, they go to the outskirts of the city, somewhere where there are some built-up areas. When they spot a cute lad, the shaykh gives the nod. He takes his kerchief, wraps it into a bundle, and sets off, the student following behind. When they get close to the boy, the shaykh's student says, "Show it to me, Master, please!" but the shaykh tells him, "My boy, this is one of Solomon's ants.[93] It weighs five hundred dirhams. It has the face of a human but it is not a human. It has the eyes of a human but it is not a human. Its nature is that of a human but it is not a human. When it glorifies God, it says, 'Glory be to God, creator of the night and the day! Glory to Him who makes water flow from stone! Glory to the Knower of Secrets! God curse the cutters of stone, the slaughterers of cattle, the male who mounts the member of a male!' I found it in a grave eating the flesh of a mortal man, and 7.2

تأكل من لحم ابن آدم فقلت لها وا لك[1] يا ملعونة يا لعينة تأكلين لحم عباد الله قالت ما أنا لعينة ولا ملعونة أنا آكل لحم من يأكل رزقه ويجحد نعمته فتكلّمت عليها بالاسم الأعظم فذلّت وخمدت

٣،٧ فإذا قال هذا الكلام لحّ عليه صاحبه بالنظر إلى هذه النملة السليمانيّة هذا وهو يتجنّب عن الطريق كي يحدث الصبيّ فإذا سمع الصبيّ ذلك طلب النظر مثلما طلب صاحبه والشيخ يهذر عليهم إلى أن يلحّوا عليه بطلب النظر إليها فيقول يا أصحابنا الساعة يجتمعون الناس علينا وأنا ما أشتهي أحدًا ينظر هذه الخلقة وقد طلبوا أن أوريهم في القلعة هذه الخلقة فما فعلت وأنتم روحوا في دعة الله فيقول صاحبه بالله يا صاحبي لا تقطع بنا قد تعلّقت قلوبنا بذلك فيقول إذا أكل واحد منكم رغيف خبز يأكله في أين فيقول في موضع مستور أو مسجد مهجور فيقول ابصروا موضع حتّى أوريكم خلقة الله وأروح فيقول صاحبه يا سيّدي أعرف هاهنا مسجد مهجور فيقول روحوا حتّى أوريكم خلقة الله تعالى ولا تعلّموا أحدًا

٤،٧ فتمّوا رائحين فيصادمهم رفيقهم الثالث فيبوس يد الشيخ ويقول يا سيّدي أنا الذي أعطيتني رزقي أوّل أمس وقد بقي لي منه عشرة دنانير فيقول أخذت رزقك فيقول نعم يا سيّدي فيقول ونفقته في الحلال فيقول نعم يا سيّدي فيقول يا سيّدي أكسيت أمّي وأختي بالذي قلت لي وتصدّقت بالذي قلت لي وقد بقي لي عشرة دنانير فيقول امشي مع إخوتك حتّى أعطيك الذي تبقى لك من رزقك فيقول له صاحبه الآخر يا سيّدي أنت تعطي الناس أرزاقهم فيقول وأنتم ما تعرفوا فيقولوا لا والله يا سيّدي

٥،٧ فيقول أنا يقال ابن العرومة بن موج[2] البحر المالح صلّوا عليه ونحن السبعة إخوة التي قال الله في حقّهم يا أيّها الذين آمنوا ﴿لَا خَوْفٌ عَلَيْكُمْ وَلَآ أَنتُمْ تَحْزَنُونَ﴾

١ ش: ذلك. ٢ الرسم غير واضح في الأصل – ش: مون.

I said to it, 'Woe unto thee, accursed one, damned one! Wouldst thou eat the flesh of mortal men?' to which it replied, 'Damned I am not and accursed I am not! I eat the flesh of those who gobble up all their God-given daily portion and are ingrates.' I then adjured it by the Greatest Name,[94] and it was cowed and became incapable of movement."

After he's said all this, the student begs him to let him have a look at this "Solomonic ant," turning off the road as he does so, so that he can speak to the boy. When the boy hears what's going on, he asks for a look too, just like the shaykh's student did, and the shaykh goes on talking nonsense to them till they pester him so much that he says, "At any moment, friends, people will gather round, and I don't want to let anyone see this creature. The people at the citadel asked me to show it to them, but I wouldn't, so run along now!" His student then says, "Please, dear teacher, don't give us the brush-off! We've set our hearts on seeing it." So the shaykh says, "When you want to eat a loaf of bread, where do you go?" and the other says, "To some spot secluded or mosque unfrequented." The shaykh says, "Look for a place where I can show you this creature of God's and then I'll be on my way." His student says, "Master, I know an abandoned mosque near here," so the shaykh says, "Let's go there so I can show you this creation of the Almighty, but don't you dare tell anyone!" 7.3

So they set off, and then they run into the third companion, who kisses the shaykh's hand and says, "Master, I'm the one to whom you delivered his divinely allotted portion of upkeep the day before yesterday, and I still have ten gold pieces left." "Did you receive your portion in full?" the shaykh asks him, and he replies, "Master, I did." "And did you spend it on things that religion permits?" the shaykh asks. "Master, I did," the man replies, going on to say, "I bought clothes for my mother and my sister in the amount you recommended and I gave alms in the amount you recommended and I have ten gold pieces left." So the shaykh says, "Come along with your brothers so that I can give you what you're still owed." His other student then says to the shaykh, "Master, do you really hand out their divinely allotted upkeep to people?" "You didn't know that?" says the shaykh. "No way, Master!" say the first student and the boy. 7.4

Then the shaykh says, "I am the one they call Ibn al-ʿArūmah, Son of the Waves of the Salty Sea (pray for him!). We are the seven brothers of whom God said, 'O You who believe, «No fear shall come upon you nor shall you grieve.»'[95] We have been instructed in God's Greatest Name and He has commissioned us 7.5

ونحن قد علمنا اسم الله الأعظم ووكّلنا على أرزاق الخلق ندور في الأرض إن وجدنا جيعان أشبعناه أو عرياناً أكسيناه أو فقير أغنيناه فيقول صاحبه وأنت تعرف الاسم الأعظم فيقول الشيخ نعم أتكلّم به على الماء يجمد وعلى النار تخمد وعلى الحديد ينغزمثل الشمع وعلى التراب يصير ذهباً وفضّة وهاتوا سلسلة يكون طولها سبعون ذراعاً وعرضها سبعون حتّى أتكلّم عليها بالاسم الأعظم أعجنها مثل الشمع فيقولوا من أين لنا الساعة سلسلة فيقول أيش عندكم صُلب قويّ فيقولوا الحجارة فيقول هاتوا حجرحتّى أتكلّم عليه أخلّيه ينعجن مثل الشمع وأخرج منه عرق النبيّ صلّى الله عليه وسلّم

٦،٧ فيجيبوا له حجر فيأخذه بيده وفي يده قطنة مشرّبة بماء الورد إن أمكن وإلّا ماء القراح فيأخذ الحجر ويقول هذا الحجر يوم شجّ جبين النبيّ صلّى الله عليه وسلّم وكسر ثنيّته وعقر جواده عرق فسقط عرقه على الحجر فإذا تكلّمت عليه بالاسم الأعظم إن أردتم أخرج لكم منه ناراً تحرق الأرض والسماء والشجر والمدر وإن أردتم أن ينزل منه عرق النبيّ صلّى الله عليه وينفع من اثنين وسبعين حاجة ينفع لمن يضربه أبوه أو عمّه أو معلّمه أو قرابته وينفع القبول وقضاء الحوائج ولمن يكون قليل الرزق ثمّ يقول افتحوا أيديكم فيفتحوا أيديهم فيعصر الحجر فينزل منه ذلك الماء الذي في القطن

٧،٧ فيقول امسحوا وجوهكم فيمسحوا به وجوههم ثمّ يبوسوا يده ويقول[١] يا سيّدي والله يا سيّدي أنا فقير وأريد من الله ومنك شيء أعيش به أنا وأمّي فيقول وأنت فقير فيقول نعم يا سيّدي فيقول فإذا طلع رزقك تصدّق منه بعشر الدنانير والباقي تنفقه في الحلال فيقول نعم يا سيّدي فيقول قول الحمد لله ثمّ يلتفت إلى الصبيّ فيقول وأنت فقير فيقول نعم فيقول إذا أعطيتك رزقك تنفقه في الحلال وتصدّق منه بخمس دنانير فيقول نعم يا سيّدي هذا ويكون قد خرجوا إلى موضع يمكن فيه الفسق بالصبيّ

١ ش: ويقولوا.

to distribute their divinely allotted portions to His creation. We roam through the land and if we find someone hungry, we feed him till he is full; if naked, we clothe him; if poor, we make him rich." His student then says, "Do you really know the Greatest Name?" "Yes indeed!" says the shaykh. "I adjure water by it and it freezes. I adjure fire by it and it dies down. I adjure iron by it and it melts like wax; dust, and it turns into gold and silver. Fetch me a chain seventy cubits long and seventy wide so that I can adjure it by the Greatest Name and knead it like wax." "Where are we supposed to find a chain right now?" they say, and he says, "So what do you have that's very hard?" "Rocks," they say. So he says, "Get a rock so I can adjure it and make it as soft as wax, and squeeze from it the sweat of the Prophet, God bless him and keep him."

So they fetch him a rock, which he takes in his hand, in which he is already 7.6
holding a piece of cotton soaked in rosewater if he can get it, or in clean water if he can't. He takes the rock and says, "One day this rock gave the Prophet, God bless him and keep him, a cut on his forehead, broke his front tooth, and hocked his horse. He sweated, and the sweat fell onto the rock. When I adjure it by the Greatest Name, I can, if you so desire, cause a fire to come out of it that will incinerate earth and sky, trees and clay; or, if you so desire, the sweat of the Prophet himself, God's blessings upon him, will come out of it, and that is good for seventy-seven things: It is good for anyone whose father, uncle, teacher, or any relative beats him, and it is good for attracting affection and taking care of various needs, and for anyone who has a hard time making a living." Then he says, "Hold out your hands!" so they hold them out and he squeezes the rock and the liquid that's in the cotton comes out.

"Wipe your faces!" he says, so they wipe their faces with the liquid and kiss 7.7
his hand. The first student then says, "Master, Master, I swear I'm poor and want something from God, and you, that my mother and I can live on." So he says to him, "You're poor?" "Yes, Master," he answers. "And if your divinely allotted portion appears before you, will you give away ten gold pieces of it in alms, and spend the rest on things that religion permits?" he asks. "Yes, Master," he replies. "Say 'Thanks be to God'!" he says. Then he turns to the boy and says, "And are you poor too?" and the boy says, "Yes." Then he says, "If I give you your divinely allotted portion, will you spend it on things that religion permits, and give five gold pieces in alms?" and he says, "Master, I will." By this time, they will have veered from the beaten track and reached a place where they can debauch the boy.

٨،٧ ثمّ إنّه خطّ خطّ في الأرض وقعدوا الجمع حوله ثمّ يقول احضروا أيّها الملٰئكة[١] الموكّلون بخزائن الأرض الذي تحت يدي حتّى أعطي لعبيد الله أرزاقهم ثمّ يقول طأمنوا رؤوسكم فيفعلوا ذلك فيقول أيّها الملك الفلانيّ توكّل بهذا وأنت بهذا ثمّ يكون معه دنانير من الرصاص المطليّة بالصندروس كأنّها ذهب فيأخذ تراب يعمله صُبّة قدّامه ثمّ يدكّ فيه ذلك الدنانير الرصاص ثمّ يقول أيّ من قام صُرع ثمّ يقول من هو أصغركم فيقولوا أصحابه هذا الصبيّ أصغر من فينا فيقول له[٢] ارفع طرف المنديل وابصر أيش تحته فيرفع طرف المنديل فيجد تحته ذلك الذهب فيذهل عقله ثمّ يقول لصاحبه قارعني فيقارعه فيقول قد طلع لك من المال خمسون ديناراً ونصف دينار وثلث دينار فيقول نعم يا سيّدي فيقول اشكر الله ثمّ يلتفت إلى الصبيّ فيقول وأين تسكن وإن كان له أب ولا يزال حتّى يعلم جميع أحواله ثمّ يقول قارعني فيقول قد طلع خمسمائة دينار وخمسين دينار وخمس دنانير قل الحمد لله وتصدّق منها بخمس دنانير والباقي انفقه في الحلال وكلّ سنة يطلع لك مثلها

٩،٧ فهو يحدّثه وصاحبه يمدّ يده إلى نحو المنديل الذي تحته الذهب الذي قد أبصره الصبيّ كأنّه يريد يأخذ منه شيء فيزعق عليه الشيخ ويقول تخطف تراب ثمّ يرفع المنديل فلا يجد تحته شيئاً فييوس يده ويقول بالله يا سيّدي لا تقطع بنا وأعطينا رزقنا ويفعل الصبيّ كذلك فيقول إنّ الملٰئكة يخبروني أنّ كلّ واحد منكم عمل ثلاث ذنوب قد سرق وقتل وزنى أو زُنِيَ به ويقول لصاحبه من زنى بك فيقول ما زنى بي أحد وأيش يكون الزناء فيقول من عمل بك مثلما يعمل الرجل بالمرأة فيقول ما عمل بي أحد شيء فيقول وا لك يا ملعون تخفي على[٣] الشيخ اسكني في رأسه هيّا فإذا قال ذلك وقع إلى الأرض وجعل يخبط ويقول تشفّعوا فيّه فيبوس يده صاحبه الآخر ويقول من شأن الله يا سيّدي أوهبنا ذنبه ويفعل الصبيّ كذلك

١ ش: ملوك. ٢ ش: فيقولوا. ٣ أضيف للسياق.

The shaykh now draws a line in the dirt and the whole gang sits down around it. "Attend," he says, "ye angels charged with guardianship of the treasure houses of the earth who are under my command, so that I may give God's slaves their portions!" Then he says, "Bow your heads!" and they do so, and he says, "Angel So-and-so, take care of this one, and you there, of that!" Now, he has on him coins made of lead coated with sandarac to look like gold, and he makes a little pile of dirt in front of him and sneaks the lead coins into it and says, "Anyone who gets up will be struck down." Then he asks, "Which of you is the youngest?" and his students say, "This boy," so he tells him, "Lift the corner of the handkerchief[96] and see what's underneath." So the boy lifts the corner of the handkerchief and finds the "gold" underneath it and his mind reels. Then the shaykh says to the student, "Hit me!" so he "hits" him and the shaykh tells him, "Fifty gold pieces plus one-half of a gold piece plus one-third of a gold piece—that's what they've sent up for you from down below," and the student says, "So be it, Master," and the shaykh says, "Give thanks to God!" Then he turns to the boy and asks him where he lives and whether his father is still alive, so as to find out everything about his circumstances. Then he says, "Hit me!" and then, "Five hundred and fifty-five gold pieces, that's what they've sent up for you. Say, 'Praise be to God!' Give the five gold pieces away as alms and spend the rest on things that religion permits. They'll be sending you up the same each year." 7.8

While he is talking to the boy, the student stretches out his hand in the direction of the handkerchief that covers the "gold" the boy saw, as though meaning to take some. "You would snatch a handful of dust?" the shaykh yells at him, and he lifts the handkerchief and there's nothing there. The student kisses his hand and says, "For God's sake, Master, don't cut us off! Give us our portions!" and the boy does the same, so the shaykh says, "The angels are telling me that each of you has committed three sins: He has stolen, he has killed, and he's either fornicated or been used for fornication." To the student, he says, "Who used you for fornication?" and the other replies, "Nobody, and what is fornication anyway?" So the shaykh says to him, "Who did to you what a man does to a woman?" and the other says, "Nobody did anything to me." "Woe unto you, accursed one!" says the shaykh. "Would you conceal things from your shaykh? Angels, go dwell in his head, pronto!" and as he says it, the student falls to the ground and starts flailing around and saying, "Intercede for me!" At this, the shaykh's other follower kisses his hand and says, "For the sake of God, Master, give him our sin!"[97] and the boy does the same. 7.9

فإذا سألوه أخذ حصوة ويوري أنّه يتكلّم عليها ويدفعها للصبيّ ويقول اجعلها على وجهه فإذا جعلها عليه قعد وباس الأرض ويد الشيخ وقال العفو يا سيّدي فيقول له هيّا حدّث أيش أبصرت فيقول العفو يا سيّدي أبصرت ناس بلا رؤوس وناس رؤوس بلا أبدان وأبدان بلا رؤوس وناس على خيول من نار وبأيديهم حراب من نار فقالوا لي يا لعين يا ملعون إن كتمت الشيخ شيء قتلناك وأحرقناك وأنا يا سيّدي أقول بكلّ ما عملت وبالله عليك لا تسلّمني إلى أولائك ١٠،٧

فيقول له الشيخ قول لي من قتلت فيقول يا سيّدي والله ما قتلت إلّا عصفور وأنا صغير عصرت عليه مات فيقول قل اللّهمّ إنّي تائب إليك فيقول نعم ثمّ يقول أيش سرقت فيقول يا سيّدي والله وقت كنت صغير كانت أمّي تبيع الغزل قرطاسين أو قرطاس أو أربع فلوس وإذا أعطوني أشتري لهم حويجاء أسرق منها فلسين ثلاثة فهذا كلّ شيء كنت أسرق فيقول الشيخ تب إلى الله ثمّ يقول ومن زنى بك فيقول يا سيّدي وقت كنت صغير كان عندنا في الدكّان صانع وكان يوهبني فليسات ويزني بي فيقول ما هو هذا ويقول آخر يبيع الحلاوة وكان يطعمني الحلاوة ويزني بي فيقول وكان يدخّل[١] ذكره كلّه فيقول أيّ والله يا سيّدي ولا يزال كذلك حتّى يعدّ سبعة ثمانية ويقول والله يا سيّدي ما بقي أحد فيقول الشيخ تتوب فيقول نعم يا سيّدي فيقول ابشر بزيادة رزقك ألف دينار زيادة قل الحمد لله ١١،٧

ثمّ يلتفت إلى الصبيّ فيقول أيش سرقت فيقول كذا وكذا فيقول تتوب فيقول نعم فيقول لمن قتلت فيقول ما قتلت أحد فيقول من زنى بك فيقول واحد صفته ونعته كذا وكذا[٢] فيقول ما هو هذا هذا آخر فيقول نعم يا سيّدي كان أمره معي كذا وكذا ولا يزال عليه حتّى يذكر كلّ من فسق به ويعلم أن ما بقي له أحد فيقول تتوب فيقول نعم فيقول قد زاد رزقك ألف دينار وفي كلّ جمعة يزداد رزقك إلّا أنتم تريدون تطهّرون من الذنوب ١٢،٧

١ ش: يداخل. ٢ كذا وكذا: أضيف للسياق.

In response to their plea, he takes a rock and makes as though he's saying a spell over it. Then he gives it to the boy and says, "Put it on his face!" and when he does so, the student sits up and kisses the ground and the shaykh's hand and says, "Forgive me, Master!" The shaykh tells him, "Go on, tell us what you saw!" and the student says, "Forgive me, Master! I saw people without heads and people who were heads without bodies and bodies that were without heads and people on horses of fire with spears of fire in their hands who said to me, 'Accursed one! Damned one! If you conceal anything from the shaykh, we will kill you and burn you!' and I will tell you, Master, everything I've done, but please, for God's sake, don't hand me over to those people!" 7.10

Now the shaykh says to him, "Tell me whom you killed!" and he says, "The only thing I ever killed was a sparrow. When I was young, I squeezed it and it died." The shaykh says, "Say, 'O God, I repent unto you!'" and the other says, "I repent." Then the shaykh says, "What did you steal?" so he says, "I swear to God, Master, when I was little my mother used to sell yarn—two copper coins' worth, one copper coins' worth, four copper coins' worth—and when a customer gave me money to buy some little thing for him, I'd steal two or three copper coins from him. That's all I ever stole." The shaykh says, "Repent unto God!" Then he says, "And who used you for fornication?" and he says, "Master, when I was little, we had an apprentice in the shop and he'd give me a few farthings and use me for fornication." The shaykh says, "Attaboy!" and the student continues, "And there was another who sold candy and used to give me free candy and use me for fornication." The shaykh says, "And did he push his member all the way in?" and the other says, "Indeed, Master, he did!" and he keeps on in the same vein till he's listed seven or eight others and says, "That's the last of them, Master, swear to God!" Then the shaykh says, "Do you repent?" and the other says, "I do, Master," and the shaykh says, "Rejoice! Your portion has been increased by a thousand gold pieces. Say, 'Praise God!'" 7.11

Then he turns to the boy and says, "And what have you stolen?" and the boy says what he's stolen and the shaykh says, "Do you repent?" and the boy says, "I do." Next the shaykh says, "And whom did you kill?" and the boy says, "I never killed anyone." Then the shaykh says, "And who used you for fornication?" and the boy says, "A man of such and such a description and such and such a condition," and he describes him. Then the shaykh says, "Attaboy! Anyone else?" and the boy says, "Yes, Master, and what he used to do with me was thus and so," and he keeps on in the same vein till he's mentioned everyone 7.12

فمن تطهّر رزقه ومن لا يتطهّر احترق الساعة أيّما أحبّ إليكم تطهّركم ملٰئكة من نار بذكور من نار لو طرح واحد منهم ذكره في النار أحرقها أو في السماء خرقها أو تطهّرون بعضكم بعض فيقول صاحبه والله يا سيّدي ما لنا طاقة بذكور الملٰئكة نحن نطهّر بعضنا بعض فيقول رضيوا فيقولوا نعم

فيقول لصاحبه خذ هذا الحصوة وانظر أيش ما أبصرت عرّفني فيأخذ الحصوة ثمّ ١٣،٧
يشخص ثم ينكب على رجل الشيخ يبوسها ويقول يا سيّدي العفو فيقول أيش أبصرت فيقول أبصرت أربعين ملكًا من نار وهم وقوف حتّى يؤذن لهم يطهّرونا وأبصرت لكلّ واحد منهم ذكر مثل النخلة العظيمة يشعل بالنار فبالله يا سيّدي لا تفعل فنحن نطهّر بعضنا بعض فيقول خذ هذه الحصوة وروح نام هاهنا وحلّ سراويلك وروح اعمل به مثلما عملوا بك سواء ثمّ يصرخ فيه فيروح يحلّ سراويله ويريد يدنو منه والشيخ يزعق عليه ويقول ركبت البحر المالح فيقول لا يا سيّدي فيقول نام لا تحترق فيزعق عليه فينام على وجهه ويقول لصاحبه قم طهّر أخوك المؤمن فيثب إليه ثمّ يولج فيه آلته والشيخ يقول للصبيّ قل حلال يا سيّدي لا زنى ولا خنى ولا يزال كذلك حتّى يفرغ منه فيقول الشيخ ارتفع يا مبارك فيقوم ويهمّ الصبيّ أن يقوم فيزعق عليه الشيخ ويقول نام لا تحترق فيتمّ نائم فيقول لصاحبه الآخر قوم طهّر أخوك المؤمن فيقوم إليه الآخر فإذا قضى شغله يقول الشيخ ارتفع يا مبارك ثمّ يقول للصبيّ قم فاغتسل فإذا قام اغتسل فيقول اقعدوا خذوا أرزاقكم

who ever debauched him and the shaykh feels sure he's told him about everyone and says to him, "Do you repent?" and he says, "I do." The shaykh then says, "Your portion has increased by a thousand gold pieces and will continue to increase every Friday. Now, never mind all that. You all need to be cleansed of your sins, for any whose portion is cleansed but is not himself cleansed shall be consumed by flames on the spot. Which would you rather: that angels of fire cleanse you with members of fire (just one of which, if its owner were to throw it into hellfire, would consume it, or into the sky, would rip it to shreds) or that you cleanse each other?" The student says, "I swear to God, Master, we don't have the stamina to take the angels' members. We'd better cleanse one another." "Agreed?" says the shaykh. "Agreed!" they say.

So he says to the student, "Take this rock, take a look, and tell me what you see!" So the student takes the rock, narrows his eyes, and then suddenly throws himself at the shaykh's feet, kissing them and saying, "Master! Forgive me!" "What did you see?" the shaykh asks, and he replies, "I saw forty angels of fire, standing erect, waiting for permission to cleanse us. And I saw that each one had a member like a mighty palm tree, burning like a torch. In God's name then, Master, don't do it! We can cleanse one another." The shaykh says to him, "Take this rock and come and lie down here and drop your drawers and do to the boy the same as the others did to you, down to the last detail!" Then he shouts at him and he comes over and drops his drawers and is trying to close in on the boy when the shaykh yells, "Have you set sail yet upon the salty sea?" and the student says, "Not yet, Master!" so the shaykh says to the boy, "Lie down lest ye be consumed by the flames!" so the boy lies down on his stomach and the shaykh says to his companion, "Cleanse thy believing brother!" and the man jumps on top of the boy and sticks his tool in him, while the shaykh says to the boy, "Say after me, 'A godly deed, Master! In no way depraved and in no way profane!'" and keeps on doing so till the other has finished. The shaykh then says, "Arise, blessed one!" and the student gets up and the boy starts to get up too but the shaykh yells at him and says, "Lie down lest ye be consumed by the flames!" so he stays on his stomach and the shaykh says to his other follower, "Arise and cleanse thy believing brother!" and the follower goes at it with him, and when he's finished his business, the shaykh says to him, "Arise, blessed one!" Then he says to the boy, "Arise and perform your ablutions!" and after he has done so, "Sit down and receive your portions." 7.13

١٤،٧ فإذا قعدوا يقول لصاحبه الذي جاء في الآخر وادّعى أن بقي له من رزقه عشرة دنانير خذ هذه الحصوة إن كنت قد كمّلت طهورك فيقول يا سيّدي فما قد طهّروني ذلك اليوم خمسة كما زنى بي خمسة فيقول صدّقت خذ هذه الحصوة وما في دارك بئر فيقول بلى يا سيّدي فيقول روح الساعة اقف على البئر ثمّ أرمي الحصوة فيه وقل يا حرحير يا حرحير أعطني رزقي من البئر وافتح يدك وغمّض عينيك فإنّه يقع في يدك عشرة دنانير قم الساعة ثمّ يصيح به فيأخذ حصوة ثمّ يبوس يده ثمّ يقول لصاحبه الآخر أنت ما وقع لك من يطهّرك فيقول يا سيّدي العفو ما لي طاقة بالملٰئكة أنا أبصر لي من يطهّرني فيقول اشكر الله ثمّ يلتفت إلى الصبيّ ويقول أنت قد بقيت ولدي يا ولدي بقي عليك كذا وكذا طهور وتأخذ رزقك فيقول صاحبه يا سيّدي ما تطهّره أنت فيقول أنا إذا طهّرت واحد يطلع الذهب الذي له كلّ دينار وزنه عشرة دنانير وأنا ما أطهّر أحد فيقول يا سيّدي صبيّ فمن شأن الله طهّره وأعطيه رزقه ودعه يروح لم يقم الصبيّ يسأله ذلك إلى يوم يطهّره ويبقى صاحبه متأسّف كيف ما وقع له من يطهّره

١٥،٧ ثمّ يعاوده صاحبه يقول للصبيّ إذا كان غداً تعال إلى هاهنا حتّى تكمل طهورك وتأخذ رزقك واحذر أن تبيح بسرّي فتهلك وما يرجع يطلع لك رزق ثمّ يقول لصاحبه وأنت غداً تكمل طهورك وتأخذ رزقك ثمّ يقول فمن فيكم يريد يبيح بسرّي ثمّ يرجمه الآخر[١] بحصاة ويقول هيّا عذّبوه فيبقى يخبط ساعته ثمّ يقول للصبيّ تسأل فيه فيقول نعم فيعطيه حصوة ويقول حطّها على رأسه فإذا فُعِلَ ذلك فاق ثمّ أقبل على الشيخ وقال العفو يا سيّدي أنا والله لي صديق وكنت أريد أن أحدّثه وأنا تائب على يد الله ويدك فيقول أبصرت سبع ملٰئكة من نار بأيديهم حراب من نار كلّ واحد هزّ حربته وجاء إليّ وقال وا لك يا لعين يا ملعون تبيح بسرّ الشيخ وهمّوا بقتلي

---

١ أضيف للسياق.

When they have sat down, the shaykh says to the follower who arrived last and pretended that he had ten gold pieces of his portion left over, "Take this rock, if you have completed your cleansing!" and the man says to him, "But Master, the number of those who cleansed me the other day was five, just as the number of those who had used me for fornication was five,"[98] and the shaykh says, "Quite right! Take this rock!" and "Doesn't your house have a well?" "Indeed, it does," says the other, so the shaykh says, "Off with you right away and stand by the well and throw this rock into it and say, 'Ḥarḥīr! Ḥarḥīr![99] My portion—from down in the well to here!' and open your hand and close your eyes and ten gold pieces will fall into it. Off you go, right now!" and he screams at him, so the man takes the rock and kisses the shaykh's hand. Then the shaykh says to the student, "You! There's no one around to cleanse you" and the student says, "Pardon, Master, I don't have the stamina to take the angels. I'll find myself someone to cleanse me," so the shaykh says, "Give thanks to God!" Then the shaykh turns to the boy and says, "Now you're my son, my child. You have to complete such and such a number of cleansings and then you can receive your portion," at which the student says, "Master, why don't *you* cleanse him?" to which the shaykh replies, "When *I* cleanse someone, every gold piece of the portion that's due him comes up weighing ten, which is why I never do it," to which the other responds, "Master, he's just a boy! For love of God, cleanse him, give him his portion, and let him go home. The boy didn't go ahead and ask his master for that, so how much longer must he wait for him to cleanse him? And his master must be sorry that it didn't fall to his lot to cleanse anyone." 7.14

The man's master now turns back to the boy and tells him, "Come back to this same spot in the morning to finish your cleansing and take your portion. Mind you don't give my secret away or you'll be destroyed and there'll be no more portions sent up to you from down below!" Then he says to his companion, "And you too will finish your cleansing tomorrow and take your portion." Next he says, "If either of you decides to divulge my secret, let the other stone him with pebbles and say, 'Go to it, angels! Torment him!'" And at that very moment, the student does indeed fall to the ground and flail around, and the shaykh says to the boy, "Are you worried about him?" and the boy says, "Yes." So the shaykh gives him a rock and tells him, "Put it on his head." When he does so, the student comes to and then turns to the shaykh and says, "Master, forgive me. I cannot lie. I have a friend and I was going to tell him but I repent, at God's hand and at yours," and he goes on, "I saw seven angels of fire with 7.15

فجاء ملك آخر قال أنا أضمنه أنّه لا يبيح بسرّ الشيخ وإن باح أنا أقتله بهذا الذي خلصني منهم وأنا تائب يا سيّدي

١٦،٧ ثمّ يصرفهم ويقول أنا الساعة رائح ما أبات الليلة إلّا في مكّة فإن قد وصل ناس إليها ولهم عندي رزق أروح أعطيهم وأروح إلى الغرب أعطي أخر أرزاقهم وأكون هنا باكر فإذا أبصرني أحد منهم احذروا أن يسلّم عليّ أو يقول لأحد هذا يعطي الناس أرزاقهم فيهلك ثمّ يقول قوموا افعلوا ما قلت لكم ثمّ يتفرّقوا أمّا صاحبه فإنّه يمشي مع الصبيّ ويأخذ خبره ويعلم ما في نفسه وما قد حصل عنده من الشيخ ثمّ يعرف صاحبه ذلك فافهم

الباب الثاني في كشف أسرارهم

١٧،٧ ومن ذلك الذين يأخذون أموال الناس بالنملة السليمانيّة وذلك أنّ سيرتهم في الحديث مثل الأوّل والفصل فيه من حيث يخرج الماء من الحجر فإذا فعل ذلك قال اعلموا أنّي أنا يقال لي الحجّاج علي بن المعلومة بن مؤذّن البحر المالح صلّوا عليه وتحت يدي أموال الأرض ونحن السبعة إخوة الذي نحن أوتاد[1] الأرض الذي قال الله في حقّنا يا أيّها الذين آمنوا ﴿لَا خَوْفٌ عَلَيْكُمْ وَلَآ أَنتُمْ تَحْزَنُونَ﴾ ونحن موكّلون على أرزاق الخلق أنا موكّل على أرزاق بني آدم وأخي موكّل بأرزاق الدوابّ والآخر موكّل بأرزاق الوحوش والآخر موكّل بأرزاق الطير والآخر موكّل بأرزاق وحش البحار والآخر موكّل بأرزاق الأسماك

١٨،٧ وأنا ما لي شغل إلّا دائر في الأرض إن لقيت فقير أغنيته أو عريان أكسيته أو جيعان أشبعته أنتم فقراء فيقول صاحبه أيّ والله يا سيّدي أنا رجل فقير وعليّ

---

١ ش: آذناه.

lances of fire in their hands and each one shook his spear and said, 'Accursed one! Damned one! Would you give away the secret of the shaykh?' And they were about to kill me when another came and said, 'I will stand surety that he doesn't give away the shaykh's secret, and if he does, I will kill him.' By the one who saved me from them, Master, I repent!"

The shaykh then sends them on their way, saying, "I'm off now. I have to spend the night in Mecca. Some people whose portions I have with me have turned up there. I'll give them their portions and then go on to the Maghreb and give another man his portion. I'll be here tomorrow, early. If either of you happens to see me, mind you don't say hello or tell anyone 'That's the one who gives people their divinely allotted portions of upkeep' or you'll be destroyed!" Then he says, "Up you get and do as I told you!" So they part ways, but the student goes with the boy and listens to what he has to say and learns what he thinks of what happened when he was with the shaykh, then tells his master. Wise up to these things! 7.16

Section Two of the Exposé of Their Tricks

Another example: Some of them use Solomon's ant to make off with people's money. 7.17

Exposé: They use the same spiel as the first lot, the difference coming at the point when the water comes out of the rock, when the charlatan says, "I am called 'Alī the Pilgrim-guide, Son of the Known Woman, Son of the Muezzin of the Salty Sea (pray for him!) and the wealth of the world is in my keeping. We are the seven brothers who are the 'stakes'[100] that hold the Earth fast, regarding whom God has said, 'O You who believe, «No fear upon you nor shall you grieve»'[101] and we are entrusted with the divinely allotted portions of upkeep of all creation. I am entrusted with the portions of humankind, one of my brothers with those of domestic animals, another with those of wild beasts, another with those of birds, another with those of the monsters of the oceans, and another with those of fish.

"My only work is to tour the earth and when I find a poor man, make him rich, or a naked man, clothe him, or a hungry man, feed him till he's full. Are you poor?" "That we are, Master," says his student. "I'm a poor man with a debt on my shoulders and no means to settle it. My creditor wants to put me 7.18

دين وما لي شيء أوفيه وصاحبه يريد يحبسني عليه فيقول اشكر الله الذي وقعت لي ثمّ يعطف إلى الآخر الخشن وهو باهت إليهما ويقول أنت فقير فيقول أيّ والله يا سيّدي فيقول اشكر الله ثمّ يقول قال النبيّ صلّى الله عليه وسلّم المال يجرّ المال والقمل يجرّ الصيبان من كان معه درهم صار عشرة دنانير من كان معه دينار صار مائة دينار وأيش معكم من مال الله

١٩،٧ فيقول صاحبه يا سيّدي معي خمسين درهم جمعتها لصاحب الدين أريد أعطيه أيّاها ثمّ يخرجها فيقول هذه تصير خمسين دينار أو لو كانت مائة صارت مائة دينار أو ألف درهم صارت ألف دينار فخلّيه معك حتّى أقول لك ثمّ يلتفت إلى الخشن ويقول أيش معك من مال الله ويكون قد دخل المدينة وأباع إمّا غلّة وإمّا شيء وهذا شيء لا يفعلوه إلّا مع فلّاح أو جبليّ أو حورانيّ أو[1] سواديّ ويرقبوه بمقدار ما يبيع ويقول حُطّوا عليه

٢٠،٧ فإذا قال أيش معك من مال الله فيقول كذا وكذا ثمّ يخرجه ويقول الوديعة الذي معك تتحوّج بها فإنّ الفلّاح لا بدّ أن يكون معه لأحد من الضيعة شيء يتحوّج به فيخرجه ويتوهّم أنّه يعلم الغيب فإذا أخرج جميع ما معه يقول له اتركه معك حتّى أقول لك أيش تعمل به ثمّ يلتفت إلى صاحبه فيقول أين الذي معك فيقول هذا الذي معي فيقول أعطيه لأخوك المؤمن فإذا أعطاه الذي معه يقول للخشن اربطه في ذيل أخوك المؤمن فيربطه في ذيل صاحبه ثمّ يقول للخشن أين الذي معك من مال الله تعالى فيخرج إليه الذي معه فيقول أعطيه في هذه الساعة لأخوك المؤمن يربطه في ذيلك ثمّ يقول لصاحبه خذ من أخوك المؤمن واربطه في ذيله كما ربط في ذيلك فيأخذ من الخشن فيدك إمّا فلوس أو دراهم أو رصاص ثمّ يربطها

٢١،٧ فإذا فعل ذلك يقول الشيخ أيّ من لمس صرّته اليوم يبست يده ثمّ يلتفت الخشن ويقول من أيّ الضياع أنت فيقول من الموضع الفلانيّ فيقول إذا وصلت إلى البلد

---

[1] ش: و.

in prison for it." The charlatan then says, "Give thanks to God that you came across me!" Then he turns to the other, the mark, who is gawping at them openmouthed, and says, "Are you poor?" and he says, "I am indeed, Master!" The charlatan says, "Give thanks to God!" and then, "The Prophet, God bless him and keep him, has said, 'Money makes money and lice make nits.'[102] He who has a single silver piece will find it has become ten and he who has a single gold piece will find it has become a hundred. How much of God's money does each of you have on you?"

The student says, "I have fifty silver pieces, Master, that I've collected for my creditor and that I mean to give him," and he produces them. The shaykh says, "These could be fifty gold pieces, or, if they were a hundred silver pieces, a hundred gold pieces! Hold on to them till I tell you." Then he turns to the mark and says, "And how much of God's money do you have on you?" (The man will have been to the city and sold grain or something of the sort. They only play this trick on a peasant or a man from the mountains or one from Hawran or the Mesopotamian plains. The more he sells in the market, the more closely they watch him, till at a certain point the charlatan says, "Have at 'im!") 7.19

When he asks him, "How much of God's money do you have on you?" the mark replies, "Such and such a sum," and produces it, deluded into thinking that the charlatan knows what goes on in the World of the Unseen. When he's produced everything he has on him, the charlatan tells him, "Hold on to it till I tell you what to do with it." Then he turns to his student and says, "Where's your money?" and the student says, "Here's what I have." The charlatan says, "Give it to your believing brother!" and when the man has done so, he says to the mark, "Knot it into the hem of your believing brother's robe,"[103] and he does so. Then he says to the mark, "Where's your money that the Almighty gave you?" so he hands over to him what he has on him. The charlatan says, "Give it this second to your believing brother so that he can knot it into the hem of your robe," and he says to his follower, "Take the money from your believing brother and knot it into the hem of his robe just like he did with yours." So he takes the money from the mark, switches it for copper, silver, or lead coins, and knots it into his robe. 7.20

As soon as he's done this, the shaykh says, "If anyone touches his money bag today, his fingers will be paralyzed." Then he turns to the mark and asks him, "What village are you from?" and the other says, "Such and such." The shaykh says, "When you get to the village, wait until nightfall, then leave the house 7.21

اصبر إلى الليل وأخرج إلى البيدر اقف فيه ووجّهك إلى الشرق وخذ هذه الحصوة أرميها من جهة الشرق وقول يا كور يا كور أعطيني من البيدر رزقي ثمّ افتح هذه الصرّة تجد كلّ درهم قد صار عشرة دنانير فخذها اشكر الله ولا تنفقها إلّا في الحلال وتصدّق منها دينار على الفقراء

٢٢،٧ فإذا فعل ذلك أومى صاحبه إلى الصرّة كأنّه يلتمسها ثمّ يصيح ويعوّج أصابعه كأنّها قد يبّست فيقول وا لك يا لعين يا ملعون ما وصّيتك وا لك تخالف الشيخ اسكني في رأسه فينصرع وتبقى أصابعه كأنّها قد يبست فيقول للخشن تسأل فيه فيعطيه حصوة ويقول اجعلها على رأسه فإذا جعلها على رأسه أفاق وبقيت أصابعه يابسة فيقول للخشن قل له لا يرجع يمسّها فيقول لا والله وقد أبصرت ملك رجليه في الأرض ورأسه في السماء ومعه مرزبّة[١] من نار فقال لي متى لمست هذه الصرّة قبل ما يأمرك الشيخ ضربتك بهذه المرزبّة على يدك يبّستها من كفك فيقول الشيخ تسأل فيه فيردّها إلى ما كانت فيقول لا ترجع تلمسها فيوصيه الخشن

٢٣،٧ ثمّ يلتفت الشيخ إلى صاحبه ويقول إذا كان ليلة الجمعة انزل اقف في مفرق ثلاث طرق ثمّ تقول يا ابو فِرَق أعطيني رزقي ثلاث طرق ثمّ افتح هذه الصرّة تجد كلّ درهم قد صار عشرة دنانير وإن أعلمت أحد أو قلت لأحد فأنت إذا فتحت الصرّة تجد بها فلوس أو رصاص وقال قوموا إلى أشغالكم أنا أريد الليلة أروح أبات في الهند أعطي الناس أرزاقهم وأصبح في مكّة ثمّ يقوموا ويثور هو يهرول قدّامهم يثور كلّ واحد منهم مع هواه فافهم ذلك وتميّز الأشياء وابصر محَال العالم

---

١ ش: مرزبّات.

and go to the threshing floor. Stand there facing the east and take this pebble. Throw it eastward, and say, 'Koor! Koor![104] My portion, from the threshing floor!' Then open this money bag and you'll find that every silver piece has turned into ten gold pieces. Take them, give thanks to God, spend them only on things that religion permits, and give one gold piece in alms to the poor."

When he has finished, his follower points at the money bag as though he had just been touching it, then screams and curls his fingers as though they had become paralyzed. "Woe is you, accursed one, damned one!" says the shaykh. "Didn't I tell you? Woe is you for disobeying the shaykh! Angels, go dwell in his head!" and the man falls down in a fit and his fingers appear to become paralyzed. Then the shaykh says to the mark, "Are you worried about him?" and he gives him a pebble and says, "Put it on his head," and when he does so, he comes around but his fingers remain paralyzed. The shaykh tells the mark, "Tell him not to touch it again!" and the other says, "I won't, I swear to God! I saw an angel whose feet were on the ground and head in the heavens, and he was holding a rod of fire and he said to me, 'If you dare touch this money bag before the shaykh has ordered you to do so, I shall strike your arm with this rod and paralyze it from the shoulder down.'" Then the shaykh says, "Are you still worried about him?" and turns the man's hand back to the way it was and says, "Don't touch it again!" and the mark likewise urges him not to do so. 7.22

Then the shaykh turns to his student and says, "On Friday eve, go stand where three roads divide and say, 'Father of Divisions, give me my portion three ways!' Then open this money bag and you'll find that each silver piece has become ten gold pieces. But if you inform anyone or tell anyone, you'll find only copper coins or lead in the money bag when you open it." Then he says, "Get up and see to your affairs! I want to spend tonight in India giving people their portions and make it to Mecca by morning." They get up and he rushes off in front of them and each of the others rushes off in his wake. Wise up to these things! Discriminate, and observe the wiles of the world! 7.23

الفصل الثامن

سبعة أبواب

في كشف أسرار أصحاب الحروب وحملة السلاح

اعلم أنّ الحرب يحتمل جميع ما يتعلّق بالخدائع والمكر والحيل ويجوز فيه جميع ذلك فإنّ من طلب يأخذ روحي فلي أن أتعلّق عليه بما قدرت عليه من جهتين أحدهما تخليص روحي منه والثاني أريد أن أنصر روحي فجاز لي عليه الخديعة ومن أجل ذلك قال النبيّ صلّى الله عليه وسلّم الحرب خدعة معناه ما انفتح لك من أبواب الخدع والمكر في الحرب فافعله فإنّه جائز لك أن تفعله ومع ذلك فإنّه يجب على الرجل أن يكون يعلم شيئاً من ذلك فهو واجب ١،٨

الباب الأوّل في كشف أسرارهم

فمن ذلك أنّ لهم مياه يسقون بها آلة الحرب مثل سقاية الحراب والسيف وأسنّة الرماح والسكاكين ونصول النشّاب فإذا أرادوا ذلك فيأخذون من البصل شيئاً فيدقّونه ثمّ يأخذون ماءه ثمّ يحلّون فيه الشبّ الجيّد ثمّ يجمعون ما أرادوا من آلة الحرب ويسقون الآلة من ذلك الماء فإنّها تكون لها فعل عظيم في مضاربها وجراحها وفعلها فافهم ٢،٨

Chapter Eight, in Seven Sections:

Exposé of the Tricks of Those Who Practice War and Bear Arms

War admits of everything that has to do with deception, cunning, and subterfuge; anything of that sort is allowed. If someone is trying to take my life, I have the right to put one over him using whatever means I have at my disposal, from two perspectives: First, to save my life from his attack; second, because I want to be the victor. That means that I'm permitted to practice deception, which is why the Prophet, God bless him and keep him, has said, "War is deception,"[105] meaning, "In war, use any variety of deception and cunning that may present itself to you: You are permitted to act in this way." Moreover, a person is obligated to know something of such matters: It is a religious duty.[106] 8.1

Section One of the Exposé of Their Tricks

Example: They have a liquid with which they quench instruments of war such as spears, swords, lance tips, knives, and arrowheads. To do so, they take a certain quantity of onions and pound them, then take the resulting juice and dissolve in it high-grade alum. They then collect whatever instruments of war they wish to treat and quench each of them in this liquid. Weapons so treated deliver highly effective blows, cause severe wounds, and generally perform to great effect. 8.2

الباب الثاني في كشف أسرارهم

٣،٨ ومنه أن يأخذون من ورق الدفلى والباذروج أجزاء سواء فيدقّونه ويجعلونه مثل الماء ثمّ يجعل فيه شحم الحنظل ويغلى عليه حتّى يذهب الربع من الماء ثمّ يحمى الحديد من أيّ شيء كان من آلة الحرب ويسقيها من ذلك الماء سقياً روياً فإنّها تقطع جميع ما يقدم لها ولا يقف قدّامها شيء فافهم ذلك

الباب الثالث في كشف أسرارهم

٤،٨ ومن ذلك عمل السيف والحراب وأسنّة الرماح وما شاكلها فمن ذلك عمل سيف قاطع يؤخذ فولاذ هنديّ أو دمشقيّ ويعمل منه سيف قويّ الوسط رقيق الجوانب ويكون مبرده مبرد شرب ويتوقّى في رفعه لا يكون موضع أقوى من موضع ثمّ يسقى من ذلك الماء المقدّم ذكره فإنّه لا يقف قدّام ضربته شيء وكذلك آلة الحرب وأسنّة الرماح

الباب الرابع في كشف أسرارهم

٥،٨ فمن ذلك عمل قوس يرمي بأربعمائة سهام وذلك أن يؤخذ قوس جَرْخ ثمّ يضع فيه جوزة واسعة الوضع ثمّ يجعل على ساعد القوس قفيز من الناحيتين بحيث أن يحفظ السهام وتكون سهام طقش ويكون مقبض واسع النقر فافهم ذلك فإنّه إذا ضربت بذلك القوس خرجت السهام جملة صائبة ولا يخطئ منها شيء فافهم ذلك

Section Two of the Exposé of Their Tricks

Another example: They take equal parts of oleander and basil and pound them till they reach the consistency of a liquid. To this they add colocynth oil and then boil the lot till it's reduced by one quarter. Then they heat any part of a weapon that is made of iron, whatever it may be, and quench it slowly in this liquid. This done, it will cut through anything that engages it or stands in its way. Wise up to these things! 8.3

Section Three of the Exposé of Their Tricks

Another example: Making swords, spears, lance heads, and the like. 8.4

Another example: To make a sword that will slice through anything, Indian or Damascene steel is used. From this can be made a sword that is tough in the middle and fine at the edges. The sword should be cooled to drinking temperature and care must be taken when removing it, so that no one place is stronger than another. Then it is quenched in the liquid mentioned above, after which nothing can withstand a blow from it. The same goes for any other weapon and for lance heads.

Section Four of the Exposé of Their Tricks

Another example: How to make a bow that shoots four hundred arrows. 8.5

Exposé: They do this by taking a wheel-powered crossbow[107] and setting within it a socket with a wide bottom. Then they place a housing on either side of the main stock of the bow in such a way that it holds together the arrows, which are made of yew.[108] The grip should have a wide space for the hand. Wise up to these things: When one shoots a bow of this sort, the arrows come out in a single unerring shower, and not one of them misses. Wise up to these things!

الباب الخامس في كشف أسرارهم

ومن ذلك عمل ترس إذا كنت تسايف أحد في الحرب أو تطاعنه يخرج من الترس نشّاب يقتل خصمك تأخذ ترس كبير واسع وتجعل عند وسطه مع الجوز جوزة بقفيز فيها السهم المذكور فإذا جال مع الخصم وجاوره فقصّ تلك الجوزة بإبهامه فيخرج السهم فيقتل خصمه واعلم أنّ هذا من أدقّ الحيل وأعظم الأسرار وأجلّها وأبلغها وأعظمها نفعاً فافهم ذلك ٦.٨

الباب السادس في كشف أسرارهم

ومن ذلك أن يُرمى بمنجنيق يرمي إلى سائر الجهات وصفة ذلك أن تعمل منجنيق مغربيّ وله بكرتين في جانبيه كمثل بكر دولاب الحمّام وفي أعلاه عند الخنزيرة بكرة كذلك فيها السهم وتكون متحصّلة بتلك الخنزيرة الذي ذكرت لك فإنّه يرمي إلى سائر الجهات بذلك اللولب والبكر وهذا المنجنيق عمله الشيخ عبد الصمد الإشبيليّ بثغر دمياط سنة سبعة عشر وستّمائة وكان للمسلمين به نفع عظيم وأنا إن شاء الله أصنع لك صفته هاهنا كما ترى ٧.٨

الباب السابع في كشف أسرارهم

ومن ذلك في حصار المدن والحصون فإذا عمل البرّانيّ مرمى أو برج على ميزان ٨.٨
صورة المدينة والحصن فينبغي أن يعمل الجوّانيّ سهمين خشب مثل الصواري أطول ما يكون ثمّ ينقرها في أطوالها مثل النهر ثمّ يجعل فيها بكرة مدفونة يكون ثلث البكرة ظاهر والثلثان مدفون في السهام فإذا فعل ذلك أسقفها بألواح مثل السقالة ثمّ جعل في رأس كلّ صاري منها حلقة وفيها سلسلة مع جنب الصاري إلى داخل ثمّ يأخذ صاريين أخر وينصبهما من داخل السور ويجعل في رؤوسها

Section Five of the Exposé of Their Tricks

Another example: To make a shield that propels darts that can kill your opponent when you're engaged in hand-to-hand combat with swords or thrusting at one another with spears, take a large, broad shield and place in the center, over the pommel, a socket and sleeve containing arrows of the kind mentioned above. When the fighter is circling his opponent and has managed to get close to him, he releases the socket with his thumb, the arrows are expelled, and the opponent killed. This is among the subtlest of subterfuges and a very prodigious, fine, effective, and useful trick. Wise up to these things! 8.6

Section Six of the Exposé of Their Tricks

Another example: Shooting with a siege engine that shoots in all directions. 8.7
One does this by constructing a Maghrebi siege engine.[109] This will have two windlasses, one on either side,[110] made like the windlasses used for the waterwheel of a bathhouse. Above, at the axle bearing, there is likewise a pulley attached to the boom; this is attached to the aforementioned axle bearing and windlasses. The axle in question allows it to shoot in all directions. Shaykh ʿAbd al-Ṣamad al-Ishbīlī made one in the port city of Damietta in 617 [1220–21][111] and it proved of great benefit to the Muslims. God willing, I shall draw it for you here, as you can see.[112]

Section Seven of the Exposé of Their Tricks

Another example: On laying siege to cities and fortresses. When the besiegers 8.8
make a shooting platform or siege tower as tall as the wall of the city or fortress, the besieged must make two wooden booms like masts and these should be as long as possible. They should make a groove, like a water channel, running the length of each, then attach each to a buried windlass, one-third of which is visible while the other two-thirds are buried at the ends of the booms. Once this is done, they should roof over the windlasses with planks, making it like a siege ladder, then at the end of each of the booms put a ring attached to a chain that runs down the side of the boom into the windlass pit. Then they take two more booms and fix them into the wall, placing at their ends windlasses

البكر وفيها حبال مرتبطة في سلاسل الإسقالة قد رفعت على السور حتّى تصل إلى فوق الخندق

٩،٨ وإذا أراد أن يدخل داخل السور دارت الرجال في اللولب دخلت الإسقالة فإذا فعل ذلك عمل السقالة دَرابْزين ثمّ سترّها كما جرت العادة لمّا جاءت المِرَمّة أو البرج الذي قد صنعه[١] البرّانيّ عليه جعل تلك الإسقالة مقابل الموضع الذي يريدون أن يقدموا له البرج ثمّ دفعوها من داخل وقد أرخوا حبال اللولب ثمّ يدفعها إلى الرجال فتمشي بتلك البكر الذي فيها إلى أن تخرج عن السور إلى أن تأخذ حدّها ثمّ يطلع الرجال فيها بالسلاح الكامل فإذا مدّوا البرّانيّ السقالة الذي للبرج حصلت على هذه السقالة ثمّ مشت الرجال إلى الرجال فيدفعوا أهل البلد الرجال الذي في البرج ثمّ ينكسروا قدّامهم ويدخلوا على سقالتهم ويقاتلونهم حتّى يعلموا أن أهل البرج البرّانيّ قد صاروا على سقالتهم أعني سقالة برجهم

١٠،٨ فإذا جُعلوا عليها دارت الرجال من داخل في لولب السقالة فإذا فعلوا ذلك دخلت السقالة على السور فإذا دخلت تبقى سقالة البرج البرّانيّ بلا شيء يمسك حبلها فتميل إلى الخندق فيسقط كلّ من عليها إلى الخندق ويكون أهل البلد قد رتّبت في باب السرّ الذي لذلك المكان الرجال بالسيف والترس فساعة ما يسقطوا إلى الخندق يخرج عليهم من الباب فلا يبقى منهم أحد إلّا أُسَر وقُتَل ثمّ إذا مالت سقالة البرج ووقعت رجعوا دفعوا سقالة البلد خارجة وفيها الرجال والزرّاقين ويأخذوا البرج ويحرقوه فافهم ذلك ولم أجد في كتب كشف أسرار الحرب والحصارات أحسن من هذا في الحيلة والمكر فافهم

١ ش: صنع.

that bear ropes, which are tied to the chains of the siege ladder. This should then be raised above the wall so that it passes over it and reaches the trench surrounding the city or fortress.

When the besiegers want to go over the wall to the inside, the besieged unfold the joint in the middle of the siege ladder, converting it into a ramp,[113] then conceal it in the usual way. When the shooting platform or siege tower made by the besiegers moves toward the wall, the besieged set this siege ladder opposite the place toward which the besiegers are trying to move the tower, then push it out from the inside, after slackening the ropes attached to the joint. They push it toward the attackers and it moves, by means of the windlass to which it is attached, until it projects to its fullest extent beyond the wall. The men of the besieged city then climb onto it, fully armed. When the besiegers extend the siege ladder belonging to their tower, it comes into contact with this other ladder and the men of each side move toward each another. The people of the town drive the men in the tower back; the latter break before them and the people of the town get onto the ladder belonging to the others and fight them till they are sure that the people in the besiegers' tower are all on their own ladder—that is, the ladder belonging to their own tower. **8.9**

Once the besiegers have been forced onto it, the besieged unfold the joint of their own siege ladder and the ladder drops inward toward the wall and the besiegers' tower's ladder is left with nothing to hold its ropes in place so it tilts toward the trench and all the men on it fall off. The people of the town will have men drawn up, at a secret door located there, with swords and shields, and the moment the others fall into the trench, these launch themselves at them through the door and fall on them; in the end, no one is left but captives and the dead. Once the besiegers' tower's ladder has tilted and fallen, they go back inside and push the town's ladder out again, with armed men and throwers of Greek fire on it, and capture the other tower and burn it. Wise up to these things! This is the most ingenious and cunning thing I've come across in the manuals on the tricks of war and sieges. Wise up! **8.10**

الفصل التاسع

وهي تسعة أبواب

في كشف أسرار الذين هم أهل الكاف وهي الكيمياء

١،٩ فمن ذلك أنّ هذه الطائفة أعظم الطوائف تسلّط على أموال الناس والواصل منهم فهو دكّاك ولو علم شيء عن يقين لما أطلع عليه أحد من العالم ولا كان له حاجة إلى الخلق أجمع لأنّ الذي يريد من الناس قد حصل له فما يريد حاجة إلى الناس فهذا مستحيل واعلم أنّ هذه الصنعة هي الصنعة الإلهيّة التي لا يقدر عليها إلّا الله عزّ وجلّ أو من ارتضاه من الأنبياء والصالحين وحاشا لله أن يطلع على هذا السرّ الأعظم من يستعين به على المعاصي والفسق بل يطلع عليها الأولياء والصالحين من خلقه وأهل هذه الدرجة لا يجوز لهم أن يظهروا على هذا السرّ أحد ولا يظهرون به للناس فهذا مستحيل

٢،٩ وأمّا هؤلاء القوم الذي يتكلّمون في هذه الصناعة فإنّهم أقوام ينصبون على الناس ويأكلون أموالهم بالباطل وهم صنّاع في صوغ الكلام والدكّ على الناس يكون مع الواحد منهم مائة درهم يدكّها على أحد من الناس يأخذ منه الألف والألفين والأقلّ والأكثر ويجعله دولاب دائر كلّما أخذ شيء دكّ شيء فأنا إن شاء الله أكشف لك أسرارهم ودكّهم حسب الاختصار والإيجاز فاعلم يا أخي أنّي كشفت لهم ثلاثمائة طريقاً في الدكّ ولا يمكن شرحها خوف الإطالة بل نذكرمنها ما يستدلّ به على الكلّ ليعلم من وقف على كتابي هذا ويعلم أنّي قد وقفت على كثير من العلوم والذي خفي عنّي أكثر

Chapter Nine, in Nine Sections:

Exposé of the Tricks of the People of the *Kāf*, That Is, Alchemy[114]

This tribe of charlatans is the most prodigious of all in terms of getting their hands on people's money, and their so-called "initiates" are simply con artists: If they really had any solid knowledge, they'd never let an ordinary person in on it and they wouldn't need anyone else at all because they'd have gotten what they wanted and wouldn't need anyone—the idea's absurd! This craft is a divine craft that only God, Mighty and Exalted, or the prophets and the Righteous whom He is pleased to select, are capable of practicing. God forbid that any who might use it for sinful purposes and debauchery should be let in on this most prodigious of secrets! Only God's wards and the Righteous among His creation are let in on it, and those of this rank are forbidden to reveal the secret to anyone or to explain it to others. The idea's absurd! 9.1

Contrariwise, those who talk openly about this profession are simply robber bands who swindle people and take their money by illicit means. They are "Men of the Craft" only in the sense that they craft words to cheat people. A person of this type will have a hundred silver pieces and use them to cheat someone out of a thousand, or two thousand, or more, or less. He uses the money as a revolving float: As soon as he's used it to take one thing, he uses it to cheat someone out of another. I intend, God willing, to provide you with an exposé of their tricks and charlatanry in an abridged and concise form, and just so you know, my brother, I have uncovered three hundred methods that they use to cheat people, though not all of these can be explained here or it would become boring. Instead, we shall cite enough cases for you to infer the nature of the rest, so that anyone who studies this book of mine may be well informed—and be aware that I have examined many sciences, though those 9.2

ممّا وقفت عليه فليتحقّق ذلك ويعلم الطالب أنّه لم يزل متعلّماً ويعترف بالعجز والتقصير وفوق كلّ ذي علم عليم فافهم

الباب الأوّل في كشف أسرارهم ودكوكهم

٣،٩ فمن ذلك أنّهم إذا أرادوا أن يدكّون شيئاً يعتمدون من يكون طالب هذه الصنعة من المياسرة ثمّ يتّفقون به ويدّعون الوصول ويقول أنا أفرّجك ثمّ يأخذ شيء من الفضّة والذهب فيدكّه عليه ويقول انزل به بيعه في السوق فيأخذ ذلك وينزل به إلى الصاغة فيبيعه بأوفى ثمن فيجيء إليه ويدفع له الثمن فيقول والله ما يدخل إلى ملكي[١] منه شيء فإنّي ما أنا محتاج إليه هذا يكون برسم الصغار والنفقة ثمّ يناسيه أيّام ثمّ يجتمعوا فيعمل شيء آخر ويدفعه إليه فيعمله ويبيعه مرّة أخرة ثانية وثالثة حتّى يسلب عقله ويتمكّن منه ويأخذ عوض الدراهم دنانير

٤،٩ فأمّا كشف دكّهم فإنّ منهم من يجعل الدكّة في فحمة ويحرّك بها البوتقة فتحترق الفحمة وينزل ما فيها إلى البوتقة ثمّ تحترق العقاقير الذي وضعها في البوتقة وتبقى الدكّة فيقلب البوتقة فتنزل سبيكة إمّا ذهب أو فضّة على قدر ما يكون قد ذكر لهم فيُذهل عقله ويسلب ماله فيطلب أن يعمل شيئاً آخر فيدّعي أنّ الإكسير الذي عنده قد نفد وما هو وقت يعمل إكسيراً ثاني فلا يزال عليه حتّى يذعن له بالعمل ثمّ يقول هذا يريد تعب وخسارة إلّا أنّه إذا انتهى صار منه مال جزيل لا يقع عليه قياس فيشرع فيه فيقيم عنده في أكل وشرب وكسوة وغير ذلك سبعة ثمانية أشهر وكلّ أيّام يطلب منه خمسين درهم وعشرين درهم وأقلّ وأكثر حتّى تحصّل له منه جملة ثمّ بعد ذلك يروح

١ ش: لي ملك.

I haven't are more than those I have, and this is a truth that must be acknowledged; the searcher after knowledge should always bear in mind that he is still learning and admit his incapacities and shortcomings. Above everyone who has knowledge is One Who Knows All. Wise up to these things!

Section One: Exposé of Their Tricks and Their Different "Sauces"

To set up a scam, they set their sights on some well-heeled would-be student of the craft and, posing as initiates, come to an agreement with him, the charlatan saying, "I'll show you everything!" Then he takes a little silver and gold, treats it with "sauce,"[115] and says, "Go sell this in the market!" So the other takes it and goes with it to the gold merchants and sells it for a most satisfactory price and comes back and gives the charlatan the money, but the latter tells him, "I swear I won't allow a penny of this money to be added to my own wealth. I don't need it. It's just small change and pocket money to me." After this, the charlatan pretends to forget about the man for a few days and then they meet and he cooks up some more and gives it to him and then cooks up still more and the man sells it and the charlatan does so again and again until the man falls completely under his spell and he can do with him whatever he wants and take gold for silver.[116] 9.3

Now to expose their chicanery. The fake alchemist introduces sauce into a piece of charcoal and then stirs the crucible with it till it is burned up by the fire and its contents are released into the crucible. Then the apothecary's simples that he has also put into the crucible are burned up too and only the sauce is left. Now he turns the crucible upside down and the ingot falls out, either as gold or as silver, depending on whatever he's told them it will be. This way, he puts the man under his spell and, by asking him to do one more thing, is able to rob him of his money. He pretends that his supply of elixir has run out and he doesn't have time to make more. The man, however, keeps on at him until the charlatan agrees to do what is asked of him. He tells him, "This will require effort and sacrifice but once done will produce vast wealth, beyond measure." So the man sets about doing what he's been asked and the charlatan moves in with him, eating, drinking, and clothing himself and so on at the other's expense for seven or eight months, each day demanding from him fifty silver pieces or twenty silver pieces, or more, or less, until he's made a tidy sum off him. Then he disappears, leaving the other to bang his head against the wall. 9.4

ويخلّيه يخبط وإمّا يدّعي أنّه فسد أو أنّه يحيّله على شيء من الزغليّات فهذه صفتهم

٩،٥ وأمّا دكّهم وصفته فهو في الفحم فما هو على ما يقول من لا يفهم ينقب الفحمة ويجعل الدكّة فيها ليس الأمر كذلك بل يأخذ الفحم يسحقه كالغبار ويعجنه بالغراء ثمّ يقلبه في دريزك حجر ثمّ يودع الدكّة فيه وهي برادة ثمّ يجففه فإذا جفّ قلّم رأس القضيب على مثال الفحم ثمّ بعد ذلك يحلّ له فحماً ثانياً ثمّ يلبسه لذلك القضيب ويفركه حتّى يجفّ ثمّ يكون مخبّى فإذا شرع في ذلك العمل دكّ الفحم الذي معه في الفحم ثمّ قال لصاحبه خذ فحمة فحرّك بها البوتقة فإذا فعل ذلك أخرج من وسطه إمّا[1] عقدة قصب وإمّا مكحلة وإمّا قرطاس وأخرج منه شيئاً على مثال الرماد أو الزعفران أو على أيّ لون كان أو شاء ثمّ يقول لصاحبه أوزن من هذا وزن أرزّة أو حبّة ولفّها في ورقة في شمعة ثمّ ألقها في البوتقة فإذا فعل ذلك قال اقلب فيقلب فيجد الدكّة سبيكة إمّا ذهب أو فضّة فيقول انزل بيع وأنت طيّب القلب واشكر الله على هذه النعمة وتصدّق منها بما سهّل الله وتنفق الباقي لأهل البيت والصغار فأنا ما لي حاجة إلى شيء من ذلك فافهم

الباب الثاني في كشف أسرارهم ودكّهم

٩،٦ ومن ذلك أنّ لهم دكّة في البندق يأخذون بندق فارغ ثمّ يودعه الدكّة ويخبأه معه فإذا كان وقت العمل طلب بندق فإذا حضر له دكّ فيه الذي معه وجعل الرصاص في البوتقة ثمّ ألحقه بدقّ الفحم وساق عليه حتّى يعلم أنّ الرصاص قد احترق ثمّ يرجمه بالبندق حتّى يعلم أن الدكّة قد دارت في البودقة ثمّ يخرج من وسطه الذي ادّعى أنّه إكسير ويقول لصاحبه ازن منه حبّة وألقيه في البوتقة ثمّ اقلب على بركة الله فإذا

[1] ش: ما.

Either he claims that the operation failed or he tricks him with a few counterfeit coins. This is the way they work.

How their trick works: The secret lies in the charcoal, but it isn't what those who don't know might expect—that he hollows out the charcoal and puts the sauce inside. Rather, he takes the charcoal, pulverizes it, and kneads the powder with fish glue. He pours this into a stone mold and introduces it into the sauce, which is in the form of filings, and dries out the resulting mixture. When it's dry, he pares the top end of the resulting bar until it looks like charcoal. Then he crumbles up some more charcoal and coats the bar with it, rubbing it until it dries, by which time the bar will be completely hidden. When he embarks on the operation, he slips the false charcoal, which he will have on him, in among the rest of the charcoal and tells his companion, "Take a piece of charcoal and stir the crucible with it." When the man does so, he takes from his waistband either a node of sugarcane, a kohl case, or a spindle of paper and from this he extracts something the color of ashes, or saffron, or any other color, whatever it may happen to be, or as the charlatan desires. He tells his companion, "Take the weight of a grain of rice, or a barley grain,[117] of this and wrap it in a bit of paper coated with wax. Then throw it into the crucible." When he has done so, he tells him, "Stir!" so the man stirs and finds the sauce, now in the form of an ingot of either gold or silver, so he tells him, "Go sell this. You're an honest fellow, so thank God for his blessings and use what you can afford of it for alms and spend the rest on your household and children. I have no need of it." Wise up to these things! 9.5

Section Two of the Exposé of Their Tricks and Their Chicanery

Another example: They have a trick they do with hazelnuts. They take empty hazelnuts, place the sauce inside them, and hide them on their persons. When the time comes for the scam, the charlatan asks for hazelnuts and when these are provided, slips those that he has on him in among the others and puts lead into the crucible. He follows this by pounding charcoal, which he blows on with the bellows till he knows the lead has melted; then he pelts the charcoal with the hazelnuts till he is sure the mixture has been distributed throughout the crucible. Next he takes from his waistband something he claims is "the elixir" and tells his friend, "Weigh out a grain and throw it into the 9.6

أقلب نزلت سبيكة على ما ذكر فيحيّر عقله وينزل إلى السوق فيبيعه بأوفى ثمن فيسلب عقله ويأخذ بها ماله

الباب الثالث في كشف أسرارهم

ومن ذلك الدكّ في البودقة أن تكون طبقتين والدكّة[1] في الطبقة السفلى مثقوبة إلّا مسدودة بشمعة فإذا جعل فيها الرصاص وساق عليها حتّى يحترق دارت الدكّة وقد ذاب الشمع فإذا أقلب نزل كلّها في البوتقة وقد صار رماد ونزلت الدكّة سبيكة إمّا ذهب أو فضّة فيذهل العقول ويفعل بهما ما أراد فافهم ذلك ترشد إن شاء الله ٩،٧

الباب الرابع في كشف أسرارهم

ومن ذلك أنّ لهم دكّة في الكلبتين وذلك أنّ هذه الكلبتين يكون العقرب الذي لها مجوّف والذي يمسك به البوتقة ثمّ يجعل الدكّة فيه ويسدّ عليها بالعجين فإذا ساق على البودقة حكّها بالكلبتين ولا يزال كذلك حتّى يعلم أنّ الدكّة نزلت في البوتقة ثمّ يسوق حتّى تذوب ثمّ يقلب فتنزل سبيكة في غاية ما يكون من الجودة فيبهت من يرى ذلك ٩،٨

الباب الخامس في كشف أسرارهم

ومن ذلك أنّ لهم دكّة في العجين وهو أن يطلب عجين فإذا حضر جعل الدكّة فيه وجعل بنادق ثمّ يرجم به البوتقة فتنزل الدكّة فإذا علم أنّها قد دارت فيقلبها فتنزل سبيكة على قدر ما ذكر إمّا ذهب أو فضّة ثمّ يقول انزل ٩،٩

١ ش: الدكّ.

crucible, turn it upside down, and may God bless the work!" When he does so, an ingot falls out, as he has said it would. The other man is nonplussed and goes to the market and sells it for a most satisfactory price. The charlatan now has him under his spell and uses the trick to take his money.

Section Three of the Exposé of Their Tricks

Another example: Fixing the crucible so that it's in two compartments, the sauce being in the lower one. The crucible is perforated but its holes are sealed with wax.[118] When he puts the lead into the crucible and blows on it with the bellows till it's molten, the sauce becomes runny, and by that time the wax will have melted and, when he turns it upside down, it all descends into the upper compartment of the crucible and turns to ashes, and the sauce comes out in the form of an ingot, either of gold or of silver. People are amazed and he can do with them whatever he wants. Wise up to this and you won't go wrong, God willing! 9.7

Section Four of the Exposé of Their Tricks

Another example: They have a kind of sauce that they put into tongs. 9.8

Exposé: the tongs are hollow pincers that are used to grip the crucible. The charlatan puts the sauce into the hollow space and seals it over with dough. Then, once he has puffed on the crucible with the bellows, he scrapes at it with the tongs, continuing to do so until the sauce is released into the crucible. He goes on puffing away at it with the bellows until it melts and then turns it over and an ingot of the highest quality falls out. Anyone who sees him do this will be flabbergasted.

Section Five of the Exposé of Their Tricks

Another example: They have a kind of sauce that they put into dough. The charlatan requests some dough and when it's brought, puts the sauce into it and makes it into balls. He throws these into the crucible, the sauce comes out, and, when he's sure that it has blended in well, he overturns the crucible and an ingot comes out, either gold or silver, depending. "Out you come!" he says. 9.9

الباب السادس في كشف أسرارهم

ومن ذلك أن يأخذون الذهب والفضّة ثمّ يحرقونه بالزرنيخ فيبقى مثل الرماد ويجعله هو الإكسير ويدّعي أنّ هذا الإكسير تدبيره خمس شهور وأنّه استعجل عليه ودبّره في خمسة عشر يوماً فإذا كملت خدمته وتدبيره يلقي منه الواحد على ألف يقوم ثمّ يأخذ منه ويلقي ثمّ يقلب ويكون قد احترق بالزرنيخ فتنزل سبيكة إلى غاية ما يكون من الجودة ثمّ يبيعها فافهم ذلك فاعلم أنّي أطّلعت لهم على ثلاثمائة دكّة لم يقف عليها أحد ١٠،٩

الباب السابع في كشف أسرارهم

ومن ذلك أنّ أعجب ما صادفته وأغرب ما وقفت عليه أن كان بدمشق رجل نصرانيّ يُعرف بابن ميسرة ففيما هو بعض الأيّام في الدكّان إذ أتى إليه رجل متميّز ثمّ سلّم عليه وناوله سبيكة فضّة مقدار ثلاثمائة درهم وقال لعلّ منادي ينادي لي على هذه السبيكة فأخذها منه وقال يا سيّدي على الحِما نبيع قال نعم وعلى الروباص فأعطاها للمنادي فباعها له المائة بمائة وعشرة هذا وقد أصعده عنده على الدكّان وأجلسه إلى جانبه فلمّا قبض الثمن دفع للمنادي أجرة وافرة ثمّ شال خمسة دراهم وقال للصائغ سيّر بعض أجراءك يشتري لنا بهذه شيء نأكل بحسب الممالحة والحرام يلزمه لا بدّ من ذلك قال فأبعث اشترى شيء أكلوا وتحدّثوا ساعة ثمّ نزل وجعل تحت نطع الصائغ عشرة دراهم وغاب أيّام ١١،٩

ثمّ عاد فسلّم عليه وقعد وقد فرح به الصائغ فتحدّثوا ساعة ثمّ أخرج من كمّه سبيكة أكبر من الأولى فلمّا دفعها إلى المنادي جابت المائة مائة وخمسة عشر درهم فقال إن ١٢،٩

Section Six of the Exposé of Their Tricks

Another example: They take gold and silver and heat them with arsenic till they turn to ashes. The charlatan claims that this "elixir" takes five months to prepare but that he's shortened the process and prepared it in fifteen days, and when it's been properly treated and prepared, he can throw in one part and out will come a thousand. Then he takes some, throws it in, and upends the crucible, and, because it's been heated together with arsenic, an ingot of the highest quality falls out, which he sells. Wise up to these things! For your information, I have familiarized myself with a further three hundred tricks of theirs that no one else has studied. 9.10

Section Seven of the Exposé of Their Tricks

Another example: The most amazing and strangest thing I've ever read is that there was once a Christian in Damascus named Ibn Maysara. He was in his shop one day when a man of distinguished appearance approached him, greeted him, handed him a silver ingot weighing three hundred dirhams, and said, "Would you mind having a public crier announce that I have this ingot for sale?" The man took it from him and said, "My dear sir, are we to sell it for a commission?" "Indeed," the other replied, "and after proof of purity." So the Christian gave it to the public crier, who sold it for him at a profit of 10 percent. The Christian, meanwhile, had invited the man to step up to where he was in the shop and sat him down next to him. When the man took his money, he paid the crier a handsome fee, then removed five silver pieces and said to the gold merchant, "Send one of your hired men with this to buy us something to eat and let us eat as brothers. It would be bad luck not to.[119] I won't take no for an answer!" So the Christian sent someone to buy something to eat, and they ate and chatted for a while. Then the man left, leaving ten silver pieces under the gold merchant's mat, and wasn't seen again for days. 9.11

Eventually the man returned, greeted the merchant, and sat down. The merchant was delighted to see him and they chatted for a while. Then the man pulled from his sleeve an ingot larger than the first and when he gave it to the crier, the latter got him an offer of 15 percent profit, but the man said to the gold merchant, "If you can use it, take it at cost." So the merchant took it from him and asked, as 9.12

كانت من حاجتك فخذها وزن بوزن فأخذها منه ثمّ عمل مثل المرّة الأولى فمنعه من ذلك فقال له يا فلان أيش تخاف عليه هذه الفضّة تقوم على المائة درهم بدرهم ونصف فما عسى أن يروح منها فلمّا سمع الصائغ ذلك عظم في عينه ثمّ إنّه انصرف وغاب أيّام ثمّ أتى ولم يصحب معه سبيكة فسلّم وصعد ثمّ تحدّثوا ساعة وكلمّا عبر شيء من مأكول إمّا حلاوة وإمّا فاكهة أو نقل فيقول حطّ ازن فيشتري ويأكل هو والمعلّم وكلّ من في الدكّان مع الجيران

١٣،٩ وقام يتردّد أيّام ولم يصحب معه شيء من السبائك فسأله الصائغ فقال له والله كنت قد عملت إكسير فرغ فلمّا سمع الصائغ ارتبط ثمّ تحدّث معه ساعة وقال أشتهي أن تجبر قلبي وتأكل معي خبز في داري فقال وما أكلّفك فأقسم عليه فقال إن كان ولا بدّ فهذه عشرين درهم اعمل لنا بها شيء نأكل والحرام يلزمه لا بدّ من ذلك ثمّ تواعدوا إلى ذلك اليوم جاء الرجل إلى الدكّان فوجد الصائغ قاعد فأخذه وراح إلى البيت فلمّا استقرّوا بالجلوس قدّم شيء كثير للأكل فأكلوا وقعدوا يتحدّثوا فقال الصائغ يا سيّدي لم لا تعمل الإكسير فقال له عندي الساعة ما أنفقه وأخرى فإنّ ما لي في البلد لا مكان ولا صاحب وأنا وحدي ما أقدر أدبّر هذا

١٤،٩ فقال الصائغ له هذه القاعة وهي ملكي وما لي فيها نساء وإنّما هي برسم صديق أو ضيف يأتي وأنا أخليّها لك وأساعدك أنا وابني يكون في الدكّان وما تحتاج فأنا أحضره فقال أمّا خسارة فما يلحقك عشرة دراهم وقد صار إكسير يعمل منه قناطير إلّا يريد تعب وطولة روح وأنا اليوم ما لي همّة للعمل لأنّ عندي ما أنفقه سنة وعشرة ثمّ إنّه يمتنع عليه وهو يرغّب إليه ويسأله ثمّ إنّه مسكه تلك الليلة عنده وتمكّن منه بالحديث ولم يزل عليه حتّى تقرّر معه الأمر ثمّ إنّهم تحالفوا بوفاء

he had the first time, if he was to sell it for a commission and after proof of purity, at which the man said, "What are you afraid of? This silver will bring one and a half silver pieces in cash for every dirham in weight, and no one can change that." When the merchant heard this, his opinion of the man went up. The man then departed and wasn't seen for days. Then he came back, but this time he didn't bring an ingot with him. He greeted the merchant, stepped up, and they chatted for a while, and every time some dish—whether halvah, or fruit, or nuts—went by, he'd say to the vendor, "Weigh us out some!" and he'd buy and he, the shopkeeper, everyone in the shop, and even the neighbors, would eat.

Thereafter and for several days, he'd drop by but not bring any ingots with him, so the merchant asked him about it, and he said, "To be honest, I had made some elixir but it's all used up." When the merchant heard this, he was hooked. He chatted with the man for a while, then said, "I'd really be pleased if you'd do me the honor of breaking bread with me at home." "I wouldn't want to put you to the trouble," said the other, but the merchant swore an oath, so the man said, "If you insist. Here are twenty silver pieces. Use them to have some dish prepared for us. It would be bad luck not to! I won't take no for an answer!" So they set an appointment for a particular day and the man came to the shop and found the merchant waiting for him, and the merchant took him home. When they were comfortably seated, great quantities of food were brought, and they ate and chatted. Then the merchant asked, "My dear sir, why don't you make some more elixir?" to which the other replied, "Right now I have money to spend on that and more, but I have no place of my own in this town and no friend, and I can't prepare it on my own." 9.13

The gold merchant said, "This apartment,[120] which is my property and isn't used by any of my women, is for the use of any friend or guest who might turn up. I'll let you use it. I'll help you and leave my son to look after the shop, and I'll fetch you anything you need." "It's a pity," the charlatan said. "You'd only have to pay ten silver pieces and there'd be enough elixir to make bushels of money. On the other hand, it needs effort and stamina and I have no enthusiasm for the work right now because I have enough money to last me for a year, or ten!" Thus the one demurred while the other tried to engage his interest and kept on pestering him. In the end, the merchant made him stay at his place for the night, kept up his attempts to talk him into it, and refused to leave him till the matter was settled. Then they swore to be faithful to their pact, the merchant saying he would "make do with the least possible quantity of the elixir 9.14

العهد وإنّ الصائغ يقنع من الإكسير بأيسر ما يكون منه والباقي لك فقال أنا أقنع منه بمثقال وخذ أنت الباقي فيفرح الصائغ رجاء أن يتعلّم الإكسير ويأخذه معمول

ثمّ اتّفقوا إلى يوم واجتمعوا واشتروا الحوائج ووزن الرجل ثمنها ولم يخلّي الصائغ يخسر شيئاً فلمّا أن حصلت الحوائج سحق منها ما أمكن سحقه وهيّأ حوائجه قال الرجل للصائغ تريد أن تعمل ذهباً أو فضّة فقال من هذا شيء ومن هذا شيء فقال له اقسم هذه الحوائج نصفين ثمّ قال هات ما أمكن من الذهب والفضّة حتّى ننقعها في الماء ثلاثة أيّام ثمّ نأخذ ماءها نسقي منه الأدوية الذهب للذهب والفضّة للفضّة فعمد إلى ستّمائة دينار فدفعها له فربطها في منديل قدّامه ثمّ جعلها في وعاء فيه ماء ثمّ قال له هات فضّة فأحضر ألف وخمسمائة ففعل كما فعل بالذهب ثمّ أقاموا سبعة أيّام ثمّ يخدمون تلك الحوائج ثمّ بعد ذلك قال قوم اطلع إلى جبل المِزّة اجمع منها حصى الذي يُعرف ببصاق القمر مقدار رطل واحد وتعال فقام الصائغ وصعد الجبل ونقّى حاجته ١٥،٩

فأمّا الرجل فإنّه فتح صرّة الذهب فأخذه ثمّ جعل مكانه فلوس وكذلك فعل بالفضّة وقعد فلمّا جاء الصائغ بالذي يريده قال لهذا يريد تكليس في أتون الزجّاج ليلة ثمّ يخدم بماء الذهب نصفه وبماء الفضّة نصفه فإذا تكلّس اقسمه ثمّ اخدمه ثمّ خرج لصلاة الجمعة ثمّ استقبل الدرب فلم يطلع له خبر فأقام ينتظره مدّة لم يفتح الذهب ولا الفضّة فقال له ابنه لا يكون أخذ الذهب وراح فقال له وحقّ المسيح يقدر يعمل خزائن أموال وذا محتاج إلى ذهبنا فقال ابنه كن عاقل وافتقد الذهب فقال أنت قصدك تفسد علينا الشغل فقال افتح الذهب وخلّي عنك الطمع فلم يفعل فقام ابنه فتح الصرّة وجدها فلوس وكذلك صرّة الفضة فقال له أنت ما تسمع منّي ابصر هذا الدهاء والمكر لهذه الطائفة ١٦،٩

and the rest is yours!," the other saying, "I'll make do with one mithkal and you take the rest!" The merchant was delighted because he hoped he'd learn how to make the elixir and get some ready-made too.

They agreed on a day and met and bought the ingredients, and the charlatan paid, and made sure they didn't cost the merchant a penny. When the ingredients arrived, he ground up as much as he could and got everything ready and asked the merchant, "Which would you like to make, gold or silver?" and the man replied, "A bit of this and a bit of that." "Divide these ingredients in two," the charlatan told him. Then he said, "Bring as much gold and silver coin as you can so we can steep it in water for three days. Then we'll take the water and soak the compounds with it, the gold water for the gold, the silver water for the silver." The merchant decided on six hundred gold pieces and gave them to the charlatan, who tied them up in a kerchief in front of him and put them in a vessel filled with water. Next, he told the man, "Get the silver," so he brought him 1,500 silver pieces and the other did with them as he had with the gold. Then they waited seven days, after which they added the ingredients they had bought. Once they'd done that, the charlatan said, "Go up to Mount Mizzah and gather there half a pound of the stones they call moon spittle and then come back." So the merchant went and climbed the mountain and picked out what he needed. 9.15

Meanwhile, the charlatan opened the bag of gold, took out the gold, and put copper coins in its place, and he did the same with the silver. Then he sat and waited till the merchant arrived with what he'd asked for and told him, "This needs to be calcined in a glass furnace for one night. Then half of it must be treated with the water from the gold, and the other half with the water from the silver. Have it calcined, divide it in two, and then treat it." Then he left to perform the Friday prayer. The merchant waited for him at the head of the street but he failed to show, so he waited for a while longer, without opening either the gold or the silver. "Couldn't it be that he's taken the gold and gone?" his son asked him. "By Christ!" swore the merchant. "He could make treasuries full of money! What does a man like that need with our gold?" "Use your head," the son said, "and take a look at the gold." "You want to ruin the whole operation for us?" asked his father. "Just open the gold, and enough of your greed!" said the son. The merchant refused to do so, so the son went and opened the bag and found it was full of copper coins, and the same with the bag of silver. "You just wouldn't listen to me!" he said. Observe the craftiness and cunning of this tribe of charlatans! 9.16

الباب الثامن في كشف أسرارهم

فمن ذلك أنّ كان لي في البقاع صاحب في ضيعة يقال لها صَغْبين وكان يُعرف بالحاجّ علاّق وكان موسراً كثير الرزق وكان يطعم الخبز لكلّ أحد فاتّفق أنّي في بعض الأيّام زرته لأجدّد به عهداً ففرح بي وقال الله جاء بك في وقت الحاجة إليك فقلت وما الحاجة فقال رجل صالح جاء عمل عندي إكسير راح ولا أتمّ ولا أعلم أيش كان منه فقلت وكيف اتّفق لك هذا العبد الصالح حدّثني من يوم اجتمعت به إلى فراقه ١٧،٩

فقال لي جاء رجل إلى المسجد الذي لي وأقام به أيّاماً ملازم الصلاة والقرآن فلمّا رأيته قلت للجارية هذا الرجل الذي في المسجد لا تغفلوا عنه من شيء يأكله في كلّ وقت ثمّ في بعض الأيّام دخلت إلى المسجد وصلّيت معهم وتحدّثت معه فوجدته وليّ من الأولياء فحلفت عليه وأخذته معي إلى الدار فأكلنا شيئاً وهو يحدّثنا ثمّ قام إلى المسجد فأقمت كذلك أيّاماً حتّى إذا جئت من شغلي جئت إلى عنده إلى المسجد وأصلّي معه ثمّ آخذه معي إلى الدار فنأكل شيئاً ونتحدّث ويروح ينام في المسجد فلا أراه قطّ إلّا واقفاً يصلّي ١٨،٩

فلمّا كان بعد أيّام قعدنا نأكل شيئاً فلمّا رفعت المائدة قال لي يا حاجّ تقدر لي على شيء من الرصاص فقلت له عندي زبديّة صغيرة فأحضرتها فقال جيّدة ثمّ أخرج من جرابه ظريف صغير ثمّ أخرج بوتقة ثمّ أخذ من تلك الزبديّة قطعة وجعلها في تلك البوتقة ثمّ نفخ عليها ساعة وأخرج من جرابه أنبوبة قصب فأخرج منها شيئاً على مثال الكحل الأغبر فأخذ منه مقدار أرزّة ووضعه في البوتقة فأقلبه فضّة كلَغَم ثمّ قال يا حاجّ قد دخلت منزلك وأكلت خبزك وصار لك عليّ حقّ فأشتهي من الله ومنك أن تأخذ هذه السبيكة وتعملها خلاخل في رجل الصغير والحرام يلزمني لا بدّ من ذلك فامتنعت من ذلك فكرّر على الأيمان فلم يمكن إلّا آخذها ١٩،٩

Section Eight of the Exposé of Their Tricks

Another example: I had a friend in the Biqāʿ, in a village called Ṣaghbīn, who was called al-Ḥājj ʿAllāq. He was well off, with a large income, and handed out bread to all and sundry. One day, I happened to visit him, to renew our acquaintance. He was delighted to see me and said, "God has brought you just when you're needed!" "Needed for what?" I asked. "A man, one of the Righteous," he said, "came and made elixir at my house. Then he left before he'd finished and I don't know what's happened to him." "And how did you happen to meet this 'Righteous Mortal'?" I asked. "Tell me everything, from the day you met him to the day he left." 9.17

"A man came to the mosque I own," he told me, "and stayed there for a number of days, devoting himself to prayer and the recitation of the Qur'an. When I saw him, I told the serving girl, 'That man in the mosque—make sure he always has something to eat.' Then one day I went into the mosque and prayed with them and talked to him. I discovered he was a Ward of God, so I swore he must come to the house and took him home with me and we ate and he talked to us. Then he got up and went to the mosque. For several days, I took to going to him at the mosque whenever I came home from work and praying with him and then taking him home with me, where we would eat and chat, after which he would go off and sleep in the mosque. Every time I saw him he was standing and praying. 9.18

"A few days later, after we had sat and eaten and the table had been removed, he said to me, 'Hajj, could you fetch me something made of lead?' 'I have a small butter dish,' I said, and I went and got it. 'Perfect,' he said. Then he took from his bag a small envelope and a crucible. He broke a piece off the butter dish and placed it in the crucible and blew on it for a while and took from his bag a cane tube from which he extracted something resembling dust-colored antimony. He took the equivalent of the weight of a grain of rice of this and placed it in the crucible and it turned into a bit of silver, like a small quantity of ointment. Then he said, 'Ḥājj, I've been to your house and eaten your bread, and I owe you. I'd really like you, for God's sake and mine, to take this bit of metal and make anklets from it for your little one's feet. It would be bad luck for me to keep it![121] I won't take no for an answer!' I protested, but he repeated his oaths, and in the end I had to. 9.19

٢٠.٩ ثمّ بعثها إلى الشعراء فعملوا منها هذه الخواتم ثمّ أوراني ذلك فرأيتها فضّة ثمّ بعد ذلك عمل مثل ذلك دفوع ثمّ تعجّبت منه ثمّ تفاتحنا في الحديث فقال والله كان معي إكسيرًا أنفع به الناس والصعاليك نفد وما بقي منه شيء وأنا مستحي منك ثمّ انبسطنا فقلت له ليش ما تعمل الإكسير فقال والله ما لي مكان فقلت قد أمكن الوقت هذه الدار لك وهذا عبد وأمة يخدموك ومهما عازك من الحوائج أحضرتها لك فاعمل شيئًا يحصل للناس من ذلك راحة فتمنّع من ذلك وأنا أرغّبه فيه إلى أن أجاب لي في ذلك

٢١.٩ فقال متى تشتري لنا الحوائج فقلت اكتب نسخة حتّى أنزل إلى بعلبكّ فأشتري لك مهما أردت فكتب لي نسخة وهي هذه ثمّ أحضر لي ورقة فيها حوائج ما خلقها الله قطّ فأخذت النسخة وركبت إلى بعلبكّ فما وجدت من تلك الحوائج شيء ثمّ رحت إلى دمشق فلم أجدها إلّا عند فرد واحد في قصر حجّاج ثمّ أخبرني عن هذه الحوائج عجائب حتّى قال إنّ نعمة الرئيس خليل بن زوكران من هذه الحوائج كانت وذلك أنّه أتى إلى عنده رجل وذكر أنّه يعمل له شيئًا يعمل منه بيوت أموال ثمّ طلب منه هذه النسخة بعينها فلم توجد إلّا عندي فأخذها منّي وعملوا منها أشياء كثيرة وهذه أصل نعمة الرئيس خليل

٢٢.٩ فلمّا سمعت منه ذلك تعجّبت ثمّ قلت له بكم تبيعها فقال بخمسمائة فلا أزال معه حتّى اتّفقنا على مائتي درهم فوزنت له المبلغ فقال ابصر أن كان لك شغل يومين ثلاثة حتّى أعبئ لك النسخة مكمّلة صبرت عليه حتّى عبّأها لي ثمّ أخذتها وركبت فرسي وجئت وأنا فرحان بما أحكي لي العطّار فلمّا وصلت إلى الشيخ أعرضت عليه الحوائج جميعها فقال من أين حصلت لك مكمّلة فقلت له إنّي لم أجدها مكمّلة في دمشق إلّا عند فرد واحد في قصر حجّاج فقال ما غشّك فيها فكم أخذ منك فأخبرته بما خبّرني به من خبر الرئيس خليل فقال سمعت ذلك

"Then he sent the metal to the goldsmiths and they made signet rings[122] from it. He showed them to me and they looked to me like real silver. Subsequently, he did this on numerous occasions and in the end I expressed my amazement and we spoke openly. He said, 'The truth is, I had some elixir that I could use for the common good and for the paupers, but it's run out. I have nothing left and I feel embarrassed to see you.' Now that we were at ease with one another, I asked him, 'Why don't make some more elixir?' and he replied, 'The truth is, I don't have a place.' 'It couldn't have happened at a better time!' I said. 'This house is yours, here are a male and a female slave to serve you, and I'll get you whatever you need by way of ingredients. This way I can do something that will bring people some comfort.' He refused, but I pressed him till he agreed. **9.20**

"'When will you get us the ingredients?' he asked. 'Write me a list and I'll go to Baalbek and buy you whatever you need,' I answered. So he wrote me a list"—and here my friend showed me the list, fetching a piece of paper containing the names of ingredients otherwise unknown to God's creation—"and I took the copy and rode to Baalbek but couldn't find a single one. Then I went to Damascus, where I found them in stock with just one person, in Qaṣr Ḥajjāj. This man told me extraordinary things about the ingredients. He said that the luxurious lifestyle of Boss Khalīl ibn Zawkarān[123] was down to these ingredients: 'A man came to me and mentioned he was going to make himself a batch of something from which he'd be able to make treasuries full of money; then he asked me for exactly the same list, because these ingredients are to be found only in my shop. He bought the stuff from me and made lots of stuff with it, and that's how Boss Khalīl got his fortune!' **9.21**

"When I heard this, I was amazed. 'How much do you sell them for?' I asked. 'Five hundred silver pieces,' he said, but I kept at him till we agreed on two hundred. I paid him the required sum and he said, 'Find yourself something to do for two or three days so that I can make up the list down to the last ingredient,' so I waited till he'd made it up for me, then took the things, got on my horse, and came back, delighted with what the apothecary had told me. When I got to the shaykh, I showed him all the ingredients and he asked, 'Where were you able to find everything down to the last ingredient?' and I told him I'd had to go to Damascus, where I'd found them with just one person, in Qaṣr Ḥajjāj. 'He didn't overcharge you?' he asked. 'How much did he take from you?' I told him what he'd told me about Boss Khalīl and he said, 'I heard that too.' **9.22**

ثمّ شرعنا في دقّ الحوائج ونخلها فلمّا فرغت قال أريد قِدْر يكون غطاءها كذا وقدرها كذا وتكون مزنّجة ويكون لها غطاء محكم وفي الغطاء أربعة أثقاب فاستعملت القِدْر كما طلب ثمّ أحضرتها فقال جيّدة ثمّ أخذ[1] رطل زيت طيّب ورطل دهن ألية ورطل سمن بقريّ ورطل شيرج ووضع الجميع في القِدْر ثمّ قال أيش معك من الدراهم فقلت كم تريد فقال هذه الطريقة كلّما كثرت الفضّة فيها كانت بالغة ومع ذلك ترجع الفضّة المائة منها تساوي مائة وخمسين درهم لأنّ يصلح بها الفضّة اليابسة وتبقى الخاصّيّة في الإكسير وكلّ مثقال منه على ألف مثقال تصير تلك الألف إكسير كلّ مثقال منه على ألف أخرى تصير إكسير كذلك تمام سبع بطون ٢٣،٩

فلمّا سمعت ذلك أحضرت له ألف درهم ومائتي درهم فأخذها وقلّبها وربطها في بوشيّة زرقاء وقال هذه القِدْر تريد تبقى تحت الصقيع سبعة أيّام وهي مكشوفة ثمّ تدبّر بعد ذلك ثمّ قال أنا أروح أزور قبر إلياس وقبر الراعي وقبر شيث وأجيء فارفع هذه البوشيّة عندك واترك القِدْر تحت الصقيع وودّعني وأنا أوكد عليه العود سرعة ٢٤،٩

ثمّ غاب عنّي ستّة أيّام وأتى في اليوم السابع فقعد وطلب الدراهم فأحضرتها على ما تركها ثمّ طلب القِدْر فأحضرتها قدّامه وأخرج كاز وجعل يقصّ الدراهم ويرميها في القِدْر والدهن إلى أن قصّ الجميع ثمّ قال أين الحوائج فأحضرتها فأرمى الجميع في القِدْر ثمّ حرّكه بعود وجعل الغطاء عليها ثمّ إنّه شدّ وصلها بطين الحكمة وبنى للقِدْر نصبة ثمّ قال لا تزال توقد عليها وبخارها يصعد حتّى إذا وضعت يدك على البخار عادت مثل الفضّة فقد استوى شغلك فاشكر الله تعالى على ذلك فإن تمّ لها على النار ثلاثة أيّام ولا تصبغ الكفّ فاجعل عليها من الأدهان الذي فيها من كلّ شيء أوقية ثمّ شدّ النار عليها يوماً وليلة فإنّها تصبغ وهي نهاية العمل فأنا قد بقي عليّ زيارة أريد أروح أكمّل الزيارة وأجيء وتكون أنت قد كمّلت الشغل إن شاء الله تعالى ٢٥،٩

---

١ ش: أخذت.

"We then set about pounding and sifting the ingredients. When they were all ready, he said, 'I need a pot with a lid of such and such a type and such and such a size. It must be glazed and the lid must be tight and have four holes in it.' So I had the pot made as he requested, and brought it, and he said, 'Perfect!' Then he took a pint of sweet olive oil, a pint of sheep's-tail fat, a pint of clarified cow butter, and a pint of sesame oil, and put the lot in the pot. 'How many silver pieces do you have with you?' he said. 'How many do you need?' I asked. 'According to this method,' he said, 'the more silver you put in the more it makes, not to mention that the silver gives a return of one hundred and fifty silver pieces on every one hundred, because it fixes the raw silver and the elixir retains its properties, which means that every mithkal of elixir makes a thousand mithkals, which means that every thousand mithkals of elixir makes a thousand more, so that, this way, the elixir ends up throwing precisely seven litters.' 9.23

"When I heard this, I got him 1,200 silver pieces, which he took, examined one by one,[124] and tied up in a length of blue cloth, saying, 'The pot needs to be kept in ice for seven days with the lid off. Then we'll prepare it.' He added, 'I'm off to visit the graves of Elias the Shepherd[125] and Seth,[126] and will be back. Put the cloth away, leave the pot in ice, and bid me goodbye. I promise I'll be back to check on it soon.' 9.24

"He was away for six days and came back on the seventh, when he sat down and asked for the silver pieces, so I brought them to him just as he had left them. Then he asked for the pot, which I brought and placed in front of him, and he took out a pair of shears and started cutting up the silver pieces and throwing them into the pot with the fat, till he had cut them all up. Then he stirred the pot with a stick, placed the lid on it, sealing the join tightly with clay-of-wisdom, and built a platform for it. 'Keep heating it,' he said, 'till the steam rises and when you put your hand in it comes out looking like silver. At that point, your work will be done, and you can thank the Almighty for it. If it's been on the fire for three days and your palm still doesn't change color, add some more of the fats that are in the pot, an ounce of each kind, and make the fire hotter for a day and a night. Then it will change color and the work will be over. I still have one more visit I want to make. Then I'll come back and you'll have finished the work, should the Almighty will it.' 9.25

٢٦،٩ فحرصت عليه أن يأخذ شيئاً ينفقه عليه فلم يفعل وراح وقد انقطع خبره عنّي وأخاف أن يكون قتل في البقاع أو وقع به أحد من الدرزيّة قتله والشغل إلى الساعة ما تكمّل ابصر أيش تعمل والنصف لك فقلت لا يكون أخذ الدراهم وراح فقال أعوذ بالله من ذلك هذا الرجل جميع ما في الدنيا ما يسوى ذرّة واحدة ومع هذا فإنّ الدراهم في أسفل القِدر ظاهرة فقلت أحضر القِدر فلمّا أحضرها ميّلت القِدر على جنبها فإذا فيها قالب أبيض مثل الملح فقال ألم أقل لك إنّه لم يتعلّق لي بشيء فقلت فرّغ ما في القِدر وأخرج الفضّة فلمّا أخرجها وإذا بها قصدير قد أخذت الأدهان وساحت[١] وقد تصفى فقلت له ذلك الشيخ الصالح أخذها وراح فقال وكيف عمل والله الدراهم ما وقعت في يده إلّا وهو يقصّ فيها قدّامي ويرمي في القِدر فانظر إلى هذه الطائفة ما أكثر مكرهم على أموال الناس

٢٧،٩ وأمّا كشف هذه الدكّة فأنا أبيّنه إن شاء الله تعالى وذلك أنّه لمّا طلب الدراهم فأحضرها له فلمّا رآها وعرف نقودها أمره أن يشدّها في البوشيّة وراح من عنده وأقلب دراهم قصدير على النقود نقدها ثمّ جعلها في بوشيّة مثل البوشيّة وربطها بخيط مثل ذلك الخيط فلمّا حضر وهي في عبّه طلب الدراهم الذي قد شالها عنده فأحضرها قدّامه ثمّ طلب القِدر فبمقدار ما قام يحضر القِدر أخذ الشيخ البوشيّة الذي فيها الدراهم الجيّدة وجعلها مكان البوشيّة الذي فيها الدراهم القصدير فلمّا حضرت القِدر فتح البوشيّة وجعل يقصّ ويرمي في القِدر ويطيّنها ورتّب ذلك الترتيب وشال وقد صحّ له الإكسير والوصول إليه فتميّزوا يا عميان القلوب بالبصائر وتفهّموا

---

١ ش: وساخت.

"I urged him to take some money to spend on himself but he declined and left. I've heard nothing from him since and I'm afraid he may have been murdered in the Biqāʿ or some Druze may have fallen on him and killed him, and the work still isn't finished. Just think of what to do and half of it is yours!" "You don't think he might have taken the silver pieces and fled?" I said. "I seek refuge with God from such an idea!" the man replied. "To a man like that, the whole world and all it holds are but a mote of dust! Not to mention that the silver pieces are still at the bottom of the pot, plain to see." "Bring me the pot," I said, and when he did so, I tipped it on its side and a white solid, like salt, appeared. My friend said, "Didn't I tell you he'd never try to put one over me?" "Empty out what's in the pot," I said, and when he did so he found tin, which had absorbed the fats, melted, and become clarified. I said to him, "That 'Righteous Shaykh' of yours has taken it and gone!" "But how did he do the silver pieces? Every one that he held, he snipped in two in front of me and threw into the pot!" Just look at this tribe of charlatans and how cunning they are at getting their hands on people's money! 9.26

I shall now reveal to you clearly how this trick was done, the Almighty willing. 9.27

Exposé: When he requested the silver pieces and the other brought them to him, and after he'd looked at them and made sure they were of proper assay, and after he'd ordered my friend to tie them up in the cloth and my friend had left him, he switched the silver pieces for tin and put them in a piece of cloth just like the other cloth and tied it with string just like the other string. Then, when my friend came back—the second bag now concealed under the front of the man's robe—he asked him to bring the silver pieces he'd set aside, and my friend brought them and set them in front of him. In other words, in the time it took him to go and fetch the pot, the shaykh had taken the cloth that held the good silver pieces and switched it with the cloth that held the tin, and when the pot was brought, he opened that cloth and started snipping away and throwing them into the pot, and then he stoppered the pot with clay and set up things up as described and made off. He really did make a proper "elixir" and crack its secrets! Use your eyes, ye blind of heart, so that ye may distinguish the good from the bad, and beware!

الباب التاسع في كشف أسرارهم

ومن أعظم ما وقفت عليه ما جرى للسلطان الملك العادل نور الدين زَنْكي رحمه الله حديث يصلح يكتب بماء الذهب وذلك أنّ بعض العجم جاء إلى دمشق فأخذ ألف دينار مصريّة فبردها برادة ثمّ أخذ لها دقّ فحم وعقاقير مجمّعة وطحن الجميع ثمّ عجنه بغراء السمك ثمّ جعله بنادق وجفّفه جفاف بالغ ثمّ لبس دلق وتزايا بزيّ الفقراء وجعل تلك البنادق في مخلاة ثمّ أتى إلى بعض العطّارين وقال له تشتري منّي هذا فقال وأيش هو هذا قال طنزبك خراسانيّ وهذه طنزبك معناها طَنَزَ بِكَ قال العطّار هذه أيش تنفع فقال تنفع من السموم وتجوز في جميع الأدوية التي تدفع الأخلاط وله نفع عظيم ولولا قد أدركني أوان الحاجّ وما أقدر على حمله ما أبعته فإنّه يسوى وزن بوزن عند من يعرفه فقال العطّار بكم هو قال عشرة دراهم فقال له ثلاثة فأبى فاشتراها منه بخمسة دراهم ثمّ جعله في برنيّة وأخذ العجميّ الدراهم وراح فانظر إلى هذا الرجل ما أجسره أباع ألف مثقال ذهب بخمسة دراهم فهذه جسارة عظيمة ٢٨،٩

وقد قال القائل من خاطر بنفيس ملك نفيس ثمّ انفصل عنه ولبس أنزه ما يرى من ملابس الوزراء وخلفه مملوك واكترى دارا تصلح لوزير أو قاضي وصار يتمشّى في الجامع ثمّ يتعرّف بالكبراء من أهل البلد ويعمل السماعات ويخسر جملة ويدّعي الوصول في علم الصنعة وأنّه يقدر يعمل في يوم واحد جملة مال وشاع ذلك في دمشق فسألوه الكبراء أن يعمل عندهم فكان يقول أنا ما احتاج إلى أحد أنا في يوم واحد أعمل بمقدار نعمة الذي يريدني أعمل عنده فأيش حاجتي إليه فإن كان من أجل مكان أعمل فيه فأقدر أشتري عشرة بساتين ومثلها دور وإن كان من أجل جاه فأنا ما أعمل شيء عليّ ٢٩،٩

Section Nine of the Exposé of Their Tricks

One of the most extraordinary things I've ever read is the story of what happened to Sultan al-Malik al-ʿĀdil Nūr al-Dīn Zangī, God have mercy on his soul—a tale fit to be written in golden ink! 9.28

Exposé: A Persian came to Damascus. He took a thousand Egyptian gold pieces and filed them down till they were nothing but gold dust. Then he got some pounded charcoal and an assortment of ingredients and ground them up together. Finally, he kneaded this with fish glue and made it into balls, which he dried very thoroughly. Then, donning a mantle, he dressed himself up in the clothes of a dervish, and put the said pellets in a sack over his shoulder. Going to one of the apothecaries, he said, "Will you buy these from me?" "What are they?" asked the man. The Persian replied, "They're Khurasani heezmaydafulautovyu" ("he's made a fool out of you").[127] "And what are they good for?" asked the apothecary. "They're good against poisons and can be added to any compound that stimulates the humors. They are very potent and if I hadn't found myself running out of time before the start of the pilgrimage season and unable to go on carrying them around with me, I wouldn't be selling them. To the cognoscenti, they're worth their weight in gold." "How much?" asked the apothecary. "Ten silver pieces," said the man. "Three," said the apothecary, but the man refused and in the end the apothecary bought them from him for five silver pieces and put them in an apothecary's pot and the Persian took the money and left. Observe the audacity of the man in selling a thousand mithkals of gold for five silver pieces! This is truly exceptional daring.

As the saying goes, "Who risks much gains much." The Persian left the man, dressed himself in the most decorous suit of clothes one could ever hope to behold, fit for a vizier, set a slave to walk behind him, rented a house that would have done a vizier or a judge proud, and then set off on foot for the mosque. There he became acquainted with the great men of the town, sponsored chanting and dancing sessions for the dervishes, spent a prodigal amount, and claimed that he had been initiated into the science of the Craft[128] and could make vast sums of money in a single day. News of this got around in Damascus and its great men asked him to come and work in their houses, but he'd say, "I need no one. I can make in a day as much wealth as the one who wants me to work in his house possesses, so what need do I have of him? If it's a question of a place for me to work, I can hire a dozen plantations and 9.29

فيه درك لأنّ الذي أعمله ما هو زَغَل ولا فيه غشّ فأطلب به جاه أحد هذه صنعة إلاهيّة وأنا آليت أن لا أعمل شيء إلّا لملك مع أنّي ما أعمل شيء حتّى يحلف لي أنه مهما عملت لا ينفقه إلّا في الغزاة في سبيل الله تعالى

٣٠،٩ وتمّ على ذلك فاتّصل خبره بالوزير المَزْدَقانيّ[١] فأحضره وآنسه ولاطفه مدّة حتّى صار بينهما صحبة ثمّ فاتحه في مثل ذلك فقال والله يا سيّدي قد كان منّي ومن أمري أنّي حلفت أن لا أعمل شيء إلّا لملك بعد أن يعاهدني أنه لا ينفق ممّا أعمله شيء إلّا في الغزاة في سبيل الله عزّ وجلّ فإن حصل هذا عملت وإلّا لا سبيل إلى عمل شيء على غير الوجه فلمّا سمع الوزير ذلك أفكر وقال والله إنّ هذه سعادة للمسلمين وللسلطان فهذه البلاد كلّها للإفرنج إلى بانِياس وكلّ يوم الغارة تصل إلى دارَيّا[٢] فإذا عملت شيئًا نفتح به هذه البلاد وهذه نعمة عظيمة

٣١،٩ ثمّ قال له أعرّف[٣] السلطان ذلك قال نعم إلى أن تجمع بيني وبينه حتّى تستوثق منه أن يفعل ما قلت فقال نعم ثمّ ركب الوزير من الغد إلى الخدمة فاختلى بالسلطان ثمّ عرّفه ذلك فقال والله لقد هدس في فكري أنّ لا بدّ من شيء يوصلنا إلى قلع شأفة هذه الملاعين فأحضر الرجل في غاية الكرامة فأخذ له خلعة حسنة وبغلة مسرّجة مليحة ثمّ أحضره وألبسه الخلعة وأركبه إلى جانبه ثمّ صعدوا واجتمع به السلطان ثمّ تحدّثا فقال صحيح ما قال الصاحب قال نعم يا مولانا إلّا أنّ الشرط وقف عليه السلطان قال نعم وهو الذي نفعله فقال الرجل حكم مولانا أنّ كلّ من ادّعى هذه الدرجة كاذبين وكّالين دكّاكين يدكّوا في كلّ شيء أنا شيء واحد أقوله لمولانا السلطان شرطي أن لا أمسّ بيدي شيئًا بل أكون بعيد عن مولانا وأقول افعل

١ ش: المزدعاني. ٢ ش: داره. ٣ ش: عرف.

the same number of houses, and if it's a question of patronage and protection, I'm not doing anything that could get me in trouble because what I make isn't counterfeit and involves no cheating, so I don't need to call on anyone to cover for me with the authorities. This is a divine craft, and I have taken an oath that I will work only for a king, and even then I will do nothing unless he swears to me that anything I make he will spend exclusively on mounting campaigns to extend the domains of the Almighty."

Things stopped there, until news of him reached the ears of the vizier 9.30
al-Mazdaqānī, who had him brought, treated him in a friendly manner, and lavished such kind attentions on him that in the end they became fast friends. The vizier then broached the matter in question and the Persian said, "To be honest, my lord, all my life I've sworn to make nothing for a king unless he first give me an undertaking to spend anything I make exclusively on mounting campaigns to extend the domains of God, Mighty and Sublime. If and when this happens, I will perform the operation. If it does not, it is out of the question that I should make anything for no good reason." When the vizier heard this, he pondered the matter, then said, "This, I swear, is a happy day for Muslims and sultan alike. All the lands up to Bāniyās belong to the Franks and every day their raids reach Dārayyā. If you make up a batch, we shall use it to reconquer these lands, which would be a mighty blessing."

"Should I inform the sultan of this?" the vizier asked. "Yes," said the man, 9.31
"and then set up a meeting between me and him so you can get his assurance that he'll do as I demand." "Very well," said the vizier and the very next morning he rode to work, closeted himself with the sultan, and told him the story. "Truth to tell," the sultan said, "I've been puzzling over what I could come up with to help us root out those devils." So the vizier had the Persian brought with great pomp, had a fine robe of honor prepared, had a mule saddled and bridled, and when he arrived dressed him in the robe and mounted him at his side. Then they ascended and met with the sultan, and the two talked. "Is what the honorable vizier says true?" asked the sultan. "Indeed it is, my lord," said the Persian, "but has the sultan been informed of the condition?" "I have," said the sultan, "and that is precisely what we shall do." The other said, "Since my lord probably thinks that all who lay claim to this rank are liars, plunderers of others' wealth, and cheats for whom everything is an opportunity for a scam, I have just one thing to say: I am making it a condition that I shall lay my own hand on nothing. I shall, in fact, keep my distance from you, my lord, and say, 'Do this, do that,'

كذا أو كذا ومولانا يفعل فلمّا تقرّر الأمر على هذه القاعدة قال له السلطان بسم الله أشرع على بركة الله

٣٢،٩ فأخذ العجميّ ورقة وكتب لهم استدعاء الحوائج فقال من العقّار الفلانيّ كذا ومن العقّار الفلانيّ كذا وذكر عقاقير شتّى ثمّ قال من الطنزبك الخراسانيّ مائة مثقال ثمّ دفعوا الورقة لأستاد الدار وقال له أحضر هذه الحوائج فأحضر الجميع ولم يعجز شيء إلّا الطنزبك فقال إنّه ما وجد في المارستان ولا عند العطّارين فقال العجميّ ومثل دمشق ما يعدم الطنزبك فقال السلطان ما لنا شيء يغني عنه فقال العجميّ لا ولا تخلو دمشق منه ومن المصلحة أن يتقدّم مولانا إلى المحتسب بأن يختم الليلة دكاكين العطّارين فأنا إذا كان الغد ركبت أنا وهو وشاهدين عدلين ونفتح حانوت حانوت ونفتّشه فلا بدّ أن نجده فقال نعم ما رأيت

٣٣،٩ وكان المحتسب يقال له القائد فأرسلوا ففعل ذلك ثمّ ركب العجميّ من الغد وأخذ معه العدول ونزلوا مع القائد ثمّ جعلوا يفتحون دكّان بعد دكّان حتّى انتهوا إلى دكّان الذي أباعه العجميّ الطنزبك فقعدوا الشهود والمحتسب والعجميّ ونزل صاحب الدكّان وجعل يحطّ قدّامهم برنيّة بعد برنيّة إلى أن جاءت البرنيّة التي فيها الدكّة فلمّا رآها العجميّ تهلّل وجهه فرحاً وقال هذا السلطان مسعود ثمّ قال للمحتسب والشهود اختموا عليها بختومكم ثمّ ابعثوا بها إلى القلعة ففعلوا ذلك

٣٤،٩ ثمّ عطف على العطّار وقال من أين لك هذا فقال ابتعته من رجل بخمسة دراهم فحلّ منديله وقال هذه عشرة دراهم من عندي ولا تبطّل شغلك وتطلع إلى الديوان ثمّ ركبوا وطلعوا جميعهم إلى القلعة وعرّفوا السلطان فقال العجميّ هذا أوّل سعد السلطان هذا يعمل شيء كثير فيشرع مولانا في العمل في هذه الليلة والتوفيق بيد الله

and my lord shall carry it out." Once things had seen settled on this basis, the sultan said, "In God's name—get to it, with His blessings!"

So the Persian took a piece of paper and wrote down an order for the ingredients, writing, "From such and such a druggist, this, and from the other, that," listing a wide variety of simples. Finally, he wrote, "And one hundred mithkals of Khurasani heezmaydafulautovyu." Then he gave the piece of paper to the steward and told him, "Bring these ingredients!" and he brought them all and none were missing except the heezmaydafulautovyu, which he said was nowhere to be found, either at the hospital or in the apothecaries' shops. "Can a place such as Damascus really have no heezmaydafulautovyu?" said the Persian, to which the sultan responded, "Don't we have something that can stand in for it?" "No," said the Persian, "and Damascus cannot be out of it. The best thing to do is for my lord to quickly send word to the market inspector to seal the apothecaries' shops. In the morning, he and I, along with legally qualified witnesses, will ride out and open each shop, one at a time, and make an inspection. We are bound to find it." "What a brilliant idea!" said the sultan. 9.32

The market inspector was called the Commander. They sent for him and he did what was asked. The next morning, the Persian rode out, taking the witnesses with him, and began opening up the shops, one at a time, until they ended up at the shop where the Persian had sold the heezmaydafulautovyu. The witnesses, the inspector, and the Persian sat down and the owner of the shop came out and placed in front of them one medicine pot after another, till finally the pot containing the alchemists' sauce was produced. When the Persian saw it, he beamed with pleasure. "This sultan has fortune on his side! Use your seals to seal it," he told the inspector and the witnesses, "and send it to the citadel," and that is what they did. 9.33

Then the Persian leaned over to the apothecary and asked, "Where did you get this?" and the man said, "I bought it from someone for five silver pieces." The Persian untied his handkerchief and said, "Here's ten silver pieces for you from me, so you don't have to interrupt your work and come to court." Then they mounted and everyone went up to the citadel and informed the sultan. "This is the sultan's first installment of good fortune," said the Persian. "It will make a great quantity. Let my lord initiate the work this very night. All success lies in the hand of God!" In the evening, they called for the equipment they needed, and the sultan and his servant sat in a vestibule, the Persian being off on his own to one side. "Let my lord weigh out so much of this simple and so 9.34

فلمّا أمسى عليهم المساء استدعوا بما يحتاجون إليه من الآلة ثمّ قعد السلطان والخادم في صفّة والعجميّ قد اعتزل عنهم ناحية ثمّ قال يزن مولانا من العقّار الفلانيّ كذا ومن الفلانيّ كذا وجعل يعدّ له العقاقير جميعها ثمّ قال ومن الطنزبك مائة مثقال ففعل ذلك وجعل الجميع في البوتقة ثمّ قال انفخ ولم يزل كذلك حتّى احترقت تلك الحوائج ودار الذهب ثمّ قال اقلب على بركة الله وعونه فأقلب فنزلت سبيكة ذهب مصريّ معلّى لا يكون شيء أعلى منه

٣٥،٩ فلمّا نظر السلطان إلى ذلك حار ودهش ثمّ قدّم له تلك الليلة شيء يساوي ثلاثة ألف دينار ولم يزالوا يعملوا حتّى فرغ ذلك الطنزبك فطلبوه فلم يجدوه فقال له السلطان كيف نعمل في طنزبك فقال العجميّ تبعث تجيب من خراسان فإنّه معدن في الجبل الفلانيّ في مغارة صفتها كذا وكذا إذا أراد إنسان[١] يحمل منها ألف حمل جمل وأنا دخلت إليها وأخذت منها شيئاً كثيراً وعندي منه مقدار قنطارين ثلاثة فلمّا سمع السلطان ذلك قال ما نجد من يروح إليه أخير منك فإن لم تقدر على الوصول إلى المغارة تحمل الذي عندك وإن وصلت إلى المغارة فتحمل منها مهما قدرت على حمله وأنا اكتب معك كتاب إلى السلطان الأعظم أن لا يمنعك الأخذ من ذلك

٣٦،٩ فلمّا سمع العجميّ ذلك قال إن رأى السلطان أن يبعث غيري يفعل فإنّي قد طابت لي دمشق وخدمة مولانا السلطان فقال لا غنى عن ذلك ولم يزل عليه حتّى أنعم عليه السفر فلمّا شرع يتجهّز جهّزه بستّين حمل شرب منها عمل تنّيس ودمياط ومن عمل إسكندريّة ومثلها سكّر جوريّ والأحمال[٢] والحمّالين والجمال ثمّ أعطاه خيمة ومطبخ ومستراح وفراش ونفقة الطريق إلى بغداد يبيع شيء يتسفّر به إلى العجم وكتب معه كتب إلى سائر البلاد بالمراعاة والخدمة والإقامة ثمّ خرج السلطان وأرباب الدولة في وداعه وراح وقد وصل إلى الحجر المكرّم وجعل له الإكسير الأعظم

---

١ ش: إنسان أن. ٢ ش: الأحمال.

much of that," said the Persian, and counted off the entire list of them for him. Then he said, "And a hundred mithkals of heezmaydafulautovyu." The sultan did as he was told and put everything in the crucible. Then the Persian said, "Blow, and keep on blowing until all the ingredients are red hot and the gold is swimming in the mixture. Then turn it upside down, with God's blessings and aid." So the sultan turned it upside down and out came an ingot of the finest imaginable Egyptian gold.

When the sultan saw this, he was astounded and confounded. That very night, he presented the Persian with a gift worth three thousand gold pieces, and they kept working till all the heezmaydafulautovyu was used up. They asked for more but none was to be found. "What are we to do about the heezmaydafulautovyu?" asked the sultan. "Send for more from Khurasan," said the Persian. "It's a mineral found on such and such a mountain, in a cave of such and such a description, and you can carry off a thousand camel loads of it if you want. I went into the cave and took a great quantity and still have two or three hundredweight left back home." When the sultan heard this, he said, "No one is better qualified to go than you. If you can't reach the cave, load up what you already have, and if you do reach it, carry off as many loads as you can. I shall write you a letter addressed to the Great Sultan[129] asking him not to stop you from taking any." 9.35

When the Persian heard this, he said, "If the sultan so please, let him send someone else to do the work, for I have grown fond of Damascus and of serving our lord the sultan." The sultan, however, said, "It cannot be otherwise!" and he kept at him until he had made the idea of traveling sufficiently agreeable to him. When the Persian set about preparing himself, the sultan equipped him with sixty loads of byssus linen, some the product of Tinnīs and Damietta, some the product of Alexandria, along with the same quantity of Gur sugar, as well as the necessary sacks, porters, and camels. He also gave him a tent, a kitchen, a toilet, bedding, and expenses for the road as far as Baghdad, where he was to sell some of the goods so as to be able to continue his journey to Persia. And he wrote him letters to take with him to all lands, requiring all and sundry to look after him well and provide him with services and a place to stay. After this, the sultan and the great men of the state went out to bid him farewell and he departed, having indeed arrived at the secret of the venerable stone[130] and made himself the most prodigious elixir! 9.36

٣٧،٩ وأعجب ما في هذه القضيّة أن كان بدمشق رجل يكتب المحارَفين فسمع هذه القصّة وتخبّر باطنها فلمّا تحقّق ذلك كتب على رأس جريدة نور الدين محمود بن زنكي رأس المحارفين فشاع ذلك ولم يعلم أحد باطن القضيّة إلّا يقال إنّ فلان قدكتب السلطان رأس المحارفين فاتّصل الخبر بالوزير فعرّف السلطان ذلك فقال وأيش أبصر من حرافي حتّى كتبني هاتوه فنزلت إليه الجنَداريّة بسم الله كلّم السلطان فأخذ الجريدة في كمّه ومشى معهم فلمّا وقف قدّام السلطان قال أنت فلان قال نعم قال وتكتب المحارفين قال نعم قال وكتبتني قال نعم وهذا اسمك فأظهره له قال وما بان لك من حرافي حتّى كتبتني فقال يكون أن جاءك واحد نصّاب وعمل عليك حيلة ودكّ عليك ألف دينار أخذ بها مال المسلمين وراح يجيب طنزبك فما يكون حراف أبلغ من ذلك

٣٨،٩ فلمّا سمع السلطان كلامه قال كأنّك به قد جاء وصحبته طنزبك نعمل منه أموال لا تقدر ولا تحصى فقال يا خَوَنْد إن رجع محيت اسمك وكتبت اسمه فما يكون في عالم الله أحرف منه إن رجع جاء قال فلمّا سمع السلطان كلامه ضحك وقال أعطوه شيء ينفق عليه فأعطوه شيء وراح وكان كلّما أفلس أخذ الجريدة ووقف على باب القلعة فإذا ركب السلطان فتح الجريدة فيقول ما جاء وهذا اسم السلطان مكتوب مثبوت فيضحك ويطلق له شيء ويروح فأقام كذلك حتّى مات السلطان والطنزبك ما جاء فانظر إلى هذه الدكّ والجسارة على بيع ألف دينار بخمسة دراهم

٣٩،٩ وقد كان عند عزّ الدين أيبك المعظّمي رجل مغربيّ يُعرف بعبد الله الغُماريّ وكان يدكّه مائة دينار يأخذ منه ألف فأقام عنده مدّة وعلى هذه الصورة فلمّا انتهى إليّ خبره علمت أنّه دكّاك فكشفت دكّه ووجدته يدكّ في البوتقة ثمّ زرّقت عليه خادم من خدّام الأمير وعرّفته الدكّة فتقرّب إليه وسأله أن يعمل عنده شيئاً فلمّا تقرّر الأمر

The most amazing part of the whole affair is that in Damascus there was a man who kept a record of the acts of fools. He heard the story and looked into it in depth, and when he had established the facts, he wrote at the top of a sheet of a piece of paper "Nūr al-Dīn Maḥmūd ibn Zangī is the Fool-in-Chief." Word of this got around but no one knew the truth of the matter beyond the fact that someone had written that the sultan was the Fool-in-Chief. News reached the vizier, who informed the sultan. "What would he know about how stupid I am that he should write about me? Fetch him!" said the sultan. So the royal guard went to him and said, "In the name of God, come talk to the sultan!" So he put the sheet of paper in his sleeve and went with them. When he stood before the sultan, the latter asked him, "Are you so-and-so?" and he said, "Yes." "And you record the acts of fools?" "Yes." "And you wrote about me?" "Yes, and here's your name," and he showed it to the sultan. "And what stupidity of mine have you uncovered to make you write about me?" "A confidence trickster came to you and put one over you and cheated you out of a thousand gold pieces, which he took from the wealth of good Muslims, and then he went off to get heezmaydafulautovyu. What greater foolishness could there be than that?" 9.37

When the sultan heard his words, he said, "I can see him as clearly as I see you, arriving and bringing with him the heezmaydafulautovyu, from which we will make wealth beyond estimation or calculation." "Prince," said the man, "if he comes back, I'll erase your name and write his, for in that case *he'd* be the stupidest person in the world!" When the sultan heard this, he laughed and said, "Give him some token he can use to get a handout," so they gave him something and he left, and whenever he ran out of money, he'd take the piece of paper and stand at the gate of the citadel, and when the sultan rode out, he'd open up the paper and say, "He hasn't come, and here's the sultan's name, written out and still firmly in place!" and the sultan would laugh and make him a gift and he'd leave. This continued until the sultan died, but the heezmaydafulautovyu never arrived. Observe the trickery, and the audacity of selling a thousand pieces of gold for five of silver! 9.38

ʿIzz al-Dīn Aybak al-Muʿaẓẓamī had in his house a Maghrebi called ʿAbd Allāh al-Ghumārī who could treat a hundred silver pieces with sauce and get a thousand. He lived with him for a while on the basis of that claim. When news of him reached me, I realized he was a charlatan, so I exposed his trickery, discovering that he was tampering with the crucible. Then I put one of the emir's servants onto him and told him how the trick was done, and the man made 9.39

فعمل بوتقة ودكّ إليها أربعين ديناراً فعمل الخادم بوتقة على مثالها ثمّ تركها في موضع بوتقة الشيخ وأخذ تلك البوطقة ثمّ شرعوا يعملوا فلمّا ساق على البوتقة وأقلب فلم ينزل شيئاً فقال الخادم وأين الشيء فقال النار أفسدت هذه الطريقة

٤٠،٩ فقال الخادم والله لا بدّ ما أخلّي الأمير يعلّقك على باب الدار ويرميك بالنشّاب يا شيخ نحس تضحك على الأمراء وتأخذ أموالهم وهذه البوتقة أوقف عليها الأمير فلمّا سمع الشيخ طار عقله خوفاً وفزعاً وأقبل على الخادم يسأله ويخدعه وهو يأبى فما كان له بدّ من إعطاء الخادم شيئاً وقال أنا أحلف لك أيّ شيء تحصّل من اليوم نصفه لك ثمّ نزل ولم يثق بالخادم وخاف من غائلته فما كان له إلّا أن هرب فهذه صفة الواصل إلى هذه الصنعة

friends with him and asked him to make up a little at his house. After they'd come to an agreement, the charlatan constructed a crucible and slipped forty gold pieces into it, unnoticed, but the servant made a crucible just like it and switched it with the shaykh's crucible, which he removed. Then they set to work, but when the shaykh blew on the crucible with the bellows and turned it over, nothing fell out, so the servant said to him, "Where's the stuff?" and the man said, "The fire wasn't right for this method."

"I swear," the servant said, "I have no choice but to advise the emir to have 9.40
you hung at the door of his mansion and shot through with arrows, you filthy shaykh! You think you can cheat the emirs and take their money? And I'm going to give the emir this crucible to examine." When the shaykh heard this, he went crazy with fear and terror, and set upon the servant, begging him and cozening him, but the other refused to go along with him, and in the end he had no choice but to give the servant money and tell him, "I solemnly promise that from now on half the proceeds go to you!" Then he left, but he didn't trust the servant and was afraid he might do him harm, so he had no choice but to flee. Such are the "initiates" of this craft.

الفصل العاشر

اثنا عشر باباً

في كشف أسرار العطّارين

اعلم أنّ هذه الصناعة أكثر دكّ وزغل من جميع الصنائع وفيها ما هو معمول معلوم ومنها ما هو معمول مجهول فأمّا المعمول المعلوم فهو الزُنْجُفُر والزنجار والإسفيداج والمرَتَك وخبز الفضّة وغيره وهذه الأشياء معمولة وقد عُلِمَتْ أنّها معلومة ولا كلام فيها ولولا أنّها عُمِلَتْ ذكرت كلّ صنف منها وكيفيّة عمله وإن كان فقد اطّلعت منها على أشياء مختلفة فلمّا علمت ذلك ضربنا عنها وإنّما نذكرما لم يصل إلى أفكار الناس أنّه يعمل مثل الفلفل والهليلج والعود والزنجبيل ودم الأخوين نوعين والنيل والمسك والعنبر والماورد والزباد والكافور وغيرهما وكلّ ذلك نذكر باب باب ليعلم من وقف على كتابي هذا أنّي أنا لم أترك شيئاً من العلوم ولا من الصنائع إلّا قد بيّنّاه وبرهنا عليه وسلكنا طريق أهله وانتظمنا في كلّ سلك فافهم ذلك ١،١٠

الباب الأوّل في كشف أسرارهم في عمل الهليلج

وذلك أنّهم[١] يأخذون من حبّ الهليلج ثمّ يرفعونه عندهم فإذا أرادوا عمل هليلج أخذوا من الصبر جزء ومن المرّ جزء ومن الصمغ جزء ثمّ يدقّون الجميع دقّاً ناعماً ثمّ يأخذون من مرائر الماعز يعجنون بها تلك الحوائج عجناً جيّداً شديداً ثمّ يكون قد عملوا لها قوالب في ٢،١٠

١ ش: أن.

Chapter Ten, in Twelve Sections:

Exposé of the Tricks of Apothecaries

This craft contains more charlatanry and fakery than all the others put together. Some of the substances in question are faked and known to be so and others are faked but not known to be so. The substances that are known to be faked are cinnabar, blue vitriol, white lead, litharge, and silver salt, and there are others. These things are faked, are known to be so, and there's no argument about them; were they not known to be faked, I would have discussed each item and how it is made, which would have forced me to digress into a review of a number of other matters—a course that, when I became aware of it, I resolutely rejected. I shall therefore list only things that people have no idea are faked, such as pepper, myrobalan, agarwood, ginger, dragon's blood (two kinds), indigo, musk, ambergris, rosewater, civet, and camphor, and there are others. I shall discuss each of these item by item; anyone who peruses this book of mine will thus be apprised that there isn't a science or a craft I have failed to elucidate, for which I have failed to provide the proof that condemns its practitioners, the path of whose practitioners I have failed to follow, or whose various branches I have failed to join. Wise up! 10.1

Section One: Exposé of How They Make Fake Myrobalan

Exposé: They take myrobalan kernels and set them aside in their shops. To make fake myrobalan, they take one part each aloe, myrrh, and gum, pounding everything together till smooth. Then they take some goat gallbladders and knead them extremely thoroughly with the said ingredients. Having earlier prepared molds in the form of lemons set into lengths of wood, they put some 10.2

ألواح خشب على شبه قوالب أقراص اللّيمو ثمّ يجعلون في القالب من ذلك الدواء ويجعلون فيه نواية هليلج ولا يزال كذلك حتّى يملأ اللوح ثمّ يردّ عليها اللوح الآخر ويثقّلونه ويتركونه يوم وليلة ويجفّفونه في الظلّ جفافًا بالغًا فإنّه يجيء أحسن ما يكون من الهليلج وأجوده وهذا باب أعرف فيه عشرة طرائق مختلفة الأنواع فافهم

الباب الثاني في عمل الماورد

٣،١٠ وذلك أنّهم يأخذون من زرّ الورد العراقيّ ينقعونه في ماء الورد الخالص النُصيبينيّ يوم وليلة ثمّ يحشونه في القرعة ويجعلون في بلبلة الأنبيق مسك ويجعلون مع زرّ الورد لكلّ رطل زنة عشرة دراهم كبّاش القرنفل ودرهمين هال ويستقطرونه بنار لينّة فإنّه يقطر فيجعل في فقّاعة زجاج ثمّ يسدّ رأسها ويلفّها في قطن ويجعلها في حُقّ ويحترز عليها من الهواء وأن لا يخرج شيء من رائحتها فإذا أراد عمل الماورد أخذ الماء العذب الصافي ثمّ جعله في طِنْجير وأغلى عليه بنار لينّة حتّى ينقص الثلث ثمّ يخرجه ويحترز عليه من الغبار فإذا برد أخذ من ذلك الإكسير الذي استقطره لكلّ رطل بالبغداديّ من الماء المغليّ وزن ثلاثة دراهم من الإكسير المذكور ثمّ يسدّ رأس الوعاء ويجعله في الشمس ثلاثة أيّام فإنّه أحسن ما يكون من الماورد وأعرف فيه أربعين طريقة مختلفة أنواعها

الباب الثالث في عمل الزنجبيل

٤،١٠ وذلك أنّهم يأخذون عرق الجرجير اليابس ثمّ يغمرونه بماء الرشاد ويعملون معه وزن درهمين زنجبيل ثمّ يغلون عليه حتّى يذهب من ذلك الماء الربع وينزلونه عن النار ويتركه حتّى ينشف الماء عنه فإنّه يكون أشدّ حرارة من الزنجبيل وأحسن وأعرف فيه ثلاثة طرائق أحسن ما يكون فافهم

of the mixture into each mold and place a myrobalan kernel in it. This is left until the first length of wood is full, whereupon another length is placed on top and weighted down, the whole then left for a day and a night, after which they dry the result thoroughly in the shade. It comes out like the best and highest quality of myrobalan. I know ten ways of fabricating different kinds of fruit by this method.

Section Two: On Making Fake Rosewater

Exposé: They take Iraqi rosebuds, steep them for a day and a night in pure water from Nusaybin, then stuff them into the still pot and place musk in the beak of the alembic. In each pound of rosebuds, they put ten dirhams by weight of cloves and two of cardamom, distilling it over a low flame until it forms droplets, which run into a glass flask. They then stopper the flask, wrap it in cotton, and place it in a box, which protects it from the air and prevents any scent from escaping. To make rosewater, the apothecary takes pure sweet water and puts it in a boiler and boils it over a low flame until it is reduced by one third. He removes this and covers it against dust. When it has cooled, he takes three dirhams by weight of the aforementioned distilled elixir for each Baghdad pint of boiled water, stoppers the vessel, and places it in the sun for three days. It comes out like the best kind of rosewater. I know forty different ways of doing this. 10.3

Section Three: On Making Fake Ginger

Exposé: They take dry arugula root, cover it with water in which cress has been steeped, and put two dirhams by weight of ginger with it. They boil this till a quarter of the water has gone, then remove it from the fire and leave it till the liquid has dried. The result is spicier and better than real ginger. I know three brilliant ways of making it. 10.4

الباب الرابع في عمل العود

٥،١٠ ومن ذلك أنّهم يأخذون حطب الزيتون ينقعونه في ماء العنب المسطار سبعة أيّام ثمّ يرفعونه على النار ويغمرونه بماء الورد وقد أخذوا برادة العود وجعلوها في الماورد ثمّ يغلون عليها بنار ليّنة حتّى يذهب ربع الماء ثمّ ينزلونه عن النار ويتركونه حتّى يشرب جميع ما عليه من الماء ويحترزون عليه من الغبار ثمّ يجفّفونه في الظلّ ويرفعونه في وعاء ويسدّون رأسه ويحترزون من الهواء فإنّه يكون عود لا يمكن شيء أحسن منه من رائحته ومن أراد جرايدي[١] يجعل عوض حطب الزيتون عود النَوْر وأعرف فيه سبعة عشر طريقة

الباب الخامس في عمل المسك

٦،١٠ ومن ذلك أنّهم يأخذون فراخ الحمام المجهولة أو العادة[٢] كما تفقس ويزقّوهم بكاش القرنفل مع الماورد مسحوق معجون مع المحلب والسنبل يفعل ذلك سبعة أيّام ثمّ يأخذون جام زجاج يدهنونه بدهن البان ثمّ يذبحون تلك الفراخ ويصفّون دماءهم فيه ويحترزون عليه من الغبار فإذا جفّ قلعه من الجام ثمّ أضاف مثل خمس الدراهم مسك ويسحقه جميعاً ثمّ يأخذ نافجة فارغة ويحشوها من ذلك المعمول ثمّ يلصق النافجة بصمغ عربيّ ويلصق معها من شعر النافجة ثمّ يبيعه فهو أحسن ما وجدت من عمله وأمشاهم فافهم

الباب السادس في عمل العنبر

٧،١٠ فمن ذلك أنّهم يأخذون حبّ العُصفور فينقعونه في ماء الورد يوم وليلة بعد أن يكون قد نزعه من حبّه فإذا كان من الغد مرثه بيده حتّى يطلع القشر ويبقى اللحم فيرمي القشر ثمّ يأخذ اللحم فيجعله على الصلاية ثمّ يلقي عليه العنبر ويسحقه بماء الورد الذي كان

---

١ كذا في الأصل. ٢ في الأصل: العداد.

Section Four: On Making Fake Agarwood

Another example: They take chunks of olive wood and steep them for seven days in the juice of musty grapes. Then they set the wood to cook over the fire and cover it with rosewater in which they have previously put agarwood sawdust. They boil this over a low fire until it has been reduced by a quarter, then take it off the fire, leave it until all the water has been absorbed, and cover it against dust. Finally, they dry it in the shade, put it in a vessel, cover its top with a lid, and put it in an airtight container. The result is agarwood of the best, and best-smelling, kind. If one of them wants *jarāyidī*,[131] he substitutes cloves for the chunks of olive wood. I know seventeen ways of doing this. 10.5

Section Five: On Making Fake Musk

Another example: They take newly hatched pigeon squabs, either wild or domesticated, and feed them with cloves and rosewater ground with mahaleb cherry and spikenard and made into a paste. They do this for seven days. Then they take a glass bowl and oil it with ben oil. Next, they slaughter the squabs, let their blood into the bowl, and cover it against dust. When the blood has dried, the apothecary removes it from the bowl and adds around five dirhams by weight of musk and grinds it all up together. Then he takes an empty musk vesicle and stuffs it with the product. Finally, he seals the vesicle with gum arabic, to which he adds some of the hairs from the vesicle, and sells it. This is the best and most salable example of the apothecary's work that there is. 10.6

Section Six: On Making Fake Ambergris

Another example: They take safflower seeds and steep them in rosewater for a day and a night, having first removed them from the flower heads.[132] The following morning, the apothecary mashes them with his hand till the husk comes off and the seed itself is left. He discards the husk, takes the seed and places it on the grindstone, sprinkles it with ambergris, and then grinds it up 10.7

منقوعاً به ولا يزال يسحق حتّى تنقطع الدَبوقاء فإذا انقطعت أخدمه بعد ذلك بدهن البان الخام ثمّ يسقيه من قشر الجوز الأخضر شيء يسير ثمّ يجعل عليه مثل ربعه عنبر خام ثمّ يخلطه جيّداً ثمّ يجعله في وعاء زجاج ضيّق الرأس ثمّ يسدّ رأسه سدّاً جيّداً ثمّ يجعله في مكان فيه نداوة أربعين يوماً ثمّ يخرجه وقد أعشب وصار أشهب وهو أحسن ما وجدت بعد معرفة ثلاثين طريقة

الباب السابع في كشف أسرارهم في عمل التوتياء

فمن ذلك أنّهم يبنون تنّوراً مربّعاً يكون ارتفاعه ثلاثة أشبار ويجعلون له إفريزاً في نصفه ٨،١٠ ثمّ يجعلون له غطاء محكماً عليه ثمّ يعملون قضباناً من طين ثمّ يشوونه فإذا انشوت مثال الفخّار يأخذون التراب الأصفر ثمّ يعجنونه بماء الهندباء عجناً جيّداً ثمّ يلبسونه تلك القضبان ثمّ يأخذون شِقاف كيزان بيض فيدقّونها مثل الدخن ثمّ يمرّغون فيها القضبان الذي يلبسونها للطين ثمّ يصفّونها في التنّور على ذلك الإفريز ويخلّون بين القضبان ليدخل الدخان بينهما ثمّ يردّون الغطاء على التنّور ثمّ يوقدون تحته بحطب الطرفاء الأخضر لا يجزي غيره فإذا احمرّت القضبان يشيلونها ثمّ يطفونها في ماء الهندباء يفعلون ذلك ثلاث دفوع وفي الثالثة يطفون القضيب ويمرّغونه[١] في الشقاف ثمّ يصفّونه في التنّور على الوصف المقدّم فلا يزالون يوقدون عليها حتّى تنسبك ثمّ يقطعون عنها النار ويخلّونها حتّى تبرد فإذا بردت أخذ القضيب ودقّ عليه بالمطرقة دقّة خفيفة فإنّه ينزل صفائح صفائح توتياء جيّدة مليحة لا بعدها شيء وهذه الطريقة أعرف فيها سبع طرق

١ ش: يمرخونه.

with the rosewater in which it was steeped. He keeps on grinding until the gluiness has broken. Once this happens, he adds unrefined ben oil, tempers it with a little green walnut husk, adds about a quarter of its mass in raw ambergris, and mixes well. Next, he places everything in a glass vessel with a narrow neck, closes it tightly, and leaves it in a cool place for forty days. Then he takes it out, and by this time it will have produced mold and turned gray. This is the best method I found after familiarizing myself with a total of thirty.

Section Seven: On Making Fake Tutty

Another example: They construct a square oven three handspans in height **10.8**
with a shelf inside and a tight-fitting lid. Then they shape mud into bars. When these have been baked till they look like earthenware, they take yellow dust, knead it well with endive water, and coat the bars with it. Next, they take shards of white milk mugs, pound them like millet, and roll the bars in them, having first coated them again with mud. They arrange these in the furnace on the shelf, leaving spaces between the bars so the smoke can pass through. They put the lid back on the furnace and light a fire under it, using green (and only green) Nile tamarisk for fuel. When the bars turn red, they remove them and extinguish them in endive water, repeating this three times and extinguishing the bars altogether on the third by rolling them in the shards. Then they arrange them in the furnace in the way described above and keep the fire going under them until they harden, at which point they douse the fire and leave them to cool. Once they are cool, the apothecary takes each bar and taps it lightly with a mallet and a lovely high-grade tutty that couldn't be bettered drops off it, flake by flake. I know seven variations on the above method.

الباب الثامن في عمل دم الأخوين القاطر وغيره

٩،١٠ وهو أن يأخذون المغرة المدنيّة وأيضاً العراقيّة الجيّدة ثمّ يسحقونها ويأخذون من دم الحجّامين ويسقونها منه شيئاً بعد شيء حتّى يعجبهم لونه ثمّ يجفّفونه فإنّه يكون أحسن شيء وهذه الطريقة أعرف منها ثمان طرق

الباب التاسع في كشف أسرارهم في عمل الزباد

١٠،١٠ ومن ذلك أنّهم يأخذون الظفر الطيّب يغسلونه غسلاً جيّداً نقيّاً ويجعلون عليه رأس الصابون ويتركونه ثلاثة أيّام فإنّه يحلّ فإذا انحلّ يرفعونه على النار ويلقون فيه وزن درهم مصطكاء ودرهم خميرة وقليلاً من شعر قطّ أسود يعود جميعه زباد جيّد وأعرف فيه ثمانية عشر طريقة هذه أجودهم وأحسنهم

الباب العاشر في عمل اللازورد وغسله

١١،١٠ ومن ذلك أنّهم إذا أرادوا غسله يأخذون الغشيم وهو تراب اللازورد الجيّد منه ثمّ يجعلونه في برام مرنّج ويجعلون لكلّ أوقيّة منه أوقيّة زفت[١] وأوقيّة قلفونية ثمّ يوقدون عليه فإذا ذاب طلع عليه الصبغ كأنّه رغوة الصابون فإذا أراد يحترق يلقون عليه قليل بورق فإنّه يستوي جيّداً وهذه الطريقة أعرف منها خمسة وهي أجودهم

الباب الحادي عشر في كشف أسرارهم في عمل اللازورد الأصل

١٢،١٠ ومن ذلك أنّهم يأخذون قشر البيض ويكلّسونه ثمّ يلقون عليه حشيشة الصبّاغين الذي تطلع على القاشي وتسمّى الوَسْمة أيضاً وتسمّى الغبيراء ويلقون عليه ماء النيل

---

١ ش: زيت.

Section Eight: On Making Fake Dragon's Blood (in Resinous or Other Form)

They take high-grade hematite, either the Medinan or the Iraqi kind. They crush it and take some cuppers' blood and moisten the hematite with it, in small doses, till they get the color they're looking for. Then they dry it. It's the best quality, and I know eight variations on this method. 10.9

Section Nine: Exposé of the Tricks They Use to Make Fake Civet

Another example: They take fragrant operculum, wash it well in clean water, pour lye over it, and leave it for three days, which makes it dissolve. Once it is dissolved, they place it over a fire and throw in a dirham by weight of mastic, the same of yeast, and a little hair from a black tomcat, and at this the whole turns into high-grade civet. I know eighteen variations on this method, this being the highest quality and the best. 10.10

Section Ten: On Making Fake Lapis Lazuli and Lapis Lazuli Wash[133]

Another example: To make a lapis wash, they take the unprocessed form, which is to say high-grade lapis powder, place it in a glazed pot, and add an ounce of tar and an ounce of resin for every ounce of lapis. Then they set it over a fire. When it melts, the pigment rises to the surface like soapsuds. If they want to use it as a polishing agent, they put a little borax on it and it comes out nicely. I know five variations, this being the highest quality. 10.11

Section Eleven: Exposé of Their Tricks for Making Fake Real Lapis Lazuli[134]

Another example: They take eggshells and calcine them. Then they toss on top of them leaves of dyers' weed, such as is found in faience tiles, also called *wasmah* and *ghubayrā'*.[135] They also toss in Indian indigo from Sarav. It then turns into high-grade fake lapis. I know forty-two methods, each producing a different type, but if I were to start listing everything I know, no book would 10.12

الهنديّ السراويّ فإنّه يعود لازورد جيّد وهذه الطريقة أعرف فيها اثنان وأربعون طريقة مختلفة الأنواع ولو ذهبت أذكر جميع ما أعرف ما وسعه كتاب بل إنّي أختصر على البعض وبه يستدلّ على الكلّ من له لبّ وفكر صائب واعلم أنّ لهم أعمال كثيرة في كلّ فنّ وفي الأمراض القاتلة ولا بدّ أن أذكر منها شيئاً يسيراً فافهم ذلك

الباب الثاني عشر في كشف أسرارهم في عمل قرص الكاكنج[1]

وهو ممّا يحل البدن ويورث الاسترخاء في المعدة ويضعف القوام وذلك أنّهم يأخذون ١٣،١٠
من الكاكنج جزء ومن حبّ الغاريقون جزء ومن الدلب جزء ومن شحم النمس جزء ويُدقّ الجميع ثمّ يحلّ بماء الدفلى فإنّه قرص قاتل جدّاً وأعرف من هذه الأقراص مائة قرص مختلفة الأنواع لم يقدر عليها حكيم من الحكماء وإنّما العاقل اللبيب يستدلّ بواحد عن أحاد فافهم ذلك

١ ش: الكاكب.

be big enough to contain it all; I shall limit myself instead to mentioning just a few, from which the man of intelligence and discernment will be able to infer the rest. These people have many fake preparations that are of use in every field, and for causing fatal diseases, one of which I am now obliged to describe. Wise up to these things!

Section Twelve: Exposé of Their Tricks for Making Alkekengi Pills

This is something that wastes the body, leaves the bowels loose, and undermines the constitution. **10.13**

Exposé: They take one part each of alkekengi, agarikon, plane fruit, and ichneumon fat, pound these all together, and then liquefy the mixture, using oleander water. The resulting pill is very deadly. I know a hundred different pills of this kind that no doctor is a match for. Any rational and intelligent person, however, can infer multiple instances from a single example. Wise up to these things!

الفصل الحادي عشر

خمسة أبواب

في كشف أسرار أصحاب الميم وهم المَطالِبيّة الذين يدّعون الوصول إلى المطالب والكنوز

١،١١ اعلم أنّ هذه الطائفة أكثر حيل وتسليط ومكر على أموال الناس ولهم أفعال لا يقع عليها قياس ثمّ إنّ جميع الخلق يرتبطون عليهم ويصغون إلى كلامهم وينطاعون لهم طمعاً في المال الذي يلعب بعقول الرجال ويذعن له الملوك وكلّ غنيّ وصعلوك وتطير له الرقاب وسأذكر بعض أفعالهم

الباب الأوّل في كشف أسرارهم

٢،١١ فمن ذلك أنّهم إذا أرادوا أن يدّعوا معرفة المطالب ويأكلون أموال الناس ويرتبطون عليهم فإذا أرادوا ذلك أتوا إلى بعض المغاير أو بعض الأودية فحفروا فيها فإذا هُمّ حفروا أخذوا رمل من غير تلك الأرض طمروه ثمّ يأخذون مفتاح حديد ويطلوه بالذهب ثمّ يأخذون صفيحة ينقشون عليها أحرف مفرّقة على مثال بعض الأقلام اليونانيّة ثمّ يطلونها أيضاً بالذهب ثمّ إنّهم يطلون الجميع بالصندروس ثمّ يدفنون أشياء كثيرة مثل ذلك ويتركونها زماناً طويلاً ويأخذون رقّ ويكتبون عليه بالأقلام العجميّة ويقولون فيها إذا سافرت إلى بلاد الفلانيّ فاسأل عن المكان الفلانيّ ثمّ ينعتون ذلك الموضع نعتاً جيّداً فإذا وصلت إليه فإنّك تجد عنده كذا وكذا وقف في موضع كذا وكذا وقس عن يمين الموضع كذا وكذا وعن يساره كذا وكذا ثمّ احفر فإنّك تجد رمل

Chapter Eleven, in Five Sections:

Exposé of the Tricks of the People of the *Mīm*[136] (Who Are Treasure Hunters Who Pretend to Have Access to Hoards of Wealth and Buried Treasure)

This is the tribe of charlatans most skilled at subterfuges and cunning ways of getting their hands on people's money; they have maneuvers beyond measure. Everyone falls for them, listens to what they say, and follows their instructions, driven by that greed for money that plays havoc with men's minds and is obeyed by potentates, plutocrats, and paupers alike, all of whom become slaves to its influence. I shall now list some of those maneuvers. 11.1

Section One of the Exposé of Their Tricks

Example: To give the impression that they know the whereabouts of hoards of buried treasure in order to be able to eat up people's money and to make them fall for their lies; to do this, as I say, they go to some cave or dry riverbed and dig a hole there. Hole dug, they fetch sand from someplace else and cover it over. Then they take an iron key and coat it with gold, after which they take a sheet of metal and inscribe it with letters that don't join up, like those of certain Greek scripts, and they coat this too with gold. Finally, they coat everything with sandarac. They bury lots of things of this sort and leave them for a long time and take a piece of parchment and write on it in non-Arabic scripts the following: "When you travel to such and such a country, ask after such and such a place"—and then they describe very precisely the place where they buried the key—"and when you get there, you will find such and such things. Stand in such and such a spot and measure so much from the right and so much from the left. Then dig and you will find sand that has been brought 11.2

منقول من غير تلك الأرض فاحفر وابشر بالوصول فإذا حفرت وجدت كذا وكذا فلا يزال يعدّ العلائم حتّى ينتهي إلى المفتاح والصحيفة

٣،١١ ثمّ يقول إذا وصلت إلى ذلك فاحذر أن تتعرّض له إلى وقت الفلانيّ حتّى تنزل الشمس في البرج الفلانيّ في الدرجة الفلانيّة ثمّ يبعد[١] إلى مقدار سبعة ثمانية أشهر مقدار ما يحصل منهم شيء على قدر ما يريد فإذا نزلت الشمس إلى ذلك البرج فاجمع هذه العقاقير وهي كذا وكذا ويذكر أشياء لا يصاب في تلك الأرض ثمّ يكون لها قيمة ومنهم من يقول اعمل صنماً من ذهب وزنه كذا وكذا وانقش عليه كذا وكذا واجعل في إصبعه خاتم بفصّ ياقوت وانقش على الخاتم كذا وكذا ثمّ قدّمه إلى المكان فإنّ الصنم يشير بالخاتم إلى نحو المكان فإذا أشار إليه انفرج المكان وظهر لك من المال ما يعجز عن حمله الجمال فخذ ما أردت ثمّ ادفع ذلك الصنم وانزع الخاتم من يده فإنّ المكان يعود إلى ما كان ولا يرجع أحد يقدر على ذلك المكان إلى مثل ذلك الوقت من السنة الآتية بذلك الصنم

٤،١١ فإذا كتب ذلك أخذ الصندروس ودهنه بعد أن عتّقه ثمّ يكون قد قطع من هوامشه مواضع فإذا فعل ذلك تحدّث مع الناس هل يعرف أحد ذلك المكان الفلانيّ ولا يزال حتّى يشيع الخبر بين الناس بذلك ثمّ يقصد بعض أصحاب الجاه والمقدرة فيقول أنا أوقفك على المكان وأحضر كتابه ونعمل ونتوكّل[٢] على الله عزّ وجلّ بشرط أنّك تحلف لي أنّك لا تغدر بي ولا تخوفني ولا ترزق على أحد ولا تحسن في أذيتي وإنّ الكتاب لا يزال معي فإنّي أنا رجل غريب ومنقطع وفد إلى باب الله وبابك فاعمل معي ما يليق بمثلك ووالله هذا الكتاب اشتريته من بلاد الروم بكذا وكذا وقد حملته إليك فافعل ما يقتضي كرمك ومروّتك

٥،١١ فإذا اتّفق الأمر وخرجوا إلى ذلك المكان وحقّقوه عادوا إلى البلد وعملوا أشغالهم ثمّ طلعوا بالرجال وحفروا فلا بدّ أن يظهر لهم ذلك الرمل فإذا ظهر ذلك وقع الوهم

١ ش: يبعده. ٢ ش: ونتكلّم.

there from someplace else, and be glad, for you have arrived, and when you dig, you will find such and such," and it goes on listing the clues, ending with the key and the metal sheet.

Next, the parchment says, "When you reach that place, mind you set about things at such and such a time, so that the sun is in such and such a sign of the zodiac and at such and such a degree." (At this point in the story, as it plays out in real time, the man will put everything on hold for some seven or eight months. The parchment continues:) "When the sun enters the specified sign, gather together the ingredients needed to make incense—namely, this and that," and it lists things that cannot be obtained in that country and are therefore of high value. Alternatively, some of them say, "Make a gold statue weighing so much and inscribe on it such and such and put on its finger a signet ring with a ruby and inscribe such and such on the stone. Then set the statue up facing the direction of the place in question and it will point toward the place with the ring, and when it points to it, the place will open up and there before you will appear a treasure hoard of such vast size that loaded camels couldn't carry off all the prize. Take what you want, knock the statue over, and wrench the ring from its hand. That way, the place will go back to what it was before, and none shall find it ever more—until the same time next year, using the statue." 11.3

Having written this, the charlatan takes the sandarac and coats the parchment (having first made it look old by cutting bits out of its edges), and then engages people in conversation, asking, "Does anyone know this place?" He goes on doing this till word gets around. Then he makes his way to some man of influence and wherewithal, and says, "I will show you the place and bring along the document that explains it all and, with God's support, we'll be able to get down to work, on condition that you swear never to play me false or seek to intimidate me or pay others to do so, or try to do me any harm, and that the document remain with me, for I am a stranger with no one to take his part presenting himself at God's door and yours; do with me, then, as seems right to you. I swear I bought this document from the land of the Greeks for such and such a price, and I have brought it to you, so do as your generosity and manliness dictate." 11.4

When a sum has been agreed on and they have made their way to the place in question and verified it, they return to the town and make their preparations. Then they set off again with men and they dig. Inevitably, they find the abovementioned sand. At its appearance, everyone is deluded into thinking 11.5

بصحّة ذلك ثمّ حفروا فيظهر شيء آخر من تلك العلائم فتحقّقوا ذلك ولا تزال العلائم تظهر على ما يذكر الكتاب حتّى تظهر الصفيحة والمفتاح فإذا ظهروا وكّد على الصنم أو على البخور وأبعد الأمر إلى وقت آخر وإن كان على الصنم فلا يزال حتّى يعمل الصنم ثمّ يأخذه ويمدّها وطنه وإن كان على البخور فإنّه يأخذ شيء يشتري به البخور ويسافر ليشتريه ولكن من أين من بلاد الهند من داخل فافهم

الباب الثاني في كشف أسرارهم

ومن ذلك أنّهم يعملون العلائم كما تمّ إذا لم يبق إلّا الدخول إلى المكان جعلوا عليه مَهْلَك منهم من يعمل مهلك الحيّات ومنهم من يعمل مهلك الأخذ بالبصر ومنهم من يعمل مهلك الأشخاص وغيرها فإذا وصلوا إلى الموضع احتجّ عليهم بالمانع الذي قد ظهر لهم وأنا أبيّن ذلك المهلك ٦،١١

فأمّا مهلك النار فإنّهم يأخذون ظرف ينفخوه ثمّ يدفنوه في الأرض في المجاز ثمّ يجعلون قدّام فم الظرف مُشاقة الكتّان محلول فيها قلفونية وكبريت ويكون الذي للظرف محكم وذلك أنّه يكون له قصبة حديد مهندم عليه كما يعمل لمنافيخ[١] الحدّادين إلّا أنّها تكون أقوى من ذلك وأضيق ويكون بعد نفخ الظرف قد سدّت بشمع رقيق فإذا جاز بالضوء يتحايد الظرف ثمّ يودع في رأس تلك المشاقة من رأس الفند الذي معه شيء لا يؤبه إليه ثمّ يقول والله ما بقي لي قدرة على العبور فليعبر غيري فإذا عبر غيره مشى على الظرف فاختنق الريح ثمّ طارت الشمعة من فم القصبة فبلغت النار في تلك المشاقة مع القلفونية والكبريب فهربوا من ذلك وتكون القصبة التي للظرف طويلة مقدار خمسة أذرع ويكون تحت المشاقة حبّ قطن مسقى ببعض الأدهان ٧،١١

١ ش: منافيخ.

that it's all true. They dig some more, and more of the abovementioned clues appear. They see this as further proof, and the clues keep on appearing just the way the document says they should, until the metal sheet and the key appear, at which point the man insists that they prepare either the statue or the incense and postpones everything till later. If it's to be the statue, he keeps at them till the statue is made, then takes it and makes a run for his home country. If it's to be the incense, he takes some money to buy it and sets off on a journey to do so—but from where? From India, and from the interior at that! Wise up to these things!

Section Two of the Exposé of Their Tricks

Another example: They fake the clues as mentioned. Then, when the only thing left to do is actually enter the place, they make a booby trap to guard it. Some use the snake trap, some the trap that blinds, some the trap with figures, and there are others. When they reach the place, the man restrains his victims, citing the thing that is going to appear and bar their way and saying, "I'll show you the trap." 11.6

For the fire trap, they take a small waterskin, inflate it, and bury it in the floor of the entrance passage. They place some linen wadding soaked in resin and sulfur in front of the mouth of the skin, which is tightly sealed. 11.7

Exposé: The mouth of the skin has a fitted metal pipe of the type made for blacksmiths' bellows but stronger and narrower, and this is stopped up with a tiny bit of wax after the skin has been inflated. When the man goes in with a light, he keeps clear of the skin but deposits on the end of the wadding a quantity of burning wax, too small to be noticed, from the tip of his taper. Then he says, "To be honest, I'm too exhausted to go any farther. Someone else can do it." When that someone does, he steps on the skin, the air is compressed, the wax flies out of the end of the pipe, the fire on the wadding ignites with the resin and sulfur, and everyone runs away. The pipe attached to the skin is five cubits in length and there are cotton bolls soaked in oil underneath the wadding.

الباب الثالث في كشف أسرارهم في مهلك الحيّات

٨،١١ وذلك أنّهم يعملون حيّة قائمة إلى صدرها ويجعلون لها عينين مزبقة وقصبة الظرف المقدّم ذكره إلى جوفها وفي جوفها المشاقة والقلفونية والكبريت كما ذكرنا فإذا وطئ على الظرف خرجت النار من جوف فم تلك الحيّة وتبقى عينها تتوقّد فلا يجسر أحد يلبث قدّامها ولو ذهبت أكثر ذكر المهالك لطال الشرح في ذلك ولكن هذا المقدار كاف

الباب الرابع في كشف أسرارهم

٩،١١ منهم من يدّعي الوصول وذلك أنّه يدّعي الوصول إلى بعض المطالب المشهورة ويريد يربط الناس على ذلك فيتقرّب إليه الخلق فكلّ منهم يسأله فيقول أنا والله أحرص على الدخول إلّا أنّي أرصد وأخاف القتل فلعلّ ينقطع عنّي الطلب وأدخل ثمّ أخرج بما يكفينا مدّة طويلة فيربط على مثل ذلك ويبقى يعلّلهم ثمّ يصف لهم ما في المطلب من الأموال والجواهر فيشوقهم إلى مثل ذلك ولا يزال كذلك وهو يجلبهم كلّ واحد على قدره ويسرّ إلى واحد واحد أنّه ما يدخل إلّا هو وإيّاه وحدهم ولا يطّلع عليهم أحد فكلّ من سمع هذا وافقه الطمع وينفق عليه ويطلب منه على مقداره ولا يزال كذلك حتّى لا يبقى إلّا الدخول

١٠،١١ فإذا تواعدوا إلى يوم يؤلّف جماعة يخرجون بالعدّة ويكمنون له عند ذلك المكان فإذا خرجوا ووصلوا إليه ثاروا عليهم وأوّل ما يبدأوا[١] بالواصل ويقولوا كم نرصدك وما تقع لنا فإذا أبصروا ذلك أصحابه تهاربوا ولا يقف معه أحد ثمّ ينقطع عنهم أيّام ثمّ يحضر وهو يتشكّى ألم الضرب ثمّ يقول من هذا كنت أخاف وأتوقّف ولكن

١ ش: يبدوا.

Section Three: Exposé of Their Trick with the Booby-Trapped Snake

Exposé: They make an artificial snake that stands erect, give it eyes filled with mercury, and put the same pipe, attached to the abovementioned skin, in its belly. In its belly too are the wadding, the resin, and the sulfur, prepared as described above. When the man treads on the skin, fire erupts from deep inside the serpent's mouth and keeps on burning. No one dares confront it. If I were to go on listing all the different kinds of booby trap, the explanations would become tedious. This is enough. **11.8**

Section Four of the Exposé of Their Tricks

Some of them pretend to have "access." **11.9**

Exposé: These claim to have access to certain famous hoards of treasure and attempt to swindle people on that basis. People curry favor with such a person, each asking him questions, and he replies, "Honestly, I'm eager to go in but I'm waiting and watching, afraid of getting killed. Perhaps if people would just stop asking me, I'd be able to slip in and then get out with enough to keep us going for a long time." He convinces people of this point of view, keeps on making excuses to them, and then describes the money and gems that make up the hoard, exciting them with the thought. He keeps on at them, drawing each one in according to his means and confiding to each, separately, that he won't go in without him and that no one must observe them. Everyone who hears this is seized by greed and gives him money, the man demanding from each according to his means, and so it goes till the only thing left to do is actually go in.

Once they've agreed on a given day, he gathers together a group of men, who set off with their gear and lie in wait for him at the place he's been talking about. Then, when the man and his dupes set off and arrive, these men set upon them, threatening them—starting with the one who claims to have access—with violence and saying, "We've been watching and waiting so long for you to fall into our hands!" Seeing this, his companions flee: Not one stands by him. After this, he doesn't go near them for a few days, then turns up complaining of what a painful beating he took. "This," he says, "is exactly what I was afraid of and why I took no action! All the same, we have to do it. I just **11.10**

لا بدّ لنا إن شاء الله ما يخلو لنا الوقت وندخل دخلة وهي تكفانا فيزدادوا القوم رباط فافهم ذلك

الباب الخامس في كشف أسرارهم في الوصول

١١،١١ وذلك أنّهم إذا ادّعوا الوصول وعملوا ما تقدّم ذكره ولم يبق إلّا الدخول إلى المطلب يكون الواصل قد عمل مقدار عشرة أرطال سبائك رصاص أو نحاس ويغشّيها بورق الفضّة أو الذهب ثمّ يدفنها في ذلك المكان فإذا أرادوا الدخول وقد ترك الذي قد خرجوا معه يحشدون ثمّ يأخذ جراب ويتسرّب في سراب ذلك المكان ويغيب مقدار ثلاث أو أربع[1] ساعات ثمّ يخرج ذلك الجراب ملآن من تلك السبائك فيُطلعهم[2] على ذلك ويقول يا أصحابنا اطلعوا[3] بنا البحر نشرب ونغتسل ثمّ نتّفق ثانية ونحلف ثمّ نتّفق على مصلحة نعملها ولا يزال عليهم حتّى يجوز إلى البحر

١٢،١١ فإذا مشوا على ساحل البحر دار بينهم الكلام فينافرهم ثمّ يغلظ عليهم فلا بدّ منهم من يرادده فإذا راددوه غضب وقال الذنب ما هو لكم الذنب لمن صاحب مثلكم ولكن يا أخي بيننا شيء إلّا هذا المبلغ الذي قد حُصّل فأنا ما أريده ولا آخذ منه شيء ويأخذ الجراب ويحذف به إلى البحر ثمّ يولّي عنهم ويكون قد أسرّ إلى بعض من هو متميّز من الجماعة بأنّ هؤلاء قد بان لي منهم الغدر وأنا إن رأيتهم قد بان لي منهم شيء أو ما لا يجب أحرمتهم أن يأخذوا منه مثقال ذرّة فأنت أيش أبصرتني أعمل لا تتكلّم وأنا وأنت نكون كتف واحد ونعيش أنا وأنت فإن أصابني شيء فهو لك ولهم مثل ذلك فنون لا يعلمها إلّا هم ولا يدركها غيرهم وهم أشدّ الطوائف مكر ونفاق فافهم ما أشرت إليك

---

١ ش: ثلاثة أذرع أو. ٢ ش: فيطلقهم. ٣ ش: اطلبوا.

hope we don't run out of time. Let's get in and out fast. It'll be enough." This makes people trust him even more. Wise up to these things!

Section Five of the Exposé of Their Tricks, on the Theme of "Access"[137]

Exposé: When they've made their claim to access and done all the things mentioned above and the only thing left to do is enter the place where the treasure hoard is, the "initiate" makes ten pounds of lead or copper ingots and wraps them in silver or gold leaf. He buries these in the place in question and when they are ready to go in (and this time he sets out with a big mob), he takes a bag and slips away into the underground tunnels of the place, disappearing for three or four hours, then reemerges, the bag filled with the aforementioned ingots. He shows these to them and says, "Friends! Let's be off to the sea, where we can drink and bathe and afterward make a second agreement, swear to it, and agree to some mutually beneficial deal." He keeps on at them like this till he makes it to the sea. **11.11**

While they are walking beside the sea, they start quarreling. He keeps his distance from them, then speaks to them harshly. Naturally, some of them have to answer back, and when they do he loses his temper and says, "It's not you that are at fault. The one at fault is the person who keeps company with people like you! Is there anything keeping us together other than this sum of money that has been collected? I don't want it and won't take a penny of it," and he takes the bag and throws it into the sea. Then he turns his back on them. Earlier, he will have confided in somebody from the group who stands out and told him, "I can see that the others intend to betray me. If I notice they're about to do me harm or anything unpleasant, I shall prevent them from taking so much as a mithkal's weight of corn from the treasure. Whatever you see me do, say nothing. You and I have to stand shoulder to shoulder if we're to come out of this alive. If anything happens to me, the treasure is yours."[138] They have techniques that only they know and no one else can fathom. They are the most cunning and hypocritical of all these tribes of charlatans. Wise up to what I have shown you! **11.12**

الفصل الثاني عشر

تسعة أبواب

في كشف أسرار المنجّمون أرباب الطريق

١،١٢ اعلم أنّ هذه الطائفة يسمّون الغرباء ولهم أحوال لا يقطع عليها قياس ولهم مَشاتين لا تحدّ ولا توصف فمنهم الذين يبلّزون السَرّماط ولهم إشعار بالسين ودُوبَيْتيّ وغيره ويجيء في موضعه ولهم أصحاب المواليد والبلهان ومنهم أصحاب الفألات والمقالب ومنهم أصحاب الحديدة[1] ومنهم أصحاب القُرَع أصنافها فمنها قرعة الفصّ المنسوبة إلى جعفر الصادق رضي الله عنه ومنها قرعة الطيور ومنها قرعة المدن ومن ذلك قرعة الأطعمة ومنها قرعة الدوائر ومنها قرعة المنازل ومنها قرعة الأسماء ومنها قرعة الكواكب اليمانيّة وقرع كثيرة لم نذكرها خوف الإطالة ومنهم أصحاب فألات الورق الذي يغمسونها في الماء فتطلع مكتوبة ومنهم أصحاب الورق الذي يحمّونها فتظهر مكتوبة بالبشارة والحذر واعلم أنّ أصحاب هذه الأوراق هم أذلّ المنجّمين وكذلك منجّمين الساعات فإنّ كلّ نفر من هؤلاء لهم مُشتان وسرّ وسوف أذكر من ذلك أنواع مختلفة مختصرة موجزة إن شاء الله

١ ش: الجريدة.

Chapter Twelve, in Nine Sections:

Exposé of the Tricks of Astrologers Who Ply Their Trade on the Highway[139]

Charlatans of this tribe are called "wonder-workers."[140] They have manifestations beyond measure and performance props too plentiful to count or calculate. Some peddle amulets and have a way of communicating using *Sīn*,[141] or by means of verse or by other systems that will be described in their proper place. Other groups are known as "birth-horoscopes-and-*Balhān* men,"[142] others as "prognostications-and-flip-box men," others as "iron men," and yet others as "fortune-casting men," the different kinds of castings being "the casting of the ring stone" (whose origin goes back to Jaʿfar al-Ṣādiq, God be pleased with him), "the casting of the birds," and the "casting of the cities," the latter being subdivided into "the casting of the foods," "the casting of the circles," "the casting of the houses," "the casting of the names," "the casting of the southern constellations," and many other castings we won't list for fear of boring you. Another group is the "paper-prognostications men," who dip papers in water, which then come out with writing on them, as well as the "paper men" who heat papers, which come out with either good tidings or warnings written on them. These paper men are the lowest class of astrologers, along with the "astrologers of the hours."[143] Every troop of these has its own prop and its own trick, and I shall now, God willing, list a variety of such types, summarized and abridged.[144] 12.1

الباب الأوّل في كشف أسرار الذين يتكلّمون على السرماط

وذلك أنّ لهم مقاريض تسمّى الطروس وهي القوالب فيطبع بها كلّ يوم ما شاء الله ٢،١٢
من السراميط ثمّ يحشونها بالزعفران والزنجار والزنجفر ثمّ يكون نوعين منها صغار ويسمّونها الشرائح ومنها كبار يسمّونها الهياكل فمنهم من يتنبّل بالتغميضة ومنهم من يتنبّل بالمقلب ومنهم من يتنبّل بالمقلمة الذي يخرج منها الأقلام ومنها من يتنبّل بالإبرة ومنهم من يخرج الضمائر إذا كان معه صبيّ فيقول كلّ من كان في قلبه ضمير يقوله في أذني وهذا الصبيّ في آخر الحلقة وهو مغمّض العينين وهو يبيّن لكم جميع ما تضمروا عليه فإذا جاء واحد إلى عند الحكيم قال ضمرت على كذا وكذا فينشد له قصيدة يخرج منها كلّ ما يُسأل عنه وأنا أبيّن جميع ذلك إن شاء الله

باب شرح كشف أسرار أصحاب التغميضة وما يفعلون من التغميضة فإنّها هذيان ويربطون بها الأخشان

وهو أن يأخذ الملح ويغمّض عينيه ويجعل الملح عليها ثمّ يعصّب عينيه بعصائب عراض ٣،١٢
ثمّ يقعد رأسه فينزل الملح أخلى له موضع الضوء فيستمدّ الضوء من جانبي أنفه نظرًا جيّدًا ثمّ يأخذ الدُخن والحبّة السوداء والسمسم وما اتّفق من البزور ثمّ يجعل الجميع على ظهر كتاب مجلّد ويأخذ السكّين ثمّ يفرّق كلّ جنس من هذه الأجناس وحده ثمّ واحد يكتب ضمائر الناس في أوراق فإنّه يدفعها إليه ثمّ يعرضها قدّامه فيقرأها ويطويها ثمّ ينادي باسم صاحبها يا فلان طلع اسمك واسم أمّك وما ضمرت عليه اقعد حتّى أبيّن لك وأبشّرك ببشارة وأحذّرك من هذا الحذر فقد ظهر لك ثمّ يعطف على الآخر بمثل ذلك حتّى يأتي على الجميع ثمّ يحلّ العصائب عن عينيه ويشرع في الهادور ولا يزال كذلك حتّى يخرج الشرائح وهي خرقة حرير أسود فيمسك طرف

Section One: Exposé of the Tricks of Those Who Say Spells over Amulets

Exposé: They have cut-out blocks called *ṭurūs*.[145] These are molds with which 12.2
they stamp out a staggering number of amulets each day, which they then stuff with saffron, blue vitriol, and cinnabar. There are two kinds of amulet—the smaller, which they call "slices," and the larger, which they call "temples."[146] Some of these people are skilled at the blindfolding game, others with the paper tetrahedron, others with the penholder that produces pens, and others with the needle. Some do mind reading: If the man has a boy with him, he says, "Anyone who is thinking privately about something should whisper it into my ear and, at the end of the session, this boy will reveal everything you're thinking about, with his eyes blindfolded." So, when someone comes up to the wise man, he says, "I'm thinking of such and such a thing," and the man produces a poem from which the boy can deduce the answer to whatever he's asked. I shall explain the whole thing below, God willing.

An Explanatory Section Consisting of an Exposé of the Tricks of the Blindfold-Men and of Their Blindfold Game (a Form of Nonsense with Which They Dupe the Marks)

Example: First, the man takes salt, closes his eyes, and puts the salt on them, 12.3
then swathes his eyes with broad bandages, and finally sits up, so that the salt falls off, leaving a place for the light to come in from either side of his nose and allowing him a good view. Next he takes millet, black seed, sesame, and any other seeds that may be to hand, places them all on the cover of a bound book, and takes a knife, with which he separates the different kinds of seed into piles.[147] Then someone writes down what everyone is thinking on pieces of paper and gives them to him, and he spreads them out in front of him, reads them, and folds them up. Then he calls out, using the name of the owner of one of the pieces of paper, "So-and-so! Your name, your mother's name,[148] and the thing you were thinking of have come up. Stay where you are while I explain everything to you, give you some good news, and warn you about the bad news, whose time has come." Then he turns to the next and tells him something similar, and keeps this up till he gets to the last of them. Finally, he

الخرقة ويقول طال والله ما بلبلتها الرياح على الكعبة ثمّ يتكلّم بالهادور فيبلّز منها ما اتّفق

٤،١٢ فيقول من أعطاني فيقول واحد أنا فيقول أيش اسمك فيكتب اسمه على الشريحة يفعل ذلك بالجميع ثمّ يقول يا أصحابنا لو اتّكلت على هذا كنت والله أشحت الخبز وإنّما اتّكالي على الله وعلى معقود أحلّه وعلى أن أفرق بين اثنين في الحرام وأجمع بين اثنين في الحلال أو على هيكل سلطانيّ جامع آخذ فيه الخلعة والمائة درهم والخمسين والأقلّ والأكثر وقد أرسل إليّ الأمير فلان الدين وقال أريد أن تكتب لي هيكل جامع الأشياء قلت السمع والطاعة أرصد لمولانا طالع سعيد وأكتب له في ذلك الطالع فمدّ يده وأعطاني شيء أنفق فيه مدّة طويلة ثمّ أعطاني المسك والعود والعنبر ثمّ عدت إلى منزلي فأخذت الأصطرلاب بيميني ووقفت على قدميّ ثمّ أخذت طالع سعيد جعلت المشتري في الطالع والقمر في السابع ثمّ أسقطت النحسين عن الطالع ثمّ بدأت على اسم الله وأطلقت البخور وكتبت في ذلك الوقت السعيد والطالع الحميد عشر هياكل جامعة أسرار الكتب المنزّلة فلمّا فرغت من كتابتها أخذت منها خمسة وحملتها إليه فلمّا وقف عليها قال لي زمان أطلب مثل هذه الهياكل حتّى وقعت ثمّ دفع لي شيء آخر فخرجت من عنده وقد قال لي بعض أصحابه يا حكيم أريد منك لي ولخشداشي هيكلين من هذه الهياكل فقلت السمع والطاعة قد تبقى عندي منها اثنين أحملها إلى خدمتكم فشال أعطاني شيء له قيمة وعندي منها ثلاثة ثمّ مدّ يده إلى خريطة فيخرج منها خرقة سوداء ثمّ يقول ولو لم يكن فيها إلّا بركة هذه الخرقة الذي طال ما حرّكتها الرياح على قبر رسول الله صلّى الله عليه وسلّم

٥،١٢ ثمّ يهدر عليها فيما تتضمّن من المنافع ثمّ يقول إذا كانت هذه منافعها وقد كتبت في ذلك الوقت وذلك الطالع السعيد كم استأهل هديّة كلّ هيكل منها استأهل

unties the bandages over his eyes and starts in on his patter, which he keeps up till he brings out the "slices," which consist of pieces of black silk cloth. Taking one by its corner, he says, "For how many a month, dear God, has this been worried by the winds that buffet the Kaaba?"[149] Then he patters on some more and peddles as many as he wants.

Next, he says, "Who gave me something?" and someone says, "I did!" 12.4
"What's your name?" he says, and writes the name on the "slice." He does this for all of them. Then he says, "Dear friends, if I were to rely on this to make my living I'd be begging for my bread but I've put my trust in God and a puzzle I'll solve and in separating two that practice abomination and bringing two together in holiness or in a universal sultanic Great Amulet which will earn me a robe of honor plus one hundred and fifty silver pieces or more or less so Emir Whatsit-of-Religion[150] summoned me and he said I want you to write me a Great Amulet that does everything and I said I hear and obey I'll keep my eye out for an auspicious ascendant for our lord and master and write the amulet at that very ascendant then he extended his hand and gave me enough to live on for a long time after which he gave me musk agarwood and ambergris and I went back to my house and took the astrolabe in my right hand and stood on both feet and found an auspicious ascendant that placed Jupiter in the first house and the moon in the seventh I canceled out the two unlucky planets[151] from the ascendant set to with an In the Name of God let the incense fly and wrote at that happy time and under that commendable ascendant ten Great Amulets that brought together the secrets of all the divinely inspired scriptures and when I was done writing them I took five of them and bore them to him and when he'd studied them he told me Long have I asked for Great Amulets such as these and now I have them in my hand and he gave me a further sum and I left his presence but not before one of his companions said to me Sage I want you to make me and my brother officer two of these Great Amulets and I said to him I hear and obey I have two left that I'll bring to serve you and before he made off he gave me something of value and I have three left"—here he reaches his hand into his sack and pulls out a piece of black cloth—"and even if the value of these amulets was only the blessing attached to this piece of cloth—so long worried by the winds that buffet the tomb of the Prophet God bless him and keep him!—they'd still be worth it!"[152]

Then he does his patter over the three amulets, using words referring to 12.5
various useful properties, saying, "If these are their properties and they were

دينار والله لو أعطيتني ملك الأرض كانت هذه أفضل ولكن كم قلت دينار طال والله ما أخذت فيها الخمسة والعشرة ولكن على قدر الكساء مددت رجلي كم ديناري خمسة دراهم أخلّي منها درهم لله ودرهم لمحمّد بن عبد الله كم يبقى أخلّي منها درهم نحاس وطلاس ورصاص يحمى في عين ذاك الشكّاك الأفّاك الذي لا يؤمن بالله ولا بكتاب الله وحاشا هذه الجماعة أن يكون هذا بينهم كم يبقى درهمين أخلّي منها نصف لهذه الجماعة يبقى منها درهم ونصف يا سماء اشهدي ويا أرض اعهدي ويا ملئكة ربّي بلّغي أنّي ما بخلت بها وقد جعلت الهديّة درهم واحد ونصف والدرهم حقّها لا والله اسم الله لا يُباع ولا يُشترى بل الدرهم حقّ هذه الخزانة

ثمّ يخرج غلاف ويتكلّم عليه ويقول ما معك درهم أهدي لي مئزر أصلّي عليه منديل أمسح به وجهي سكّين أبري بها قلم مقصّ أقصّ به ورقة ما معك تراب من تحت قدمك اجعله على رأسي وأملّكك ختمة جامعة ثمّ يهدر ويقول ويقرأ ما في الهيكل فإن مشت تلك الثلاثة أخرج ثنتين أخر وقال هذه الذي كنت أوعدت بها ذلك الطواشي وما كانت من رزقه فسبحان مقسّم الأرزاق من يقول اكتبها على اسمي ويهدر عليها إلى أن يبلّزها وهذه طريقة الذين يتكلّمون على السرماط وهادورهم ٦،١٢

الباب الثاني في كشف أسرارهم

فمن ذلك أصحاب المقلمة الذي تصدر منها الأقلام وهذه المقلمة لا يمكن أن تكون إلّا جلدة مبسوطة وتكون لها طبلة في نصفها داخل وهي مُحكَّمة الأقلام ولها عروة ورؤوس الأقلام منزّلة فيها وفيها خيط وفي طرف الخيط لوح رصاص وهو في الطبلة من ناحية والأقلام في الناحية الأخرى وإذا عصر المقلمة بيده اتّسع ذلك ٧،١٢

written out at such a time and under such an auspicious ascendant how much would each of these Great Amulets be worth by way of a gift it would be worth a gold piece I swear if you were to grant me kingship over the earth this would still be better but what am I saying one gold piece for ages I've been getting five and ten but I cut my coat to fit my cloth however many gold pieces I may have I set aside a silver piece out of every five for God and a silver piece for Muḥammad ibn ʿAbd Allāh[153] but still many are left over I set aside a silver piece worth of copper a silver piece worth of paper and a silver piece worth of lead to burn in the eye of every doubter and lie-spouter who doesn't believe in God or God's Book God forbid there should be any such among present company time and time again there's a couple of silver pieces left over I set half a silver piece aside for you guys what's left one and a half silver pieces Heavens bear witness Earth take note angels of My Lord pass on the message that I have never been miserly with them and I've set the gift at a silver piece and a half but is a silver piece its proper price no by God such things cannot be bought or sold a silver piece is the price of the box!"

Then he pulls out a receptacle, says a spell over it, and says, "If you don't have a silver piece give me a garment to pray on a hankie to wipe my face a knife to sharpen a pen scissors to cut paper with take the dust that's beneath your feet and put it on my head and I'll make you the owner of a Universal Seal." Then he rattles on some more, speaking and reading what's in the Great Amulet: "And if these three take off I'll produce two more" and "This is the one that I promised to that eunuch but it wasn't destined for his livelihood glory be to Him who apportions men's livelihoods who's going to tell me to write it in his name?" and he keeps reciting his patter over it till he can flog it. This is the practice of those who say spells over amulets and the patter they use. 12.6

Section Two of the Exposé of Their Tricks

Another example: The penholder men, whose penholders produce pens. The holder in question has to consist of a single continuous piece of leather, with an insert in the middle on the inside, which is the restrainer for the pens and has a slit beneath which sit the tops of the pens. A thread is attached to the restrainer, with a lead plate at the end of the thread, this being on one side of the insert, while the pens are on the other. When the man squeezes the 12.7

المكان على اللوح الرصاص فينزل إلى أسفل المقلمة وتصعد الأقلام إلى رأس المقلمة فيربط الأخشاب

الباب الثالث في كشف أسرار الذين يتنبّلون بالمقلب

٨،١٢ وذلك أنّهم يأخذون ورقة يطوونها مثلّثة الجوانب والأسفل ثمّ يقطعون ورقة ثانية على مثال الأوّل لا زائد ولا ناقص ثمّ يلصقونها في أسفلها في المثلّث الأوسط واحدة على واحدة لصاق محكم بحيث أنّها لا تبان فإنّها تبقى لها بيتين فيأخذ أوراق صغار تسع كلّ ورقة سطرين وتكون على قدر البيت الواحد وعددها سبعة أوراق فيكتب بعضها بمداد وبعضها بزعفران ثمّ يجعلها في البيت الواحد ثمّ يأخذ أوراق بياض على قدرها فيجعلها في البيت الآخر من المقلب فإذا ألّف الهنكامة وهي الحلقة قال كلّ من كان في قلبه ضمير عن بيع أو شرى أو أخذ أو عطاء يتقدّم أفسّر له اليوم سبع ضمائر لا فضّة ولا ذهب للثواب

٩،١٢ ثمّ يفتح البيت الذي فيه أوراق البياض من المقلب ويقول لواحد من الجماعة اضمر أيش ما كان في قلبك على هذه الورقة فيأخذها ويتكلّم عليها ثمّ يردّها إليه فيقول أيش اسمك فيقول فلان فيكتب على رأس الورقة حرف من حروف اسم صاحبها وهو آخر حرف من اسمه فيستدلّ به يفعل ذلك بالسبعة أوراق ثمّ يردّها في مكانها ثمّ يشغل الناس ويحدّثهم والمقلب في يده قدّام الجماعة ثمّ يفتح المقلب فتطلع تلك الأوراق مكتوبة بعضها بالمداد وبعضها بالزعفران فيطلع ورقة في يده ويقول يا فلان هذه ورقتك وقد طلع اسمك وضميرك اقعد حتّى أقول جميع ما طُلب لك ثمّ يفعل

penholder, this space opens out under the lead plate, which slips down to the bottom of the penholder while the pens themselves rise to its top. The marks are fooled.

Section Three: Exposé of the Tricks of Those Who Are Skilled with the Flip Box[154]

Exposé: They take a piece of paper and fold it into a tetrahedron. Then they cut out a second piece of paper of the same size as the first, neither larger nor smaller. They glue this tightly and precisely onto the bottom of the central triangle[155] in such a way that the division doesn't show; the flip box now has two chambers. The man now takes small pieces of paper, each large enough to hold two lines of writing and of a size to fit inside a single chamber. There are seven of these pieces of paper. He writes in ink on some of them and in saffron on the others, then puts all of them into one of the chambers. Next, he takes blank pieces of paper of the same size and puts them into the flip box's other chamber. When he's gathered his *hankāmah*—his circle of spectators[156]—around him, he says, "Let anyone who's worrying over some plan he has in mind concerning buying or selling, or trade, or commerce, come forward and I'll lay out for you today seven possible outcomes—no silver or gold required, just for the heavenly reward!" 12.8

Now he opens the chamber of the flip box holding the blank pieces of paper and says to someone in the crowd, "Write down on this piece of paper whatever it is you're worrying about without anyone seeing." Then he takes it from the man, says a spell over it, and gives it back to him. Next, he says to him, "What's your name?" and the other says, "So-and-so," so he writes one of the letters (it has to be the last) of the name of the person to whom the paper belongs at the top of the paper and uses this as a guide. He does this with all seven pieces of paper, then puts them back where they were. Next, he distracts everyone by talking to them, holding the flip box in his hand. Then he opens the flip box and out come the pieces of paper that are written on, in some cases with ink and in others with saffron. He takes one in his hand and says, "So-and-so, this is your paper—your name and what you're worried about have come up. Sit down so I can tell you what you have to do." Then he does the same with the next person and so on for all seven pieces of paper. Next, he spouts some 12.9

بالآخر مثله كذلك السبعة ثمّ بعد ذلك يطلق الهادور ويتكلّم على السرماط بما سبق في الباب الأوّل فيبلّز الشرائح ثمّ يرجع إلى الهيكل فيتكلّم عليه ويبلّزه

الباب الرابع في كشف أسرار الذين يخرجون الضمائر بالصبيّ

وذلك أنّ لهم خمس أبيات شعر يخرج بها الحروف ويجمعها فيخرج الضمير وذلك أنّه ١٠،١٢
يعصّب عيني الصبيّ ثمّ يجعله في آخر الحلقة وظهره إليه ثمّ يقول من كان له ضمير يتقدّم فيقول اسمه واسم أمّه وضميره في أذني حتّى يبيّنه له هذا الصبيّ فإذا قال ضميره للمعلّم أنشد الشعر إلى البيت الذي فيه أوّل حرف من اسمه فيقول للصبيّ اجعل بالك فيأخذ الحرف ثمّ إلى البيت الذي فيه الحرف الثاني فيقول ما قلت لك اليوم أغلبك فيقول الصبيّ يا معلّم ظهر اسمه واسم أمّه وضميره ويقول بيّن فيقول اسمه فلان وأمّه فلانة وقد ظهر ضميره ويصبر حتّى أبيّن له ضميره ثمّ يفعل بالجماعة مثل ذلك فيتعجّب الناس من ذلك ويبلّز السرماط

وهذه جملة الأبيات الذي تخرج الضمائر والأسماء وغيرها يقول شعر [هزج] ١١،١٢

أَطَاعَ ٱلدَّهْرُ فِي ٱلْجَدِّ ٱلسَّنِيِّ صَفَا جَدُّ ٱلْفَتَى جَدُّ عَلِيِّ
لِمَنْصُورٍ شَذِيهُ خَنْدَرِيسٌ مُلَازِمُهُ لَمَلِكٌ لُؤْلُؤِيِّ
فَوَجْهٌ صَفْحُهُ... شَفَقًا جَلَاهُ حَبِيبٌ عَزِيزٌ سَحْسَحٍ غَوِيِّ
قَوِيٌّ لَا يُغَفِّلُ عَنْ ضَعِيفٍ كَظِيمٌ غَيْظُهُ عَنَفٌ وَطِيِّ[1]

١ في الأصل: اطاع الدهر في الجد السنى صفى حدا فى حد على لمنصور شدبه خندريس ملازمه لملك لولوى فوحه (. . . .) نفحه سععا حلاه حبيب عرز سحسح غوى قوى لا نغفل عى ضعيف كظيم غيظه عنف وطى.

patter and says a spell over the "slice."[157] He peddles the slices and then he goes back to the Greater Amulet and flogs that.

Section Four: Exposé of the Tricks of Those Who Are Skilled at Mind Reading Using a Boy

Example: They have five lines of verse[158] from which they extract and string together letters. Exposé: They blindfold the boy and place him at the end of the ring of onlookers, with his back to the charlatan. The charlatan then says, "If anyone is thinking of something, he can come forward and whisper his name, the name of his mother, and what he's thinking about in my ear, and this boy will state them clearly." When the mark has told the boss what he's thinking about, the latter recites the verses up to the word[159] containing the first letter of the mark's name and says, "Concentrate!" so the boy gets that letter. Then he continues up to the word containing the second letter and says, "Didn't I tell you I'd get the better of you today?"[160] to which the boy replies, "Boss, I've got his name, his mother's name, and what he's thinking of," so the other says, "Out with them!" and the boy says, "His name is so-and-so, his mother's is so-and-so, and I've got what he's thinking about too. If he can just hold on, I'll tell him what it is." Then the man does the same with the rest of the crowd and everyone is amazed and he flogs the amulet. **12.10**

The following is the full set of lines used to deduce what people are thinking about as well as their names and other things: **12.11**

aṭāʿa l-dahru fī l-jaddi l-saniyyī
ṣafā jaddu l-fatā jaddun ʿaliyyī
li-manṣūrin shadhīhū khandarīsun,
mulāzimuh la-malikun luʾluʾiyyī
fa-wajhun ṣafḥuhu . . . shafaqā jalāhu
ḥabīb ʿazīz saḥsahin ghawiyyī
qawiyyun lā yughaffil ʿan ḍaʿīfin
kaẓīmun ghayẓuhu ʿanfun waṭiyyī[161]

فهذه الخمسة أبيات يخرج بها الأسماء والضمائر وكلّ ما أراد شرح العمل بها

١٢،١٢ وذلك أنّهم قسموا حروف أ ب ت ث على هذه الخمسة أبيات الأوّل أحد والثاني اثنين والثالث أربعة والرابع سبعة والخامس خمسة عشر ويجمعون منها الحروف ولهم قصيدة أخرى تخرج بها الحروف والضمائر وهذه أوّلها [طويل]

خَلِيلَيَّ هَلْ هَـٰذَا ٱلْغَـزَالُ تَظُنُّهُ يُزِيلُ شَقَائِي إِنْ قَضَى ٱللهُ لِي نَجَا

الباب الخامس في كشف أسرار الذين يتنبّلون بالأوراق الذي يغمسونها في الماء فتطلع مكتوبة

١٣،١٢ اعلم أنّ هذه الأوراق أعرف منها سبعين نوعًا بل نذكر بعضها فمن ذلك أن يكتب الأوراق بماء الزاج ويجعل في الكوز ماء عفص فإذا غمس الورق فيها اسودّ موضع الزاج ومنهم من يكتب بماء العفص ويجعل في الكوز ماء الزاج ومنهم من يكتب بماء النشادر ويغطس في الخلّ فافهم ذلك

الباب السادس في كشف أسرار الذين يتنبّلون بالأوراق الذي يجعلونها على النار فتظهر الكتابة فيها

١٤،١٢ وذلك أنّي أعرف منه تسعة أنواع فنذكر البعض فمن ذلك أنّهم يكتبون بماء البصل فإذا كان على النار ظهرت الكتابة وهذه الطريقة تحبّ نار قويّة فإذا كان مع ماء البصل نشادر ظهرت الكتابة سوداء فإذا كان ماء البصل وحده ظهرت الكتابة حمراء وإذا كان معه مرارة كبش ظهرت الكتابة صفراء ومنهم من يكتب باللبن الحليب ويقدّمه إلى النار فتظهر الكتابة حمراء ومنهم من يدفع لكلّ واحد من الجماعة ورقة مكتوبة

Using the five lines, the charlatan can deduce names, things people are thinking about, and anything else he needs in order to get the answer to whatever stunt it is he's pulling.

Exposé:[162] They have divided the letters *ʾ*, *b*, *t*, *th*, and so on among these five lines as follows—first line one letter, second line two, third line four, fourth line seven, fifth line fifteen—and from these they string the letters together.[163] They also have another poem they use to deduce letters and read minds, the first line of which is: 12.12

khalīlayya hal hādhā l-ghazālu taẓunnuhu
yuzīlu shaqāʾī ʾin qaḍā llāhu lī najā[164]

Section Five: Exposé of the Tricks of Those Skilled in the Use of Papers That They Dip in Water and That Come out with Writing on Them

For your information, I am familiar with seventy ways of using these papers, of which I'll mention just a couple. 12.13

Example: One way is to write on the papers with a solution of vitriol and put oak gall water in the jug. When the paper is dipped in this, where the vitriol is turns black. Some of them write with oak gall water and put vitriol water in the jug and some write with liquid ammonia and dip the paper in vinegar. Wise up to these things!

Section Six: Exposé of the Tricks of Those Who Are Skilled in the Use of Papers That They Hold over Fire, Causing the Writing to Appear on Them

Exposé: I know nine ways, so let me mention just a few. They write with onion juice. When this is held over fire, the writing appears (this method prefers a hot fire). If ammonia is used along with the onion juice, the writing comes out black, and if it's just onion juice the writing comes out red. If ram's bile is used with it, the writing comes out yellow. Some write with milk and then hold it close to the fire, and then the writing comes out red. Some charlatans give everyone in the crowd a piece of paper written on in milk. The charlatan 12.14

باللبن فيقول اضمر على هذه الورقة ويجمع الأوراق ويخطّ خطّة في الشمس الحارّة وتكون الأوراق مفرقة بعضها من بعض ويوري أنّه يعزّم عليها ويحرّك شفتيه ثمّ يقول أيّها الخدّام الصالحين بحقّ ما كتبت به عليكم اكتبوا أسماء هؤلاء وأسماء أمّهاتهم فإنّ هذه الأوراق إذا حميت ظهرت فيها الكتابة فيتنبّل كيف شاء ويربط كيف أراد فافهم ذلك

الباب السابع في كشف أسرار الذين يكتبون بالحديدة

وذلك أن يكون لهم مُهابِرين قيام على رؤوسهم فإذا جاء الخشن يقعد المهابر ويحطّ إصبعه على الحديدة ثمّ يرمي له فرد أعني درهم أو شطر أعني نصف ويقول أخرج لي ضميري فيقول أريد مع ذلك ضمير آخر حتّى نتفرّج عليه فيقعد الخشني ويضع يده على الحديدة فيضمر ويقول للمهابر خذه واخرج إلى هناك واسمع ضميره ويسمع ضميرك حتّى لا ينكر أحد فيأخذه ويخرج عنه فيقول المهابر أنا ضمرت كذا وكذا وأنت عن أيش ضمرت فيقول عن كذا وكذا فيموس دانكه ثمّ يعودوا إليه فيقول للخشن سمعت ضميره فيقول نعم فيقول اقعدوا فإذا قعدوا قدّم الحديدة ويقول اضمروا فيضمر فيقول للخشن أخرج كرامتي فإن طلع ضميرك جيّد أخذت منك وإن طلع رديّ ما آخذ منك شيء ١٥،١٢

فيخرج له ما تيسّر فيقول للمهابر أنت ضمرت كذا وكذا ثمّ يلتفت إلى الخشن فيقول هكذا ضمر[١] فيقول نعم هذا الضمير فيقول إن قربت هذا الأمر فإن عاقبته غير صالحة وهذا يدلّ على الشرّ والنكد والضرب والحبس فاترك هذا وخذ فضّتك فهي عليّ حرام فيقول خذها فيأبى ثمّ يقول أنت ضمرت كذا وكذا ويكون المهابر قد بلّغ له بالضمير فإذا قال نعم قال طيّب قلبي حتّى أبيّن لك جميع ما يطلع فإنّ هذا الضمير فيه إشارة ١٦،١٢

١ ش: ضمرت.

says, "Think of something!" and then collects the pieces of paper, draws a line on the ground under the hot sun, having first spread out the papers so they aren't touching one another, and makes a display of reciting spells over them, moving his lips. Then he says, "O Righteous Servitors, by the power of what I have written to bind you, write the names of these people and the names of their mothers!" and, when they are heated, the writing appears on these pieces of paper. In this way, he works his tricks as he wishes and dupes people as he wants. Wise up to these things!

Section Seven: Exposé of the Tricks of Those Who "Write with the Iron"

Exposé: They have shills who stand nearby. When a mark comes along, the **12.15**
shill sits down and places a finger on the iron. Then he throws the charlatan a "single," meaning a silver piece, or a "semi," meaning half a silver piece, and says, "Tell me what I'm thinking about," so the charlatan says, "To divine, I need something else that someone's thinking about," so the mark sits down and places his hand on the iron and thinks of something. The charlatan tells the shill, "Take him over there and get him to tell you what he's thinking about, and you tell him what you're thinking about, so that no one can deny the truth when I say it." So the shill takes him away from the charlatan and says, "I was thinking of such and such. What were you thinking of?" and the other says, "Such and such." This way he finds out what's on his mind. Then they go back to the charlatan, who says to the mark, "Did he tell you what he's thinking of?" and he says, "Yes," so he says, "Sit down!" and when they've sat down, he pushes the iron forward and says, "Concentrate on what it is you're thinking about!" and each does so. Then he says to the mark, "Show me what you're going to tip me. If what you're thinking about comes out right, I'll take it, but if it comes out wrong, I won't take a penny from you."

So the mark shows him some money. The charlatan says to the shill, "You **12.16**
were thinking about such and such," then turns to the mark and says, "Is that what he was thinking of?" and the mark says, "Right! That's what he was thinking of." The charlatan then says to the shill, "If you do anything like what you were thinking of, the outcome will not be good; it points to evil, misfortune, beating, and imprisonment, so have nothing to do with it and take back your

عظيمة وقال النبيّ صلّى الله عليه وسلّم أكرموهم وسائلوهم فيطلب[١] منه شيء آخر ويقول أقدم على هذا الضمير فإن لك فيه راحة صالحة جيّدة وأمور راجحة وأحوالك مستقيمة وتجارتك رابحة فابشر بما بشّر به فألك ثمّ يهدر عليه بما وافق ذلك الضمير ثمّ يقول قم على فألك

الباب الثامن في كشف أسرار الذين يكسبون بالبلهان ويتكلّمون على المسئلة الاثنا عشريّة

وذلك أنّهم يعملون كتابًا كبيرًا قطع البغداديّ ثمّ يصوّره ويذهّبه ويجعلون في أوّله صفات الأقاليم وعجائبها وما فيها ثمّ يجعلون فيه بعد ذلك صور الجنّ وملوكهم وأعوانهم وخواتمهم وحرابهم ثمّ بعد ذلك يعملون فصول الزمان وصور الكواكب ثمّ يعملون المنازل القمريّة وجميع ذلك مصوّر مذهّب ثمّ بعد ذلك يصوّرون البروج الاثنا عشر كلّ برج منها بثلاث وجوه وخمس حدود وتسع نُوبَهْرات وثلاث مثلّثات وثلاثين درجة واثنا عشر حالة جميع ذلك مذهّب مليح ثمّ يبسط البساط ويجعل الكتاب على كرسيّ ويجعل الكرسيّ قدّامه ١٧،١٢

ثمّ يفتح ورقة ورقة ويقول هذه صفة الإقليم الفلانيّ وهذه بلاده وهذه عجائبها ويتكلّم عليها ثمّ يفتح ورقة أخرى ويقول هذه أعجب وأغرب هذه صفة الإقليم الفلانيّ وعجائبها وغرائبها فيتكلّم عليها ولا يزال كذلك حتّى يؤلّفها[٢] فإذا ألّفها وهي الهنكامة ١٨،١٢

١ ش: فيعبوا. ٢ ش: يلقّها.

silver. I cannot take it in good conscience." "You take it!" the shill says, but the man refuses. Then the charlatan says to the mark, "You were thinking of such and such" (the shill having previously told him what it is). When he says, "That's right!" the charlatan, soliciting more money from him, says, "Give me a sweetener, and I'll tell you everything that's going to happen. What you were thinking of points to great matters. The Prophet, God bless him and grant him peace, has said, 'Honor them and question them.'"[165] Then he says, "Go for what you have in mind—you will feel so blessed; plus, it's excellent business. Things will go to plan and your commercial ventures will turn a profit. Now, a gift, for the gifts you've been promised!" Then he rattles off a patter appropriate to whatever it is the mark was thinking of and says, "Off with you now! Go live your dream!"

Section Eight: Exposé of the Tricks of Those Who Use the *Balhān* to Make Predictions and Who Speak of "the Dodecatemorian Question"[166]

Exposé: They make a large Baghdad-cut book. This they have illustrated and illuminated in gold. At the beginning, they put descriptions of the various climes and their wonders and what they contain; next, pictures of jinn and their kings, assistants, signet rings, and lances; next, they make a section on the seasons and the planets; then they put in the mansions of the moon. All of this is illuminated in gold. After this, they draw pictures of the twelve houses of the zodiac, each house having three decanal faces, five decanal hours, nine ninth-parts, three triangles, thirty degrees, and twelve aspects, all illuminated in gold and looking very nice. The man rolls out his rug, puts the book on a bookstand, and places the bookstand in front of him. **12.17**

He opens each page, one after the other, saying, for example, "This is a description of such and such a clime. These are its towns and these are its wonders," and reciting spells over it. Then he turns to another page and says, "These are even more wonderful and strange! This is the description of such and such a clime, with its wonders and marvels," and recites spells over it. He keeps on like this till he's gathered it—the *hankāmah*, his circle of spectators—together, and when he's done so, he opens the first house of the zodiac. He says, "This is the House of the Ram from the first decanal face and this from the second **12.18**

يعني الحلقة فتح أوّل البروج ثمّ قال هذا برج الحمل من الوجه الأوّل وهذا الثاني وهذا الثالث فصاحب الحمل والمرّيخ في الحبس وصاحب الحمل والمرّيخ قدّامه خلعة وفائدة وهو ماتت زوجته وصاحب الحمل والمرّيخ الليلة يموت وصاحب الحمل والمرّيخ الليلة يولد له ولد فيا من يقول نجمي الحمل والمرّيخ إنّما هو من هذه الصفات نجمك تقدّم حتّى أبيّن لك نجمك ودرجتك وما هو أخير أيّامك وما يتمّ عليك وما يوافقك من النساء والصنائع والملابس والمواكيل والمشموم والأدهان وأيش تكون أمراضك وما يوافقك من الأدوية

١٩،١٢ فإذا قعد قال أيش اسمك قال فلان قال وأمّك قال فلانة وهذا الهذيان الذي لا يكون قطّ ولا يصحّ نجم إلّا بمولد رصديّ أو نَموداري أو ما يقارب ذلك من المولد القدريّ أو الجبريّ[١] وإن كان هذا لا يصحّ بل هو أصلح من هذا الهذيان الذي قد ارتبطوا[٢] عليه الأخشان ثمّ يقول أيش[٣] اسم أبوك فيقول فلان فيقول أنت من الوجه الثاني من الدرجة الفلانيّة وهذا الهذيان والمحال إلّا أنّه لا يصحّ منه شيء إلّا بما قدّمنا من العمل في المواليد

٢٠،١٢ وإذا كان المكتسب منهم حاذق مناسب يكون يعرف حساب الجمل الصغير والكبير فأمّا الصغير فيخرج منه النجم وأمّا الكبير فيخرج منه الوجه والدرجة ولا يحتاج إلى ذلك إلّا أنّ رزق أَبي العَنْبَس ورزق أبو مَعْشَر فإنّه إذا قرأهما أو أحداهما تكلّم مع كلّ أحد بما في قلبه فإنّه يذكر فيه رزق الجنديّ كذا ورزق التاجر كذا ورزق الفلّاح كذا ورزق الخادم ورزق المملوك ولا يخلّي شيء حتّى يذكره فإذا تحدّث معه بما هو فيه ارتبط عليه ولا يكون من أحكام ما قال شيء واعلم أنّ هذه المبشكين لا يقال

---

١ ش: الحوريّ. ٢ ش: ربطوا. ٣ ش: أيش اسمك و.

and this from the third. He whose house is the Ram and Mars is in prison; he whose house is the Ram and Mars has a robe of honor and some great advantage coming to him; he whose house is the Ram and Mars, his wife has died; he whose house is the Ram and Mars will die tonight; he whose house is the Ram and Mars will have a son born to him. Anyone who says, 'My star is the Ram and Mars,' behold the characteristics of your star! Step up so I can give you a reading for your star and your degree and tell you how your days will end and what will happen to you and what women, actions, garments, sources of livelihood, sweet-smelling flowers, and unguents are good for you and what your diseases are and what medicines suit your constitution."

If someone then comes and sits down, the charlatan asks, "What's your name?" and the man replies, "So-and-so." The charlatan says, "And your mother's?" and he replies, "So-and-so." (This is nonsense that shouldn't be allowed: It is improper for him to practice astrology without a birth-date reading using either documentation or calculation or something of that sort based either on observation of the stars or an animodar. However, proper or not, it is at least less pernicious than the earlier nonsense with which the marks have been duped.) Then he asks, "What's your father's name?" and the mark says, "So-and-so," and he says, "you belong to the second decanal face of such and such a degree" (which, again, is meaningless nonsense; in fact, nothing he says is proper unless done using birth dates, as mentioned above). 12.19

If one of these astrologers is sharp and fit for purpose, he will know the *jummal* system of calculation, both the lesser and the greater. The lesser gives one the stars; the greater the decanal face and degree, neither of which are needed: All he needs is to read the *Livelihood* of Abū ʿAnbas and the *Livelihood* of Abū Maʿshar. If he's read both of these, or even just one, he'll be able to talk to anyone about what matters to him, for each specifies the divinely allotted livelihood of the soldier as such and such, of the merchant as such and such, of the peasant as such and such, of the servant as such and such, and of the slave as such and such, covering everything. Thus, when he talks to the mark about his actual situation, the mark will be taken in, though what the charlatan says will have nothing to do with the rules. It cannot be said that there's a single scholar, or even a craftsman, among these bunglers; the most one can say is that so-and-so "speaks well." The only "scholars" they have are those who've completed their studies in how to get their hands on silver specie by any means 12.20

بينهم عالم ولا صانع بل يقال فلان يتكلّم جيّد ليس عندهم عالم إلّا من يحصل الفضّة بأيّ وجه كان ويقال بينهم اكفر وهات شيء فافهم ذلك

الباب التاسع في كشف أسرار الذين يتكلّمون على الرمل وعلمه

اعلم أنّ علم الرمل علم شريف من أجلّ العلوم وهو علم علّمه الله عزّ وجلّ لنبيّه إدريس صلّى الله على نبيّنا وعليه وبه أظهر الله نبوّته وذلك لمّا بعث الله إدريس كان ذلك الزمان من ادّعى النبوّة قبل إدريس وكان إدريس لا يظهر نبوّته ولا يلفظ بها خوفاً من القتل وكان يختلس من قومه ويعبد الله على ساحل البحر فهو ذات يوم يعبد الله عزّ وجلّ إذ تمثّل له جبريل عليه السلام في صورة آدمي فسلّم عليه ثمّ جلسا يتحادثان فبسط جبريل الرمل ثمّ خطّ ثمّ نظر إلى إدريس وقال اسمك إدريس قال نعم قال وأنت نبيّ وتكتم نبوّتك قال نعم وتمّ لك كذا وكذا قال نعم قال ستظهر نبوّتك ويكون من أمرك كذا وكذا ثمّ حدّثه بكلّ ما هو فيه ٢١،١٢

فلمّا سمع إدريس كلامه تعجّب منه وقال يا أخي ومن أين لك هذا قال هذا شيء يقال له علم الرمل وإنّما سمّي علم الرمل بحيث أنّ جبريل وضعه على الرمل فصار يُعرف بذلك وإنّما كان سمّاه جبريل علم الدمّ ثمّ قال سألتك بالله أن تعلّمني ممّا علمت فقال حبّاً وكرامة فإذا أردت ذلك نجتمع كلّ يوم هاهنا ثمّ أعلّمك فانصرف عنه فإدريس قد تعلّق قلبه بذلك فلمّا كان من الغد أتى إلى المكان فوجد جبريل عليه السلام واقف يصلّي فصلّى معه ثمّ جلسا فشرع جبريل يعلّم إدريس أيّاماً حتّى علم أنّه قد كمّل العلم قال له إن كنت قد ايتقنت هذا العلم[١] فخطّ على جبريل هل هو في هذه الساعة في السماء أو في الأرض فخطّ ونظر ثمّ قال جبريل في هذه الساعة في الأرض فقال انظر ٢٢،١٢

---

١ ش: العمل.

possible, a procedure that they refer to among themselves as "Bend over and cough up!" Wise up to these things!

Section Nine: Exposé of the Tricks of Those Who Recite Spells over Sand and an Account of the Science of Sand

For your information, the science of sand is a noble science, one of the most sublime. It is a science that God, Mighty and Exalted, taught His prophet Idrīs, God bless and keep both our prophet and him, and which He used to show that he was a prophet. This came about because when God sent Idrīs, it was at a time when there were others who had already laid out their claims, before Idrīs, to be prophets, and Idrīs neither manifested nor announced his prophethood for fear of being killed. Instead, he held himself aloof from his people and worshipped God on the seashore alone. One day, when he was worshipping Mighty and Exalted God, Gabriel, eternal peace be his, appeared in human form. Idrīs greeted him, and they sat down and talked. Gabriel smoothed the sand, then "cast the line"[167] and looked at Idrīs and said, "Your name is Idrīs." "True," he said. "And you are a prophet but you keep silent about your prophethood." "True," he said. "And this, that, and the other have happened to you." "All that is true," he said. "And you will manifest your prophethood and things will be thus and so for you," said Gabriel, who then proceeded to tell him everything else about him. **12.21**

When Idrīs heard his words, he was amazed. "Where did you get all this, brother?" he asked, and Gabriel replied, "It's called the science of sand" (this is what it's called, because Gabriel laid it out on sand and that gave it its name; Gabriel himself, however, referred to it as "the science of smoothing"). Then Idrīs said, "I beseech you in God's name to teach me some of what you know," and Gabriel said, "With all my heart! If that's what you want, let's meet right here every day, and I'll teach you." Then he left. Idrīs had set his heart on it, so the following day, he went to the same place and found Gabriel standing and praying, and he prayed with him. Then they sat and Gabriel began teaching Idrīs, and this went on for days until Gabriel was sure he had learned the science fully and said to him, "If you really have achieved mastery of this science, make a casting to find out about Gabriel—is he in Heaven right now or on **12.22**

في أيّ الأقاليم هو فنظر في الرمل ثمّ نظر إليه فقال إن يكن جبريل آدميّ فأنت جبريل فطلبه فلم يجده فتعجّب من ذلك

ثمّ أتى قومه واجتمع بأكابرهم ثمّ قال لهم قد تعلّمت علم نفيس فمن كان في قلبه ضمير أو أمر من الأمور يضمره أبيّنه له فأضمر كلّ منهم ما في قلبه فجعل يحدّثهم بما في قلوبهم وهم يتعجّبون منه ثمّ قالوا له سألناك أن تعلّمنا هذا العلم فاصطفى منهم أربعين الذين هم رؤوس القبائل ثمّ شرع في تعليمهم وهم الهرامسة المذكورة وهم تلامذة إدريس عليه السلام ولم يزل يواظبهم حتّى علم أنّهم صاروا في طبقته في العلم ٢٣،١٢

فلمّا علم ذلك جمعهم وقال اعلموا أنّي أمس لمّا انفصلت منكم خطّيت في الرمل فظهر لي أنّ الله تعالى قد أرسل نبيّ وهو نبيّ صادق فخطّوا كلّ واحد منكم على ذلك فخطّوا الجميع واتّفقوا على ذلك فقال إدريس إذا اتّفق ذلك وصحّ فخطّوا في أيّ الأقاليم هو حتّى نقصده ثمّ نؤمن به فخطّوا جميعاً وقالوا في إقليمنا الذي نحن فيه فقال الحمد لله الذي لم يتعبنا فخطّوا في أيّ البلدان هو فقالوا في هذا البلد الذي نحن فيه فقال في أيّ الدور فقالوا في هذه الدار الذي نحن فيها ولم يزالوا حتّى قالوا هو فينا فقالوا أنت هو فقال[1] نعم فقالوا اكتموا ذلك حتّى نتفرق إلى القبائل الذي لنا ونعيد عليهم ذلك فمن آمن حلّفناه وأحضرناه إليك ومن أبى أو خالف قتلناه ٢٤،١٢

ثمّ تفرّقوا على قومهم وقصّوا عليهم القصّة فأكثر الناس قالوا أنتم ساداتنا وما رضيتم لأنفسكم فنحن لكم تبعاً فآمن أكثرهم بإدريس عليه السلام وأظهر الله تعالى نبوّته بالرمل وقد قلت في الأرجوزة الذي عملتها في علم الرمل حيث أقول [رجز] ٢٥،١٢

---

١ ش: فقالوا.

Earth?" So Idrīs cast the sand and looked. Then he said, "Gabriel is on Earth right now." "Look," said the other, "to see what clime he's in." So he looked at the sand, looked at him, and said, "If Gabriel may be a man, then you are Gabriel." Then he sought him but couldn't find him, and was left to marvel.

Next, Idrīs went to his people, met with their elders, and told them, "I have learned a science of great value. If anyone is holding a secret in his heart or privately pondering a business matter, I shall reveal it to him." Each of them thought of something and he began to talk to them of the secrets they held in their hearts and they were amazed that he could do so. "We beg you!" they said. "Teach us this science!" So he chose forty of them who were the chiefs of the tribes and began teaching them. They are the Hermeses who are mentioned in the books and who are the pupils of Idrīs, eternal peace be his. He continued giving them regular lessons until he was sure that they had reached the same level in the science as he.[168] 12.23

When he was indeed sure, he gathered them and said, "Yesterday, after I left you, I cast the sand and I saw that the Almighty has sent a prophet, one who speaks the truth, so let each of you cast the sand now with that in mind." So they all cast the sand and came to the same conclusion he had. Idrīs then said, "This being agreed upon and therefore true, now cast to see which clime he is in so that we can go to him and believe in him." So they cast the sand and said, "He is in the very same clime as us!" "Thanks be to God for not setting us too daunting a task!" said Idrīs. "Now cast to see what country he is in." "He's in the very same country that we're in!" they said. "In which territory?" he asked. "In the very territory that we are in!" they said, and they kept on casting till they said, "He is among us!" and then, "You are he!" and he said, "Right!" Then they said, "Let's keep this quiet until we have gone our separate ways to the tribes that follow us and passed this on to them. We shall take the oath of allegiance of all who put their faith in you and bring them to you, and all who refuse or cavil we shall kill." 12.24

So they split up and went to their peoples and told them the story, and most people said, "You are our masters, so whatever you're happy with, we're with you!" Thus, most of them placed their faith in Idrīs—the one whose prophethood God Almighty made manifest through sand—eternal peace be his. In an *urjūzah* I made up about the science of sand, I say: 12.25

وَأَظْهَـرَ اللّٰهُ بِهِ لِهِرْمِسَا   دَعْوَتَهُ وَكَانَ مِنْهُ مُوئِسَا

وقد قال سيّد المرسلين وخاتم النبيّين محمّد الأمين وسُئِلَ[١] عن علم الرمل فقال كان ٢٦،١٢
نبيّاً يخطّ الرمل فمن وافق خطّه فقد أصاب ثمّ إنّ الذين يكسبون به لا يحصل أحد
منهم على شيء منه سوى معرفة الضرب والتوليد فإذا[٢] أقام ستّة عشر صورة ترك
العلم ورجع إلى الحمق ولا يحصل منه على طائل وذلك أنّ جميع كلام الناس يجمعهم
أربع كلمات وهي أن يقول سؤالك في بيت الحركات متّصل لبيت العاقبة تدلّ على
حركة تطلب فيها الاتّصال وتسأل عن العاقبة في ذلك ثمّ يسمع ويأخذ منه ويردّ عليه
ولا يعتمد على شيء من أصول العلم بل على الحمق[٣] فمن أجل ذلك نبذوا العلم وراء ظهورهم
وتعلّقوا بالباطل فضاع العلم[٤] ونحسب[٥] أنّ لا تمّ علم والعلم صحيح لا طعن فيه بل الطعن
في من يدّعيه ولا يعمل بمقتضاه وكذلك أقول في جميع العلوم

١ ش: سأل. ٢ ش: فإذ. ٣ ش: الخفق. ٤ ش: العمل. ٥ ش: ونسب.

Through it God to a Hermes made his mission clear,
rescuing him thus from long despair.

The Lord of Messengers and Seal of the Prophets, Muḥammad the Virtuous, on being asked about the science of sand, said, "There was once a prophet who divined from sand, so anyone who does it as he did does well."[169] None of these charlatans who use it to make astrological predictions, however, have acquired any more knowledge of that science than how to set up the rows in the sand and generate patterns from them. Thus, when a person of this sort sets up sixteen patterns, he leaves all science behind, reveals his essential imbecility, and ends up with no significant results. **12.26**

Exposé: This is because everything these people say boils down to four phrases—namely, "Your question concerns the position of 'movements,'" or "is connected to the position of 'outcomes,'" or "You are pointing to a movement for which 'interconnection' is required," or "You are asking about the 'outcome' of this."[170] The practitioner listens, gathers information from the mark, and responds to him, not basing himself on the proper rules of this science but on imbecility. In so doing, they throw science to the dogs and cling to invalid premises. The science is lost; indeed, according to our reckoning, no science has taken place. The science itself is true and beyond criticism; the criticism attaches to those who pretend to practice it but don't work according to its rules, and the same may be said of all the sciences.

الفصل الثالث عشر

ثلاثة عشر بابًا

في كشف أسرار المعزّمين

اعلم وفّقك الله أنّ لهذه الطائفة أمور عجيبة وأحوال غريبة لا تحدّ ولا تعدّ ولا يكون شيء أعجب من أفعالهم وذلك أنّهم إذا خلوا بمن كان من الرجال والنساء أظهروا لهم أحوال لا تلتفت ولا تدرك فيذهبون عقل من حضر فإذا أرادوا عزبرة على أحد من الرجال أو النساء خيّلوا لهم أشياء فيُذهلوا عقولهم وأنا إن شاء الله أبيّن بعض ذلك فافهم ما أشرحه لك في هذا الفصل فإنّه عجيب ١،١٣

الباب الأوّل في كشف أسرارهم

فمن ذلك أنّهم إذا أرادوا أن يعزبروا على أحد ضربوا له مَنْدَل فيأخذون قدح زجاج بلا تدخين ثمّ يختزنه في القطن فإذا أرادوا أن يضربوا المندل وأن يعزبروا على أحد أخرجوا ذلك القدح وملؤوه ماء ثمّ أطلقوا البخور وشرعوا في العزائم فبمقدار ما يستقرّ الماء في القدح ثمّ يقول هيّا احضروا وبيّنوا البرهان بحضوركم الوَحا العَجَل فإنّ القدح إذا تشرّب الماء قعقع وتكسّر فيحسب من حضر أنّ الجنّ حضروا فيعزبر عليهم كيف شاء على قدر غرضهم في ذلك ٢،١٣

Chapter Thirteen, in Thirteen Sections:

Exposé of the Tricks of Spirit Conjurors

You should be aware, God grant you success, that this tribe of charlatans is involved in marvelous machinations and wondrous workings beyond enumeration or calculation, and there is nothing more dumbfounding than their deeds. 13.1

Example: When they seclude themselves with some group of people, be they men and women, they show them supernatural states beyond anything that can normally be observed or comprehended, leaving them confounded; and to screw with someone's mind, be it a man or a woman, they make them think they're seeing things, and send their wits packing. God willing, I shall reveal the true facts behind some of these things. Wise up to what I explain in this chapter! It's quite extraordinary!

Section One of the Exposé of Their Tricks

Exposé: To screw with somebody's mind, they "strike the *mandal*" for him. 13.2
They obtain a goblet of unsmoked[171] glass and pack it for safekeeping in cotton wool. When they want to strike the *mandal* and start screwing with somebody's head, they take out the goblet and fill it with water, then light the incense and start in on their conjurations. As soon as the water in the goblet has stilled, the conjuror says, "Arise! Attend, and by your presence proclaim the proof, lickety-split!" and the moment the goblet absorbs the water, it gives out a loud bang and shatters. Those present think the jinn have arrived. Then the charlatans screw with their minds any way they please and in accordance with whatever goal they have set themselves.

الباب الثاني في كشف أسرارهم

وذلك أنّهم إذا أرادوا أن يظهروا على سحر يأخذون شمع لم يستعمل يعملون فيه شيئاً من الملح الناعم ثمّ يعملون منه صورة ذلك الشخص الذي زعموا أنّ عليه السحر ثمّ يكتبوا على الصورة أسماء فيسيّة ثمّ يقولون له خذ هذه الصورة وبيّتها تحت رأسك وقل يا صالحين يا مصلحين بيّنوا سحري في هذه الصورة بحقّ هذه الأسماء فإذا أصبحت رشّ عليها الماء فإن تفتّت فأنت مسحور وتعود الصورة تراباً ورماداً فإنّه إذا رشّ عليها الماء تعود تراباً فيتوهّم ذلك الشخص أنّه مسحور حقّاً فيرتبط عليه فيقول أنا أبطّل ذلك عنك فيأكله به ٣،١٣

الباب الثالث في كشف أسرارهم

ولهم في ضرب المندل أمور عجيبة فمن ذلك أن يأخذون جرّة جديدة لطيفة يملؤوها ماء ويجعلون تحتها حصوة نشادر لا يراها أحد ثمّ يطلقون البخور ويندفع في العزيمة ثمّ يقول احضروا مندلي هذا وأعلموني حضوركم فإنّ الجرّة تميل وتسقط فيتبدّد الماء منها فيقول حضروا[١] وذلك أنّ الوعاء من الفخّار الأبيض إذا كان جديد يرشح فإذا رشح يشربه النشادر الذي عمله تحته فينحل فتميل الجرّة وتسقط فيظنّ من حضر أنّ الجنّ قد حضروا وأقلبوها فيرتبط عليه ويعزبر[٢] كيف شاء فافهم ذلك ٤،١٣

الباب الرابع في كشف أسرارهم

ومن ذلك أنّ لهم منجنيق من الحديد ويسمّى جدار ويسمّى منج[٣] وفي رأسه حجر ملح وهو يمسكه قدر حبّة القمح فإذا أرادوا عزبرة أحد فيوهّموه أنّهم يحضروا الملوك من الجنّ ٥،١٣

---

١ ش: احضروا. ٢ ش: ويعزّم. ٣ في الأصل: محح.

Section Two of the Exposé of Their Tricks

To reveal the presence of a magic spell, they obtain unused wax and mix into it a small amount of fine salt, then mold it into the image of the person they claim is under the spell and write made-up names on the image. They tell the person, "Take this image, sleep with it under your pillow, and say, 'O Righteous, O Restorers of Righteousness, make the spell on me appear in this image, by the power of these names!' and the next morning sprinkle water on it. If it breaks into little pieces, you're under a spell and the image will turn to dust and ashes." When the person in question sprinkles the water on it, it turns to dust, so he's deluded into thinking he truly is under a spell and he's taken in. "I'll remove it from you," the charlatan says, and takes him for whatever he's worth. 13.3

Section Three of the Exposé of Their Tricks

They have some marvelous ways of "striking the *mandal*." 13.4

Example: They obtain a finely made new pot, fill it with water, and place a crystal of sal ammoniac out of sight underneath it. Then they light the incense and the charlatan sets about the invocation. He says, "Come to this *mandal* of mine, and inform me of your presence!" and the pot tilts and falls over and the water in it all spills out, at which he exclaims, "They are come!"

Exposé: The vessel is made of white earthenware. Being new, it sweats and when it sweats, the ammonia he has placed underneath it absorbs the sweat, and the pot thins, sags to one side, and falls over. Those present believe the jinn have come and toppled it, so they're taken in, and he screws with them as he wishes. Wise up to these things!

Section Four of the Exposé of Their Tricks

Another example: They have a contrivance made of iron called a *judār* or a *manj* that has a piece of salt at its top that keeps it closed; the salt is about the size of a grain of wheat. To screw with someone's mind and con him into thinking they can make the kings of the jinn come so that they can then ask them the whereabouts of lost property, they take a shallow drinking bowl and put 13.5

ويسألوهم عن الحوائج يأخذون[1] طاسة يجعلون فيها ماء ويكون في رأسه من الناحية الأخرة دم يابس ثمّ يجعلون المنجنيق في الطاسة ثمّ يغطّونها بمنديل ويطلقون البخور ويتكلّمون بالعزائم ثمّ يقولون الوحا الوحا العجل العجل احضروا وبيّنوا البرهان وأسمعوا صوت الإجابة فإنّ الملح إذا ذاب ينفقس ذلك المنجنيق ويذوب الدم[2] فإذا انفقس طلع له صوت شديد فعند ذلك يكشف المنديل فيجد الماء أحمر فيقول هذا علامة الإجابة وقضاء الشغل ونجاح العمل ويعزبر كما يريد

٦،١٣ والامرأة يجعل الطاسة في عبّها فإذا كان المكان خالي وهو آمن على روحه أمرها أن تخلع السراويل من وسطها والطاسة من تحتها فإذا انفقس المنجنيق صاح عليها نامي ولا تحترقي ويبطل نصفك ثمّ نهرها بصوت آخر نامي حتّى تنام ويقوم إليها ويقول هذا ملعون لا يدفعه إلّا النجاسة ولولا هذا بطل نصفك وبعد ذلك تقضى حاجتك

الباب الخامس في كشف أسرارهم

٧،١٣ ومن ذلك أنّهم إذا جاء إلى عندهم أحد وأرادوا أن يعزبروا فيأخذون الهاون أو طاسة أو مهما كان من النحاس ويجعلوه في مجلس أو خزانة ويأخذون يد الهاون ويربطونها بخيط مسدّس ثمّ يفتلونه حتّى يرجع طوله شبر ثمّ يربطون طرفه في مسمار مسمّر في الحائط ثمّ يجعلون الهاون أو ما اتّفق من النحاس تحته ويكون الخيط على طول المكان ثمّ يخرجون ويكون قد أخذ ذلك الشخص الذي يريد عزبرته وأدخله البيت ثمّ يقول قول أنا فلان صاحب هذا الشغل وأريد من الله ومنكم قضاءه يا صالحين مراد بذلك لا يتوهّم أنّ في البيت أحد فإذا عمل هذا جعل على الباب ستر ثمّ يطلق البخور ثمّ يعزّم فيقول احضروا وأعلمونا بالحضور الوحا العجل فهذا وفتل الحبل منحلّ

١ ش: ويأخذون. ٢ ش: الملح.

water in it. In the top of the contrivance, on the other side, is dried blood. They place the contrivance in the bowl, cover it with a kerchief, light the incense, and perform their conjurations. Then they say, "Lickety-split! Lickety-split! Attend and proclaim the proof, and let us hear your answer to my call!" When the salt dissolves, the contrivance springs open, making a loud noise as it does so, and the blood dissolves. He removes the kerchief, finds that the water has turned red, and says, "This proves that they have answered my summons, and that the work is complete and the operation successful," and he proceeds to screw with their heads as he pleases.

If the mark is a woman, he puts the bowl in the front of her robe and when 13.6
the place is empty and he has no fears for his safety, he orders her to undo her drawers at the waist and place the bowl underneath her. When the contrivance springs open, he yells at her, "Lie down, so that you won't be burnt and one half of you destroyed!" Then he speaks roughly to her in another voice,[172] saying, "Lie down!" so she does so and he gets on top of her and says, "Only foulness can drive this miscreant off. If I don't do this, one half of you will be destroyed. Afterward, you will get your wish."

Section Five of the Exposé of Their Tricks

Another example: When someone whose mind these charlatans want to screw 13.7
with comes to their house, they get hold of a mortar or a drinking bowl or any other bronze object that may be lying around and place it in a parlor or a closet. Then they get a pestle and attach six-ply string to it, braiding it till it's no more than a handspan in length. The end of this they tie to a nail that's been inserted into the wall and they place the mortar, or anything of brass that's to hand, underneath it, the length of the string being equal to that of the space between the pestle and the mortar. Now they leave, the charlatan having previously brought the person whose mind he wants to screw with inside the house. The charlatan orders him to say, "I am so-and-so. I commissioned this work and I ask God and you, O Righteous Ones, to bring it to its conclusion!" the point being to delude the man into thinking that there is some presence in the house. Having done this, the charlatan places a curtain over the doorway and lights the incense. Then he makes his conjurations, saying, "Attend and give a sign that you are here, lickety-split!" This done, the braiding of the rope

فإذا وصل إلى النحاس ضربه ضرباً شديداً يسمعوه الحاضرين فإذا سمعوا ذلك توهّموا أنّ الجنّ حضروا وقد علّموا بحضورهم

٨،١٣ فإن كانت إمرأة أرادوا لَقْيَها فإذا سمّع الجنّ قفز إلى البيت وصاح يا فلانة اسرعي الحضور ويكرّر عليها حتّى تدخل إلى عنده فإذا دخلت يعزبرها كيف شاء ولقد حدّثني بعض من كان يتعانى هذا الباب أنّه اجتمع عنده في يوم خمس نسوة وكان كلّما دقّ الهاون قفز إلى المجلس ثمّ قال هذه زاوية فلانة ثمّ يصيح بها فتدخل إليه فيلقّيها ثمّ يمست البانوك ويخرج يعزّم فإذا دقّ قفز إلى المجلس[١] ثمّ قال هذه زاوية فلانة ثمّ يفعل كما فعل أوّل مرّة إلى أن أتى على الخمسة فانظر إلى هذه العزبرة وما أشدّها واعلم أنّ لهم أمور عجيبة

الباب السادس في كشف أسرارهم

٩،١٣ ومن ذلك أنهم إذا أرادوا عزبرة أحد يقولون نحن نخلّي الجنّ يحضرون ويورونك صورهم وتراهم عياناً فإذا أرادوا ذلك يظهرون الجنّ وجنودهم وعساكرهم فيأخذون من حشيشة البَرْشاوُشان ومن السنا ومن السيكران ومن حبّ البان ومن ورق الغبيراء ومن الرامك المصريّ من كلّ واحد جزء ثمّ يدقّ الجميع ويعمله بنادق ويجفّفه في الظلّ ثمّ يبخّر به بين يدي من يريد يعزبر عليه فإنّه يخيّل له أنّه قد حضر بين يديه ملوك الجنّ وأجنادهم وعساكرهم وقبائلهم فيبهت من ذلك ويعزبر كما يشتهي ويريد فافهم ذلك الدهاء

١ ش: البيت.

is released[173] and when the pestle reaches the brass, it strikes it hard. Those present hear this and conceive the deluded notion that the jinn have arrived and given a sign of their presence.

If one of these charlatans wants to fuck some woman, he sets up the arrange- 13.8
ments for making the jinn audible and then immediately hops over into the main house[174] and yells her name, saying, "Hurry up and come!" He keeps telling her to do this till she goes to the room where he is, and once she's inside he screws her as he pleases. One of those who practice this form of chicanery told me once that five women had meets with him in one day, and every time the mortar sounded, he'd hop along to the parlor and say, "This is such and such a woman's corner"; then he'd yell for her, she'd come in, and he'd fuck her. Then he'd hang the hammock in another place and emerge, making conjurations. When it sounded again, he'd hop back to the parlor and say, "This one is so-and-so's corner" and do as he'd done the first time, and so on till he got up to five. Observe this ability to screw with people's minds and how powerful it can be, and be on guard against the extraordinary things they get up to!

Section Six of the Exposé of Their Tricks

Another example: To screw with someone's head, they say, "We can make the 13.9
jinn come and show you all their various shapes: You will see them in front of you with your very own eyes." To do this (that is, to make the jinn, accompanied by their cavalry and soldiers, appear), they get hold of one part each of maidenhair fern, senna, stinking nightshade, ben nut, marijuana leaves, and Egyptian ramek. The charlatan pounds these all together, makes them into balls, and dries them in the shade. Then he burns the stuff as incense in the presence of the one he wants to screw with and the latter imagines that the kings of the jinn, with their cavalry and soldiers and their various tribes, are present before him, and he's stunned, and the other screws with him however he wishes and desires. Be on your guard against such cunning!

الباب السابع في كشف أسرارهم

ومن ذلك أنّهم إذا أرادوا أن يوهّموا أحد أنّهم يحضرون ملوك الجنّ وقبائلهم وعساكرهم ويراهم عيانًا فيأخذون من حبّ البان جزء ومن الباذروج جزء ومن حبّ القَنّا جزء ومن بزر القرع جزء ومن الغافت جزء ومن ذات الأسرّة جزء يدقّ الجميع ثمّ يجعل بنادق ويبخّر به بين يدي من أراد فإنّهم يرون قد حضر لهم جميع الجنّ والإنس وعساكرهم وقبائلهم وأجنادهم فيذهل من ذلك ١٠،١٣

الباب الثامن في كشف أسرارهم

وذلك أنّ منهم من يدّعي أنّه يقتل الجنّ بمثل ما يقتل عامر الدار وعارض قد عرض لبني آدم أو ما أرادوا أن يعزبروا عليه فإذا أرادوا ذلك يأخذون من الضفادع مهما أرادوا ثمّ يقتلونه ثمّ يجفّفونه ويخبّئونه معهم فإذا أرادوا أن يعزبروا على أحد فينبغي أن تكون لهم حربة للقتل يكون نصابها منها وبها وهي مجوّفة ثمّ يجعلون فيها دم الأخوين ثمّ يدخل إلى بعض البيوت ويغلق عليه الباب وليس معه غير مجمرة البخور ثمّ يقعد كأنّه يعزّم ويطلق البخور ثمّ يجعل من ذلك الضفدع المجفّف قطعة في النار فإنّهم يسمعون لها صياح عظيم جدًّا فإذا سمعوا ذلك أخرج من دم الأخوين وجعله في طست أو طاسة ثمّ يبول عليه فيبقى كأنّه دم عليه رغوة فيقول اقتلوه يا أعوان القتل بحقّ هذه الأسماء ثمّ يفتح الباب ويخرج بذلك الدم فمن رآه لا يشكّ فيه أنّه قتل الجنّيّ فيعزبرهم على حسب ما يريد وما ربطهم عليه ١١،١٣

الباب التاسع في كشف أسرارهم

ومن ذلك أنّهم يؤلّفون لهم ناظر ويكون يعرف الخطّ ولهم معه إشارة في إخراج الخبايا فإذا أرادوا عزبرة أحد من الناس يربطونه على ضرب المندل فإذا حضروا من ١٢،١٣

Section Seven of the Exposé of Their Tricks

Another example: To make someone believe these charlatans can summon the kings of the jinn with their tribes and soldiers, and that he will be able to see them with his own eyes, the charlatan takes one part each ben nut, basil, galbanum granules, calabash seed, agrimony, and line plant, and pounds them all together. Then he makes balls and burns them as incense in front of whomever he wants, and they think that everyone, jinn and men, have come to them with their soldiers, tribes, and cavalrymen, and are astounded. 13.10

Section Eight of the Exposé of Their Tricks

Exposé: Some of them claim they can kill jinn, such as a house demon or some phantom that appears to humans or anything else they wish to use to screw with the mark's mind. To do this, they take as many frogs as they have a mind to, kill them, dry them, and hide them on their persons. To screw with somebody's mind, they have to have a lance ("for the killing") whose shaft is all of one piece and hollow. Inside this they put dragon's blood resin. Then the charlatan enters a house and locks the door, taking only his incense brazier with him. He sits as though making conjurations, lights the incense, places a dried frog in the fire, and everyone hears it make a very loud screaming sound. Once they've heard that, he takes out the dragon's blood and puts it in a metal basin or shallow drinking bowl and urinates on it, which turns it into something that looks like blood with froth on it. "Kill it, my murderous assistants, by the power of these names!" he says, and he opens the door and brings out the supposed blood, and none of those who see him are in any doubt that he's killed a jinni. He can now screw with their minds however he wants, using whatever trick he has in mind to dupe them. 13.11

Section Nine of the Exposé of Their Tricks

Another example: They team up with a "seer," who must also know the science of sand and with whom they will have worked out a signal for the revelation of secrets. If they want to screw with the mind of a particular person, they talk 13.12

أجل ضربه قال المعزّم لصاحب الشغل اعلم أنّ هذا الناظر ما في زمانه مثله ومع[١] ذلك أنّه في بعض الأوقات يختلّ نظره وإنّه خلاف غيره وأنت منزلتك عندي خلاف الغير وما أنت عندي قليل حتّى أخسّرك وما ينقضي لك شغل فنريد أنا وأنت نمتحن هذا الناظر فإن نظر قضينا الشغل وإن لم ينظر يقول اليوم ما نقدر نعمل شيء إلى أغداً فيقول صاحب الشغل وكيف نمتحنه فيقول أخبأ له خبيئة فإن أظهرها قضينا الشغل فيقول أنا والله كنت أريد أن أقول لك هذا من قبل وهذا مراد المعزّم يخاف لا يخبأ خبيئة ولا يطلع عليها فيدكّون عليه ثمّ يتّفق معه على شيء يخبّئونه

فإذا علم ذلك أطلق البخور واندفع في العزيمة إلى أن يصل إلى اسم منها يكون آخر حرف فيه أوّل من حروف الخبيئة فيقول اجعل بالك فيحفظ ذلك الحرف حتّى يصل إلى اسم آخر فيه حرف ثاني من حروف الخبيئة فيقول حضر أحد فيأخذ الحرف الثاني ولا يزال كذلك حتّى تكمل حروف الخبيئة فيقول إن كان ما حضر لك أحد ما بقيت اليوم أتكلّم فيقول قد حضر الملك الفلانيّ ومعه خلق كثير يسلّم عليك فيقوم له المعزّم ويخدمه ويقول للخادم اخدمه عن فلان يعني صاحب الشغل فيقول الناظر الملك يخدمك وقد أحضر أيضاً حاجتك فيقول له المعزّم هذه درجة عاليّة ثمّ يقول للناظر اخدم الملك وعرّفه أنّ فلان خبئ له[٢] خبيئة ويسأل من إحسانك لي أن تظهرها لي حتّى أخبرهم عنها وأعرّفهم ما هي ثمّ ينظر ساعة ويضحك فيقول المعزّم ممّ تضحك فيقول إنّ الملك أخبرني أنّ المخبئ[٣] أنت وهو خبّأتموها لي على سبيل الامتحان وأنا أفرح بذلك فأمّا هذه الخبيئة فهي كذا وكذا فإذا سمع صاحب الشغل فرح وارتبط عليهم ١٣،١٣

١ ش: بعد. ٢ ش: لي. ٣ ش: الخبيئة.

him into sponsoring a session of "striking the *mandal*." When the two of them present themselves, the conjuror says to the sponsor, "Bear in mind that even though this seer has no equal in these times, his visionary powers do not always work. Now he's one of a kind, and you, given my respect for your station, are the same and not so unimportant to me that I'd risk losing your friendship and see the session you've sponsored come to nothing. You and I need to put this seer to the test. If he can see, we'll go through with the work, but if he's having difficulty, he'll say, 'I can't do anything today. Let's put it off to tomorrow.'" "And how are we to test him?" the sponsor asks, and the other says, "I'll hide something for him to find. If he discovers what it is, we'll go through with the business." "To be honest," says the sponsor, "I've been wanting to ask you to do that all along"—and this is what the fake conjuror is hoping for: He's afraid the man will hide something and the seer won't be able to find it, so he tricks him. They then agree on something for them to hide.

Once the charlatan knows what the thing is, he lights the incense, and sets **13.13** about his conjurations till he comes to a name of a jinni whose last letter is the first letter of the name of the thing that has been hidden, at which point he says, "Concentrate!," so the seer commits that letter to memory. The conjuror then continues till he gets to another name, one that contains the second letter of the name of the thing hidden, at which point he says, "I see one of them now!," so the seer gets the second letter, and the conjuror keeps going like this till the name has been spelled out in full. He then says to the other man, "If none of them has appeared to you, I won't speak another word for the rest of the day," to which the seer replies, "King So-and-so has appeared, and with a great crowd of folk, who send you their greetings." The conjuror rises to greet and commune with the king and tells the servant,[175] "Commune with him on behalf of so-and-so (meaning the sponsor)," so the seer says to the sponsor, "The king would like to commune with you and he's brought what you need as well." "This is premium service!" the conjuror says to the sponsor. Then he tells the seer, "Commune with the king and inform him that so-and-so has hidden something for him to find and asks, as a kindness to me, that you reveal it to me so I can tell those present about it and inform them as to what it is." The seer peers about for a while and then laughs, so the conjuror asks him, "What are you laughing at?" and the seer says, "The king has informed me that you're the one who hid the thing—along with that guy. The two of you hid it from me as a test, which is why I'm happy. As to the thing you hid, it's such and

فيقول المعزّم وجب تطييب قلب هذا الناظر فإنّه معدوم المثل فإذا طاب قلبه نصح في النظر فيوهبه شيء آخر غير ما جعل له ويعزبره كما يريد فافهم

الباب العاشر في كشف أسرارهم

١٤،١٣ فمن ذلك أنهم إذا أرادوا رباط أهل مدينة أو بلد وأخذ أموالهم إمّا البلد الذي هم فيه أو غيرهم من البلاد فإن كان غير الذي هم فيه فيسيّرون إلى ذلك البلد واحد أو اثنين ويدّعون الصرع ويصرعون في كلّ وقت وفي كلّ محفل من الخلق وفي الأسواق وعلى أبواب الأمراء إذا نزلوا من الركوب وفي الجوامع والمحافل ويكونوا قد ماشوا بعد سعداء أهل البلد فيتحدّثون في الصرع بذلك ثمّ يتبعونها بأشياء مدغمة ثمّ يعوّجون أيديهم وأرجلهم ويخرجون الزبد على أشداقهم وكلّ ذلك عزبرة وفيس فيعرفهم أهل البلد وكبراءها فيحملوهم إلى معزّمين ذلك البلد فلا يقدر أحد يعمل فيهم عمل

١٥،١٣ ثمّ بعد ذلك يسافر المعزّم الذي أرسلهم ثمّ يدخل ذلك البلد ويدّعي التعزيم فيقال إنّ عندنا واحد صفته ونعته[١] كذا وكذا وما يقدر أحد يخلّصه وهو رجل غريب وقد تعصّب معه الأمير الفلانيّ وقال أيّ من أبرأه أعطيته ما أراد فيقول أحضروه حتّى أبصره فإذا أحضروه نظر إليه وقال له كيف صورة ما يأخذك العارض وما ترى وأيش الذي يحلّ بك فيحدّثه فيقول هذا عارض ما يقدر يخلّصه أحد إلّا أنا وما أعالجه إلّا قدّام هذا الأمير الذي تقولون عنه وبحضور معزّمين كثير من بلدكم فيقول له المجنون يا معلّم كثير قد جاءني مثلك وادّعى أنّه يخلّصني وعجز عن ذلك فيجعل المعزّم في كمّه خاتم من النحاس منقوش ويقول للمصاب انظر في كمّي فينظر فيه ثمّ يقلّب عيناه

---

١ ش: نعته.

such." When the sponsor hears this, he's delighted and places his faith in them, and the conjuror says, "You ought to give the seer something to make him feel appreciated. After all, he's the best there is and when he feels appreciated, he'll report what he sees honestly"—so the sponsor gives the man something extra on top of what he's already paid, and the charlatan screws him over as he wishes. Wise up to these things!

Section Ten of the Exposé of Their Tricks

Another example: To gain the confidence of the people of some city or town (whether the one they're in or any other) and take their money, if it's a town other than the one they're in, they send one or two of their number on ahead, claiming to be epileptics.[176] These constantly throw fits wherever people are gathered—in the markets, at emirs' gates when the latter are dismounting, in mosques, and at public events—having previously followed wealthy members among the townsfolk about, which is something they speak of during their fits, followed by obscure mutterings, after which they curl their hands and feet and foam at the mouth, all of which is nothing but humbug and screwing with people's minds. This way, the people of the town, including their great men, become aware of them, and they carry them to the town's conjurors of spirits, though none of the latter will be able to do anything for them. 13.14

The conjuror of spirits who sent them now sets off and, on entering the town, claims he can perform exorcisms, so people tell him, "We have someone here whose description and situation are such and such, and no one can free him. He's a stranger and Emir So-and-so has taken an interest in his case and declared he will give anyone who can cure him whatever he likes." "Bring him, so I may see him!" says the conjuror. When they bring him, he looks at him and asks him, "What does the demon that takes possession of you look like? What do you see? What is it that has taken up residence inside you?" The man answers, and then the conjuror says, "This is a demon only I can free him from, and I can only treat him in front of the emir of whom you speak and in the presence of a gathering of your town's own conjurors of spirits." The madman says, "Many like you, boss, have come to see me, claimed they could free me, and failed!" The conjuror then places an engraved copper seal on his sleeve and says to the afflicted man, "Look at my sleeve!" He looks, and his eyes roll back inside his head. He peers this way and that, makes distorted movements with 13.15

ويقلّب بصره ويلوّق فكّه ويعوّج يديه ويصيح صياح منكر يرمى نفسه إلى الأرض فيتعجّب من حضر من الناس من ذلك

فإذا وقع إلى الأرض قعد عند رأسه وقال خلّيه يا ملعونة ثمّ يزعق فيه فيقعد ويبوس يده ويتعلّق به ويبكي ويقول يا سيّدي أنا في حسبك أنا رجل غريب وما لي أحد وقد تصدّق عليّ الأمير فلان الدين بأنّ من خلّصني أيش ما طلب يعطيه ويتعصّب له من الحاضرين بعضهم فيواعدهم إلى يوم معلوم وقد ارتبط عليه خلق كثير ويحدّث الناس بعضهم لبعض ثمّ يحضر في ذلك اليوم الذي قد واعدهم فيه خلق من كبراء أهل البلد ثمّ يحضرون ويحضروه بين يديه فيعقده ويكتب في كفّه ويوريه الخاتم في كمّه ويطلق البخور ويقول هيّا الأرض به يا ملعونة فيتكلّم ويصيح عليه فيقع إلى الأرض فيقول أنطقي وقولي ما اسمك ودينك وقبيلتك ولماذا أخذتي هذا الجثّة فيسكت ولا يردّ عليه جواب فيكتب في ورقة أو في كفّ نفسه ويضعها على جبينه فعند ذلك يستغيث ويقول العفو النار ويخبط وتمنّع[1] من الخروج منه فيقول هذا يحتاج إلى أن يعمل له خاتم من الذهب ودملج من سبع معادن وينقش عليه العهد ثمّ ينجّم سبع ليال ثمّ يحتاج إلى معالجته بالشراب أربعين يوماً ويحتاج إلى كذا وكذا وهذا إذا برئ يفتقر إليه الملوك وينفع الناس ١٦،١٣

وذلك أنّ صاحبته تأتيه فتخبره بما يكون في العالم من غير أن تصرعه وتخبره بما يسأل عنه من أمور الدنيا لأنّ هذا القبيل هذا فعلهم وهذا يكون قليل المثل إذا برئ معدوم فمن أنس إليه نفعه وكان عنده جميع أخبار الدنيا ويتحصّل لهم بذلك مبلغ ويقول ذلك الأمير هذا يكون ينفعني فيرتبط عليه فافهم ما أشرت به إليك وكن شاطر ذكيّ خبير بجميع أعمال الناس واختلاف فعلهم وتميّز الأشياء بعين القلب والفكر الصائب لا بعين الرأس والفكر البارد الخائب وقد قال الحكيم شعر [طويل] ١٧،١٣

---

١ ش: ويتمنع.

his jaw, twists his hands, lets out an appalling cry, and throws himself to the ground. Everyone present is amazed.

When the man falls to the ground, the charlatan sits down at his head and says, "Leave him, accursed woman!" and the man screams at him, kisses his hand, and clings to him, saying, "Master, I beg you! I'm a stranger and have no one. Emir Whatsit-of-Religion has charitably offered to give anyone who releases me whatever he asks for." Some of those present now take up his cause and the charlatan agrees to meet with them on a certain day; many are taken in by him and everyone talks to everyone else. On the agreed day, a large number of important people from the town turn up. Then the other conjurors come and bring the man before him, and the charlatan sits him down and writes things on the man's hand, shows him the seal on his sleeve, sets light to incense, and says, "Get to it! Throw him to the ground, accursed woman!" and he speaks to him and yells at him and the man collapses. The charlatan now says, "Speak, woman! Say your name, your religion, your tribe, and why you have taken possession of this body!" The man falls silent and answers not a word, so the charlatan writes something on a piece of paper or on his own hand and places it on the man's forehead, at which the man begs him for mercy and says, "Mercy! The fire!" and flails around, the female spirit refusing, all the same, to leave him. So the charlatan says, "You must make him a gold signet ring and an armlet of seven metals with the Covenant[177] engraved on it, and then he must watch the stars for seven nights, after which he will need to be treated with wine for forty days; plus, he'll need this and he'll need that, and then, when he recovers, he'll be the cynosure of kings and a resource for the common good. 13.16

"Why? Because his lady friend will come to him and tell him everything that's going on in the world without making him have a fit. She'll tell him anything he cares to ask about the affairs of this world because, this tribe of hers—well, it's their job! Someone like him will be a rare thing if he recovers but stays dead. In that condition, he'll be useful to anyone who befriends him: His befriender will have all the world's news at his disposal and be able to make a killing." "This man may be of use to me!" thinks the emir in question and is snared. Take note of what I have shown you and be sharp, smart, and informed of all the tricks people get up to and the range of the things they do. Judge with the eye of rationality and judicious calculation, not that of passion and foolish, inconsequential speculation! As a wise man has said: 13.17

أَفِيقُوا بَنِي ٱلْأَنَامِ مِنْ سِنَةِ ٱلْكَرَى   فَكُلُّ ٱلَّذِي يَدْعُو إِلَيْهِ نَوَامِيسَا

أراد بذلك أنّ جميع هذه الطوائف يتمنّسون على الحقّ بالباطل

الباب الحادي عشر في كشف أسرارهم في إظهار السرقة

١٨،١٣ وذلك أنّهم يعملون خاتم من نحاس يكون وزنه دانق ونصف ثمّ يفرغون منه ويركّبون عليه فصّ من حجر الصندروس ثمّ يخبّئونه معهم ويعملون خاتم آخر مثله إلّا أنّ هذا الخاتم يكون ثقيل وفصّه حجر كاربا فإذا جاءهم إنسان وقال ضاع لي ضائع فقال أنا أخرجه وأظهره ثمّ يجمع جميع المتهومين ثمّ يأخذ طاسة يملأها ماء صافي[١] ويطلق البخور ويعزّم ويخرج الخاتم الثقيل ويقول إن كان هذا الاسم الذي ذكرته هو السارق عوّموا الخاتم على وجه الماء ثمّ يرمي الخاتم فيغطس يفعل ذلك مرّتين ثلاثة

١٩،١٣ ثمّ يدكّ الخاتم ويخرج الخاتم الخفيف فيقول إن كان هذا اسم السارق فعوّموه ثمّ يرمي به فيعوم في الطاسة على وجه الماء فيقول هذا اسم السارق قد ظهر ثمّ يأخذ الخاتم كأنّه يمسحه ثمّ يجعل عوضه الخاتم الثقيل فيقول إن كان السارق فغطسوه ثمّ يرميه فيغطس فيقول إن كان هذا هو السارق فعوّموه ثمّ يرمي بالخفيف فيعوم يفعل ذلك مرّتين ثلاثة ثمّ يدكّ الخاتم ويرمي الآخر فيقول قد طلع اسم السارق وقد عرفته ولا يمكن أن أهتكه إلّا بعد ثلاثة أيّام فقد أمهلته ثلاثة أيّام فإن لم يردّ القماش وإلّا عرّفتكم باسمه وقلت لكم أين خبأه فيتوهّم السارق أنّ اسمه قد ظهر فيردّ القماش خوفاً من الفضيحة فافهم ذلك

---

١ ش: ماء صافي ثمّ يجمع المتهومين.

Awake, mankind, from your deep slumber
for all that the man claims is true is illusion!

—meaning that all such tribes of charlatans dress up falsehood to look like truth.

Section Eleven: Exposé of Their Tricks for Bringing Theft to Light

Exposé: They make a copper signet ring weighing three carats, hollow it, and mount a bezel of sandarac on it. This they conceal upon their persons. Then they make another ring just like it; the second, however, is solid, and the bezel is made of amber. When someone comes to the conjuror of spirits and says, "I've lost something," he tells him, "I'll get it back, wherever it may be hiding." He then gathers all the suspects together, takes a shallow drinking bowl, and fills it with clean water. He lights incense, recites his conjurations, takes out the heavy ring, and says, "If the name that I am about to mention to you is the thief's, make it float, O spirits, on the surface of this water!" and he throws the ring into the water and it sinks. He does this two or three times. 13.18

Then he palms the heavy ring and brings out the light ring and says, "If this is the thief's name, make it float!" and he throws it in and it floats on the surface of the water in the bowl, so he says, "The name of the thief is now revealed!" and he takes the ring as though to wipe it dry and swaps it for the heavy ring, saying, "If this is the thief, O spirits, make it sink!" and throws it in again, and it sinks. Then he says, "If this is the thief, make it float!" and he throws in the light ring and it floats, and he does the same thing two or three more times, then palms the ring again and throws in the other. Now he says, "The name of the thief has now been revealed to me and I know who he is but I won't out him without giving him three days in which to return it. If he doesn't return the cloth, I shall announce his name and tell you where he's hidden it." The thief imagines that his name has been revealed and returns the cloth for fear of scandal. Wise up to these things! 13.19

الباب الثاني عشر في كشف أسرارهم

ومن ذلك أنّهم يأخذون ديك ثمّ يكتبون ورقة فيسيّة ويجعلونها في عنق الديك ويجعلونه تحت طاسة كبيرة في بيت مظلم يلطخون ظهر الطاسة بشيء من الثوم من حيث لا يعلم به أحد ثمّ يخرجون يقفون على الباب ويقولوا للمتهومين اعبروا واحد واحد يضع يده على ظهر الطاسة فإنّ السارق إذا وضع يده عليها فإنّ الديك يصيح ويصفّق بجناحيه ثمّ يصيح ثلاثة أصوات إذا قال ذلك توهّم السارق ولا يجسر يضع على الطاسة يده فإذا دخل واحد وخرج يقول له افتح كفّك فإذا فتحه شمّه فإن كان بريء فقد طرح يده وإنّ رائحة الثوم تظهر في كفّه وإن كان السارق لا يجسر يضع يده على الطاسة فإذا شمّ يده لم يجد فيها شيء فيعلم أنّه هو السارق ويقول إلى أغداً يظهر القماش ٢٠،١٣

فإذا خلا به يقول أعلم أن ما أخذ القماش إلّا أنت وأنا فما أشتهي أفضحك والمصلحة أن تردّ ما أخذت من حيث لا يعلم أحد وأنا والله ما أعلم بذلك مخلوق فإن لم تردّه وإلّا أعلمتهم بك وأنا أشهد عليك والسلام فإذا سمع ذلك احتاج يردّ ما أخذ فافهم ذلك واعلم وتدبّر ما أشرت به إليك واعلم أنّني أعلم لهم من هذا الفنّ مائة وعشرة أبواب منها تخرج الضائع وغيره ٢١،١٣

الباب الثالث عشر في كشف أسرارهم

ومن ذلك أنّي استنبطت شيئاً مليحاً في استخراج السرقة لم يُسبق إليه وذلك أنّني أخذت بيضة ثقبتها خفيّاً ثمّ استخرجت ما فيها ثمّ جعلت فيها ماء الطلّ و سددت الثقب وكتبت على ظهرها الواحد باللبن الحليب من حيث لا يعلم أحد ثمّ جمعت المتهومين وقلت أنا أكتب رسالة على هذه البيضة إلى الملك الموكّل بالأرواح فأعرّفه صورة الحال فهو يردّ الجواب ويعرّفنا من هو السارق ٢٢،١٣

Section Twelve of the Exposé of Their Tricks

Another example: They take a rooster and write something meaningless on a piece of paper and place it around its neck. Then they put the rooster underneath a large bowl in a dark room, having first, without anyone noticing, smeared the back of the bowl with a bit of garlic. They leave the room and stand at the door and say to the suspects, "You must each go in one at a time and place your hand on the back of the bowl. When the thief places his hand on it, the rooster will crow, beat its wings, and then crow three more times." When he says this, the thief thinks he'll be caught and so he doesn't dare put his hand on the bowl. As each goes in and comes out, the charlatan tells him, "Open your palm!" and when he does so, sniffs it. If he's innocent, he pushes the man's hand aside as the smell of the garlic on his hand will be noticeable. If the thief hasn't dared to place his hand on the bowl, the charlatan finds nothing when he sniffs it and knows he's the thief. He tells everyone, "Wait until tomorrow and the cloth will appear." 13.20

When he is on his own with the man, he tells him, "I know it was you and nobody else who took the cloth. I personally have no desire to expose you, and the best option is for you to put back what you took without anyone noticing. I will not, I swear, tell a single creature. If you don't, though, I will inform on you and bear witness against you and there's an end to it." When the thief hears this, he has to return what he took. Wise up to these things! Ponder the things I've pointed out to you, and be aware that I know 110 ways they use to discover lost articles and suchlike. 13.21

Section Thirteen of the Exposé of Their Tricks

Another example: I came up with a smart trick, never used before, for exposing theft. 13.22

Exposé: I got an egg and made an invisible hole in it, then extracted its contents. Then I put dew in it, sealed the hole, and wrote in milk on one side, without anyone noticing. Next, I gathered the suspects and said to them, "I shall write a letter on this egg to the king who's in charge of the spirits and inform him of the situation, and he'll write back and tell me who the thief is."

٢٣،١٣ فإذا تقرّر ذلك أخذتهم وجئت إلى الشمس والفضاء ثمّ خطّيت[1] خطّة ثمّ أخذت البيضة فكتبت على جانبها الآخر بحضور الجماعة أوّل رسالة من فلان إلى الملك الموكّل بالأرواح أنّ فلان قد ضاع له قماش وقد حار لمن يتّهم فعرّفنا من أخذه وانظر فيما ترى ويكون مقتضى الذي كتبته أنا باللبن الحليب أوّل قرأت الكتاب وفهمت الخطاب وقد عرفت سارق القماش فقد أمهلته ثلاثة أيّام فإن ردّه وإلّا لعنته وخزيته وقلت اسمه وأين خبأه فإذا كتبت عليها بالمداد بحضور الجماعة وجعلتها في الخطّة ثمّ أوهمت أنّي أعزّم عليها فإنّها إذا حمي الشمس عليها ارتفعت حتّى تغيب عن العيون فإذا نشف الطلّ منها وقعت وقد احمرّت كتابة اللبن ثمّ تظهر على البيضة فإذا قرأت الجواب على الجماعة قلت يا أصحابنا من كان أخذ هذا الضائع يردّه وإن جاءت عليه ثلاثة أيّام ولا يردّه لُعِنَ على الأشهاد وبطلت يده التي سرق بها هذا الضائع ومع ذلك فإنّ الملك سلام الله عليه يعرّفنا أين خبأه فإنّ السارق يتوهّم ويردّ ما أخذه فافهم ذلك

٢٤،١٣ واعلم أنّ لهم أمور لا تعدّ ولا تحدّ ولا يقع أحد[2] لها على إحصاء ولا يقف عليها غيرهم ولولم قد وسمت نفسي أنّني منهم ذكرت لهم أموراً لا تكيّف وأظهرت لهم ألف باب وإن كان أعلم من فيهم يعلم منها أقلّ ما يكون فيعلم من وقف على كتابي هذا أنّني لم أترك شيئاً ما وقفت عليه وجمعت طرفيه وما وضعت هذا الكتاب إلّا بعد مطالعة كتب كثيرة ومصاحبة سائر أرباب العلوم والحيل بل والله العظيم معلّ العلل وأزليّ الأزل لم تطاوعني نفسي ولم أحسّن إليها أن تفعل شيئاً من ذلك بل أنزّهها عن ذلك ولقد قال الأمير سيف الدين قِليج يا فلان هذا العلم ما يحصّل به آخرة فحصّل به دنيا فقلت والله إنّي أنزّه نفسي عن ذلك وعن الدخول في الأدناس بل معرفة الأشياء

---

١ ش: خطبت. ٢ أضيف للسياق.

This being settled, I took them with me outdoors where it was sunny, and there I made a furrow in the sand. Then I took the egg and wrote on its other side for all to see: "To begin: Letter from So-and-so to the king in charge of the jinn to inform him that so-and-so has lost some cloth and has no idea who took it, so look and see!" Now, what I had written in milk was, "To begin: I have read your missive, I have understood your message, and I have discovered who stole the cloth but have given him three days to return what he took. If he does so, well and good. If he does not, I shall denounce him and shame him and state his name and where he has hidden it." After I'd written on the egg in ink in the presence of everyone and placed it in the furrow, I made a pretense of adjuring the spirits to appear, and when the sun heated it, what I had just written faded till there was nothing left to see, but when the dew dried out, the egg, on which by this time the writing in milk had turned red, fell over and the writing was revealed. Reading the response to my audience, I declared, "Dear friends! Whoever took the missing item should return it. If three days have passed and he has not done so, he will be denounced before witnesses and the hand with which he stole the missing item will be cut off. In addition, the king of the jinn, God's eternal peace be his, will tell us where he has hidden it." The thief then believes he'll be exposed and returns what he took. Wise up to these things! 13.23

They get up to things too numerous to enumerate, things beyond calculation, of which none but they have cognition. Were it not that I would never demean myself by descending to their level, I'd mention a number of other unpleasant things they do and set out a thousand methods they use, even though the most learned among them knows fewer than there actually are. Contrariwise, anyone who peruses this book of mine will be aware that I have left out nothing I have looked into and have given a thorough account of everything. I wrote this book only after reading many others and keeping company with all the masters of these sciences and subterfuges. Despite this, I swear by Mighty God, Causer of Causes, Sempiternal of the Sempiternal, that my soul never gave in to me and I was never able to persuade it that it was in its interest to do such things; I declare it innocent of involvement in anything of the sort! Emir Sayf al-Dīn Qilīj once told me, "Fellow! This science cannot win one the things of the next world. It can win one only those of this world," to which I replied, "I swear I am innocent of any such things and of any involvement with filth! On the other hand, it is better to know things 13.24

خير من الجهل بها فهذا مراد المملوك من هذه العلوم فتعجّب من ذلك وأنعم وتفضّل أدام الله إنعامه

than to be ignorant of them. This is your slave's goal with regard to these sciences." He was deeply impressed and gave generously and graciously, God prolong his munificence!

الفصل الرابع عشر

اثنان وعشرون باباً

في كشف أسرار أطبّاء الطرق

اعلم أن هذه الطائفة كثيرة المكر والكذب والمحال وهم أجناس كثيرة وضروب شتّى ١،١٤ لا يقع عليهم إحصاء بل نثبت منهم ما سهل على طريق الاختصار والإيجاز اعلم أنّ هذه الطائفة منهم من يتكلّم على العقاقير وهم أكثر كذب على الناس ومنهم من يتكلّم على الشلب وهو المعجون ومنهم من يتكلّم على الدود ومنهم من يتكلّم على الأدهان ومنهم من يتكلّم على السفوفات ومنهم من يتكلّم على أدوية الشعر ومنهم من يتكلّم على الترياق ولو ذهبت أصف الجميع لطال الشرح ومنهم من يتكلّم على الوُشّق ومنهم من يتكلّم على منفحة الدبّ ومنهم من يتكلّم على مرارة الضبع فكلّ صنف من الأصناف لهم دكّ وفعل وأنا إن شاء الله أكشف بعض أسرارهم على حسب ما وقع عليه العيان وقام عليه الدليل والبرهان

الباب الأوّل في كشف أسرار الذين يتكلّمون على الحشائش والعقاقير

اعلم أنّ فيهم فضلاء وسادة وفيهم من له معرفة بجميع النبات ومنافعه ومضارّه ٢،١٤ ومعرفة الأرض الذي ينبت فيها كلّ نبات ثمّ يعرفونه بعينه واسمه وصفته فهم من الحكماء الطبائعيّة وذلك أنّ الطبائعيّ لا يعرف النبات بعينه فقط[1] بل يعرف اسمه

[1] أضيف للسياق.

Chapter Fourteen, in Twenty-Two Sections:

Exposé of the Tricks of the Doctors Who Practice on the Highways

This tribe of charlatans is very cunning, mendacious, and tricky. They come in too many shapes and sizes to be comprehensively surveyed; instead, we shall give details of the ones that are easy to describe, so as to keep things brief and concise. The tribe includes those who say spells over apothecary's simples (these are the biggest liars), over *shalab*—meaning "electuaries"—over worms, over essential oils, over powders, over hair treatments, over antidotes to poison; were I of a mind to describe them all, the list would go on forever ("over ammoniac, over bear's rennet,[178] over hyena gall . . . !"). Every single article is faked and fabricated, and I shall, God willing, expose some of their tricks, citing only what I've seen with my own eyes and things for which I have evidence and proof. **14.1**

Section One: Exposé of the Tricks of Those Who Say Spells over Herbs and Apothecary's Simples

You should be aware that among those who know plants there are learned scholars and masters, and then there are others who are familiar with each and every plant, including its uses and dangers, as well as with the kind of soil in which each plant grows; they know the nature of the plant, its name, and what it looks like. The latter are the physicians, the essential difference between them and the scholars being that the physician knows not only the **14.2**

ومنفعته والحشائشيّ يعرفها بالنظر ويعرف أين تنبت وهذا دليل على أنّه أفضل من الطبائعيّ فإنّ الطبائعيّ يقرأها من الكتب ويصفها من الكتب من غير توقيف ومنهم من لا يفهم شيء من ذلك بل يفهم أسماء العقاقير ويتكلّم عليها بالهادور ويجمع الناس عليها ويتعيّش

الباب الثاني في كشف أسرارهم في اليَبْروح الصنميّ والكلام عليه

٣،١٤ اعلم أنّ هذا العقّار يسمّى تفّاح الجنّ ويسمّى اليبروح ويسمّى المَنْدَغورة وأمّا الصنميّ فإذا مكث في الأرض أربعين سنة تصوّر منه صورة صنم وأمّا الطُرُقِيّة فإنّهم يمكرون عليه وعلى قلعه ويقولون إن ما يقدر أحد يقلعه إلّا يموت في وقته فيرتبطون الناس على ذلك ويزعمون أنّهم إذا أرادوا قلعه يحفرون حوله حتّى يبلغون أقصاه ثمّ يربطون فيه حبل ويتكلّمون بالعزائم المخرّفات ثمّ يأخذون كلب ويربطون الحبل في عنقه ويزعقون عليه فيجذب الحبل فيقلع الحشيشة ثمّ إنّ الكلب يموت من ساعته وهوكلّه فيس وهادور

٤،١٤ فاعلم أنّك متى أردت قلعه قلعته ولا تخاف فإنّ جميع ما يقال فيه هادور ورباط يربطون الأخشان ولهم فيه سرّ وأنا أكشفه وذلك أنّهم يجيئون في أيّام الخريف إلى الحشيشة الرُكُف ثمّ يحفرون على عِرقها ثمّ يأخذون السكّين ويصوّرون فيها صورة آدميّ تامّ الخلقة ويعملون له ذكر وجبهة وشعر ويدين ورجلين وجميع خلقة بني آدم فيه فمنهم من يعمل صورتين ذكر وأنثى متعانقين فإذا صنع ذلك ذرّ عليها التراب من غير أن يقلعها من أصلها ثمّ يتركها إلى الربيع إلى أوان قلع الحشائش ثمّ يجيء يحفر عليها فيجدها قد تربّت كما قد صوّرها وهي خلقة بني آدم فيقلعها ثمّ يتكلّم عليها بالهادور فإذا رآها إنسان لا يشكّ أنّها خلقة ثمّ يبيعها وزن بوزن لا يقدّر عليها

plant's essential nature but also its name and its uses. The herb gatherer, in contrast, knows plants by sight and where they grow, which means that he's better than the physician, as the latter reads about them in, and describes them from, books, without ever studying them in the field. Finally, there are those who know nothing about any of that; they just know the names of the apothecary's simples and say spells over them using a special patter so as to get people to gather round and look, and who scrape a living by this means.

Section Two: Exposé of Their Tricks Using Humanoid Mandrake Root and Saying Spells over It

This apothecary's simple is called "apple of the jinn," "mandrake," and "man- 14.3
dragora." If the humanoid variety stays in the ground for forty years, it takes the shape of a doll. Itinerant quacks tell lies about it and about how it is uprooted, claiming that anyone who does so drops dead on the spot. They use this belief to ensnare people, pretending that to uproot it they dig around it until they reach its farthest point of growth, then tie a rope to it and say nonsensical spells over it. Then they take a dog, tie the rope round its neck, and yell at it, causing it to pull on the rope and uproot the plant, after which the dog drops dead. This is all drivel and lies.

The truth is, if you want to uproot it, you just uproot it. There's nothing to 14.4
be afraid of. Everything said to the contrary is twaddle and a pack of lies to dupe the mark. They have a trick, which I shall now reveal.

Exposé: In the fall, they go to a cyclamen,[179] dig up the root, take a knife, and carve into it the shape of a perfectly formed human being, giving it a penis, a forehead, hair, two hands and two feet, and everything else a human has. Some of them make two different shapes embracing, male and female. Having done this, they sprinkle the soil back around the plant, leaving the roots in the ground, and leave it alone till spring and the time for pulling weeds. The charlatan now comes, digs around it, and finds that it has grown the way he fashioned it—namely, in the shape of a human. He uproots this and recites his patter over it, and no one who sees it can doubt that it's a real creature. He then sells it for its weight in gold, for its value is inestimable.

الباب الثالث في كشف أسرارهم

ومن ذلك أنّهم يأخذون هذه الحشيشة الذي يقال لها الركف ثمّ يصوّرون فيها صورة كلب على ما ذكرناه فيما تقدّم من ذكر اليبروح ثمّ يجعلون ذلك الكلب كأنّه أرمى في فمه شيء وهو ينظر إليه ثمّ يحسّن الصورة جُهْدَه فإذا فعل ذلك ردّ عليه التراب ويتركه يتربّى إلى أوان قلع الحشائش ثمّ يقلعه وهو صورة كلب ثمّ يدّعي أنّ هذه الحشيشة تنفع من عضّة الكلب الكَلِب إذا شرب الآدميّ منها وزن نصف مثقال فإنّه يبرأ من الكلب ويتكلّم عليها بالهادور كيف شاء ويبلّزها وزن بوزن فافهم هذه الأسرار ١٤،٥

الباب الرابع في كشف أسرار الذين يتكلّمون على الشلب

فمن ذلك أنّهم يأخذون إمّا عسل قُطارة وإمّا ربّ العنب ثمّ يغلونه على النار حتّى يأخذ قوام ثمّ يأخذ الطحين ويلفّون به لفّاً جيّداً ثمّ بعد ذلك يعجنه بالزنجبيل ومنهم من يعجنه بعود القرح ومنهم من يضيف إليه دارفلفل ويقرّصه أقراص ثمّ يجعله في حُقّ ثمّ يلفّ الهنكامة ويحكي حكاية ثمّ يتكلّم على الأمراض ودواءها ثمّ يخرج ذلك الشلب الذي معه ويبلّزه كما يحبّ[١] ويدّعي أنّه ينفع لكلّ علّة ١٤،٦

الباب الخامس في كشف أسرارهم

ومن ذلك أنّ لهم معاجين كثيرة مختلفة يطول فيها الشرح والجميع من تلك النسبة وقد كان لي صاحب بالديار المصريّة منجّم يتكلّم على السرماط وكان سيّداً في شغله ظريف وقته وإنّه أحكى حكاية عجيبة قال كنت في سنة غلاء يقطع حلقتي كلّ يوم ثلاثمائة درهم ويزيد عن ذلك أحياناً فقلت له ومن كان في ذلك الوقت ينجّم وعلى من ١٤،٧

١ ش: يجب.

Section Three of the Exposé of Their Tricks

Another example: They take some of that same plant called cyclamen and fashion it into the shape of a dog just as we described when speaking of the mandrake above. They make the dog look as though the charlatan had thrown something into its mouth and the dog is looking at him, the charlatan making the shape as perfect as he can. Having done so, he puts the soil back over it and leaves it to grow until it is the time for pulling weeds. He pulls it up and it will have taken on the shape of a dog. He claims that the plant is good against the bite of a rabid dog: If you drink half a mithkal, you will recover from rabies. He repeats his patter over it any way he pleases and peddles it for the equivalent of its weight in gold. Wise up to these tricks! 14.5

Section Four: Exposé of the Tricks of Those Who Say Spells over Electuaries

Another example: They take either a syrup of sugar and honey or some thickened grape juice and boil it over the fire till thick. Then they take flour and mix it in well. Next, they knead this with ginger (some knead it with pyrethrum, some add long pepper) and make it into pills, which they place in a box. Then they gather a crowd and tell a story, followed by a discussion of illnesses and their treatment. The quack then takes out the electuary, which he has on him, and peddles as much of it as he wants, claiming it works for every disease. 14.6

Section Five of the Exposé of Their Tricks

Another example: They have so many different pastes it would take too long to describe them, but all are of the type described above. I had a friend once in Egypt who was an astrologer who recited spells over amulets.[180] He was both a master of his craft and the greatest wit of his day and he told me an amazing story. "During a certain year of high food prices,"[181] he said, "my crowd used to bring in three hundred silver pieces a day, sometimes more." "And who," I asked, "would want to have his future read at a time like that? Who could you 14.7

كنت تبلّز سرماطك قال كنت أتّكل على الشلب وكنت أخرج كلّ يوم إلى أرض الطبّالة ومعي هذه الزنجلة يعني الطاسة ثمّ أخرج لي طاسة إسبادريّة تسع خمس أرطال بالمصريّ قال كنت أملأها طين إبْليز ثمّ أجيء إلى داري فآخذ العسل القصب ثمّ أعقده على النار ثمّ ألقي عليه ذلك الطين وأعجنه عجنًا جيّدًا ثمّ أضيف إليه أيْش ما كان من الطحين ثمّ أعجنه ومعه الكمّون المطحون ثمّ أجعله أقراص كلّ قرص مثقالين

٨،١٤ ثمّ أنزل وألّف الهنكامة وأتكلّم عليه أنّه يمنع من أكل الطعام ويحفظ القوّة ويحسّن الصورة وهذا المعجون إذا أكل الإنسان منه قرص بالغداة أغنى عن الطعام بالعشاء وإذا أكل منه العشاء أغناه عن الطعام إلى الغداة ثمّ إنّه يحفظ القوّة والصحّة فكنت أتكلّم عليه بما يليق وكنت أبلّز منه القرص بدرهم فأخرج كلّ يوم ثلاثمائة قرص وما يزيد عنها حتّى كانوا الناس يقعدون ينتظرون حتّى أبسط وكان كثيرًا من الناس يأخذ الخمسة والستّة والأقلّ والأكثر فإذا أكل منه قرص تغذّت الأعضاء من ذلك العسل والطحين وينزل ذلك الطين إلى فم المعدة فيسدّها فلا يرجع يشتهي من الطعام ولا تدفع المعدة في ذلك اليوم

الباب السادس في كشف أسرارهم

٩،١٤ ومن ذلك الذين يتكلّمون على دواء الدود فمن ذلك الوَخْشيزَك الخُراسانيّ ما فيه شكّ أنّه إذا عالج به الدود مع القِنّبِيل الطائفيّ مع حبّ النيل مع ورق الخوخ فإنّ هذه أدوية الدود مع الترمس البرّيّ إلّا أنّهم يأخذون بزر الشيح فهو شبه بزر الوخشيزك ثمّ يأخذ البرنيّة فيسحقونها سحقًا جيّدًا فلا يشكّ من رآها أنّها قنبيل طائفيّ ثمّ يأخذ حبّ زبيب الجبل فلا يشكّ من رآه أنّه حبّ النيل ثمّ يهدر عليه ويبلّزونه فإذا أرادوا رباط الأخشان يأخذون من الرقّ البياض الصافي وهو رقّ الضأن ثمّ يقدّ منه قدّة ويقصّ منه شيء على مثال حبّ القرع ثمّ يبلّه بالماء ويغسله[1] ويتركه حتّى

[1] ش: يفتله.

peddle your amulets to?" "I depended on electuaries," he replied. "Every day, I'd go to Arḍ al-Ṭabbālah, taking a *zanjalah* (meaning a metal bowl) like this with me. I'd take out a bronze bowl of this type, holding nine-fifths of an Egyptian pint, fill it with Nile mud, go home, take cane syrup, boil it over the fire till it coagulated, then throw in the mud and knead it all well. Then I'd add whatever flour was around and knead it with ground cumin. Finally, I'd make it into pills, each weighing two mithkals.

"After that, I'd leave, get my circle to gather round, and claim that the pills 14.8
eliminated appetite, kept up one's strength, and improved the appearance, and that if a person ate one at lunch, he wouldn't need food at dinner, and if he ate one at dinner, he wouldn't need food at lunch, not to mention that it conserved strength and health. I'd say whatever spells were appropriate over them and flog a pill for one silver piece, and I'd be producing three hundred or even more pills a day. People used to sit and wait for me to set up, many of them taking five, or six, or more or fewer, pills, because when someone ate a pill, his limbs would be nourished by the honey and the flour, and the flour would descend to the mouth of the stomach and block it. He wouldn't keep wanting food, and for the rest of that day his stomach wouldn't keep urging him to eat."

Section Six of the Exposé of Their Tricks

Another example: Some say their spells over worm medicine,[182] such as san- 14.9
tonica from Khurasan. There is no doubt that when the practitioner treats worms with this, plus kamala from Taif, plus indigo seed, plus plum-tree leaves, the worms will die—these, along with wild lupin, are indeed the treatments for worms. These quacks, however, get wormwood seed, which looks like santonica seed, then bring the medicine pot and grind it well, after which no one who sees it doubts that it's kamala from Taif. Next, he takes lousebane seed, which everyone who sees it is sure is indigo seed, prattles his patter over it, and peddles it. To dupe the marks, they get hold of some unblemished white parchment, made from sheepskin, cut a strip from it, and snip it into something resembling calabash seeds. They moisten these in water, wash them, and leave till they are dry. Then they add them to the medical mixture, where

يجفّ ثمّ يضيفه إلى الدواء فيبقى مثال السمسم ويمعكه في البرنيّة فلا يبان ثمّ إذا جاء إليهم صاحب الدود يأخذون من تلك العقاقير التي وصفناها ثمّ يجعلونها في شيء من المعاجين ثمّ يطعموه ذلك ويقولون إذا كان أغدًا فإنّك ترمي الدود فإنّ ذلك الرقّ يرميه وهو أبيض كأنّه دود لا يغادر منه شيء افهم ذلك الدهاء والزغل وتميّز هذه الأحوال

الباب السابع في كشف أسرارهم

ومن ذلك أنّهم إذا أرادوا أن يظهروا للإنسان أنّهم يسقونه دواء يرمي الدود ١٠،١٤ فيأخذون عصب الجمال ويعملون منه هيئة الدود ثمّ يأخذون شيئًا من الحشائش المسهلة ويضيفون إليها تلك الأعصاب من حيث لا يعلم بها الخشن فإذا أكلها انسهل فيبقى الطبع مثال الماء وتلك الأعصاب فيه مثال الدود ولا ينكر منه شيئًا فافهم ذلك واعلم أنّي لو شرحت جميع ما اطّلعت عليه لما وسعه مجلّدات كثيرة ولكن ببعض الشيء يستدلّ به على الكلّ ويعلم من وقف على هذا الكتاب أنّ ما كلّ ما يعلم يقال بل هذا القدر كاف ولله درّ[١] الشيخ أبو القاسم الحريريّ صاحب المقامات حيث يقول

فَـإِنْ فَطِـنْتُمْ لِلَحْنِ[٢] ٱلْقَوْلِ بَانَ لَكُمْ   فَضْـلِي ودَلَّكُمْ طَلْعِي عَلَى رُطَبِي
وَإِنْ شُدِهْتُمْ فَإِنَّ ٱلْعَارَ فِيهِ عَلَى   مَنْ لَا يُمَيِّزُ بَيْنَ ٱلْعُودِ وٱلْحَطَبِ

١ لله درّ: أضيف للسياق. ٢ ش: قَضَيْتُمْ بِلَحْنِ.

they take on the appearance of sesame seeds, and rub a medicine pot with it, though it doesn't show. When someone with worms comes to them, they take some of the ingredients we have listed and introduce them into certain pastes and give him these to eat, telling him, "You'll expel the worms tomorrow," and he does indeed expel the pieces of parchment, which are white, like worms, leaving none behind. Wise up to such craftiness and counterfeiting and learn to spot such cases!

Section Seven of the Exposé of Their Tricks

Another example: To demonstrate that the medicine they are giving someone 14.10
will indeed expel worms, they get camel sinew and make out of it things that look like worms. Then they get a quantity of laxative herbs and, unbeknownst to the mark, mix the bits of sinew in with these. When the mark eats them, his bowels open and his stools become watery, with bits of sinew with an undeniably wormlike appearance in it. Wise up to these things, and bear in mind too that numerous volumes would be insufficient to contain everything I have observed, were I to analyze it all; a certain amount, though, should allow one to deduce the rest. Likewise, those who have looked into this book will be aware that not everything that is known may be said and that this much will do. How well Shaykh Abū l-Qāsim al-Ḥarīrī put it when he said:[183]

> Pay but heed to the meaning of my words and you'll find clear evidence
> of my erudition, while my sprouting spathes the presence of my ripe dates proclaim.
> Should you nevertheless get confused, the blame must go
> to him to whom agarwood and firewood are one and the same.

الباب الثامن في كشف أسرار الذين يتكلّمون على الأدهان

ومن ذلك أنّ هذه الطائفة لهم أمور ذاهلة ومحال لا يدركه أحد غيرهم وذلك أنّ ١١،١٤ العالم منهم يأخذ من حشيشة يقال لها العُبَب وهذه الحشيشة مشهورة أنّها تنفع من الأخلاط المزمنة فالعالم منهم يأخذ منها شيء كثير عند ما تبلغ وتنتهي فإذا أراد يجعلها في دست كبير ثمّ يغمره بالماء ويغلي عليه ويشدّ النار حتّى تهرأ على مثال ما يعمل اللاذَن ثمّ يعمل منها أقراص ويجفّفها وتكون عنده فإذا جاء من به وجع أو خلط أو ضربان أخذ من ذلك القرص ثمّ حلّه في الماء حتّى يختر ذلك الماء ثمّ يسقي منه قطنة ثمّ يعصرها على موضع المرض ثمّ يدلك بها ذلك الموضع ويديم ذلك ساعة جيّدة فإنّ كثرة الدلك تخدّر المرض فلا يحسّ به ولا يجده فيتوهّم من ذلك فاعلم أنّ سائر الأمراض إذا طال المعك عليها والدلك تخدّر ولا يحسّ بها في ذلك الوقت فافهم وتميّز ذلك وكن ذا فهم ولبّ وعقل ثابت صائب

الباب التاسع في كشف أسرارهم

ومن ذلك أنّهم إذا أرادوا الكلام على الأدهان وأن يبلّزوها على الأخشان فيأخذون ١٢،١٤ من شحم الجمل ثمّ يحلّونه بدهن الحلّ حتّى يعود مثال الدهن[١] الجامد الدقيق ثمّ يسحقون قلب المحلب ويستخرجونه في ذلك الدهن ويضربونه معه ضربًا جيّدًا ثمّ يصبغونه بالورس صبغًا خفيفًا ثمّ يتكلّمون عليه إذا دهن منه الزَمِن وداومه يبرأ وينسبه أنّه دهن سبع عقاقير من جملتها دهن الصنوبر ويتكلّم عليه كيف شاء ويهدر عليه بالهادور

١ ش: الذهب.

Section Eight: Exposé of the Tricks of Those Who Say Spells over Ointments

This tribe of charlatans is distinguished by baffling and seemingly impossible feats that only they can comprehend. **14.11**

Exposé: One of their experts will take a plant called ashwagandha, well known as an effective treatment for chronic abscesses. The expert takes a large amount of it when it's ripe and almost rotten. To do the trick, he puts it in a large vessel, covers it with water, and boils it, keeping the fire high so that it disintegrates like labdanum. From this he makes pills, which he dries and puts aside. When someone who is in pain or has an abscess or a throbbing wound comes to him, he takes one of these pills, dissolves it in water until the water becomes ropy, soaks a bit of cotton wool in it, and squeezes it over the place where the sickness is located. Then he massages the place with it, keeping at it for a good while, since prolonged rubbing numbs the pain and the patient ceases to either feel it or be able to locate it. This gives him false notions, but you should be aware that any painful place, if rubbed and massaged long enough, will go numb and cease to manifest sensation for as long as the rubbing continues. Wise up, learn to detect such things, and be a person of understanding, intelligence, and unwavering discrimination!

Section Nine of the Exposé of Their Tricks

Another example: To perform spells over ointments so as to peddle them to the marks, they take camel fat and dissolve it with oil of unhulled sesame seeds till it turns into a fine hard kind of fat. Then they grind mahaleb cherry kernels, add the extract to this fat, and mix the two together well. Next, they tint the mixture with *waras*, and finally they say spells over it. If a chronically sick person rubs himself with this and continues doing so for some time, he will be cured, and the charlatan will claim that this is because the ointment is composed of seven apothecary's simples, including pine-nut oil.[184] He says over it whatever spells he feels like and prattles his patter. **14.12**

الباب العاشر في كشف أسرارهم

ومن ذلك أنّهم يأخذون زيت الفجل ثمّ يصبغونه بعقّار يسمّى ساق الحمام ثمّ يزيّتون لهم مرّيخين فإذا هنكم الهنكامة تكلّم على ذلك الزيت ثمّ ادّعى أنّ هذا الدهن يقال له دهن الآجرّ وأنّه يبرئ الزمن فإذا هدر عليه بالهادور يأتوا المرّيخين فمنهم من يأتي وهو يمشي على عصاة فيتقدّم إليه ويدهنه من ذلك الدهن ويطيل المعك ثمّ يقول قم امشي فيقوم ثمّ يمشي خلقاً سويّاً فيأخذ العصاة منه ويقول له روح في حال سبيلك فإنّ هذا المرض لا يعاودك إن شاء الله ١٣،١٤

الباب الحادي عشر في كشف أسرار الدهن المشار إليه وهو الدهن المتقدّم وهو دهن الآجرّ

وأمّا صفة إخراجه فإنّ هذا الدهن من أعظم الأدهان فعلاً وأكثرها نفعاً وله قوّة عظيمة في الأخلاط[١] والبرودات وتصرّفها وذلك إذا أراد استخراجه يأخذ الآجرّ المشويّ البالغ في الشيّ المصريّين يسمّونه الطوب والمشارقة يسمّونه القرميدة يؤخذ فيهرس مثال الفلفل ثمّ يمعك بالزيت العتيق معكاً جيّداً ثمّ يحشى في قرعة ويُركَّب عليها أنبيق ثمّ يستقطر بنار مقلوبة فإنّه يقطر دهناً على مثال العقيق فهو دهن المنفذ المتقدّم ذكره ومن فعله أنّه إذا تركت في كفّك منه نقطة نفذت من ظاهر كفّك ولأجل ذلك سمّي دهن المنفذ ١٤،١٤

الباب الثاني عشر في كشف أسرارهم

ومن ذلك أنّهم يأخذون زيت البُطم ويضيفون إليه شيئاً من الدهن ويصبغونه أخضر ثمّ يتكلّمون عليه ويقولون أنّه دهن يقال له دهن الغار ويُعرف بالرند ثمّ يهدرون عليه بالهادور ويبلّزونه ولهم من هذا أشياء كثيرة لا يقدر عليها أحد سواهم ١٥،١٤

---

١ ش: الاختلاط.

Section Ten of the Exposé of Their Tricks

Another example: They take radish-seed oil and color it with an apothecary's simple known as "pigeon's leg,"[185] and have "oilers" whom they anoint with it, as follows. When an audience has gathered round, the quack says spells over the oil and then claims that it's what is called "baked-brick oil" and that it cures the chronically sick. When he's said his patter over it, the "oilers" come, some walking with sticks. The quack goes over to one of them, anoints him with this oil, and rubs it in for a good while. Then he says, "Walk!" and the man gets up, moving as though his body was sound. The quack takes the man's stick from him and tells him, "Be on your way! God willing, the disease will never return." 14.13

Section Eleven: Exposé of the Tricks Related to the Oil Mentioned above (That Is, the Aforementioned Baked-Brick Oil)

How it is extracted: This oil is in fact one of the most prodigious and effective oils, with a very strong action against abscesses and cold sores. To extract it, the quack takes well-baked brick, of the sort Egyptians call *ṭūb* and easterners *qirmīdah.* This is taken and milled like pepper, rubbed well with aged oil, and stuffed into a still pot with an alembic on top. This is then distilled over a gradually reduced fire and produces an oil resembling agate. This is the aforementioned "penetrating oil,"[186] one of whose effects is that if you leave a drop of it on your palm, it will penetrate through to the back of your hand, which is how it gets its name. 14.14

Section Twelve of the Exposé of Their Tricks

Another example: They take terebinth oil, add a little of the aforementioned oil to it, and dye it green. Then they say spells over it and claim that it's an oil called laurel oil, also known as bay oil. They then speak their patter over it and peddle it. They have so many things of this kind that only they can understand them all. 14.15

الباب الثالث عشر في كشف أسرارهم

١٦،١٤ ومنهم من يتكلّم على منفحة الضبع للأرياح المزمنة وغيرها ومنهم من يتكلّم على حشيشة السلحفاة إنّها تنفع في المحبّة والعطف وإجلاب القلوب ولقد كشفت عن ذلك الحشيشة فوجدت لها فعل عظيم في هذا المعنى لأنّ هذه الحشيشة لا يقدر عليها إلّا من رصد الفحل للسلحفاة إلى حين هياجه فإذا هاج طلب الأنثى فإذا جاء إليها تمنّع منه وتدافعه فإذا علم منها المنع ذهب إلى هذه الحشيشة قطعها ثمّ أتى بها إلى الأنثى فوضعها على ظهرها فانطاعت له ثمّ يرمي الحشيشة فإذا أرماها أخذها الذي قد رصدها فاعلم أنّها بالغة وأن لا يوجد في هذه الحشيشة إلّا فرد ورقة وهي الذي يأخذها الفحل وما سواها فلا يسوّي شيء بل هؤلاء الغرباء يهدروا عليها ويبلّزوها وأمّا بيض السلحفاة ومنفحة الضبع والمرارة التي لهم فافهم فكلّ ذلك مصنوع وانقد الأشياء بعين القلب

الباب الرابع عشر في كشف أسرار الكحّالين

١٧،١٤ وذلك أنّ هذه الطائفة لهم أشياء عظيمة وأنّهم إذا عنوا بإنسان قرّبوا دواءه بأقرب ما يكون من الأكحال ما يوافقه وما يوافق ذلك المرض وداووه بأقرب ما يكون من الأدوية ومنعوه من أكل ما يضرّه وإذا أرادوا جعلوه مقثأة كلّ يومين يستغلّوه كحّلوه بكحل يوافقه يومين ثلاثة فإذا وجد الراحة قليل خلط عليه الكحل فلا يجد له برء وقابلوا المرض بما لا يستحقّه من الدواء فذلك أعظم ما يكون من طلب الحرام وقلّة الدين وذلك أنّهم يبطّلونه عن تصرّفاته ويأكلون ماله واعلم أنّ لهم في كتاب التذكرة أكحال جيّدة تذهب البياض من العين وكذلك الغشاوة وكذلك الظلمة وتزيل جميع أوجاع العين فمن ذلك الكحل اللؤلؤيّ الملكيّ وكذلك الروشانايا إلّا أنّ الملوكيّ أشدّ نفعاً وكذلك مرارة الضبع وغيرها وسوف أذكر في هذا الفصل الأكحال النافعة

Section Thirteen of the Exposé of Their Tricks

Some say spells over hyena's rennet[187] to treat chronic sores and other conditions, and some say spells over alyssum, which is good for affection, sympathy, and the winning of hearts. I looked into this plant and found that it's extremely effective for such things because the only people who can obtain it are those who watch the male turtle and wait for him to come into rut. When he does so, he looks for a female; when he finds one, though, she will have nothing to do with him and pushes him away. When the turtle realizes that she's unreceptive, he goes to this plant, cuts it, brings it to the female, and places it on her back. The female then submits to him. The male throws the plant aside and when he does so, the person who's been observing him takes it. Note that it is extremely powerful, and that the plant has only a single leaf, which is what the male takes. The rest of the plant is of no value, despite which these "wonder-workers" prattle their patter over it and peddle it. As for their turtle eggs, hyena rennet, and gall, wise up—it's all artificially made! Look at things critically, with a rational eye! 14.16

Section Fourteen: Exposé of the Tricks of Quack Eye Doctors

Exposé: This tribe of charlatans knows how to do extraordinary things. If they want to take care of someone properly, they shorten his treatment by using the fastest-working collyriums for the eyes appropriate to his constitution and the disease, and treat him with the fastest-working medicines while forbidding him to eat anything that might do him harm. If they want to, though, they can also turn him into a nice little pumpkin patch for them to crop every couple of days by treating him with a collyrium that works for two or three days but which, as soon as he finds a little relief, they adulterate with something. The patient then finds that he isn't cured and that they are treating the disease with an inappropriate medication. This is the worst example of the pursuit of illicit profit, combined with indifference to the strictures of religion, that there can be. Such people both prevent the patient from going about his legitimate business and devour his wealth. At the same time, they have available to them, listed in the *Memorandum*, excellent collyriums that rid the eye of cataracts, conjunctivitis, and blindness, and relieve all kinds of eye pain. These include 14.17

الأشياف وكذلك الأكحال الذي يعملونها ويبلّزونها على الناس ثمّ أذكر شيء من غدرهم ومكرهم في مكايدهم

الباب الخامس عشر في كشف أسرارهم

١٤،١٨ فمن ذلك إذا أرادوا عمل الأكحال أيّ كحل أرادوا فيأخذون من النشاء ما أرادوا ويسحقونه حتّى يعود كالغبار وينخلونه ثمّ يأخذون من الملح الأَنْدَرانيّ مع الدارفلفل فيسحقونه ثمّ ينقعونه مع الملح المذكور ويسقونه لذلك النشاء ويسحقونه ثمّ يجفّفونه ثمّ يعيدونه إلى السحق فإذا أرادوا أن يعملونه أغبر أضافوا إليه قليل من الدخان الذي يجمع على المداخن أدنى ما يكون من ذلك فإن أرادوه ملوكيّ يجعلون فيه صدف الجوهر مسحوقاً ثمّ يعملون منها أصفر ويصبغونه بالورس ثمّ يعملون منه أحمر فيسقونه دم الأخوين ثمّ يعملون منه عزيزيّ يصبغونه بالمغرة المدنيّة ثمّ يتركون منه أبيض بلا صبغ يقولون مَلَكايا واعلم أنّ النشاء يشدّ عصب العين والدارفلفل يأكل الجرب والحُكاك ويقطع الدمعة ولهم أمور عجيبة لا تعدّ ولا تحدّ فهذا من أكحال الذرورات ولهم أشيافات عدّة وسوف أكشف أسرارها فافهم ذلك

الباب السادس عشر في كشف أسرارهم

١٤،١٩ ومن ذلك أنّهم يعملون أشيافاً يسمّونه أشياف المرائر فهذا الأشياف أعظم الأشيافات وذلك أنّه يعمل من سبع مرائر وهم مرارة بن آوى[١] ومرارة العقاب ومرارة الضبع ومرارة القنفذ ومرارة الباز ومرارة السلحفاة ومرارة البقريّ فهذه أسماء المرائر النافعة من جميع الأمراض في العين ثمّ إنّها تزيل البياض

---

١ ش: مرارة بن آدم.

"royal nacreous" and "*rawshanāyā*"[188] collyrium (the "royal" is the more effective); likewise, hyena gall and so on. In this chapter, I shall list the beneficial dry collyriums as well as the collyriums that quacks make and peddle to people. After that, I shall say something about the treachery and cunning they employ in their games.

Section Fifteen of the Exposé of Their Tricks

Another example: To make collyriums of any kind they have a mind to, they take as much starch as they feel they need, grind it till it has the consistency of dust, and sift it. Then they take pure rock salt, along with long pepper, grind it all, steep this in water with said salt, feed it into said starch, and grind it again. They dry this and then grind it yet again. To make "dust-colored," they add a little of the lampblack that gathers in chimneys (the smallest possible amount of this). To make "royal," they put ground-up mother-of-pearl into it. They also make "yellow," which they color with *waras,* and "red," which they tint with dragon's blood. Precious collyrium they dye with hematite from Medina, and "white" they leave undyed and call "*malkāyā*."[189] The starch tightens the ocular nerve, while the long pepper eats away the scabbiness and the itching and prevents tearing. They know how to do extraordinary things, too many to count or quantify. The preceding are powdered collyriums, but they also have numerous other dry collyriums, whose secrets I shall lay bare. Wise up! 14.18

Section Sixteen of the Exposé of Their Tricks

Another example: They make one collyrium of this sort that they call "the collyrium of many galls" and this is the most powerful of them all. 14.19

Exposé: It is made from seven galls—jackal gall, eagle gall, hyena gall, hedgehog gall, hawk gall, turtle gall, and bovine gall. These are the galls that are good against all eye diseases; they also get rid of cataracts.

الباب السابع عشر في كشف أسرارهم

١٤،٢٠ وأمّا عمل الأشيافات التي يبيعونها على الطريق فإنّهم يأخذون الجولان يسحقونه ناعماً ثمّ يعجنونه بمرائر الماعز ويقطعونها على مثال الأشياف فإذا أرادوا عمل أشياف أبيض يأخذون النشاء ويعجنونه بماء الصمغ العربيّ مع قليل ملح أندرانيّ وماء الزنجبيل فإن أرادوه أحمراً صبغوه بماء البَقَّم أو بساق الحمام وإن أرادوه أزرق صبغوه بماء النيل

الباب الثامن عشر في كشف أسرارهم
في عمل الأكحال النافعة

١٤،٢١ صفة كحل يذهب البياض من العين نافع يأخذ مرارة الضبع وكحل إصبهانيّ فيسحقه بتلك المرارة سحقاً ناعماً ثمّ يجفّفه في الظلّ ثمّ يكتحل به صاحب البياض يذهب بإذن الله ويطلع البياض كأنّه قشر الثوم فالحسه بلسانك فإنّه يذهب ثمّ اكحله بكحل حادّ فإنّه يبرأ بإذن الله صفة إذهاب الشعرة من العين وذلك أن يأخذ النحاس الطالِقون فيعمل منه ملقط ثمّ يقلع به الشعر من العين ثمّ يأخذ كحل إصبهانيّ فيسقيه بماء الرمّانين ومرارة الضبع ثمّ يكحّل به العين فإنّها تبرأ بإذن الله صفة كحل يذهب جميع أوجاع العين يؤخذ كحل إصفهانيّ فيسحق بماء العوسج مع التوتياء وحيّ العالم[1] ثمّ يجعله أشيافاً ويشيّف به العين فإنّه يزيل جميع ما يكون في العين من الأمراض والأوجاع بإذن الله صفة كحل آخر يذهب جميع أوجاع العين من سائر الأمراض يؤخذ التوتياء القلميّ[2] يسقى بماء حصرم العنب ثمّ يؤخذ من الهليلج الأصفر فيسحقه سحقاً بالغاً مع ذلك التوتياء ويسقيه مرائر الماعز حتّى يعود أشياف ثمّ يحكّه على المسنّ ثمّ يكحّل به العين فإنّه يذهب جميع أمراضها صفة كحل آخر يذهب جميع أمراض العين يؤخذ من خرء الحرذون جزء ومن التوتياء جزء يدقّان وينخلان بحريرة ويؤخذ من الملح الأندرانيّ جزء مدقوق ناعم أنعم ما يكون ثمّ يكحّل به العين فإنّه يذهب جميع ما فيها من الأمراض

---

١ ش: الحيّ علم. ٢ ش: التوتياء العلم.

Section Seventeen of the Exposé of Their Tricks

When it comes to the dry collyriums they sell on the highway, though, they take dry dirt, grind it till smooth, knead it with goat's gall, and chop it till it resembles a genuine preparation of this type. To make "white," they take starch and knead it with a solution of gum arabic plus a little pure rock salt and ginger juice. To make "red," they dye it with a decoction of sappanwood or alkanet and, to make "blue," with a decoction of indigo. **14.20**

Section Eighteen: Exposé of Their Tricks for Making Medically Efficacious Collyriums

A collyrium that removes cataracts from the eye (efficacious): The maker takes hyena's gall and collyrium of Isfahan and grinds the latter with the gall till smooth, dries it in the shade, then uses it to anoint the eyes of the cataract patient. The cataract will then disappear, God willing. The cataract itself rises like a garlic skin; lick it with your tongue and it comes off. Then the practitioner anoints the patient with an astringent collyrium and the man recovers, God willing. How to get rid of an eyelash in the eye: The practitioner takes some of the copper amalgam called *ṭāliqūn*, makes tweezers from it, and removes the lash from the eye. Then he takes collyrium of Isfahan, dilutes it with juice of "the two pomegranates"[190] plus hyena gall, and anoints the eye with it; the eye will be cured, God willing. How to make a collyrium that relieves all eye pains: Collyrium of Isfahan is taken and ground up with an infusion of boxthorn plus antimony and houseleek; the practitioner makes this into a gall-based preparation and treats the eye with it; it removes from the eye any sickness or pain there may be, God willing. How to make another collyrium that relieves all eye pains, irrespective of the disease that has caused them: Calamine dust is taken and moistened with unripe grape juice; then some yellow myrobalan is taken and the practitioner grinds this thoroughly with antimony and adds goat galls, thus making it into a dry collyrium, and rubs it against a whetstone; when he anoints the eye with it, it eliminates all morbid conditions. How to make another collyrium that relieves all eye pains: One part stellion feces plus one part antimony are taken, pounded, and passed through a silk strainer, and to these one part pure rock salt, pounded till as smooth as possible, is added. This gets rid of all eye diseases. **14.21**

الباب التاسع عشر في كشف أسرار عدّة الكحّالين

٢٢،١٤ وذلك أنّ لهم عدّة كثيرة لكلّ مرض فمن ذلك المكاحل ثمّ ملقط السَبَل ولهم أيضاً كلاليب يرفعون بها الأجفان وقت قبض السبل ولهم أيضاً مكاوي يكوون بها أصحاب الأمراض فأوّل ذلك مكوى يعملونها لكيّ نزول الماء الأصفر في العين ولهم مكاوي آخر يعملونه لنزول الماء الأبيض في العين ولهم أيضاً مكوى آخر يعملونه لأجل كيّ الأصداغ[١] ولهم مكوى آخر يعملونه لأجل الكيّ إذا أبروا العين من السبل وهو مسيل الماء الأسود ونزوله من الدماغ إلى العين ولهم مكوى آخر يعملونه لأجل أرياح تعرض في العين فيكوي بها الصدغين إذا كانت في الاثنين وإن كانت في صدغ واحد ولهم أيضاً مكوى يعملونه لتغيّر الأعين ومسيل الدمعة والرطوبة في الأجفان ولهم مكوى آخر يعملون للقروح التي تعرض في الأعين فإنّها تزول ولهم مكاوي أيضاً لسائر الأوجاع لا تحدّ ولا يعلّمها[٢] إلّا العلماء ثمّ الحكماء وقد ذكرت منها ما يستدعي على معرفة الجميع ويعلم من وقف على كتابي هذا أنّي لم أترك شيئاً من العلوم لم أقف عليها

الباب العشرون في كشف أسرار الذين يخرجون الصيبان من الجفن

٢٣،١٤ اعلم وفّقك الله أنّ هذا أعظم ما يكون من الدهاء والمَرَض فإنّ هذا المَرَض ما خلقه الله تعالى فإنّ هؤلاء القوم إذا عجزوا عن جميع الأشياء ينظروا من في عينيه بعض الأمراض المزمنة يقولون هذا فيها صؤاب[٣] وما يعرف هذا المرض إلّا كلّ واصل في هذه الصناعة فإنّ هذا مرض يسمّى الآكلة وهو عفونة تنصب في العين فيتولّد فيها صيبان يسكن في الجفن فإذا كحّل صاحبه أحسّ الصيبان بحادّيّة الكحل كمن في

١ أزيل للسياق: ولهم مكوى آخر يعملونه لأجل تزول الماء الأبيض في العين. ٢ ش: يعلها. ٣ ش: صور.

Section Nineteen: Exposé of Tricks Related to Quack Eye Doctors' Instruments

Exposé: They have a large set of instruments covering all diseases. Among them are collyrium containers and aneurism tweezers, as well as pincers for raising the eyelid when an aneurism is to be seized and cauterizing irons for cauterizing their patients. The first such instrument is an iron they make themselves for cauterization when a yellow cataract descends and covers the eye. They have other cauterizing instruments too that they make—to cauterize the descent of white cataract over the eye, to cauterize the temples, for cauterizing when curing the eye of an aneurism (which is created when black water flows down from the brain into the eye), and for sores that appear in the eye, with which they cauterize both temples if the sore is in both eyes, or just one, if it is in just one eye. They also have an iron they make for corruptions in the eye and liquid tearing and moisture in the lids; one they make for the ulcers that appear in the eye, resulting in blindness; and likewise irons for every kind of pain, too many to count. The making of these instruments should be taught only by professionals and, after them, physicians. I have mentioned enough of them to imply my acquaintance with the rest, and any who has perused this book of mine will be aware that I have left no science unexamined. **14.22**

Section Twenty: Exposé of the Tricks of Those Who Extract Nits from the Eyelid

You should be aware, God grant you success, that this trick is an example of the greatest cunning and hypocrisy, for the disease in question isn't even one created by the Almighty![191] This company, when at a loss for anything better to resort to, looks at a person with chronic eye disease and says, "The man has nits in his eyes!" Only doctors who are truly learned in their craft understand the genuine disease, which is called canker and consists of a painful putridity, inside of which are generated "nits" that then live on the eyelid. When the sufferer puts collyrium on his eye, these "nits" react to the astringency of the collyrium, become embedded in the eyelid, and remain there. From then on, **14.23**

الجفن وسكن فيه فعند ذلك يصعب برؤه ولا يقدم عليه حكيم إلّا أن يكون فاضل في هذه الصناعة فإنّه يعالجه ويتساقط من الأجفان على مثال الصيبان فيقاطع عليه بما اتّفق أنّه يخلّيه يقع

٢٤،١٤ فإذا اتّفق ذلك أخذ بيض النمل يضعه في مكحلة ثمّ يضع مكحلة أخرى بماء الرمّان الحامض قد عقّد بالسكّر حتّى يبقى على مثال اللعوق ثمّ يكحّله سبعة أيّام بما أراد من الأكحال فإذا كان اليوم السابع أخذ المِرْوَد وغمسه في المكحلة الذي فيها ماء الرمّان ثمّ يردّه إلى المكحلة الذي فيها بيض النمل ثمّ يكحّله في كلّ عين ثلاث مراود ولا يخلّيه يفتح عينه فإذا كحّله انحبس الدمع في العين ساعة وسبح بيض النمل وتساقط مع الدمعة ومنهم من يأخذ بزر الرشاد فينقعه في ماء حارّ ثمّ يمعكه بيده معكاً ليّن حتّى ينزع جميع قشره ثمّ يجفّفه جيّد ثمّ يودعه بعض الأكحال وقد أضاف إلى الكحل قليل صمغ عربيّ ثمّ يكحّله بما اتّفق من الأكحال سبعة أيّام ثمّ يدخل الحمّام فيغسل ثمّ يخرج فيعمل على شيء من الأدوية الحادّة حتّى يحمى الجفن ثمّ يكحّله من ذلك الكحل المدبّر ويقول نام فإذا نام انحلّ الصمغ فلصق أجفانه ومسك عليها بمقدار ما ينحلّ البزر وقد انحبست الدمعة في عينهم يفتح عينه يتساقط ذلك البزر مع الدمعة فلا يشكّ أنّه صيبان

الباب الحادي والعشرون في كشف أسرارهم في قلع الناصور من العين

٢٥،١٤ وذلك أنّه يأخذ ريشة حمام أبيض ويقصر سفلها بمقدار شعيرة ثمّ ينقعه في الخلّ الحاذق مع البورق سبعة أيّام حتّى يعود مثل العلك ثمّ يكحّل المريض بما اتّفق من الأكحال فإذا علم أنّ الريشة قد انحلّت كحّله تلك الليلة بكحل حادّ ومن الغد يأتي يأخذ تلك الريشة يلبّسها رأس المرود ثمّ يغطّ المرود في المكحلة فيها كحل ثمّ يكحّله ويدير المرود

it becomes difficult to cure the eyelid. Only a doctor who is learned in this craft will take the case on; when, however, a qualified person does treat it, the matter in question will fall from the lids in a form resembling nits, which the doctor scrapes off using anything to hand that will do the job.

When a case of the disease in question turns up, the quack takes ants' eggs 14.24
and puts them in a container for collyrium, puts sour pomegranate juice, stiffened with sugar till it's like a thick syrup, into another such container, and then anoints the patient's eyes with whatever collyriums he likes for seven days. On the seventh day, he takes the collyrium applicator, dips it into the container that holds the pomegranate juice, and then again into the container holding the ants' eggs. He anoints each of the man's eyes with three applicators' worth and forbids him to open his eyes. When he anoints him, the tears are retained in the eye for a while and the ants' eggs float around and later fall out with the tears. Or a quack of this sort may take cress seed, steep it in hot water, rub it gently between the fingers till all the hulls come off, and then dry it well. He puts this into certain collyriums, to which he may add a little gum arabic. Then he anoints the patient for seven days with whatever collyriums he happens to have to hand, after which the patient goes to the bathhouse and washes, then leaves. The quack now makes a batch of astringent medications to protect the eyelid. He anoints the patient with the aforementioned specially prepared collyrium and tells him to lie down, and when he does so, the gum runs and it seals his eyelids and keeps them closed for as long as it takes for the seed to be released. The tears having been retained in the man's eyes, when he opens them the said seed falls out along with the tears, and the patient never doubts that they are in fact "nits."

Section Twenty-One: Exposé of Their Tricks for Extracting Fistulas from the Eye

Exposé: They take the feather of a white dove and cut a piece the size of a grain 14.25
of barley from its bottom end.[192] This they steep in acidic vinegar and borax for seven days till it turns into something like a chewy gum. The quack then anoints the patient's eyes with whatever collyriums are to hand and, when he sees that the piece of quill has dissolved, does so again that same night with an astringent collyrium. The next morning, he takes the same piece of quill and

في عينه حتّى يعلم أنّ الريشة قد علقت في الجفن ويتركه ساعة بمقدار ما يتجمع الدمع في العين ثمّ يفتح عينه فإنّ تلك الريشة تنزل مع الدمعة وقد ألقى الدموع في إناء من الزجاج فإذا علم أنّ الريشة قد نزلت ألقى عليها ماء بارد فإنّها ترجع إلى حالتها الأولى فإذا رآها أحد فلا يشكّ أنّها ناسور ثمّ يكحّله سبعة أيّام بكحل يقطع الدمعة ثمّ يسكن المرض ويتركه فافهم ذلك ترشد

الباب الثاني والعشرون في كشف أسرار الذين يقلعون الشرناق من العين

اعلم أنّ هذا المرض لا يزول أبدًا إلّا بالقطع فمن قطعه عن صحّة فقد أبرأ صاحبه ولكن هؤلاء القوم أكثر معاشهم على صاحب هذا المرض يجعلونه مقثأة كلّ من جاء استغلّه وإذا أرادوا أن يتعيّشون عليه يأخذون مصران الغنم ثمّ يجرّدونه من لحمه بالظفر حتّى لا يبقى شيئًا منه إلّا الغشاوة على نحو ما يعملون مصران النقانق ثمّ يقطّعونه حلق حلق كلّ حلقة على قدر قلامة الظفر فإذا أرادوا قطع الشرناق أخذوا من ذلك حلقة ثمّ جعلها تحت لسانه حتّى تلين ثمّ يجعلها بين أصابعه لاصقة ثمّ يخرج الجفن بالحديد ويشرط فيه بالحديدة ويأخذ تلك الحلقة يمعكها في الدم على جفنه ثمّ يأخذ الميل فيرفعها به ثمّ يعصب العين فإذا أبصروا الحاضرين ذلك[١] فلا يشكّوا أنّه قطع من الشرناق ثمّ إنّه لم يقطع منه شيئًا فافهم ذلك ٢٦،١٤

١ ش: فإذا أرادوا الحاضرين ذلك أبصروه.

mounts it on the end of the collyrium applicator. Now he dips the applicator into a container holding collyrium and anoints the patient's eyes, turning the applicator in the eye until he is sure that the quill has stuck to the eyelid and leaving it there as long as is needed for tears to gather in the eye. Then he opens the man's eye and the quill comes out along with the tears, which he puts into a glass vessel. When he's sure that the quill has come out, he pours cold water on it and it reverts to its previous state. No one who sees it can doubt that it was a fistula. He then anoints the patient's eyes for seven days with a collyrium that prevents tearing, after which the morbid condition[193] subsides and leaves the patient. Wise up to this and you can't go wrong!

Section Twenty-Two: Exposé of the Tricks of Those Who Remove Tapeworms from the Eye

This disease can be put an end to only by incision. If a practitioner cuts the **14.26** tapeworm out correctly, he will cure the patient, but this band of quacks makes most of their living off patients with this disease, whom they turn into nice little pumpkin patches that anyone who comes along can crop. To make their living off a patient of this sort, they take sheep's intestines and strip the meat off them with their fingernails, leaving only the membrane, as one would when making sausage cases. They slice this into rings, each the size of a fingernail clipping. Now, to "cut out the tapeworm," the quack takes one of these rings and puts it under his tongue till it softens, then places it between his fingers, where it sticks. Next, he pulls the eyelid outward using his metal instrument, cuts into it using the same instrument, takes the ring, rubs it in the blood on the eyelid, and then takes the probe, removes the ring with it, and bandages the eye. Seeing this, the onlookers never doubt that he has cut out a tapeworm, though in fact he has cut out nothing! Wise up to this!

الفصل الخامس عشر

ستّة أبواب

في كشف أسرار الذين يقلعون الدود من الضرس

اعلم أنّ هذه الطائفة أشدّ محال من غيرهم وذلك أنّهم يدّعون علم ما لا يكون ١٫١٥
فيوهمون الناس أنّهم يقلعون من أضراسهم الدود فإنّهم يكذبون ويعملون للناس أدوية لا تسوى شيء وأنا أبيّن ذلك وأكشف بعض أسرارهم

الباب الأوّل في كشف أسرارهم

وذلك أنّهم إذا أرادوا يظهرون للناس أنّهم يقلعون الدود من الضرس يأخذون من ٢٫١٥
الحشيشة المعروفة باللاعِية الصفراء ثمّ يجفّفونها في الظلّ ثمّ يسحقونها ثمّ يأخذون من الدود الذي يكون في الفواكه ثمّ يلفّون الدودة في ورقة من بعض أوراق الثمر دمجًا جيّدًا ثمّ يلفّون عليها خيطًا ثمّ يتركونها حتّى تجفّ الورقة عليها وتمسك الدودة مسكًا جيّدًا ثمّ يعجنون ذلك الحشيش ويعملون منه أقراص ثمّ يأخذون ذلك الحشيش الذي فيه الدود ويجعلونه في جوانب الأقراص ويجفّفونها في الظلّ ويبقى الدود يأكل من تلك الحشيشة من الورق الذي هو فيها فإذا أرادوا أن يقلعوا الدود من الضرس يأخذون من تلك الأقراص بطرف أناملهم ثمّ يقطعون من حافته بسنّه قدر الموضع الذي فيه الدود ثمّ يجعلها على الضرس ويقول اطبق فمك فإذا فتح مدّ يده بالملقط أخذ الدودة عليه وأخرجها قدّام الحاضرين فيخيّل لهم أنّه قد أخرج الدودة من الضرس فافهم ذلك

Chapter Fifteen, in Six Sections:

Exposé of the Tricks of Those Who Extract Worms from Teeth

This tribe of charlatans is trickier than any other, because they claim to know things that cannot be known and give people to believe they can extract worms from their teeth. They are liars who concoct medications that do nothing for people. I shall show you how they do this and provide an exposé of some of their tricks. 15.1

Section One of the Exposé of Their Tricks

Exposé: To make people think they're pulling worms out of their teeth, they get hold of some of the weed known as yellow spurge, dry it in a shady place, and grind it to a powder. Next, they get some worms of the kind you find in fruit. They wrap each worm in the leaf of a certain fruit, pressing it well down inside, wind a thread round it, and leave it till the leaf dries over it, gripping the worm tightly. Now they make a paste from the grass powder, shape it into pills, take the leaves that contain the worms, insert them into the pills from the side, and dry them in the shade. The worms feed on the green leaves in which they're contained, and when the charlatans want to extract a worm from a tooth, they take one of these pills between the tips of their fingers, bite off a little piece where the worm is, and place it on the tooth, saying, "Close your mouth!" When the patient opens his mouth again, the quack inserts his hand with the tweezers, grips the worm with them, and pulls it out in front of those present, who think he's pulled a worm from the tooth. Wise up to these things! 15.2

الباب الثاني في كشف أسرارهم

٣،١٥ ومن ذلك أنّهم يأخذون أعصاب الجمال ينشرونها على قدر الدود وهي رطبة ثمّ يقرضونها بالمقراض على قدر الدود الصغار ثمّ يجفّفونها فإذا جفّت يجعلونها مثال[١] الأقراص فإذا أرادوا خروج الدود من الضرس أخذوا من ذلك القرص شيء يسير ثمّ تركه على الضرس فإذا حمي العصب في الفم فتحه فيخرجه فلا يشكّ فيه أحد أنّه دودة قد أخرجها من الضرس فيتوهّم له الناس ثمّ يبلّز عند ذلك الدواء

الباب الثالث في كشف أسرارهم

٤،١٥ ومن ذلك أنّهم يدّعون أنّهم يقلعون الضرس بلا حديد ولا كلَبات ولا مشراط فإذا أرادوا ذلك يأخذون صمغ الزيتون ثمّ يجعلونه على النار بلبن اللاعية ويجعلونه أقراص فإذا أرادوا قلع ضرس أحد أخذ المشراط وشرط على الضرس من بينين ثمّ يجعل عليه من ذلك الدواء ثمّ يمعكه به معكاً جيّداً فإذا فعل ذلك خلا لحم الضرس عنه فانقلع بلا كلبات ولا وجع وهذا ما يعمله إلّا رجل فاضل حكيم وهو من سرّ العلم

الباب الرابع في كشف أسرارهم

٥،١٥ فمن ذلك أنّهم يعملون سفوف ويوهّمون أنّه ينفع من الحفر[٢] والبخر ونزف الدم وأنّه يزيل الرائحة الكريهة من الفم وهذا واقع فإذا عمل على الوجه الصحيح وقد ذكر سابور في أقراباذينه شيئاً من ذلك ثمّ إنّهم يأخذون من قرن أيّل محرق وهليلج أصفر وملح أندرانيّ وحافر حمار محرق وشبّ يمانيّ وعفص أخضر ورؤوس الرمّان الحلو وحبّة سوداء وزرّ ورد وجُلّنار مصريّ وقرض وسمّاق وزرنيخ ورؤوس الإبار من كلّ واحد جزء ثمّ يسحقونه سحقاً ناعماً ويستاك به فإنّه نافع لما ذكرناه من أمراض الأسنان

---

١ ش: مع. ٢ الرسم غير واضح في الأصل – ش: الجصّ.

Section Two of the Exposé of Their Tricks

Another example: They take camel sinew and while it is still supple spread open a piece of it large enough to accommodate the worms. Then they snip it with scissors into pieces the size of the little worms and dry it. When it's dry, they make it into something resembling pills. To extract the worms from the tooth, they take a few of the pills and stick one onto the tooth. When the sinew has warmed up inside the patient's mouth, they open it and pull out the worm. No one doubts that the man has pulled the worm out of the tooth. Everyone thinks he's a real dentist and on that basis he peddles them the medication. 15.3

Section Three of the Exposé of Their Tricks

Another example: They pretend they can pull teeth without using metal instruments, pincers, or a scalpel. To do so, they take olive gum, place it over the fire with spurge milk, and make it into pills. To extract a tooth, they take a scalpel, make a cut on either side of the tooth, then put some of this preparation on the place and rub it in well. When the practitioner does so, the flesh around the tooth recedes and the tooth can be extracted without pincers or pain. Only one who is learned and wise can do this because it is a secret peculiar to this science. 15.4

Section Four of the Exposé of Their Tricks

Another example: They make powders and claim they're good against caries, bad breath, and bleeding and that they deodorize the mouth, which is in fact the case if done properly, for Sābūr mentions something of the sort in his *Pharmacopoeia*. They take burnt stag's horn, yellow myrobalan, pure rock salt, burnt donkey's hoof, Yemeni alum, green oak galls, sweet pomegranate fruit, black seed, rosebuds, Egyptian pomegranate blossom, acacia pods, sumac, arsenic, and palm spadices—one part each. They grind this till smooth and use it to clean their teeth. It works for the dental conditions we list above. 15.5

الباب الخامس في كشف أسرارهم

ومن ذلك أنّهم يعملون سفوفاً مجهول ويتكلّمون عليه ويبلّزونه على الأخشان وهو أن يأخذون فحم وسمّاق وقشور رمّان ويتكلّمون عليه فاعلم أنّ الفحم يجلو الأسنان والملح والسمّاق وقشور الرمّان لنزف الدم ويبلّزونه كما يريدون ٦،١٥

الباب السادس في كشف أسرارهم

ومن ذلك أعجب ما صادفته أن كان لي صاحب من أهل بُصْرَى يُعرف بعليّ البصراويّ وكان خبير بالأمور فدخل إلى الديار المصريّة في سنة عشرين وستّمائة وكنت بها فكان أهلها يستخفّون به وبأهل الشام ويقولون بقر الشام فقال أنا أبيّن من هم البقر ثمّ اجتمع بي فقال لي انقدح لي خاطر وأترك كلّ من في الديار المصريّة يلوك القذر فقلت كيف تعمل فقال بعد ثلاثة أيّام يبان لك الخبر ثمّ شرع عمل له مَجْمَع شبيهاً بالبيزرانيّة ثمّ جعل فيها عقاقير جملة برسم السَنون ثمّ أخذ من القذر اليابس وسحقه وجعله في حُقّ ثمّ بسط بساط بين القصرين وعمل حلقة ولفّها ثمّ إنّه تكلّم على دواء الفم وإنّه يظهر للعالم الأمراض الكامنة في أفواههم نظر العيان ومن أراد يجلس ٧،١٥

فجلس واحد ثمّ تقدّم فقبّله ذلك الحُقّ الذي فيه القذر وقال له خذ من هذا الدواء على إصبعك ثمّ استاك به وأطل المعك فأخذ منه وجعل في فمه ثمّ استاك وأطال المعك فانحلّ القذر وظهر له رائحة كريهة ثمّ قال ابصق في كفّك فجعله في كفّه فيقول ابصق وشمّ رائحة مرضك فشمّ تلك الرائحة التي تصرع الطير فقال خذ هذه الإبريق وتمضمض ونظّف قال ففعل ذلك ثمّ أخذ من ذلك السفوف الطيّب الذي في المجمع وقال استاك بهذا الدواء وأطل المعك وقال ابصق في كفّك واشتمّ رائحة كفّك فشمّ رائحة الطيّب فقال الآن خلصت من الموادّ الرديئة في الفم ٨،١٥

Section Five of the Exposé of Their Tricks

Another example: They make powders out of mystery ingredients, say a spell over them, and peddle them to the marks. What they do is they take charcoal, sumac, and pomegranate rinds and say a spell over them. Mind that the charcoal polishes the teeth, while the salt, sumac, and pomegranate rinds are for the bleeding. They can peddle this stuff for any price they care to name. 15.6

Section Six of the Exposé of Their Tricks

The most amazing thing of this type I came across was that I had a friend from Bosra called ʿAlī al-Buṣrāwī, who was a real expert. In 620 [1223–24], he came to Egypt while I was there. The Egyptians used to make fun of him and of Syrians in general, calling them "Syrian cows." "I'll show them who the cows are!" he said. Then he ran into me and said, "I've got a bright idea for how to make everyone in Egypt chew filth." "What are you going to do?" I asked him. "Three days from now you'll see," he said. He set to and had a compartmented box similar to a seed box made. In this he placed a bunch of apothecary's simples made up into tooth powder. Then he took dry filth, ground it up, and put it in another box. Now he rolled out a carpet in Bayn al-Qaṣrayn and gathered a circle of people around him and gave a spiel about his "mouth medicine" and how it revealed to people the diseases hidden in their mouths so they could see them with their own eyes, and that anyone who felt so inclined should take a seat. 15.7

One of them did, and ʿAlī leant forward and placed the box with the filth in it in front of him and told him, "Take some of this medicine on your finger and rub it over your teeth. Keep doing it for a while." The man took some, put it in his mouth, rubbed his teeth with it, and kept doing it till the filth disintegrated and he smelled a revolting smell. "Now," said ʿAlī, "spit in your palm" and the man did so. Then ʿAlī said, "Spit and smell your sickness," so the man took a good whiff of that well-known smell that makes flies drop dead. Then ʿAlī said, "Take this jug and rinse your mouth out with its contents," and the man did so. Next, ʿAlī took some of the sweet-smelling powders that were in the compartmented box and said, "Clean your teeth with this medication, and make a good job of it." Then, "Spit in your palm and see what it smells like." The man smelled the good smell. Then ʿAlī said, "You are now free of the foul 15.8

فلو دامت هذه الموادّ حصل لك منها البخر وفساد المعدة وكمد اللون وقلع الأسنان ثمّ أخذ منه نصف درهم كامل وأعطاه من هذا السفوف شيء يسير ثمّ فعل بآخر كذلك ولم يزل يفعل ذلك بهم مدّة سنة كاملة وكانت حلقته تقلع كلّ يوم من أوّل النهار إلى آخر النهار ستّين سبعين درهم سوداء يسوّك كلّ يوم جماعة بالقذر ويأخذ فضّتهم ثمّ بعد ذلك بطّل وجلس يحدّث في سيرة البطّال وكلّ ليلة يعرّض لهم أنّهم يستاكون بالقذر ويؤدّون الجعل إلّا أنّه يحكي لهم نوادر من مثل ذلك ولا يفهمون معناه

matter that was in your mouth. If it had been allowed to remain, you'd have bad breath and stomach upsets, your complexion would have lost its color, and your teeth would have fallen out." He took a whole half-silver-piece from the man and gave him a few of the powders, and he did the same with another, and he went on treating them to the same for an entire year, the circle of customers around him providing a take, from first thing in the day to the end, of sixty to seventy "black" silver pieces,[194] while every day he made a bunch of people clean their teeth with filth and hand him their money. Afterward, he gave that up and instead sat and recounted *The Legend of al-Baṭṭāl*, and every night he'd make some allusion to the fact that they were cleaning their teeth with filth and they'd give him baksheesh, even though he was telling them anecdotes to this effect. They never got it!

الفصل السادس عشر

باب واحد

في كشف أسرار أصحاب الحديد من الكحّالين

وقد ذكرنا ذلك في الفصل الرابع عشر إذ ذكرنا فيه أطبّاء الطريق وهذا الفصل قد ١،١٦
جمعهم ونظمهم في جملة أطبّاء الطريق إذ لا يكون لحّال صاحب حديد إلّا طُرُقيّ
فبهذا السبب ضمّهم الفصل الرابع عشر مع جملة أطبّاء الطريق ولا فائدة في إعادته

Chapter Sixteen, in One Section:

Exposé of the Tricks of Eye Doctors Who Use Metal Instruments

We have already dealt with this topic in the chapter on quacks who practice on the highway, where these are brought together and placed in the same class as the other itinerant quacks, since an eye doctor who uses metal instruments can only be a "highwayman." This is why Chapter 14 lumps them in with the rest of the itinerant quacks, and there's no point going over it again.[195] **16.1**

الفصل السابع عشر

ستّة أبواب

في كشف أسرار الذين يصبغون الخيل

اعلم أنّ هذه الطائفة أشدّ دهاء ومكر وتسلّط على أموال الناس فأكثرهم دكاشرة أو مواطئون الدكاشرة وذلك أنّهم يأخذون فرس واحد ويصبغونها ويُبَيعونها عليه وهذا أشدّ ما يكون من البهت والدهاء وقد اجتمعت منهم بجماعة في أرض الصعيد وعَيْذاب وفي بلاد الغرب رأيت ذلك عيانًا وفي تونس وصحبني بعضهم ١،١٧

الباب الأوّل

من ذلك أنّهم يغيّرون الجواد الأدهم فيعيدونه أبيضاً وهذا أبلغ ما يكون فإذا أرادوا ذلك يأخذون من خرّوب المعز وقثّاء الحمار ومن الباذروج ومن الخردل الأبيض ومن حبّ النارنج من كلّ واحد جزء فيدقّ الجميع ويغمر بماء حُمّاض الأُتُرُجّ ويغلى حتّى ينقص الربع ويحمّ به الجواد الأدهم فإنّه يعود أبيضاً شديد البياض فافهم ذلك ٢،١٧

الباب الثاني في كشف أسرارهم

ومن ذلك أنّهم يعيدون الجواد الأبيض أدهم فإذا أرادوا ذلك يأخذون من ورق الحنّاء ومن حشيشة الصبّاغين ومن حبّ الباذروج ومن القلقند ومن الفِرصاد الشاميّ ومن حبّ الإذخر ومن ورق الغبيراء من كلّ واحد جزء يدقّ الجميع ويغمر بماء السمّاق ٣،١٧

Chapter Seventeen, in Six Sections:

Exposé of the Tricks of Those Who Dye Horses

This tribe of charlatans is extremely crafty, cunning, and audacious in taking people's money. Most of them are crooked horse copers or people in cahoots with them. 17.1

Exposé: They get a horse, dye it, and change its color, which is one of the most astonishing and ingenious things anyone can do. I hung out with a group of them in Upper Egypt and at ʿAydhāb. I saw these things with my own eyes in the Gharb too, as I did in Tunis, and some of them became my friends.

Section One

Another example: They can change the color of a black horse and turn it white, which is as clever as it gets. To do this, they get bean clover, squirting cucumber, basil, white mustard, and bitter orange pips, one part each, pound them together, cover them in citron-pulp water, and boil everything till reduced by a quarter. A black horse washed with this turns the whitest of whites. Wise up to these things! 17.2

Section Two of the Exposé of Their Tricks

Another example: They can turn a white horse into a black horse. To do this, they take equal parts henna leaves, dyers' weed, basil seed, vitriol, Syrian mulberry, fever grass seed, and folded croton. All this is pounded and covered with sumac water. They boil this till reduced by a quarter, then wash 17.3

ثمّ يغلونه حتّى يذهب الربع ثمّ يحمّون به الجواد فإنّه يعود أسود شديد السواد حسن اللون فافهم ذلك

الباب الثالث في كشف أسرارهم

٤،١٧ وذلك أنّهم إذا أرادوا أن يصبغوا أحمر شديد الحمرة يأخذون من الحنّاء الطيّب أربعة أجزاء ومن ساق الحمام جزء ومن الجلّنار المصريّ جزء ومن ورق الحنّاء أيضاً جزء ومن ورق النَوْر الأحمر جزء ومن الشبّ اليمانيّ جزء فيدقّ الجميع ناعماً ثمّ يغمره بالماء ثمّ يغلى عليه حتّى يذهب الربع ثمّ يحمّ به الجواد فإنّه يعود أحمر شديد الحمرة أحسن ما يكون

الباب الرابع في كشف أسرارهم

٥،١٧ فمن ذلك أنّهم إذا أرادوا أن يصبغوه أصفرًا فيأخذون من ساق الحمام جزء ومن الحنّاء جزء ومن الزعفران جزء ومن الشبّ الأحمر جزء ومن الرامك المصريّ جزء ومن حبّ الباذروج جزء ويدقّ الجميع ناعماً ويغمر بالماء ويغلى عليه حتّى ينقص الربع ثمّ يحمّ به الجواد فيعود أصفرًا حسن الصفرة ولا يمكن أن يكون صبغ الجواد أحمرًا ولا أصفرًا إلّا أن يكون أصله أبيضاً

الباب الخامس في كشف أسرارهم

٦،١٧ ومن ذلك أنّهم يصبغون الجواد أبرشاً[١] وذلك أنّهم يأخذون من ورق الخِطْميّة جزء ومن القلقند جزء ومن الزاج جزء ومن ساق الحمام جزء ومن حشيشة الصبّاغين جزء ومن الحنّاء جزءين ومن الباذروج جزء ومن حبّ البان جزء يدقّ الجميع ويغمر بماء الهندباء مع الماء العذب ثمّ يغلى عليه حتّى يذهب الربع ثمّ يحمّ به الجواد فإنّه يعود أبرش اللون

---

١ ش: أسودًا.

the horse with it and it turns a very deep black, of a fine tone. Wise up to these things!

Section Three of the Exposé of Their Tricks

Exposé: To dye a horse a very deep dark red, they take four parts sweet henna, one part alkanet, one part Egyptian pomegranate blossoms, one part henna leaves, one part leaves of cloves,[196] and one part Yemeni alum. All this is pounded till smooth, then covered with water and boiled till reduced by a quarter. The horse will turn an intense red, as pretty as can be. 17.4

Section Four of the Exposé of Their Tricks

Another example: To dye a horse yellow, they take one part alkanet, one part henna, one part saffron, one part red alum, one part Egyptian ramek, and one part basil seed. All this is pounded till smooth, covered with water, and boiled till reduced by a quarter. The horse is washed with this and it turns a beautiful yellow. A horse can only be dyed red or yellow if it was white to begin with. 17.5

Section Five of the Exposé of Their Tricks

Another example: They dye horses a speckled color. 17.6

Exposé: They do this by taking one part leaves of marshmallow, one part vitriol, one part alum, one part alkanet, one part dyer's weed, two parts henna, one part basil, and one part ben nut. All this is pounded and covered with endive water mixed with drinking water, then boiled till reduced by a quarter. They wash the horse with it and it comes out speckled with whitish spots.

الباب السادس في كشف أسرارهم

ومن ذلك أنّ الدكاشرة إذا اشتروا الفرس الكبير وأرادوا أن يجعلوه رَباع يأخذون الفرس ويشكّلوه ثمّ يرموه إلى الأرض ثمّ يأخذون خازوق يجعلونه في فمه ثمّ يأخذون المبرد يبردون أنيابه ويدوّرونها حتّى يبقى كأنّه رباع لا ينكر منه شيئاً وكذلك يعملون بأسنانه ٧،١٧

Section Six of the Exposé of Their Tricks

Another example: When these crooked copers buy an old horse and want to turn it into a four-year-old, they take the animal and hobble it, then throw it to the ground and get a stake and put it in its mouth. Next, they take a file and file down its wolf teeth, rounding them off till the animal resembles a four-year-old so closely that nothing about it raises suspicion. They do the same with its other teeth too. 17.7

الفصل الثامن عشر

عشرة أبواب

في كشف أسرارهم ومن ذلك الذين يصبغون بني آدم

رأيت في بلاد الروم أقواماً يصبغون بني آدم وذلك أنّهم يصبغون الغلمان ويصبغون ١،١٨
من يكون عليهم طلابة ويريدون الهرب ويسرقون البنات والصبيان ثمّ يصبغونهم ويبيعونهم ويخرّجونهم من البلاد ولا ينكر أحد عليهم في ذلك فكشفت أسرارهم في ذلك وبيّنته

الباب الأوّل في كشف أسرارهم

ومن ذلك أنّهم إذا أرادوا أن يتركون الأبيض أسودًا حبشيّاً أو نوبيّاً أو زنجيّاً يأخذون ٢،١٨
من حشيشة الصبّاغين جزء ومن القلقنت جزء ومن الزاج جزء ومن العفص الأخضر جزء ومن الشبّ الزَفَر جزء ومن عروق الجوز جزء وقشوره جزء ومن ورق الفرصاد جزء يدقّ الجميع ناعماً ويغمره بماء السمّاق ثمّ يغلى عليه حتّى يذهب الربع ثمّ يحمّ به ابن آدم فإنّه يعود أسود شديد السواد فافهم ذلك

الباب الثاني في كشف أسرارهم

ومن ذلك أنّهم إذا أرادوا أنّ الإنسان يعود حبشيّاً أو نوبيّاً أو زنجيّاً فإنّهم يأخذون ٣،١٨
من ورق الفرصاد الشاميّ جزء ومن حشيشة الصبّاغين جزء ومن القلقنت جزء ومن الزاج جزء ومن الخرّوب الشاميّ جزء يدقّ الجميع ناعماً ويغمر بماء السمّاق

Chapter Eighteen, in Ten Sections:

Exposé of Their Tricks; Example: Those Who Dye Humans

In Anatolia, I came across bands who dyed humans. 18.1

Exposé: They dye slaves and any wanted persons who wish to flee. They steal girls and boys, whom they dye, sell, and smuggle out of the country without anyone thinking to stop them. I got to the bottom of their tricks and revealed how they work.

Section One of the Exposé of Their Tricks

Example: To make a white person into a black Abyssinian, Nubian, or Negro, 18.2
they take one part dyers' weed, one part vitriol, one part verdigris, one part green oak gall, one part stinking alum, one part walnut roots, one part walnut shells, and one part mulberry leaves. All these are pounded together till smooth, covered with sumac water, then boiled till reduced by a quarter. When they bathe a man in this, he turns extremely black. Wise up to these things!

Section Two of the Exposé of Their Tricks

Another example: To turn someone into an Abyssinian, a Nubian, or a Negro, 18.3
they take one part Syrian mulberry leaves, one part dyers' weed, one part vitriol, one part verdigris, and one part Syrian carob. All this is pounded together till smooth, covered with sumac water, then boiled till reduced by a quarter.

ثمّ يغلى عليه حتّى يذهب الربع ثمّ يحمّون به ابن آدم فإنّه يعود حبشيّاً أو نوبيّاً أو زنجيّاً فافهم ذلك

الباب الثالث في كشف أسرارهم

ومن ذلك أنّهم إذا أرادوا أن يصبغون الآدميّ حبشيّاً أو زنجيّاً أو نوبيّاً حتّى ينكره ٤،١٨ أهله وأبوه وأمّه فإذا أرادوا ذلك يأخذون من ورق حشيشة الصبّاغين جزء ومن القلقنت جزء ومن الزاج جزء يدقّ الجميع ثمّ يغمر بماء الشبّ المحلول ثمّ يغلى عليه حتّى يذهب الربع ثمّ يحمّون به الآدميّ فإنّه يعود حبشيّاً أو نوبيّاً ثمّ ينكروه أهله وغيرهم فافهم ذلك

الباب الرابع في كشف أسرارهم وتغيير لحاهم

وذلك أنّ هذه الطائفة يفعلون ما لا يقدر عليه أحد فمن ذلك أنّهم إذا أرادوا أن ٥،١٨ يغيّروا خلقهم ويدخلون في كلّ باب كما قال الله ﴿فِيٓ أَىِّ صُورَةٍ مَّا شَآءَ رَكَّبَكَ﴾ فمن ذلك صبغ ألوانهم وصبغ لحاهم ومن أعجب ما صادفته لهم أنّي رأيت بمدينة هندبار غلام شابّ حسن الشمائل يُعرف بمحمود بن شاباش وكان من شطّار زمانه فلمّا كان بعد أيّام وأنا عند صاحب لي نجّار[١] ونحن نتحدّث إذ قدم علينا رجل أسود إلّا أنّه شيخ قد أنقى فسلّم ثمّ جلس فردّ عليه النجّار السلام وجعل يحادثه ساعة ثمّ وثب قائماً وراح إلى سبيله

فقلت لصاحبي وكان هذا الشيخ عنده شيء من العلوم فضحك فقلت ما ٦،١٨ يضحكك فقال ما تعرف هذا الشيخ قلت لا والله فقال ما هذا محمود بن شاباش فقلت هوّن الله عليك فقال والله ما قلت إلّا حقّاً فقلت لا تفعل فقال هذا والله

١ ش: من النجّار.

They bathe a human in this and the person turns into an Abyssinian, a Nubian, or a Negro. Wise up to these things!

Section Three of the Exposé of Their Tricks

Another example: To dye a client to look so like an Abyssinian, Negro, or Nubian that his wife, his father, and his mother will all refuse to have anything to do with him—to do this, as I say, they take one part dyers' weed, one part vitriol, and one part verdigris. These are pounded together, covered in water in which alum has been dissolved, then boiled till reduced by a quarter. They bathe the client in it and he turns out looking so much like an Abyssinian or a Nubian that neither his wife nor anyone else will have anything to do with him. Wise up to these things! 18.4

Section Four of the Exposé of Their Tricks and How They Change the Color of Their Beards

Exposé: This tribe of charlatans does things no one else can. 18.5

Example: To change their appearance so as to pass for any kind of person they want—as though in imitation of God's words «and He composed thee after what form He would»[197]—they may go so far as to change the color of their skin and dye their beards. The most amazing example I ever came across of what they're able to do was in the city of Hindibār, when I saw a youth with handsome features called Maḥmūd ibn Shābāsh, who was one of the leading "wiseguys"[198] of his day. A few days later, I was at the shop of a friend of mine, a carpenter, and we were chatting, when a black man of venerable appearance and white hair suddenly appeared in front of us, greeted us, and sat down. The carpenter returned his greeting and talked with him for a while. Then the man jumped up and went his way.

I asked my friend, "Is that shaykh a master of any of the sciences?" and he laughed. "What makes you laugh?" I asked. "Didn't you recognize him?" he said. "Certainly not!" I said, to which he responded, "It's Maḥmūd ibn Shābāsh!" "Don't be stupid!" I said. "I swear I'm telling the truth!" he replied. "No you're not!" I said, but he said, "That, I swear, was our friend Maḥmūd ibn 18.6

محمود بن شاباش صاحبنا فقلت وما الذي جعله على هذه الصفة أمّا السواد فإنّه يمكن بل الشيب كيف فيه الحيلة فقال أَوَما علمت صفة الشيب كيف هو فقلت لا والله ولا سمعت به إلى وقتي هذا فقال أنا أعرّفك ذلك اعلم أنّهم إذا أرادوا أن يصبغون اللحية حتّى تبقى كأنّها اللجين يأخذون من ماء السمّاق جزء ومن اللبن الحامض جزء ومن حبّ الليمو جزء ومن الراوندان جزء فيدقّونه ويعلفون به اللحية فإنّها تعود بيضاء شديدة البياض فتعجّبت من ذلك وقال لهم صفة أحسن من ذلك فقلت وما هي قال يجعلون اللحية السوداء[1] شقراء لها صفة لا يكون أحسن منها فافهم ذلك

الباب الخامس في كشف أسرارهم

٧،١٨ ومن ذلك أنّهم إذا أرادوا أن يجعلون اللحية شقراء فيأخذون من الحنّاء جزء ومن الفوّة المدقوقة جزء ثمّ يعجنونها عجنًا جيّدًا ويخمرونها ثمّ يعلفون بها اللحية فإنّها تعود شقراء شديدة الشقرة والصهوبة

الباب السادس في كشف أسرارهم

٨،١٨ ومن ذلك أنّهم إذا أرادوا أن يسوّدوا وجه إنسان حتّى يعود وجهه أسود دون يديه ويمّسون عليه ما أرادوا فإذا أرادوا ذلك فيأخذون من العفص المحرق جزء ومن الشبّ المرايش جزء ومن الزاج جزء يدقّ الجميع ثمّ يعملون أقراص بعد أن تهابا ويبيّتونه على الوجه فإنّه يسودّ ويكمّده

الباب السابع في كشف أسرارهم

٩،١٨ ومن ذلك أنّهم إذا أرادوا يسوّدون وجه إنسان ولا يزال كذلك مع الدوام يأخذون من الكاكنج جزء ومن ورق لسان الحمل جزء ومن الغبيراء جزء ومن عصارة لحية

---

١ ش: سوداء.

Shābāsh!" "How did he get to look like that?" I asked. "The black skin I can see, but what's the trick with the white hair?" "You never learned the recipe for white hair?" asked my friend. "No, I didn't," I replied, "and I've never heard of such a thing." "I'll tell you how it's done," he said. "To dye a beard to make it look like pure silver, they take one part sumac water, one part sour milk, one part lemon pips, and one part rhubarb. They pound this and dress the beard with it, and it turns a brilliant white." I was amazed. He went on to say, though, "They have an even better recipe than that!" "Which is what?" I asked. "They can turn a black beard blond," he said, "and that's the best recipe there can be!" Wise up to these things!

Section Five of the Exposé of Their Tricks

Another example: To turn a beard blond, they take one part each of henna and crushed madder, knead this well, and let it ferment. Then they dress the beard with it and it turns a very intense reddish blond. 18.7

Section Six of the Exposé of Their Tricks

Another example: To turn a man's face but not hands black and trick the client with an illusion—to do this, as I say, they take one part burnt oak gall, one part halotrichite, and one part verdigris. They make this into pills, the ingredients having first been ground to the consistency of dust, and they leave it on the face overnight. The man's face turns black and he uses it as a poultice.[199] 18.8

Section Seven of the Exposé of Their Tricks

Another example: To make a person's beard permanently black, they take one part alkekengi, one part broadleaf plantain leaves, one part dyers' croton, and one part goat's beard sap. All this is pounded together till smooth and placed 18.9

التيس جزء يدقّ الجميع ناعماً ويكمّد به الوجه ليلة فإذا أصبح غسله فإنّه يعود أسود سواد عظيم فافهم ذلك

الباب الثامن في كشف أسرارهم

١٠،١٨ ومن ذلك إذا أرادوا يغيّروا لحية إنسان ويخرجونه من حال إلى حال وكذلك جسده فإذا أرادوا ذلك من إزالة سائر العيوب يأخذون من ورق الفرصاد الأبيض جزء ومن ورق العنّاب جزء ومن الغبيراء جزء وورقها ويدقّها ومن حبّ البان جزء ومن حبّ المحلب جزء ومن الخردل الأبيض جزء ومن البورق الأرمنيّ جزء يدقّ الجميع ناعماً ثمّ يلبّس به الوجه ليلة فإذا أصبح دخل الحمّام ثمّ غسله فإنه يبقى نقيّاً صافياً لا فيه أثر أبداً ولا جدريّ ولا نمش ولا شيء من العيوب فافهم ذلك

الباب التاسع في كشف أسرارهم

١١،١٨ ومن ذلك إذا أرادوا أن يبقى على الوجه نوراً ساطعاً وبهاء لامعاً حتّى يذهب عقل من ينظر إليه ويبهت من يراه فيأخذون من بزر الخسّ جزء ومن حبّ الخروع جزء ومن الرامك المصريّ جزء ومن العفص الهنديّ جزء ومن الفوذنج النهريّ جزء ومن الجلّنار المصريّ جزء ومن الزاج الصينيّ جزء ومن البورق الأرمنيّ جزء ومن خبز الفضّة جزء ومن زرّ الورد الأحمر جزء ومن الخردل الأبيض جزء يدقّ ناعماً ويعجن بماء الهندباء ويكمّد به الوجه ليلة فإذا أصبح غسله بدقيق الشعير فافهم ذلك

الباب العاشر في كشف أسرارهم

١٢،١٨ ومن ذلك أنّهم إذا أرادوا أن يغيّروا حلية إنسان ويخرجونه من حال إلى حال وذلك أن يكون بوجه إنسان بهقاً أو نمشاً أو برصاً أو جدريّ فيبدلونه[١] حتّى ينكره من

---

١ ش: فيبلّزنه.

over the face at night in the form of a poultice. In the morning, it is washed off and the beard will have turned dark black. Wise up to these things!

Section Eight of the Exposé of Their Tricks

Another example: To blacken a person's beard and change it completely, or to get rid of any blemishes on his body, they take one part leaves of white mulberry, one part jujube leaves, and one part dyers' croton with the leaves, all of which are then pounded together; then one part ben nut, one part mahaleb cherry seed, one part white mustard, and one part Armenian borax. All this is pounded together till smooth and the subject applies it to his face at night, and in the morning he goes into the bathroom and washes it off, after which his face will be left white and clear, with no trace of anything—no pox, no freckles, no blemish of any kind. **18.10**

Section Nine of the Exposé of Their Tricks

Another example: To create a light coming from the face that shines so brightly it drives everyone who looks at it crazy and leaves everyone who sees it speechless, they take one part lettuce seed, one part castor seed, one part Egyptian ramek, one part Indian oak gall, one part water mint, one part Egyptian pomegranate blossom, one part Chinese verdigris, one part Armenian borax, one part silver salt, one part red rosebuds, and one part white mustard. All this is pounded together till smooth, kneaded with endive water, and applied to the face overnight as a poultice. The next morning the subject washes it off using barley flour. Wise up to these things! **18.11**

Section Ten of the Exposé of Their Tricks

Another example: To change a person's countenance and transform it completely—for instance, when a person's face is marked by tetters, freckles, vitiligo, or leprosy—they switch the new for the old so skillfully that his accompanying acquaintances and family members refuse to believe that it is he. **18.12**

يحضر معه من المعارف والأهل وذلك أنهم يأخذون من الرامك المصريّ جزء ومن الخردل الأبيض جزء ومن حشيشة الزجاج جزء ومن حبّ البان جزء ومن الفوذنج النهريّ جزء يدقّ الجميع ناعماً وينخل بحريرة ويلبّس به الوجه فإذا أصبح باكر أتى الحمّام فإنّه يذهب جميع ما ذكرناه من الوجه ويصقله وينقيه من جميع العيوب فافهم ذلك

Exposé: They do this by taking one part Egyptian ramek, one part white mustard, one part pellitory-of-the-wall, one part ben nut, and one part water mint. All this is pounded together till smooth, passed through a silken sieve, and applied to the face. Early the next morning, the subject goes to the bathhouse. The preparation removes from his face everything we listed above, polishes it, and cleanses it of all blemishes. Wise up to these things!

الفصل التاسع عشر

ثلاثة أبواب

في كشف أسرار الذين يلعبون بالنار ويمنعون حرّها

١٬١٩ اعلم أنّ هذه الطائفة ألعن الطوائف وأخبثهم وأكذبهم وأكثرهم تسلّط على مثلهم وأكثرهم فساداً وأشدّهم نفاقاً وأعظم كفراً وهم طوائف المجوس وهم الذين يعبدون النار ويسجدون للشمس حين طلوعها ولهم نبيّ يعرفون به وهو زَرادُشْت وهذا الرجل كان خبيراً بجميع الترابيص وجميع الموانع التي تمنع من حريق النار وكان قد جعل له عيداً في كلّ سنة فإذا كان قبل العيد بسبعة أيّام لا يبقى أحد من أهل ملّته حتّى يحمل إلى بيت النار من الأحطاب ما أمكنه فإذا كان قبل العيد بثلاثة أيّام أضرموا النار في تلك الأحطاب فتظلّ تأكل بعضها بعضاً إلى أن تعود جمراً فلا يستطيع أحد أن يدنو منها لوهجها فإذا كان يوم العيد أقبل زرادشت إليها والخلق خلفه ثمّ سجد إليها وتبعه جميع رهطه فإذا رفع رأسه من السجود وهجم عليها فخاضها كخوض الماء ولا يزال في النار إلى الساعة الثالثة من النهار ثمّ يخرج فيقرّب لها قربان من الأغنام ثمّ الأبقار وغيرها من الحيوان ويمّس بهذا الناموس العظيم

الباب الأوّل في كشف أسرارهم

٢٬١٩ فمن ذلك أنّهم إذا أرادوا الدخول في النار فلا تضرّهم شيئاً ولا تأذيهم فيأخذون ضفدع فيقتلونه ويقلونه حتّى يخرج الدهن ثمّ يأخذون ذلك الدهن ويجعلونه مع

Chapter Nineteen, in Three Sections:

Exposé of the Tricks of Those Who Manipulate Fire and Can Block Its Heat

This is the most despicable, vile, and mendacious of all the tribes of charlatans, the most absolute in their control over their own kind, the most corrupt, the most hypocritical, and the most prodigious in their lack of true belief. They are the Magians, the ones who worship fire and prostrate themselves to the sun on its rising, and they have a prophet, Zoroaster, by whose name they are also known. This man was well versed in all agents and retardants effective against the incendiary power of fire. An annual celebration was held for him, seven days before which every member of his religion would carry as much fuel as he could to the fire temple. Three days before the celebration, they would light this fuel, which would consume itself until nothing was left but embers so hot no one could get near them. On the day of the celebration, Zoroaster would approach the embers, the people following. He would then bow down to the embers, along with all his company. Finally, when he raised his head, he would charge at the embers, wading through them as though through water and remaining in the fire until the third hour of the day, after which he would emerge. Sheep, goats, cows, and other animals were then sacrificed to the fire, and he used this prodigious illusion to delude people. 19.1

Section One of the Exposé of Their Tricks

Example: To be able to go through fire without it harming or hurting them in any way, they take a frog, kill it, and fry it till the fat comes out. Then they take the fat, mix it with saltpeter, and rub it till it turns into a kind of ointment, with 19.2

البارود الثلجيّ ثمّ يمعكون حتّى يعود كالمرهم ثمّ يلطخون بذلك المرهم أجسادهم ويدخلون النار فإنّها لا تضرّهم ولا تأذيهم واعلم أنّ هذا المرهم المذكور من أعظم الأسرار فافهم ذلك

الباب الثاني في كشف أسرارهم

وذلك أنّهم إذا أرادوا أن يلعبون بالنار فلا تضرّهم شيئاً فيأخذون من الطلق الجيّد ٣،١٩
النقيّ ثمّ ينقونه ويغسلونه في خرقة كتّان ثمّ يربطونها ويجعلونها في قِدْر فيها باقلّى ويتركونه حتّى ينسلق الباقلّى ثمّ يخرجونها ويمرسونها بين أيديها حتّى يخرج جميع ما فيها ثمّ يأخذون شحم اللَّجَاة ويمعكونه بذلك الطلق حتّى يعود كالزبد ثمّ يلطخون به أيديهم ويلعبون بالنار كيف شاء فلا تضرّهم شيئاً

الباب الثالث في كشف أسرارهم

ومن ذلك أنّ من جملة ما رأيت بمدينة هندبار رجل نجّار مجوسيّاً يُعرف بعبد النار ٤،١٩
وهو شيخ يعمل الأصنام الصغار برسم الحمل تكون معهم في جيوبهم يبيع الصنم بخمسة دنانير مالكيّة وذلك أنّهم يضعون الصنم في النار فلا تحرقه ولا تضرّه شيئاً مع أنّه خشب فلم أزل أدنو منه وأتقرّب إليه وأرادده وأوريه شيء بعد شيء من أصناف العلوم بما يخرق عقله ولم أزل حتّى ربطته أنّي أعرف شيئاً يدهن[1] به جدارات الدار فلا تزال الجدارات تشعل نار ولا تضرّ الأخشاب

فلمّا سمع ذلك ارتبط عليه والتمسه منّي فقلت فائدة بفائدة فما عندك من الفوائد ٥،١٩
فقال معالجة هذه الأصنام فلا تعمل النار فيها شيئاً فقلت له ذلك داخل في الذي قد ذكرته لك فأعرض عليّ أشياء فلم أعتني بها فأخذه القلق إلى معرفة ما ذكرته له وجدّ

١ ش: يذهب.

which they smear their bodies. Then they enter the fire, which neither harms nor hurts them. The aforesaid ointment is one of the most prodigious of tricks. Wise up to this!

Section Two of the Exposé of Their Tricks

Exposé: To manipulate fire without it harming them in any way, they take pure, high-grade talc, purify it further, and strain it through a linen rag. Next they tie it into bundles, place these in earthenware pots containing beans, and leave them till the beans are cooked through. They then take the beans out and mash them by hand in water till their contents have been completely extruded. Then they take frog[200] fat and rub it into the talc till it turns into a kind of scum. They smear this on their hands and can then do what they like with fire without it harming them in any way. 19.3

Section Three of the Exposé of Their Tricks

Another example: One of the things I saw in the city of Hindibār was a Magian woodworker whose name was Fire-Worshipper. He was an old man who made little idols in the shape of lambs, which the Zoroastrians used to carry around in their pockets. He sold the idols for five Mālikī gold pieces each. He was able to ask that much because they could put the idols in the fire and it wouldn't burn them or harm them in any way even though they were made of wood. I approached him persistently, cozied up to him, visited him, and showed him scientific feats that blew his mind, and it wasn't long before I'd duped him into thinking that I knew something one could use to paint the walls of a house that would prevent them from catching fire but wouldn't harm the timbers. 19.4

When he heard this, he fell for it and begged me to tell him, so I said, "One good turn deserves another. What can you do for me?" He said, "I can tell you how to treat these idols so that fire doesn't do anything to them." "That's already part of what I said I'd tell *you*!" I replied. So then he offered me some tips, which I showed no interest in, and that made him even more anxious to learn about the thing I'd said I'd tell him, and even more importunate. I told 19.5

في الطلب فقلت إذا لم يكن عندك فائدة فابدل الذهب فقال كم مقدار ما يرضيك فقلت مائة دينار فقال كثير عليّ اقتصر معي فاتّفق الحال على خمسين مثقال

فلمّا قبضت المبلغ قلت أطلعني على سرّ هذا الصنم حتّى أزيدك فيه علم فقال إذا أردت ذلك أخذت الخشب الرخو الميّت ثمّ اعمل منه واهيئه فإذا تمّ عمله ولا يبقى فيه عمل أخذت الكسفرة الرطبة مع حشيشة حيّ العالم فادقّ الجميع ثمّ استخرج ماءهما ثمّ اصعّده بالقرعة والأنبيق ثمّ آخذ ذلك الماء واجعل فيه الأصنام مقدار ما يغمرها واتركهم أربعين يوماً ثمّ أخرجهم من ذلك واجفّفهم في الظلّ فإذا جفّوا أخذت شحم الضفدع وشحم الترمس ودهن الحنطة ودهن الأرزّ أجزاء متساوية ثمّ اجعل الجميع في قِدر مزجّجة واجعل الأصنام فيها وأغلي عليها غليان جيّد إلى أن تشرب ذلك الدهن ثمّ ارفعها واجعلها في نخالة الأرزّ ثلاثة أيّام ثمّ امسحها واصقلها فإذا وضعت في النار فلا يعمل فيها شيئاً فهل عندك فيها زيادة علم فقلت نعم لو أنّك تجعلها في الطلق المحلوب عوضاً عن الأرزّ كان ذلك أبلغ وأشدّ فعل ودفعاً للنار فلمّا سمع ذلك قال وحقّ النار والنور والظلّ والحرور ما أنت إلّا فاضل ٦،١٩

him, "If you don't have any information that's of use to me, give me gold instead." "What kind of money would make you happy?" he asked, and I said, "One hundred gold pieces," but he said, "That's too rich for my blood. Go easy on me!" so we settled on fifty mithkals.[201]

Once I had the money in my hands, I told him, "Show me the trick with 19.6
the idol, so I can suggest improvements." So he said, "To do it, I take soft, dry wood, which I shape and prepare. When it's properly shaped and there's nothing left to do, I take cilantro plus houseleek and pound them together. Then I extract their juices and distill them, using the still pot and the alembic. I take the resulting liquid, place the idols in it so that they're covered, and leave them for forty days, then remove them and dry them in the shade. Once they've dried, I take equal parts of frog fat, lupine-seed oil, wheat oil, and rice oil[202] and put all of them in glazed pots along with the idols and boil them well till all the fats and oils are absorbed. Then I remove them and place them in rice bran for three days. Then I wipe them and polish them, and when I put them in the fire, it does nothing to them. Do you have any improvements to suggest?" I said, "Yes. Put them in talc soaked in milk instead of the rice. The effect will be stronger and more intense, and it will make a better retardant." When he heard this, he said, "By fire, light, and heat, I swear you truly are a man of learning!"

الفصل العشرون

ثمانية أبواب

في كشف أسرار الذين يعملون الطعم

اعلم أيّها الأخ أيّدك الله وإيّانا بروح منه أنّ هذه الطائفة أشدّ الناس زغل ١،٢٠
وأكثرهم أكلاً للحرام ولهم أمور لا تعدّ ولا تحصى ولا يقع عليها عيار ولا يقدر أحد على إدراكها ولا الإحاطة بها بل نذكر منها ما تيسّر لأنّ هؤلاء القوم لم يتركون شيئاً من الطعم حتّى يعملونه ثمّ يبلّزونه على المسلمين ولهم في ذلك أشياء عجيبة وأمور غريبة تحيّر فيها العقول وتدهّش فيها الأفكار وأنا إن شاء الله أكشف أسرارهم مختصراً موجزاً

الباب الأوّل في كشف أسرارهم

فمن ذلك أنّهم إذا أرادوا أن يعملون العسل الجيّد السميقيّ ويبلّزونه فيأخذون من التين ٢،٢٠
المعرّيّ الجيّد فيجعلونه في شيء ثمّ يلقون عليه من الماء العذب ما يغمره ويتركونه حتّى يعود مثل الحلاوة ثمّ يغلون عليه غلياً جيّداً ثمّ يرفعونه عن النار ويتركونه حتّى يبرد ثمّ يمرسونه بأيديهم مرساً جيّداً ثمّ يصفّونه ثمّ يأخذون الثفل يلقون عليه ماء فاترًا يمرسونه حتّى لا يبقى فيه شيء من الحلاوة ثمّ يصفّونه على الأوّل ثمّ يرفعون الجميع على النار الليّنة حتّى يأخذ له قوام ثمّ يلقون عليه الصمغ العربيّ وقليل من الكَثيراء الشقراء وشمع خام ويغلون عليه ثمّ يرفعونه في أوعية فخّار جديدة ويتركونه سبعة أيّام فإنّه يعود

Chapter Twenty, in Eight Sections:

Exposé of the Tricks of Those Who Concoct Artificial Foodstuffs

20.1 Note, dear brother, may God strengthen us both with His spirit,[203] that this is the tribe of charlatans that goes to the most extreme lengths in counterfeiting and is the greediest when it comes to feeding off ill-gotten gains. They get up to things too numerous to count or calculate, too bizarre to measure by any ordinary standard, and which they alone are fully apprised of and capable of understanding. We shall list here only a limited number of such items as there is no foodstuff of which this company has not concocted an artificial version and then peddled to the Muslims. In this area they have amazing practices and do extraordinary things that boggle the mind and astonish the intellect. God willing, I shall provide an exposé of their tricks in condensed, summarized form.

Section One of the Exposé of Their Tricks

20.2 Example: To make up a batch of artificial, pure, high-grade honey to peddle, they take high-grade figs from al-Maʿarrah, put them in a container, add enough sweet water to cover them, and leave them till they look more or less like halvah. They boil this thoroughly, remove it from the fire and leave till cool, then mash it well with their hands. Next, they strain it, take the solid matter, add warm water, and mash till nothing of its halvah-like consistency remains. Then they strain it again, in the same way as before, place it over a gentle heat till it starts to thicken, add gum arabic, a little light-colored tragacanth and raw wax, and boil this. They set this aside in new earthenware containers and leave it for seven days, and it comes out as high-grade honey, which they peddle. Furthermore, I've seen them make it from wheat and from watermelon, and

عسلاً جيّداً فيلزّونه ثمّ رأيتهم يعملون من القمح ومن البطّيخ الأخضر فيجيء أحسن ما يكون ولولا خوف الإطالة ذكرت جميع أعماله وأصنافه فافهم ذلك

الباب الثاني في كشف أسرارهم

٣،٢٠ ومن ذلك عمل السمن إذا أرادوا أن يعملون سمناً جيّداً يأخذون من دِهْن الألية فيذيبونه فإذا ذاب يلقون عليه من الحلبة المدقوقة الناعمة مثل الهباء[١] ومن الكثيراء الشقراء أجزاء متساوية ثمّ يضربونها مع الدهن ضرباً جيّداً فإنّه يعود سمناً أحسن ما يكون من السمن الغنميّ الجيّد فافهم

الباب الثالث في كشف أسرارهم

٤،٢٠ ومن ذلك عمل سمن بقريّ جيّد فإذا أرادوا يعملونه يأخذون من الدهن البقريّ السمين الجيّد ثمّ يلقونه كما ذكرنا أوّلا ثمّ يأخذون من الورس المدقوق ناعماً مثل الهباء جزء ومن الصمغ العربيّ جزء ثمّ يخلطون الجميع مع الدهن ويضربونه ضرباً جيّداً فإنّه يعود الجميع سمناً أجود ما يكون من السمن البقريّ الجيّد

الباب الرابع في كشف أسرارهم

٥،٢٠ ومن ذلك عمل الزبد الجيّد إذا أرادوا أن يعملون زبداً جيّداً من اللبن فيغلون اللبن بنار ليّنة ثمّ يلقون عليه من البورق جزء ومن الصمغ العربيّ جزء ومن حشيشة المصطكى[٢] جزء ثمّ يتركونه ساعة فإنّه يعود زبداً أحسن ما يكون من الزبد ويعملونه بمرارة سمكة الرعّاد فيجيء أحسن ما يكون فافهم

---

١ ش: الهواء. ٢ ش: الحشيشة السطلى.

it came out as fine as could be. If I weren't afraid of boring you, I'd list all the different recipes and kinds. Wise up to these things!

Section Two of the Exposé of Their Tricks

Another example: Making artificial clarified butter. To make up a batch of artificial high-grade clarified butter, they take some sheep's-tail fat and melt it. When it has melted, they add equal parts of fenugreek ground as fine as dust and light-colored tragacanth. They mix this well with the fat and it comes out as the finest sheep's butter there could be. **20.3**

Section Three of the Exposé of Their Tricks

Another example: Making artificial high-grade clarified butter from cow's milk. To make up a batch of this, they take some high-grade, rich cow's fat and add the ingredients mentioned in the preceding item. Then they take one part *waras*, pounded till fine as dust, and one part gum arabic. They put all this together with the fat and mix it well. The whole thing comes out like a high-grade clarified butter as fine as the finest cow butter. Wise up! **20.4**

Section Four of the Exposé of Their Tricks

Another example: Making artificial high-grade butter. To make up a batch of artificial high-grade butter from milk, they boil milk over a gentle heat, then add one part borax, one part gum arabic, and one part mastic leaf. They leave this for a while and it comes out like the finest butter there is. They also make it from electric-ray bile and it comes out as fine as can be. Wise up to these things! **20.5**

الباب الخامس في كشف أسرارهم في عمل الخلّ

٦،٢٠ وذلك أنّهم إذا أرادوا أن يعملون خلاًّ حاذقاً جيّداً يأخذون من الزبيب الأسود رطل فينقعونه في رطل خلّ حامض ويتركونه في ذلك يوماً وليلة ثمّ يسقونه رطلاً ثانياً كذلك أربعة أيّام أربعة أرطال خلّ ثمّ يغمرونه بذلك الخلّ ثمّ يزيدونه شيء ثمّ يرفعونه على النار ويغلونه حتّى ينهرس ذلك الزبيب حتّى يتغدّد ثمّ يقلبونه على بلاطة بعد أن يلقون عليه نصف رطل زيت السكّر ثمّ يقطّعونه شوابير من على البلاطة ويرفعونه فإذا أرادوا عمل خلاًّ حامضاً يأخذون خمسة أرطال من الماء العذب ثمّ يجعلون فيها من هذا الدواء المعمول أوقيّة وأوقيّة زيت السكّر ثمّ يجعلونه في الشمس الحارّة ثلاثة أيّام وفي الشتاء سبعة أيّام على ملاك النار فإنّه يعود خلاًّ حاذقاً يعمل عملاً عظيماً لا يكون شيئاً مثله فافهم ذلك

الباب السادس في كشف أسرارهم

٧،٢٠ ومن ذلك أنّي رأيتهم يعملون خلاًّ حاذقاً يهضم الطعام وذلك أنّهم يأخذون من النعناع البريّ جزء ومن النعناع الجويّ جزء ومن بزر الحمّاض جزء ثمّ يجعلون الجميع في إجّانة ويغمرونه بالماء ويغلون عليه حتّى يذهب الربع ثمّ يرفعونه ويصفّونه فإذا أرادوا عمل خلّ أيضاً قاطعاً فيأخذون من ذلك أوقيّة فيجعلونها على ثلاثة أرطال ماء عذب ثمّ يجعلونه في الشمس الحارّة ثلاثة أيّام وفي الشتاء على ملاك النار خمسة أيّام فإنّه يعود خلاًّ حاذقاً ولونه أحسن ما يكون على مثال الورد ويعملون من الخرّوب أيضاً خلاًّ حامضاً ويعملونه أيضاً من الكمّثرى ويعملونه من سَقَط التين اليابس ويعملونه من التمر ويعملونه من الجمّيز ويعملونه من المشمش اليابس ويعملونه من السفرجل ومن التفّاح فافهم ذلك

Section Five: Exposé of Their Tricks for Making Artificial Vinegar

Exposé: To counterfeit high-grade sour vinegar, they take a pound of black raisins and steep them in a pint of acidic vinegar, leaving them for a day and a night. Then they pour a further pint of vinegar onto the raisins, a total of four pints of vinegar over four days, covering them in said vinegar. Next, they add a little more to the raisins and place them over the fire and boil them until said raisins have turned mushy. They now turn them out onto a tile, after first adding half a pint of sugar oil,[204] and cut them into pieces a handspan in width, trimming them off the tile, and set them aside. Then, to make an acidic vinegar, they take five pints of sweet water and add a twelfth of a pint of this faked-up medication,[205] plus a twelfth of a pint of sugar oil, and place it in the hot sun for three days, or, in winter, on the trivet by the fire for seven days, after which it comes out as an acidic vinegar of unparalleled efficacy. Wise up to these things! 20.6

Section Six of the Exposé of Their Tricks

Another example: I have seen them make an artificial sour vinegar that promotes digestion. 20.7

Exposé: They take one part wild mint, one part valley mint, and one part sorrel seed, place everything in a glass bowl, cover with water, and boil till reduced by a quarter. Then they remove it and strain. To make a different artificial digestive vinegar, they take one-twelfth of a pint of the preceding and add it to three pints of sweet water. They set this in the hot sun for three days, or, in the winter, on the trivet by the fire for five days, and it comes out as a sour vinegar of the finest rosy color. They also make an artificial acidic vinegar from carob, another from pears, and others from dry fallen figs, dates, sycamore figs, dried apricots, quinces, and apples. Wise up to these things!

الباب السابع في كشف أسرارهم
في عمل الزيت والشيرج

٨،٢٠ فإذا أرادوا أن يعملون أُنفاق جيد[١] أو شيرج جيّداً فإنّهم يأخذون رطل شيرج أو سَلْجَم أو زيت خصّ[٢] أو ما كان من الأدهان ووزن أوقيّة ونصف شحم كلى ماعز مذاباً وخمسة أرطال ماء ويرفع على النار في دست ثمّ يغلى عليه حتّى يصير الجميع أربعة أرطال ثمّ يأخذون وزن درهم بقل ويبذرونه عليه ورطل زيت طيّب إن يريدونه زيت طيّب وإن كانوا يريدونه شيرج فيجعلون عوض الزيت شيرج ويبرّدونه ثمّ يرفعونه على النار ثانياً فإنّه يكون أحسن ما يكون من الأنفاق فافهم ذلك

الباب الثامن في كشف أسرارهم
في عمل اللبن من غير ضرع

٩،٢٠ وهذا باب معدوم ولا يعمل هذا إلّا كلّ فاضل فإذا أرادوا أن يعملون لبن من غير ضرع فيأخذون من الجوز الهنديّ ويقشرون عنه القشرة السوداء تقشيراً جيّداً ثمّ يخرطونه في إناء أو[٣] قوارير ثمّ يضعون عليه ماء ثمّ يمرسونه باليد مرساً جيّداً حتّى إذا ذاقونه يجدونه مثل اللبن فعند ذلك يعصرونه عصراً جيّداً ثمّ يجعلون ما خرج منه مع الماء الذي كان فيه ويصبّونه فإنّه يعود خاثراً كثير الدسم فيجعلونه في إناء ثمّ يكمرونه قليلا كما يكمر اللبن حتّى يصير حامضاً فإنّه يكون لبناً جيّداً ولو ذهبت أشرح لك جميع أحوال الطعم لما وسعها مجلّدات كثيرة ولكن قصدنا في ذلك الاقتصار فإنّ هذا القدر كاف للعاقل اللبيب ومن البعض يستدلّ على الكلّ لمن له رأي وفكرة وبصيرة فافهم ذلك

١ ش: جيّد أنفاق. ٢ ش: خاصّ. ٣ أضيف للسياق.

Section Seven: Exposé of Their Tricks for Making Fake Olive or Sesame Oil

To make an artificial high-grade early-harvest olive or sesame oil, they take a pint of sesame, turnip-seed, lettuce-seed, or any other oil, plus one-and-a-half twelfths of a pound's weight of melted goat-kidney fat, plus five pints of water, and place it over the fire in a tub, boiling it till the whole thing has been reduced to four pints. Then they take a dirham's weight of nuts and scatter these over it, plus a pint of olive oil (or sesame oil if they want that rather than olive oil) and cool it. Then they hang it over the fire again and it comes out like the finest early-harvest oil there is. Wise up to these things! 20.8

Section Eight: Exposé of Their Tricks for Making Fake "Udder-Free" Sour Milk

This is a rare art: Only the truly well versed are capable of making an artificial version of it. To make artificial "udder-free" milk, they take some coconut, thoroughly peel away the black outer shell, mince it, and place it in a container or bottles, then put water on it and mash it well by hand. When they taste it, they get the flavor of sour milk. They then squeeze it thoroughly, add the liquid that emerges to the water it was sitting in, and pour it out; it now comes out clotted and rich. They put this in a vessel. Next, they cover it long enough to turn sour, as one does with the real thing. It makes an excellent sour milk. If I were to lay out all the different fake foodstuffs, it would be too much to fit in even several volumes. However, I've done my best to deal with the matter concisely, and this should be enough to allow the reader of intelligence and insight to derive a multiplicity of instances from a single example. Wise up to these things! 20.9

الفصل الحادي والعشرين

خمسة أبواب

في كشف أسرار الذين يمشّون بالعَلَفات

١،٢١ اعلم أنّ هذه الطائفة ألعن الناس وأخبث وقتلهم مباح وذلك أنّ جميع الطوائف الذي قد ذكرناهم في كتابنا هذا فإنّهم ينصبون على الناس ويأخذون ما يقدرون عليه من أموال الناس ولا يستحلّون دماءهم وإنّ هذه الطائفة يستحلّون المال والروح فمن أجل ذلك قلنا أنّ قتلهم مباحاً ولهم أمور لا يعلم أحد آخرها

٢،٢١ فإنّهم يضعون[١] العلفات في الخبز ثمّ يرمونه على الطريق ويرقبون من يأكله ويعملونها في التين وفي جميع الطعم فمنهم من يرافق في الطريق ويطرح عينه على من معه شيء فلا يزال معه حتّى يلوح له منه مَضرِب ثمّ يعلفه ويأخذ ما معه ومنهم من يسافر في زيّ الأجناد ويفعل ذلك ومنهم من يتزايا في زيّ التجّار ويوهّم أنّ لهم في البلاد الفلانيّة تجارة مخزونة وهو رائح إليها ومنهم من يتزايا بزيّ المكارية فلا يكري إلّا لمن يعلم أنّ معه شيء ومنهم من يجهّز العَلَفة مع النساء الملاح ثمّ يتزيّنون ويلبسون ويمشون في الشوارع ويتحدّقون على الناس ثمّ ينطلقون لمن يعلمون أنّه غريب مثل تاجر أو جنديّ ويعلمون أنّه موسراً وهو وحده

٣،٢١ فإذا انطاع لها[٢] جرّته إلى بعض الأزقّة ثمّ قالت له أين موضعك ومن عندك فأنا والله ما هذا شغلي بل إنّ زوجي عشق على واحدة كانت تخدمني فمن الغيرة فعلت هذا فإن كنت وحدك في بيت فأنا أجيء معك بحسب أن يكون مستوراً وإن كان

١ ش: يصنعون. ٢ ش: انطاعت له.

Chapter Twenty-One, in Five Sections:

Exposé of the Tricks of Those Who Work Knockout Drugs and Stupefacients

The members of this tribe of charlatans are the vilest and most hateful of people, and killing them is no sin. The rest of the tribes we have listed in our book swindle people and take whatever money they can from them, but they don't claim to have the right to shed their blood. These, however, believe that both blood and mortal souls are theirs for the taking, which is why we say that to kill them is no sin. There is no known limit to the things they will do. 21.1

They put knockout drugs in bread, throw the bread onto the highway, and watch who eats it, and the same with figs and any other foodstuff. Some of them take up with others on the highway, watch out for anyone who has anything on him, stick with that person till it seems he's going to pitch his tent for the night, and then feed him a knockout drug and take whatever he has on him. Some travel in soldier's uniform and do the same. Some dress up as merchants and give others to think they have stores of goods in some country or other and that they're heading there. Others dress up as muleteers but only hire out their animals to those they know have something on them. Some of them supply the drug to pretty women who then put on makeup, dress, and walk the streets, scanning the people there, and finally throwing themselves at someone, such as a merchant or a soldier, whom they think must be a stranger and whom they believe is well-heeled and alone. 21.2

When she has him wrapped round her little finger, she drags him into some alley and asks, "Where's your place? Do you live with anyone? This isn't what I do for a living, I swear. My husband fell in love with a girl who used to be my servant, so I'm doing it out of jealousy. If you're in a house on your own, I'll go with you, so long as no one can see who goes in and out, but if you have someone at 21.3

عندك أحد فما أقدر أجيء فلا يكون إلّا أنت[١] ولد حلال وأنا والله إذا أبصرت منك ما يعجبني فإذا رحتَ إلى بيتي أخذتَ منه شيء له قيمة وأجيء معك حيث رحت فإنّ الغيرة تعمل أكثر من هذا وهي التي أحوجتني أن أقف معك وأحدّثك وتبكي وتتوجّع فإن كان له مكان أخذها وراح وتكون العلفة معها في خُشْكُنانِكة أو حلاوة فإذا استقرّ بهم الجلوس أخرجت الذي معها وأكلت ولقّمته منه وقالت له أنت ما ضيّفتنا نحن نضيّفك فلمّا[٢] يستقرّ في جوفه يسقط إلى الأرض فتقوم إليه فإن كان على وسطه شيء أخذته ومهما كان في البيت يُحمل حملته وراحت وإن كان ما له مكان تقول له روح إلى ظاهر البلد فما نغلب عن مكان وبعد ذلك أنا أحصّل مكان يكون نجتمع فيه فإذا خرجوا إلى ظاهر البلد ووجدوا مكان تكون تعرفه قبل ذلك فإذا جلسوا أخرجت الذي معها وأكلت ولقمّته ثمّ وثبت إليه فمهما كان معه تأخذه ثمّ تعمد إلى ما كان عليه من الملبوس فتسلبه عنه وتروح ولهم في ذلك فنون لا تذكر

الباب الأوّل في كشف أسرارهم وصفات العلوفات

٤،٢١ فمن ذلك أنّهم إذا أرادوا أن يعملوا علفة يأخذون من بزر الخسّ جزء ومن بزر الخشخاش جزء ومن بزر البصل جزء فيدقّونه ويجعلونه في أيّ طعام أرادوه كان فإنّهم يعلمون أنّ من أكل منه نام لوقته

الباب الثاني في كشف أسرارهم

٥،٢١ ومن ذلك يأخذون البنج الأزرق جزء ومن الأفيون جزء ومن بزر الخسّ جزء ومن بزر الرشاد جزء ومن لبن التين جزء ومن الجندبادستر جزء يدقّ الجميع ويعمل في أيّ طعام كان فأيّ من أكل منه نام لوقته

---

١ أضيف للسياق. ٢ ش: فكما.

home, I can't come. You look like a decent guy, and if you treat me right and come to my house, you'll get the goods, I swear. I'll follow you wherever you go—jealousy makes people do worse than this and it was jealousy that made me stop and talk to you," and so she keeps on, weeping and agonizing. If he has a place, he takes her along, the drug being concealed on her person in a stuffed cookie or some halvah. When they've sat down, she pulls out the stuff she has on her, eats a little, and feeds him mouthfuls, saying, "I'm not your guest, you're mine!" When it settles in his belly, he falls to the ground, and she approaches him. If he has anything round his waist,[206] she takes it, picks up anything that's in the house that can be carried, and leaves. If he doesn't have a place, she tells him, "Go to the outskirts of town. We're sure to find a place there, and later I'll come up with somewhere we can meet regularly." When they reach the outskirts of town and have "found" a place—which she already knows—and they sit down, she pulls out the stuff she has with her and eats some herself, but feeds it to him by the mouthful. Then she jumps on him and takes whatever he's carrying, after which she turns her attention to the clothes he's wearing, strips him of them, and leaves. They have innumerable techniques for doing such things.

Section One of the Exposé of Their Tricks and of Their Recipes for Knockout Drugs and Stupefacients

Exposé: To concoct a knockout drug or stupefacient, they take one part let- 21.4
tuce seed, one part poppy seed, and one part onion seed. They pound this and put it in any food they have a mind to, knowing that anyone who eats it will fall asleep on the spot.

Section Two of the Exposé of Their Tricks

Another example: They take one part blue henbane, one part opium, one part 21.5
lettuce seed, one part cress seed, one part fig milk, and one part castoreum. Everything is pounded together and mixed into any foodstuff, and anyone who eats it falls asleep on the spot.

الباب الثالث في كشف أسرارهم

٦،٢١ وهو السرّ الأكبر والمُرْقِد الأفخر وهو البنج الأَقْرِيطِشيّ الأزرق فإذا أرادوا أن يعملون علفة قاطعة إلى غاية ما يكون يأخذون من البنج الأزرق البالغ وزن خمسة دراهم ومن بزر الخشخاش الأسود وزن أربعة دراهم ومن الأفيون ثلاثة دراهم ومن الأَفْرَبْيُون أربعة دراهم ومن الحبّة السوداء خمسة دراهم ومن الغاريقون ستّة دراهم ومن بزر الخسّ أربعة دراهم ومن حبّ الباذروج درهمين ومن اللُفّاح خمسة دراهم ومن جوزة ماثل درهمين يدقّ الجميع ويعجن بماء الكرّاث ويعمل أقراص ثمّ يبخّر بالكبريت الأزرق ولا يعمل أقراص إلّا حتّى يسحق ناعماً فإذا أراد أن يعلفون إنساناً أطعموه من ذلك في طعام أو شراب أو حلاوة فإنّه ينام من وقته ولا يعلم أيش يعمل به حتّى يسعطه بالخلّ ويشمّمه بالحُرّاق الأزرق فإنّه يتقايأ العلفة وهو من أعظم ما وجدته

الباب الرابع في كشف أسرارهم

٧،٢١ فمن ذلك يأخذون من الغاريقون جزء ومن الكاكنج جزء ومن البنج الأصفر جزء يدقّوا الجميع ويعمل في أيّ طعام كان ويطعمونه لمن أرادوا فإنّه يبقى باهت لا يعلم ما يُفعل به ولا له لسان ينطق به فافهم ذلك

الباب الخامس في كشف أسرارهم

٨،٢١ ومن ذلك أنّ لهم علفات غير منوّمة وهي تبهت الإنسان فيبقى شاخصاً ولا يردّ جواباً ولا يعلم ما يعمل به فإذا أرادوا ذلك يأخذون من الكاكنج جزء ومن حبّ البلاذر جزء ومن الغاريقون جزء يدقّ الجميع ناعماً ثمّ يطعمونه لمن أرادوا فإنّه يبقى باهت إليك ولا يقدر على ردّ الجواب ولا يعلم ما يراد منه

Section Three of the Exposé of Their Tricks

This is their most prodigious trick and the classiest of the sleeping pills—"blue Cretan" henbane.[207] To concoct the most effective possible knockout drug, they take five dirhams by weight mature blue henbane, four dirhams black poppy seed, three dirhams opium, four dirhams euphorbium, five dirhams black seed, six dirhams agarikon, four dirhams lettuce seed, two dirhams basil seed, five dirhams mandrake apple, and two dirhams datura nut. All of this is pounded together, kneaded with leek juice, and made into pills, which are then fumigated with blue sulfur;[208] the pills can be made only after it has been crushed to a powder. To drug a person, they give it to him to eat in some food, drink, or halvah, and he falls asleep on the spot and has no idea of what's been done to him till he's revived by the administration of vinegar via the nose or is given blue tinder[209] to sniff, after which he vomits up the drug. This is one of the most effective things of its kind I've come across. 21.6

Section Four of the Exposé of Their Tricks

Another example: They take one part agarikon, one part alkekengi, and one part golden henbane, pound them all together, put this in any food they have a mind to, and feed it to whomever they please. The latter then becomes stupefied and doesn't know what's being done to him, and his tongue fails to obey him. Wise up to these things! 21.7

Section Five of the Exposé of Their Tricks

Another example: They have preparations that, rather than putting a person to sleep, stupefy him, so that his eyes glaze, he's speechless, and he has no idea what's happening to him. To do this, they take one part alkekengi, one part anacardium nut, and one part agarikon. These are all pounded together till smooth, after which they feed it to whoever they want, who then looks at one stupidly; he can't answer a question and doesn't even understand what he's being asked. 21.8

الفصل الثاني والعشرون

ستّة أبواب

في كشف أسرار الكتّاب وهم أصحاب الشروط

١،٢٢ اعلم أنّ هذه الطائفة عندهم من الدهاء والحيل والمكر ما لا يعلمه غيرهم وهم أخبر العالم بالأمور الشرعيّة وغيرها وهم أشرّ خلق الله في الظاهر وفي الباطن ولهم في الظاهر إقامة الحدود الشرعيّة والنواميس السياسيّة[١] ولهم أسرار غامضة لا يعلمها إلّا هم وإذا أرادوا أبطلوا الحقّ وأقاموا الباطل بأمور شرعيّة وأثبتوا الحقّ لغير مستحقّه وأقاموا عليه البرهان بالباطل

الباب الأوّل في كشف أسرارهم

٢،٢٢ وذلك أنّهم إذا كتبوا مكتوبًا لمبيع[٢] حصّة شائعة في ملك يقولون ووقفنا على ذلك فإذا ذكروا ذلك كان البيع مفسوخًا والدليل عليه أنّ الحصّة لا تكون معيّنة حتّى يقفون عليها بل هي من شيء فلا يقع ثمّ تعيين إلّا على الأصل فإذا قالوا ووقفنا على ذلك كان العقد مفسوخ فمتى ما أرادوا تعلّق المبيع ذكروا ذلك ومنهم من لا يعلم هذه المسئلة ثمّ يبصرون من هو النادم من البائع والمشتري فيقولون كم تزن حتّى نفسخ هذا العقد بالشرع فيتّفقون معه على شيء ثمّ يفسخون العقد بهذه النكتة بالشرع لأنّ[٣] الكاتب إذا لم يقل ووقفنا على منه ذلك كان العقد مفسوخًا فإذا قال ذلك كان العقد صحيحًا

١ ش: الساسانيّة. ٢ ش: مبيع. ٣ ش: لا.

Chapter Twenty-Two, in Six Sections:

Exposé of the Tricks of Notaries, That Is, of the People Who Draw Up Contracts

This tribe of charlatans is possessed of a cunning, a wiliness, and a deviousness found among no others. They are the most knowledgeable of men in terms of legal and similar affairs, and the worst of God's creatures both inside and out. On the surface, their role is to uphold the penalties imposed by the laws of God and the regulations of the secular authorities, yet they play arcane tricks comprehensible only to them. If they want to, they can, using legal means, make what's valid invalid and what's invalid valid, successfully asserting rights for one who has none and proving he's right by invoking what's wrong. 22.1

Section One of the Exposé of Their Tricks

Example: When they draw up a document for the sale of a share in something that is owned in common, they write, "and we have inspected that share." However, when they state this, the sale is rendered null and void, on the grounds that the share is not properly defined and they cannot therefore claim to have inspected it: It is a part of a larger thing and there can be no definition beyond that of the original item. It follows that when they say, "and we have inspected it," the contract is nullified. It's what they write when they want to hold in reserve the possibility of annulling the sale later. Sometimes some of the parties involved are unaware of this issue, so the notaries look to see who—seller or buyer—is unhappy with the contract and ask him, "How much will you pay to annul the contract legally?" They agree on a price, then annul the contract using this method to breach it legally, because if the notary doesn't write "and we have inspected *the whole of which this is* a share," the contract 22.2

لا كلام فيه والمعنى في ذلك أنّه وقفنا[1] على الذي منه جميع تلك الحصّة ولم يذكرون الحصّة فإنّها غير معيّنة

الباب الثاني في كشف أسرارهم

٣،٢٢ ومن ذلك أنّهم إذا أرادوا أن يكتبون على إنسان مكتوباً صحيحاً ولا فيه كلام وفيه خطوط الشهود يأخذون حجّة على ميت إمّا شيء يكون مبلغه قليل فيجعلونه كثيراً أو كتاب ملك أو صداق يزيدونه فإذا أرادوا ذلك فإنّهم يقلعون الكتابة من ذلك المكتوب ويبقون خطوط الشهود ثمّ يكتبون ما أرادوا على ذلك الشخص فتبقى الحجّة عليه وخطوط الشهود لا ينكرون الشهود خطوطهم فإذا أرادوا ذلك فإنّهم يأخذون من الكاربا خزء ومن النشاء جزء ومن حبّ القنا جزء ومن حبّ الخروع جزء ومن حبّ القطن جزء ثمّ يبخّرون به الكتاب فإنّ الكتابة تنقلع من الكتاب فيكتبون ما أرادوا

الباب الثالث

٤،٢٢ ومن ذلك أنّهم يأخذون من الكاربا ومن حبّ الباذروج جزء يدقّون الجميع ويبخّرون به الكتاب فإنّه لا يبقى للكتابة أثر فافهم

الباب الرابع في كشف أسرارهم

٥،٢٢ ومن ذلك أنّهم يأخذون قِلِي مبيّض فيسحقونه بماء حمّاض الأترنج حتّى يرقّ ثمّ يلطخون به الكتابة ويدعونه حتّى يجفّ فإنّه يُمحى أثرها ولا يبقى لها أثر وهو أحسن ما كشفت

١ ش: وقفا.

is annulled; if he writes it, though, the contract is sound and cannot be challenged. The sense of the phrase is that he has inspected the whole entity to which this share belongs, but if he doesn't mention the share, what he has inspected remains unspecified.

Section Two of the Exposé of Their Tricks

Another example: To draw up a contract that is sound and binding and cannot be challenged,[210] with witnesses' signatures, they take an IOU drawn on a dead person—it may be for a small sum, in which case they make it for a large one—or a document relating to property or a dower, whose value they increase. To do this, they erase the writing from the document and leave the witnesses' signatures. Then they write whatever they care to as the obligation of the person in question, and the binding language and the witnesses' marks remain; the witnesses cannot repudiate their signatures. To do this, they take one part amber, one part starch, one part galbanum granules, one part castor seed, and one part cottonseed. They fumigate the document with this, the writing is erased, and they write whatever they want. 22.3

Section Three

Another example: They take one part each amber and basil, pound the whole together, fumigate the document with it, and none of the writing is left. Wise up to these things! 22.4

Section Four of the Exposé of Their Tricks

Another example: They take house painters' potash and grind it up with citron-pulp water till runny, then smear the document with this and leave it till it dries. All traces of writing will be obliterated and no sign of it will remain. This is the best method I have come across. 22.5

الباب الخامس في كشف أسرارهم

ومن ذلك أنّهم يأخذون الشبّ اليمانيّ وحبّ العفص والكبريت الأبيض من كلّ واحد جزء يدقّونه ناعماً ثمّ يسقونه خلّ خمر ثمّ يسحقونه حتّى يصير مثل المرهم ثمّ يعملونه على مثال البلّوطة ويجفّفونه في الظلّ ثمّ يحكّون به الحبر وما أرادوا من الدفاتر تمحى الكتابة فإنّه يزول ولا يبقى له أثر البتّة ٦،٢٢

الباب السادس في كشف أسرارهم

ومن ذلك أنّهم يقلعون الكتابة من الكتب ويأخذون إسفيداج الرصاص وصمغ عربيّ من كلّ واحد جزء يُدقّ الإسفيداج ويُنخل ويذاب الصمغ ثمّ يعجن به الإسفيداج ويجعلونه بنادق ويجفّفونه في الظلّ فإذا أرادوا ذلك أخذوا من تلك البنادق بندقة ثمّ يجعلون عليها شيء من الماء ويحرّك بطرف القلم ثمّ يطلون به موضع الكتابة الذي يريدون قلعها ويتركونه حتّى يجفّ ويكتبون عليه ما أرادوا فافهم أسرار هذه الطائفة وميّز فعالهم وأعمالهم حتّى يخرجون صاحب الحقّ بلا حقّ ويردّون الحقّ على من لا حقّ عليه ولهم أبواب لا يعلمها غيرهم فافهم ٧،٢٢

Section Five of the Exposé of Their Tricks

Another example: They take Yemeni alum, oak galls, and white sulfur, one part each, and pound them till smooth. Then they add wine vinegar and grind it till it becomes like an ointment, which they then make into things like acorns and dry in the shade. They rub one of these over the ink in whatever ledgers they fancy and the writing is erased; it disappears, leaving no trace at all. 22.6

Section Six of the Exposé of Their Tricks

Another example: They remove the writing from documents. They take white lead and gum arabic, one part each. The white lead is pounded and strained, and the gum melted. Then they knead the latter into the white lead, make it into balls, and dry these in the shade. To concoct an ink remover, they take one of these balls, pour a little water on it, stir it with the tip of their pen, paint over the writing they want to remove, and leave it till it dries. Then they write anything they like. Be alert to the tricks of this tribe of charlatans! Learn to detect their deeds and the things they do to deny the wronged their rights and assign rights to those who have none! They have dodges only they know. Wise up to these things! 22.7

الفصل الثالث والعشرون

ثمانية أبواب

في كشف أسرار المشعوذين

١،٢٣ اعلم أنّ هذه الطائفة لهم أمور عجيبة وأحوال غريبة وهم أشدّ الناس كذب وأخذ بالنظر وهم أصلح من جميع هذه الطوائف وذلك أنّهم لا يتعرّضون لأخذ أموال الناس ولا يستحلّون دماءهم كبعض الطوائف والناس يعلمون أنّ كل شيء يعملوه دك وخفّة ورشاقة وبعد ذلك يرجعون إلى المروّة ومكارم الأخلاق لمن يقف عليهم ولا يحلفون على شيء يزغلوه على الناس بل جميع ما هم فيه دكّ وشعوذة وكذلك لعبهم بالأحقاق وهو أوّل دكّهم ولهم آلة جملة وأنا أذكر بعضها

الباب الأوّل في كشف أسرارهم في لعب الأحقاق

٢،٢٣ وذلك أنّهم يجعلون الجوزة تحت إصبع الخنصر مع أسفل الحُقّ فافهم ذلك ويحتمل أن يكون عنده رشاقة يلعب كيف شاء

الباب الثاني في كشف أسرارهم

٣،٢٣ فمن ذلك لعب المخلاة وتكون ثلاث طبقات مخيّطة الرأس مسيّبة الأسفل من داخل فإذا جعلوا فيها بيضة أو غير ذلك وكبّوها على رأسها طلعت البيضة إلى رأس المخلاة ولا يبقى في أسفلها شيء فيتوهّم الإنسان أنّه حقّ فافهم ذلك

Chapter Twenty-Three, in Eight Sections:

Exposé of the Tricks of Prestidigitators

This tribe of charlatans is involved in marvelous machinations and wondrous workings. They are the greatest of liars and exhibitionists but are more innocent than the rest: They don't devote their time to swindling people out of their money and they don't regard other people's blood as fair game, as do some. People are aware that everything they do is by sleight of hand, dexterity, and nimbleness; after that, it's up to the generosity and decency of the bystanders. They don't swear that the things they counterfeit are genuine in order to cheat people; everything they do depends, rather, on sleight of hand and prestidigitation. Their routine with the cups, the best known of these sleights of theirs, is of this type, but they have a whole battery of such props, some of which I shall discuss.[211] 23.1

Section One: Exposé of Their Tricks Regarding the Cup Routine

Exposé: They place the nut under their little finger, next to the bottom of the cup. Wise up to these things! The practitioner should have manual dexterity so he can manipulate things the way he wants.[212] 23.2

Section Two of the Exposé of Their Tricks

Another example: The feed-bag routine. On the inside are three layers, which are sewn together at the top and left unsewn at the bottom. When they put an egg or something similar inside the bag and turn it upside down, the egg goes to the top of the bag and there is nothing left at the bottom, so everyone is tricked into thinking that it really has disappeared. Wise up to these things! 23.3

الباب الثالث في كشف أسرارهم
في لعب حُقّ الغطاء

اعلم أنّ لهم حُقّ بغطاء ملبّس بغطاء من خارجه كمثل المنخل[1] لا يؤبه لأجل القمح والدقيق ولهم أسرار عجيبة في لعب الخاتم والنارنجة والسمكة وذلك أنّهم من أعجب الأشياء وأجلّها ولولا خوف الإطالة ذكرت فيها أشغال كثيرة لا يدركها كلّ أحد منهم ٤،٢٣

الباب الرابع في كشف أسرارهم في لعب المَجَرّ

وذلك أنّهم يعملون مجرّ له ستّة أبيات وله بطانة من داخل فيها الأبيات تلعب البيوت جميعها وله أسفل مجرى فإذا أرادوا تغيير البيوت ونقل ما فيها جرّوا ذلك الدفّ فعند ذلك تلعب البيوت وجرّت إلى مكان يريده ٥،٢٣

الباب الخامس في كشف أسرارهم
في كوز يُعرف بالمسحور

وصفته أنّه كوز مثقوب من أعلاه وأسفله فإذا أرادوا أن يقلبون فيه شيء ولا ينزل منه شيء فيثقبون جانبه ثمّ يثقبون أعلاه فإذا أقلبوا ذلك الماء سدّوا ذلك الثقب ٦،٢٣

الباب السادس في كشف أسرارهم في كوز المائين

وذلك أنّهم إذا أرادوا أن يعملون كوز فيه مائين يكون أبيض وأحمر فيأخذون كوز فيقسمونه من داخل نصفين ثمّ يثقبونه ثقبين في أعلاه عند الرقبة وثقبين عند العروة ٧،٢٣

---

١ ش: المرسل.

Section Three: Exposé of Their Tricks Regarding the Covered Cup Routine

They have a cup with a cover—that is, a cup covered in an outer, undetectable, envelope, like the diaphragm of a sieve for wheat or flour. They also perform wonderful tricks using the ring routine, the orange routine, and the fish routine. These are some of the most marvelous and impressive there are, and if I weren't afraid of boring you, I'd detail many more, some of which not even all of them are familiar with. 23.4

Section Four: Exposé of Their Tricks Regarding the Production Box Routine

Exposé: They make a production box with six compartments that has a lining to which the boxes are attached and that manipulates them. The box has a slit in the bottom. To switch the compartments and move their contents around, they draw this underside back, and then the compartments may be manipulated and dragged to wherever they want them.[213] 23.5

Section Five: Exposé of Their Tricks Regarding the Jug Known as "the Bewitched"

This is a jug that is pierced at the top and bottom. In order to be able to pour into it something that won't come out, they pierce its side and then its top. When they tip out the water they've put in, they block the hole.[214] 23.6

Section Six: Exposé of Their Tricks Regarding "the Jug of Two Waters"

Exposé: To create a trick jug that can contain two liquids, one white, one red, they take a jug and divide it inside into two halves. They make two holes in the top at the neck and two at the handle. To fill the red side, they block the right 23.7

فإذا أرادوا أن يملؤون الجانب الأحمر سدّوا الجانب الأيمن وصبغوه بماء ساق الحمام وذلك إذا أرادوا يملؤون الجانب الأيسر وإن أرادوا يفرّغونه

الباب السابع في كشف أسرارهم في عمل كوز

٨،٢٣ إذا أقلبته على رأسه فلا يجري فإذا أقلبته على جانبه جرى وذلك أنّهم يأخذون كوز واسع الرأس كبير البطن طويل ويجعلون في وسطه أكرة بلولبين على منجرة العراض فإنّهم إذا أقلبوها يصير أعلاها أسفلها ولا يقع منها شيء وإذا أقلبوها على جانبها بطل لعب اللولبين فيقع جميع ما فيها

الباب الثامن في كشف أسرارهم في عمل كوز الدينار[١]

٩،٢٣ واعلم وفّقك الله أنّ لهم كوز يقال له كوز الدينار[٢] وهو مفتوح القاع وله صفيحة خفيفة رقيقة جدًّا مريّحة إذا جعل يده تحت قاعها وقرصها ارتفع ذلك الدينار إلى الجوّ لأجل قوّة فعل تلك القطعة وريحها وهو كوز على معنى الكوز الذي يقلب على رأسه وهو أصغر منه ولهم عدّة كثيرة لا تحصى ولولا خوف الإطالة ذكرتها قطعة قطعة ولكن بهذا المقدار يفهم الباقي

---

١ ش: الدنيا. ٢ ش: الدنيا.

side, and dye the liquid with alkanet juice. They do the same to fill the left side. They can then empty out either color as they wish.

Section Seven: Exposé of Their Tricks for Fixing a Jug

When you turn it upside down, the water doesn't run out, but if you lay it on its side, it does. Exposé: They take a tall jug with a wide top and a big belly. In its middle they put a curved piece with two hinges on a crossbar.[215] Thus, when they turn it upside down, its top becomes its bottom and nothing comes out. If they lay it on its side, though, the flaps stop working and everything comes out. 23.8

Section Eight: Exposé of Their Tricks for Fixing "the Jug with the Golden Coin"

You should be aware, God grant you success, that they have a jug called "the jug with the golden coin." Its bottom has been removed and replaced with a very delicate and thin metal sheet with some play to it. When the practitioner puts his hand under its bottom and prods it, the coin shoots up into the air because of the springiness and give of the piece of metal. The jug itself is of the same type as the jug they turn upside down but smaller. They have too many such tricks to enumerate—if I weren't afraid of boring you, I'd list them device by device, but this should give you enough to infer the nature of the rest. 23.9

الفصل الرابع والعشرون

أحد عشر باباً

في كشف أسرار الجوهريّة وأعمالهم

اعلم أنّ هذه الطائفة أكثر الطوائف زغل وأكثرهم محالاً وأعظمهم مكرًا وتسلّطًا على أموال الناس وأيّ شيء أرادوا من الجواهر والفصوص صنعوها[1] وأباعوها بجُمَل ويصنعون ألوان الفصوص ولهم أمور لا يطّلع عليها إلّا كلّ عالم بعلمهم وقد ينصبون على الناس ويدّعون أنّهم يفعلون ذلك ومنهم من يعلم علم ذلك ويعمل ويبيع ومنهم من لا يعلمه بل يدّعي أنّه يعلمه ويأكل أموال الناس بالباطل فكيفما دارت القضيّة فإنّهم يأكلون أموال الناس بالباطل من الوجهين فهم إذاً أخبث الناس وأشدّ دهاء ١،٢٤

الباب الأوّل في كشف أسرارهم

فمن ذلك الدرّ والجوهر فإنّهم إذا أرادوا أن يعملوا الدرّ والجوهر وهو اللؤلؤ حتّى لا ينكره أحد أنّه معدنيّ فإنّهم يأخذون من اللؤلؤ الصغار ومن الصدف الجوهريّ ثمّ ينقّونه من جميع السواد الذي عليه من خارج ثمّ يسحقونه سحقاً ناعماً ثمّ يسقونه ماء حماض الأترجّ أعني يحلّونه به فإذا انحلّ وصار مثل العجين يلقون عليه من غراء الحلزون ومنهم من يضيف إليه الطلق المحلول ومنهم من يضيف إليه الفرّار المطهّر ثمّ يعملون ملعقة من الفضّة صغيرة فيأخذون الدواء بها بمقدار ما يريدون قدر اللؤلؤ ٢،٢٤

١ ش: صبغوها.

Chapter Twenty-Four, in Eleven Sections:

Exposé of Jewelers and Their Fake Products

This is the charlatan tribe most given to counterfeiting and trickery, most prodigious in its cunning, and most audacious in getting its hands on other people's money. They know how to manufacture and sell for huge sums any kind of jewel or ring stone they have a mind to, and how to color ring stones. They have techniques that only those truly well versed in their science learn and may use this knowledge to swindle ordinary people while claiming that their use of such techniques is legitimate. Others know the science that underlies these techniques and use it to fake things and sell the results. Yet others know nothing about these techniques but pretend they do and thus swindle people out of their money without any justification. Whatever the details of the matter, one way or another, they get their hands on people's money by foul play.[216] They are, it follows, the vilest and craftiest of people. **24.1**

Section One of the Exposé of Their Tricks

Example concerning the large pearls called *durr* and the ones called *jawhar*: **24.2** To make either fake *durr* or fake *jawhar* (here meaning small pearls)[217] of such quality that no one would deny that they are true mineral pearls, they take small real pearls and mother-of-pearl, clean them of any blackness on the outside, crush them till smooth, and temper (by which I mean dissolve) them in citron water. When the ingredients have dissolved and turned into a kind of paste, they add snail slime; some also add a solution of talc, others purified quicksilver. Next, they make a silver spoon (a small one), take as much of the mixture as they need to make a pearl of the size they want, put it into an eggshell, and roll it back and forth with their hand till it's smooth and round.

ثمّ يجعلونه في قشر بيضة ثمّ يدلكونه فيها حتّى يسكن فإذا صار كما يريدون يجفّفونه في الظلّ ويحرزون عليه من الغبار فإذا جفّ قليلاً أخذوا له شعرة من شعر الخنزير يثقبونه بها ثمّ يتركونه حتّى يجفّ جفافاً جيّداً ثمّ يعقدونه

٣،٢٤ صفة عقده[١] فمنهم من يجعله في عجين ثمّ يبلّعه لطير حمام أسود ثمّ يذبحه من الغد ومنهم من يبلّعه لطير وزّ ويحرز عليه لا يطعمه شيء في ذلك اليوم فإنّه في اليوم الثاني يرميه فيأخذونه ويجلونه ويبيعونه ومنهم من يجعله في شحم دجاجة ويلفّون عليه خرقة من الأطلس الأحمر ثمّ يأخذون فرخ سمك طريّ كما طلع من الماء ثمّ يشقّون جوفه وينظّفوه ولا يتركوا فيه سوى النفّاخة الذي في جوفه الذي يسمّونه العوّامة ثمّ يشقّونها ويودعون ذلك الحبّ فيها ثمّ يردّونها إلى جوف السمكة ثمّ بعد ذلك يخيّطون جوفها ثمّ يجعلونها في طاجن ويجعلونها في الفرن حتّى تستوي السمكة ثمّ يرفعونه فإنّه يكون منه لؤلؤ جيّد مليحاً ومن الناس من يعمل عوض غراء الحلزون الطلق المحلوب أو المحلول واعلم أنّي أعرف في عمله[٢] تسعة وأربعين طريقاً مختلفة الأنواع كلّ منها يكون في غاية الجودة

الباب الثاني في كشف أسرارهم في جلاء اللؤلؤ

٤،٢٤ إذا خرج فيه صفرة أو جرب فيأخذون ماء الليمو ونشارة العاج ثمّ يبلّون بماء الليمون خرقة رفيعة ويجعلون فيها نشارة العاج مع اللؤلؤ ثمّ يدلكونه بذلك دلكاً جيّداً فإنّه يكون أحسن ما يكون من النقاء والبياض والجوهريّة فافهم ذلك ترشد

الباب الثالث في عمل الفصوص وصباغها

٥،٢٤ وذلك أنّهم يأخذون فصّاً من العقيق فيجعلونه ياقوت أحمر فإذا أرادوا ذلك يأخذون من العقيق ما أرادوا ثمّ يذيبونه في مقعرة حديد نقيّة من الأوساخ فإذا ذاب يأخذون من البقّم جزء ومن الزنجفر جزء ومن ساق الحمام جزء فيدقّون الجميع ناعماً ثمّ يلقونه على

١ ش: عقدة. ٢ ش: علمه.

When it's how they want it, they dry it in the shade, having first scattered dirt over it to protect it. Once it has partially dried, they take a pig's bristle to it and pierce it, then leave it until it has dried completely. Then they string it onto a necklace.

How to harden a pearl: Some of them place it in dough, then force-feed it 24.3
to a black dove, which they slaughter the next day. Some feed it to a goose, making sure it doesn't eat anything else that day, and next day discard the goose, take the pearl, clean it off, and sell it. Some place it in chicken fat and wrap the whole in a piece of red satin, then take a young fish, as fresh as it was the moment it came out of the water, slit open its stomach, and clean it, leaving only the inflatable membrane in its stomach that they call "the float." They slit this open and place one of the seed pearls inside it, then put the float back inside the fish's stomach. After this, they sew the fish's stomach up, place the fish in a casserole, and put it in the oven till the fish is cooked. They now remove the seed pearls, which will have turned into lovely high-grade pearls. Some people, instead of adding snail slime, use emulsified, or dissolved, talc. Note that I know forty-nine ways to make pearls of different kinds, all of them of extremely high quality.

Section Two: Exposé of Their Tricks for Polishing Pearls

If pearls display any yellowness or pitting, they take lemon juice and ivory 24.4
shavings, wet a thin rag with the lemon juice, and place the shavings on it with the pearls. They rub the pearls well with this mixture and they come up as fine as can be in terms of purity, whiteness, and gemlike appearance. Wise up to this and you can't go wrong!

Section Three: On Making and Coloring Fake Ring Stones

Exposé: They can take an agate ring stone and turn it into red ruby. To do this, 24.5
they take as much agate as they care to and melt it in an iron casting vessel from which any old castings have been cleaned out. When it melts, they take one part sappanwood, one part cinnabar, and one part alkanet, pounding everything together till smooth. To this they add the agate, which turns into red

ذلك العقيق فإنّه يعود ياقوتاً أحمراً ثمّ يتركونه على بلاطة مانع نقيّة ويقطّعونه على قدر ما يريدوا من الصغر والكبر فافهم ذلك ترشد

الباب الرابع في كشف أسرارهم

ومن ذلك أنّهم يعملون فصّ ياقوت أصفر مليح جيّد فإذا أرادوا ذلك فيأخذون من البلّور ما أرادوا ثمّ يدقّونه ثمّ يذيبونه في مقعرة ثمّ يأخذون من الزعفران جزء ومن القيسا جزء يذيبونه ويجعلونه فوق ذلك البلّور ويطرحونه على بلاطة فإنّه يعود ياقوت أصفر لا شيء أحسن منه ثمّ يقطّعونه على ما يريدون منه ما أرادوا ثمّ يبيعونه بأوفى ثمن فافهم ذلك ٦،٢٤

الباب الخامس في كشف أسرارهم
في عمل الياقوت الأخضر الزمرّدي

فإذا أرادوا ذلك يأخذون من البلّور ما أرادوا فيذيبونه في مقعرة نقيّة فإذا ذاب يأخذون من الزنجار الحمّصيّ جزء ومن النيل الجيّد جزء ومن الحبّة الخضراء جزء ومن ورق الحنّاء جزء يدقّ الجميع ثمّ يطرحونه على ذلك البلّور فإنّه يعود ياقوت أخضر لا يكون شيء أحسن منه ولا يشكّ فيه أحد أنّه زمرّد ٧،٢٤

الباب السادس في كشف أسرارهم
في صنع الياقوت السماويّ

وذلك أنّهم يأخذون ياقوتة صفراء يجعلونها في بوتقة ويجعلون من تحتها النشادر ومن فوقها ثمّ يطيّنوها بطين الحكمة ثمّ ينفخون عليها حتّى تحمرّ ثمّ يخرجونها بعد ما تبرد فإنّ الصفرة تنسلخ وتبقى حجراً أبيضاً فيصبغونه بما شاء من الألوان فإنّه يجيء كما يريدون والله اعلم ٨،٢٤

ruby. Then they leave it on a clean heat-resistant tile and cut it into pieces as small or large as they want. Wise up to this and you can't go wrong!

Section Four of the Exposé of Their Tricks

Another example: They can fake a pretty, high-grade topaz ring stone. To do this, they take as much rock crystal as they have a mind to, pound it, and melt it in a casting vessel. Then they take one part saffron and one part buckthorn, melt this, put it on top of the rock crystal, and pour it out onto a tile. It will turn into a yellow topaz of the finest possible kind. Thereafter, they cut it up into as many sizes and as many pieces as they like and sell them for a very good price. Wise up to these things! 24.6

Section Five: Exposé of Their Tricks for Faking Emerald-Green Gems

To do this, they take as much rock crystal as they have a mind to and melt it in a clean casting vessel. Then they take one part green-chickpea verdigris, one part high-grade indigo, one part terebinth seeds, and one part henna leaves and pound them all together. Next, they pour this over the rock crystal and it comes out as a green gem of the finest possible kind that no one can believe is anything but emerald. 24.7

Section Six: Exposé of Their Tricks for Manufacturing Sapphires

Exposé: They take a topaz and put it in a crucible, placing ammonia below it and above it, then seal it with clay-of-wisdom. After this, they puff at it with the bellows till it glows red. Once it has cooled, they take it out, the yellowness flakes off, and it turns into a white stone that they can dye any color they have a mind to as it will come out however they want it (though only God knows how this can be). 24.8

الباب السابع في كشف أسرارهم في عمل الفصوص وصباغها وكمال شغلها وخدمتها[1]

اعلم أنّ هؤلاء القوم يعملون الفصوص من الكاربا ومن المَرْقَشيثا ومن اللازورد ومن السُنْباذَج ومن العقيق ومن الزجاج ومن البلّور ومن كلّ ما يقع عليه اسم الفصوص فأمّا ماكان منها من الزجاج فيصبغونه على وجهين أحدهما يصنعون فرناً من نخالة الشعير مثلما يصنعون الصيّاغ ويأخذون بلاطة من الطين الأحمر المعمول بالشعير ثمّ يعملون فصوصاً مربّعة مدوّرة معمولة[2] على أيّ شيء أرادوا ويطبعون بها في البلاطة حتّى يبقى مكان الفصّ فارغ في البلاطة فيكون مثل الدريزك فيها خمسة أو ستّة فيأخذون الزجاج المصبوغ أيّ لون أرادوه ثمّ يدخّلونها في الكلّاب في فرن النخالة المقدّم ذكرها ثمّ ينفخون عليه حتّى يذوب ويخرجونها ويتركونها ثمّ يحكّونها بالماء وحجر الرحى ويصقلونها بخشب الجوز فيأتي أحسن ما يكون من الياقوت الجيّد فافهم ذلك وانظر ما عند هؤلاء القوم من الدكّ والزغل والدهاء واعلم أنّي أطلعت لهم على أشياء تنافر العقول وأمّا الوجه الثاني في عمل الفصوص فإنّه يطول الشرح فيه فإنّ هذا المقدار كاف للعاقل اللبيب ويعلم أنّه لم يعدم شيئاً ممّا يعملون ولو ذهبت أن أكمّل كشف أسرارهم لمّا وسعه كتابي بل إنّا كتبنا من كلّ شيء بعضه ليستدلّ به على الكلّ ٩،٢٤

الباب الثامن في كشف أسرارهم

إذا أرادوا أن يردّون إلى الياقوت مائيّته فإنّهم يأخذون الجزع فيحرقونه ثمّ يسحقونه سحقاً جيّداً ثمّ يشرّبون به الياقوت بالماء على خشب الصفصاف أو خشب الدفلى فإنّه يكسب مائيّة عظيمة ويزداد في قيمته زيادة جيّدة فافهم ذلك ١٠،٢٤

١ ش: وحكمتها. ٢ ش: معمولة مدوّرة.

Section Seven: Exposé of Their Tricks for Making Fake Ring Stones and Coloring Them, and of Every Stage of Their Processing and Care

This company makes fake ring stones resembling amber, marcasite, lapis lazuli, emery, agate, glass, rock crystal, and anything else to which the term "ring stone" might be applied. Glass they color using one of two methods. According to the first, they fashion a barley-bran-fired oven the way goldsmiths do and take a tile made of red clay mixed with barley bran, then fake up ring stones—squared, rounded, worked any way they please—and stamp the tile with them, leaving the imprint of the ring stone as a hollow on the tile, so it looks like a mold with five or six compartments. Now they take the glass, which has been colored any color they want, put it into the previously mentioned bran-fired oven with the tongs, and blow on it with the bellows till it melts, at which point they take it out and leave it. Thereafter, they grind it, using water and a hand-mill pounding stone, and polish it with walnut wood. In the end, it turns out as fine as any high-grade gem. Note this and observe the cheating, counterfeiting, and cunning this company employs! I have watched them do things the rational mind would reject as impossible. The second method for making fake ring stones would take too long to explain. The above should suffice for any person of intelligence and insight, who should be aware that none of their doings has escaped my notice and that if I were to set about making a complete exposé of all their tricks, this current book of mine would be too small to hold them. Instead, we have taken a different approach, setting down enough examples of each kind of trick to allow the reader to infer the rest. **24.9**

Section Eight of the Exposé of Their Tricks

To restore a gemstone to its original brilliance, they take onyx, burn it, and crush it well. Then they heat the gemstone with this in water over willow or oleander wood till it has absorbed it. This process imparts to it a prodigious brilliance and increases its value significantly. Wise up to these things! **24.10**

الباب التاسع في كشف أسرارهم في صباغ العقيق والكتابة عليه والنقوش حتّى أنّ من نظر إليها لا يشكّ أنّها خلقة

١١،٢٤ ورأيت جماعة من أهل صناعة التنجيم والتعزيم يعملون من ذلك أصنافاً ويعزبرون بها الناس على قدر ما يريدون فإذا أرادوا ذلك يأخذون ورق الأثل ويجفّفونه ويجعلون معه من القلي مثله ثمّ يسقونه بالماء حتّى يعود مثل المرهم ثمّ يأخذون الفصّ أو الحجر وينقشون عليه ما أرادوا من النقوش والصور والتماثيل ويكون النقش خطّ حسن ثمّ يحشونه من ذلك الدواء ثمّ يجفّفونه ويجعلونه في خرقة ثمّ يجعلونها في قِدْر على نار ليّنة ثمّ يخرجون منها فصّاً فإن رأونه قد ابيضّ مواضع الكتابة بياضاً جيّداً وإلّا تركوه ساعة أخرى حتّى يبلغ ما يريدون ثمّ يخرجونه ويغسلونه فيرون كلّ ما كان تحت الدواء قد ابيضّ والباقي أحمر على ما كان عليه

الباب العاشر في كشف أسرارهم في عمل المها ياقوت

١٢،٢٤ وذلك أنّهم يأخذون من المها على قدر ما يريدون ثمّ يعملون منه فصوصاً ثمّ ينقعونها في ماء الرأس وهو رأس الصابون ثلاثة أيّام ثمّ يرفعونها ويتركونها حتّى تجفّ ثمّ يسحقون رهج الغار بالبول ثمّ يرمون تلك الفصوص فيه ثلاثة أيّام ثمّ يطبخون الغاسول حتّى يصفرّ ثمّ يسحقون الأشنان المروّق بالخلّ ثمّ يغلونه فيه غلية فيخرج ياقوت أحسن ما يكون

الباب الحادي عشر في كشف أسرارهم في عمل البلّور زمرّد

١٣،٢٤ فإذا أرادوا ذلك يأخذون البلّور الصافيّ الجيّد فيجعلونه في قِدْر حجر ثمّ يعصرون عليه من ماء الدفلى قدر ما يغمره بأربع أصابع ثمّ يجعلون فيه قيراط من الزنجار الحمّصيّ ثمّ يطبخونه بنار متوسّطة حتّى يخضرّ ويحسن لونه فإنّه يخرج أحسن ما يكون من الزمرّد

Section Nine: Exposé of Their Tricks Regarding How to Color, Write On, and Carve Agate so That No One Who Sees It Will Have the Slightest Doubt That It Is Natural

I have seen how a bunch of astrologers and conjurors of spirits fake agate in different ways and screw people over to their hearts' delight. To do so, they take athel leaves, dry them, and add an equal quantity of alkali. This they temper with water till it reaches the consistency of ointment. Then they take the ring stone or the uncut stone and carve whatever designs or pictures or figures they want on it, using a handsome style. Next, they insert the stone into the mixture, dry it, and place it in a rag. After this, they put the stones in pots over a low flame. Finally, they extract one stone from the pots. If they find it's turned a good white where the inscriptions are, they set it aside; if not, they leave it a while longer till it reaches the state they want, then take it out and wash it. They will find that all the bits that were covered with the mixture have turned white, while the rest remains the same red as before. 24.11

Section Ten: Exposé of Their Tricks for Turning Quartz into Fake Rubies

Exposé: They take as much quartz as they care to and fashion ring stones from it. These they steep for three days in lye water, remove, and leave to dry. Next, they crush together realgar and urine, and throw the ring stones into this mixture, leaving them for three days. Then they cook potash till it turns yellow, grind up old waterskins that have been cleaned with vinegar, and finally boil everything well. They then extract rubies as fine as can be. 24.12

Section Eleven: Exposé of Their Tricks for Turning Rock Crystal into Fake Emeralds

To do this, they take high-grade pure rock crystal, place it in a stone pot, then squeeze over it enough oleander water to cover it to a depth of four fingers. Next, they place a carat of green-chickpea verdigris in the pot and cook it over a medium flame till it turns an attractive green. It comes out as the finest possible emerald. 24.13

الفصل الخامس والعشرون

ستّة أبواب

في كشف أسرار الصيارف ودكّهم والدكّ عليهم

١،٢٥ اعلم أنّ هذه الطائفة من جملة الحراميّة وقطّاع الطريق ولهم أمور لا يعلمها إلّا كلّ فاضل وأحوال لا يطّلع عليها إلّا من كان راجح العقل وهم أشدّ الناس حرام وأصنعهم في أخذ أموال الناس مع أنّهم متميّزين وذو هيبة وسكينة ووقار ومع ذلك أنّهم أصنع[1] من غيرهم ولهم في الدكّ أبواب

الباب الأوّل في كشف أسرارهم

٢،٢٥ فأوّل ما رأيت في بلاد الهند رجل صيرفيّ عليه من الحشمة شيئاً عظيماً وجميع التجّار تورّد عنده أموالهم ويستعيدونها قليلاً قليلاً ثمّ رأيته قد صنع شيء لم يسبق أحد إليه ولا إلى معرفته وذلك أنّي رأيت في يده خاتم بفصّ وعليه نقش ثمّ أدمت الجلوس عنده وأدمت النظر إلى الخاتم فرأيته إذا قبض الذهب من التاجر يجعل فصّ الخاتم من قدّام لسان الميزان إلى ناحية السنج فإذا دفع للتاجر الذهب حوّل فصّ الخاتم إلى ناحية الذهب ثمّ رأيت لسان الميزان إذا قرب للخاتم لعب لعباً زائداً فعلمت أنّ هذا الخاتم فيه شيء من الدكّ

١ ش: أصلح.

Chapter Twenty-Five, in Six Sections:

Exposé of the Tricks of Money Changers, of Scams They Pull and Scams Pulled on Them

This tribe of charlatans should be considered as part of the larger category that includes thieves and highwaymen. They get up to things that only the most erudite can fathom and are involved in matters to which only the most distinguished minds can be privy. They are the worst offenders against the laws of religion and the most artful in getting their hands on people's money, even though they are noted members of society, full of gravitas, poise, and dignity; despite this, they are the cleverest swindlers of all and have a variety of scams with which to cheat people. 25.1

Section One of the Exposé of Their Secrets

The first of this kind that I saw was in India, a money changer who, to all appearances, was a man of the greatest respectability and one with whom the merchants all lodged their money so that they could later withdraw it little by little. With time, I noticed that he'd come up with a trick no one had ever pulled, or even heard of, before. 25.2

Exposé: I observed that he wore on his hand a seal ring with an inscribed bezel. I took to spending a good deal of time with him, keeping my eye on the ring, and I noticed that whenever he took in gold from a merchant, he'd hold the bezel in front of the arm of the scales that was on the side with the weights. Then, on returning the gold to the merchant, he'd switch the bezel to the side with the gold. I then noticed that, when the ring came close to the arm, the latter moved more than it should, so I realized that there must be something fishy about the ring.

٣،٢٥ لم أزل أبحث عنه وأنا مفكرٌ فيه ثمّ في بعض الأيّام انفرج لي فيه شيء وقلت والله هذا دكّ لم يسبق أحد إليه وإذا فصّ الخاتم من حجر المغنطيس فإذا قبض الذهب أدار الخاتم إلى ناحية السنج فيأخذ لسان الميزان هواءه ويمتنع من النزول بمقدار ما يجذب الحجر فيكون في الوزنة المثقال والأكثر من ذلك فلمّا علمت ذلك خلوت به وقلت له والله إنّي قد درت البلاد وكشفت أسرار جميع الأشياء فلم أجد أحد قد سبقك إلى ذلك يا عفيف الدين

٤،٢٥ فلمّا علم أنّي قد كشفت عنه ما هو فيه خجل وخاف جانبي ثمّ قال الحرّ من كتم وستر عيوب الناس فاكتم عنّي ذلك بمروّتك وكرمك مع أنّ الحكيم لا يجوز عنده إفضاح الصورة ومن شيم الحكيم كتمان السرّ مع أنّ والله لهذا الخاتم في يدي خمسة وعشرين سنة ما علم أحد سرّه غيرك مع ذكاء أهل الهند ومن يجلس عندي من أهل الفضل والعلم فبالله عليك اكتم عنّي ذلك فقلت والله لا أظهرت ذلك في الإقليم أبدًا ولا ذكر فتكون منزلة سيّدنا كما هي وتكون من ذلك على يقين وقد تمثّلت بما قال الحريريّ منزلة منزلة أهل الفضل وسدلت الذيل على مخازي الليل

٥،٢٥ فعند ذلك تهلّل وجهه ومال إلى صندوقه فأخرج منه صرّة وقال أشتهي أن تقبل منّي هذه النفقة في هذا الوقت وأنا أقسم لا بدّ منها ولك على ما يتحصّل كلّ جمعة يوم بما يحصل فيه وإنّك الأخ الشفيق ونعم الصاحب الرفيق فأبيت قبول ذلك فزاد في الأيمان وقال ما كان نيّتك لي صالحة وهي علامة امتناعك عن قبول خدمتي فلمّا سمعت أخذتها على وجه الهديّة ثمّ تحدّثنا ساعة ثمّ جاءه بعض التجّار بذهب فاشتغل معه فقمت أنا وودّعته وهو يجهد عليّ أن لا أنقطع عنه

٦،٢٥ فلمّا حصلت في منزلي فتحت الصرّة فإذا فيها خمسين دينارًا مسعوديّة يعمل كلّ دينار أربعة دراهم ناصريّة ثمّ إنّي صرت عنده أحظى أصحابه ثمّ بعد ذلك أخذني

I kept searching for the answer and turning it over in my mind. Then one day I had a brain wave. I thought, "For sure, there must be some scam going on here that no one ever thought of before. If the bezel in the ring were magnetic, and if, when he took in the gold, he turned the ring in the direction of the weights, the arm of the scales would be attracted to it and prevented from descending, in proportion to the degree of attraction exerted by the bezel. This would add a mithkal or more to the weight." When I realized this, I got him on his own and said, "I swear I've been all over the world and uncovered all kinds of secrets, but you, ʿAfīf al-Dīn, are the first I've come across to pull this one!"[218] 25.3

When he realized I'd caught on to what he was up to, he became embarrassed and scared, and said, "The noble man keeps his counsel and hides the faults of others. Be a decent fellow, and generous, and don't show me up—not to mention that the wise man never allows a good reputation to be sullied, and another of his qualities is to keep secrets—even though, I swear, this ring has been on my hand for twenty-five years and you're the first to discover the trick of it, for all that the Indians are so clever and for all the men of learning and science who have kept me company! For God's sake, then, keep my secret!" "I swear," I responded, "never to give your secret away, or even refer to it, anywhere in these parts. Our Master's high standing shall remain as it is, you can be sure of that, for I shall take my cue from the words of al-Ḥarīrī: 'Your standing as a virtuous man remains quite certain—on any nocturnal embarrassments I've lowered the curtain.'"[219] 25.4

His face brightened at this and he turned to his chest and took out a money bag, saying, "I'd like you to accept this gift from me for now—no, really, you must!—and one day's worth of each week's take shall be yours. You shall be to me a compassionate brother, a companion like no other!" I refused, but he swore yet mightier oaths, saying, "You're not playing straight with me, as witness your refusal to do me this service." When I heard that, I took the money as a gift. Afterward, we chatted for a while and then a merchant came along with his gold and he set to work with him, so I rose and bid the man farewell, and he begged me not to be a stranger. 25.5

When I reached my house, I opened the bag and found fifty Masʿūdī gold pieces, each worth four Nāṣirī silver pieces, and from then on I was his most favored companion. Once, he took me to his house, treated me to his hospitality, and revealed to me all his secrets. He put one of his rooms at my 25.6

إلى داره وأضافني وأكشفني على أسراره وبعد ذلك أخلى لي بيتاً عنده وفرح بمعرفتي ثمّ عرّفني بكبراء أهل البلد وصرت كواحد منهم فافهم

الباب الثاني في كشف أسرارهم في تثقيل الذهب فتزيد المائة مثقال خمس مثاقيل

وذلك أنّه كان يأخذ الذهب ويعمله على صفيحة حديد ويصفّه شيئاً تحت شيء صفّاً جيّداً ثمّ يدخّل الصفيحة إلى النار وينفخ عليها حتّى يحمرّ الذهب ثمّ يأخذ الدينار ويطفئه في أمياه مستقطرة من عقاقير ثمّ يرفعها ويعبّرها وقد زادت المياه خمس مثاقيل وفهمت الأمياه وهي أربعة أمياه من عقاقير وهي ماء الرجلة الحمقاء مقطّرة الثاني ماء ورق الآس مقطّر وقد سترت المائين الباقيّين ٧،٢٥

الباب الثالث في كشف أسرارهم

ومن ذلك أنّ لهم ميزان مجوّف القصبة وفيه الزيبق فإذا أرادوا أن يدفعون لواحد ذهب يمسكون الكفّة الذي فيها الذهب فيجري الزيبق إلى قدّام ويأخذون بوزن الزيبق ذهب وإن أرادوا أن يقبضون الذهب يمسكون الكفّة الذي فيها السنج فيأخذون من الذهب بوزن الزيبق ٨،٢٥

الباب الرابع في كشف أسرارهم في السنج

إنّ لهم سنج مختومة بختم المحتسب صحاح الوزن فإذا أرادوا أن يثقّلون بها ويخفّفون بها فيأخذون سنبكة فولاذ مدوّر ثمّ يحمّونه وينزّلونه في جنب الصَنجة فإذا أرادوا يثقّلونها ملؤوا ذلك الخلوّ رصاص على قدر ما يريدوا من الثقل ثمّ يحشونه بالشمع ثمّ يلصقون عليه قشر توبال الحديد فلا يعلم أحد ذلك وإن أرادوا تخفيفها فإنّهم ٩،٢٥

disposal and was delighted to have made my acquaintance. He introduced me to the town's leading lights and soon it was like I was one of them. Wise up to these things!

Section Two: Exposé of Their Tricks for Increasing the Weight of Gold so That Five Mithkals Are Added to Every Hundred

Exposé: They take the gold pieces and put them on a metal sheet, placing them on top of each other in carefully arranged layers. Then they put the sheet into the oven and blow on it with the bellows till the gold turns red. Next, they take a gold piece and douse it in solutions distilled from certain apothecary's simples. Finally, they remove it and weigh it, and the solutions will have added five mithkals. I worked out what the solutions were and they turned out to be four in number, consisting of simples, the first being filtered purslane water, the second distilled myrtle-leaf water, and the other two I won't reveal.[220] 25.7

Section Three of the Exposé of Their Tricks

Another example: They have scales with a hollow arm that contains mercury. When paying out gold, they hold the pan with the gold in it in such a way that the mercury runs forward, so they gain gold equal to the weight of the mercury. When taking in gold, they hold the pan with the weights in it the same way and again acquire gold equal to the weight of the mercury. 25.8

Section Four: Exposé of Another of Their Tricks, Regarding Weights

They have accurate weights, stamped by the market inspector. To make these heavier or lighter, they take a round steel punch, heat it, and drive it into the side of the weight. To make the weight heavier, they fill the space that has been made with as much lead as they need to get the weight they want; then they fill up the rest with wax and apply iron hammer paint over it; no one can tell. If they want to make it lighter, they take a round file and file the sides of 25.9

يأخذون مبردًا مدوّر يبردون جوانب ذلك الخلوّ الذي فتحوه بالسنبك على قدر ما يريدون من الخفّة ثمّ يحشونه كما فعلوا في سَنجة التثقيل ثمّ يغشون عليه بالتوبال المذكور

الباب الخامس في كشف أسرارهم

ومن ذلك أنّي وجدت بمدينة الرُهاء رجل صيرفيّ اسمه رجب وقد رأيته يأخذ نواة الخرّوب ينقعه في الماء عشرين يوماً ثمّ يرفعه ويأخذ نواة ويشدّ عليها إصبعه فإنّ العَجَمة تطير منها ثمّ يحشوها بما يثقّلها به ثمّ يلصقها بغراء السمك ويجعلها تحت يده ١٠،٢٥

الباب السادس في كشف أسرارهم الذين يدكّون على الصيارف

اعلم أنّ هذه الطائفة لم يكن في الطوائف أرجل منهم وذلك أنّهم يدكّون على من هم أشطر الطوائف فإنّ الصيارف يتعيّشون على كلّ الناس وهؤلاء يتعيّشون عليهم فهذه عين الرُجلة والشطارة وقد رأيت بدمشق رجل من أهل حلب يُعرف بجمال الدين يوسف بن المنقّش وهو متميّز وله حشمة ظاهرة ورأيته يدكّ على الصيارف الذهب والفضّة ١١،٢٥

فإذا أراد[١] ذلك أتى إلى الصيرفيّ وفي خنصره دينار أو درهم فيكون نحاس ثمّ إنّه يكون معه إمّا دينار وإمّا درهم جيّد على قدر ما يريد يدكّ ويكون على قدر ذلك الزغل الذي معه لا يُعرَف ذلك إلّا بحسن النقد فيقف على الصيرفيّ ثمّ يدفع له الدينار الجيّد فيقول ادفع لي به دراهم فيأخذ الصيرفيّ الدينار ثمّ ينقده ويزنه ويدفع له الدراهم فيقول كم وزنت لي فيقول كذا وكذا فيقول ما آخذ إلّا كذا وكذا فيقول ما أدفع لك إلّا هذا فيقول هات الدينار فيناوله الدينار فبمقدار ما يحصل في يده قد جعله في ١٢،٢٥

١ ش: أرادوا.

the space that they opened with the punch until they reach the desired reduction in weight. Then they fill it up as they did the weight whose weight they increased and smear the abovementioned hammer paint over it.

Section Five of the Exposé of Their Tricks

Another example: In the city of Urfa, I came across a money changer called Rajab. I saw him take carob seeds, steep them in water for twenty days, take them out, pick up a seed, and squeeze it in his fingers. This made the insides squirt out. He would then fill the seeds with something to make them heavier, seal them with fish glue, and keep them at the ready.[221] 25.10

Section Six: Exposé of the Tricks of Those Who Scam Money Changers

There is no tribe ballsier than this, for they scam the cleverest of all the tribes of charlatans: money changers make their living by fooling everyone, while these make their living by fooling money changers, which is the ne plus ultra of balls and skill. In Damascus, I came across a man from Aleppo called Jamāl al-Dīn Yūsuf ibn al-Munaqqish. He was a man of distinction and outward respectability, and I watched how he scammed the money changers who worked with gold and silver. 25.11

To do this, he'd go to a money changer with a gold or silver piece, but made of copper, tucked under his little finger. He'd also have with him either a good gold or a good silver piece, depending on how much he wanted to score, the good coin being of the same face value as the bad—only proper testing could show it was fake. So Jamāl al-Dīn would stand in front of the money changer and give him a good gold piece to change, saying, "Give me the equivalent in silver pieces." The money changer would take the gold piece, test it, weigh it, and pay out the silver pieces. Jamāl al-Dīn would then ask him, "How many silver pieces did you give me?" The man would say how many it was. Jamāl al-Dīn would say, "I won't take less than such and such," and the man would say, "And I won't pay more than I already did." So then Jamāl al-Dīn would say, "Give me back the gold piece," and the money changer would hand him back the gold piece. The second Jamāl al-Dīn had it in his hand, he'd switch it for the 25.12

موضع الدينار المبهرج[1] وحلّق له المبهرج[2] وقال هذا ناقص عن حقّي فيكون الصيرفيّ قد وزن الدينار ونقده ويأخذه ويرميه في صندوقه ثمّ يدفع له الدراهم طيّب القلب أنّه قد وزن ذلك ونقده وكذلك الدرهم فافهم ذلك

١ ش: البهرج. ٢ ش: البهرج.

"dressed" piece and throw that down in front of the money changer, saying, "I still say it's less than what you owe me."[222] The money changer would have weighed and tested the piece, so he'd take it and throw it into his coffer, and then pay over the silver pieces, perfectly happy in his own mind that it was the one he'd weighed and tested. It was the same if the coin was silver. Wise up to these things!

الفصل السادس والعشرين

باب واحد

في كشف أسرار الذين يدبّون على المردان في السماعات وفي الأفراح وفي الأسفار وغيرها

١،٢٦ اعلم أنّ هذه الطائفة يتمسّون بالفقر ثمّ يحضرون السماعات وفي الأفراح وفي الأسفار وقد كنت في مدينة أنطاكيّة من الروم وقد عمل بعض التجّار سماع فدعاني فيه وكان من أهل إسكندريّة فحضرنا[١] وكان قد جاء إلى المدينة رجل من أهل حرّان ومعه ولد عمره خمسة عشر سنة لم يكن في عصره أحسن منه ومعه مملوكه تركيّ اسمه أيبك ويلقب بالأغيد يضاهي ابن أستاذه في الحسن وكان الصبيّ مغنّي بالدفوف والشبابات وقد أفتن أهل البلد بحسنه وحسن غنائه وحسن المملوك وكان لا يعمل السماع إلّا بمائة درهم سلطانيّة وكان التاجر قد تلف به وبذل شيء كثير ولم يصل إليه فعند ذلك صار يعمل السماعات رجاء أن ينال منه غرض ولم يصل إلى شيء منه

٢،٢٦ فلمّا كان تلك الليلة عمل السماع وأحضرني[٢] فلمّا طاب الشغل ودار السماع جعل ينقّط بخمسة سلطانيّة خلف خمسة إلى أن نقّطه بجملة ولم يزل كذلك إلى وقت الصبح فلمّا عزموا على النوم والراحة قام المغنّي أخذ مملوكه وجعله مع الحائط وجعل ابنه إلى جانبه ونام الشيخ في جنب ابنه وناموا الناس فلم يبق فيهم إلّا من قد غرق في النوم قام الإسكندريّ ودبّ إلى عند رجل المغاني وأنا ألاحظه ثمّ نام لحظة

١ ش: فلما حضرنا. ٢ أزيل للسياق. وكان صاحبي من الإسكندريّة.

Chapter Twenty-Six, in One Section:

Exposé of the Tricks of Those Who Creep Up on Beardless Boys at Music and Chanting Performances and Weddings and on Journeys and So On

This tribe of charlatans puts on a show of being dervishes and in this guise they attend music and chanting performances and weddings, and make journeys. Once I was in the city of Antioch, in Anatolia, and a merchant was putting on a performance, so he invited me. He was from Alexandretta, so we went. A man, a native of Ḥarrān, had come to the city, bringing with him a son of his aged fifteen, the handsomest boy of his day. With him too was a Turkish slave called Aybak, known as "the Willow Waisted," who rivaled his master's son in beauty. The boy sang to the tambourines and the pipes, and everyone in town was entranced by his beauty and that of his singing, as they were by the beauty of the slave. The boy wouldn't take less than a hundred royal silver pieces for a performance, and the merchant had paid out a fortune and spent vast sums of money but still hadn't gotten anywhere with him, and he went on sponsoring performances in the hope that one day he would. 26.1

He was sponsoring a performance that particular night and had me come along. When things started to heat up and the chanting was in full swing, my friend began handing out tips of five royal silver pieces, one after another, till he'd given away a huge sum, and he kept this up till morning. Then, when everyone had decided to turn in and take a rest, the head musician took his slave and placed him next to the wall, put his son next to him, and himself lay down next to his son. Everyone lay down and there wasn't a soul who wasn't fast asleep when the Alexandrettan got up and crept over to the leader of the band—observed, however, by me. He lay down for a moment, then sat up and took from his waist sash a box containing a bit of cotton wool soaked in I know 26.2

ثمّ قعد وأخرج من وسطه حُقّ فيه قطنة مسقاة لا أعلم ما فيها ثمّ إنّه مسح بها أنوف الجماعة من المغاني

٣،٢٦ ثمّ أخرج من وسطه ظرف صغير فجعله بين المملوك وبين الصبيّ ثمّ جعل رأس الظرف إلى عنده وجعل في رأسه أنبوبة نحاس ونفخ في تلك الأنبوبة فكلّما صار في الظرف شيء من الريح قد أخلى بين الصبيّ وبين المملوك إلى أن أخذ ذلك الظرف حقّه من الريح وقد صار بين الصغير وبين المملوك مكان يسع من يريد ينام بينهما فلمّا فعل ذلك صبر لحظة ثمّ ترك رأس الظرف إلى أن خلا من الريح ثمّ جمعه وردّه إلى مكانه ثمّ أخرج صنّارة على مثال مخالب القصّاب ثمّ علّق بها ذيل الصبيّ وعلّقها إلى حلوقه فبقي الصبيّ مكشوف إلى نصفه ثمّ أخرج حُقّ ثاني وأخرج دهن دهن به مشقّ الصبيّ ثمّ إنّه جعل نفسه[١] بين الصبيّ وبين المملوك واستعمل الصبيّ مرّتين ثمّ عدل إلى المملوك وفعل به كما فعل بالصبيّ ولم يزل على هذه الصفة إلى باكر ثمّ انسلّ من بينهم بعد ما مسحهما ثمّ ربط حِزَزهما ثمّ انسلّ إلى موضعه

٤،٢٦ فلمّا صار فيه قلت له صحّة صحّة هناك فقال وأنت منتبه فقلت نعم لأنّك أنت استأجرتني ليلة وما كان يمكنني النوم فقال الحمد لله الذي لم يطّلع على حالي أحد غيرك فقلت له والله لقد كان من حقّي عليك المواساة فقال المائدة منصوبة والطعام حاضر بسم الله فقلت من عادتي أن لا آكل فضلة ولا نوالة فقال ليلة بعد أغداً نعمل سماع وتكون أوّل من يقعد على المائدة فقلت والله إلى ذلك الوقت يكون سيّدنا قد جاع وقد حلّت له الميتة فضحك وقمنا إلى أشغالنا فهذا أعجب ما رأيت من صناعة من يدبّ على المردان وإنّما كان مرادي أن أذكر ذلك لأجل أنّي لم يفتني شيء ولم أترك شيء فافهم ذلك

---

١ أضيف للسياق.

not what, with which he proceeded to wipe the noses of the whole troupe of musicians.

Next, he took a small leather waterskin from his waist and placed it between the slave and the boy. He turned the top end of the skin toward himself and inserted a copper tube, into which he blew, and the more the skin filled with air, the more space it created between the boy and the slave, till it was completely filled with air and there was enough space to accommodate anyone who wished to lie between them. He waited for a moment, then allowed the waterskin to empty of air, folded it up, and put it back where it came from. Next, he took out a hook like the ones butchers use, snagged the back of the boy's robe with it, and raised it to the level of his collar, leaving the boy half naked. Then he took out another box and removed from it some ointment with which he smeared the boy's crack, and he placed himself between the boy and the slave and used the boy twice, after which he turned to the slave and did to him the same as he had done to the boy, keeping this up till morning. In the end, he slipped out from between them, after first wiping them off and tying the strings of their drawers back up. Then he slipped back into his place. 26.3

When he got back, I said to him, "In good health! In good health!" to which he replied, "You were awake?" "Yes," I said. "You hired me for the night, so of course I couldn't sleep." "Thank God you were the only one who saw what I was up to!" he said. I responded, "I swear, you owe it to me to go even steven!" to which he replied, "The table's set, the food's ready, go right ahead and say grace!" I told him, "It's not my way to eat leftovers or handouts." "The night after tomorrow," he said, "I'll put out another serving, and you can be the first to sit down to table." "By that time," I replied, "my lord will surely have gotten hungry enough to eat a corpse!" He laughed, and we set off to see to our daily affairs. This is the most amazing example I've seen of the craft of those who creep up on beardless boys. The only reason I mention it is to show that nothing escapes my notice and that I've left nothing unrecorded. Wise up to these things! 26.4

الفصل السابع والعشرين

اثنان وثلاثون باباً

في كشف أسرار أرباب الصنائع

١،٢٧ اعلم أنّ هذا الفصل لا يُحدّ ولا يقع عليه احتواء ولا يحُصى جميع ما يتضمّن فإنّ دائرته واسعة الأكناف بعيدة الأطراف لا تجمعها الأوصاف وإنّما نذكرمنها ما سهل على سبيل الاختصار والإيجاز إن شاء الله تعالى وقد تقدّم ذكر الصنّاع مفصّلاً وهاهنا نجمل ما نذكرمنه فأمّا صنعة الكيمياء فهي من الدكّ وغيره واعلم أنّ فيها حقّ وباطل فلمّا طلب الحقّ جهل فاستعمل الباطل

الباب الأوّل في كشف أسرارهم في حقائق علم الصنعة

٢،٢٧ إذ كان الذي ذكرناه فيما تقدّم في الدكّ وهو باطل فأنا أذكرمن ذلك ما يؤكل منه فمن ذلك أعمال البياض فإذا أردت ذلك فتأخذ من الزرنيخ الأحمر والأصفر ما شئت فتدقّهما دقّاً ناعماً ثمّ تسقيهما الخلّ والنطرون عشرة أيّام ثمّ تستنزلها فتنزل لك رصاصة بيضاء صافية البياض ثمّ تعقد لها الزيبق وذلك أن تأخذ من الزيبق خمسة دراهم ومن العَنْزَروت درهمين ومن اللبانة المغربيّة درهمين ونصف ومن البارود خمسة دراهم يدقّ الجميع دقّاً ناعماً ثمّ يجُعل من فوق الرصاصة[١] ومن تحته ثمّ يثبّت

---

١ ش: الزيبق.

Chapter Twenty-Seven, in Thirty-Two Sections:

Exposé of the Tricks of "the Masters of the Crafts"

27.1 This chapter contains charlatans too numerous to count and too various to confine, and the compass of its content escapes calculation. Its scope is too broad, its limits too large to be gathered under any one rubric, so we shall mention here only what may be summarized with ease and brevity, the Almighty willing. We have spoken of "the Craftsmen" before, in detail. Here, we shall provide a summary of what we still have to say about them.[223] The craft of alchemy, for example, encompasses both chicanery and honest dealing: It contains things that are genuine and things that are false. When one of these charlatans strives for the genuine, he fails, so he resorts to the false.

Section One: Exposé of Their Secrets Regarding the True Nature of the Science of "the Craft"

27.2 Given that what we have described above involves chicanery, which is dishonest, let me mention here a few things from which an honest living may be made. One of these is production of "the white."[224] To do this, take as much realgar and orpiment as you like and pound them till smooth. Next, steep them in vinegar and natron for ten days, then purify them. You will be left with a very pure white nugget. Quicksilver is now added for thickening, which is done by taking five dirhams by weight of quicksilver, two of sarcocolla, two and a half of Maghrebi styrax, and five of saltpeter. These are pounded together till smooth, then placed above and below the quicksilver. This is firmly set in a banked fire, as is, for seven days. When you see that it has hardened and you

في نار دمس هكذا سبعة أيّام فإذا رأيته قد ثبت وجرّبته فالقمه تلك الرصاصة وألق منه واحد على عشرين يقوم الجميع فضّة نقيّة

الباب الثاني من الصنعة في التحمير

٣،٢٧ ومن ذلك إذا أردت أن تعمل ذهباً خالصاً إبريزاً فتأخذ من الراسُخت المغربيّ جزء فتستنزله ثمّ تأخذ من التوتياء الخضراء جزء ومن الزنجفر جزء ومن الزنجار جزء ثمّ تلحف به ذلك الراسخت وتسبكها ثلاث مرّات فتعود ذهباً ولا بدّ من الزاج

الباب الثالث في كشف أسرار مقادير النيران

٤،٢٧ اعلم أنّ النيران لها مقادير تزيد وتنقص على قدر الأعمال واستعمالها فمنها أعمال الأرواح فإنّها يجب أن تكون نار لطيفة جدّاً ثمّ يقوّيها بالتدريج على قدر تلك الروح وأمّا النار التي تكون في الأجساد فإنّها تكون قويّة أشدّ من نار الأرواح وأمّا نار الأنفاس فإنّها تكون نار معتدلة وأمّا نار التكليس فإنّها تكون أقوى ما تكون من النيران وقد بيّنت لك كلّ فنّ مليح واعلم أنّ النار هي التي تضرّ الأعمال وتفسدها وهي التي تصلح وتنفع واعلم أنّها هي القاضي في علم الصنعة وهي العلم كلّه

الباب الرابع في كشف أسرار عدّتهم وما يحتاجون إليه من الأعمال بالآلات

٥،٢٧ اعلم أنّ هذه الصناعة جليلة المقدار ولا يقع لها على حدّ ولا عيار وأهلها على الحقيقة هم أهل الله عزّ وجلّ فإنّ هؤلاء القوم لا يظهرون لأحد من الناس فأمّا من تعلّق بها غيرهم فإنّهم أصحاب دكّ ومكر وقد وضعت لها آلة وصارت معروفة بينهم فمن ذلك الزُنجُفْرِيّات والقرعات والأنابيق لأجل التصعيد والتقطير ولهم أيضاً

have tested it, cut the nugget into pieces, discard a twentieth, and the rest will come out pure silver.

Section Two on "the Craft," on "Reddening"[225]

If you want to make pure unalloyed gold, take one part Maghrebi antimony 27.3
and purify it. Then take one part green tutty, one part cinnabar, and one part blue vitriol. Cover the antimony with this, smelt it three times, and it will come out as gold. The vitriol is essential.

Section Three: Exposé of the Secrets Regarding the Different Intensities of Fire

The intensity of the fire used will be higher or lower depending on the scale of 27.4
the operation and how it is to be managed. Operations to produce "spirits"[226] require a very gentle flame that is increased by degrees depending on their quantity, while the flame used to produce "bodies"[227] should be strong and fiercer than that required for spirits. The fire for "souls"[228] should be moderate and that for calcining should be the strongest possible. In the same spirit in which I've laid out for you the core principles of every other agreeable art, you need to know that it is fire that impairs and corrupts alchemical operations, just as it serves and benefits them. Note well—fire is the determining factor in the science of the Craft; indeed, it is the whole of that science.

Section Four: Exposé of the Secrets Regarding Their Tool Kit and of the Operations They Perform That Require Instruments

This craft is of sublime scope; no one knows its end or its extent, and its true 27.5
practitioners are people of God, Mighty and Glorious. They are a company who do not show themselves to ordinary people. The others, however, who ride on their coattails, are scammers and cheats. A set of instruments has been devised for this science that they all now know well and that includes cinnabar retorts, still pots, and alembics for sublimation and distillation.

أقداح التشميع وقناني وفيّاشات ولهم زباديّ التصعيد لأجل تبييض الزرنيخ وتصعيد الزيبق ولهم أيضاً عدّة غير هذه العدّة ولهم عدد شتّى للتكليس وغير ذلك وأمّا ما يحتاجون إليه عند السحق فهي الصلاية أعني بلاطة مانع أو حجر أسود ثمّ الفِهْر وهو الذي يسحقونه على تلك الصلاية ولهم أيضاً في عقد الزيبق وتكليسه وما أشبه ذلك فافهموا فقد بيّنت لكم وكشفت جميع الأعمال ودكّها حتّى لا يخفى عليكم شيء من الأمور ولو قصدت أن أبيّن كلّ فصل بجميع معانيه لطال الشرح في ذلك وما ذكرت من كلّ شيء إلّا أيسره والمقصود منه وما يستدلّ به على غيره

الباب الخامس في كشف أسرار جرهم الأكبر

٦،٢٧ اعلموا أيّها[١] الواقفون على كتابي هذا أنّ خادمكم عبد الرحيم بن عمر مؤلّف هذا الكتاب قد اجتمع بفضلاء هذه الصنعة فرأيت كلّ قوم قد ذهبوا إلى شيء وأثبتوا أنّ هذا الحجر المكرّم وأقاموا عليه البرهان والدليل على قدر مبلغهم في العلم فمنهم من قال إنّه الملح وقد قيل هو ذلك لأنّه دليله أنّه أوّل ما يحتاج إليه المولود وآخر ما يحتاج إليه الميّت وقالوا إنّ الله عزّ وجلّ قد ذكّر به بني آدم كلّما[٢] خرج من بطن أمّه ونبّه عليه وقال أناس إنّه البيض وذهب إلى أنّه يمكن ذلك لأنّه يجيء منه ممّا تختلف ألوانه ويعمل[٣] جميع الأعاجيب وقال قوم إنّه الشعر وقد رأيته ورأيت له برهاناً ظاهراً ولعمري إنّه الخرّاج الولّاج والمؤلّف وله ممّا تختلف ألوانه وقال يوشع بن نون عليه السلام إنّه الدم وقد قال لي بعض مشايخ هذا العلم إنّه أصحّ ما وجدناه وأقام عليه دليل أنّه حياة الآدميّ فإذا مات ذهب منه الدم وتصريفه عجيب في تكليسه وعمله وقال قوم البول وقال قوم العذرة وقال قوم العظام وقال قوم حجارة المعادن وقال قوم عيون الحيوان

---

١ ش: أنّ هذه. ٢ ش: كما. ٣ ش: يقول.

In addition, along with their many other instruments, they use waxing cups, bottles, and flasks, as well as sublimation dishes for turning arsenic into silver[229] and sublimating quicksilver, plus their various instruments for calcification and so on. When it comes to pulverization, they use the *ṣalāya*, a resistant slab of black stone,[230] and the rounded pounding ball, which is what they use to crush things on the *ṣalāya*. They also have things for thickening and calcining quicksilver and so on. Wise up! I am setting out and explaining all these operations and their scams to you so that none remains a mystery to you. I don't intend to lay out every single category of trick with all its branches, as it would take too long. I have just mentioned the more accessible examples of everything, the purpose of each, and enough of everything to allow you to infer the rest.

Section Five: Exposé of the Secrets of Their "Great Stone"[231]

All you who peruse this book of mine need to be aware that its author, your servant ʿAbd al-Raḥīm ibn ʿUmar, met with the most learned practitioners of this craft. He noted that each group had followed its own path and asserted that this or that particular thing was the Venerable Stone, each providing proof and evidence to that effect commensurate with their degree of attainment in the science. Some said it was salt, basing their claim perhaps on the evidence that that is the first thing a newborn child needs and the last thing a dead man needs; they claimed that God, Mighty and Glorious, reminds humans of it and draws their attention to its importance every time one of them exits its mother's belly. Others claimed it was the egg; they believed this might be the case because different-colored things come out it and because it performs every kind of wonder. Another group stated it was hair; I met them and thought they had clear proof of what they said, for hair is indeed, I swear, something that is always going out and in and is produced in the thousands, just as it has a variety of colors. Joshua son of Nun, eternal peace be his, said that the Venerable Stone is blood, and one doyen of this science told me this was the truest thing he'd found, citing as proof that blood is a human's vital force, for when he dies, his blood leaves him, and the way it changes from state to state when calcined and processed is extraordinary. Others said it's urine, others feces, others bones, others mineral ore, yet others animals' eyes. Each of them came 27.6

وكلّ منهم دبّر شيء وقال هذا هو الحجر المكرّم وقد يحملون الكلّ على الصدق لأنّهم يكرّمونه ونعوتهم كثيرة وصفاتهم تطول

الباب السادس في كشف أسرارهم التي تتعلّق ببني ساسان

فهو أبو أرباب هذه الصنائع جميع ما يتعلّق منها يدخل فيما وضعه وهو الذي فتح هذه الأبواب وسلّك[١] الناس فيها وأوضح لهم الطرق وبيّن لهم سبيل المعرفة والتسلّط المختلف الأنواع على أخذ أموال الناس واعلم أنّ جميع أرباب هذه الصنائع إنّما هم غلمانه وعلى آثاره يمشون ٢٧،٧

ولقد رأيت منهم نفرًا يعملون أشياء من أنواع الحلي من النحاس ثمّ يطلونها بالذهب والفضّة شيئًا إذا كان ذهب يساوي خمسمائة دينار ودراهم ثمّ يخرجون إلى ظاهر البلد إلى بعض الطرق المنقطعة القليلة الخاطر ثمّ يكون ذلك في شيء ثمّ يرمونه على جنب الطريق فيروحون عنه ثمّ يرقبون من يعثر عليه فهو يراه قد مدّ يده إليه وقد شاله وهو يحطّ عليه ويقول شركة بلا كلام ثمّ ينعزل به عن الطريق ويقول يا أخي من هاهنا اصطحبنا ومن هاهنا نفترق إمّا أن تبيعني وإمّا أن تشتري منّي نصيبي فيقول له بكم نصيبك فيقول أنا أشتري منك فيقول بكم فإذا كان يسوى خمسمائة فيقول مائة درهم فيقول أنت مجنون هذا يسوى كذا وكذا أبيعك بهذا المقدار فيقول والله ما معي غير الذي قلت لك فإن أخذت فبسم الله فيقول الخشن تبيعني أنت نصيبك فيقول بكم يصلح لك فيقول خذ مائة وعشرة بزائد عشرة فيقول ما هو مليح تأخذ منّي بلا ثمن فيقول وعشرين فيبيعه نصيبه ويأخذ ما حصل ويشيل ولا يلتفت فهذا من بعض صناعتهم ٢٧،٨

---

١ ش: سلّط.

up with something and said, "This is the Venerable Stone!" and it may be that all of them are right, for they do venerate it. Their descriptions of it are diverse; their accounts would take long to rehearse.[232]

Section Six: Exposé of Tricks That Relate Specifically to the Banū Sāsān

Sāsān is the father of the masters of these crafts; everything that has to do with them falls within the scope of his invention. He is the one who opened these doors, led his people through them, showed them the way, and laid out for them the path that leads to all the various forms of knowledge and control required to get one's hands on people's money. All the masters of these crafts are his servants and follow in his footsteps. 27.7

I saw a group of them who make different kinds of copper-ornament-type things, then coat them with a little gold and silver so they look like they'd be worth five hundred gold pieces and change, if they really were gold. Then they leave the city for its outskirts, where the roads are isolated and have little traffic. He throws the ornament, which will be wrapped in something, down at the side of the road and removes himself but watches to see who comes upon it. When he sees someone stretch out his hand to take it, he falls on him and says, "It belongs to us both, no two ways about it!" Then he leaves the highway with the man and says, "Brother, here we met and here we go our separate ways. Either you sell it to me or you buy me out." "How much to buy you out?" says the mark. "I'll buy it from you," says the charlatan. "For how much?" says the mark. If it looks as though it's worth five hundred gold pieces, the charlatan says, "One hundred silver pieces." "Are you crazy?" says the mark. "It's worth such and such. I'll sell it to you for that." The charlatan says, "I swear, that's all I have on me. Take it or leave it." So the mark says, "How about I buy you out?" so the charlatan says, "How much is it worth to you?" so the first says, "Here's a hundred and ten. That's ten over the odds." The other says, "It's not nice of you to take it off me for nothing!" so the first says, "Make it a hundred and twenty!" So the other lets him buy him out, takes what he's made, and hightails it without looking back. This is just one example of their craft. 27.8

الباب السابع في كشف أسرارهم

ومن ذلك أنّهم يأخذ أحدهم درموت ويأتي إلى الفاخورة ويملأه شقاف ويغطّيه بكساء ويحمله إلى بعض المواضع ويوري أنّه قد تعس ثمّ يرمي بالدرموت عن رأسه ثمّ يدقّ يد على يد ويوري أنّه يبكي ويحولق أيّ من رآه عبر يقول أسعدوني في ثمنه فوالله ما أملك قوت العائلة في يومي هذا ولا يزال يتسأسأ حتّى يحصل القَشْمة والصَميّة واللقية ثمّ يمدّها فافهم ذلك ٩،٢٧

الباب الثامن في كشف أسرارهم

ومن ذلك أنّهم يرسلون صغيرة بنت عشر سنين فتقف على بعض الشوارع معها قنّينة مكسورة وقد يبقى في يدها حلق القنّينة وهي تبكي وتبحث في التراب كأنّ قد وقع منها شيء وهي تفتّش عليه وتبكي فيجتمع عليها الناس ويقولون ما لك أيش ضاع لك فتقول[1] والله أعطتني أمّي نصف نُقْرة والله باعت به غزل قالت اصرفيه خذي منه بقرطيس زيت والباقي خبز وقعت وكان في يدي طار منّي وانكسرت القنّينة فلا تزال تبكي حتّى يعطيها واحد نصف نقرة فتأخذه وتشيل ويكون لها أخ أو أخت قد عملت كذلك في موضع آخر ١٠،٢٧

الباب التاسع في كشف أسرار الذين هم العطّارين

وقد رأيت في ساحل جدّة رجل نوبيّ يعمل الفلفل فيجيء جيّد وقد تموّل منه وذلك أنّه يأخذ من البسيل رطلاً جيّداً ثمّ يغمره بالماء المستخرج من الجرجير ويجعل فيه أوقيّة فلفل حارّ ثمّ يغلي عليه حتّى يذهب الثلث من ذلك الماء فإنّه يعود فلفلاً جيّداً ثمّ يرفعه ويجفّفه جفافاً جيّداً وهو مليح ١١،٢٧

---

١ ش: فيقول.

Section Seven of the Exposé of Their Tricks

Another example: One of them takes a container, goes to the potters' field, fills it with broken shards, covers it with a cloth, and carries it off with him someplace, where he makes himself out to be a pauper, throws the container down off his head, slaps his hands in grief, and pretends to weep, crying out, "Power and strength come from God alone!" [233] To any passerby he sees, he says, "Give me something to help me buy another! I swear to God, this lousy day I don't have enough to buy food for the family!" and keeps bleating till he's got his hands on some half-ripe dates, wine, and fried offal. Then he hotfoots it out of there. Wise up to these things! 27.9

Section Eight of the Exposé of Their Tricks

Another example: They send a child, a girl of ten, and she stands in the street holding just the broken neck of a bottle in her hand, while she cries and searches in the dust as if she's dropped something and is looking for it everywhere, weeping. People gather round and ask, "What's wrong? What have you lost?" She says, "My mother gave me half a silver penny I swear she got it from selling yarn I swear she told me change it into smaller coins and get oil for two farthings and spend the rest on bread but I fell and it was in my hand but it shot off and the bottle broke,"and keeps crying till someone gives her half a silver penny, which she takes and makes off with. And she most assuredly has a brother or a sister who's pulled off the same scam in some other part of town. 27.10

Section Nine: Exposé of the Tricks of the Ones Who Are Apothecaries

On the coast, I saw a Nubian who made fake pepper. It was a good earner and he'd made a lot of money off of it. 27.11

Exposé: He'd take a good pound of peas, cover them with juice extracted from arugula, add an ounce of hot pepper, then boil till the liquid was reduced by a third. It turned into high-grade pepper, which he'd set aside and dry well. It's a smart trick.

الباب العاشر في كشف أسرارهم

١٢،٢٧ ومن ذلك عمل الفلفل من الماش من حبّه وجاء حسن ولم أقدر له على الجرجير فأخذت بزر رشاد وسحقته سحقاً ناعماً ثمّ نقعته في الماء يوماً وليلة ثمّ صفّيت الماء وأغليت به الماش فجاء أحسن ما يكون وكنت قد أخذت من الدخان الذي يكون على طاقة الفرن شيء يسير ثمّ جعلته في ماء الرشاد فجاء أسود

الباب الحادي عشر في كشف أسرارهم

١٣،٢٧ اعلم أنّ لهم أقراص جملة من القواتل يعملونها وهي تذهب بالعمر والحياة ثمّ تكون عندهم لمن يقصدهم فيها فيأخذون منها ما أرادوا فمن ذلك قرص قاتل وهو أن يأخذون من ورق رجل الغراب جزء ومن حشيشة ذات الأسرّة جزء ومن الشيح جزء يدقّون الجميع ويعملون أقراص فإنّها من القواتل

الباب الثاني عشر في كشف أسرارهم

١٤،٢٧ ومن ذلك أنّهم يعملون قرصاً قاتلاً وذلك أنّهم يأخذون من حبّ النارنج جزء ومن ورق الدفلى جزء ومن حبّ الفلفل الذي هو لاعية الأخواص جزء يدقّ الجميع ثمّ يجعلونه قرص فإنّه يفعل في إسقاط القوّة فعلاً عظيماً فافهم ذلك ترشد

الباب الثالث عشر في عمل الزنجار

١٥،٢٧ ومن ذلك إذا أرادوا يعملون زنجاراً جيّداً فيأخذون من النحاس الأحمر فيرقّونه صفائح ثمّ يطلونه بالخلّ والنشادر المعدنيّ ثمّ يجعلونه في الندى أيّاماً فإنّه يعود زنجاراً جيّداً وإن أرادوا حمّصيّ فيرقّونه ويلوّثونه بالخلّ والنوشادر ويعلّقونه في دنّ الخمر أو في جوانبه فإنّه يعود أحسن ما يكون

Section Ten of the Exposé of Their Tricks

Another example: Making fake pepper from mung beans, which turned out well, though I couldn't obtain any arugula for it so I used cress seed instead, which I crushed till smooth, then steeped in water for a day and a night. Then I strained the liquid and boiled the beans in it and it turned out as fine as could be. I'd previously taken a little soot from the mouth of the oven and put it in the cress water, so it turned black. 27.12

Section Eleven of the Exposé of Their Tricks

They concoct pills using multiple deadly ingredients that will put an end to anyone's life. They keep these on hand for anyone who comes to them and asks for them, who can then buy as many as he pleases. Among them are a certain deadly pill that they make by taking one part leaves of buckhorn plantain, one part line plant, and one part wormwood. They pound these all together and make pills, which are deadly.[234] 27.13

Section Twelve of the Exposé of Their Tricks

Example: They know how to concoct deadly poisonous pills. 27.14

Exposé: They take one part bitter-orange seeds, one part oleander leaves, and one part "pepper seed," which is the same as caper spurge seed, and pound them together. They make this into a pill that is very effective for sapping strength. Wise up to this and you can't go wrong!

Section Thirteen: On Making Artificial Verdigris[235]

Another example: To concoct high-quality verdigris they take copper and beat it into sheets that they coat with vinegar and niter, then put out in the dew for several days. These then turn into high-grade verdigris. To make green-chick-pea verdigris, they beat out the copper, spatter it with vinegar and ammonia, and hang it in, or on the side of, a wine barrel. It comes out as fine as can be. 27.15

الباب الرابع عشر في عمل الزنجفر

وهو أحسن شيء وقفت عليه من أعمالهم وذلك أنّهم يأخذون من الزرنيخ جزء ومن الكبريب جزء ومن الزيبق جزء فيقتلون[1] الزيبق في الزرنيخ والكبريب والخلّ ثمّ يجعلونه في زنجفريّة مطينة إلى حدّ الدواء ولها طوق من الطين ثمّ يجعلون لها تنورًا على قدرها من أسفله واسع وأعلاه ضيّق على قدر الزنجفريّة ثمّ يكون لها بابان أحد الأبواب للنار والثاني معلّق فيه ورقة فإذا كان النار قويّة تحرّكت الورقة جدًّا كثيرًا فيحدّون عليه عند ذلك الحريق وإذا بطل التحريك من الورقة كانت النار ضعيفة فيقوّيها كي لا تجيء فطير فافهم ما أشرت إليك في النار ترشد ١٦،٢٧

الباب الخامس عشر في كشف أسرارهم في عمل الإسفيداج

وذلك أنّهم يأخذون من الرصاص القَلَعيّ فيجعلونه في إناء مزجّج ويجعلون من فوقه شيئًا ثمّ يجعلون عليه النار من فوقه ومن أسفله كذلك ثلاثة أيّام فإنّه يتكلّس إسفيداج جيّد فافهم ذلك ترشد ١٧،٢٧

الباب السادس عشر في كشف أسرارهم في عمل النيل

إذا أرادوا أن يعملونه يأخذون قشر البيض يكلّسونه تكليسًا جيّدًا ثمّ يسحقونه ثمّ يسقونه ماء ساعة ثمّ بعد ذلك يسقونه بماء حشيشة الصبّاغين وهي الوسمة وكلّما أسقونه فمّ يتركونه حتّى يجفّ ثمّ يسقونه فم آخر ثمّ يرفعونه ويجففونه ثمّ يكسّرونه ١٨،٢٧

---

[1] ش: يقلبون.

Section Fourteen: On Making Artificial Cinnabar

This is the best operation of theirs I've observed. 27.16

Exposé: They take one part arsenic, one part sulfur, and one part quicksilver, and dilute the quicksilver in the arsenic, sulfur, and vinegar. They then place this in a cinnabar retort that has been packed with clay to the level of the mixture and has a clay ring. Next, they make a clay oven fitted to the retort, which is wide at the bottom and as narrow as the retort at the top. This oven has two openings. One is for the fire; in the other a piece of paper is hung. If the fire is too fierce, the paper moves violently and when this happens they reduce the heat. If the paper stops moving, the fire is too low, and they increase it so it doesn't come out underdone. Bear in mind what I told you about fire[236] and you can't go wrong!

Section Fifteen: Exposé of Their Tricks for Making Artificial White Lead

Exposé: They take some tin and place it in a glazed vessel and put something over it. Then they expose it to fire from both above and below for three days, at which point high-grade white lead is calcined out. Wise up to this and you can't go wrong! 27.17

Section Sixteen: Exposé of Their Tricks for Making Artificial Indigo

To make it they take eggshells, calcine them well, then soak them in water for an hour. Next, they soak them in dyers' weed, which is the same as dyers' croton, leaving them to dry out after each soaking. Then they give them a final soaking, set them aside, and dry them out, after which they break them up into small pieces. 27.18

الباب السابع عشر في كشف أسرارهم

١٩،٢٧ وهم الذين يدّعون المشيخة من الفقراء في منع المطر حتّى أنّهم يتوهّم فيهم الصلاح وذلك إذا أعاقهم المطر عن تصرّفاتهم فيشتكون ذلك إلى الشيخ فيقوم كأنّه يدعو الله عزّ وجلّ ثمّ يأخذ ناراً فيطرح فيها من ورق الدفلى جزء ومن اليبروح جزء ومن الرامك المصريّ جزء ومن الغبيراء جزء ويكون ذلك كلّه مدقوقاً ناعماً ثمّ يبخّر به ويقف كأنّه يدعو الله تعالى فإنّ المطر يرتفع عن تلك الأرض فافهم وأعرف من هذا النوع أربعة عشر نوعاً مختلفة الفعال

الباب الثامن عشر في كشف أسرارهم في نبع الماء

٢٠،٢٧ اعلم أنّ هذا الباب من الأسرار العجيبة الخفيّة الذي يستعملونها أصحاب النواميس في الأسفار وهي أعجب ما رأيت حتّى كدت أن أرتبط عليهم وذلك أنّهم يأخذون من حبّ الرشاد جزء ومن[١] برشاوشان جزء ومن حبّ الإذخر جزء يدقّون الجميع ويجعلونه أقراصاً فإذا أرادوا معرفة الأرض الذي فيها الماء يبخّروا بتلك الأقراص فإنّه يظهر لهم شبه السحاب فيحفروا قليلاً فإنّ الماء يطلع فيتوهّم الناس من ذلك وهذا من أجلّ النواميس الملاح

الباب التاسع عشر في كشف أسرارهم

٢١،٢٧ ومن ذلك أنّي رافقت في أرض الحجاز رجل اسمه سليمان وكان يدّعي المشيخة وكان يُعرف بحسن السائح اسمه الصحيح سليمان فكان معه ثلاثون فقراء فشرع ينومس على شيء من النواميس وأنا قد انطعت له وقد وقع له أنّه قد ربطني فقلّ علينا الماء ولم نجده فشكوا أصحابه إليه فقال أوقدوا نارا فأضرموا النار ثمّ أخرج من وسطه

١ أضيف للسياق.

Section Seventeen of the Exposé of Their Tricks

This is about dervishes who claim to be Sufi masters on the basis of their ability to stop it raining, which causes people to believe mistakenly that they number among the Righteous. This comes about when said people are inconvenienced by rain in the pursuit of their affairs, causing them to complain to the shaykh. He sets about making as though he was praying to God, Mighty and Glorious, then gets some fire and throws into it one part oleander leaves, one part mandrake root, one part Egyptian ramek, and one part marijuana, pounded together till smooth. He uses this as incense and stands as though praying to the Almighty, at which point the rain removes itself from the land in question. Wise up to these things. I know fourteen variants of this, each with a different effect. 27.19

Section Eighteen: Exposé of Their Tricks Regarding Springs of Water

This section concerns an amazing cryptic trick that illusionists use on journeys and is the most extraordinary thing I ever saw, to the degree that I was almost taken in by these charlatans myself. 27.20

Exposé: They take one part cress seed, one part maidenhair fern, and one part fever grass seed, pound these all together, and make them into pills. To discover where water lies underground, they use these pills as one would incense, the fumes rising before them like clouds. Then they dig a little and the water rises up to the surface, which makes everyone believe in them. This is one of the finest of all enchanting illusions.

Section Nineteen of the Exposé of Their Tricks

Another example: In the Hejaz, I hung out with a man called Sulaymān. He claimed to be a Sufi master and went by the name of Ḥasan the Journeyer;[237] his real name, though, was Sulaymān. He had thirty dervishes with him. He started going on about practicing certain illusions at a time when I'd placed myself under his command and he imagined I'd believe anything he said. One day, we ran low on water and couldn't find any, so his companions complained to him. "Light a fire!" he said, so they lit a fire. Then he produced some pills—I have no idea what they were—from his waistband and put one in 27.21

أقراص لا أعلم ما هي فجعل في وسط النار منها قرصاً ثمّ قال أمّنوا على الدعاء وجعل يرفع يديه إلى نحو السماء ويدعو سرّاً في قلبه فلمّا ارتفع الدخان طلع من السماء غمامة ولم تزل تدور على ذلك المكان ثمّ وقفت قريباً منه فقال احفروا فحفرنا بالعكاكيز مقدار شبر ونصف وإذا بالماء قد صعد مثل الفوّارة فقال اشربوا وتوضّؤوا للصلاة ففعلنا ثمّ أقمنا يومنا على ذلك الماء ثمّ بتنا عليه وحملنا كلّ واحد وعاءه ورحلنا طالبين المدينة

٢٢،٢٧ فلمّا وصلنا واسترحنا شرعت في أشياء من نواميس المشايخ فقال فلان كان ينزل في التنّور ولا تؤذيه النار فقلت نعم ثمّ إنّها ثلاثة تنانير فقال والله أحبّ أن أقف على شيء من ذلك فقلت نعم حبّاً[1] وكرامة فقال ولعلّ شيء آخر نذكرك به في مدّة حياتنا فقلت وما تريد قال كنت سمعت أنّ بعض المشايخ كان يظهر الفواكه في غير أوانها وفي أماكن لا توجد فيها فقلت نعم وهي ستّة وثلاثين نوعاً قال شيء في هذا الحجاز أقابلك به فقال كنت عزمت أنّي أصيدك فصدتني فقلت له أريد منك صفة نبع الماء الذي أظهرته لنا في ذلك الموضع والله أعرف منه تسعة أنواع ولعلّ يكون ذلك من الجملة فقال والله ما قلت أنّ فكرك يذهب إلى ذلك فما أنت إلّا فاضل ولو كنت تلبس خرقة الفقراء كنت أشيخ أهل عصرك فقلت هذا لا يمكن

٢٣،٢٧ فقلت أطلعني على ذلك وإن كان من جملة ما أعرفه فكان ما كان غير ذلك فأنا لا بدّ أن أعرض عليك الذي أعرف فقال حبّاً وكرامة أمّا الذي أعمل أنا به فإنّي آخذ من بزر السلجم جزء ومن المُستَعجِلة جزء ومن بزر السيكران جزء فأدقّ الجميع ثمّ أجعله أقراص فإذا أردت ذلك بخّرت به كما رأيت فقلت والله هذا ما كنت أعلمه وهذه فائدة منك وأنا أعرّفك غيرها أليق منها ثمّ علّمته من هذا النوع ثلاثة وعلّمته ما طلب منّي وأقمنا في المدينة مدّة أربع شهور وقد أقبلوا عليه أهل المدينة إقبال كلّيّ وهو عندهم أعظم من الجنيد وكنت أنا كلّما حضر من الأشراف لا أبرح واقف في خدمته فكنّا

[1] أضيف للسياق.

the center of the fire. "Repeat 'Amen' after my prayers!" he said, and raised his hands toward the sky, praying inaudibly. As the smoke rose, a cloud appeared in the sky and kept circling round that very place, then came to a halt close by him. "Dig!" he said, and we dug with our staffs to a depth of about one and a half handspans, and lo and behold the water rose up like a fountain. "Drink," he said, "and perform your ablutions for the prayer!" so we did, and we spent the rest of the day beside the water, and slept next to it too. Then each of us filled his water flask and we set off for Medina.

When we got there and had rested, I started shooting the breeze regarding some of the illusions performed by various shaykhs, and he said, "So-and-so used to go into the oven and the fire wouldn't harm him," and I said, "Right. It's a question of using three ovens." He said, "I'd really like to learn something about that," so I said, "Sure, with the greatest of pleasure!" Then he said, "Maybe something else too, for me to remember you by after we've gone our separate ways?" "What are you interested in?" I asked. He said, "I heard once there was this shaykh who could produce fruit out of season and in places where it wasn't to be found." "Right," I said. "Thirty-six kinds!" "Is there anything here in the Hejaz I can give you in return?" he asked, and went on: "I'd made up my mind I was going to put you in a corner, but you've cornered me!" I told him, "What I want from you is your recipe for the water spring you produced for us in that place yesterday. I already—please take my word for it—know nine. I want to know if yours is one of them." "Seriously," he said, "I didn't think you'd be so well informed. You're a real scholar. If you'd just put on dervish patchwork,[238] you'd be the shaykhliest man of the age." "That," I said, "isn't going to happen." 27.22

Then I said, "Show me the trick. If it's one I know, well and good. If it isn't, I promise I'll show you what I know." "With the greatest of pleasure!" he said. "What I do is, I take one part turnip seed, one part lizard orchid, and one part stinking nightshade seed, which I pound all together and make into pills. To do the trick, I burn one as incense, the way you saw." "By God," I said, "that's a new one to me. You've given me something I can use, so in return I'll teach you something different, and slicker," and I proceeded to instruct him in three ways of doing the same and taught him what he'd asked me to. We stayed in Medina for four months, where its inhabitants lionized him and thought he was greater than al-Junayd. For my part, whenever a descendant of the Prophet arrived,[239] I would spend the whole time on my feet, waiting on him; later, when we were 27.23

إذا خلونا يقول يا أخي أسألك أن لا تفعل ذلك فوالله أنا أحقّ بالوقوف في خدمتك فأقول هذا هو الواجب فلا تغيّر ما نظمت

الباب العشرون في كشف أسرار المطالبيّة في إبطال المهالك

٢٤،٢٧ اعلم أنّ هؤلاء القوم عندهم جبروت عظيم ولهم تقدّم على كلّ أمر صعب مثل الدخول في السروب ومعالجة تلك المضايق ثمّ الهجوم على المهالك وإن كان فيها التلاف ولهم الصبر على العمل بالفاعل والجوع فإنّ في طلب المال تذهب الأنفس بالطمع واعلم أنّ لهم آلة يطول شرحها بل نذكر شيئاً من إبطال المهالك اعلم أنّ من يمشي في هذا الباب لا غنى له من أن يكون يعرف شيئاً من الهندسة حتّى يقوى على فتح الكنوز فمن ذلك إبطال المهالك منهم مهلك الماء اعلم أنّ هذا مهلك عظيم وهو من أشدّ المهالك وذلك أنّهم إذا أرادوا فتح المطلب فرأوا إنّ قد ظهر عليهم الماء فينظرون من أيّ جهة يكون جريانه فإن كان جريه من أعلاه فيحفرون عن شرقيّه فيجدون قناة عظيمة فيخطونها فيجدون حجرًا وهو جُرنًا عظيماً فتنزل تلك القناة فيه وينقطع الماء وإن كان عن يمينه فيحفرون إلى جانبه فيجدون الجرن وكذلك عن شماله أيضاً وإن كان أسفله فيحفرون عند باب المطلب فإنّهم يجدون جرناً كما ذكرنا بلا زيادة ولا نقصان وذلك حسب ما وقع عليه التجاريب فافهم ذلك

الباب الحادي والعشرون في كشف أسرار إبطال مهلك الأشخاص

٢٥،٢٧ وذلك أنّك إذا دخلت المطلب رأيت دهليزًا مادّ وفيه أشخاص بأيديهم السيوف فإذا دخلت لعبت تلك الأشخاص بما في أيديها فاحفر قدّامك وذلك أنّك تأخذ عكّازًا وتتوكّأ عليه فأيّ مكان لعبت عليه فاحفره فتجد فيه مزاريب مملوءة زيبقا

on our own, the man would say to me, "Please, brother, don't do that! Honestly, I'm the one who should be on his feet waiting on you!" but I'd say, "Duty requires it, so don't try and change my way of doing things!"

Section Twenty: Exposé of the Tricks of Treasure Hunters for Disarming Booby Traps

This company is prodigiously arrogant and shows no reluctance when it comes 27.24
to formidable undertakings such as entering tunnels, navigating their narrow spaces, and tackling the booby traps that have been set there, even if they risk death and destruction in so doing. Since people are willing to die in pursuit of wealth, they will put up patiently with physical labor and hunger. They have a tool kit that would take too long to describe, so we will limit ourselves to discussing a few of their methods for disarming traps. Anyone who becomes involved in this kind of activity has to know something about engineering so as to be savvy enough to get into the troves of treasure, and this includes disarming the traps. Among these is the water trap—a prodigious trap, one of the deadliest.

Exposé: To get into the treasure, they look to see if there is any moisture on them, then look to see from which direction the moisture is dripping. If it's dripping from above, they dig to its east, where they will find a mighty channel. They step over this and then find a stone, which is a large basin into which the channel runs and the water ends. If it is to their right, they dig next to it and find the basin, and the same to the north. If it is underneath it, they dig at the door to the treasure and find the basin, exactly as mentioned, neither more nor less. This is based on what actual attempts have shown to be the case. Wise up to these things!

Section Twenty-One: Exposé of Their Tricks for the Disarming of Traps in the Form of Human Figures

Another example: When you enter a place where treasure is hoarded, you will 27.25
see a corridor stretching ahead of you where there are idols with swords in their hands. When you enter, these idols will make play with the things in their hands, so dig in front of where you are standing.

وسلاسل ملتفّة على تلك الأشخاص فإذا مشى الإنسان التفّت تلك السلاسل على الأصنام فلعبت تلك الأشخاص فتهلكه فافهم وحينئذ اقلع تلك السلاسل وقد بطلت الحركة وهو أقرب ما يعمل فاعمل في أعناقها حبلاً تعمله بشوطة[١] ثمّ تلقيه في أرقاب الأصنام وتجذبها فتكسرها وهذا أقلّ خطر وأقرب إلى إبطال فعل الأشخاص فافهم ذلك

الباب الثاني والعشرون في كشف أسرار إبطال مهلك النار

وهذا المهلك يكون من جهة عُمّار ذلك المكان فإبطاله بالبخور والعزائم والإصرافات والإحرافات والحجب ورأيت مهلك آخر وهو عجيب وذلك أنّا حفرنا على مطلب بالديار المصريّة في بريّة في أرض الحاجر فلمّا وصلنا إلى الباب وجدنا ثلاث درجات إذا طرح الإنسان رجله على باب أحدهما لعبت تلك الدرجة مثل ما يلعب البرجاس فيقع إلى جبّاً عميقاً فيهلك فلمّا أردنا أن نعبر منعنا ذلك فاحتجت إلى إبطاله فعمدنا إلى العكّاز المتقدّم ذكره ثمّ توكّئنا عليه إلى حين رأينا تلك البلاطة تلعب فأخذنا النار ثمّ وقّدناها على تلك البلاطة ثمّ ألقينا الرصاص وسبكناه فلمّا ذاب الرصاص جرى ونزل في الخلوّ الذي للبلاطة فسدّ الخلوّ للولب وبطلت حركته ٢٦،٢٧

الباب الثالث والعشرون في إبطال مهلك الرمل

وذلك أنّهم إذا دخلوا بعض المطالب فجرى عليهم الرمل حتّى يغطّيهم فيهلكهم فيحتاجون حينئذ إلى إبطاله فإن كان جريانه عن يمين المطلب فيحفرون عن يساره ٢٧،٢٧

١ ش: بشوطة أنشوطة.

Exposé: You take a staff and rest your weight on it, and wherever you find movement, you dig. You'll find pipes filled with quicksilver and chains attached to the idols in question in such a way that, when a person moves, the chains turn this way and that around the idols, and the figures move and destroy him. Be on your guard, and when this happens, pull out the chains and they will stop moving. This is the easiest thing to do. You may also put a rope around their necks, which you do by making a noose with a knot and throwing it over the idols' necks and pulling them toward you so you break them. This is a less dangerous and more certain way of stopping the figures from operating. Wise up to these things!

Section Twenty-Two: Exposé of Their Tricks for Disarming the Fire Trap

This trap belongs to the demons of the place, so it has to be disarmed using incense, conjurations, repellent devices, magic squares, and charms. I saw another trap that was amazing. 27.26

Exposé: We were digging for a treasure in Egypt, in the desert in the area of al-Ḥājir. When we reached the door, we found three stairways constructed so that if anyone placed his foot on the first step, the stairway would give way beneath it, like a jousting target,[240] and the person would fall into a deep pit and perish. This stood in our way when we wanted to cross over, so I needed to disarm it. We resorted to the aforesaid staff and pressed down on it until we saw the slab moving, so we got kindling and lit it on the same slab. Then we cast some lead and made it into ingots, and when the lead melted, it ran down into the empty space beneath the slab and blocked it where the roller was so it stopped moving.

Section Twenty-Three: Exposé of Their Tricks for Disarming the Sand Trap

Exposé: When they enter some locations where treasure is hoarded, sand runs down on top of them till it buries and kills them. They need therefore to disarm this. If the sand runs from the right of the treasure, they dig to its left, causing vast quantities of sand to flow into the opening, leaving an area of worked sand 27.27

فيجرون شيئاً عظيماً من الرمل إلى تلك الطاقة وإلى جانبه قَليب فحينئذ يحتالون إلى الصعود إليه ويحفرون إليه طريقاً فحينئذ ينزل جميع ذلك الرمل إليهم فافهم ذلك وكذلك إن كان عن شماله فيحفرون عن يمينه وكذلك إن كان عن شرقيّه فيبطلونه

الباب الرابع والعشرون في كشف أسرارهم وما يعملون

اعلم أيّها الأخ أنّ هؤلاء القوم أقلّ دين وأمانة ووفاء بالعهد من جميع الطوائف وذلك أنّ الذي يكون منهم قد يوهم أنّه يصل إلى بعض المطالب إمّا إلى نواويس[١] وإمّا إلى خبيّة وإمّا إلى ضريح فإن كان عنده دين وخوف من الله فإنّه لا يخرج إلى ذلك المكان إلّا ومعه المرقد في شيء من المأكول ٢٨،٢٧

فإذا تبعه إنسان أو أراد أن يأخذ منه شيء فيقول يا أخي إنّ هذا المكان الذي أنا واصل إليه فيه من المال ما لا يقع عليه عيار وما عسى أن ينقص منه إذا أخذت حملك إلّا أنّ النفس أمّارة بالسوء وأنا رجل وحيد وأريد منك أن تحلف لي أن لا تغدرني ولا تخونني ثمّ أخرج من جيبه مصحفاً وهو مسقيّ بالمرقد ثمّ يقول احلف بهذا المصحف أنّك لا تغدرني ولا تعرّف أحداً بهذا المكان ومهما أردت منه خذ فيحلف وهو يقدّمه إلى وجهه ثمّ يبوسه ويقول بوس كلام الله وهو الشاهد بيننا فعند ما يقبله يتصعّد البخار إلى دماغه فيقع إلى الأرض ولا يحسّ ما يعمل به ويقوم الواصل يروح في شغله ومنهم من يعمل المرقد في خبز أو كعك أو في تين فإذا أراد أن يرقّد أحداً قال له بعد الأيمان حتّى نتمالح فإنّ الخبز له حرمة فيأخذ الذي معه ثمّ يخرجه وهو آخر عهده بالدنيا ٢٩،٢٧

وهذه صفة المرقد وهو أن يؤخذ من بزر البنج الأزرق البالغ خمس الدراهم ومن الخشخاش الأسود أربع دراهم ومن الأفيون ثلاثة دراهم ومن الفُرْبيون أربعة دراهم ومن ٣٠،٢٧

---

١ الرسم غير واضح في الأصل – ش: بوليس.

next to it. When this happens, they work out a way to get up to it and dig a path to it. Then all the rest of the sand descends to where they were. Wise up to these things! Similarly, if it's to its left, they dig to its right, and if to its east, they disarm it using the same method.

Section Twenty-Four: Exposé of Their Tricks and of the Concoctions the Same People Put Together

Note, brother, that of all the charlatan tribes, this company has the least conscience, is the least honest, and is the least likely to keep its word. 27.28

Exposé: One of them will give people to think, deceitfully, that he has found his way to a certain hoard of treasure, among graves or in a hiding place or tomb. Having neither conscience nor fear of God, he never goes there without taking along some kind of knockout drug, concealed in something to eat.

If someone follows him or wants to rob him, he tells him, "Brother, this place I've found out how to get into holds more money than anyone can count. Why, it's perfectly possible that if you carried off everything you could, it would make no difference to how much there is! On the other hand, the carnal soul urges us to evil, I'm one man on his own, and I want you to swear to me that you won't betray me or play me false." Then he pulls from his pocket a copy of the Qur'an that has been soaked in the knockout drug and says, "Swear on this Qur'an you won't betray me or tell anyone about this place! After that, whatever you want you can take." So the man swears, bringing the Qur'an close to his face and kissing it, while the other says, "Kiss God's word and let Him be our witness!" When the man kisses it, though, the fumes rise up into his brain and he falls to the ground, insensible to whatever the other may do to him. The "initiate" who supposedly knows how to get to the treasure then gets to work.[241] Another may work the knockout drug into bread, or shortcake, or figs. To put someone to sleep, he says to him, "Now that we've sworn our oaths, let's eat bread and salt together, for bread is a sacred bond." Then he takes the man and goes out with him, and that's the last thing he knows of this world. 27.29

This is the recipe for the knockout drug: five dirhams by weight of mature blue henbane, four of black poppy, three of opium, four of euphorbium, six 27.30

الجندبادستر ستّة دراهم ومن الحبّة السوداء خمسة دراهم ومن الغاريقون ستّة دراهم ومن بزر الخسّ أربعة دراهم ومن جوزة ماثل درهمين ومن بزر السيكران درهمين يدقّ ذلك جميعه ويجن بماء الكرّاث ويعمل أقراص ثمّ يبخّر بالكبريت الأزرق ولا يعمل أقراص حتّى يسحق ناعماً مثال الهباء فإذا أرادوا يعملونه في المصاحف يحلّوا ذلك القرص بماء قد نقع فيه جوزة ماثل مهرسة مثال الحمّص ثمّ بعد ذلك يصفّونه بخرقة رفيعة ويعصرونه عصراً جيّداً ثمّ يأخذون ذلك ويسقونه للورق والمصحف فافهم ذلك

وإن كان الواصل قليل الدين فإنّه يعمل فيه شيء من السمومات فمتى وضع عينه ووقع على من عرف الموضع أطعمه من ذلك فإنّه يقتله من ساعته ولا يجد ألم ولا وجع ومنهم من يعمل هذا السمّ في الكعك وفي الخبز ثمّ يرميه في أثره ثلاثة أربعة مواضع فأيّ من جاء على أثره فيأكل ذلك المرقد الذي في الكعك فيرقد قبل وصوله إليه فافهم ذلك الدهاء والمكر واحذر إن تقع عليه ٣١،٢٧

الباب الخامس والعشرون في كشف أسرار المنجّمين وما لهم من الإشعار الذي يسمّونه السين

وهو البلاغ الذي يتكلّمون به ولا يفهمه إلّا هم ومن صاحبهم فافهم ذلك فمن ذلك يقول سعموى كسحاب سهت ما ابهله فى سسى فرحات ومطى شن ... ورح فى الطلموت ىربد فى صهوتى سعا للبر ... فيه كدى[1] ولهم في السين أشياء كثيرة لا تعدّ ولا تحدّ ولهم مجالس لم تكن للملوك وأوقات عجيبة ولولا خوف الإطالة ذكرت لهم نوادر لا تحصى وذلك أنّهم يعرفون بين الطوائف بالغرباء وهي لغة عجيبة واعلم أنّهم سمّوا بالغرباء لأنهم يأتون بالغرائب من كلّ الفنون بما يعجز عنها غيرهم وأمثالهم ٣٢،٢٧

١ كذا في الأصل.

of castoreum, five of black seed, six of agarikon, four of lettuce seed, two of datura nuts, and two of stinking nightshade seed, pounded all together, kneaded with leek juice, and made into pills. These are then fumigated with blue sulfur. To be made into pills, they first have to be crushed to a powder as fine as motes of dust. To get this into copies of the Qur'an, they dissolve the pill in question in water in which datura nut, milled to the size of chickpeas, has been steeped. They strain this through a cloth with a fine mesh and squeeze well. Then they take this and soak pieces of paper and copies of the Qur'an in it. Wise up to these things!

If the "initiate" has no conscience, he will add some poisonous ingredients, **27.31** and when he spots someone who knows the location of a treasure and gains his confidence, he'll feed him the drug and kill him then and there; the man will feel no pain and will not suffer.[242] Some of them put the same poison in shortcake or in bread, then throw it behind them in two or three places, so anyone who's following them will consume the drug that's in the cake and pass out before he gets to them. Wise up to this cunning and wiliness, and if you come across anything like it, watch out!

Section Twenty-Five: Exposé of the Tricks of Astrologers and the System They Use to Communicate with One Another, Which They Call the *Sīn*[243]

This is a form of communication they use for speaking to one another that only **27.32** they and those who hang out with them understand. Wise up to these things!

Example: They say, *Saʿamūnī kashḥāb bihit mā ablahu fī sinnī farḥāt wa-maṭā shan . . . wa-ramaḥ fī l-ṭalmūt yurīd fī ṣahwatī saʿā lil-bar . . . fīhi kaddinī.*[244] They can say lots of things in the *Sīn*, too many to count or calculate. And they have get-togethers better than any king's, and amazing good times. If I weren't afraid of boring you, I could tell you endless anecdotes about them; not for nothing are they known among the charlatan tribes as "wonder-workers."[245] The *Sīn* is an amazing language. They're called wonder-workers because they come up with wonderful things in every field, things no one else could.

الباب السادس والعشرون في كشف أسرار الذين يدّعون النبوّة

٣٣،٢٧ ومن جملة ما رأيت لهم أنّهم يقطعون رأس الآدميّ ويحضرونه لهم في صينيّة والدماء عليها ثمّ يقولون للرأس أخبر بما رأيت فيقول وقفت بين يدي الله عزّ وجلّ فقال ما تقول في هذا الرجل فقلت وما عسى أن أقول في أنبياء الله جلّ جلاله أنا مؤمن بما جاء به من الرسالة وأداء الأمانة فقال الله جلّ اسمه للملائكة اعرضوا عليه ما أعدّ الله له في الجنّة من النعيم المقيم والقصور والولدان والحور العين واعرض عليّ ملك بقدر ملك الدنيا سبع مرّات

٣٤،٢٧ ثمّ يقول قال الله تعالى تعرف فلاناً الذي كذّب رسلنا فقلت نعم يا ربّ أعرفه فقال أوقفوه عليه ليعاين ما وقع فيه من العذاب فأوقفني على شفير جهنّم ثمّ قالوا يا مالك إنّ الله عزّ وجلّ أمرك أن توقف هذا المؤمن على فلان لينظر ما أعدّ الله له من أنواع العذاب ثمّ يخبر الناس بما رأى فعند ذلك كشف لي مالك عن طبقات النيران إلى الدرك الأسفل منها فإذا أنا بفلان في سلسلة من نار لو وُضِع كعباً من كعابها على الجبال الشوامخ تدكدكت وعن يمينه حيّات تنهش من لحمه كلّ حيّة مثل النخلة العظيمة وعن شماله عقارب كلّ عقرب مثل الرامي وله رائحة لا يقف عليها أحد إلّا انصرع من نتنها والزّبانية بأيديهم مقامع من حديد يضربونه ويقولون هذا جزاء من عصى الله ومن كذّب الرسل وهو في عذاب سرمد وبلاء متجدّد

٣٥،٢٧ فهذا الذي رأيت فالحذر الحذر يا إخوتي في الدين من مخالفة الرسل فوالله لو رأيت منابر الأنبياء لقد رأيتها جميعاً في الجنّة وعلى كلّ منبر اسم صاحبه وفيها شيء أرفع من شيء ورأيت منبر هذا المصطفى صلوات الله عليه أرفع المنابر وهو منصوب تحت ساق العرش وقد احتفّت به الملئكة وقد احتمله ملك من الملئكة وهو يطوف به حول العرش وهذه درجة لم أرها إلّا له ولا خصّ بها غيره وأنا مؤمن به صلّى الله عليه فمن آمن به فله الجنّة ونعيمها ومن تولّى وكفر فله النار

Section Twenty-Six: Exposé of the Tricks of False Prophets

27.33 One of the things I saw them do was cut off a man's head, bring it in on a tray with the blood still on it, and then say to it, "Tell us what you saw!" to which the head would respond, "I stood before God, Mighty and Glorious, and He said, 'What have you to say about that man?' and I said, 'What can one say of the Prophets of God, His glory be extolled? I believe in the message he brought, and that he did what God charged him to.' Then God, exalted be His name, said to the angels, 'Give him a preview of what God has prepared for that man in Paradise by way of comfort everlasting and palaces, handsome lads and pretty dark-eyed lassies!' and one of the angels showed me wealth equal to seven times that of this world."

27.34 The head went on, "The Almighty then asked me, 'Do you know so-and-so, who called our prophets liars?' I said, 'Yes, Lord. I know him,' so God continued, addressing the angels, 'Let him see him, so he may behold the torment that other man has suffered!' so one of the angels stood me on the edge of Hell and the angels said, 'Mālik! God, Mighty and Glorious, commands you to let this believer have a look at so-and-so, so he can see the different kinds of torment that God prepared for that man, and tell people what he saw.' At this, Mālik peeled back for me the layers of fire down to their lowest level and there I saw so-and-so in a chain of fire any one of whose links, if placed on the peak of a towering mountain, would level it. To his right were serpents, each the size of a mighty palm tree, that tore at his flesh, and to his left were scorpions, each the size of Sagittarius, and he smelled so foul none could go near him without falling to the ground in a fit. Meanwhile, the angels of Hell, iron crooks in their hands, beat him and said, 'This is the reward of those who disobey God and call his prophets liars. He lives in sempiternal torment and ever-renewed affliction.'

27.35 "This is what I witnessed, so beware, beware, O my brothers in religion, of disobeying God's messengers! Could you but behold the pulpits of the prophets, you would see that they are all in Heaven, each one bearing the name of the prophet for whom it is waiting. Some, though, are raised higher than others, and I saw that the pulpit of this Chosen One was the highest of all; it had been set up right under the leg of the Throne, ringed by angels, and was borne by an angel who carried it around the Throne: That is a rank I saw accorded to no other and by which no other was distinguished. I believe in him, God bless him, and I believe that Paradise and its comforts will be the lot of all who believe in

وسعيرها فإذا سمعوا القوم ذلك من رأس مقطوع يتوهّمون منه الأوهام ويقولون إنّ هذه معجزة بالغة

٣٦،٢٧ وقد ظهر في سنة ثلاث وخمسين وخمسمائة صاحب من الإسماعيليّة يقال له سِنان ونزل بمَصْياف وحكم فيها وما لها من القلاع وكان خبيرًا بالحيل والنواميس الأفلاطونيّة وسمع له أهل تلك الجبال وأطاعوه طاعة لا حدّ لها حتّى أنّه كان يقول أريد الساعة عشرة من الرجال تصعد إلى السور ويرموا أرواحهم إلى الخندق فإنّهم يسابقون إلى تلاف أرواحهم وهذا رباط لا يقدر عليه أحد وكان يعمل لهم هذا الباب ويستعبدهم به وهذا مشهور عن سنان

٣٧،٢٧ وهذه صفة العمل بهذا الباب وهو أجلّ الحيل وذلك أنّه كان حفر في مجلسه عند الطرّاحة التي يجلس عليها فحفر هنالك حفيرة يكون مقدارها إذا جلس الإنسان فيها جاءت إلى رقبته ثمّ حسّنها وبلّطها وعمل لها غطاء من الخشب الدقيق مقوّر قدر ما يسع رقبة الرجل ثمّ أخذ طبق نحاس فيقوّره في وسطه ثمّ جعل له مصراعين ولم يطلع عليه أحد فكان إذا أراد أن يفعل ذلك أخذ الذي يختار من أصحابه وأوهبه شيء جيّد ثمّ يوصيه ما يقول وينزله الحفرة ويغطّي عليه ويخرج رأسه من القُوارة ثمّ يأخذ الطبق المقوّر فيجعله في رقبته ثمّ يسقط عليه السواقط فلا يرجع يبان منه إلّا رأسه ثمّ يجعل في الطبق شيئًا من الدم ثمّ إنّه يشيع[١] أنّه قد ضرب رقبته ثمّ يدعو أصحابه إليه

٣٨،٢٧ فإذا حضروا أمرهم بالجلوس فإذا جلسوا واستقرّ بهم الجلوس قال لمملوكه اكشف هذا الطبق فيكشفه فيجدوا فيه رأس صاحبهم فيقول له حدّث أصحابك بما عاينت وما قيل لهم فيحدّثهم بما قد وصّاه من الكلام فيذهل عقولهم من ذلك ثمّ في آخر الكلام يقول له أيّما أحبّ إليك ترجع إلى أهلك وإلى ما كنت فيه من الدنيا أو تسكن الجنّة فيقول وما حاجتي بالرجوع إلى الدنيا والله إن خرذلة ممّا أعدّ لي في الجنّة ما أبيعها

١ ش: يشنع.

him, but anyone who turns away from him and does not believe will go to the Fire and its flames." When the company hears this from a severed head, they conceive fantastical ideas and say, "This is indeed a mighty miracle!"

In the year 535 [1140–41], an Ismaili master called Sinān appeared. He took up residence at Maṣyāf and ruled over the town and its fortresses. He was well versed in tricks and Platonic illusions,[246] and the people of the mountains there obeyed him and offered him their unqualified allegiance. He would even say, "I need ten men to climb up onto the wall right away and cast themselves into the moat," and they would race one another to throw away their lives, which demonstrates a degree of mind control no one else has ever achieved. Sinān used to perform for them the trick described in this section, using it to make them worship him. He was famous for it. 27.36

Here is how the trick described above—and it is the most impressive trick of all—is done. Exposé: He dug a hole in his assembly chamber near the carpet on which he sat, making an excavation deep enough to come up to the neck of anyone sitting in it. Then he leveled it, tiled it, and made a cover of thin wood with an opening carved out of its middle wide enough to accommodate a man's neck. Next, he took a copper plate and made a hole in the middle, fashioning it so that it had two leaves. No one was permitted to look at it. To perform the trick, he'd take whomever of his companions he chose, give him a costly gift, and instruct him in what to say. Then the man would go down into the hole, which Sinān would then close, leaving the man's head poking up through the hole in the wooden cover. Sinān would then take the plate with the hole in the middle, place it around his neck, and close the clasps, after which nothing would remain visible but the man's head. He'd put some blood in the plate and spread the word that he'd decapitated him. Then he'd invite his followers over to see. 27.37

When they arrived, he'd order them to sit down, and once they'd done so and were settled, he'd tell his slave, "Uncover the plate!" and the man would do so and they'd find the head of their friend on it. Sinān would then tell the head, "Speak to your friends of what you saw and of the message that was sent them!" so he'd tell them whatever he'd been told to and they'd be astonished. Following this speech, Sinān would say to the head, "Which would you rather do? Return to your family and the earthly life you once led, or dwell in Paradise?" and the head would say, "Why would I need to go back to the life of the world? I wouldn't sell one mustard seed's-worth of what has been prepared for me in Paradise for seven times the value of a world like this. Pay heed, my friends, and greetings to 27.38

بمثل هذه الدنيا سبع مرّات فانتهبوا[١] يا أصحابي وأنتم على كلّكم سلامي وارجوا في الجنّة فالله الله الحذر من المخالفة لهذا الصاحب فإنّه خليفة الإمام وسيّد الحكّام في الموقف كما قال لي الخالق جلّت قدرته والسلام[٢] فإذا سمعوا ذلك قوي ربطهم ثمّ انصرفوا فإذا انصرفوا عنه أطلعه من الحفرة ثمّ يحيّيه إلى الليل ثمّ يضرب رقبته ويدفنه فبهذا استعبد أهل تلك الجبال إلى مدّة حياته وإلى يومنا هذا ذكره باقي

الباب السابع والعشرون في كشف أسرار نوادر من ادّعى المشيخة

وقد ظهر في ساحل عَيْذاب رجل من النوبة وادّعى المشيخة وسمع له خلق كثير ٣٩،٢٧
ومعه جماعة من التَكرور وبني له زاوية في جانب البحر وكان يعمل السماع فإذا طرب[٣] في السماع في الليل رقص ساعة ثمّ خرج من الزاوية إلى جانب البحر فأرمى سجّادته على الماء وصعد فوقها وهو يرقص ويجوز في البحر مقدار رمية سهم هذا والفقراء على الساحل يعملون السماع وهو يرقص ثمّ يعود إليهم وقد ارتبط عليه جميع البجاوة والتكرور والنوبة والحبشة وقالوا إنّه تكروريّ ويُعرف بعبد الله التكروريّ وكان جميع تجّار الهند واليمن يقبلون إليه ويهدون له من كلّ الطرف المعدومة في البلاد وتحصل له بهذا الناموس وهذه الحيلة جملة كبيرة وقُتل في اليَنْبُع سنة خمس عشر وستّمائة وأخربت الزاوية التي له بعيذاب

وهذا كشف أسرار مشيه على الماء وذلك أنّه كان واسع الحيلة فأخذ ثلاث ظروف ٤٠،٢٧
ماعز فدبغها ثمّ أملأها ريح واستوثق وكائها ثمّ ربط أيديها وأرجلها إلى بعضها بعض ثمّ أخذ ألواح من الرصاص وجعلها تحت تلك الظروف معلّقة فيها بمقدار معايير إذا وقف[٤] على الظروف لا ترجع تبان وعمل في أجنابها سُكّان لا يراها أحد فإذا وقف على تلك الظروف جعل رجليه على تلك السكّان وكيفما أراد سيّرها بها

---

١ ش: فانتهوا. ٢ ش: والسلم. ٣ ش: طاب. ٤ ش: وقع.

one and all! Set your sights on Paradise! And I swear and swear again, beware of opposing this master! He is the imam's successor[247] and his status is that of lord over all other rulers, as I was informed by the Creator, His might be extolled. Farewell!" When they heard this, their attachment to their master would grow stronger and they'd go their different ways. As soon as they'd done so, however, he'd lift the man out of the hole, let him live till night, and then cut off his head and bury him. This is how he made the people of those mountains worship him till the day he died, and his memory survives to this day.

Section Twenty-Seven: Anecdotes Regarding the Exposure of Fake Shaykhs

A man of Nubian origin once appeared on the coast at ʿAydhāb claiming to be a shaykh, and many listened to him. With him was a band of people from Takrūr. A lodge was built for him next to the sea, where he held devotional singing and dancing sessions. By night, transported by the music, he'd dance for a while, then leave the lodge, go down to the sea, throw his prayer mat onto the water, climb on board while still dancing, and go a bowshot out to sea. The dervishes on the seashore, meanwhile, would keep up the singing and dancing; he'd dance, then return to them. All the Beja, Takrūr, Nubians, and Abyssinians became his followers. They said he was a Takrūrī and he was known as ʿAbd Allāh al-Takrūrī. All the merchants of India and Yemen, from every benighted part of the land, would come to him and give him gifts, and he made a huge pile with this illusion and cunning deception. He was murdered in al-Yanbuʿ in 615 [1218–19] and his lodge at ʿAydhāb fell into ruin. 27.39

This is an exposé of how he walked on water. 27.40

Exposé: He was very ingenious. He took three waterskins made from goat hide and had them tanned, then filled them with air and made sure they were well sewn. Next, he tied the forelegs and back legs of the skins together, took lead plates, and hung them beneath the skins, suspended at measured distances in such a way that, when he stood on the skins, the latter disappeared from sight. He also attached a hidden rudder to the side of the skins and when he stood on them, he placed his feet on the rudder and used it to move the raft any way he pleased.

الباب الثامن والعشرون في نوادرهم

وقد كان ظهر في قَلْهات في بلاد اليمن رجل علويّ يُعرف بالشيخ حسن وادّعى المشيخة ٤١،٢٧
وسمع له خلق كثيرة من أوباش تلك البلاد وكان معه عكّاز إذا وضعه يصلّي يورق
تلك العكّاز وهي كان معجزته وتبعه خلق كثير من أهل اليمن فلمّا استفحل أمره ادّعى
أنّه المهديّ وخرج من البلاد وقتل وسبى وملك أطراف بلاد اليمن وفتح حصون وكسر
عساكر الملك وقُتل في سنة أحد وعشرين وستّمائة

وأمّا كشف أسرار العكّاز وكان يسمّيه قضيب الطاعة وذلك أنه أخذ عوداً من ٤٢،٢٧
خشب الدلب وعمل منه عكّازاً في غلظ الإصبع الإبهام ثمّ قرض فيه من جانبه
قرضين ثمّ عمل في تلك القرضين قصبتين من رقيق الخيزران ثمّ ركّب لها أوراقاً من
ورق الكاغذ وصبغها أخضر وجعلها واقفة فيه ثمّ عمل لهذا العكّاز رح من الحديد
طوله شبراً ثمّ عمل له كرسيّ منه وبه وترك العكّاز الخشب فيه وقوّاه تقوية جيّدة
ثمّ عمل له قطعة من خشب القنا مجوّفة وجعل الخشب فيها من داخل وشقّ لها
في جوانبها موضعين تحت تلك القصبتين ثمّ عمل طبلتين خفيفتين لا يدركها أحد
ثمّ جعلها أقصر من العكّاز الخشب الذي من داخلها

فإذا أراد العكّاز يورق أغرز العكّاز في الأرض فإذا فعل ذلك سحبت القطعة القنا ٤٣،٢٧
ونزلت حذاء الكرسيّ الحديد فإذا صارت عليه صعدت تلك القصبتين الخيزران التي
لها الأوراق فخلّت الطبلتين فانفتحت وطلعت تلك الأغصان منها فيخيّل لمن يراها
أنّها ورق الآس فيذهل وهذا ناموس عظيم لا يدركه إلّا كلّ ذكيّ

الباب التاسع والعشرون في نوادرهم

وقد اجتمعت في ساحل جدّة من أرض الحجاز برجل كان شيخ ثمّ صار سالوس فرأيته ٤٤،٢٧
وقد حضر في الموقف وكان من عادته أن يقف في أفراد الأيّام ويورد أخبار عن

Section Twenty-Eight: Some Anecdotes About Them

In Qalhāt, in Yemen, a man appeared—an ʿAlawī called Shaykh Ḥasan—who claimed to be a Sufi master. Many of the rabble of that country followed him. He had a staff which, when he placed it in the ground so he could pray, would produce foliage. This was his miracle, and large numbers of Yemenis followed him. When his cause had gathered enough momentum, he declared himself the Mahdi and rose in rebellion, killing and taking prisoners, and took control of the marches of Yemen, conquering castles and scattering the king's armies. He was killed in 621 [1224–25]. 27.41

Now to reveal his trick with the staff, which he called "the Rod of Obedience." 27.42

Exposé: He'd take the branch of a plane tree and make a staff from it about as thick as one's thumb. Then he'd make two holes in the side of this staff and insert into each a length of thin reed to which he'd attach leaves made of paper that had been dyed green, arranging these so that they stood upright. Next, he'd make an iron ferrule for the staff a handspan in length and make a socket that was attached to the ferrule and was an integral part of it and set the wooden staff in this, making sure it was very firmly fixed. Then he'd fashion a hollow piece of giant fennel stalk, insert the staff into it, and make slots in the sides of the stalk in two places below the two aforementioned holes. Finally, he'd fabricate two membranes too fine for anyone to see, making them shorter than the wooden staff they enclosed.

When he wanted the staff to produce foliage, he'd plant it in the ground. As he did so, the fennel stalk would slide down toward the iron socket, and when it reached it the reeds with the leaves would rise, the membranes would break and part, and the branches would emerge through them. Anyone who saw this would think they were myrtle leaves and be amazed. This is a prodigious illusion, one that only the truly intelligent can see through. 27.43

Section Twenty-Nine: More Anecdotes about Them

On the coast at Jeddah in the Hejaz, I met a man who was first a shaykh, then a hustler. I observed him at his post. It was his custom to stand on particular days and narrate stories of the Righteous and tales of the Prophet, eternal peace be his. He'd speak of the everlasting ease God has prepared for His 27.44

الصالحين وأحاديث الرسول عليه السلام ويذكر ما أعدّ الله من النعيم المقيم للذي أعدّه لعباده الصالحين وما ابتلى به من شرّ العذاب المجرمين[١] ويذكر الجنّة ونعيمها والنار وسعيرها كذلك حتّى يدمع العيون ويوجل القلوب وبعد ذلك لا يلتمس من أحد شيئاً البتّة ولا يقبل ما يدفع له وهذا هو الناموس العظيم والرباط

٤٥،٢٧ ثمّ رأيته في الموقف وهو يتكلّم على حسب عادته وقد اجتمع عليه الخلق من كلّ مكان فلمّا شوّقهم وحذّرهم قال يا أصحابنا ألم تعلموا أنّي رجل مسلم مثلكم سلام عليكم اعلموا أنّي رجل لا ألتمس شيئاً من هذه الدنيا لما ثبت عندي أنّ حلالها حساب وحرامها عقاب وقطعت منها عِلَقي وعلائقي ونبذتها خلف ظهري وانقطعت إلى الله عزّ وجلّ فهو متولّي أمري وأنا لا أعيش إلّا من نبات الأرض وهذه نعمة من الله عليّ لا أقدر أقوم بشكرها

٤٦،٢٧ فلمّا كان أمس بعد صلاة المغرب ورد عليّ أربعين فقيراً وقالوا نحن نريد نتوجّه إلى الشام وقد نزلنا بك ونريد منك الزاد فأوضحت لهم عذري فلم يقبلوه بل قالوا أنت رجل معروف في هذه الديار ولو طلبت شيئاً جاءك فقلت إنّ[٢] في هذه الديار منزلي[٣] لم ألتمس منه شيء وذلك أنّ ما لي في الدنيا علاقة ورزقي قد يسّره الله من نبات الأرض فلا أريد شيئاً آخر فقالوا قد نزلنا بك ولا بدّ من تسفيرنا وقد ألحّت الضرورة إلى أن أتكلّف لهم هذا الأمر وقد أتيتكم بتحفة لا بل بتحفتين

٤٧،٢٧ أحدهما أنّي قد حملت لكم هديّة من الله عزّ وجلّ والأخرى أنّي قد سقت لكم أجري عند الله فأمّا الهديّة فإنّها اسم الله العظيم الأعظم الأكرم الجليل الأجلّ وهو ممّا يظهر لكم برهانه في هذه الليلة لأنّه من جعله تحت رأسه في الليل فإنّه يرى سيّد المرسلين وخاتم النبيّين محمّد الصادق الأمين ويوريه ما قد أعدّ الله له في جنّته من النعيم المقيم وهذا أقلّ فائدة في الاسم الأعظم وهو واسطة بينكم وبينهم

١ ش: للمجرمين. ٢ ش: إنّي. ٣ ش: منذ لي.

righteous slaves and the terrible torment the evildoers will suffer, as well as of Heaven and its comforts and Hell and its flames, till the eyes of the onlookers gushed tears and their hearts filled with dread. Afterward, he wouldn't ask anyone for anything and would refuse anything that was offered him. That is how truly great trickery and conning is achieved!

Once I saw him at his post and he was giving his usual speech and people from all over the place had gathered around him. After he'd aroused their longings and given them his warnings, he said, "Friends, you know, do you not, that I am an honest Muslim like you. Greetings to all! Just so you know, I am a man who has never asked for anything from this world, convinced as I am that what is permitted is subject to account and what is forbidden is subject to punishment. I have cut myself free from all I hold dear in it and from all for whom I care, casting them behind me and devoting myself rather to God, Mighty and Glorious. I have consigned myself to Him and live off nothing but the plants of the earth, which are a blessing to me from God, for which I cannot thank Him enough. 27.45

"Yesterday, after the evening prayer, forty dervishes presented themselves to me and said, 'We want to make our way to Syria. We've come to stay with you and want you to provide us with the provisions we need for our journey.' I explained to them that I was unable to oblige, but they refused to take no for an answer. On the contrary, they said, 'You are a man well known in this country and what you ask for, you receive.' 'This is the land in which I have my home,' I said, 'and I have never asked anything of it. I have nothing to tie me to this world, my livelihood is vouchsafed to me by God from the plants of the earth, and I want nothing more.' They repeated, 'We have come to stay with you and you have to provide for our journey!' Necessity therefore dictates that I take care of this matter for them, and I have brought you all a treat—or, in fact, two treats! 27.46

"One of them is that I've brought you a gift from God, Mighty and Glorious. The other is that I'm consigning to you the reward that I myself would have gained from God. Now, the gift is the mightiest mighty, noblest, greatest great name of God, and the proof of its efficacy will appear to you tonight, because if any of you puts it under his head at night, he will behold the Lord of the Messengers and Seal of the Prophets, Muḥammad, the Trusted and Trustworthy, who will show him what he has prepared for him in His heaven by way of everlasting ease—though this is the least of the benefits of the Greatest Name. 27.47

فمن ساعدهم بشيء من تسفيرهم جعلته هديّة هذه الاسم وإنّه يرى برهانه الليلة في نفسه وولده وماله

٤٨،٢٧ ثمّ أخرج من جرابه أوراق كلّ ورقة قدر إصبعين مكتوبة بالزعفران والمسك والماورد ثمّ جعل يقبّلها ويجعلها على رأسه وقال هذه اسم الله الأعظم فمن كان يجد في جسده مرض فيمسح به عليه يزول من وقته ثمّ هدر عليه بالهادور وقال قد جعلت هذا الاسم واسطة بينكم وجعلت هديّته مسعوديّ ولا أطلبه صدقة بل هديّة بهديّة ومن أخذ منه شيء في هذه الليلة يرى برهانه فأخرج منها مقدار عشرين فلم يرضيه ذلك فقال يا أصحابنا من أخذ منّي يعيده حتّى أقول لكم كيف تعملون بهذا الاسم ثمّ استعاد الأوراق وجعلها في كفّه ورفع رأسه إلى نحو السماء وقال اللّٰهمّ إن كان هذا اسمك العظيم الأعظم الذي فضّلته على سائر الأسماء كلّها وأودعته سرّ قدرتك وإنّ هؤلاء العصابة من عبيدك قد حصل عندهم منه وفيه شكّ ولم يكن عندهم له قبول ولا يقين صادق وإنّك لا ترضاهم لحمل اسمك وغرت على اسمك أن لا يملكه لمن يشكّ فيه فخذ باسمك إليك يا ربّ

٤٩،٢٧ ثمّ فتح كفّه فجعلت تلك الأوراق تطاير وارتفعت حتّى غابت عن الأبصار ثمّ ركب قصبته وهرول مدبرًا فلحقه الناس وجعلوا يسألونه فقال زال ما عندكم من الشكّ وضعف اليقين وضعف الظنّ فقالوا نعم فقال ارفعوا أيديكم وقولوا يا الله ثمّ جعل يدعو ويقول اللّٰهمّ إن كان قد سبق في علمك أنّك تمحو ما في قلوب هؤلاء الذين هم عبيدك من الشكّ وسوء الظنّ وضعف اليقين وأن تصفّي قلوبهم ونيّاتهم وترضاهم لاسمك فاردد عليهم ما سلبتهم يا الله فأنت قلت وقولك الحقّ ﴿يَمْحُو اللَّهُ مَا يَشَاءُ وَيُثْبِتُ وَعِندَهُ أُمُّ الْكِتَابِ﴾ ثمّ جعل يدعو وتلك الأوراق تتقاطر عليه نازلة فلمّا رأوا ذلك تعجّبوا فأخرج منها في ساعة واحدة خمسمائة شريحة بخمسمائة درهم ولقد

This gift shall also be a bond between you and them, and I shall make a gift of it to any who helps them with anything by way of provisions for their journey, and he will experience proof of its efficacy this very night, on himself, on his offspring, and on his wealth."

Then he took out of his purse a number of papers, each the size of two fingers, with writing in saffron, musk, and rosewater, and started kissing them and placing them on his head, saying, "This is God's Greatest Name. If anyone discovers a disease in his body, he has only to wipe a paper over it and it will go away immediately." Then he recited some patter over the papers and said, "I hereby make this name a bond between you and have fixed the donation for it at one Masʿūdī dinar. I'm not asking for alms, just a gift for a gift, and anyone who takes some will discover its efficacy for himself tonight." He handed out about twenty such pieces of paper, but then decided he was unhappy with what he'd done and said, "Friends! Any of you who took papers from me should give them back so that I can tell you how to use the name," and he recovered the pieces of paper, took them in his hand, raised his face toward the sky, and said, "O God, if this be Your mightiest mighty name that You have preferred over all Your other names and within which You have deposited the secret of Your power, and if this band of slaves of Yours has managed to get hold of some of it and harbors some doubts and isn't wholly and truly satisfied and You aren't comfortable with them carrying Your name about and care too deeply about Your name to let anyone who has any doubt about it possess it—then take back Your name, O Lord!" 27.48

And he opened his hand and the pieces of paper started flying away in all directions, rising in the air till they had disappeared from sight, after which he mounted his reed[248] and galloped off, turning his back on them. Everyone ran after him and began asking him what was going on, and he said, "Do you still have any doubt, uncertainty, or suspicion?" and they said, "Yes!" so he said, "Raise your hands and say, 'O God, if You ever remember previously having erased whatever doubt or suspicion or weakness of faith may have been in the hearts of these slaves of Yours and having purified their hearts and intentions and made them accepting of Your name, return to them whatever You wrested from them, O God, for You have said—and Your words are Truth—«God erases and confirms what He will, and with Him is the Essence of the Book.»'"[249] Then he began praying and the pieces of paper began falling down upon him in a continuous stream. When they saw this, they marveled, and in 27.49

رأيت من الناس من يأخذ منه الشريحة والمثلّثة ولو كان معه أكثر من هذا بلزه فافهم عظم هذا الباب

٥٠،٢٧ وهذا كشف سرّ تطيير هذه الأوراق وذلك أنّهم إذا أرادوا يأخذون من الندى وهو الطلّ الذي يقع على أوراق الشجر ثمّ على الزرع فيجمعون ذلك ثمّ يسقون به تلك الأوراق فلا يرجعون يمسونها حتّى تجفّ في الظلّ ثمّ يبقى فيها رطوبة يسيرة ثمّ يأخذها ويقف بها في الشمس وجعلها في كفّه ثمّ فتح كفّه فإذا حميت الأوراق ارتفعت بما فيها من الرطوبة التي هي من الطلّ فإن الطلّ إذا حمي ارتفع ولا تزال الأوراق مرتفعة حتّى تجفّ الرطوبة منها فعند ذلك تنزل إلى الأرض وهذا من النواميس الكبار وهو عظيم فافهم

٥١،٢٧ صفة كشف أسرار تطيير الأوراق نوع آخر وذلك أنّهم إذا أرادوا أن يطيّرون الأوراق أو بما أرادوا من ذلك فيأخذون الصمغ العربيّ ويحلّونه على قوام ما يكون العسل القويّ ثمّ يقتلون فيه الزيبق ويكون من الصمغ جزء ومن الزيبق خمسة أجزاء فإذا فعلوا ذلك أخذوا الورق وقشّروه وقطّعوه كلّ قطعة مقدار إصبعين أو ثلاثة ثمّ يلطخ الورقة من ذلك ثمّ يردّ قشرها عليها ثمّ يلصقها لصاق جيّد ثمّ يتركها حتّى تجفّ فإذا جفّت صقلها جيّداً برفق ثمّ تركها عنده في مكان لا حرّ فيه فإذا أراد تطييرها يقف بها في الشمس فمتى ما حميت الأوراق وحمي الزيبق طلب العلوّ فارتفع فرفعها وهذا أعجب شيء يكون

الباب الثلاثون في كشف أسرار نوادرهم في علم الغيب

٥٢،٢٧ اعلم أنّ الأوائل الذين كانوا يشتغلون بالكهانة وكانوا يخبرون بالحوادث من قبل وقوعها من جميع ما يحدث في العالم من خير وشرّ وغلاء ورخص وأمن وخوف فكان يحصل عند الناس منها وهم عظيم ويمتثلون ما يأمرونهم به من خبر ويطيعونهم فيما يعملون ولهم في ذلك أحوال عجيبة ولقد رأيت بالديار المصريّة ديرًا يقال له دير

one hour he moved five hundred strips for five hundred silver pieces. I saw people who took both the slice and the triangle,[250] and if he'd had more, he would have unloaded them too. Wise up to just what a prodigious trick this is!

This is how the trick of the flying paper works.

Exposé: To do it, they take some dew, which is the fine mist that falls onto the leaves of trees and then onto crops. They collect this and soak the papers in it and don't touch them again until they have dried in the shade and only a little moisture is left. The fake Sufi master now takes them and stands outside with them, in the sun, holding them in his palm, then opens his palm. The papers, having grown warm, rise up through the action of the moisture within them (which is because of the dew, for as dew warms, it rises) and the papers stay high up until the moisture dries out; then they come back down to the ground. This is one of the major illusions, and a prodigious one. Wise up to these things! 27.50

Exposé of another recipe for making papers fly: To make papers or anything similar fly, they take gum arabic and liquefy it to the consistency of thick honey. Then they dilute quicksilver in it (one part gum arabic to five parts quicksilver) and, when they've done so, take paper, peel off its upper layer, and cut it into pieces, each the size of two or three fingers. They then smear with this one of the pieces of paper that have been so prepared, replace the upper layer, stick the two together well, and leave them until the paper is dry. When the papers are dry, the fake shaykh irons them out well, but gently, then leaves them in his house in a cool place. To make the papers fly, he stands outside with them in the sun, and when the papers have warmed up and the quicksilver has warmed up, the latter seeks elevation, so it rises, lifting the papers with it. It's the most extraordinary thing you can imagine. 27.51

Section Thirty: Exposé of Anecdotes Told about Them Concerning the Science of the Unknown

People used to be greatly deluded by the ancients who worked using divination and who would provide information about every event that would take place in the world—good things or bad things, high prices or low prices, security or fear—before it occurred. People would do whatever they commanded and obey them in everything. Some remarkable doings are attributed to such 27.52

القَلَمون وهو من بلاد البَهْنَسا ورأيت فيه راهب يقال له أَشْمُونِيت قد مرّ عليه من العمر مائة وستّون وهو من أعظم فلاسفة وقته وكان في أوّل كلّ يوم من كلّ شهر يقول لمن حضر عنده من اليوم الفلانيّ يتمّ كذا وكذا وفي اليوم الفلانيّ من هذا الشهر يحدث كذا وكذا

ثمّ امتحنت ذلك فوجدت جميع ما يذكره يقع كما نطق به فسألت عنه فقيل لي من أبناء رجل كان من عظماء الكهّان وهذه الكهانة موجودة في ذرّيّتهم وكلّ من قام في هذا الدير من نسل ذلك الرجل يفعل ذلك فتعجّبت من ذلك ولم أزل عنده حتّى كشفته بعد المدّة ثمّ إنّي اجتمعت براهبة كان الراهب اصطفاها لنفسه وأطلعها على سرّ ذلك فحصل لها عندي غرض يكون أنّها لا تقدر تطرف عينها عمّا تريد فلمّا تحقّقت منها ذلك ذكرت لها شيء من ذلك فقالت إنْ أنت طاوعتني على ما ألتمس منك أطلعتك على سرّ ذلك فحلفت لها على ما أرادت فقالت اعلم أنّ هذا الشيخ فيلسوف حاذق وقد اطّلع على أسرار الكهنة المتقدّمين وقرأ كتبهم وحلّ رموزهم وفهم وعلم علومهم ٥٣،٢٧

فإذا أراد أن يعلم[١] الأشياء ويخبر بالمغيّبات فإنّه يأخذ خلد فيغرّقه في الماء حتّى يموت فإذا مات أخذ ذلك الماء وأعزله عنده ثمّ يدقّ ذلك الخلد دقًّا جيّدًا مع مثل وزن نصفه من لحم الكروان ومع ربع وزنه من قلب قرد ومثله من ببغاء ناطق ذكر ثمّ يعجن الجميع بذلك الماء المعزول الذي غرّق فيه الخلد ثمّ يعمل منه طوابع الطابع وزنه مثقال وهو طريًّا فإذا جفّ رجع وزنه درهم ثمّ يجفّف تلك الطوابع في الظلّ ويرفعها في حُقّ ويستوثق من رأسها لا يدخل فيه الهواء فإذا أراد أن يعلم ما يحدث في ذلك السنة من خير وشرّ فيشرب من تلك الطوابع طابعاً واحداً يكون وزنه درهماً فإنّه يخبر بما يكون في العالم فلمّا سمعت ذلك منها أعرضته على ما كشفته فوجدته ذلك بعينه لم أُخُلَّ فيه بشيء إلّا[٢] المقدار الذي يشرب منه في كلّ شهر فعلمت صحّة ما قالته الراهبة ٥٤،٢٧

١ ش: يعمل. ٢ أضيف للسياق.

persons in this regard. In Egypt, I saw a monastery called al-Qalamūn, in the district of al-Bahnasā. There I met a monk called Ashmūnīt, who was 160 years old and one of the greatest philosophers of his time. On the first day of each month he'd say to those with him, "Starting on such and such a day, such and such will happen, and on such and such a day of this month, such and such will happen."

I put this to the test and I found that everything he mentioned came about 27.53
the way he'd said it would. I asked about him and was told that he was a son of a man who had been one of the greatest diviners and that the gift of divination was present in all his offspring, and that all the progeny of this man who lived in the monastery could do the same. This amazed me, so I stayed there till I was able, after some time, to find out more about him. Then I met a nun whom the monk had picked out for himself and to whom he'd revealed the trick behind all this. She happened to want something from me and was incapable of tearing her eyes away once she'd set her heart on having something. When I was certain that this was how things stood, I mentioned to her some of what I've described, and she said, "If you obey me and give me what I want from you, I'll let you in on how the trick is done." So I swore I'd give her what she wanted, and she said, "This shaykh is a skilled philosopher who has pored over the secrets of the earliest diviners, read their books, deciphered their symbols, and understood and learned their sciences.

"When he wants to know things and to provide information about what 27.54
lies hidden in the future, he takes a mole, holds it underwater till it dies, and when it's dead, takes the water and sets it aside. Then he pounds the mole well, together with half its weight of the flesh of a curlew and a quarter of its weight of the heart of an ape and the same of a male talking parrot. He kneads all of this together with the water he's set aside, in which he drowned the mole, and makes pills from this, each of which weighs one mithkal when soft but only a dirham when dry. He dries these pills in the shade and sets them aside in a pill-box whose lid he closes so tightly no air can get in. To find out what good and bad things are going to happen that year, he swallows one of those pills, whose weight will be a dirham, and then he is able to give information on what is going on in the world." When I heard this from her, I reviewed it against what I'd found out and discovered it was the very same. The only thing I'd missed was the amount of it that he took each month. Thus I confirmed the truth of what the nun had said.

الباب الحادي والثلاثون في كشف أسرار نوادر الطرقيّة في كشف أسرار الذين يعملون القرون للحيّة ويلفّ الهنكامة عليها

وذلك أنّه يأخذ الحيّة المعروفة بالدفانة الذي تسكن الرمل وتسمّى ذنب الثعلب وهي حيّة صفراء يرى طولها شبر واحد ونصف وهي كما رأسها كما ذنبها فيأخذ هذه الحيّة ويشمّمها شيء من المخدّرات ويكون ذلك في شهر كانون الأصمّ ثمّ يعمد إلى رأسها ويأخذ إبرة ويخيط في رأسها ثقبين ثمّ يأخذ شعر فرس وتعبر الشعرة في ذلك الثقب ثمّ يجمع رأسها ويعقد فيها عقدة طول الإصبع الخنصر ودونها قليل ويقطع الشعرة من فوق العقدة ثمّ يفعل بالناحية الأخرى كذلك ثمّ يأخذ القير يلبّسه لذلك الشعر بعد أن يكون حلّه بقليل شمع وزيت ثمّ يعمل على هيئة القرون مُلَس دِقاق من أعلاها فلا يشكّ أحدًا فيه[1] أنّها خلقة فيلفّ عليها الهنكامة ويهدر عليها بما أراد ٥٥،٢٧

وكذلك يعملون بالصلّ فإنّهم يأخذون جلد حيّة من هذه الحيّات الحمر الكبار ثمّ يحشونه بشيء ثمّ يطوّقونه كما تطوّق الحيّة ثمّ يعمدون إلى رقّ الضأن ويصوّرون فيه وجه ابن آدم ورأسه وشعره على مقدار تلك الحيّة ثمّ يحشونه ويتركونه على تلك الحيّة بهندام مليح حتّى لا يبان ثمّ يجعله في كيس ويظهر الوجه وعليها خرقة ثمّ يهدر عليها ويلفّ الهنكامة وهو بلهانة ٥٦،٢٧

واعلم أنّ كلّ شيء من هذه البلهانات لها هادور مختصّ بها فأمّا هادور الحيّات وهي حكاية يخبر الذي خبأ الحيّة في جوفه وأحادها عن عدوّها وهي حكاية تليق بهذا الموضع وأمّا الهادور على الصلّ فهي حكاية بُخْت نَصَر وما ورد عنه من حديث ابنته مع عبيد الساحر الأنصاريّ وكيف كان كلّ ليلة يحضرها من بلاد الفرس إلى صعيد مصر إلى أنصِنا ثمّ يعيدها إلى المكان الذي فيه وهي حكاية تليق بهذا المكان فيلفّ عليها الهنكامة ويهدر عليها بالهادور ويشكر الأخشان ٥٧،٢٧

---

١ ش: في.

Section Thirty-One: Exposé of Anecdotes Concerning Itinerant Quacks

Exposé of the ones who put horns on snakes to draw a crowd. 27.55

Exposé: A charlatan of this type takes the snake known as a *daffānah*, which lives in the sand and is also called a foxtail. It's a yellow snake one and a half handspans in length and its head is identical to its tail. He takes this snake, gives it some kind of soporific to sniff (this should be in the month of Kānūn the Speechless),[251] then turns his attention to its head and, taking a needle, makes two holes in it. Next, he takes horsehair and passes a hair through one of the holes, holds its head, and ties a loop in the hair the length of his little finger or a little less and cuts off the hair above the loop. He does the same with the other side. Then he takes pitch, which he first dilutes with a little wax and oil, and makes smooth, slender things in the shape of horns on the top of its head, which no one doubts are natural. This allows the quack to gather a crowd and he can then go ahead with his patter at his leisure.

They do the same with the *ṣill*.[252] They take the skin of one of these large red 27.56
snakes, stuff it, coil it the way a snake coils itself, then work on a piece of sheep parchment, drawing the face of a human being on it, with a head and hair, to the same scale as the snake. They stuff this too and put it onto the snake, nicely set so it's easy to see. Next, they place the whole thing in a bag with the head sticking out but covered by a cloth. Then they make their patter and gather their crowd. It's what they call a crowd-drawer.

Each of these crowd-drawers has its own special patter. The patter for 27.57
snakes is a story that tells of the man who hid a snake in his belly and saved it from its enemy ("which is a story well suited to this place"),[253] while the patter for the *ṣill* is the story of Nebuchadnezzar and the story that has come down about the conversation between his daughter and ʿUbayd, the Anṣārī sorcerer, and how every night he would send her from Persia to Upper Egypt, to the town of Anṣinā, then return her to where he was ("which is a story well suited to this place"). In this way, he gathers a crowd around it, does his patter, and gets the marks to loosen the strings of their moneybags.

الباب الثاني والثلاثون في نوادر المشعوذين

وذلك أنّهم يزرعون المقثأة فتنبت من ساعتها فيعجب من ذلك فإذا أرادوا ذلك ٢٧،٥٨ يأخذون بزر البطّيخ الأصفر أو بزر القثاء أو بزر الخيار إحدى هذه البزور ثمّ ينقعونه في دم ابن آدم مع قليل ماء فاتر أربعون يوماً ثمّ يرفعونه ثمّ يجفّفونه في الظلّ ويكون عندهم فإذا أرادوا أن يزرعون المقثأة يأخذون تراب جزء ويعملونه على هيئة المقثأة ثمّ يغرزون فيه ذلك البزر المدبّر في الدم ثمّ يجعلون عليه ماء فاتر ويغطّونه بمنديل ويشغلون الناس ساعة بحركة أخرى بمقدار ما يحلّ ذلك البزر فيكشفونه فيجدونه قد طلع ذلك البزر وقد أورق أوراق كبار فيتعجّب الناس من ذلك وكذلك يعملون بالقِنَّب وبالرشاد وبغيرهما من البزور ولهم زرع الأرض مثال النجيل الأخضر وهو مليح

ولهم وهمة عظيمة وهو أن يأخذ خيط حرير أحمر وأصفر يكون طوله شبرين ٢٧،٥٩ ثمّ يبلعه قدّام الحاضرين ويوري أنّه قد بلعه ثمّ يخبأه في فيه ثمّ يكشف عن بطنه ويجذب ذلك الخيط فتراه قد برز من خاصرته طالع إلى أن يبرز جميعه وهذه وهمة عجيبة فإذا أراد فإنّه يأخذ خيط حرير على مقدار ذلك الخيط الذي يوهم أنّه يبلعه وعلى لونه ثمّ يجعله في إبرة غير مسقيّة ثمّ يجمع خاصرته بيده ثمّ يثقبها بتلك الإبرة ثمّ يطلّع برأس الخيط ويقلب خاصرته فإنّه يبقى رأس الخيط الواحد بارز من الثقب الواحد والطرف الآخر نازل عنه مقدار شبر أو أقلّ فيحصل الطرف النازل السفلانيّ تحت سراويله والطرف الفوقانيّ ظاهر فإذا جذبه فلا يشكّ أحداً أنّه طلع من بطنه وهذه وهمة مليحة

ولهم في ذلك فنون كثيرة واعلم أنّي لو أرخيت عنان الكلام في هذا الفصل لطال ٢٧،٦٠ الشرح فيه لأنّي قادر أن أكمل هذا الفصل ألف باب تتضمّن أمور لهم لم يقف عليها الغير بل هذا القدر كاف وبه يستدلّ على ما سواه فافهم ذلك

Section Thirty-Two: Anecdotes Regarding Prestidigitators

Exposé: They sow a cucumber patch, which immediately proceeds to sprout, impressing people. To do this, they take seeds of yellow melon, Armenian cucumber, or regular cucumber—any of the preceding. They steep them in human blood with a little tepid water for forty days, then dry them in the shade and set them aside. To sow the patch, they take a small quantity of soil and spread it out in the shape of a cucumber patch. Then they plant in it the seeds that have been prepared with the blood and run tepid water over it and cover it with a kerchief and occupy everyone for a while with some other distraction, keeping it up for as long as it takes the seeds to unfurl. Then they uncover the patch and discover that the seeds have come up and formed large leaves. Everyone finds this amazing. They do the same with cannabis, cress, and other seeds. They also know how to sow the ground with green grass, which is a nice trick. 27.58

They know an extraordinary hoax, which is to take a red or yellow silk thread two handspans in length, then swallow it in front of the onlookers, demonstrating clearly that they have done so. The charlatan keeps this hidden in his mouth. Then he uncovers his stomach and pulls out the same thread, which looks as though it's exiting from his side and keeps on coming till all of it is out. This is a marvelous hoax. To do it, he takes a silk thread of the same length and color as the one he pretends to swallow. He threads this onto an untempered needle, gathers the flesh of his side in his hand, and pierces it with the needle. Then he pulls the top end of the thread through and rolls the flesh over. Thus, one end of the thread comes out of the one visible hole and the other end dangles down for a hand's breadth or less, with the lower end going under his drawers and the upper end visible. When he pulls on it, everyone thinks it's coming out of his stomach. It's a nice trick. 27.59

They know so many arts in this field. If I allowed myself to run on in this chapter, all the explanation would become tedious, because I'm capable of adding a thousand more sections to it, each one covering something they do that no one else has ever studied. This, however, is enough, and from it other similar things may be inferred. Wise up to these things! 27.60

الفصل الثامن والعشرون

ثلاثة أبواب

في كشف أسرار الهجّامين الذين يهجمون البيوت من اللصوص

اعلم أنّ هذه الطائفة أخبث الناس وأدهى وأسرع بطش من اللصوص أصحاب القتل والنقب وسيأتي ذكرهم وهؤلاء الهجّامين لم يكن لهم يد في النقوب ولا في التسليق في الحيطان بل فعلهم الهجم ونتش ما حصل بسرعة ولهم في ذلك طرائق شتّى يطول شرحها وسنذكر بعضها ١،٢٨

الباب الأوّل في كشف أسرارهم

وذلك أنّهم يأخذون طير حمام يكون مقصوص الجناح ثمّ يدورون به في الأزقّة فأيّ باب وجدوه مفتوح سيّب فيه ذلك الطير الحمام ودخل خلفه فإن وجد أحدًا يقول لعلّ تمسكوا لي الطير الحمام وإن لم يجد أحدًا علّق مهما قدر عليه وشالها ٢،٢٨

الباب الثاني في كشف أسرارهم

ومن ذلك أنّهم يأخذون قطّ وقطعة لحم تكون كبيرة ثمّ يدورون في الشوارع فأيّ باب وجدوه مفتوح أرمى القطعة اللحم والقطّ خلفها فأخذها وزعق عليها فهم داخل إلى الباب وهو خلفه فإن وجد أحد يقول امسكوا لي القطيطة وخلّصوا منه اللحمة وإن لم يجد أحدًا خطف ما قدر عليه وتمّ هارب ٣،٢٨

Chapter Twenty-Eight, in Three Sections

Exposé of the Tricks of Sneak Thieves (Thieves Who Enter Houses Unlawfully)

This tribe is the lowest of the low and they are craftier and more violent than the thieves who commit murders or the ones who remove bricks to get through walls (whom we shall get to later). Sneak thieves have nothing to do with tunneling through walls or climbing them. Their MO is to enter a place without permission and quickly snatch anything they can lay their hands on. It would take too long to describe all the ways they have of doing this, so we shall list just a few. **28.1**

Section One of the Exposé of Their Tricks

Exposé: They take a pigeon with clipped wings and go around the alleyways and whenever they find an open door slip the pigeon in and go in after it. If he finds anyone at home, the thief says, "Would you be so kind as to grab that pigeon for me?" If he doesn't, he seizes what he can and makes off with it. **28.2**

Section Two of the Exposé of Their Tricks

Another example: They take a cat and a piece of meat, preferably large, then roam the streets. Anytime they find an open door, they throw the meat inside and the cat after it. The cat takes the meat and lets out a loud meow. By now they're through the door, the man behind the cat. If he finds anyone there, he says, "Grab me that kitty and get the meat away from it!" and if he doesn't, he snatches whatever he can and makes off. **28.3**

الباب الثالث في كشف أسرارهم

ومن ذلك أن يكون بعضهم معه صغيرًا أو صغيرة ابن سبعة ثمان سنين ثمّ يكون موصّى توصية جيّدة وهو دائر به في الدروب فإن وجد باب مفتوح دكّ الصغير دخل وهو يبكي وهو خلفه فإن وجد أحد يقول أخرجوا هذا الولد الزناء فإنه قد ضيّع عليّ كذا وكذا فمنهم من يخرجه ومنهم من يرحمه فيقول بالله عليك خلّيه عندنا الساعة حتّى يسكن روعه فقد قطعت قلبه بالفزع ثمّ يقول وا لك روح البيت ثمّ يتركه ويخرج يقعد بعيد عن الباب فيسألوه النساء فيقول لهم ما وصّاه به ثمّ يطعموه شيء ويبقى عندهم فإن هم غفلوا عن شيء خطف مهما قدر عليه وطلب الباب وذلك قاعد له فيخطفه منه مثل مرجونة الحمام ثمّ يمدّها وإن لم يقدر على شيء أقام عندهم[1] ساعة ثمّ يخرج يغيب عنهم جمعة ثمّ يجيء ويقول والله ضربني أبي أو عمّي ثمّ أراد يعلّقني وقد هربت منه ثمّ إنّه يقعد عندهم ولا يزال حتّى يلوح له شيء فيلفّه ويشيل فافهم واعلم أنّ الذي دكّ أكثر ٤،٢٨

١ ش: عنده.

Section Three of the Exposé of Their Tricks

Another example: One of them will have a little boy or girl with him, seven or eight years old, who has been well coached and with whom he roams the neighborhoods. If he finds an open door, he shoves the child through and the child enters, crying, the man in pursuit. If the man sees anyone, he says, "Chase that little brat out! He's cost me a load of money!" Some people do as he says but others have pity on the child and say, "Please leave him with us for a while till he calms down. You've scared him to bits!" When this happens, the thief says, "Kid, go into the house!" and he leaves him and goes out and sits down some way from the door. In the house, the women question the child, and he tells them what he's been told to, so they give him something to eat and he stays with them. As soon as they take their eyes off something, though, he snatches whatever fate may put in his way and asks to be let out the door. The man is sitting waiting for him and grabs from him whatever it is—a basket of pigeons, for example—and makes off with it. If the child can't get his hands on anything, he remains in the house awhile, then makes tracks. He stays away from them for a week, then goes back and says, "Swear to God! My father (or uncle) beat me and was going to hang me up by my feet, so I'm running away from him." Then he stays with them till another opportunity to take something presents itself and he swipes it and makes off. Wise up to these things—and don't forget that these are only a few of their scams! 28.4

الفصل التاسع والعشرون

أربعة أبواب

في كشف أسرار اللصوص
أصحاب النقوب والقتل

١،٢٩ اعلم أنّ هذه الطائفة مجمعة على أكل الحرام وقتل النفس التي حرّم الله عزّ وجلّ وذلك أنّ أيّ مكان دخلوه وحسّ بهم صاحبه ثمّ تكلّم قتلوه لا محالة فهم يأخذون المال والروح ولا يردّون أيديهم عن أحد يقعوا به

الباب الأوّل في كشف أسرارهم

٢،٢٩ وذلك أنّ أهل هذه الصنعة يحتاجون إلى عدّة فمن ذلك عدّة النقب مثل العتلة والسكّة والصفيحة والفشّاشة وكفّ حديد بأصابع حديد ولا بدّ من السلّم وكيس فيه رمل وسلحفاة صغيرة ولهم من العدّة ما يطول شرحها وأكثر الناس يحملوها فإذا أرادوا النقب ثقبوا بالعتلة والسكّة والكفّ فإنّ العتلة من شأن خلع الأبواب وإذا أنفذوا النقب أخذوا عصاة ثمّ يلفّون عليها قطعة قماش يعبرونها في النقب مخافة أن يكون قد فطن عليهم أحد[1] في الدار فيقف داخل النقب فإذا أدخل اللصّ برأسه في النقب ضربوه بدبّوس أو بعصا أو بسيف فيهلك فيجعل اللصّ تلك العصاة وعليها قطعة قماش عوضاً عنه فإن وقع ضرب كان على تلك العصاة فعلم اللصّ أن قد فطن به وإن لم يجد من يسمعه دخل إلى المكان وعمل ما أراد

١ أضيف للسياق.

Chapter Twenty-Nine, in Four Sections

Exposé of the Tricks of the Thieves Who Enter Houses by Making Holes in Walls and Committing Murder

This tribe of charlatans believes that living off ill-gotten gains and taking human life—which God, Mighty and Glorious, has declared sacrosanct—are permitted. 29.1

Exposé: If they enter a place and its owner hears them and opens his mouth, they kill him and that's the end of it. They will take property and life alike and not stay their hands from anyone who may fall into their clutches.

Section One of the Exposé of Their Tricks

Exposé: Those who practice this craft have need of a tool kit. This consists in part of tools for making holes in walls, such as a crowbar, an iron spike, a metal plate, a lock breaker, and an iron hand with iron fingers. A ladder, a bag of sand, and a small turtle are also essential. They have so many tools it would take forever to go through them all, but most of them carry them. To pierce a wall, they make a hole with the crowbar, the spike, and the iron hand (the crowbar is also used for prizing open doors). Once they've made the hole, they take a stick, wrap a piece of cloth around it, and push it through the hole to test whether their presence has been detected inside the house. If that is the case, someone may stand next to the hole on the inside and when the thief sticks his head through it, hit him with a club, stick, or sword, so that he dies. The thief therefore uses the aforementioned stick with the cloth to substitute for himself and if a blow is delivered, it falls on the stick, not him; this shows the thief that he has been discovered. If he finds that no one there has heard him, he goes in and does what he pleases. 29.2

الباب الثاني في كشف أسرارهم في السلحفاة

٣،٢٩ ومنهم إذا نقب النقب وأراد يأخذ أخبار الدار ويعلم أحوال من فيها ويعلم أيش الشيء الذي يريد يأخذه وكيف الطريق إليه وبعد ذلك يدخل وذلك أنّه يكون معه الزناد فيقدح ثمّ يكون معه شمعة على قدر الخنصر فيوقدها ثمّ يلصقها إلى ظهر السلحفاة ثمّ يرسل السلحفاة في النقب فيدور جميع الدار وهو يشاهد كلّ ما في البيت ويعلم أين يذهب هذا وهو خارج عن النقب فإن فطن به أحد خلا وراح وإن لم يكن فطن به وإلّا يكون قد عرف جميع الدار وما فيها وأين يسلك ولا يخفى عليه شيء منها فإذا انطفت الفتيلة دخل من النقب ومشى إلى موضع يريد وأخذ ما أراد وخرج سالمًا فافهم

الباب الثالث في كشف أسرارهم

٤،٢٩ وذلك أنّ منهم من يكون معه كيس فيه رمل فإذا نقب النقب دخل ثمّ جلس داخل النقب ثمّ أخذ حفنة من ذلك الرمل وبذرها في البيت ثمّ صبر ساعة ثمّ أخذ حفنة أخرى وبذرها كذلك أربع دفوع فإن كان في الدار أحد منتبه علم به وسمع حسّه وكلامه وإن لم يكن أحد منتبه إطمأنّ قلبه ثمّ دخل وامتدّ في الدار وفعل ما أراد وأخذ ما اشتهى وخرج سالمًا وقد يكون مع اللصّ الخبز اليابس والباقلّى فإن طلع له حسّ أو جلبه إخفاء الحسّ ثمّ شرع يأكل من ذلك الخبز اليابس ويقرش فيه فيظنّ صاحب البيت أنّ القطّ قد أخذ فأر وهو يأكله فلا يلتفت ثمّ يهمل أمر اللصّ ثمّ يخلّيه حتّى يهجع ويتمّ شغله ويروح سليم فاعلم أنّي قد طالعت لهم ستّمائة نوع من هذه الصناعة ولولا خوف الإطالة ذكرت ما يعجز الغير عنه فاعلم ذلك ترشد

Section Two: Exposé of Their Trick with the Turtle

Some of them, having made the hole in the wall, like to test the waters in the house, find out first something about the people inside, decide what it is that they want to take and how to get to it, and only then enter. 29.3

Exposé: The man will have a flint with him, which he strikes. He will also have a candle the size of a little finger, which he lights and sticks to the turtle's back. Then he sends the turtle through the hole and the turtle takes a turn around the whole house while the man observes what's there and finds out where to go. All this is while he's still on the outside of the hole. If anyone becomes aware of his presence, he withdraws and leaves. If not, he will have become familiar with the whole house and its contents and what route he should take, and everything about it will be familiar to him. When the candle goes out, he enters through the hole, goes where he wants, takes what he wants, and comes out unharmed. Wise up to these things!

Section Three of the Exposé of Their Tricks

Exposé: One of them will have a bag containing sand. When he's made his hole in the wall, he enters, sits down on the other side of the hole, takes a handful of the sand, and casts it into the house. He waits for a while, then takes another handful and casts that the same way, repeating this four times. If anyone in the house is awake, the thief will become aware of him, hear his voice, and hear him speaking. If there isn't, he'll stop worrying, go in, and walk around the house; he'll do whatever he pleases, take whatever he wants, and leave unharmed. The thief may also have dry bread and beans. If he makes a noise, or finds having to not make a noise inconvenient, he starts eating some of the dry bread, crunching it between his teeth, and the owner of the house thinks the cat has caught a mouse and is eating it, so pays no attention and fails to discover the thief. The thief leaves him till he goes to sleep, then gets on with the job and leaves unharmed. I have observed six hundred techniques that they use in this craft, and if I weren't afraid of boring you, I'd give you a list no one else could. Wise up to this and you can't go wrong! 29.4

الباب الرابع في كشف أسرار الذين يسلكون البرّ من اللصوص

وهذه الطائفة يسمّون المداورين ومنهم السلاّلين وهم الذين يداورون الأكراد والتركمان والعربان وأمّا السلاّلين فهم الذين يسلّون الخيل الجيّدة الأصيلة السابقة ويسافرون خلف الفرس من بلد إلى بلد مسيرة الشهر والشهرين والثلاثة ولا يزالون حتّى يسلّونها وأمّا المداورون الذين يداورون العربان والتركمان والأكراد فإنّ منهم من يأخذ الكُسْب ويعجنه بمشاقة الشعر ويكون معه فإذا أتى إلى الدور ثمّ أخذت عليه الكلاب أخرج ذلك الكسب المعجون فأرمى لكلّ كلب قطعة منه فإذا أكلها تعلّق الكسب مع الشعر في أسنانه وسقف لهاته فيظلّ يعالجه ليلة ويشتغل بروحه فعندها يتمكّن الدوّار من الذي جاء في طلبه وأمن غائلة الكلاب ومنهم من يلبس جلود الوحوش المزنجة ثمّ يمشي على أربع فتجفل منه الدوابّ والرعاة وهذا لا يفعلوه إلّا في البرّ والمُراحات ولهم أمور يطول شرحها ٥،٢٩

وأمّا السلاّلين فإنّهم أشدّ تسلّط وأقدم على كلّ أمر صعب وأكثر خطر ومع ذلك فإنّ واحد منهم يرمي روحه في الهلاك واعلم أنّ هذه الطائفة يتزايّون بكلّ زيّ ويتقلّبون في كلّ قالب فمنهم من يتزايا بزيّ الشعراء ومنهم من يتزايا بزيّ الفقراء ومنهم من يتزايا بزيّ الحدّادين ومنهم من يتزايا بزيّ الوعّاظ ولا يزال حتّى يعرف موضعه وأينه ومن يحفظه ويعرف جميع أحواله فمنهم من يكون معه المبرد ويبرد به القيد ومنهم من يكون معه الفشّاشة فيفشّ بها القيود جميعهم ومنهم من يكون معه مفاتيح جملة فينزل على القيد مفتاح بعد مفتاح ولا يزال حتّى يقع عليه مفتاح فيركّبه عليه فيأخذ الجواد ويخرجه من الحلّة ثمّ يركبه ويطلق رأسه فافهم ذلك وقد اختصرت ٦،٢٩

Section Four: Exposé of the Tricks of the Kind of Thieves Who Crisscross the Countryside

This tribe of charlatans is known as "camp followers" and includes the ones called "extraction men." Camp followers are the ones who follow the Kurds, Turkmen, and nomadic Arabs around, while the extraction men are those who slip away with fine horses of good pedigree, following the horse from town to town for as much as a month, or two, or three, keeping this up till they are able to slip away with it. A camp follower of the sort that hangs around the encampments of the nomadic Arabs, Turkmen, and Kurds will take oil cake, knead it with wadded hair, and keep it with him. Then, when he arrives at the encampment and the dogs attack him, he takes out the oil-cake paste and throws a piece to each dog. When the dog eats it, the oil cake sticks to its teeth and the roof of its mouth, and the dog will spend the whole night trying to remove it, preoccupied with its own problems. Once this is achieved, the camp follower can get his hands on whatever he came for, having rendered the dogs harmless. Some of them put on frightening wild-animal skins and walk on all fours, which startles the beasts and their minders; they only do this in the countryside and the animal enclosures. They get up to things it would take too long to describe. 29.5

Extraction men are more audacious, readier to take on stressful tasks, and more dangerous than the foregoing, for they are, to a man, willing to risk even their lives. This tribe of charlatans will adopt any form of dress and put on any disguise. Some of them dress up as itinerant minstrels, some as dervishes, some as blacksmiths, and some as preachers, and they keep up the pretense till they have discovered what town the horse is in, where it's being kept, and who's looking after it, so they know everything about it. One of them will carry a file on him and file through horses' fetters, another a jimmy good for forcing them open, another skeleton keys and will try key after key on the fetter till he finds one that fits and then open it with it. Then he'll take the horse, move it out through the encampment, and finally mount and give it its head. Wise up to these things (even though what I've mentioned is just a summary)! 29.6

الفصل الثلاثون

بابان

في كشف أسرار النساء وما لهم من الحيل والمكر والخداع

اعلم أنّ النساء أكثر مكر وحيل وخداع وتسلّط وقلّة حياء من الرجال ولهم ١،٣٠
قلوب لا يخافون بها وذلك أنّهم ناقصات عقل ودين وقلّة المروّة والأمانة فإنّ الرجل إذا أراد أن يفعل شيئاً أو يقدم على شيء من الأمور الصعاب منعه عنه إمّا الخوف من الله عزّ وجلّ وإمّا خوف السيف وإمّا الحياء وإمّا المروّة وقد قال الحكيم الفاضل أرسطاطاليس حيث يقول الظلم من طبع النفوس وإنّما يصدّها عنه أحد علّتين إمّا علّة ديانة لخوف معاد وإمّا علّة سياسة لخوف السيف وأمّا النساء فلا[1] يخافون شيئاً من ذلك وقد عدموا المروّة والحياء فلمّا عدموا هذه الخصال الحميدة قدروا على الأفعال الرديئة وتسلّطوا عليها فمتى أقدروا وصلوا[2] إلى كلّ رذيلة من الرذائل فإنّهم أوصل إليها من الرجال فإنّ من لا لها مروّة على أن تحفظ نفسها لا تؤمن على بائقة تفعلها ورذيلة تصدر عنها وقد ذكرت شيئاً ممّا وقفت عليه

١ ش: لا. ٢ ش: وصل.

Chapter Thirty, in Two Sections

Exposé of the Tricks of Women, and of Their Cunning, Craftiness, and Duplicity

Women are more cunning, devious, treacherous, audacious, and immodest 30.1
than men. Their hearts know no fear. This is because they are both mentally and morally defective, and lack manly honor and trustworthiness. When a man wants to do something or set off on some pernicious enterprise, he will be restrained either by fear of God, Mighty and Glorious, or by fear of the sword, or by modesty or manly feeling. Aristotle, that learned sage, expresses this idea when he says, "A proclivity for evil is inborn and only two motivations can divert a person from it: a religious motivation (fear of what may befall him in the next world) or a political motivation (fear of the sword)."[254] Women fear neither. They have no manly feeling or modesty and, absent these praiseworthy qualities, are capable of evil deeds, which they undertake audaciously, there being no vile act they will hesitate to perform, given the chance. And they are more likely to perform them than men, for a woman who lacks the decency to refrain from getting involved in things that don't concern her cannot be trusted not to create mischief, and vile deeds will emanate from her naturally. In what follows, I list just a part of what I have observed.

الباب الأوّل في كشف أسرارهم ممّا وقفت عليه

٢،٣٠ فمن ذلك أنّا كنّا في بعض الأيّام في مجلس لهو وقصف ونحن جماعة وكان لي صاحب من أهل حلب وكان له واحدة وقد هجرته وكنّا متوجّهين إلى اليمن فجعلنا ذلك اليوم لهو ووداع ممّن نحبّه من الأصحاب والأصدقاء ولمّا اجتمعنا فكلّ من كان له صاحب أو صاحبة أحضره فلمّا كان ذلك قلت لصاحبي وكان اسمه عيسى فقلت له أنفذ أحضر فلانة نودعها ونستجعل منها في حلّ فقال ما تفعل تجيء فقلت لغلامي خذ هذا الخاتم وروح إلى فلانة وقول سيّدي يخدّمك ويقول لك نحن أغداً رائحين إلى اليمن وقد اجتمعنا اليوم برسم الوداع وإنّي أشتهي حضور الأخت لنودعها ونستجعل منها في حلّ ولا بدّ من حضورك

٣،٣٠ فأخذ الغلام الخاتم وراح غاب ساعة وقال هذه جائية فما كان إلّا لحظة وقد دخلت ونحن في حجرة وفيها مجلس وفي جنب المجلس صفّة فدخلت قعدت على الصفّة تخلع من رجلها وهي قد خلعت الفردة من رجلها إذ نظرت زوجها قاعد معنا في المجلس فلمّا رأته لم تفزع ولا خبت وجهها ولا ردّت عنه بل أخذت فردة الخفّ وهجمت عليه والأخرى في رجلها ثمّ لم ترتدّ ولم تخاف بل قبضت بشاشيته وجعلت تصقّله بالخفّ حتّى غاب عن رشده ثمّ مسكت بذقنه وخرجت به من المجلس وهي تقول يا قوّادكم تنحشر في موضع بعد موضع وهذه ثلاثة عشر مشربة قد درت فيها اليوم عليك فكم تنحشر

٤،٣٠ ثمّ أنزلته إلى الزقاق وقالت لواحد خذ هذا الدرهم[1] هات لي غلام القاضي فنزلنا إليها وسألنها[2] وبسنا بيديها وهي تقول أنتم الذي تفسدوا زوجي وهذه القحبة الذي عندكم هي له فخلفنا لها وسألناها فقالت ما أتركه حتّى يحلف بالطلاق أنّه لا يرجع يعبر في هذا الدرب فحلف لها ثمّ قال لها روحي إلى البيت فقالت والله ما أطلع لك اليوم بيت ولا الليلة أنا طالعة إلى مصر عند أختي فخذ مفاتيحك وروح والله

[1] ش: درهم. [2] ش: سألتها.

Section One: Exposé of Some of Their Tricks That I Have Observed Personally

Example: One day we were at a party, to drink and carouse. We were a group of buddies, and I had a chum from Aleppo who had a girlfriend but she'd given him the cold shoulder. We were about to set off for Yemen so we'd taken the day off to feast and say farewell to our good buddies and friends, and so everyone who had a buddy or a girlfriend brought them along. So, at the party, I said to my buddy—whose name was ʿĪsā—I said to him, "Look lively and fetch so-and-so, so we can say goodbye to her and she can absolve us from our vows." "She'll never come," he said. So I said to my servant, "Take this signet ring and go to so-and-so's house and say, 'My master sends his respects and says, "We're leaving for Yemen tomorrow and having a gathering today to say goodbye and I'd love our sister to come so that we can say goodbye to her and receive from her absolution from our vows—so you have to come."'" 30.2

So the servant took the ring and set off. He was gone awhile, then returned and said, "She's coming," and a moment later she entered. We were in a room and in the room was a sitting area and to the side of that there was a bench. She sat down on the bench and began taking off her shoes. She'd taken off one when she caught sight of her husband sitting right there with us! When she saw him, she showed no fear, didn't hide her face, and didn't back away from him. On the contrary, she took one of her boots and attacked him with it, while the other was still on her foot. She didn't hold back and showed no fear, but grabbed him by his cap and kept beating on him with the boot till the man almost passed out. Then she took hold of his beard and dragged him out of the sitting area, saying, "Pimp! You're always stuffing yourself into some place or other. This makes thirteen watering holes you've stuck your nose into today! How many more are you going to stick it into?" 30.3

Then she dragged him down into the alley and said to a man, "Take this silver piece and fetch me the judge's servant!" We went down to her, asked her to come back up, and kissed her hands, while she exclaimed, "You're the ones who are corrupting my husband, and that whore you have with you[255] is his!" We swore to her it wasn't true and asked her to go back with us but she said, "I won't leave him till he's sworn, on threat of divorce, that he'll never set foot on this street again!" So the man swore this and told her, "Go home!" but she said, "I swear to God, I'll never enter your house again, by day or by night! 30.4

ما تجيء خلفي أو تبعث لي شيء وترجع تشمّ لي عقصة عمرك كلّه وأطالبك بمائة دينار مصريّة

٥،٣٠ فقلت له[١] خلّيها تروح إلى بيت أختها حتّى ينكسر غيظها وتكسّر عليها النُسَيّات وتجيء من الغد فقال خذي أدي عشرة الدراهم اشتري بها شيء معك وروحي فأخذتهم وقالت روح اخرج قدّامي أنا ما أخرج ربّما تأخذ القحبة وتروح ولم تزل عليه حتّى خرج ثمّ طلعت إلى عندنا وقلعت وقعدت وقالت لغلامي خذ هذه الفضّة واشتري لنا بها شيء نتنقّل ففعل وأقامت عندنا ذلك اليوم وتلك الليلة فافهم هذا المكر وفعل هذه القحبة وقلّة الحياء والتسلّط والجسارة على كلّ أمر صعب منهم واعلمه

الباب الثاني في كشف أسرارهم

٦،٣٠ ومن ذلك كان لي صاحب من أهل دمشق جَنْدار ثمّ ترك الجندرة وفتح له دكّان نقل في القاهرة فجاءته إمرأة عجوز وصارت تشتري من عنده النقل وتتردّد إليه وصارت زبونة فقال لها ذات يوم ما تقدري تبصري لي واحدة طفيلة لا تكون من هذه القحاب الذي كسروا فإنّ ما لي عادة أن تكون عندي واحدة ولها التفاتة إلى موضع آخر فتعلمي أنّ الشيء كثير إلّا أريد من تكون مصانة وأنا أقنع منها بساعة تقعد عندي وتروح وإذا علمت أنها لي أنا أكسيها وما أحوجها إلى شيء فقالت كرامة أنا أفتّش على غرضك

٧،٣٠ ثمّ غابت عنّي يوم ثمّ عادت وقالت قد حصلت لك واحدة بنت خمسة عشر سنة لا تعرف يمينها من شمالها ولها في بيتها شهر ونصف إلّا أنها لا تقدر تطلع ولا تنزل ولا برحت عليها حتّى لأنت فقالت إذا كان ولا بدّ فإنّ زوجي شغله في

---

١ ش: لها.

I'm off to Cairo, to my sister's. Take your keys and go! I swear, if you follow me or try to get at me in any way, the next thing you'll feel will be a slap the like of whose sting you've never in your life felt before and I'll sue you for a hundred Egyptian gold pieces!"

"Let her go to her sister's house," I told him, "till she's calmed down and the girls have given her a talking to. She can come back tomorrow." So he told her, "Here's ten silver pieces. Buy something to take with you and go," and she took them and told him, "You go! Let me see you get out of here first! I'm not going to leave before you do, as you might take that whore and go off with her," and she kept on at him till he left. Then she came back upstairs to us, took off her street clothes, sat down, and said to my servant, "Take this silver piece and buy us something to snack on," which he did, and she stayed with us for the rest of the day and the night too. Wise up to this kind of cunning and the things this whore did; immodesty, audaciousness, and the daring to undertake any pernicious enterprise are part of their makeup, so be warned! 30.5

Section Two of the Exposé of Their Tricks

Another example: I had a friend, a Damascene, who was a member of the royal guard, who left that line of work and opened a shop selling nuts and other snacks in Cairo. An old woman came along, took to dropping by and buying nuts from him, and became a regular customer. One day, he asked her, "Could you find me a young girl who isn't one of those raddled whores? I'm not accustomed to keeping a woman who's always looking over her shoulder to someplace else. As you know, there's plenty of it around but I want a girl who's been respectably kept. I'd be happy to have her stay with me for just an hour and then go. If I know she's mine only, I'll buy her clothes and she won't go without a thing." "With the greatest of pleasure!" the old woman said. "I'll look around for what you want." 30.6

"After that," the man told me, "I didn't see her for a day, but then she returned and said, 'I've found one for you. A girl of fifteen who doesn't know her right hand from her left. She only moved to her husband's house a month and a half ago, so she can't go anywhere, but I wouldn't leave her alone till she gave in. She told me, "Since it must be so, my husband's work is in Cairo[256] and every day he gets up early and doesn't come back till the end of the evening 30.7

مصر وكلّ يوم يطلع من الصبح ما يجيء إلى عشاء الأخير وما معي في الدار أحد فإن كان هو يجيء إلى عندي وإلّا نزول ما أقدر أنزل من البيت فإن كنت تشتهي فأنا آخذك وأروح فقلت أنا أروح فقالت أنا أجيء إليك غداً فلمّا كان الغد جاءت فأخذت معي من الدكّان شيء ومشيت معها فأتت بي إلى زقاق

٨،٣٠ وقالت إذا أبصرتني دخلت في الباب فادخل خلفي ثمّ دخلت وأنا خلفها فأطلع أصيب قاعة معلّقة إيوان وصفّتين لا غير وهو موضع طيّب إلّا أنّه حَرِج ثمّ ألقى صبيّة كما قالت العجوز فجلست معها وقامت العجوز راحت والصبيّة حرجت[١] من الحياء فمال قلبي إليها ثمّ أقمت عندها ساعة ونزلت وجعلت في كلّ يوم في وقت القائلة آخذ معي شيء نأكل وأقيم عندها إلى العصر فأقمت كذلك مدّة ثلاث شهور

٩،٣٠ فنحن في بعض الأيّام جلوس وإذا بزوجها قد دخل في باب الدرب فقالت[٢] جاء زوجي قال فوثبت ووثبت أنا قائم فقالت اقعد واسكت ثمّ عمدت إلى مسمارين فسمّرتهما في زوايا الإيوان وعقدت عليها ملحفة وقالت جوز اقعد فدخلت ومداسي معي وأنا خائف فلمّا دخل قال لها من عندك قالت يا رجل بنت خالتي ضربها زوجها وجاءت إلى عندي وما كان عندي شيء أطعمها فأخذ زبديّة وتمّ نازل إلى السوق فلمّا نزل قمت من تحت الملحفة طالب الباب فقالت لي إلى أين قلت أروح قبل ما يجيء قالت والله ما تروح حتّى تأكل معه اقعد واسكت ثمّ تركت الملحفة على حالها وأخرجت مداسي جعلته تحت الإيوان وعملت على رأسها بوشيّة وقعدت عند الملحفة وهو قد طلع

١٠،٣٠ فلمّا سمعت حسّه قالت أيْ والله تأخذ أنت واحدة تعمل بها هذا العمل وترجع تجيء خلفها هذا وزوجها قد طلع وقد بدرته وقالت يا مولاي ضربها ذاك الضرب وقال لها قومي روحي عنّي ورجع جاء خلفها فقال لي[٣] زوجها هذي طفلة وما لها

---

١ ش: خرجت. ٢ ش: فقال. ٣ ش: له.

and there's no one else in the house besides me. So he has to come to me—no going out. There's no way I can leave the house." So if you want,' continued the old woman, 'I can take you and go there.' 'I'll go,' said I. 'I'll come to you tomorrow,' said the old woman. The next day she came, so I took a few things from the shop and went with her, and she brought me to an alleyway.

"'When you see me go through a door,' she said, 'go in behind me.' Then she went through, with me behind her. I went up some stairs and straightaway found myself in a chamber with a raised recess, two benches, and nothing else. It was a nice place, if a bit cramped. There I found a girl who was just as the old woman had described her. I sat down with her and the old woman got up and left, though the girl was so modest she became quite embarrassed, which made me like her. I spent an hour with her and left, and I took to taking something with me that we could eat each day at midday and going to her and staying till the afternoon prayer. I did this for three months. 30.8

"One day we were sitting together, when suddenly we learned that her husband had passed through the gate at the end of the street leading to her alley. 'My husband has come,' she said, so I leapt up, but she said, 'Sit down and shut up!' Then she took two nails, hammered them into the corners of the recess, hung a blanket from them, and told me, 'Get in there and sit down!' so I went in, carrying my shoes and scared stiff. When her husband entered, he asked her, 'Who's here with you?' 'Don't even go there!' she replied. 'My cousin got a beating from her husband, so she came to me, but I don't have anything for her to eat.' So the man took a pot and set off for the market. When he'd gone, I came out from behind the blanket, making for the door. 'Where are you off to?' she asked me. 'Home,' I said, 'before he comes back.' 'Swear to God,' she said, 'you're not going anywhere until you've had a meal with him! Sit down and shut up!' She left the blanket as it was, took my shoes out, placed them at the foot of the recess, placed a waist wrapper in front of them, and sat down next to the blanket, by which time her husband was on his way back up. 30.9

"As soon as she heard his voice, she said, 'Swear to God, you'd better believe it! You think you can take a woman and do something like that to her and then come running after her?' By this time, her husband had come back up, and she rushed over to him and said, 'My lord, that man there beat her really badly and then he told her, "Get out of my sight!" and now he's come running after her!' 'She's just a kid and doesn't know any better,' her husband said to me. 'She needs to be humored, and if you have a quarrel, don't let things get out of 30.10

عقل وتحتاج إلى المداراة فإذا جرى بينكم كلام اكسر الشرّ وانزل غيب عنها ساعة وقد انكسر الشرّ فقالت قال ذا لا إلّا يقعد يمرّث قلبها ويضربها وجعلوا يكسّرون عليّ ثمّ شالت من الذي قد جاء به حطّته تحت الملحفة وقالت كلي وشرعنا نحن نأكل أنا وهو ونتحدّث

فلمّا رفع الأكل قال[1] لها خلّيها تلبس وتنزل قالت روح أنت انزل أنا آخذها وأجيء ١١،٣٠
وأبصر البيت ونوصي عليها أهل الدار وإن حلفوا علينا بتنا عندهم وإلّا جئنا ثمّ أخذ يده في يده ونزلوا يتحدّثون فقال زوجها أنا ما أنزل من مصر إلى غلوق السوق فكن خلّيها تجيء تظلّ عندها يتوانسوا وكن خذها وتعالوا ناموا عندنا قال وانصرفت جئت إلى الدكّان والعجوز قد جاءت قالت أين البنت[2] قلت في الموضع الفلانيّ فقالت اقف لي على الباب فقمت وإذا بهم قد جاءوا فبتنا في ليلة طيّبة وتعجّبت من ذلك الفعل على صغر سنّها وعلمت أنّ المكر مع النساء خلقة لا اكتساب

قال وأقمنا على ذلك مدّة ثمّ مرضت وانتقلوا إلى مصر ولم أرجع أراها وبقيت ما ١٢،٣٠
لي من يخدمني فشاروا عليّ الأصدقاء بالزواج فخفت من ذلك ثمّ قلت ابصروا لي واحدة بنت خمسة عشر سنة لا تعرف شيء وأقيم معها حتّى أعلم أنّها قد تخرّجت وأسيبها فإنّ النساء يخرّجوا بعضهم بعض وفي أقلّ من سنة وثنتين ما تتخرّج فخطبوا لي واحدة بنت ستّة عشر سنة وقالوا كان أبوها رجل إمام وهي خاتمة القرآن وأقامت أمّها مع أبوها في داره أربعين سنة ما فتحت لها طاقة وذكروا أحوال حسنة فتزوّجت بها ودخلت عليها فرأيت منها أمور تسرّ ولا تقطع لها صلاة وكلّ يوم تقرأ سبع من القرآن ففرحت بذلك وأقمنا كذلك ستّ شهور

فبعض الأيّام جئت إلى البيت أصيب الملحفة معلّقة في زوايا البيت فقلت من ١٣،٣٠
عندك وقد خفق قلبي فقالت بنت أختي تزورني فخلعت مداسي ثمّ شلت الملحفة أصيب تحتها واحد قاعد فقلت قم يا نحس إن كنت ابن أختها أنا والله كنت ابن

---

١ ش: قلت. ٢ ش: البيت.

hand. Leave the house and let her alone for a while and you'll find things have calmed down.' 'Not that one!' said the woman. 'The best he could come up with was to hurt her feelings and beat her,' and they went on scolding me. Then she took some of what her husband had brought, set it behind the blanket, and said, 'Eat something!' while her husband and I set about eating and chatting.[257]

"After the food had been cleared away, her husband told her, 'Tell her to dress and go downstairs,' but she said, 'You go down. I'll get her and go see the house and tell the folks there to make a fuss over her, and if they insist, I'll stay the night with them. If not, I'll come home.'" Then, according to my friend, the husband took my friend's hand in his and they went out, chatting. The woman's husband told my friend, "I don't leave Cairo till the market closes. Let my wife go stay with yours so they can keep each other company, or you could bring her and come and spend the night with us." I left and came to the shop, where I found the old woman. "Where's the girl?" she asked, and I answered, "In such and such a place." "Wait here at the door!" she said. "So I waited, and lo and behold they came, and we spent a lovely night. I was amazed that she'd do such things even though she was so young, and learned that, for women, cunning is an inborn trait, not something acquired." 30.11

My friend continued, "We went on like this for a while and then she got sick and they moved to Cairo and I never saw her again. I had no one to look after me so my friends advised me to get married but I was afraid to do so. Finally, I said, 'Find me a fifteen-year-old girl who knows nothing and I'll live with her till I find out she's gotten smart and then leave her, for women make sure to clue their sisters in, and they get smart in a year or two, tops.' So they engaged me to a girl of sixteen, whose father, they said, had been an imam, while she herself had memorized the Qur'an, not to mention that her mother had lived with her father in his house for forty years, during which time she had never even opened a window; in other words, they made her sound like a paragon of virtue. So I married her and consummated the marriage, and I found only good things in her: She never missed a prayer and every day she would read a seventh of the Qur'an. I was delighted and we lived like this for six months. 30.12

"Then one day I came home and found myself confronted with the blanket, hung up in the corner of the house. 'Who's here with you?' I asked, my heart beating wildly. 'My niece,' she said, 'who's visiting with me.' So I took off my shoes, lifted the blanket, and found myself face to face with a man, sitting there. 'Get up, you wretch!' I said. 'You may be the son of her sister, but I'm 30.13

خالتها ثمّ أنزلته وحلفت بطلاقها وسيّبتها وحلفت أن لا أرجع أطلب النساء ولقد تمّت لي آناء ووقائع [1] مع النساء يطول شرحها كلّ وقعة منها أغرب من الأخرى هذا ومن أراد يتفرّج على مكرهنّ فعليه بكتاب الجاحظ في مكر النساء فإنّ فيه فنون ومع ذلك فلا تدرك نهاية مكرهم ودهاءهم هذا القول عن الحرائر وأمّا المباحات فإنّ لهم أمور قباح لا يمكن شرحها فافهم ذلك

---

١ ش: وقائع.

the son of her uncle!'[258] Then I threw him out of the house, swore the oath of divorce, and released her." And I myself have experienced situations and misadventures with women that it would take too long to explain, each stranger than the first. But enough of that: Anyone who wants to get an overview of their cunning ought to read al-Jāḥiẓ's book on the wiles of women.[259] It contains many examples, though you still won't get to the bottom of their cunning and craft. The preceding applies to freeborn women; when it comes to those who may be made use of without legal formalities,[260] they get up to things too appalling to be described. Wise up to these things!

واعلم أنّي قد مارست لهم أشياء واطّلعت على كلّ فنّ من دقيقها وجليلها ولم أترك شيئاً لم أقف عليه ولو شرحت جميع ذلك لطال الشرح بل هذا المقدار دالّ على ما ذكرت ولو غشيتني السعادة وشملتني عناية الإرادة لم أتعلّق بما تعلّقت ولا أظهرت ما قد سُتر عن أعين الخلق ولكن لله في ذلك مشيئة وألطاف خفيّة يفعل ما يشاء ويحكم ما يريد ونسأله أن يتجاوز عن الهفوات ويمحو عنّا عظائم السيّئات فإنّا نلجأ في كلّ حال إليه ونعتمد في كلّ الأمور عليه فإنّه الجواد المفضال الكبير المتعال وهو حسبنا ونعم الوكيل ١،٣١

تمّ الكتاب وكمل

والحمد لله ربّ العالمين

وصلواته وسلامه على سيّدنا محمّد خاتم النبيّين وشفيع المؤمنين

وعلى آله وعشيرته الطاهرين وصحابته أجمعين

وسلّم تسليماً كثيراً

Always bear in mind that I have had practical experience of much of what they do, have observed every one of these crafts, whether paltry or sublime, and have left nothing unconsidered. To have laid them out in their entirety, however, would have taken too long, albeit this much is ample evidence of my claim. Had I been born enveloped in a caul of good fortune, embraced by the solicitude of the Divine Will, I would never have written the commentaries that I have or brought to public attention matters over which a veil of decorum has otherwise been drawn. In allowing me to do so, though, God has manifested a specific wish and hidden graces—He acts as He wills and judges as He pleases. We ask Him to overlook our venial slips and wipe clean the slate of our mortal offences, for we take refuge with Him in every situation and depend on Him in every matter. He is the Magnanimous, the Beneficent, the Great-Beyond-Measure, the Most Sublime, and He is our sufficiency and our best advocate. **31.1**

This book is at an end
and
now complete
thanks be to God, Lord of All the Worlds—
may He bless and keep
Our Master Muḥammad
Seal of the Prophets, Intercessor for the Believers
and likewise his pure family, clan, and companions
one and all
and
may His blessings
be manifold!

Notes

1 In the original, "260 sections." However, a count of the sections yields a total of 279. The reason for the discrepancy is unknown.

2 The Tablet and the Pen are the media on and by which the decisions of the divine will are recorded (Q Burūj 85:22).

3 The following works, many of which have obscure or ambiguous titles, all appear to deal with the occult sciences. In his seventeenth-century booklist, Ḥājjī Khalīfah (*Kashf al-ẓunūn*, 2:1436) refers to *The Book of the Released* as a work on conjurations and ascribes it to Āṣaf ibn Barakhyā; he also mentions *The Book of Lamps*, describing it as a work on the science of letters (see n. 5) without ascription (*Kashf al-ẓunūn*, 2:1702). Ṣaṣah ibn Ḍāmir al-Hindī, in a collection on astrology and magic titled *Sharḥ al-ṣūrah al-khāmisah wa-hiya al-maʿrūfah bi-dhāt al-dhawāʾib min al-sabʿ wa-huwa al-maʿrūf bi-Sirr al-sirr* (*A Commentary on the Fifth Image—Namely, That Known as "That of Liquids," from [the Book of] the Seven [Images], Known as "The Innermost Secret"*) (*GAS*, 7:94–95), mentions six works with titles identical or similar to those in al-Jawbarī's list (*Kitāb al-Jamharah*, *Kitāb al-Ajnās*, *Kitāb al-Usṭuwānah* [*sic*, see n. 4], *Kitāb al-Afāliq* (*sic*, cf. *Kitāb al-Afālīq* below), *Kitāb al-Ṭawāliq*, and *Kitāb al-Muṣḥaf al-khafī*), referring to them as works of special importance in the field.

4 The word *aṣṭannah* is obscure, perhaps a distortion or miscopying of *usṭuwānah*, meaning "column; cylinder; portico; penis." A *Kitāb al-Usṭuwānah* is referred to by Ṣaṣah al-Hindī (see n. 3).

5 Ḥājjī Khalīfah classifies the following five books as belonging to "the science of letters and names" (*ʿilm al-ḥurūf wa-l-asmāʾ*), i.e., the making of talismans out of magic squares formed of letters and the use of the names of God for magical purposes (*Kashf al-ẓunūn*, 1:655).

6 The name Idrīs, though not Arabic in origin, has been associated by some with the Arabic root *d-r-s*, meaning "to study/teach."

7 "A[ristotle] is without reservation considered by most Arabic philosophers as the outstanding and unique representative of philosophy"; he was referred to as "the philosopher," and was thought of as "the first teacher" (Walzer, "Arisṭūṭālīs or Arisṭū," in *EI2*). His thinking was regarded by the Arabs as largely congruent with or at least

complementary to that of Plato, as they understood him (see the Glossary); hence perhaps his presence in this list of hermetic philosophers.

8 The work appears not to have survived.

9 The author mentions and quotes from this later (§12.25), referring to it as an *urjūzah*, or didactic poem written in *rajaz*, a meter that lends itself to memorization.

10 A term taken from the jargon of the Banū Sāsān that covers many types of charlatan (see also Chapter 27).

11 The chapter titles given here vary in detail in some cases from those used for the chapters as they occur below.

12 An ungrammatical variant of an accepted hadith (for which see al-Hindī, *Kanz al-ʿummāl fī sunan al-aqwāl wa-l-afʿāl*, vol. 1, no. 78, *Kitāb al-Īmān wa-l-Islām*).

13 Q Āl ʿImrān 3:19.

14 Q Aḥzāb 33:40. The verse runs in full: «Muhammad is not the father of any one of your men, but the Messenger of God, and the Seal of the Prophets» (trans. Arberry, *The Koran Interpreted*, 432).

15 A canonical hadith (al-Hindī, *Kanz*, vol. 15, no. 43638, *Kitāb al-Mawāʿiẓ wa-l-raqāʾiq wa-l-khuṭab wa-l-ḥikam*).

16 The hadith has not been identified.

17 "Isḥāq the Mute" bears a resemblance to Abū ʿĪsā al-Iṣfahānī, a Jewish sectarian leader who, after a career that spanned the last years of the Umayyad and first of the Abbasid caliphates, led his followers into a futile armed conflict with Abbasid forces in which he was killed. He has been described as "the most important Jewish heresiarch of that period" (Friedlaender, "Shiitic Elements III," 284) and his movement, the ʿĪsāwiyyah, as "the most important Jewish sect (after the Karaites) in the millennium from the rise of Islam until the tenth/sixteenth century" (Wasserstrom, "The ʿĪsāwiyya Revisited," 57). From the text, it appears that the author thought of Isḥāq the Mute as a Muslim rather than a Jew.

18 Abū ʿĪsā al-Iṣfahānī instituted ten, or, according to another source, seven, daily prayers (Friedlaender, "Shiitic Elements III," 298) and prohibited the eating or harming in any way of birds and other animals (296).

19 Al-Shahrastānī states that Abū ʿĪsā al-Iṣfahānī was killed by the forces of al-Manṣūr (r. 136–58/754–75), successor to al-Ṣaffāḥ, at Rayy, on an unknown date (Friedlaender, "Shiitic Elements I," 203–4).

20 The fake prophet evokes the Qur'an, Q Āl ʿImrān 3:185: «He who is kept away from the Fire and is admitted to Paradise, will surely triumph» (trans. Wahiduddin Khan: http://tanzil.net/#3:185).

21 Since *sayyid* ("lord, master") is a title normally reserved for descendants of the Prophet Muḥammad, the implication is that Abū Saʿīd's followers regarded him as the latter's equal.

22 Elsewhere in the book (§§27.52–54), the term "philosopher" is associated with "the ancients who worked using divination" and who "greatly deluded" people.

23 I.e., 3 parts fat + 1 part pharaoh glass + 1 part cinnabar + 1 part quicksilver + 1 part verdigris (= 7 parts) + (half of the preceding =) 3 ½ parts dung + (one quarter of the preceding, i.e., of the 7 parts =) 1 ¾ parts forelocks = 12 ¼ parts.

24 This Jewish miracle worker and sectarian leader saw himself as a precursor of the Messiah. His movement originated in the reign of the Umayyad caliph Sulaymān ibn ʿAbd al-Malik (r. 96–99/715–17). He was imprisoned in Damascus and, according to some accounts, it was there that he vanished. Sean Anthony notes that "The preaching of the Shepherd and the movement it inspired marks the first known messianist apocalypticist movement to take root among the Jewish populations in the Islamic Near East" (Anthony, "Who Was the Shepherd of Damascus?" 54) and that he strongly influenced Abū ʿAlī al-Iṣfahānī (see n. 17).

25 No such device is described in the known works of the Banū Mūsā, such as the famous *Book of Ingenious Devices* (*Kitāb al-Ḥiyal*); most of their twenty or so titles are, however, lost. A staff that bursts into leaf is described later on (§§27.41–43).

26 See Q Qamar 54:1: «The Hour has drawn nigh: the moon is split» (trans. Arberry, *Koran*, 553). According to many commentators, this refers to a miracle performed by the Prophet Muḥammad to demonstrate his prophethood; according to others, it is a phenomenon that will occur on the Day of Judgment.

27 The "fake shaykhs and illusionists" to whom this chapter and a few later paragraphs (§§27.21–23, 27.39–51) are devoted represent a movement within Islam that was relatively new in the author's day, having come into being around the turn of the seventeenth/thirteenth century. This movement was identified with three widespread dervish groups—the Rifāʿīs (see §§2.22 and 2.32, where Abū l-Fatḥ al-Wāsiṭī, an early leader of the order is mentioned); the Ḥaydarīs (see §2.33); and the Qalandarīs (who are not referred to here by name, but the followers of one of whose leaders, Ḥasan al-Jawāliqī, are mentioned at §2.34). These groups were characterized by "social and religious antinomianism and a predilection for thaumaturgical practices. . . . They explored with great zest the border regions of the social and natural orders and consistently and deliberately violated conventional boundaries. The antinomian nature of their religiosity manifested itself especially in the form of mendicancy and other forms of social deviation (for instance, nudity, or improper clothing, shaving, promiscuity, use of hallucinogens and intoxicants) as well as in their preoccupation with working wonders (fire-walking,

self-cauterization and self-laceration, as well as the subjugation of wild animals)" (Karamustafa, "The Antinomian Dervish as Model Saint," 241–42). Most of these practices are alluded to by al-Jawbarī in what follows. Despite the frequent pigeonholing of such movements as manifestations of "popular" religion, they attracted members of all social classes (same reference, 254) and were often favored by the political elite (255). Karamustafa sees them as "radical protest movements that were directed against medieval society at large but, more specifically, against the kindred institution of 'respectable' Sufi orders" (258).

28 "The Righteous" (*al-ṣāliḥūn*) is a term with religious overtones, occurring several times in the Qur'an (e.g., Q A'rāf 7:168 and Q Anbiyā' 21:105). Ibn Taymiyyah saw the Righteous as one of the categories of persons who would be saved (see Ory, "Al-Ṣāliḥūn," in *EI2*).

29 Al-Junayd and the following all belong to the early, ascetic, "sober" school of mysticism acceptable to orthodox Muslims (see the Glossary).

30 Variant of a recognized hadith (see al-Hindī, *Kanz*, vol. 3, no. 5923, *Kitāb al-Akhlāq*, and vol. 13, no. 36851, *Kitāb Faḍā'il al-ṣaḥābah*).

31 Q Yūnus 10:2.

32 The breakdown given in this section conforms to the conceptualization of magic attributed by Lane to early nineteenth-century Egyptians (Lane, *An Account of the Manners and of the Customs of the Modern Egyptians*, 263–64).

33 Most of these figures cannot be identified. By Buhlūl may be meant Yaḥyā al-Buhlūl, a "wise fool" whose verses are quoted by the sixteenth-century Sufi 'Abd al-Wahhāb al-Sha'rānī (*Lawāqiḥ al-anwār fī ṭabaqāt al-akhyār*, 1:58). Juḥā is the name of a famous jester of countless anecdotes.

34 'Alī ibn 'Īsā, who was a cousin of one of al-Ḥallāj's supporters (Massignon and Gardet, "al-Ḥallādj," in *EI2*) and who may even have had a "secret sympathy" for him, in fact put an end to al-Ḥallāj's first trial in 301/913 and declined to try him when he was further accused in 306/918 (Bowen, "'Alī ibn Īsā," in *EI2*). Al-Ḥallāj was tortured and eventually executed in 309/922 in Baghdad. This poem is not in his collected works as published.

35 Cf. al-Ḥallāj, *Dīwān*, 39–40, verses 172a–174b.

36 In the sense intended here, "the science of letters" (*al-sīmiyā'*) means the exercise of control over the material world through the exploitation of the powers innate in the letters that make up the ninety-nine names of God, and is thus akin to the Jewish science of the kabala. It was considered a licit practice for pious Muslims (see further MacDonald and Fahd, "al-Sīmiyā'" in *EI2*).

37 Such miracles are perhaps the equivalent for the Righteous of the fraudulent shaykh's producing fruits and vegetables out of season described below (e.g., §§2.17–19).

38 These verses are found with differences in al-Ḥallāj's *Dīwān* (39, verses 169a–171b), but Louis Massignon, the great scholar of al-Ḥallāj, traces them to the present work and describes them as "certainly apocryphal" (Massignon, "Le *Dīwān* d'al-Ḥallāj, essai de reconstitution, édition et traduction," 36, verses 1a–3b).

39 In gnostic doctrine, the "drop" is described as "the pneumatic particle in the Gnostic through which he has the possibility of knowledge" and as "a dew of light [that has] been loosened, and [come] down into chaotic matter" (Zandee, "Gnostic Ideas on the Fall and Salvation," 67, 71); it has been equated with "the spark of life . . . the sperm" (Zandee, n37).

40 Retreats, during which the Sufi isolated himself from the world either alone or with pupils, were intended to facilitate the practice of spiritual exercises. For vivid accounts of abuse of the practice by shaykhs seeking to seduce gullible boys, see al-Shirbīnī, *Brains Confounded by the Ode of Abū Shādūf Expounded*, 1:317–19 and 1:335–37.

41 A debate over the permissibility of listening to music and of using it in, for example, the recitation of the Qur'an, has persisted in Islam for centuries (see Nelson, *The Art of Reciting the Qur'ān*, 32–51).

42 Stefan Wild comments: "In this instance [al-Jawbarī] refrains in a rather tantalizing manner from disclosing the secret, although he leaves no doubt that the pretended miracle is only a clever trick. This must mean that either [al-Jawbarī] himself did not know how it was worked, or that for the choicest of effects he preferred not to divulge the secret" (Wild, "Jugglers and Fraudulent Sufis," 60).

43 Edward Lane describes the type of baking pit (*tannūr*) intended here as "a hole made in the ground, and lined with bricks or tiles or the like, against which the bread is stuck, to bake; and sometimes flesh-meat, cut into small pieces, is roasted in it, or upon it, on skewers" (Lane, *An Arabic-English Lexicon*, 318).

44 The trick seems to work as follows: A fireproofed metal sheet fits into the upper part of the pit; the sheet has a portion removed from its side, which allows the shaykh to descend past it to a chamber beneath, the shaykh presumably depositing the dish to be cooked on the fire on his way down. He stays in the cool chamber, holding the fireproofed sheet in place with his hand. When the dish is ready, he reemerges, retrieving the dish on the way.

45 Presumably so that attention will be focused on the place where the shaykh is about to appear.

46 The gesture is perhaps to be interpreted as one of prayer or invocation. At some point, however, he must close his arms again as he has to open the mouth of the waterskin (see next paragraph).

47 "waterskin" (*sirdāb*): the translation is contextual since the common meaning of the word is "underground tunnel"; perhaps there is a scribal error.

48 The role of the oil of violets may have been to mask the smell of the narcotic mixture. Violet essence from Kufa, in Iraq, was considered to be of high quality (Lindsay, *Daily Life in the Medieval Islamic World*, 97).

49 Cf. Q Naml 27:88: «He [God] is aware of the things you do» (trans. Arberry, *Koran*, 390).

50 See §§2.10, 2.11.

51 "Salmagundi" (*khilāṭ*): from the root *kh-l-ṭ* ("to mix"), exact meaning unknown. Dozy, whose definition "a dish that is acrid and excites the thirst" perhaps derives from this passage, spells the word as given and opines that it may be "a kind of *potpourri* or *salmigondis*" (*Supplément aux dictionnaires arabes*, 1:394a). Salmagundi is "a mixed dish consisting of chopped meat, anchovies, eggs, onions, oil, etc." (Random House, *Dictionary*, 1262c).

52 Literally "pebbles of the Euphrates" (*al-ḥaṣā al-furātī*); the translation is tentative.

53 The name of an ingredient is missing here: Below, the beaten yolk is referred to as still being "set aside."

54 The word appears to be the Syriac *ṭaybūtha*, meaning "grace, kindness, favor" (https://sedra.bethmardutho.org/lexeme/get/1203 accessed 17 October 2018); the transfer to "glowworms" is unexplained.

55 I.e., the specific form of prostration mandated for the performance of ritual prayer in which the body rests on the forehead and nose, while the palms of both hands, both knees, and both feet touch the ground. That the tree touches his feet can only be explained by supposing that the shaykh has straightened up again by the time that happens; this is made clearer a little further on.

56 This and other references in al-Jawbarī's work to *ḥashīshah* (as here) and *ḥashīsh* (elsewhere, e.g., §2.33) constitute the first unambiguous use of these terms in Arabic to refer to cannabis. All occur in passages referring to antinomian dervishes. Both words mean literally "weed, grass" and, like these English terms, referred at this period to the leaves and buds of the plant and not to the prepared cannabis resin now called in English "hashish"; the latter seems to have arrived in the Arab world in the late seventeenth century, subsequent to the arrival of tobacco and smoking pipes earlier in the century. In al-Jawbarī's day, cannabis leaves and buds were eaten either roasted, with other

ingredients such as sesame seeds to make them more palatable, or made into an electuary (Daniel Jacobs, personal communication).

57 A variant of these verses is quoted by the eighth/fourteenth-century topographer al-Maqrīzī and the ninth/fifteenth-century poet Abū Bakr al-Badrī, both of whom attribute them to the otherwise unknown Aḥmad ibn Muḥammad al-Ḥalabī, known as Ibn al-Rassām or Ibn al-Zammām (Rosenthal, "The Herb," 292–93).

58 "calumniating" (*mutanammisī*): a possible alternative translation would be "hypocritical" (see Dozy, *Supplément*, 2:725a, against which Lane, *Lexicon*, 2854a *nammasa bi-ṣāḥibihi* "he calumniated his companion").

59 I.e., how to use cannabis, with its five-fingered leaf.

60 Q Ḥujurāt 49:13. The author presumably means that these shaykhs are one kind of people and true shaykhs are another, very different, kind, though the actual thrust of the verse cited is otherwise, in that it continues «that you may know one another».

61 The Rifāʿīyyah order, one of the largest and most influential in the history of Arab Sufism and still active today, was relatively new in the author's time, its spread dating to the assumption by Aḥmad ibn ʿAlī al-Rifāʿī (512–78/1106–82) of the leadership of his uncle's religious community in the southern Iraqi marshes. Writing around 654/1256, the biographer Ibn Khallikān stated that "His followers experience extraordinary states during which they eat living snakes and enter ovens blazing with fires that are thereupon extinguished" (Trimingham, *The Sufi Orders in Islam*, 38).

62 Among the antinomian dervishes of the period (see n. 33), shaving of the beard was a departure from the example of the Prophet Muḥammad and contravened established social custom; piercing of the body was a manifestation of deviation from established religious custom that increased the distance between dervish piety and social convention; and piercing of the genitals was designed to encourage celibacy. These and related practices (the use of drugs, sodomy as an alternative to socially productive sex, the use of singing and musical instruments in religious ceremonies, poverty and the rejection of property, mendicancy, etc.) were all part of the "renunciation of society through outrageous social deviance" that expressed the dervish's belief that "social life inevitably distanced humanity from God" (Karamustafa, *God's Unruly Friends*, 13ff.). According to a fifteenth-century source, however, a shortcut to asceticism was available in the case of body piercing, in that "the secret consists very simply in a hook or loop of the supposedly straight nail, lance or ring" (Wild, "Juggler's Programme," 356).

63 Followers of Ḥasan al-Jawāliqī (d. 622/1225), an Iranian antinomian Sufi, whose Qalandarī order was based in Egypt and had close relations with the Ḥarīrīs (Trimingham,

Sufi Orders, 39n8); al-Jawāliqī was so called either because he was a maker of sacks (*jawāliq*) or because he initiated the practice of wearing them, or both.

64 I.e., of the sort from which a number of lamps may be hung.

65 Preachers of this sort (*wuʿʿāẓ*) appeared from the fourth/tenth century and were distinguished from preachers who delivered sermons in mosques (*khuṭṭāb*) by the fact that they could preach anywhere and at any time. Thus, their appearance might attract huge masses of people. See further Radtke and Jansen, "Wāʿiẓ," in *EI2*.

66 Q Shuʿarāʾ 26:226 (trans. Arberry, *Koran*, 381).

67 I.e., he waits to make sure that the preacher is having some success.

68 Jesus is referred to as "a spirit from [Allah]" in the Qurʾan (Q Nisāʾ 4:171).

69 Islam holds that the religions of the People of the Book are corrupted forms of the one true religion; thus, a Christian does not convert to Islam but rather returns to it.

70 I.e., they would come to Cairo (al-Qāhirah), the Fatimid royal settlement and location of the mosque of al-Azhar, from the older settlement of Miṣr (now called Miṣr al-Qadīmah) or its surrounding settlements (Miṣr al-Fusṭāṭ, etc).

71 The Arabic *ṭarabrūb* (here translated "ukulele") may be a nonce derivation from Perso-Arabic *barbaṭ* ("Persian lute") or a playful form evoking *ṭarab* ("ecstasy brought on by listening to music").

72 "pork bellies": the Arabic (*awsāṭ khāthūniyyah*) is obscure; *awsāṭ* can mean "the middle of the body, where the belt is" (De Biberstein-Kazimirski, *Dictionnaire arabe-français*, 2:1533b); *khāthūniyyah* has not been found in any lexicon and is translated here in the spirit of the story.

73 "bile": literally "humor" (*khilṭ*, singular of *akhlāṭ*, "the (four) bodily humors"). The term apparently refers to one of the bodily humors other than phlegm, perhaps yellow or black bile.

74 A legal maxim.

75 "The Lover . . . the Beloved": the Sufi devotee and the Prophet Muḥammad.

76 The cutting by popular preachers of the hair of members of their congregations excited to repentance was a common feature of public sermons that appeared at this period. The penitent was sometimes awarded a new head covering (see Katz, "The 'Shearing of Forelocks' as a Penitential Rite").

77 It must be assumed that the preacher played the ukulele while singing the words that follow.

78 A reference to the Muslim claim that Christians have changed and distorted passages in the Bible, including those referring to the divine nature of Christ and anticipating the prophecy of Muḥammad.

79 I.e., the Church of the Holy Sepulcher; see the Glossary.

80 According to Orthodox Christian belief, the Miracle of the Holy Fire occurs each year on the day before Easter. The fire appears first in the form of a column of light that rises off the slab beneath which Christ is said to have been buried; from this fire, candles are lit, the first by the Orthodox patriarch, from whose candles those inside the church light their own candles, the fire then spreading swiftly to the candles of the crowd in the courtyard outside the church. In keeping with the description given by the author here, lamps and candles in the church are said to ignite spontaneously at the same moment.

81 Throughout this section, the author refers to as idols what others might describe as statues or automata.

82 The author appears to be unaware that the church of Ṣaydnāyā to which pilgrimage is made is in fact a convent (the Convent of Our Lady of Ṣaydnāyā) run by nuns. The miracle mainly associated with the church today is the production of oil by the breasts of the Virgin in an ancient icon.

83 The reference is to Stavrovouni, a hill whose name means "Mountain of the Cross" in Greek. The Stavrovouni Monastery is on the summit of the mountain, so may not be the one referred to by the author. The monastery does, however, have satellites elsewhere on the mountain and it may be one of these that is intended.

84 I.e., the mercury expands, as in a thermometer, forcing the water out through the eyes and also making the head move.

85 Muslim polemicists argue that the Gospels were deliberately changed, with "the meaning or words distorted, passages suppressed, others added, etc. They said that Jesus had never stated that he was God; the Trinity and the Redemption were doctrines invented by St. Paul" (Carra de Vaux and Anawati, "Indjīl," in *EI2*).

86 Despite the all-encompassing definition the author gives here, the list of activities of the Banū Sāsān detailed in the sections that follow is relatively short (eight, to which another two are added later on (§§27.7–8)) and consists of the faking of diseases and physical handicaps and the performance of elaborately staged confidence tricks; other groups, such as false apothecaries and doctors, jewelers, horse thieves, and so on, do not feature. The narrower concept may represent what the author saw as the fundamental profile of the Banū Sāsān, the broader definition a more literary extension thereof, or perhaps an attempt to find a unifying element to justify the scope of the book. Ḥājjī Khalīfah quotes Abū l-Khayr, who may be the person of that name referred to by the author as his teacher (§0.6), as describing the Banū Sāsān as practicing "a branch of the science of magic" (*Kashf al-ẓunūn*, 1:694).

87 "vagabonds" (*zuṭṭ*): the Arabic word derives from "Jat," the name of a people from northwestern India, some of whom were brought to Khuzistan and the Gulf before Islam, while others migrated or were moved in early Islamic times to Persia, the marshes of Iraq, and Syria (see Bosworth, "Zuṭṭ" in *EI2*). However, given that, despite his interest in criminal groups, the author devotes no discussion to the term, it would seem likely that he is using it here in a generalized sense, i.e., to mean simply "vagabonds"; the apparently related word *z*ṭāṭ* is used similarly elsewhere (§2.41).

88 Lane, writing in the first half of the nineteenth century, remarks that most of these "apes" were "of the cynocephalus kind" (*Manners*, 388), i.e., baboons, and therefore, technically speaking, monkeys.

89 Meaning perhaps that it threw its cloak or outer garments off its shoulders.

90 One has to assume that the carpet is on top of a dais or bench or the like.

91 The word is unclear in the original manuscripts. "Pazarköy," name of at least two villages in Anatolia, is one possible reading, though the context seems to indicate somewhere larger and wealthier.

92 Islam's first caliph (r. 11–13/632–34), who was called Dhū l-Khilāl because he wore a cloak whose edges were held together with a wooden pin (*khilāl*) (see al-Zabīdī, *Tāj al-ʿarūs*, 3:801).

93 The association of Solomon with ants is established in the Qur'an: «And his hosts were mustered to Solomon, jinn, men and birds, duly disposed; till, when they came on the Valley of Ants, an ant said, "Ants, enter your dwelling-places, lest Solomon and his hosts crush you, being unaware!" But he smiled, laughing at its words, and he said, "My Lord, dispose me that I may be thankful for Thy blessing wherewith Thou hast blessed me and my father and mother, and that I may do righteousness well-pleasing to Thee; and do Thou admit me, by Thy mercy, amongst Thy righteous servants"» (Q Naml 27:18–19, trans. Arberry, *Koran*, 383–84).

94 Of this name of God, which, unlike His other ninety-nine names, is thought to be known only to prophets and perhaps also the specially favored "wards" of God, Lane reports that "A person acquainted with it can . . . merely by uttering it, raise the dead to life, kill the living, transport himself instantly wherever he pleases, and perform any other miracle" (*Manners*, 264).

95 Q Aʿrāf 7:49.

96 The shaykh must have covered the pile of dirt with a handkerchief, though the author does not say so.

97 Apparently meaning "Let us take on his guilt (so that he be spared)."

98 By "the other day" the student means the day on which he received the portion he refers to above (§7.4). On the day of the events described, however, while each of the shaykh's companions has "cleansed" the boy, neither has himself been cleansed. Thus the follower hopes to be sodomized four times on this occasion and receive four times as much money.

99 The name of a jinni.

100 The phrase *awtād al-arḍ* ("the stakes of the Earth") may be taken figuratively to mean "the mountains" but here also evokes the Sufi hierarchy of "the men of the unseen" (*rijāl al-ghayb*), whose hidden influence helps to preserve the order of the universe; in this hierarchy, the "stakes" are generally considered to be the third rank after the "pole" (*al-quṭb*) who heads it (see Goldziher, "Awtād," and Goldziher and Kissling, "Abdāl," in *EI2*).

101 Q Aʿrāf 7:49 (trans. Arberry, *Koran*, 149).

102 The saying is of dubious status as a hadith but well known in the Levant as a proverb.

103 I.e., the robe is to be hitched up and tied into a knot, as is often done when a man wants to free his legs for work or to avoid getting the robe dirty, and the money (contained in a money bag, which will be referred to later) is secured inside the knotted part.

104 The name of a jinni.

105 See al-Hindī, *Kanz* 4, nos. 10887 and 11396, *Kitāb al-Jihād*.

106 Under Islamic law, war is a collective duty (*farḍ al-kifāya*), binding on the community as a whole (Khadduri et al., "Ḥarb," in *EI2*).

107 This crossbow (*qaws jarkh*, from Arabic *qaws* "bow" plus Persian *charkh* "wheel") was a one-pedal arbalest whose bow was pulled back by a wheel, allowing the firing of arrows the length of javelins (see Boudot-Lamotte, "Ḳaws," in *EI2*).

108 The word used here for yew (*taqsh*) is assumed to be a variant of the more common *ṭakhsh*; however, since *takhshīqiyūn* (from Greek *toxikon*) means "poison used for arrows" (Dozy, *Supplément*, 2:29a), it may be that "poisoned arrows" are meant.

109 The Maghrebi, or North African, siege engine was a form of counterweighted catapult or trebuchet (see Hill, "Mand̲j̲anīḳ," in *EI2*). The author's description is hard to follow and, insofar as it can be followed, problematic, not least because the Maghrebi trebuchet is normally portrayed as mounted on a trestle, which argues against it being able to "shoot in all directions."

110 A photograph of the trebuchet with double windlass at Middelaldercentret in Denmark can be seen at Wikipedia, art. "Trebuchet" (http://en.wikipedia.org/wiki/Trebuchet#CITEREFChevedden2000, accessed March 26, 2018).

111 In this year, the Ayyubid ruler al-Malik al-Kāmil (r. 615–35/1218–38) set siege to and recovered Damietta, seized by the Crusaders two years earlier.

112 The manuscripts used for this edition do not contain an illustration at this point.

113 I.e., they open out the ladder, which is jointed in the middle and originally folded, to make it into a single rigid structure like a ramp.

114 *Kāf*, the twenty-second letter of the Arabic alphabet, is the first letter of *kīmiyā'* ("alchemy"), from the Greek *khēmia*, meaning "the art of casting or alloying metals" (Ullmann, "al-Kīmiyā'" in *EI2*).

115 "sauce" (*dakkah* or *dukkah*): a jargon word for a substance that somehow "stretches" gold and silver (as here) to greater than their original bulk or (as in most of the following examples) makes base metal appear to be gold; it is the false alchemists' equivalent of the true alchemists' "elixir." The real aim of the scam is not, however, the seeming production of gold but the impression this leaves on those who witness it and their consequent hosting and funding of the false alchemist, as described below.

116 I.e., pay out a little to gain a lot.

117 A standard weight of the time (around 0.05 grams).

118 I.e., the apparent bottom of the crucible, which is in fact the bottom of its upper compartment, is perforated.

119 The man who has sold the ingot at a profit is guilty of practicing usury, a sin in both Islam and Christianity, as he has made money from money. The money gained above the approved price must therefore be rendered religiously acceptable by using it for a charitable act, such as feeding others.

120 "Apartment" (*qā'ah*): the word implies a lofty room in the upper, private, quarters of a large house (see Lane, *Manners*, 16).

121 See n. 119.

122 Above, 'anklets.'

123 Unidentified, and perhaps a fictitious personage invented by the shopkeeper, who appears to be in cahoots with the false alchemist.

124 To make sure that there were no clipped or counterfeit coins among them.

125 See n. 24; the Shepherd is usually described as having disappeared in Damascus, leaving no trace.

126 The third son of Adam and Eve, who is said, however, to have lived and died in Mecca.

127 "heezmaydafulautovyu" (*ṭanazbak*): part of the appeal of this name, which is made up of *ṭanaz* ("he's made a fool") and *-bak* ("out of you"), is that, even though it is made up, it is evocative of genuine but exotic and non-Arabic-sounding plant names such as *wakhshīzak* (santonica) (see §14.9), which is also described as coming from Khurasan.

128 I.e., alchemy.

129 I.e., the Seljuk ruler in Khurasan, Nūr al-Dīn Zangī's overlord.

130 I.e., the philosopher's stone; see further §27.6.

131 Meaning unknown.

132 In the Arabic, "from the grains," apparently in error for "flower head" or something similar.

133 Lapis lazuli was used to treat a wide variety of ailments. The fourteenth-century physician Dāwūd al-Anṭākī, for instance, prescribed it for leprosy and other skin diseases, to help mad people, to remedy eye ailments, to improve the general health of the body, and to make people happy (Lev and Amar, *Practical Materia Medica of the Medieval Eastern Mediterranean According to the Cairo Genizah*, 196).

134 Perhaps meaning lapis lazuli in rock form as opposed to the previously described wash.

135 "Dyers' weed" (*ḥashīshat al-ṣabbāghīn*) is not found elsewhere in the literature; it may be a generic vernacular or local term covering *wasmah* and *ghubayrā'*, two plants that themselves have multiple identifications, of which the most likely in the context of dyestuffs, is dyers' croton (*Chrozophora tinctoria*). The issue is further complicated by the occurrence below (§17.3) of *ghubayrā'* alongside dyers' weed in a recipe; what is meant in that case may be the closely related folded croton (*Chrozophora plicata*), which is also used as a dye.

136 From the first letter of *maṭālib*, meaning "treasure hoards" (Dozy, *Supplément*, 2:52b); such treasure hunters were also known as *maṭālibiyyah*.

137 Despite the new heading and the wording ("Exposé"), what follows is a continuation of the preceding story.

138 Presumably, the plan is to retrieve the bag of money from the sea later.

139 The term "astrologers" (*munajjimūn*) is used loosely here, with the trades discussed below covering not only activities that involve stars or planets but also prognostications using other means, such as geomancy and even mind reading.

140 According to Dozy, astrologers are called *ghurabā'* "because they do extraordinary things" (*Supplément*, 2:205) rather than because they are "strangers" (the more common sense of the word); see also §27.32 below. Later on (§17.16), the term is applied to "doctors who practice on the highway" and, in some other sources, to the Banū Sāsān in general (as in Ibn Dāniyāl's shadow play *'Ajīb wa-Gharīb*, where the eponymous hero Gharīb "in some sense embodies the entire profession . . . of the Banū Sāsān" (Jacob, *Ein ägyptischer Jahrmarkt im 13. Jahrhundert*, 6)) and where the latter's jargon, or cant, is called *lughat al-ghurabā'* ("the language of the wonder-workers") (see Bosworth, *Underworld*, 1:158).

141 The author says more about *Sīn* at §27.32 below.

142 I.e., astrologers claiming skill in interpreting the significance of birth dates and, it would seem, in the use of the *Book of Balhān* (or *Bulhān*). Such a book is alluded to by Ṣafī al-Dīn al-Ḥillī in his *Qaṣīdah Sāsāniyyah*, as "my *balhān*," which Bosworth translates as "my book of magical drawings and incantations" (Bosworth, *Underworld*, 2:298). A manuscript in the Bodleian Library with the same title, authored by the otherwise unknown ʿAbd al-Ḥasan (?) ibn Aḥmad ibn al-Ḥasan al-Iṣfahānī al-Baghdādī, dates from the ninth/fifteenth century and contains descriptions of "numerous astrological and divinatory practices, as well as many exotica. . . . It begins with explanations concerning birth dates. . . ." (Ullmann, *Die Natur- und Geheimwissenschaften im Islam*, 344–45).

143 This class of astrologers is not further described.

144 It is worth noting that all these "props and tricks," no matter how elaborate, simply serve to soften up the charlatan's audience and convince its members that he has sufficient occult power to make his amulets effective and worth buying.

145 The term *ṭurūs* used here appears in other sources as *ṭurūsh* (singular *ṭarsh*) (e.g., Bosworth, *Underworld*, 2: verse 39; see also Bulliet, "Ṭarsh," in *EI2*).

146 Or "large imposing buildings"; used elsewhere in the book in another specialized sense—namely, "the great magic formulas" (§0.4).

147 The point of this preparatory exercise must be to convince the onlookers that the man has supernatural vision, which allows him to perform such a delicate operation even while blindfolded.

148 The name of a person's mother (which is routinely requested during these tricks, see §§12.10, 12.14, 12.19) is believed to have more power than that of their father and is also used in blessing and cursing.

149 Implying that the pieces of cloth from which the amulets are made are taken from the covering of the Kaaba at Mecca, which is changed annually.

150 I.e., an emir named Sayf al-Dīn ("Sword of Religion") or Shihāb al-Dīn ("Star of Religion") or something similar.

151 Saturn and Mars (see Wahrmund, *Handwörterbuch der neu-arabischen und deutschen Sprache*, 2:992a).

152 The words "they'd still be worth it" are not in the Arabic but seem to be required.

153 I.e., the Prophet Muḥammad, whose father's name is traditionally given as ʿAbd Allāh.

154 The term *maqlab* (plural *maqālib*), describing a two-chamber paper box made of two tetrahedrons glued together, is not known from other sources but must derive from *qalaba* ("to turn over"); "flip box" seeks to reflect this.

155 Presumably meaning the largest of the four sides of a pyramid.

156 The author glosses *hankāmah* (from Persian "circle") for his lay readership because it is a jargon term.

157 See §§12.2–6.

158 Only four lines are provided below.

159 In the text, "line" (*bayt*), but only "word" makes sense in the context of the trick. It is also presumably the case that the letter in question is either the first or the last letter of the word, depending on what has been previously agreed.

160 At this point, one would expect, but does not find, a phrase such as "and so on through the poem."

161 The Arabic is illegible in places and seems to be corrupt. The meaning, so far as it can be reconstructed, is: Fate made obeisance to glorious fortune / the young man's fortune was unclouded, an elevated fortune / For one victorious, his aroma like wine / his boon companion a king of pearly hue / And a face whose side . . . / a beloved, a dear one, wide (?), seduced / Strong, one who does not neglect a weak man / A suppressor of his anger, whose anger is vehement, low (?).

162 It seems likely, though the text is not absolutely clear, that what follows is a second, separate, method for producing the illusion of mind reading, using the same lines of verse.

163 The values given for the numbers of letters (1 + 2 + 4 + 7 +15) add up to 29, which is the number of letters in the Arabic alphabet if one includes (as is traditionally the case) the grapheme *lā*. The application, however, remains obscure.

164 "My two dear friends, do you believe this gazelle / will cure my anguish? Should God judge in my favor, he will be spared!"

165 The hadith is unidentified. Its relevance lies in a double entendre, as the sentence may also be understood to mean "Tip them and beg from them."

166 Though the dodecatemoria are a concept in genuine astrology, being any of twelve segments into which a zodiacal sign may be divided (and as such parallel to the "ninth-parts," see the Glossary), the term seems to be used here merely as an example of the jumble of terms listed in this section as being misused by fake astrologers.

167 I.e., made four rows of holes in the sand and derived a reading from them.

168 The story contains two unusual elements. First, no other references to forty Hermeses (as distinct from three, see the Glossary, *Hermes Trismegistus*) have been found in the literature. Second, geomancy was not one of the sciences taught in the books attributed to Hermes. More broadly, the story may represent an attempt by al-Jawbarī's source to attenuate the potentially problematic identification of the prophet Idrīs with the pagan sage Hermes. Despite this, al-Jawbarī has made that connection earlier (see §0.3) and confirms it immediately below (§12.25).

169 A version of a hadith whose more common form runs *kāna nabiyyun mina l-anbiyāʾ yakhuṭṭu fa-man wāfaqa khaṭṭahu fa-dhāka* (or *fa-dhālika*), the last word apparently meaning "then that is acceptable" (see al-Hindī, *Kanz,* vol. 15, nos. 28365 and 29144, *Kitāb al-ʿIlm wa-l-ruqā wa-l-ṭāʿūn* and *Kitāb al-ʿIlm*). Some commentators, however, have reached the opposite conclusion to that drawn by al-Jawbarī, stressing that it would be impossible for any ordinary person to do it "as [the prophet] did" because that skill was a gift granted the latter by God to prove his prophethood; according to this interpretation, the practice is effectively prohibited (see, e.g., http://islamport.com/w/aqd/Web/1809/706.htm, accessed November 28, 2018).

170 A "position" (*bayt*) is one of the sixteen component parts, each occupied by a geomantic figure, of the design from which a geomancer derives his divination (see Savage-Smith and Smith, *Islamic Geomancy and a Thirteenth-Century Divinatory Device,* 11). The terms "outcome" and "interconnection" are also technical terms of geomancy.

171 I.e., probably, of a (clear) glass and not of the then-common dark-green or brown cut glass.

172 As though one of the jinn were speaking.

173 How the braided string is released is not specified.

174 The scenario described seems to require that the conjuror is in the "parlor" (*majlis*), i.e., a room to which he as a guest would have access, while the women are in the main part of the house.

175 I.e., the seer.

176 Epilepsy was believed to be caused by spirit possession and treatable by exorcism.

177 It is unclear which covenant is referred to; the word may be used simply for effect.

178 Perhaps meaning bear bile, or simply invented.

179 Cyclamens have large tubers from which the roots grow and which lend themselves to carving. They are widely distributed around the Mediterranean and are dormant in summer.

180 See §12.1 ff.

181 Catastrophic spikes in food prices occurred when the Nile flood either failed to rise high enough, or rose too high, to irrigate the land properly. During the likely lifetime of the author, the flood failed in the three years 587–89/1191–93, when a third of the population died, and again in 597/1201 and 627/1230, in both of which years there was famine (Toussoun, *Mémoire sur l'histoire du Nil,* 2:474–75).

182 The worms referred to are those that were believed, in the Middle East as elsewhere, to cause dental caries. See also Chapter 15.

183 The verses are from al-Ḥarīrī's forty-fourth *maqāmah*, *al-Maqāmah al-shatawiyyah* ("the Winter Maqāmah") (see al-Ḥarīrī, *Maqāmāt*, 390).

184 The point seems to be that the quack uses, and charges for, expensive ingredients while using cheap ones.

185 I.e., alkanet (*Alkanna tinctoria*).

186 "Penetrating oil" has not, in fact, been mentioned and is not referred to later on.

187 Perhaps meaning bile (see §14.1 and n. 178).

188 From *rawshanā'ī*, Persian for "brilliant". These and the "dust-colored" and other names for collyrium mentioned further on (§§14.18, 14.20) seem to be commercial appellations.

189 The word is Syriac and means "royal."

190 The term occurs elsewhere in medieval medical works and apparently means "sweet and sour pomegranates" (see, e.g., Ibn al-Bayṭār, *al-Jāmiʿ*, II:142–143).

191 The author regards the disease he calls "canker" (Arabic *ākilah*) as a genuine disease, difficult to treat, that results in the presence of something resembling nits on the eyelids. The quack eye doctor's crime is to claim that this putrid matter is indeed nits and to introduce something resembling nits into the cankered eyelids so that he can subsequently remove them. In such cases, then, the disease is of the quack's making, not the Almighty's.

192 Though the Arabic refers throughout the rest of the paragraph to "the feather" as the object that is introduced into, and then removed from, the eye to produce the false impression that a fistula has been discovered and excised, the statement further down that this object "returns to its former state" seems to imply that it is this snippet of quill that is so used; the translation follows this interpretation.

193 I.e., the inflammation caused by the fake treatment.

194 Silver pieces with a high copper content.

195 Uniquely, in this section, the author explicitly discusses the organizing principle of a part of the work. Perhaps he originally wrote up this category of charlatan here as a separate item, then decided to incorporate it with other similar categories. On "quacks who practice on the highway," see §§14.1–26.

196 "leaves of cloves" (*waraq al-nawr al-aḥmar*): the identification is tentative and based on the parallel at §10.5 with *ʿūd al-nawr*, meaning "cloves" (Dozy, *Supplément*, 187a, where the name is given in the form *ʿūd al-nuwār*). Clove flowers are bright red.

197 Q Infiṭār 82:8, trans. Arberry, *Koran*, 634.

198 The "wiseguys" (*shuṭṭār*; literally "clever ones") were members of hunting fraternities who had come to constitute disreputable militias; in the *Thousand and One Nights*, the term is used more loosely to mean a "crafty rogue" (Irwin, *Arabian Nights*, 148).

199 The text appears confused and is perhaps corrupt, but the sense seems to be that a mixture is made, used on the face as a poultice, and then made into pills (which can presumably be dissolved and used the same way). This is in keeping with the methods described in the following paragraphs.

200 Or perhaps "turtle fat" (see Lane, *Lexicon*, 7:2651c).

201 I.e., 234 grams of gold.

202 "wheat oil" and "rice oil": presumably, wheat-germ oil and rice-bran oil.

203 A Qur'anic echo: «and [We] strengthened him with the holy spirit» (Q Baqarah 2:253, trans. Wahiduddin Khan, tanzil.net, accessed June 19, 2018); the admonition is presumably addressed to the emir Rukn al-Dīn, who commissioned the book.

204 The meaning is unclear—perhaps sugar mixed with olive oil.

205 Vinegar was used widely in medications (see Lev and Amar, *Materia Medica*, 176 passim).

206 Money and valuables were carried concealed in the waistband.

207 "'Blue Cretan' henbane" (*al-banj al-azraq al-Aqrīṭishī*): according to Dozy, the description "Cretan" was conventionally associated with the narcotic *banj* ("henbane") and could even stand for it (*Supplément*, 1:30a). At the same time, there is no plant conventionally known as "blue henbane." The term "blue Cretan" henbane may thus have been a nickname, or a commercial name, for this particular concoction, perhaps because of the association of blueness with darkness, and even with the Devil (see Dozy, *Supplément*, 588b).

208 I.e., burning sulfur, because of the color of the flame emitted.

209 I.e., "sulfur" (see preceding note).

210 Understanding, "even though it is false."

211 Some of the subsequent descriptions of tricks and devices are difficult to follow and the translations are tentative. As Stefan Wild writes, "These technical descriptions are a great problem in al-Djaubarī as well as in the other sources. The authors lacked the technical vocabulary and skill to give a description of the niveau of the Banū Mūsā or al-Djazarī. In many cases even the description of the effect of the instrument is obscure, and the instruction how to make it, is hopeless" ("Juggler's Programme," 359n11a).

212 The reference seems to be to a form of the routine nowadays called "cups and balls." From the reference to concealing the ball (here, a nut) under the little finger close to the bottom of the cup, one infers that the magician makes the ball pass through the supposedly solid bottom of the cup. Wild mentions that in medieval Europe, as here (based on the fact that the author lists it first), this trick was "considered the most famous and characteristic feat in a juggler's programme" and that a description of its execution by a

Greek juggler has come down to us from the second century AD (Wild, "Juggler's Programme," 354).

213 The trick appears to be the same as that described by Edward Lane in the early nineteenth century: "Taking a silver finger-ring from one of the bystanders, he puts it in a little box, blows his shell, and says, 'Efreet, change it!' He then opens the box, and shows in it a different ring: shuts the box again; opens it, and shows the first ring; shuts it a third time; opens it, and shows a melted lump of silver, which he declares to be the ring melted, and offers to the owner. The latter insists upon having his ring in its original state. The Háwee [conjurer] then asks for five or ten faddahs [copper coins] to recast it; and having obtained this, opens the box again (after having closed it, and blown his shell) and takes out of it the perfect ring" (Lane, *Manners*, 385).

214 Wild points out with respect to this and the following three tricks that "the construction of such vessels stands in a very respectable tradition, that of pneumatical instruments, mostly working according to the principle of *horror vacui*, as described by Heron of Alexandria, Philo, Appolonius of Tyana, and others. Such Greek writings had been translated by Syrian Christians such as Thābit ibn Qurra and this tradition was then taken over by Arab scientists like the Banū Mūsā" ("Juggler's Programme," 355).

215 "a curved piece with two hinges on a crossbar" (*ukrah bi-lawlabayni ʿalā manjarat [?] al-ʿirāḍ*): the Arabic is obscure and, in the case of the word transcribed as *manjarat*, not even entirely legible. One envisages a metal disk divided in half and hinged (creating two flaps), and capable of being threaded onto a crossbar set athwart the inside of the jug. The flaps would hang down from the crossbar when the jug is upright, but would fall open, blocking the passage of liquid, when it is turned upside down.

216 I.e., some jewelers are well versed in and use scientific methods to cheat people, presumably by selling at a high price material they know to be fake; others use their scientific knowledge to actually manufacture items such as fake gemstones; and yet others are ignorant of these techniques and resort to simpler tricks, such as simply passing off as gems colored glass that they themselves have not manufactured.

217 The author clarifies the meaning of *jawhar* because the latter can also mean "gemstones." That said, his identification of *jawhar* with *lu'lu* ("small pearls") and contrasting of it with *durr* ("large pearls") does not conform to standard usage (cf. Abul Huda, *Arab Roots of Gemology*, 84).

218 There is irony in the fact that the man's name means literally "Upright in His Religion."

219 A misquotation from al-Ḥarīrī's twenty-eighth *Maqāmah* (al-Ḥarīrī, *Maqāmāt*), in which the narrator, al-Ḥārith, discovers that the hero, Abū Zayd, despite preaching by day in the mosque of Samarqand, drinks wine at night; Abū Zayd asks him to keep his hypocrisy

secret, and not only does al-Ḥārith do so, he even goes around telling everyone that Abū Zayd is as abstemious as the ascetic Hadith transmitter al-Fuḍayl ibn ʿIyāḍ (187/803).

220 This reticence on the author's part should perhaps be taken in the context of the alchemical principle of the "dispersal of knowledge," which dictated that the entire undivided truth should never be revealed in one place (Ullmann, *Geheimwissenschaften*, 1–2, 4).

221 Carob seeds were used as standard weights, equivalent to one twenty-fourth of a dinar.

222 I.e., Jamāl al-Dīn would concede and take the money, though under protest.

223 Thus, what follows is not a resumé of material already covered, but a presentation, in summary form, of new material on categories of charlatan, all but one of which (diviners and fortune tellers) has already been encountered. The categories are alchemists (§§27.2–6), members of the Banū Sāsān (§§27.7–10), apothecaries (§§27.11–18), dervishes (§§27.19–23), treasure hunters (§§27.24–31), astrologers (§27.32), false prophets (§§27.33–38), false Sufi masters (§§27.39–51), diviners and fortune tellers (§§27.52–54), itinerant quacks (§§27.55–57), and prestidigitators (§§27.58–60).

224 "the white" (*al-bayāḍ*): an alchemical term for silver (Ullmann, *Geheimwissenschaften*, 260).

225 "reddening" (*al-taḥmīr*): an alchemical term meaning "the making of gold" (Ullmann, *Geheimwissenschaften*, 262).

226 "spirits" (*arwāḥ*): an alchemical term for substances that become volatile when exposed to heat (Ullmann, *Geheimwissenschaften*, 141).

227 "bodies" (*ajsād*): an alchemical term for substances that remain stable when heated and do not change color or evaporate (Ullmann, *Geheimwissenschaften*, 141, 149).

228 "souls" (*anfās*): an alchemical term apparently covering a category parallel to the "spirits" (volatile substances) and "bodies" (metals) referred to above; Rhazes too refers to a third category, which he calls "stones" (*aḥjār*) and which consists of "stones, vitriols, borates, and salts" (Garbers and Weyer, *Quellengeschichtliches Lesebuch zur Chemie und Alchemie der Araber im Mittelalter*, 2–5 (Text 2), 8–9 (Text 5)), and this may be what is meant here.

229 I.e., for whitening both realgar and orpiment (see §27.2).

230 I.e., a particular kind of pounding surface used for braying walnuts, perfumes, etc., especially one made of basalt.

231 This great (or, below, venerable) stone is the philosopher's stone of European alchemy—a substance capable of transforming base metals into gold and bestowing immortality.

232 Of the philosopher's stone, al-Khawārazmī states in his *Mafātīḥ al-ʿulūm*: "According to [the alchemists], it is the thing that makes the Craft possible, which is to say it is that from which the elixir is produced. It is of two kinds, animal and mineral. The animal is

better. Its subcategories are the hair, the blood, the urine, the eyes, the gall, the brain, the brainpan, the ear, and the horns" (see Wiedemann, *Schriften*, 1:208–10).

233 I.e., he pretends to drop and break the container, revealing the broken potsherds inside and making people think he has smashed a container's-worth of pottery.

234 Since neither buckhorn plantain nor wormwood are in themselves poisonous, the deadly effect must come either from the unidentified "line plant" (also referred to at §13.10 as a hallucinogen) or from a reaction produced by the combination of the three plants.

235 Artificiality here lies in the fact that the verdigris is produced through human intervention rather than forming naturally, for example by weathering.

236 Probably a reference to §27.4 above.

237 Meaning that he journeyed as a devotee from one saint's tomb to another.

238 Dervishes often wore coats made of pieces of clothes donated to them and then torn up and restitched, as a token of their rejection of worldly belongings and concerns.

239 Given that they were in the city in which the Prophet Muhammad raised his family, this would no doubt have happened frequently.

240 The jousting target (*birjās*), used in the training of Mamluk cavalry, consisted of a ball or plate mounted on a pole, which the trainee had to hit with his lance; no exact description of the device exists but it may have first given way and then sprung back into place, as one would expect the false step described by the author to do.

241 I.e., sets about robbing him.

242 In this case, the perspective has shifted: Now the charlatan, rather than luring and robbing people who believe he has found treasure (which he has not) finds someone who knows the location of a real treasure, gets him to tell him its location, and kills him. In the next sentence, the narrative reverts to the original perspective.

243 *Sīn* is the twelfth letter of the Arabic alphabet and the first letter of *sīmiyā'*, meaning "natural magic," which may explain its use, as here, to mean "argot, cant" (see Rowson, "Cant and Argot in Cairo Colloquial Arabic," 16).

244 As the short vowels and in some cases even the dots necessary to transcribe these words are not supplied, as the ductus of certain words is illegible, and as the author does not explain their meaning, the transcription given here is somewhat arbitrary. However, given that the *Sīn*, like cant in other languages, is not a complete language but a set of lexical items (despite the fact that the author appears to believe the opposite), it may be that some of the words should be understood as ordinary Arabic. The likeliest candidates are *mā* ("what?" or negative particle), *fī* ("in"), and *yurīd* ("he wants").

245 See §12.1 above.

246 I.e., illusions in the style of those described in the pseudo-Platonic *Book of Illusions* (see the Glossary).

247 Sinān was in fact the chief lieutenant of the Nizārī imam of Alamut rather than his successor.

248 "Wise fools," of the kind this man appears to portray himself as being, were associated with vagrancy (represented here by his living off the land) and holding or riding a staff or reed like a hobbyhorse (see, e.g., al-Shirbīnī, *Brains Confounded*, 2:187 and n. 304).

249 Q Raʻd 13:39.

250 A "slice" (*sharīḥah*) is jargon for a small amulet (see §§12.2–6). The term "triangle" (*muthallathah*) has not occurred before; perhaps what is meant is a triangular leather pouch in which to put the slice.

251 I.e., January; Kānūn al-Awwal (Kānūn the First) and Kānūn al-Thānī (Kānūn the Second) are the twelfth and first months, respectively, of the Syriac solar calendar used in the eastern Arab countries for agricultural and other purposes. In post-classical usage, Kānūn al-Thānī is sometimes referred to, as here, as Kānūn al-Aṣamm, meaning "the Speechless," supposedly because "people are quiet during it, owing to the copiousness of the rains and the extreme cold" (al-Bustānī, *Kitāb Muḥīṭ al-muḥīṭ*, 1:1309a; see also Popper, *Egypt and Syria under the Circassian Sultans, 1382–1468 A.D.*, 2:30).

252 According to Lane, summarizing a number of dictionaries, the *ṣill* is "[a serpent against which charming is of no avail . . . or a serpent that kills at once when it bites . . . or a yellow serpent . . . in the case of which charming is of no avail . . . or a yellow serpent that is found in the sand; when a man sees it, he ceases not to tremble until he dies" (Lane, *Lexicon*, 1710b).

253 This clause (and the same further down in this paragraph) are hard to interpret; here, they have been taken to be quotations from the quack's patter.

254 The words, though attributed to Aristotle by certain medieval Arab scholars and used by poets such as al-Mutanabbī (see, for example, Ibn Ḥamdūn, *al-Tadhkirah al-Ḥamdūniyyah*, 1:278–79), belong to the vast corpus of pseudo-Aristotelian writings.

255 Perhaps a reference to the narrator's own girlfriend.

256 Apparently, the family lives in the suburbs and the husband commutes.

257 I.e., the man's girlfriend put food behind the curtain for her imaginary cousin to eat, and the men sat and ate together in the room.

258 I.e. "I'm her husband"; parallel cousin marriage being traditionally favored in Arab societies, the term "my paternal cousin" is often used to mean "my spouse."

259 Probably meaning his *Kitāb al-Maḥāsin wa-l-aḍdād* (*Book of Virtues and Their Opposites*), which contains chapters entitled "The Virtues of Women's Wiles" and "The Vices of Women's Wiles."

260 I.e., slaves.

Glossary of People, Places, and Little-Known Simples

For plants and fungi, see "Appendix 2: Plants and Fungi Mentioned in *The Book of Charlatans*" on the Book Supplements page of the Library of Arabic Literature website, at www.libraryofarabicliterature.org/extra-2/.

ʿAbd Allāh al-Ghumārī an unidentified member of the Berber tribe of the Ghumārah, of western Morocco, whose members are said to have had a talent for magic.

ʿAbd Allāh ibn Hilāl al-Kūfī perhaps the same as Abū Naṣr Aḥmad ibn Hilāl al-Bakīl, a maker of spells of the kind permitted by the Qurʾan, who is mentioned by fourth/tenth-century bibliographer Ibn al-Nadīm.

ʿAbd Allāh ibn Maymūn ibn Muslim ibn ʿAqīl i.e., ʿAbd Allāh ibn Maymūn al-Qaddāḥ, supposedly the great-grandson of ʿAqīl ibn Abī Ṭālib, brother of ʿAlī ibn Abī Ṭālib, nephew and son-in-law of the Prophet Muḥammad. He was regarded by some as the founder of the Qarmatian-Ismaili doctrine and was the grandfather of ʿUbayd Allāh al-Mahdī, first caliph of the Fatimid Dynasty (r. 297–322/909–34).

al-Abshīṭ an ancient and still-existing village in the district of al-Maḥallah al-Kubrā in Egypt's central Delta.

Shaykh ʿAbd al-Ṣamad al-Ishbīlī an individual credited by the author with having constructed a "Maghrebi siege engine" that was used at Damietta in 617/1220–21.

Abū Bakr al-Ṣiddīq (r. 10–12/632–634) the first caliph, successor to the Prophet Muḥammad as leader of the Muslim community.

Abū l-Fatḥ al-Wāsiṭī (d. 615/1218–19) a leader of the Rifāʿiyyah Sufi order, which he brought to Egypt from its birthplace in Wāsiṭ in southern Iraq. Despite the author's claim that al-Wāsiṭī was a fake shaykh, his order was well established in the author's day and survives to the present.

Abū l-Khayr perhaps the Abū l-Khayr cited by the eleventh/seventeenth-century bibliographer Ḥājjī Khalīfah as his sole authority on the Banū Sāsān.

Abū l-Qāsim Dhā l-Nūn al-Ikhmīmī (ca. 180–246/796–861) also known as Abū l-Farḍ Thawbān ibn Ibrāhīm Dhū l-Nūn al-Miṣrī or simply Dhū l-Nūn al-Miṣrī (Dhū l-Nūn the Egyptian), born in Ikhmīm (today, Akhmīm) in Upper Egypt; Dhā l-Nūn is a vernacular form of the name. As one of the first mystics to systematize Sufi thought, he is regarded as a founding father by many Sufi traditions. Much legend has accrued around him, such as that early in life he worked as a guard at a temple at Ikhmīm and knew the language of the Ancient Egyptians and that he practiced alchemy and magic. He has shrines in Cairo and al-Lidd, Palestine.

ʿAdawī a member of the ʿAdawī clan of the Quraysh, who were assigned to guard the Kaaba.

agarwood agarwood, also known as aloeswood or aloe wood, is formed in the heartwood of aquilaria trees (*Aquilaria* spp.) that have been infected with a type of mold (*Phialophora parasitica*).

Akhnūkh the biblical Enoch, a figure who, it is claimed, entered Heaven as a mortal.

ʿAlawī a descendant of ʿAlī ibn Abī Ṭālib, the Prophet Muḥammad's cousin and son-in-law, who is specially revered by Shiites.

Alexander Alexander the Great (356–323 BC), mentioned in the Qur'an (Q Kahf 18:83, 86) under the name of Dhū l-Qarnayn ("the Two-Horned"). He is accepted as a Muslim and, by some, as a prophet.

Alexandretta a small town near Antakya, in southeast Turkey, now called Iskenderun.

Āmid a city in southeast Turkey, now called Diyarbakir.

animodar a set of rules for choosing an imaginary ascendant for the nativity of the subject of an astrological reading, required because the determination of the exact moment of birth is close to impossible.

Anṣinā Arabic name of the ancient city of Antinopolis, now the village of Shaykh ʿIbādah, on the east bank of the Nile near Mallawi, al-Minya, Upper Egypt.

antimony a chemical element with symbol Sb found in nature as a lustrous gray metalloid, mainly as the sulfide mineral stibnite.

Apollonius (Arabic, Balīnās and Balīnūs) probably Apollonius of Tyana (ca. AD 15–100), a shadowy neo-Pythagorean philosopher from Anatolia to whom in the Western tradition miracles are attributed and who in the

Arabic tradition is regarded as an expert on magic and talismans and as the author of *The Book of the Seven Idols* (*Kitāb al-Aṣnām al-sabʿah*).

ʿArabā see *fortess of ʿArabā*.

Aratos Aratos of Silo, a Greek didactic poet of the fourth to third century BC, whose best-known work is the *Phenomena* (*Appearances*), which describes the constellations.

Arḍ al-Ṭabbālah literally "the Drummer-Woman's Ground," after a piece of land given in 450/1058 by the Fatimid caliph al-Mustanṣir to a woman who led a troupe of drummers that played before him on formal occasions. The land lay between the Egyptian Canal (al-Khalīj al-Miṣrī) to its east and the Nile in the area of today's Fajjālah District and would have been subjected in the author's day to annual flooding and annual deposits of Nile silt.

Āṣaf ibn Barakhyā ibn Shamwīl King Solomon's maternal nephew, vizier, and confidant.

ʿAydhāb a port on the Red Sea coast in Egypt's far southeast that served the Yemen trade from perhaps as early as the Ptolemaic period and became the point of departure for pilgrims from East Africa going to Mecca until it was destroyed by Mamluk sultan Barsbay in AD 1426.

al-Azhar see *mosque of al-Azhar*.

Badal an unidentified Turkmen Sufi shaykh, present in Egypt at the same time as the author. As a term among Sufis, *badal* (literally "substitute") refers to one of the company of forty saints who form the second tier in the hierarchy of mystical leadership under the *quṭb*, or "pole."

Baghdad cut a paper size of one cubit by one and a half cubits "of the Egyptian cloth cubit," i.e., probably fifty-eight by eighty-seven centimeters, or more than 50 percent larger than today's folio size. It was used in Mamluk times for certificates of allegiance to the caliph and similar documents.

al-Bahnasā ancient Oxyrhynchus, a town on the Nile, in Middle Egypt, in the district of Banī Mazār, province of al-Minya.

the Baḥriyyah an unidentified subsection of the Ḥaydarī dervishes; the literal meaning is "those of the sea; the navy," though it may equally well derive from the male given name Baḥr, in which case they would be "the Followers of Baḥr."

baked-brick oil olive oil in which glowing fragments of brick have been quenched and which is then cooked along with the bits of pulverized brick.

balsam of Mecca the resinous exudate of the Arabian balsam tree (*Commiphora gileadensis*); called in the Bible "balm of Gilead."

Bāniyās an ancient city in the Golan Heights southwest of Damascus (not the modern city of Baniyas on the Syrian coast).

Banū Mūsā "the Sons of Mūsā": three brothers (in order of seniority, Muḥammad, Aḥmad, and al-Ḥasan), who played a leading role in the intellectual life of Baghdad in the third/ninth century as patrons of scientists and translators and who are known to have themselves written some twenty works on mathematics, astronomy, and mechanics.

Banū Sāsān "the Sons of Sāsān," i.e., the followers of a certain Sāsān, often called Shaykh Sāsān, who is said by the Persian writer Ibn al-Muqaffaʿ (early second/eighth c.) to have been the son of a Persian emperor who, deprived of the succession, traveled the world and gathered around him a following of like-minded roamers. In *The Book of Charlatans*, the term seems to be used in two ways: In its narrower definition, it includes beggars (especially those who affect diseases and physical impairments) and charlatans who stage elaborate scams; in its wider definition, it covers most of those who practice deceit and trickery, among them fire-and-brimstone preachers, false apothecaries, and alchemists.

Banū Shaybah a clan of the Prophet's tribe of Quraysh, who were the traditional keepers of the Kaaba of Mecca and whose revenue derived from the sale of fragments of the *kiswah*, the covering on the Kaaba, which was replaced each year.

Bayn al-Qaṣrayn "Between the Two Palaces"; a large square in medieval Cairo between the western and eastern palaces of the Fatimid caliphs.

Beja a people of the west coast of the Red Sea.

ben oil a pleasantly flavored edible oil obtained from the seeds of *Moringa oleifera* (ben oil tree or drumstick tree).

Biqāʿ a valley in eastern Lebanon, between Mount Lebanon to the west and the Anti-Lebanon mountains to the east.

The Book of al-Hādīṭūs (Kitāb al-Hādīṭūs) a pseudo-Aristotelian work on the cutting of gems for the manufacture of talismans and the creation of illusions; one of the earliest works on talismanic magic in Arabic, dating from ca. AD 800. Generally regarded as being of unknown authorship, it is attributed by al-Jawbarī to the Qurʾanic figure Idrīs. As in the case of *The*

Book of al-Mīlāṭīs the Great, with which it is associated by the author, the pseudo-Greek title was probably invented to lend it an air of antiquity.

The Book of the Drawing Aside of Curtains and Screens to Expose Deceptive and Crafty Schemes (Kitāb Irkhā' al-Sutūr wa-l-kilal fī kashf al-midakkāt wa-l-ḥiyal) a work by Muḥammad ibn Muḥammad ibn Sulaymān ibn Ghālib ibn al-Dahhān (wrote after 591/1195).

The Book of Ingenious Devices (Kitāb al-Ḥiyal) a work by the Banū Mūsā brothers comprising descriptions of approximately one hundred small machines, of which about eighty are ingenious trick vessels.

The Book of Illusions (Kitāb al-Nawāmīs) a pseudo-Platonic work, translated from the Latin by Ḥunayn ibn Isḥāq (194–260/809–73) and well known to Muslim writers, that deals with tricks such as walking on water, flying, appearing in the form of an animal, speaking to the dead, making the moon appear to split in two, and turning snakes into sticks. The author of *The Book of Charlatans* may have been unaware that the last dialogue of the true Plato, on the philosophy of government, is likewise titled in Arabic *Kitāb al-Nawāmīs* (*The Book of Laws*) (from Greek *nómoi*) and had long existed in Arabic translation.

The Book of the Mighty One (Kitāb al-ʿAzīz) a book belonging to a subsection of the Banū Sāsān known as Those Who Work Solomon's Ant; otherwise unidentified.

The Book of al-Mīlāṭīs the Great (Kitāb al-Mīlāṭīs al-Akbar) a work on spells for attracting love and controlling the vital spirits of animals, generally regarded as being of unknown authorship but attributed by al-Jawbarī to the Qur'anic figure Idrīs. As in the case of *The Book of al-Hādīṭūs*, with which it is associated by the author, the pseudo-Greek name is probably intended to give it an air of antiquity.

Bosra a town in southern Syria, capital of the Ḥawrān region.

The Brilliant (Kitāb al-Bāhir) a book, perhaps either *The Brilliant Book on the Wonders of Ingenious Devices* (*al-Kitāb al-Bāhir fī ʿajā'ib al-ḥiyal*) by Ibn al-Shuhayd al-Andalusī (382–426/992–1035) or *The Brilliant Book* (*al-Kitāb al-Bāhir*) of Jābir ibn Ḥayyān, an early alchemist.

byssus linen a very fine type of linen (*Linum tenue*).

castoreum a resinoid extract produced when beaver castor (a yellowish secretion contained in an anal sac used by beavers to mark their territories) is dried and tinctured with alcohol.

cinnabar mercury (II) sulfide, the historic source for the pigment vermilion.

clay-of-wisdom an alchemical term denoting a sealant made of clay and animal hair, used to seal distillation vessels.

collyrium a liquid or unguent used to cleanse or treat diseases of the eye.

the Craft alchemy.

Damietta an Egyptian city on the eastern branch of the Nile, about nine miles from the Mediterranean.

Daʿmiyūs perhaps a scribal error for Zūsimūs, i.e., Zosimos of Panopolis, known in Latin as Zosimus Alchemista (fl.. ca. AD 300), a gnostic from the city in Upper Egypt today called Akhmīm and author of the oldest known works on alchemy.

Dārayyā a village southwest of Damascus, in the Ghouta area (now a suburb of the city).

decan from Greek *dekanoi* ("tenths"); any of thirty-six groups of stars into which the houses of the zodiac were divided and that rise consecutively on the horizon during each rotation of the earth; so called because each new group appears heliacally every ten days. Three decanic "faces" (or "phases") were assigned to each zodiacal sign, each covering ten degrees of the zodiac and ruled by a planetary ruler. The rising of each decan marked the beginning of a new decanal hour of the night.

dragon's blood a bright-red resin made in the author's day from sap collected from the trunk and branches of two related trees—*Draecana cinnabari* (native to Socotra) and *Draecana draco* (native to Morocco and the Canary Islands).

dirham (1) a weight equal to 3.14 grams in sixth/twelfth-century Aleppo; (2) a silver coin.

Druze followers of a monotheistic religion found in Syria, Lebanon, and Palestine.

electuary a paste containing honey or other sweet ingredients by which an otherwise unpalatable medication or other substance, such as marijuana, is administered.

Elias the biblical Elijah, revered by both the Muslims and Christians of the Levant and the subject of numerous popular beliefs, among them that he entered Heaven as a mortal.

the "Enthusiasts" a subsection of the Ḥarīrīs, a sect of antinomian dervishes. The Arabic—al-Ghuwāh—means in the classical language "Those Who

Deviate from the Right Path"; however, if the term was one they applied to themselves, the members of the group presumably understood it in the common modern sense of "those who give themselves over entirely (to some calling), enthusiasts, fans."

euphorbium resinous gum made from the inspissated latex of spurge (*Euphorbia resinifera*).

Fakhr al-Dīn al-Rāzī (d. 606/1210) a celebrated theologian and polymath with interests in alchemy, astrology, and palmistry.

Fāris ibn Yaḥyā al-Sābāṭī an unidentified false prophet who appeared in Egypt during the fourth/tenth century; the name "al-Sābāṭī" may indicate that his or his ancestors' origins lay in the town of Sābāṭ in Transoxiana, twenty miles from Samarqand.

Fīshat al-Manārah a village in al-Minūfiyyah governorate, near Ṭanṭā, Egypt, so-called because of its conspicuously tall minaret (*manārah*); now called Fīshat Salīm.

the five ʿAbd Allāhs unidentified writers on the occult sciences mentioned, according to the author, in an unpublished work by Fakhr al-Dīn al-Rāzī and classified as "modern" by the author.

the fortress of ʿArabā (or [the town of] Ḥiṣn ʿArabā) unidentified in either case; the voweling of ʿArabā is also unconfirmed.

galbanum an aromatic gum resin produced from the plant *Ferula galbaniflua*, which grows in northern Iran.

galia moschata a perfume made of musk, ambergris, camphor, and ben oil.

geomancy the science of predicting the outcome of events, or locating lost items, using rows of holes made in sand, or rows of pebbles or grains.

the Gharb an important agricultural area on the northwest coast of Morocco.

the Ghouta an irrigated ring of gardens encircling Damascus.

Greek fire an incendiary compound, often containing bitumen, used as a weapon.

Gur an ancient city in southern Iran near modern Firuzabad, famed for its "damask" roses.

Gur sugar presumably sugar scented with damask rose petals (see *Gur*).

hadith a report of something the Prophet Muḥammad said or did.

Hajar an obsolete name referring both to the third/ninth-century capital of Bahrain and to the area of eastern Arabia on the seaboard of the Gulf adjacent to Bahrain now called al-Qaṭīf.

al-Hājir two places of this name may be identified: one in the district of Imbābah, on the west bank of the Nile, opposite Cairo, the other in the district of al-Balīnā, in Upper Egypt.

al-Ḥājj "the Pilgrim," an honorific form of address and reference used for men who have performed the annual pilgrimage to Mecca (if Muslim), or to Jerusalem (if Christian).

al-Ḥallāj, al-Ḥusayn ibn Manṣūr (d. 309/922) an influential Muslim mystic whose name is linked to the doctrine of self-identification with God engendered by supreme love; he was executed in Baghdad as a heretic.

halotrichite a highly hydrated sulfate of aluminum and iron; also called "feather alum."

al-Ḥarīrī, al-Qāsim ibn Muḥammad (d. 516/1122), a writer and official, celebrated for his fifty *maqāmah*s, stories, composed in dazzlingly ornate rhymed prose and verse, about an itinerant confidence trickster.

al-Ḥarīrī, Shaykh ʿAlī (d. 645/1247–48), founder of an offshoot of the antinomian Rifāʿiyyah Sufi order, which introduced the latter's practices into Syria. The shaykh came from the Hawran region and died in its capital, Bosra.

Ḥarīrīs followers of Shaykh ʿAlī al-Ḥarīrī.

Ḥarrān an ancient northern Mesopotamian settlement (Carrhae to the Romans) in modern-day Turkey; the city was destroyed by the Mongols in or soon after 670/1271.

al-Ḥasan al-Baṣrī (d. 110/728), an early model of Muslim piety and righteousness, claimed by Sufis as a precursor of the mystical approach to devotion.

Ḥawrān the region separating central Syria from Transjordan; known for its fertile basaltic soil.

Ḥaydar (d. ca. 618/1221–22) Quṭb al-Dīn al-Zāwujī, an Iranian who founded an antinomian offshoot of the Rifāʿiyyah Sufi order, which also flourished in Syria, Turkey, and India.

Ḥaydarīs followers of Ḥaydar.

Hejaz the northwestern part of the Arabian Peninsula, containing the Islamic holy cities of Mecca and Medina.

hematite the mineral form of iron (III) oxide.

Hermes Trismegistus (meaning originally "Hermes-threefold-in-wisdom") the Hellenistic name both of the Egyptian god Thoth and of the supposed author of a number of philosophical, scientific, and magical works.

Arabic tradition, however, perhaps influenced by a misunderstanding of the epithet, distinguished three persons named Hermes, of which the one referred to by al-Jawbarī is chronologically the first. This earliest Hermes is said to have lived in Egypt and to have built the pyramids and temples on whose walls he described the scientific achievements of ancient men so that knowledge of them would not perish with the Flood. The second and third Hermeses lived in Babylon after the Flood, and in Egypt, respectively.

Hindibār a city mentioned by the author, though it is not clear which (presumably Indian) city is meant.

Ḥiṣn Kayfā a town in southeast Turkey, now called Hasankeyf.

Homs a city in western Syria.

Hurmuzān perhaps al-Hurmuzān ibn al-Kardawal, a vizier of King Solomon.

Ibn Khaṭīb al-Rayy (ca. 250–313/854–925) Abū Bakr Muḥammad ibn Zakariyyā ibn Khaṭīb al-Rayy al-Rāzī, known in the West as Rhazes; a physician, philosopher, and alchemist with an interest in magic. Regarded by some as the founder of modern chemistry.

Ibn Qannān according to fourth/tenth-century bibliographer Ibn al-Nadīm, the cognomen of one Khalaf ibn Yūsuf al-Dastamīsānī, a writer on talismans.

Ibn Shuhayd al-Maghribī (d. 426/1034–35) Aḥmad ibn ʿAbd al-Malik ibn Shuhayd al-Ashjaʿī, a poet and prose writer of Cordoba, best known for his *Epistle on Attendant Jinns and Whirling Winds* (*Risālat al-tawābiʿ wa-l-zawābiʿ*), in which the author's personal daemon (*tābiʿ*) vaunts his talent.

Ibn Shuhayd al-Nīsābūrī perhaps a scribal error for Abū Saʿīd al-Nīsābūrī, who wrote a *Book of Ingenious Devices*.

Ibn Sīnā (370–428/980–1037) Abu ʿAlī al-Ḥusayn ibn ʿAbd Allāh ibn Sīnā, known in the West as Avicenna, a Persian polymath and above all philosopher and physician, regarded by many as the father of early modern medicine.

Ibn Tamīm probably Muḥammad ibn Tamīm, author of a commentary on a well-known late fourth/tenth-century poem on alchemy by Abū l-Iṣbaʿ ʿAbd al-ʿAzīz ibn Tammām al-ʿIrāqī.

Ibn ʿUṣfūr unidentified (a writer on the occult sciences considered "modern" by al-Jawbarī).

Ibn Waḥshiyyah a figure whose historical existence is debatable but to whom a number of works on hermeneutical topics, including cryptic alphabets, astrological divination, alchemy, and poisons, many of which their author claims to have translated from Nabatean, are attributed. His best-known work is *The Book of Nabatean Agriculture* (*Kitāb al-Filāḥah al-Nabaṭiyyah*).

Ibrāhīm ibn Adham (d. 161/777–78) an early ascetic, born into an Arab tribe that had settled near Balkh; in legend, he was a king of Balkh who, on hearing a voice calling on him to repent, abandoned his throne for the life of a mendicant.

Idrīs a person referred to twice in the Qur'an, as "a man of truth, a prophet" (Q Maryam 19:56), and as "one of the patient" (Q Anbiyā' 21:85). Later Muslim legend claims that Idrīs entered Heaven as a mortal and never left.

Imāmīs Shiites.

Ishrāsīm a fictitious Indian woman, supposedly a concubine of the Abbasid caliph Hārūn al-Rashīd (r. 170–193/786–809), to whom an important work on magical and scientific topics is attributed.

Ismaili member of a major branch of Shiite Islam named after Ismāʿīl ibn Jaʿfar al-Ṣādiq.

Isṭakhr perhaps a scribal error for Arisṭarkhus, i.e., Aristarchus of Samos (ca. 310–230), a Greek astronomer, the first to hypothesize that the earth revolves around the sun and rotates on its axis.

ʿIzz al-Dīn Aybak al-Muʿaẓẓamī an army commander of the Ayyubid prince al-Malik al-Muʿaẓẓam ʿĪsā (r. 615–24/1218–27). Al-Muʿaẓẓamī was governor of the city of Ṣarkhad in the Druze highlands of southern Syria.

ʿIzz al-Dīn Balabān master of the hunt to the Ayyubid ruler of Egypt al-Malik al-Kāmil I (r. 615–35/1218–38).

Jābir ibn Ḥayyān Abū Mūsā Jābir ibn Ḥayyān al-Ṣūfī, known in the West as Geber; probably a pseudonym concealing the identity of a group of authors whose concerns covered the whole range of the ancient sciences, with a special emphasis on alchemy.

Jaʿfar al-Ṣādiq (ca. 82–148/702–765), sixth Shiite imam, also revered by Sunnis as a jurist, mystic, and transmitter of hadith. A large number of pseudepigraphic works on fortune-casting, auspicious omens, and astrology are attributed to him.

al-Jāḥiẓ (d. 255/868–69) ʿAmr ibn Baḥr, a brilliant and prolific prose writer of the early Abbasid period.

al-Jamāl Muḥammad ibn ʿAtamah a member of the Banū Sāsān from Damascus and friend of the author; otherwise unidentified.

Joshua biblical figure, son of Nun.

Jubbat ʿAssāl perhaps the village of al-Jubbah, in the countryside surrounding Damascus close to the village of ʿAssāl al-Ward.

al-Junayd (d. 298/910) Abū l-Qāsim ibn Muḥammad, a celebrated Sufi of the moderate Baghdad school of Islamic mysticism, which eschewed the effacement of the boundary between creation and Creator.

Kafr Sūsiyyah a village outside Damascus.

Kanakah an Indian writer of whom little is known; the fourth/tenth-century bibliographer Ibn al-Nadīm lists four works on astrology by him translated into Arabic.

Khalaf ibn Saʿīd ibn Yūsuf perhaps the same as Khalaf ibn Yūsuf al-Dastamīsānī, known as Ibn Qannān.

Khālid ibn al-Walīd (d. 21/642) an early Muslim general, best known for his defeat of would-be prophet Musaylimah and for his campaigns in Syria.

al-Khawārazmī (fourth/tenth century) Abū ʿAbd Allāh Muḥammad ibn Yūsuf al-Khawārazmī, author of the oldest Islamic encyclopedia of the sciences, *The Keys to the Sciences* (*Mafātīḥ al-ʿulūm*), the final chapter of which deals at length with alchemy.

Khurasan a loosely defined historical region northeast of Persia that included parts of central Asia and Afghanistan.

labdanum a sticky brown resin obtained from the shrub *Cistus creticus*, a species of rockrose.

Lādhan a student of the physician Hippocrates (ca. 460–370 BC); known also as Lādan.

Lawhaq ibn ʿArfajah according to fourth/tenth-century bibliographer Ibn al-Nadīm (who gives his name as Lawhaq ibn ʿArfaj), author of a work on jinn and "crazy spirits."

Legend of al-Baṭṭāl a popular romance, also called *The Legend of Dhāt* (or *Dhū*) *al-Himmah and al-Baṭṭāl*, based on the exploits of the Umayyad warrior ʿAbd Allāh al-Baṭṭāl in the wars against Byzantium.

litharge lead monoxide; one of the natural mineral forms of lead (II) oxide, a secondary mineral formed from the oxidation of galena ores.

Livelihood of Abū ʿAnbas, The (Rizq Abī ʿAnbas) i.e. *The Book of the Merits of Livelihood* (*Kitāb Faḍāʾil al-rizq*) of Abū ʿAnbas Muḥammad ibn Isḥāq al-Ṣaymarī (213–75/828–88), on telling the future using astrology.

Livelihood of Abū Maʿshar, The (Rizq Abī Maʿshar) an unidentified work of Abū Maʿshar Jaʿfar ibn Muḥammad ibn ʿUmar al-Balkhī (171–272/787–886 (?)), the most famous of Arab astrologers, known in the West as Albumasar.

al-Maʿarrah also called Maʿarrat al-Nuʿmān, a city in northwest Syria.

Maghreb North Africa from Morocco to Tunisia.

Magian a follower of Zoroaster.

al-Maḥallah also called al-Maḥallah al-Kubrā, a town in Egypt's central Delta, known for centuries as a textile-manufacturing center.

the Mahdi literally "the rightly guided one"; the restorer of religion and justice who will rule before the end of the world.

al-Malik al-ʿĀdil Najm al-Dīn (r. 592–615/1196–1218) "Just King" Abū Bakr Muḥammad ibn Ayyūb, Ayyubid ruler of Damascus.

al-Malik al-ʿĀdil Nūr al-Dīn Zangī (r. 541–69/1147–74) "Just King" Abū l-Qāsim Maḥmūd ibn Zangī, Zangid dynasty ruler of Aleppo and then Damascus.

al-Malik al-Ashraf (r. 626–34/1229–37) "Most Noble King" Muẓaffar al-Dīn, Ayyubid ruler of Damascus.

Mālik the angel guarding Hell (Q Zukhruf 43:77).

al-Malik al-Masʿūd (r. 619–29/1222–32) "Fortune-Favored King" Rukn al-Dīn Mawdūd ibn Nāṣir al-Dīn, last of the Turkmen Artuqid dynasty of Ḥiṣn Kayfā and Āmid. Imprisoned by the Ayyubid ruler of Damascus al-Malik al-Kāmil I when the latter took over his territory, he fled on al-Kāmil's death in 635/1238 to Ḥamā, where he probably died during the Mongol invasion. He commissioned *The Book of Charlatans*.

al-Malik al-Muʿaẓẓam ʿĪsā governor of Damascus from 597/1201 and ruler of all of Syria from 615/1218 until his death in 624/1227.

Mālikī gold pieces a specie said by the author to be in circulation in Hindibār, minted in Yemen, equivalent in value to less than a quarter of an Egyptian gold piece.

al-Maʾmūn (r. 197–218/813–33) seventh caliph of the Abbasid Dynasty.

mandal (1) "striking the *mandal*": a divinatory or spirit-conjuring practice involving, in some forms, the drawing of a circle in sand and in others the use of a reflecting surface such as a mirror or pool of ink into which a medium peers in order to read minds, discover hidden things, etc.; (2) the object or objects possessed by jinn summoned by a conjuror.

Māriyā a figure, identified by some in antiquity as a Copt, by others as the sister of Moses, and eventually confused with the mother of Jesus, who plays a large role in gnostic, magical, and alchemical literature. Muslim scholars sometimes identified her with "Maria the Copt," a slave woman sent by the ruler of Alexandria to the Prophet Muḥammad as a diplomatic gift, or even with the landowner of the same name who accosted the caliph al-Ma'mūn during his visit to Egypt in 217/832 and demonstrated to him her (figurative) ability to convert the rich soil of Egypt into gold.

Maʿrūf al-Karkhī (d. 200/815–16), an influential mystic of the Baghdad school of moderate Sufism, which eschewed the effacement of the boundary between creation and Creator; teacher of Sarī al-Saqaṭī.

Masʿūdī gold pieces presumably Indian coins, perhaps named after one of the three Ghaznavid rulers named Masʿūd.

Maṣyāf a town in the Jabal al-Anṣariyyah (Nuṣayrī Mountains) in central Syria, twenty-eight miles east of Bāniyās and thirty-three miles west of Hama; also called Maṣyād.

al-Mazdaqānī The name is unclear in the Arabic manuscripts and the identification is tentative. Abū ʿAlī Ṭāhir ibn Saʿd (or Saʿīd) al-Mazdaqānī served as vizier for Ẓahīr al-Dīn Ṭughtakīn (r. 497–522/1104–28), a Seljuq atabeg who established the semi-independent Burid emirate in Damascus; the author's characterization of him as a vizier of the Zengid sultan al-Malik al-ʿĀdil Nūr al-Dīn (§9.28) would, according to this identification, be wrong.

The Memorandum i.e., *The Eye Doctors' Memorandum* (*Tadhkirat al-kaḥḥālīn*) by Sharaf al-Dīn ʿAlī ibn ʿĪsā al-Kaḥḥāl (d. ca. 400/1010), a four-volume work that discusses the anatomy of the eye and its most important diseases, and lists cures.

mithkal a weight equal to 4.427 grams in twelfth-century Aleppo.

al-Mizzah in the author's day, one of the largest villages of the Ghouta, near Damascus.

moon spittle selenite, a usually transparent and colorless form of gypsum.

mosque of al-Azhar a mosque and center of religious learning founded by the Fatimids in their royal capital of al-Qāhirah (Cairo) in 359/970.

Mount Mizzah the hill today called Qalabāt Mizzah, west of the village of al-Mizzah.

al-Muʿizz al-Muʿizz li-Dīnillāh (r. 341–65/953–75), fourth caliph of the Fatimid Dynasty and the first to rule from Egypt, where he founded Cairo.

myrobalan the edible fruit of a tree (*Terminalia* spp.) with medicinal properties, also used in the production of ink and in tanning and dyeing.

Najdah ibn ʿĀmir al-Ḥanafī an Umayyad-period leader of a group of Kharijites or "those who went out" (participants in the earliest schism in Islam, which had its roots in the rejection by certain Muslim soldiers of the claims to the caliphate of both ʿAlī ibn Abī Ṭālib and ʿUthmān in ca. 37/657). Najdah conquered Bahrain and established his capital at al-Qaṭīf. However, in his account of this figure, al-Jawbarī confuses him with Abū Thumāmah Musaylimah ibn Ḥabīb, a man of the Banū Ḥanifah tribe, which controlled the trade routes of central Arabia during the lifetime of the Prophet Muḥammad. Musaylimah made a bid for the leadership of his tribe on the basis of his supposed prophethood. He is said to have offered to share power with Muḥammad and to have led his people into open revolt against the Islamic state following Muḥammad's death. His rebellion was crushed and he was killed by Khālid ibn al-Walīd in 12/634.

Nāṣirī silver pieces half silver, half copper dirhams first minted in 585/1187–88 by Saladin, whose regnal title was al-Nāṣir ("the Victorious").

ninth-part segments into which each of the signs of the zodiac are divided, each segment associated with a sign; the planet that is the lord of this sign is the lord of the corresponding ninth-part.

Nubians a people inhabiting the Nile Valley from the first to the fifth cataracts.

Nūr al-Dīn Maḥmūd ibn Zangī see *al-Malik al-ʿĀdil Nūr al-Dīn Zangī.*

Nusaybin a city in Turkey's Mardin province, on the border with Syria.

operculum a kind of plug that closes over the aperture of certain mollusks; it may be crushed and used in perfumes.

orpiment a deep orange-yellow arsenic sulfide mineral formed as a byproduct of the decay of realgar.

People of the Book Christians, Jews, and members of other religions recognized in the Qur'an as having received revealed scriptures.

pharaoh glass a highly prized yellowish-green glass made in Alexandria from at least Roman times to at least early Mamluk times.

Plato Plato was known to medieval Arab scholars largely through the lens of his Neoplatonic interpreters and as a result was associated with the magic, astrology, and alchemy that had become an integral part of the teaching of most of the Neoplatonic schools.

Ptolemy a Greco-Egyptian astronomer and geographer (ca. AD 100–170) who had a profound influence on Arab and other medieval scholars. His *Four Books* (*Tetrabyblos*) attempted to reconcile horoscopic astrology with Aristotelian natural philosophy.

al-Qalamūn Deir al-Qalamun, the Monastery of St. Samuel the Confessor, in the desert west of Beni Suef.

Qalhāt a major monsoon-trade port on the Indian Ocean, in today's southwest Oman.

al-Qarmaṭī, Abū Saʿīd al-Ḥasan ibn Saʿīd al-Jannābī the founder in eastern Arabia of the rule of the Qarmatians, a branch of the Ismaʿīlī Shiites. The descriptor "al-Qarmaṭī" is usually said to be taken from the name of one putative founder of the Qarmatian movement, Ḥamdān Qarmaṭ. In stating that Abū Saʿīd "violated Islam's holiest site," the author is confusing him with his second successor, his youngest son Sulaymān, better known as Abū Ṭāhir (d. 332/943–44), who took Mecca in 317/930 and carried off the Black Stone.

Qaṣr Ḥajjāj a district immediately southwest of the wall of the old city of Damascus.

al-Qifṭī al-Shaybānī unidentified (a poet, according to the author, of the third to fourth/ninth to tenth centuries).

Qumāmah Church the church known to Christian Arabs as Kanīsat al-Qiyāmah ("the Church of the Resurrection") and called in English the Church of the Holy Sepulcher. The best-known meaning of *qumāmah* is "sweepings, trash," and the use of this name—which is to be found as early as the writings of al-Jāḥiẓ (second to third/seventh to eighth century)—to designate one of the holiest churches in Christendom has been attributed to either Muslim or Jewish anti-Christian polemic. One scholar, however, argues that Qumāmah here is a well-attested, if antique and uncommon, male proper name (e.g., Waqqāṣ ibn Qumāmah, a Companion of the Prophet Muḥammad), from the root *q-m-m*, whose sense is "elevation, lifting"; this theory is strengthened by the fact that the name of the church most often occurs, as here, as Kanīsat Qumāmah, without the definite article.

ramek an astringent compound made from pomegranate rind with oak galls and other ingredients.

realgar an arsenic sulfide mineral, also called "ruby sulfur" or "ruby of arsenic."

Rifāʿīs members of the Rifāʿiyyah Sufi order, one of the largest and most influential in the history of Arab Sufism and still active today. Its spread dates to the assumption by Aḥmad ibn ʿAlī al-Rifāʿī (d. 578/1182) of the leadership of his uncle's religious community in the southern Iraqi marshes. Thus the order was relatively new to Syria in al-Jawbarī's time.

the River Kawthar a river that waters Paradise, according to a popular understanding of the words of God to the Prophet Muḥammad: "Surely, we have given thee abundance (*kawthar*)" (Q al-Kawthar 108:1).

Sābūr (d. 255/869) Sābūr ibn Sahl, a Christian physician at the hospital of Jundīshāpūr and author of the first widely used pharmacopoeia, *al-Aqrābādhīn* (from the Syriac for "small treatise").

al-Saffāḥ (r. 132–36/749–54), first caliph of the Abbasid dynasty.

al-Ṣafṣāf a district outside Damascus, precise location unidentified.

Ṣaghbīn Saghbine, a village in Lebanon's western Biqāʿ region, seventy-three kilometers southeast of Beirut.

Ṣāliḥ ibn Abī Ṣāliḥ al-Mudaybirī according to fourth/tenth-century bibliographer Ibn al-Nadīm, a practitioner of magic of the sort permitted by the Qur'an.

saltpeter the mineral form of potassium nitrate.

sandarac a yellow-tinged resin used in varnishes, derived from the arar, or Barbary thuja, tree (*Tetraclinis articulata*), a species of juniper.

Sarav an unidentified town, by implication in India.

Sarī al-Saqaṭī (d. 251/865) an influential mystic of the Baghdad school of moderate Sufism, which eschewed the effacement of the boundary between creation and Creator; a pupil of Maʿrūf al-Karkhī.

Ṣaṣah probably the same as the Ṣaṣah al-Hindī ("Ṣaṣah the Indian") described by fourth/tenth-century bibliographer Ibn al-Nadīm as practicing conjuration by black magic, and as Ṣaṣah ibn Ḍāmir al-Hindī, author of a collection on astrology and magic titled *Sharḥ al-ṣūrah al-khāmisah wa-hiya al-maʿrūfah bi-dhāt al-dhawāʾib min al-sabʿ wa-huwa al-maʿrūf bi-Sirr al-sirr* (*A Commentary on the Fifth Image, Namely, That Known as "That of Liquids," from the [Book of the] Seven [Images], Known as "The Innermost Secret"*).

Saturday of Light Easter Saturday.

Ṣaydnāyā (Saydnaya, Sednaya) a largely Christian town in the mountains some seventeen miles north of Damascus. The Convent of Our Lady of Ṣaydnāyā was reputedly established by Byzantine emperor Justinian I in AD 547 following visions of the Virgin Mary. Its famous icon of the Virgin remains to this day the object of pilgrimage by both Christians and Muslims.

Sayf al-Dīn Qilīj (d. 645/1247), an emir of the Ayyubid prince al-Ẓāhir Ghāzī (r. 589–613/1193–1216), ruler of northern Syria and governor of the fortress of Raʿbān, on a tributary of the Euphrates between Aleppo and Sumaysāṭ.

Sharaf an otherwise unidentified "ancient sage" whose works the author consulted.

Shaykh Sāsān putative first leader of the Banū Sāsān.

Sieve-Makers' Market (Arabic: Sūq al-manākhiliyyīn, or Sūq al-manākhiliyyah) a market located in an arcade running between the inner city and the northwestern suburbs of Damascus.

silver salt silver halide.

the Sīn a secret language or argot that the author associates specifically with astrologers.

simples the unmixed ingredients from which an apothecary creates compounds.

Sinān (d. 588/1192 or 589/1193) chief proselyte of the Nizari Ismailis in central Syria and one of the sect's most important and successful leaders; known to the Crusaders as "the Old Man of the Mountain."

Sīrā an otherwise unidentified "ancient sage" whose works the author consulted.

Sivas a city in central Anatolia.

stellion a lizard (*Stellio vulgaris*), olive green with small stellate spots, common in the eastern Mediterranean region.

stinking alum a form of alum with a dirty yellowish appearance, also called "mountain butter."

storax a resin derived from trees of the genus *Styrax*.

Sulaymān al-Dārānī properly, Abū Sulaymān al-Dārānī (d. 215/830–31), an ascetic and hadith transmitter.

Taif (Arabic: al-Ṭāʾif) a city in Arabia southeast of Mecca.

Takrūr the name by which a Muslim state and city—perhaps modern Podor in northern Senegal—was known to the Arabs in al-Jawbarī's time; also, natives of Takrūr (singular, *Takrūrī*).

Ṭālaqān a town in northeast Afghanistan known for its fine felts.

ṭāliqūn a name common to three separate copper amalgams all distinguished by their hardness.

Tiberias (Arabic: al-Ṭabariyyah) a town in Palestine, on the edge of the Sea of Galilee in the Jordan Valley.

Tinnīs a medieval port close to the estuary of the main branch of the Nile on Lake Manzalah. Tinnīs served as a major entrepôt for Mediterranean trade, especially in the textiles manufactured in the city. It was abandoned in the late sixth/twelfth century.

Ṭumṭum the Philosopher a figure associated in early Hellenistic circles with mainly astrological magic; called elsewhere Ṭumṭum al-Hindī ("Ṭumṭum the Indian").

tutty oxide of zinc.

verdigris a green pigment, usually a basic copper carbonate, obtained through the application of acetic acid to copper plates or in the form of the natural patina formed when copper, brass, or bronze is weathered and exposed over time to air or seawater. The term "green-chickpea verdigris" (Arabic, *al-zinjār al-ḥimmiṣī*) may refer to a particularly brightly colored form of verdigris. However, the Arabic also allows the reading *al-zinjār al-ḥimṣī* or "verdigris of Homs."

vitriol sulfate, qualified as "green" (iron sulfate) and "blue" (copper sulfate).

Urfa a city in southeast Turkey; ancient Edessa.

urjūzah a poem in *rajaz* meter, often with rhyming hemistichs.

ūqiyyah a weight, one-twelfth of a rotl and therefore variable: approximately 37 grams in Egypt, 154 grams in Damascus, and 190 grams in Aleppo.

waras (also *wars* and *warss*) a resinous powder obtained from the fruits of *Memecylon sphaerocarpum*, used as a brilliant-yellow dyestuff.

Ward of God a person who enjoys God's special favor and to whom miracles are often attributed; in the literature on Sufism, the term is sometimes rendered "Friend of God."

The Well-Kept Secret (al-Sirr al-Maktūm) i.e., *The Well-Kept Secret Concerning Converse with the Stars* (*al-Sirr al-maktūm fī mukhāṭabat al-nujūm*), a work by Fakhr al-Dīn al-Rāzī on astrological magic.

white lead basic lead carbonate.

al-Yamāmah in early Islamic times, a region of Najd in central Arabia.

al-Yanbuʿ a port on the Red Sea coast of the Hejaz in western Arabia and the main point of disembarkation for Medina.

Yathrib the ancient name for Medina, in western Arabia.

al-Zanātī (probably sixth/twelfth or seventh/thirteenth century) Muḥammad ibn ʿUthmān Abū ʿAbd Allāh ibn al-Zanātī, a writer of Berber origin whose works on geomancy are known only through references in other works.

Zuṭṭ a word derived from "Jat," the name of a northwest Indian people, some of whom were brought to Khuzistan and the Gulf before Islam, while others migrated or were moved in early Islamic times to Persia, the marshes of Iraq, and Syria. According to some, they are the ancestors of at least a part of the modern Romani population of the Middle East. It is unclear what the term, used only once in the book, meant to the author.

Bibliography

Abrahams, Harold J. "Al-Jawbari on False Alchemists" in *Ambix* 31, no. 2 (July 1984): 84–88.

Abul Huda, Samar Najm. *Arab Roots of Gemology: Ahmad ibn Yusuf Al Tifaschi's Best Thoughts on the Best of Stones.* Lanham, MD: The Scarecrow Press., 1998.

Anthony, Sean W. "Who Was the Shepherd of Damascus? The Enigma of Jewish and Messianist Responses to the Islamic Conquests in Marwānid Syria and Mesopotamia." In *The Lineaments of Islam: Studies in Honor of Fred McGraw Donner*, edited by Paul Cobb, 21–59. Leiden: E. J. Brill, 2012.

Arberry, Arthur J. *The Koran Interpreted.* Oxford: Oxford University Press, 1982.

Banū Mūsā Ibn Shākir. *Kitāb al-Ḥiyal.* Translated by Donald R. Hill. *The Book of Ingenious Devices (Kitāb al-Ḥiyal) by the Banū (sons of) Mūsā bin Shākir.* Dordrecht: D. Reidel, 1979.

Al-Baghdādī, Ismāʿīl Pāshā Bābānī. *Hadiyyat al-ʿārifīn: Asmāʾ al-muʾallifīn wa-āthār al-muṣannifīn.* Edited by Mehmed Šerefeddin Yaltkaya et al. 2 vols. Baghdad: Maktabat al-Muthannā, 1972. Reprint of 1950–55 reprint of Istanbul: Wikālat al-Maʿārif al-Jalīlah, 1920–1921.

Behrnauer, W. "Mémoire sur les institutions de police chez les Arabes, les Persans, et les Turcs" in *Journal Asiatique* 5:17, Paris: 1861, 5–76.

Bosworth, Clifford E. "Jewish Elements in the Banū Sāsān." In C. E. Bosworth, *Medieval Arabic Culture and Administration*, VI:1–17. London: Variorum Reprints, 1982.

———. *The Mediaeval Islamic Underworld: The Banū Sāsān in Arabic Society and Literature.* Part 1: *The Banū Sāsān in Arabic Life and Lore.* Part 2: *The Arabic Jargon Texts; The Qaṣīda Sāsāniyyas of Abū Dulaf and Ṣafī d-Dīn.* Leiden: E. J. Brill, 1976.

Al-Bustānī, Buṭrus. *Kitāb Muḥīṭ al-muḥīṭ, ay, Qāmūs muṭawwal lil-lughah al-ʿarabiyyah.* Beirut: n.p., 1876.

Cheikho, Louis, and Eilhard Wiedemann. "Die Auswahl über die Enthüllung der Geheimnisse al Maschriq (arabisch)" in *Mitteilungen zur Geschichte der Medizin und Naturwissenschaften* 9 (1910): 386–90.

De Biberstein-Kazimirski, A. *Dictionnaire arabe-français.* 2 vols. Paris: Editions G.-P. Maisonneuve, 1870.

Dozy, Reinhart Pieter Anne. *Supplément aux dictionnaires arabes.* 2 vols. Leiden: E. J. Brill, 1881. Offset, Beirut: Librairie du Liban, 1968.

EALL = *Encyclopedia of Arabic Language and Linguistics*. Edited by Kees Versteegh. 5 vols. Leiden: E. J. Brill, 2006–9.

EI2 = *Encyclopaedia of Islam*. 2nd ed. Edited by H. A. R. Gibb et al. 13 vols. Leiden: E. J. Brill, 1960–2009.

Fischer, Wolfdietrich. "What Is Middle Arabic?" In *Semitic Studies in Honor of Wolf Leslau*, edited by Alan S. Kaye, vol. 1, 430–36. Wiesbaden: Otto Harrassowitz, 1991.

Friedlaender, Israel. "Jewish-Arabic Studies; Shiitic Elements" (I and III). *The Jewish Quarterly New Series 1* (1910–11):183–215 (I) and 3.2 (October 1912):235–300 (III).

GAL = Brockelmann, Carl. *Geschichte der arabischen Litteratur*, vols. 1 and 2. Leiden: E. J. Brill, 1943, 1949; Suppl. vols. 1–3. Leiden: E. J. Brill, 1937–42.

Garbers, Karl, and Jost Weyer. *Quellengeschichtliches Lesebuch zur Chemie und Alchemie der Araber im Mittelalter*. Hamburg: Helmut Buske Verlag, 1980.

GAS = Sezgin, Fuat. *Geschichte des arabischen Schrifttums*. 17 vols. Leiden: E. J. Brill, 1967–2015.

Ḥājjī Khalīfah. *Kitāb Kashf al-ẓunūn ʿan asāmī l-kutub wa-l-funūn*. Edited by Muḥammad Sharaf al-Dīn Yāltaqāyā and Rifʿat Bīlkah al-Kilīsī. 2 vols. [Istanbul?]: Wikālat al-Maʿārif al-Jalīlah, 1941–43.

Al-Ḥallāj, al-Ḥusayn ibn Manṣūr. *Dīwān*. Edited by Abū Ṭurayf Kāmil ibn Muṣṭafā al-Shaybī. Cologne: Manshūrāt al-Jamal, 1997.

Al-Hamadhānī, Abū l-Faḍl Badīʿ al-Zamān. *Maqāmāt*. Edited by Muḥammad ʿAbduh. Beirut: al-Maṭbaʿah al-Kāthūlīkiyyah, 1924. Offset of edition of 1889.

Al-Ḥarīrī, Abū l-Qāsim. *Maqāmāt al-Ḥarīrī*. Beirut: Dār Ṣādir, n.d.

Al-Hindī, ʿAlī al-Muttaqī ibn Ḥusām al-Dīn. *Kanz al-ʿummāl fī sunan al-aqwāl wa-l-afʿāl*. Edited by Maḥmūd ʿUmar al-Dumyāṭī. 18 vols. Beirut: Dār al-Kutub al-ʿIlmiyyah, 2017.

Höglmeier, Manuela. *Al-Ǧawbarī und sein Kašf al-asrār—ein Sittenbild des Gauners im arabisch-islamischen Mittelalter (7./13. Jahrhundert): Einführung, Edition und Kommentar*. Berlin: Klaus Schwarz Verlag, 2006.

Horovitz, Josef. *Spuren griechischer Mimen im Orient: Mit einem Anhang über das egyptische Schattenspiel von Friedrich Kern*. Berlin: Mayer und Müller, 1905.

Ibn Dāniyāl, Shams al-Dīn Muḥammad. *Khayāl al-ẓill wa-tamthīliyyāt Ibn Dāniyāl*. Edited by Ibrāhīm Ḥammādah. Cairo: al-Muʾassasah al-Miṣriyyah al-ʿĀmmah li-l-Taʾlīf wa-l-Tarjamah wa-l-Nashr, 1963.

Ibn Ḥamdūn, Muḥammad ibn al-Ḥasan ibn ʿAlī. *Al-Tadhkirah al-Ḥamdūniyyah*. Edited by Iḥsān ʿAbbās and Bakr ʿAbbās. 10 vols. 3rd ed. Beirut: Dār Ṣādir, 2009.

Ibn al-Nadīm, Abū l-Faraj Muḥammad ibn Isḥāq. *Kitāb al-Fihrist*. Edited by Riḍā Tajaddud. Tehran: n.p., 1391/1971.

Irwin, Robert. *The Arabian Nights: A Companion*. London: Tauris Parke Paperbacks, 2008.

Jacob, Georg. “Ein ägyptischer Jahrmarkt im 13. Jahrhundert.” In *Sitzungsberichte der Königlich Bayerischen Akademie der Wissenschaften, Philosophisch-philologische und Historische Klasse, Jahrgang 1910*, part 10. Munich: Verlage der Königlich Bayerischen Akademie der Wissenschaften, 1910.

Al-Jāḥiẓ, ʿAmr ibn Baḥr. *Al-Kitāb al-Musammā bi-l-maḥāsin wa-l-aḍdād.* Edited by Gerolf van Vloten. Amsterdam: Oriental Press, 1974. Offset of Leiden edition, 1898.

Al-Kaḥḥālah, ʿUmar Riḍā. *Muʿjam al-muʾallifīn: tarājim muṣannifī l-kutub al-ʿarabiyyah.* 15 vols. Damascus: al-Maktabah al-ʿArabiyyah, 1376-1381/1957-1961.

Karamustafa, Ahmet T. “The Antinomian Dervish as Model Saint.” In *Modes de transmission de la culture religieuse en Islam*, edited by Hassan Elboudrari, 241–60. Cairo: Institut Français d’Archéologie Orientale au Caire, 1993.

———. *God’s Unruly Friends: Dervish Groups in the Islamic Later Middle Period: 1200–1550.* Salt Lake City: University of Utah Press, 1994.

Katz, Marion Holmes. “The ‘Shearing of Forelocks’ as a Penitential Rite.” In *The Heritage of Arabo-Islamic Learning: Studies Presented to Wadad Kadi*, edited by Maurice A. Pomerantz and Aram A. Shahin, 191–206. Leiden: E. J. Brill, 2016.

Khawam, René R. *ʿAbd al-Rahmāne al-Djawbarī. Le Voile arraché. L’autre visage de l’Islam. Traduction intégrale sur les manuscrits originaux par René R. Khawam.* Translated by Abd al-Rahmāne al-Djawbarī. 2 vols. Paris: Phébus, 1970–80.

Lane, Edward William. *An Account of the Manners and Customs of the Modern Egyptians.* Introduced by Jason Thompson. Cairo: American University in Cairo Press, 2003. Reprint of the fifth edition of 1860.

———. *An Arabic-English Lexicon.* 8 vols. London: Williams and Norgate, 1865. Offset, Beirut: Maktabat Lubnān, 1968.

Lev, Ephraim, and Zohar Amar. *Practical Materia Medica of the Medieval Eastern Mediterranean According to the Cairo Genizah.* Leiden, Boston: E. J. Brill, 2008.

Lindsay, James E. *Daily Life in the Medieval Islamic World.* Westport, CT: Greenwood Press, 2005.

Littmann, Enno. *Zigeuner-Arabisch: Wortschatz und Grammatik der arabischen Bestandteile in den morgenländischen Zigeunersprachen.* Bonn: Kurt Schroeder Verlag, 1920.

Massignon, Louis. “Le *Dīwān* d’al-Ḥallāj, essai de reconstitution, édition et traduction.” *Journal asiatique* 218 (1931): 1–158.

Muḥammad, Zakariyyā. “Aṣl al-tasmiyah li-Kanīsat al-Qiyāmah.” *Hawliyyāt al-Quds* 13 (2012): 58–61.

Nelson, Kristina. *The Art of Reciting the Qurʾān.* 2nd ed. Cairo: American University in Cairo Press, 2001.

Pertsch, Wilhelm. *Die arabischen Handschriften der Herzoglichen Bibliothek zu Gotha*. 5 vols. Frankfurt am Main: Institut für Geschichte der Arabisch-Islamischen Wissenschaften an der Johann Wolfgang Goethe-Universität, 1987. Reprint of the Gotha edition of 1878–92.

Popper, William. *Egypt and Syria under the Circassian Sultans, 1382–1468 A.D.: Systematic Notes to Ibn Taghrî Birdî's Chronicles of Egypt*. 2 vols. Berkeley: University of California Press, 1955–57.

The Random House Dictionary of the English Language. New York: Random House, 1966.

Rosenthal, Franz. "The Herb." In *Man versus Society in Medieval Islam*, edited by Dimitri Gutas, 131–334. Leiden: E. J. Brill, 2015.

Rowson, Everett. "Cant and Argot in Cairo Colloquial Arabic." *American Research Center in Egypt Newsletter* 122 (Summer 1983): 13–24.

Savage-Smith, E., and M. B. Smith. *Islamic Geomancy and a Thirteenth-Century Divinatory Device*. Malibu, CA: Undena Publications, 1980.

Al-Shaʿrānī, ʿAbd al-Wahhāb. *Lawāqiḥ al-anwār fī ṭabaqāt al-akhyār (al-Ṭabaqāt al-kubrā)*. Cairo: al-Maṭbaʿah al-ʿĀmirah al- Sharafiyyah, 1315/1897.

Al-Shirbīnī, Yūsuf. *Brains Confounded by the Ode of Abū Shādūf Expounded*. Edited and translated by Humphrey Davies. 2 vols. New York: New York University Press, 2016.

Steinschneider, M. "Gauberi's 'entdeckte Geheimnisse,' eine Quelle für orientalische Sittenschilderung." *Zeitschrift der Deutschen Morgenländischen Gessellschaft* 19 (1865): 562–77.

Thompson, Jason. *Edward William Lane 1801–1876: The Life of the Pioneering Egyptologist and Orientalist*. Cairo: American University in Cairo Press, 2010.

Toussoun, Prince Omar. *Mémoire sur l'histoire du Nil*. 3 vols. Cairo: Institut Français d'Archéologie Orientale, 1925.

Trimingham, J. Spencer. *The Sufi Orders in Islam*. Oxford: Clarendon Press, 1971.

Ullmann, Manfred. *Die Natur- und Geheimwissenschaften im Islam*. Leiden: E. J. Brill, 1972.

Wahrmund, Adolph. *Handwörterbuch der neu-arabischen und deutschen Sprache*. 3 vols. Beirut: Maktabat Lubnān, 1985.

Wasserstrom, Steven M. "The ʿĪsāwiyya Revisited." *Studia Islamica* 75 (1992): 57–80.

Wiedemann, Eilhard. *Aufsätze zur arabisch-islamischen Wissenschaftgeschichte*. Edited by W. Fischer. 2 vols. Hildesheim: Olms, 1970.

Wiedemann, Eilhard. *Gesammelte Schriften zur arabisch-islamischen Wissenschaftsgeschichte*. 2 vols. Frankfurt am Main: Institut für Geschichte der Arabisch-Islamischen Wissenschaften an der Johann Wolfgang Goethe-Universität, 1984.

Wild, Stefan. "Jugglers and Fraudulent Sufis." In *Proceedings of the 6th Congress of Arabic and Islamic Studies. Visby 13–16 August, Stockholm 17–19 August 1972*, 58–63. Stockholm: Almqvist & Wiskell International, 1975.

Wild, Stefan. “A Juggler’s Programme in Medieaval Islam.” In *La Signification du Bas Moyen Âge dans l’Histoire et la Culture du Monde Musulman: Actes du 8ème Congrès de l’Union Européenne des Arabisants et Islamisants. Aix-en-Provence Septembre 1976*, edited by Robert Mantran, 353–60. Aix-en-Provence: Edisud, 1978.

Al-Zabīdī, al-Murtaḍā al-Husaynī. *Tāj al-ʿarūs*. Beirut: Dār Ṣādir, 2011.

Zandee, J. “Gnostic Ideas on the Fall and Salvation.” *Numen* 11, Fasc. 1 (Jan. 1964):13–74.

Further Reading

Al-Aḥnaf al-ʿUkbarī. *Al-Qaṣīdah al-Sāsāniyyah*. Quoted in part in *Yatīmat al-dahr fī maḥāsin ahl al-ʿaṣr*, by ʿAbd al-Malik ibn Muḥammad al-Thaʿālibī, edited by Muḥammad Muḥyī l-dīn ʿAbd al-Ḥamīd. 4 vols. Beirut: Dār al-Kutub al-ʿIlmiyyah, 1979. Offprint of Mecca: np, 1947. [A fourth/tenth-century beggar's poem.]

Al-Azdī, Abū l-Muṭahhar Muḥammad ibn Aḥmad. *Abulḳâsim, ein bagdâder Sittenbild* [*Ḥikāyat Abī l-Qāsim al-Baghdādī*.] Edited by Adam Mez. Heidelberg: Carl Winter's Universitätsbuchhandlung, 1902. [An early fifth/eleventh-century work, in which the hero, Abū l-Qāsim, poses as a charlatan in Baghdad.]

Al-Bābilī, ʿAbd Allāh ibn Hilāl. *Nūr al-muqal fī l-dakk wa-l-ḥiyal*. Ms. Berlin 5568 (Landberg 161). [A work of unknown date that presents a range of tricks practiced by different kinds of swindlers, from quack doctors and false astrologers to horse-fakers.]

Badīʿ al-Zamān al-Hamadhānī, Abū l-Faḍl Aḥmad ibn Ḥusayn. *Al-Maqāmāt*. Beirut: al-Maṭbaʿah al-Kāthūlīkiyyah li-l-Ābāʾ al-Yasūʿiyyīn, 1924. [A fourth/tenth-century collection that depicts the experiences and records the speeches of highly educated vagabonds.

Banū Mūsā ibn Shākir. *The Book of Ingenious Devices (Kitāb al-Ḥiyal) by the Banū (sons of) Mūsà bin Shākir [Kitāb al-Ḥiyal]*. Translated and annotated by Donald R. Hill. Dordrecht, Boston and London: D. Reidel Publishing Company, 1979. [A third/ninth-century work that includes precise illustrated instructions for making bowls and utensils used in tricks.]

Al-Bayhaqī, Ibrāhīm ibn Muḥammad. *Kitāb al-Maḥāsin wa-l-masāwī*. Edited by Friedrich Schwally. Giessen: Richer, 1902. [A fourth/tenth-century work that reproduces and expands on al-Jāḥiẓ's third/ninth-century list of beggars.]

Al-Ḥarīrī, Abū Muḥammad al-Qāsim ibn ʿAlī ibn Muḥammad ibn ʿUthmān. *Maqāmāt al-Ḥarīrī*. 3rd ed. Būlāq: Dār al-Ṭibāʿah al-ʿĀmirah, 1288/1871. [A sixth/twelftho-century collection that depicts the experiences and records the speeches of highly educated vagabonds.]

Ibn Dāniyāl, Shams al-Dīn Muḥammad. *'Ajīb wa-Gharīb*. In *Khayāl al-ẓill wa-tamthīliyyāt Ibn Dāniyāl*, edited by Ibrāhīm Ḥammādah. Cairo: al-Mu'assasah al-Miṣriyyah al-'Āmmah li-l-Ta'līf wa-l-Tarjamah wa-l-Ṭibā'ah wa-l-Nashr, 1963. [A seventh/thirteenth-century shadow play depicting scenes of the everyday life of vagabonds and containing elements of the jargon of the Bānū Sāsān.]

Ibn al-Razzāz al-Jazarī, Ismā'īl. *The Book of Knowledge of Ingenious Mechanical Devices* [*Kitāb fī-Ma'rifat al-ḥiyal al-handasiyyah*]. Translated by Donald R. Hill. Dordrecht, Boston: D. Reidel Publishing Co., 1974. [An illustrated treatise from the sixth/twelfth to seventh/thirteenth century on automata and conjurors' bowls.]

Al-'Irāqī, Abū l-Qāsim Aḥmad ibn Muḥammad, known as al-Sīmāwī. *Kitāb 'Uyūn al-ḥaqā'iq wa-īḍāḥ al-ṭarā'iq*. Hs. Berlin 5567 (Wetzstein 1375). [A seventh/thirteenth-century work that includes sections on magic, amulets, conjuring tricks, and scams.]

Al-Jāḥiẓ, 'Amr ibn Baḥr. *Kitāb al-Bukhalā'*. Edited by Ṭāhā al-Hājirī. Cairo: Dār al-Ma'ārif, n.d. [A third/ninth-century work that contains a list of kinds of beggars.]

Al-Rāghib al-Iṣfahānī, Abū l-Qāsim Ḥusayn ibn Muḥammad. *Muḥāḍarāt al-udabā' wa-muḥāwarāt al-shu'arā' wa-l-bulaghā'*. Edited by Riyāḍ 'Abd al-Ḥamīd Murād. 5 vols. Beirut: Dār Ṣādir, 2012. [A sixth/twelfth-century compendium that includes anecdotes about robbers and thieves.]

Al-Zarkhūrī al-Miṣrī, Muḥammad ibn Abī Bakr. *Zahr al-basātīn fī-'ilm al-mashātīn*. Ms. Leiden Or. 119 (2), 38-87. [A work of unknown date on props, by a juggler. The author devotes the last of the ten chapters of his book to the Bānū Sāsān and their associates.]

Index

About the NYU Abu Dhabi Institute

NYU
ABU DHABI
INSTITUTE

The Library of Arabic Literature is supported by a grant from the NYU Abu Dhabi Institute, a major hub of intellectual and creative activity and advanced research. The Institute hosts academic conferences, workshops, lectures, film series, performances, and other public programs directed both to audiences within the UAE and to the worldwide academic and research community. It is a center of the scholarly community for Abu Dhabi, bringing together faculty and researchers from institutions of higher learning throughout the region.

NYU Abu Dhabi, through the NYU Abu Dhabi Institute, is a world-class center of cutting-edge research, scholarship, and cultural activity. The Institute creates singular opportunities for leading researchers from across the arts, humanities, social sciences, sciences, engineering, and the professions to carry out creative scholarship and conduct research on issues of major disciplinary, multidisciplinary, and global significance.

About the Typefaces

The Arabic body text is set in DecoType Naskh, designed by Thomas Milo and Mirjam Somers, based on an analysis of five centuries of Ottoman manuscript practice. The exceptionally legible result is the first and only typeface in a style that fully implements the principles of script grammar (*qawāʿid al-khaṭṭ*).

The Arabic footnote text is set in DecoType Emiri, drawn by Mirjam Somers, based on the metal typeface in the naskh style that was cut for the 1924 Cairo edition of the Qurʾan.

Both Arabic typefaces in this series are controlled by a dedicated font layout engine. ACE, the Arabic Calligraphic Engine, invented by Peter Somers, Thomas Milo, and Mirjam Somers of DecoType, first operational in 1985, pioneered the principle followed by later smart font layout technologies such as OpenType, which is used for all other typefaces in this series.

The Arabic text was set with WinSoft Tasmeem, a sophisticated user interface for DecoType ACE inside Adobe InDesign. Tasmeem was conceived and created by Thomas Milo (DecoType) and Pascal Rubini (WinSoft) in 2005.

The English text is set in Adobe Text, a new and versatile text typeface family designed by Robert Slimbach for Western (Latin, Greek, Cyrillic) typesetting. Its workhorse qualities make it perfect for a wide variety of applications, especially for longer passages of text where legibility and economy are important. Adobe Text bridges the gap between calligraphic Renaissance types of the 15th and 16th centuries and high-contrast Modern styles of the 18th century, taking many of its design cues from early post-Renaissance Baroque transitional types cut by designers such as Christoffel van Dijck, Nicolaus Kis, and William Caslon. While grounded in classical form, Adobe Text is also a statement of contemporary utilitarian design, well suited to a wide variety of print and on-screen applications.

Titles Published by the Library of Arabic Literature

For more details on individual titles, visit www.libraryofarabicliterature.org

Classical Arabic Literature: A Library of Arabic Literature Anthology
Selected and translated by Geert Jan van Gelder (2012)

A Treasury of Virtues: Sayings, Sermons, and Teachings of ʿAlī, by al-Qāḍī al-Quḍāʿī, with the **One Hundred Proverbs** attributed to al-Jāḥiẓ
Edited and translated by Tahera Qutbuddin (2013)

The Epistle on Legal Theory, by al-Shāfiʿī
Edited and translated by Joseph E. Lowry (2013)

Leg over Leg, by Aḥmad Fāris al-Shidyāq
Edited and translated by Humphrey Davies (**4 volumes**; 2013–14)

Virtues of the Imām Aḥmad ibn Ḥanbal, by Ibn al-Jawzī
Edited and translated by Michael Cooperson (**2 volumes**; 2013–15)

The Epistle of Forgiveness, by Abū l-ʿAlāʾ al-Maʿarrī
Edited and translated by Geert Jan van Gelder and Gregor Schoeler (**2 volumes**; 2013–14)

The Principles of Sufism, by ʿĀʾishah al-Bāʿūniyyah
Edited and translated by Th. Emil Homerin (2014)

The Expeditions: An Early Biography of Muḥammad, by Maʿmar ibn Rāshid
Edited and translated by Sean W. Anthony (2014)

Two Arabic Travel Books
Accounts of China and India, by Abū Zayd al-Sīrāfī
Edited and translated by Tim Mackintosh-Smith (2014)
Mission to the Volga, by Aḥmad ibn Faḍlān
Edited and translated by James Montgomery (2014)

Disagreements of the Jurists: A Manual of Islamic Legal Theory, by al-Qāḍī al-Nuʿmān
Edited and translated by Devin J. Stewart (2015)

Consorts of the Caliphs: Women and the Court of Baghdad, by Ibn al-Sāʿī
Edited by Shawkat M. Toorawa and translated by the Editors of the Library of Arabic Literature (2015)

What ʿĪsā ibn Hishām Told Us, by Muḥammad al-Muwayliḥī
Edited and translated by Roger Allen (2 volumes; 2015)

The Life and Times of Abū Tammām, by Abū Bakr Muḥammad ibn Yaḥyā al-Ṣūlī
Edited and translated by Beatrice Gruendler (2015)

The Sword of Ambition: Bureaucratic Rivalry in Medieval Egypt, by ʿUthmān ibn Ibrāhīm al-Nābulusī
Edited and translated by Luke Yarbrough (2016)

Brains Confounded by the Ode of Abū Shādūf Expounded, by Yūsuf al-Shirbīnī
Edited and translated by Humphrey Davies (2 volumes; 2016)

Light in the Heavens: Sayings of the Prophet Muḥammad, by al-Qāḍī al-Quḍāʿī
Edited and translated by Tahera Qutbuddin (2016)

Risible Rhymes, by Muḥammad ibn Maḥfūẓ al-Sanhūrī
Edited and translated by Humphrey Davies (2016)

A Hundred and One Nights
Edited and translated by Bruce Fudge (2016)

The Excellence of the Arabs, by Ibn Qutaybah
Edited by James E. Montgomery and Peter Webb
Translated by Sarah Bowen Savant and Peter Webb (2017)

Scents and Flavors: A Syrian Cookbook
Edited and translated by Charles Perry (2017)

Arabian Satire: Poetry from 18th-Century Najd, by Ḥmēdān al-Shwēʿir
Edited and translated by Marcel Kurpershoek (2017)

In Darfur: An Account of the Sultanate and Its People, by Muḥammad ibn ʿUmar al-Tūnisī
Edited and translated by Humphrey Davies (2 volumes; 2018)

War Songs, by ʿAntarah ibn Shaddād
Edited by James E. Montgomery
Translated by James E. Montgomery with Richard Sieburth (2018)

Arabian Romantic: Poems on Bedouin Life and Love, by ʿAbdallah ibn Sbayyil
Edited and translated by Marcel Kurpershoek (2018)

Dīwān ʿAntarah ibn Shaddād: A Literary-Historical Study
By James E. Montgomery (2018)

Stories of Piety and Prayer: Deliverance Follows Adversity, by Muḥassin ibn ʿAlī al-Tanūkhī
Edited and translated by Julia Bray (2019)

The Philosopher Responds: An Intellectual Correspondence from the Tenth Century, by Abū Ḥayyān al-Tawḥīdī and Abū ʿAlī Miskawayh
Edited by Bilal Orfali and Maurice A. Pomerantz
Translated by Sophia Vasalou and James E. Montgomery (2 volumes; 2019)

Tajrīd sayf al-himmah li-stikhrāj mā fī dhimmat al-dhimmah: A Scholarly Edition of ʿUthmān ibn Ibrāhīm al-Nābulusī's Text
By Luke Yarbrough (2020)

The Discourses: Reflections on History, Sufism, Theology, and Literature—Volume One, by al-Ḥasan al-Yūsī
Edited and translated by Justin Stearns (2020)

Impostures, by al-Ḥarīrī
Translated by Michael Cooperson (2020)

Maqāmāt Abī Zayd al-Sarūjī, by al-Ḥarīrī
Edited by Michael Cooperson (2020)

The Yoga Sutras of Patañjali, by Abū Rayḥān al-Bīrūnī
Edited and translated by Mario Kozah (2020)

The Book of Charlatans, by Jamāl al-Dīn ʿAbd al-Raḥīm al-Jawbarī
Edited by Manuela Dengler
Translated by Humphrey Davies (2020)

English-only Paperbacks

Leg over Leg, by Aḥmad Fāris al-Shidyāq (2 volumes; 2015)

The Expeditions: An Early Biography of Muḥammad, by Maʿmar ibn Rāshid (2015)

The Epistle on Legal Theory: A Translation of al-Shāfiʿī's *Risālah*, by al-Shāfiʿī (2015)

The Epistle of Forgiveness, by Abū l-ʿAlāʾ al-Maʿarrī (2016)

The Principles of Sufism, by ʿĀʾishah al-Bāʿūniyyah (2016)

A Treasury of Virtues: Sayings, Sermons, and Teachings of ʿAlī, by al-Qāḍī al-Quḍāʿī with the **One Hundred Proverbs**, attributed to al-Jāḥiẓ (2016)

The Life of Ibn Ḥanbal, by Ibn al-Jawzī (2016)

Mission to the Volga, by Ibn Faḍlān (2017)

Accounts of China and India, by Abū Zayd al-Sīrāfī (2017)

A Hundred and One Nights (2017)

Consorts of the Caliphs: Women and the Court of Baghdad, by Ibn al-Sāʿī (2017)

Disagreements of the Jurists: A Manual of Islamic Legal Theory, by al-Qāḍī al-Nuʿmān (2017)

What ʿĪsā ibn Hishām Told Us, by Muḥammad al-Muwayliḥī (2018)

War Songs, by ʿAntarah ibn Shaddād (2018)

The Life and Times of Abū Tammām, by Abū Bakr Muḥammad ibn Yaḥyā al-Ṣūlī (2018)

The Sword of Ambition, by ʿUthmān ibn Ibrāhīm al-Nābulusī (2019)

Brains Confounded by the Ode of Abū Shādūf Expounded: Volume One, by Yūsuf al-Shirbīnī (2019)

Brains Confounded by the Ode of Abū Shādūf Expounded: Volume Two, by Yūsuf al-Shirbīnī and **Risible Rhymes**, by Muḥammad ibn Maḥfūẓ al-Sanhūrī (2019)

The Excellence of the Arabs, by Ibn Qutaybah (2019)

Light in the Heavens: Sayings of the Prophet Muḥammad, by al-Qāḍī al-Quḍāʿī (2019)

Scents and Flavors: A Syrian Cookbook (2020)

Arabian Satire: Poetry from 18th-Century Najd, by Ḥmēdān al-Shwēʿir (2020)

In Darfur: An Account of the Sultanate and Its People, by Muḥammad al-Tūnisī (2020)

Arabian Romantic, by ʿAbdallah ibn Sbayyil (2020)

About the Editor

Manuela Dengler studied Arabic in Damascus and Cairo and received her Ph.D. in Oriental Philology and Islamic Studies from the University of Cologne (Germany). She is the author of the first text-critical edition based on a wide examination of the existing manuscripts of the *Book of Charlatans* by the thirteenth-century Syrian author al-Jawbarī, which she has now re-edited for the Library of Arabic Literature. Besides her research activity, she works in the fields of foreign cultural policy, the dialogue between Western and Muslim societies, and refugee policy.

About the Translator

Humphrey Davies is an award-winning translator of some twenty-five works of modern Arabic literature, among them Alaa Al-Aswany's *The Yacoubian Building*, five novels by Elias Khoury, including *Gate of the Sun*, and Aḥmad Fāris al-Shidyāq's *Leg over Leg*. He has also made a critical edition, translation, and lexicon of the Ottoman-period *Brains Confounded by the Ode of Abū Shādūf Expounded* by Yūsuf al-Shirbīnī, as well as editions and translations of al-Tūnisī's *In Darfur* and al-Sanhūrī's *Risible Rhymes* from the same era. In addition, he has compiled with Madiha Doss an anthology in Arabic entitled *Al-ʿāmmiyyah al-miṣriyyah al-maktūbah: mukhtārāt min 1400 ilā 2009* (*Egyptian Colloquial Writing: selections from 1400 to 2009*) and co-authored, with Lesley Lababidi, *A Field Guide to the Street Names of Central Cairo*. He read Arabic at the University of Cambridge, received his Ph.D. from the University of California at Berkeley, and previous to undertaking his first translation in 2003, worked for social development and research organizations in Egypt, Tunisia, Palestine, and Sudan. He is affiliated with the American University in Cairo.